Tensor Decompositions for Data Science

Tensors are essential in modern-day computational and data sciences. This book explores the foundations of tensor decompositions, a data analysis methodology that is ubiquitous in machine learning, signal processing, chemometrics, neuroscience, quantum computing, financial analysis, social science, business market analysis, image processing, and much more. In this self-contained mathematical, algorithmic, and computational treatment of tensor decomposition, the book emphasizes examples using real-world downloadable open-source datasets to ground the abstract concepts. Methodologies for 3-way tensors (the simplest notation) are presented before generalizing to d-way tensors (the most general but complex notation), making the book accessible to advanced undergraduate and graduate students in mathematics, computer science, statistics, engineering, and physical and life sciences. Additionally, extensive background materials in linear algebra, optimization, probability, and statistics are included as appendices.

Grey Ballard is Associate Professor of Computer Science at Wake Forest University. He specializes in numerical linear algebra, high-performance computing, and computational science, with much of his work focusing on numerical methods and software for tensor decompositions. His work has been recognized with a National Science Foundation (NSF) Faculty Early Career Development (CAREER) award, a SIAM Linear Algebra Best Paper Prize, and conference best paper awards at the ACM Symposium on Parallelism in Algorithms and Architectures (SPAA), IEEE International Parallel & Distributed Processing Symposium (IPDPS), and IEEE International Conference on Data Mining (ICDM).

Tamara G. Kolda is an independent consultant under the auspices of her company, MathSci.ai. Her research background is in numerical linear algebra, optimization, data science, and scientific software, and she is well known for her pioneering algorithmic and software work in tensor decompositions. She has been honored with various recognitions, notably her appointments as member of the US National Academy of Engineering (NAE), Fellow of the Society for Industrial and Applied Mathematics (SIAM), and Fellow of the Association for Computing Machinery (ACM). She helped to create and served as founding editor-in-chief of the *SIAM Journal on Mathematics of Data Science*.

"*Tensor Decompositions for Data Science* by Grey Ballard and Tamara G. Kolda is a much-needed contribution to the field of tensor analysis. This book starts from ground zero and carefully builds up to the core tensor decompositions for data science, with just the right amount of intuition and several practical exercises. This book presents a carefully designed, clear, and intuitive system of notation that will become the standard notation for tensors, making an intimidating subject approachable for new researchers. It will serve as an excellent reference for an advanced undergraduate or early graduate course in tensor decompositions, as well as a trusted guide to tensor decompositions for working researchers."

Rachel Ward, *University of Texas at Austin*

"Tensors arise naturally in many applications, but proper handling of them can be exceedingly difficult compared to matrices. This book provides a deep understanding of how to work with tensors, while also being accessible to students. On top of that, the mathematical typesetting is delightfully precise and readable, while each concept has exactly the right Tikz illustration."

Art Owen, *Stanford University*

"Ballard and Kolda masterfully lay out a step-by-step introduction to tensor decomposition methods, combining mathematical rigor with practical applications across disciplines. *Tensor Decompositions for Data Science* stands out not only as an excellent course companion, but also as an inspiring reference for data scientists and engineers committed to advancing their analytic toolkit."

Alex Williams, *New York University*

"This essential guide demystifies tensor algebra, providing insights into high-dimensional data analysis for both learning and advanced applications."

Jack Dongarra, *University of Tennessee*

"This book provides an accessible entry point into the realm of tensor decompositions, emphasizing practical algorithms, applications and approximations. It guides readers through the essential decompositions, inviting further exploration and setting them off on a wonderful journey into this fascinating field."

Nick Vannieuwenhoven, *KU Leuven*

"Tensors play a crucial role in numerous aspects of data science, including machine learning, computer vision, natural language processing, data compression, anomaly detection, social science, computational neuroscience, materials science, microbiology, and many others. This book provides an accessible yet thorough exploration of tensor representations for complex data. The authors meticulously cover key variants, foundational theories, and practical algorithms, making complex concepts understandable for readers at different levels of expertise."

Rebecca Willett, *University of Chicago*

Tensor Decompositions for Data Science

GREY BALLARD
Wake Forest University

TAMARA G. KOLDA
MathSci.ai

CAMBRIDGE
UNIVERSITY PRESS

CAMBRIDGE
UNIVERSITY PRESS

Shaftesbury Road, Cambridge CB2 8EA, United Kingdom

One Liberty Plaza, 20th Floor, New York, NY 10006, USA

477 Williamstown Road, Port Melbourne, VIC 3207, Australia

314–321, 3rd Floor, Plot 3, Splendor Forum, Jasola District Centre, New Delhi – 110025, India

103 Penang Road, #05–06/07, Visioncrest Commercial, Singapore 238467

Cambridge University Press is part of Cambridge University Press & Assessment, a department of the University of Cambridge.

We share the University's mission to contribute to society through the pursuit of education, learning and research at the highest international levels of excellence.

www.cambridge.org
Information on this title: www.cambridge.org/9781009471671

DOI: 10.1017/9781009471664

When citing this work, please include a reference to the DOI 10.1017/9781009471664

First published 2025

Printed in the United Kingdom by CPI Group Ltd, Croydon, CR0 4YY

A catalogue record for this publication is available from the British Library

Library of Congress Cataloging-in-Publication Data

ISBN 978-1-009-47167-1 Hardback

Contents

Preface xiii

I Tensor Basics

1 Tensors and Their Subparts 3
1.1 What Is a Tensor? 4
1.2 Slices and Hyperslices 5
1.3 Tensor Fibers 8
1.4 Tensor Mode-k Unfolding 10
1.5 Example Tensors 11
1.5.1 Miranda Scientific Simulation Data 11
1.5.2 EEM Fluorescence Spectroscopy Data 13
1.5.3 Monkey BMI Neuronal Spike Data 15
1.5.4 Chicago Crime Count Data 16
1.6 A First Look at Tensor Decompositions 18
1.6.1 A First Look at Tucker Decomposition 19
1.6.2 A First Look at CP Decomposition 19

2 Indexing and Reshaping Tensors 21
2.1 Linear Indexing 21
2.1.1 Natural Order Linear Indexing 22
2.1.2 Reverse Ordering Linear Indexing 25
2.1.3 General Ordering 29
2.2 Vectorization 31
2.2.1 Vectorizing 3-way Tensors 31
2.2.2 Vectorizing d-way Tensors 32
2.2.3 Representing Tensors in Computer Memory 33
2.3 Unfolding or Matricization of a Tensor 33
2.3.1 Unfolding 3-way Tensors 34
2.3.2 Unfolding d-way Tensors 36
2.3.3 Structure of Mode-k Unfoldings 40
2.4 Permuting a Tensor 41
2.4.1 Permutations and Unfoldings 43
2.4.2 Tensor Perfect Shuffle Matrix 43
2.4.3 Linear Indexing and Permutations 44

3 Tensor Operations 47
3.1 Inner Products 47
3.1.1 Inner Products for 3-way Tensors 47
3.1.2 Inner Products for d-way Tensors 48
3.2 Outer Products 49
3.2.1 Outer Product of Three Vectors 49
3.2.2 Outer Product of d Vectors 50
3.2.3 General Outer Products 52
3.2.4 Tensor–Tensor Outer Products 53
3.3 Tensor-Times-Matrix Products 54
3.3.1 TTM for 3-way Tensors 55
3.3.2 TTM for d-way Tensors 59
3.4 TTM in Multiple Modes 61
3.4.1 Multi-TTM for 3-way Tensors 61
3.4.2 TTM with Multiple Matrices for d-way Tensors 63
3.4.3 Efficient Multi-TTM Computation 64

3.5 **Matricized Tensor Times Khatri–Rao Product** . . . 65
3.5.1 MTTKRP for 3-way Tensors . . . 65
3.5.2 MTTKRP for d-way Tensors . . . 68
3.6 **Sequences of Multi-TTM and MTTKRP Operations** . . . 71
3.6.1 Multi-TTM Sequence . . . 71
3.6.2 MTTKRP Sequence . . . 74
3.7 **Sparse Tensors and Operation Efficiencies** . . . 79
3.7.1 Coordinate Format for Sparse Tensors . . . 79
3.7.2 Norm of a Sparse Tensor . . . 81
3.7.3 MTTKRP for 3-way Sparse Tensors . . . 81
3.7.4 MTTKRP for d-way Sparse Tensors . . . 82
3.7.5 Other Data Structures for Sparse Tensors . . . 83
3.8 **Tensor Contraction** . . . 84
3.8.1 Tensor Contraction for 3-way Tensors . . . 84
3.8.2 Tensor Contraction for d-way Tensors . . . 85
3.8.3 Tensor Network Diagrams . . . 86
3.8.4 Batched Tensor Contractions . . . 87
3.8.5 Einstein Notation . . . 88

II Tucker Decomposition

4 **Tucker Decomposition** . . . 91
4.1 **Formulation of Tucker Decomposition** . . . 91
4.1.1 Tucker Decomposition for 3-way Tensors . . . 92
4.1.2 Tucker Decomposition for d-way Tensors . . . 94
4.2 **Choosing the Tucker Decomposition Rank** . . . 94
4.2.1 Specified Multirank . . . 95
4.2.2 Specified Accuracy . . . 95
4.3 **Methods for Computing Tucker Decomposition** . . . 95
4.3.1 Higher-Order SVD . . . 96
4.3.2 Sequentially Truncated HOSVD . . . 97
4.3.3 Higher-Order Orthogonal Iteration . . . 98
4.3.4 Choice of Method . . . 99
4.4 **Reconstruction from Tucker Decomposition** . . . 99
4.4.1 Full Reconstruction . . . 99
4.4.2 Partial Reconstruction . . . 100
4.5 **Example: Tucker Compression of Miranda Scientific Simulation Tensor** . . . 100

5 **Tucker Tensor Structure** . . . 103
5.1 **Tucker Tensor Format** . . . 103
5.1.1 Tucker Format for 3-way Tensors . . . 103
5.1.2 Tucker Format for d-way Tensors . . . 104
5.2 **Unfolding a Tucker Tensor** . . . 105
5.2.1 Vectorizing or Unfolding 3-way Tucker Tensors . . . 105
5.2.2 Vectorizing or Unfolding d-way Tucker Tensors . . . 107
5.3 **Nonuniqueness** . . . 108
5.4 **Imposing Orthonormal Factor Matrices** . . . 108
5.5 **Full Reconstruction** . . . 109
5.5.1 Full Reconstruction for 3-way Tucker Tensors . . . 110
5.5.2 Full Reconstruction for d-way Tucker Tensors . . . 110
5.6 **Partial Reconstruction** . . . 111
5.6.1 Partial Reconstruction of 3-way Tucker Tensors . . . 111
5.6.2 Partial Reconstruction of d-way Tucker Tensors . . . 112
5.7 **Operations on Tucker Tensors** . . . 112
5.7.1 Inner Products and Norms of Tucker Tensors . . . 113
5.7.2 TTM for Tucker Tensors . . . 115
5.7.3 MTTKRP with Tucker Tensors . . . 115

6 **Tucker Algorithms** . . . 117
6.1 **Optimization Formulation** . . . 117
6.1.1 Tucker Optimization Problem for 3-way Tensors . . . 117
6.1.2 Tucker Optimization Problem for d-way Tensors . . . 119
6.1.3 Modewise Optimization . . . 120

6.2 **Higher-Order SVD** 122
6.2.1 HOSVD for 3-way Tensors 122
6.2.2 HOSVD for d-way Tensors 123
6.3 **Sequentially Truncated HOSVD** 125
6.3.1 ST-HOSVD for 3-way Tensors 125
6.3.2 ST-HOSVD for d-way Tensors 127
6.4 **Higher-Order Orthogonal Iteration** 128
6.4.1 HOOI for 3-way Tensors 128
6.4.2 HOOI for d-way Tensor 130
6.5 **Other Methods** 131

7 **Tucker Approximation Error** 133
7.1 **Decomposing the Approximation Error** 133
7.2 **HOSVD Error** 134
7.2.1 HOSVD Error for 3-way Tensors 135
7.2.2 HOSVD Error for d-way Tensors 135
7.3 **ST-HOSVD Error** 136
7.3.1 ST-HOSVD Error for 3-way Tensors 136
7.3.2 ST-HOSVD Error for d-way Tensors 136
7.4 **Quasi-optimality** 137

8 **Tensor Train Decomposition** 141
8.1 **Formulation of the TT Decomposition** 142
8.1.1 TT Decomposition of 3-way Tensors 142
8.1.2 TT Decomposition of 4-way Tensors 143
8.1.3 TT Decomposition of d-way Tensors 144
8.2 **Algorithm and Error Analysis** 145
8.2.1 TT-SVD Decomposition for 4-way Tensors 146
8.2.2 TT-SVD for d-way Tensors 149
8.3 **Example: TT of Discretized Function Tensor** 154

III **CP Decomposition**

9 **Canonical Polyadic Decomposition** 157
9.1 **Formulation of CP Decomposition** 158
9.1.1 CP Decomposition for 3-way Tensors 158
9.1.2 CP Decomposition for d-way Tensors 160
9.1.3 Connection to Matrix Low-Rank Approximation 160
9.2 **Properties of CP Decompositions** 161
9.2.1 Inherent Ambiguities 161
9.2.2 Fundamental Challenges 161
9.2.3 Uniqueness 162
9.3 **Overview of Methods for Computing CP** 163
9.3.1 Alternating Least Squares (CP-ALS) 163
9.3.2 All-at-Once Optimization (CP-OPT and CP-NLS) 164
9.3.3 Direct Computation via Simultaneous Diagonalization 164
9.4 **Practical Considerations** 165
9.4.1 Choosing the CP Rank 165
9.4.2 Regularization 166
9.4.3 Initialization and Multiple Runs 166
9.4.4 Preprocessing 167
9.4.5 Postprocessing 167
9.4.6 Comparison of Methods 168
9.5 **Extensions of CP** 168
9.5.1 Nonnegativity and Other Constraints 168
9.5.2 Methods for Incomplete Data (EM and CP-WOPT) 169
9.5.3 Other Loss Functions with Generalized CP 170
9.5.4 Methods for Symmetric Tensors 170
9.6 **Example: CP on EEM Tensor** 171
9.6.1 Comparing to EEM Ground Truth 172
9.6.2 Interpreting CP Factors for EEM Tensor 172
9.7 **Example: CP on Monkey BMI Tensor** 174
9.7.1 Nonnegative CP on Monkey BMI Tensor 174
9.7.2 Clustering Monkey BMI Trials 176

9.8 Example: GCP on Chicago 2019 Crime Tensor . . . 177
9.8.1 Choosing the Objective Function . . . 177
9.8.2 Choosing the Model Rank . . . 177
9.8.3 Interpreting the Decomposition . . . 177
9.9 Origins of the Name "CP" . . . 180

10 Kruskal Tensor Structure . . . 181

10.1 Rank-1 Tensors . . . 181
10.1.1 Rank-1 3-way Tensors . . . 181
10.1.2 Rank-1 d-way Tensors . . . 182
10.2 Kruskal Tensor Format . . . 182
10.2.1 Kruskal 3-way Tensor Format . . . 182
10.2.2 Kruskal d-way Tensor Format . . . 184
10.2.3 Kruskal 3-way Tensor Format with Component Weights . . . 184
10.2.4 Kruskal d-way Tensor Format with Component Weights . . . 185
10.3 Unfolding a Kruskal Tensor . . . 186
10.3.1 Vectorizing or Unfolding a 3-way Kruskal Tensor . . . 186
10.3.2 Vectorizing or Unfolding a d-way Kruskal Tensor . . . 188
10.4 Kruskal Tensor Ambiguities . . . 190
10.4.1 Permutation Ambiguity . . . 190
10.4.2 Scaling Ambiguity . . . 190
10.5 Kruskal Tensor Uniqueness . . . 191
10.6 Full Construction from Kruskal Tensors . . . 193
10.6.1 Full Construction from 3-way Kruskal Tensors . . . 193
10.6.2 Full Construction from d-way Kruskal Tensors . . . 194
10.6.3 Masked Full Construction from a Kruskal Tensor . . . 195
10.7 Operations with Kruskal Tensors . . . 196
10.7.1 Inner Products and Norms of Kruskal Tensors . . . 197
10.7.2 Approximation Error . . . 198
10.7.3 MTTKRP with Kruskal Tensors . . . 200
10.7.4 TTM with Kruskal Tensors . . . 201
10.8 Measuring Similarity of Kruskal Tensors . . . 202
10.8.1 Measuring Similarity of 3-way Kruskal Tensors . . . 202
10.8.2 Measuring Similarity of d-way Kruskal Tensors . . . 203

11 CP Alternating Least Squares Optimization . . . 205

11.1 CP-ALS for 3-way Tensors . . . 205
11.1.1 Least Squares Subproblem for 3-way Tensors . . . 206
11.1.2 CP-ALS Algorithm for 3-way Tensors . . . 207
11.2 CP-ALS for d-way Tensors . . . 209
11.2.1 Least Squares Subproblem for d-way Tensors . . . 209
11.2.2 CP-ALS Algorithm for d-way Tensors . . . 210
11.2.3 Complexity Analysis for CP-ALS . . . 210
11.2.4 CP-ALS with Sparse and Structured Tensors . . . 212
11.3 Further Notes on CP-ALS . . . 213
11.4 CP-ALS on Data Tensors . . . 213

12 CP Gradient-Based Optimization . . . 219

12.1 CP Optimization Problem . . . 219
12.1.1 CP Optimization Formulation for 3-way CP . . . 220
12.1.2 CP Optimization Formulation for d-way CP . . . 221
12.2 Gradients for CP . . . 222
12.2.1 Preliminaries for Computing CP Gradients . . . 222
12.2.2 CP Gradient for 3-way Tensors . . . 223
12.2.3 CP Gradient for d-way Tensors . . . 226
12.2.4 Complexity Analysis for Computing CP Gradient . . . 227
12.3 CP-OPT Method . . . 228
12.4 CP-OPT on Data Tensors . . . 230

13 CP Nonlinear Least Squares Optimization . . . 233

13.1 CP Nonlinear Least Squares Problem . . . 233
13.1.1 CP Jacobian for 3-way Tensors . . . 234
13.1.2 CP Jacobian for d-way Tensors . . . 234

13.2 Solving the Gauss–Newton Linear System 235
13.2.1 Applying Approximate CP Hessian for 3-way Tensors 236
13.2.2 Preconditioning in Approximate Gauss–Newton for 3-way Tensors 237
13.2.3 Applying Approximate CP Hessian for d-way Tensors 239
13.2.4 Preconditioning in Approximate Gauss–Newton for d-way Tensors 242
13.3 CP-NLS on Data Tensors 242

14 CP Algorithms for Incomplete or Scarce Data 245
14.1 Representing Incomplete or Scarce Data 246
14.1.1 Known Value Indicator Set 247
14.1.2 Known Value Selection Matrix 247
14.1.3 Known Value Weight Tensor 248
14.2 Missing Data CP Function and Gradient 249
14.2.1 Missing Data CP Function and Gradient: 3-way 249
14.2.2 Missing Data CP Function and Gradient: d-way 250
14.3 Weighted All-at-Once Optimization 251
14.3.1 CP-WOPT Method 251
14.3.2 Special Handling of Scarce Tensors 252
14.4 Weighted Alternating Optimization 253
14.5 Example: CP-WOPT on EEM Tensor 254
14.5.1 Computing CP on EEM with Missing Data 254
14.5.2 EEM Tensor with Even More Missing Data 256

15 Generalized CP Decomposition 257
15.1 Generalized Loss Functions 257
15.2 Choices for Loss Functions 258
15.2.1 Sum of Squared Errors (Normal-Distributed Data) 259
15.2.2 Logistic Regression (Binary Data) 259
15.2.3 KL Divergence (Count Data) 261
15.2.4 Loss Functions for Nonnegative Data 262
15.2.5 Robust Loss Functions 264
15.2.6 Summary of Loss Functions 265
15.3 Optimization Formulation 266
15.3.1 GCP for 3-way Tensors 266
15.3.2 GCP for d-way Tensors 266
15.3.3 Properties and Extensions of GCP Decompositions 266
15.4 GCP Gradient and First-Order Optimization 266
15.4.1 GCP Gradient for 3-way Tensors 266
15.4.2 GCP Gradient for d-way Tensors 267
15.5 GCP-OPT Method 268
15.6 Example: GCP-OPT on Monkey BMI Tensor 269
15.7 Example: GCP-OPT on Chicago Crime Tensor 271

16 CP Tensor Rank and Special Topics 273
16.1 Tensor Rank 273
16.2 Tensor Rank is NP-Hard 274
16.3 Maximum Rank 274
16.4 Typical Rank 275
16.5 Border Rank 276
16.6 Connections to Arithmetic Complexity 277
16.6.1 Multiplying Complex Numbers 278
16.6.2 Strassen's 2×2 Matrix Multiplication 280
16.6.3 3×3 Matrix Multiplication 282
16.6.4 General Matrix Multiplication 282
16.6.5 Arbitrary Precision Approximating Algorithms 284
16.7 CP Uniqueness 285
16.8 Direct Computation of Rank for Certain Tensors 287
16.8.1 Rank-1 Tensors 287
16.8.2 Rank of $2 \times 2 \times 2$ Tensors 289
16.8.3 Rank of $n \times n \times 2$ Tensors 293
16.8.4 Direct Computation of CP for Certain $m \times n \times p$ Tensors 294
16.9 Greedy Computation 296

IV Closing Observations

17 Closing Observations . . . 301
17.1 Comparing Matrix and Tensor Decompositions . . . 301
17.1.1 Decomposition Overview . . . 301
17.1.2 Decomposition Size . . . 303
17.1.3 Computability and Quasi-Optimality . . . 303
17.1.4 Factor Orthogonality . . . 304
17.1.5 Uniqueness . . . 304
17.1.6 Interpreting CP as Tucker . . . 304
17.1.7 Interpreting Tucker as CP . . . 305
17.1.8 CP and Tucker Equivalence for Orthogonally Decomposable Tensors . . . 305
17.1.9 Comparing Matrix and Tensor Decomposition . . . 305
17.2 CANDELINC: Tucker Preprocessing for CP . . . 306
17.3 Symmetric Tensors . . . 308
17.3.1 Symmetric Tucker Decomposition . . . 310
17.3.2 Symmetric CP Decomposition . . . 310
17.3.3 Tensor Eigenproblems . . . 311
17.4 Other Tensor Decompositions . . . 312
17.4.1 Tensor SVD (t-SVD) . . . 312
17.4.2 Hierarchical Tensor Decomposition . . . 312
17.4.3 Tensor Ring Decomposition . . . 313
17.4.4 CP–Tucker Hybrid Block Decomposition . . . 314
17.4.5 Infinite Dimensional Decompositions . . . 314

Appendices

A Numerical Linear Algebra . . . 319
A.1 Complexity and Big-O Notation . . . 319
A.2 Finite Precision and Numerical Stability . . . 320
A.3 Vectors and Matrices . . . 321
A.3.1 Definitions . . . 321
A.3.2 Vector Inner Product and Norms . . . 322
A.3.3 Matrix Inner Product and Norms . . . 323
A.3.4 Vector Outer Product . . . 324
A.3.5 Matrix–Vector Product . . . 324
A.3.6 Matrix–Matrix Product . . . 324
A.3.7 Matrix Inverse . . . 325
A.3.8 Positive Definiteness . . . 325
A.3.9 Vector Span and Subspace Dimension . . . 326
A.3.10 Matrix Range and Rank . . . 327
A.3.11 Orthonormal and Orthogonal Matrices . . . 328
A.3.12 Permutation Matrices . . . 329
A.4 Other Matrix Products . . . 330
A.4.1 Gram Matrix . . . 330
A.4.2 Matrix Hadamard Product . . . 330
A.4.3 Matrix Kronecker Product . . . 331
A.4.4 Matrix Khatri–Rao Product . . . 334
A.5 Matrix Decompositions . . . 336
A.5.1 LU and Cholesky Decompositions . . . 337
A.5.2 QR Decomposition . . . 338
A.5.3 Singular Value Decomposition . . . 338
A.5.4 Symmetric Eigenvalue Decomposition . . . 340
A.5.5 Detailed Costs of Computing the SVD . . . 341
A.6 Solving Linear Equations . . . 342
A.6.1 Solving Diagonal Linear Equations . . . 343
A.6.2 Solving Orthogonal Linear Equations . . . 343
A.6.3 Solving Triangular Linear Equations . . . 343
A.6.4 Solving Symmetric Positive Definite Linear Equations . . . 343
A.6.5 Solving Nonsymmetric Linear Equations . . . 344
A.7 Linear Least Squares Problems . . . 345
A.7.1 Solving Least Squares via Normal Equations . . . 345
A.7.2 Solving Least Squares via QR . . . 346
A.7.3 Solving Least Squares via SVD . . . 347
A.7.4 Choice of Least Squares Solver . . . 347
A.7.5 Multiple Right-Hand-Sides Version of Least Squares . . . 348

A.8 Low-Rank Matrix Approximation . . . 348
A.8.1 Specified Rank . . . 349
A.8.2 Specified Error . . . 350
A.8.3 Extensions of Low-Rank Matrix Approximation . . . 351
A.9 Software Libraries for Linear Algebra . . . 351
A.9.1 Representing Matrices in Memory . . . 351
A.9.2 BLAS Hierarchy . . . 352
B Optimization Principles and Methods . . . 355
B.1 Multivariable Calculus . . . 355
B.1.1 First Derivatives . . . 355
B.1.2 Second Derivatives . . . 358
B.1.3 Matrix Calculus . . . 359
B.2 Principles of Unconstrained Optimization . . . 361
B.2.1 Gradients and Stationary Points . . . 363
B.2.2 Hessians and Optimality Conditions . . . 365
B.2.3 Convex Functions . . . 366
B.3 Unconstrained Optimization Methods . . . 367
B.3.1 Using Optimization Methods . . . 367
B.3.2 Gradient Descent . . . 368
B.3.3 Newton's Method . . . 369
B.3.4 BFGS Optimization Method . . . 370
B.3.5 L-BFGS Optimization Method . . . 371
B.3.6 Damped Gauss–Newton for Least Squares Problems . . . 371
B.3.7 Block Coordinate Descent . . . 373
B.4 Example: Two-Dimensional Optimization . . . 373
B.5 Constrained Optimization . . . 376
C Statistics and Probability . . . 379
C.1 Random Variables . . . 379
C.1.1 Discrete Random Variables . . . 379
C.1.2 Continuous Random Variables . . . 380
C.2 Maximum Likelihood Estimator . . . 380
C.3 Useful Distributions . . . 381
C.3.1 Gaussian Distribution and Sum of Squared Errors . . . 381
C.3.2 Bernoulli Distribution and Logistic Regression for Binary Data . . . 381
C.3.3 Poisson Distribution and KL Divergence for Count Data . . . 382
C.3.4 Gamma Distribution for Continuous Nonnegative Data . . . 382
C.4 Principal Component Analysis . . . 383
C.4.1 Computing PCA . . . 384
C.4.2 Example of PCA . . . 385

References . . . 389
Index . . . 401

Preface

Tensors are essential in modern-day computational and data sciences. In this book, we explore the foundations of tensor decomposition, which is the art of disassembling multi-dimensional arrays into smaller parts. Applications of tensor decomposition are ubiquitous in machine learning, signal processing, chemometrics, neuroscience, quantum computing, financial analysis, social science, business market analysis, image processing, and much more. Our goal is to provide a self-contained mathematical, algorithmic, and computational treatment of tensor decomposition, with an emphasis on examples using real datasets to ground the abstract concepts.

Organization

To ensure the book is accessible to a broad audience coming from different technical backgrounds, review material on linear algebra, optimization, and statistics is included in the appendices. These review chapters can be used to fill in any gaps in the reader's background. Key theorems, propositions, and definitions are rendered differently to standard ones, including demarcation with a key symbol (🔑).

The main part of the book is organized into four parts:

- Part I focuses on the basics of tensors. We consider how tensors are organized and give several examples that will be revisited in later parts of the book. We formalize reshaping tensors into vectors and matrices and explain how this relates to their representation in computer memory. We consider key tensor operations, their computational complexity, and their mathematical properties, and we discuss how to implement the tensor operations efficiently using high-performance matrix computation subroutines. This early treatment of tensor operations enables the rest of the book to remain at a higher conceptual level.

- Part II focuses on the Tucker decomposition, which produces a smaller *core* tensor together with linear transformations to convert the original tensor to the core tensor. The Tucker decomposition has utility for compressing massive tensor datasets, as well as the ability to reconstruct portions of the full dataset using only the time and memory needed for the portion being reconstructed. We demonstrate the utility of Tucker decomposition for compressing data from a scientific simulation of the mixing of fluids of different densities, including the speed advantage of reconstructing only portions of the dataset. More generally, we describe how to work with tensors in Tucker-compressed form, discuss both direct and iterative algorithms for computing the Tucker decomposition, and develop the theory to explain the quasi-optimality of Tucker decomposition. We also have a chapter (Chapter 8) devoted to the tensor train (TT) decomposition.

- Part III focuses on the canonical polyadic (CP) tensor decomposition, also known as CANDECOMP/PARAFAC, which reduces a tensor to a summation of rank-1 tensors (i.e., vector outer products). In unsupervised learning, the CP decomposition is used for interpretation and for downstream tasks, such as clustering. In comparison with low-rank matrix approximations, such as principal component analysis (PCA) or nonnegative matrix factorization (NMF), the CP decomposition is generally unique and does not have constraints such as orthogonality, which makes the interpretations more meaningful. CP has proven to be an essential tool in multiway data analysis, spawning numerous variants. It can be applied to datasets with missing data, uncovering meaningful patterns even when a large majority of the tensor entries are unknown. Generalized CP (GCP) is a variant that can use distribution-specialized loss functions, which is important for count and network-science data. We consider the manipulation of tensors in CP-decomposed format, the formulation of the CP optimization problem and its variants, and a variety of algorithms. We demonstrate the utility of the CP tensor decompositions on data from computation chemistry (fluorescence emission–excitation data from multiple samples), neuroscience (neural activity from a brain–machine interface device), and criminal activity (crime reports from the city of Chicago). We also cover special topics osuch as the known results for tensor rank (the minimal number of summands required to exactly reproduce a given tensor), the connections to efficient computations such as fast matrix–matrix multiplication (e.g., Strassen's algorithm), and direct computation of the CP decomposition for certain 3-way tensors.

- In Part IV, we provide closing observations on the tensor decompositions we have discussed. We compare Tucker, TT, and CP tensors decompositions to one another in the hopes of guiding users on which decomposition is most appropriate in which circumstance. We also explain how these compare to matrix decompositions such as PCA and NMF. We explain how to combine CP and Tucker, using Tucker decomposition to compress tensors before applying CP. We briefly discuss symmetric tensors, their decompositions, and the tensor eigenproblem. This book is devoted to the Tucker and CP decompositions, since they are arguably the two most useful decompositions for real-world applications. But there are many more decompositions of interest for specific applications, so we conclude with a survey of other decompositions: tensor SVD (t-SVD), hierarchical tensor decomposition, tensor ring decomposition, block CP decompositions, and infinite dimensional tensor decompositions.

Target Audience

This book is targeted at a graduate-level or advanced undergraduate-level course in a data science or related curriculum in mathematics, statistics, computer science, engineering, neuroscience, biostatistics, etc. The background material is primarily at an undergraduate level, but requires breadth of knowledge across a number of topics. Since most readers will not have all the background required, we include extensive review material in linear algebra, optimization, and statistics to fill in any gaps.

To keep the notation and concepts both accessible and general, we provide every definition and result for both 3-way tensors (the simplest notation) and d-way tensors (the general case, but complex in notation). This book will provide a starting point for beginning researchers in tensor decompositions, as well as an essential reference for advanced researchers.

A distinguishing feature of this book that makes it appropriate for instruction is its emphasis on practical applications of tensor decompositions. The examples are based on real-world datasets curated especially for this book. The introduction of each tensor decomposition is general, including visualization and interpretation of results. We separate advanced topics, such as the details of algorithms, into their own independent chapters to allow flexibility in course design.

At its heart, this is a book about algorithms for tensor decompositions, helping readers to understand the most studied and used methods and trade-offs among them. Understanding algorithms requires understanding the theoretical nature of tensor decompositions. Certain tensor problems are known to be computationally difficult, but there are strategies for addressing many of the challenges. In the case of Tucker decomposition, for example, we show that some of the methods are quasi-optimal.

For those focused on tensor computations, there is a chapter that breaks down the computational kernels needed for tensor methods and explains how to achieve high performance. Further, the book covers the role of structure in computations, such as for sparse and specially structured tensors, which can improve efficiency.

Course Options

A course based on this book can be offered in data science, computer science, applied mathematics, engineering, statistics, biostatistics, or neuroscience. It can easily fill a semester-long topics course at the graduate level and is designed to be adapted for other scenarios.

This book is organized into four main parts. Part I (Tensor Basics) is introductory. The discussion of Tucker and CP (Parts II and III) are independent, so a course can focus on solely one or the other. Part IV (Closing Observations) is primarily for perspective and is entirely optional.

A mini-course can be based on three chapters designed to stand apart and be usable independently of the rest of the book:

- Chapter 1: Tensors and Their Subparts
- Chapter 4: Tucker Decomposition
- Chapter 9: Canonical Polyadic Decomposition.

A comprehensive introductory course can be formed from the following 12 chapters, requiring only background in numerical linear algebra:

- Appendix A: Numerical Linear Algebra
- Chapter 1: Tensors and Their Subparts
- Chapter 2: Indexing and Reshaping Tensors
- Chapter 3: Tensor Operations
- Chapter 4: Tucker Decomposition
- Chapter 5: Tucker Tensor Structure
- Chapter 6: Tucker Algorithms
- Chapter 8: Tensor Train Decomposition
- Chapter 9: Canonical Polyadic Decomposition
- Chapter 10: Kruskal Tensor Structure
- Chapter 11: CP Alternating Least Squares Optimization
- Chapter 17: Closing Observations.

For a course emphasis on algorithms, we recommend including the optimization-based methods for CP, requiring background in optimization:

- Appendix B: Optimization Principles and Methods
- Chapter 12: CP Gradient-Based Optimization
- Chapter 13: CP Nonlinear Least Squares Optimization
- Chapter 14: CP Algorithms for Incomplete or Scarce Data.

For more emphasis on statistical modeling of data, adding GCP is useful:

- Appendix C: Statistics and Probability
- Chapter 15: Generalized CP Decomposition.

More theory-inclined classes will want to also cover

- Chapter 7: Tucker Approximation Error
- Chapter 16: CP Tensor Rank and Special Topics.

Topics Not Covered

It is impossible to do justice to the entire field of tensor decompositions in a one-semester course. We ultimately hope to provide more material in future editions, perhaps requiring two semesters for complete coverage.

We provide only superficial coverage of symmetric tensor factorization and tensor eigenproblems. We only briefly survey other decompositions, such as tensor singular value decomposition (t-SVD) and hierarchical tensor (HT) decomposition.

We do not cover randomized algorithms for tensor decomposition, though this is a fast-growing area of importance. For instance, some of the most useful methods for TT decomposition are randomized. We do not consider high-performance computing (HPC) implementations of all key computational kernels for tensors since this requires significant additional background knowledge. For Tucker decomposition, we do not cover nonnegative decompositions, tensor completion, or decompositions for sparse and incomplete tensors.

Additional Resources

We have curated several datasets for use with this textbook:

- Miranda Scientific Simulation Data ($2048 \times 256 \times 256$):
  `https://gitlab.com/tensors/tensor_data_miranda_sim`

- Excitation–Emission Matrix (EEM) Fluorescence Data ($18 \times 251 \times 21$):
  `https://gitlab.com/tensors/tensor_data_eem`

- Monkey Brain–Machine Interface (BMI) Neuronal Spike Data ($52 \times 200 \times 88$):
  `https://gitlab.com/tensors/tensor_data_monkey_bmi`

- Chicago Crime Count Data ($365 \times 24 \times 77 \times 12$):
  `https://gitlab.com/tensors/tensor_data_chicago_crime`.

We do not prescribe a specific computational platform, but everything described here can be computed using the Tensor Toolbox for MATLAB at `www.tensortoolbox.org`. Much of the same functionality is available in its Python clone, the Python Tensor Toolbox (PyTTB) at `https://github.com/sandialabs/pyttb`.

Acknowledgments

This book is the culmination of our 35+ collective years of research in tensor decompositions. We have had the good fortune to work with and be inspired by the best and brightest minds in the field. We are indebted to these luminaries. We especially want to acknowledge Brett Bader, TK's coauthor on the *SIAM Review* article on tensor decompositions that is a clear precursor to this book. We want to further acknowledge so many amazing colleagues who have inspired us throughout the years, especially the following: Evrim Acar, Hussam Al Daas, Woody Austin, Casey Battaglino, Stephen Becker, Austin Benson, Rasmus Bro, Gabriel Brown, Eric Chi, Andrzej Cichocki, Jeremy Cohen, Pierre Comon, Jim Demmel, Karen Devine, Hans De Sterck, Jack Dongarra, Petros Drineas, Lars Elden, Rob Erhardt, Christos Faloutsos, David Gleich, Gene Golub, Alex Gorodetsky, Laura Grigori, Sammy Hansen, Koby Hayashi, David Hong, Lior Horesh, Daniel Hsu, Ruhui Jin, Nick Johnson, Ramakrishnan Kannan, Joe Kileel, Misha Kilmer, Alicia Klinvex, Hemanth Kolla, Suraj Kumar, Daniel Kressner, J. M. Landsberg, Brett Larsen, Lieven De Lathauwer, Jiajia Li, Lek-Heng Lim, Michael Mahoney, Osman Malik, Carla D. Martin, Jackson Mayo, Rachel Minster, Martin Mohlenkamp, Cleve Moler, Morten Mørup, Jim Nagy, Elizabeth Newman, Jiawang Nie, Jorge Nocedal, Luke Oeding, Dianne O'Leary, Ivan Oseledets, Vagelis Papalexakis, Haesun Park, João Pereira, Anh Huy Phan, Eric Phipps, Todd Plantenga, Bob Plemmons, Prashant Rai, Jill Reese, Kathryn Rouse, Arvind Saibaba, Berkant Savas, Martin Schatz, Oded Schwartz, Anna Seigal, Teresa Selee, Samantha Sherman, Nikos Sidiropoulos, Amit Singer, Shaden Smith, Edgar Solomonik, Gil Strang, Bernd Sturmfels, Jimeng Sun, Jos ten Berge, Christine Tobler, Joel Tropp, Shashanka Ubaru, Bora Uçar, Madeleine Udell, Robert van de Geijn, Charlie Van Loan, Nick Vannieuwenhoven, Alex Vasilescu, Steve Vavasis, Nico Vervliet, Rich Vuduc, Rachel Ward, Alex Williams, Kina Winoto, Barry Wise, and Steve Wright.

Much of this work has been inspired by tutorial and course presentations. Thus, we are grateful to have had the opportunity to present in various tutorials (TK with Jimeng Sun and Christos Faloutsos at SDM07, ICML07, KDD07; TK with Danny Dunlavy and Kina Winoto at SDM18; GB at AN21; GB and TK with Danny Dunlavy at MDS22), short courses (TK at 2017 Trier Autumn School and TK at 2019 Gene Golub SIAM Summer School), a mini-course (TK at Northwestern, spring 2022), and a full-semester course (GB at Wake Forest, fall 2021 and fall 2023). Huge thanks to our audiences.

Special thanks to many persons who read and provided feedback to our questions and on drafts of this book, in particular John Billos, Gabriel Brown, Jeremy Cohen, Claude Greengard, Zitong Li, Joe Kileel, Joah Macosko, Art Owen, João Pinheiro, Todd Plantenga, Nico Vervliet, and Qingjia Xu.

We thank the many brave souls who did not already know all the answers and asked questions. Hearing the same questions over and over again convinced us of the need for a textbook like this one.

Finally, we thank our families, mostly for believing that we could do this!

Grey Ballard
Winston-Salem, NC

Tamara G. Kolda
Dublin, CA

Part I

Tensor Basics

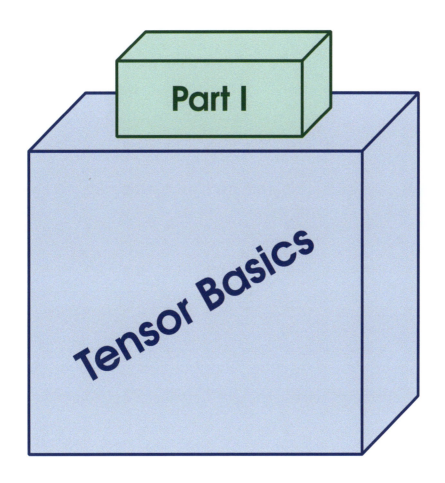

1 Tensors and Their Subparts

Tensors are multiway arrays and serve as useful tools for data representation and analysis. Tensor decompositions are similar in spirit to matrix decompositions, such as principal component analysis (PCA), singular value decomposition (SVD), and nonnegative matrix factorization (NMF). If we consider that a matrix might generically represent objects (rows) and attributes (columns), the addition of multiple measurements at different times or in different scenarios can produce a multiway array that we refer to as a tensor. In 1952, Cattell proposed that data might be organized as

$$\boxed{\text{object}} \times \boxed{\text{feature}} \times \boxed{\text{scenario}} \,.$$

The tensor in this case might look like what we see in Fig. 1.1.

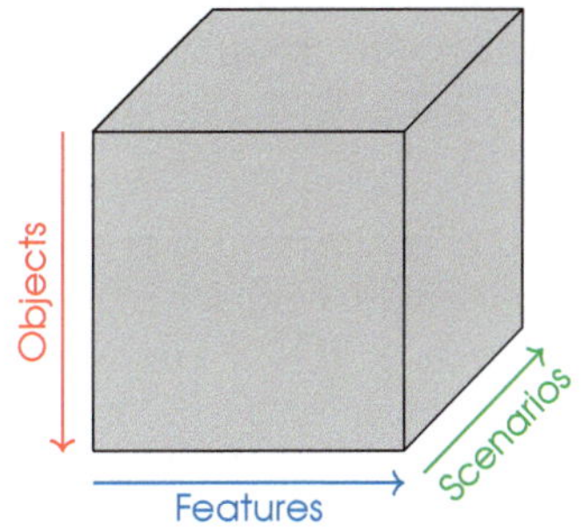

Figure 1.1 Prototypical format of the tensor in data analysis.

The different scenarios might consist of measurements at different times or under different conditions. Furthermore, there is no reason to be constrained to organizing data into 3-way arrays.

The focus of this chapter is on understanding and manipulating tensor objects. A tensor is a multidimensional array, but it is oftentimes useful for considerations of storage or computation to view it in other ways, rearranging its entries as a vector or a matrix. We can potentially exploit structure such as sparsity or symmetry. Moreover, we can consider particular subparts of the tensor, called fibers, slices, and hyperslices. We describe several example tensors that we will revisit throughout the book. We close this chapter with a preview of the two main tensor decompositions discussed in this book: Tucker and CP.

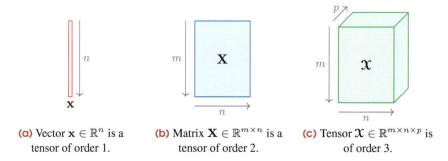

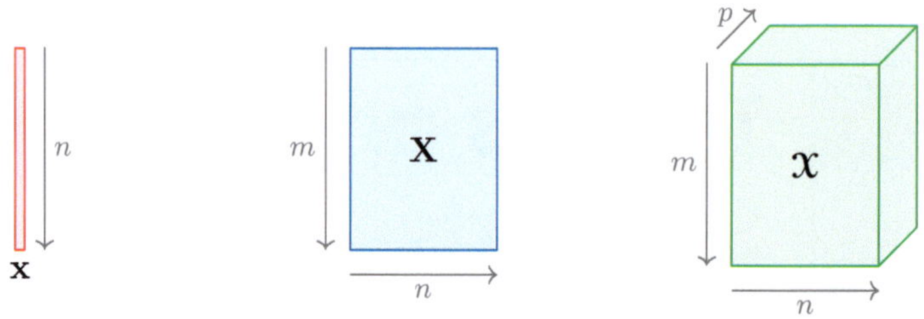

(a) Vector $\mathbf{x} \in \mathbb{R}^n$ is a tensor of order 1.

(b) Matrix $\mathbf{X} \in \mathbb{R}^{m \times n}$ is a tensor of order 2.

(c) Tensor $\mathcal{X} \in \mathbb{R}^{m \times n \times p}$ is of order 3.

Figure 1.2 Tensors of order one, two, and three.

1.1 What Is a Tensor?

A **tensor** is a d-way array, where d is referred to as the **order** of the tensor. Let's talk about how tensors relate to the known realm of vectors and matrices. First, a bit of notation. We denote the set of real values as $\mathbb{R}$. We represent scalars throughout as lowercase letters. We generally use the letters i, j, k, ℓ as indices into arrays and the letters m, n, p, q, r, s to represent sizes. We assume that indices start from 1 (rather than 0). Additionally, we use the shorthand $[n] \equiv \{1, \ldots, n\}$, and we write $[m] \otimes [n] = \{(i,j) \mid i \in [m], j \in [n]\}$.

Definition 1.1 (Tensor) A **tensor** is a d-way array, and d is the **order** of a tensor.

A **vector** is a one-dimensional array of numbers that represents a collection of measurements. In machine learning, a *feature vector* is the set of measurements that is used to characterize an object. We represent vectors throughout by lowercase boldface roman letters. If $\mathbf{x}$ is a real-valued vector of size n, then we write $\mathbf{x} \in \mathbb{R}^n$. Entry $i \in [n]$ of $\mathbf{x}$ is denoted as $\mathbf{x}(i)$ or compactly as x_i. A vector is a tensor of order 1.

A **matrix** is a two-dimensional array of numbers, such as a collection of feature vectors. We represent matrices throughout by uppercase boldface roman letters. If $\mathbf{X}$ is a real-valued matrix of size $m \times n$, then we write $\mathbf{X} \in \mathbb{R}^{m \times n}$. For instance, given a set of m objects, each of which has n features, the matrix entry $\mathbf{X}(i,j)$ would represent the jth feature of object i. More generally, entry $(i,j) \in [m] \otimes [n]$ of $\mathbf{X}$ is denoted as $\mathbf{X}(i,j)$ or compactly as x_{ij}. A matrix is a tensor of order 2.

Definition 1.2 (Higher Order) A d-way tensor is called **higher order** if $d \geq 3$.

If we have a three-dimensional array of numbers, then we have a **higher-order tensor**. Tensors of order 3 or greater are denoted throughout by uppercase bold Euler roman letters: $\mathcal{X}$. Figure 1.2 shows a vector, a matrix, and an order-3 tensor. If $\mathcal{X}$ is a real-valued tensor of size $m \times n \times p$, then we write $\mathcal{X} \in \mathbb{R}^{m \times n \times p}$. For instance, given a set of m objects, each of which has n features, measured under p different scenarios, the tensor entry $\mathcal{X}(i,j,k)$ would represent the jth feature of object i measured in scenario k. More generally, entry $(i,j,k) \in [m] \otimes [n] \otimes [p]$ of $\mathcal{X}$ is denoted as $\mathcal{X}(i,j,k)$ or compactly as x_{ijk}. We refer to each dimension as a **mode**. We say that mode 1 is of size m, mode 2 of size n, and mode 3 of size p. If all modes have the same size, we call the tensor **cubical**.

> A **tensor** is a d-way array. We refer to d as the **order** of the tensor and the different ways as **modes**. We say a tensor is **higher-order** if $d \geq 3$.

Table 1.1 Notation for scalars, vectors, matrices, and higher-order tensors

Description	Size	Order	Notation	Entry
Scalar	1	0	x	x
Vector	n	1	$\mathbf{x}$	$\mathbf{x}(i)$ or x_i
Matrix	$m \times n$	2	$\mathbf{X}$	$\mathbf{X}(i,j)$ or x_{ij}
3-way tensor	$m \times n \times p$	3	$\mathcal{X}$	$\mathcal{X}(i,j,k)$ or x_{ijk}
4-way tensor	$n_1 \times n_2 \times n_3 \times n_4$	4	$\mathcal{X}$	$\mathcal{X}(i_1,i_2,i_3,i_4)$ or $x_{i_1 i_2 i_3 i_4}$
d-way tensor	$n_1 \times n_2 \times \cdots \times n_d$	d	$\mathcal{X}$	$\mathcal{X}(i_1,i_2,\ldots,i_d)$ or $x_{i_1 i_2 \cdots i_d}$

Example 1.1 (Tensor Entries) As an example, consider the $2 \times 2 \times 2$ tensor $\mathcal{X}$, such that

$\mathcal{X} =$ 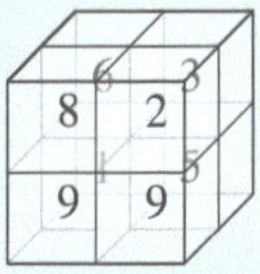 .

It has eight entries:

$$x_{111} = 8, \quad x_{211} = 9, \quad x_{121} = 2, \quad x_{221} = 9,$$
$$x_{112} = 6, \quad x_{212} = 1, \quad x_{122} = 3, \quad x_{222} = 5.$$

Exercise 1.1 How many entries are in a tensor of size $100 \times 80 \times 60$?

Tensors can go beyond third order. If we have a fourth-order tensor, we begin to run out of letters. So, for a fourth-order tensor, we would likely resort to *subscripts* on the sizes and indices. If $\mathcal{X} \in \mathbb{R}^{n_1 \times n_2 \times n_3 \times n_4}$, then $\mathcal{X}$ is a fourth-order tensor. This is difficult to visualize, but we can think of it as an array of third-order tensors or a matrix of matrices. Its entries are indexed as (i_1, i_2, i_3, i_4) or $x_{i_1 i_2 i_3 i_4}$. For a d-way tensor $\mathcal{X}$, its size can be specified as $n_1 \times n_2 \times \cdots \times n_d$, and its entries would be indexed by d-tuples of the form $(i_1, i_2, \ldots, i_d) \in [n_1] \otimes [n_2] \otimes \cdots \otimes [n_d]$. In this case, mode 1 is size n_1, mode 2 is size n_2, and so on. More generally, the size of mode $k \in [d]$ is n_k.

Exercise 1.2 (a) Consider a 3-way tensor of size $512 \times 512 \times 512$. If each entry is a double precision value that requires 8 bytes of memory, how many gigabytes of memory are need for a tensor (note that a gigabyte is 2^{30} bytes). (b) What about a 4-way tensor of size $512 \times 512 \times 512 \times 512$?

We summarize the notation for tensors in Table 1.1. Because of the awkwardness of tensor notation using many levels of subscripts, this book will generally describe things first in terms of 3-way tensors of size $m \times n \times p$ to establish the concepts, and then generalize to d-way tensors of size $n_1 \times n_2 \times \cdots \times n_d$.

1.2 Slices and Hyperslices

A slice of a tensor is a 2-way subtensor, which is a matrix. For a third-order tensor, we can give names to all the different 2-way slices.

Definition 1.3 (Slices of 3-way Tensor) Let $\mathcal{X}$ be a 3-way tensor of size $m \times n \times p$. The ith **horizontal slice** is a matrix of size $n \times p$ given by $\mathcal{X}(i, :, :)$. The jth **lateral slice** is a matrix of size $m \times p$ given by $\mathcal{X}(:, j, :)$. The kth **frontal slice** is a matrix of size $m \times n$ given by $\mathcal{X}(:, :, k)$.

The three types of slices for 3-way tensors are shown in Fig. 1.3. For a tensor of size $m \times n \times p$, the horizontal slices are $\mathcal{X}(i, :, :)$ for all $i \in [m]$ and of size $n \times p$. Likewise, the lateral slices are $\mathcal{X}(:, j, :)$ for all $j \in [n]$ and of size $m \times p$. Finally, the frontal slices are $\mathcal{X}(:, :, k)$ for $k \in [p]$ and of size $m \times n$. The frontal slices can be denoted as $\mathbf{X}_k$ if there is no ambiguity. Tensors are often displayed in terms of their frontal slices.

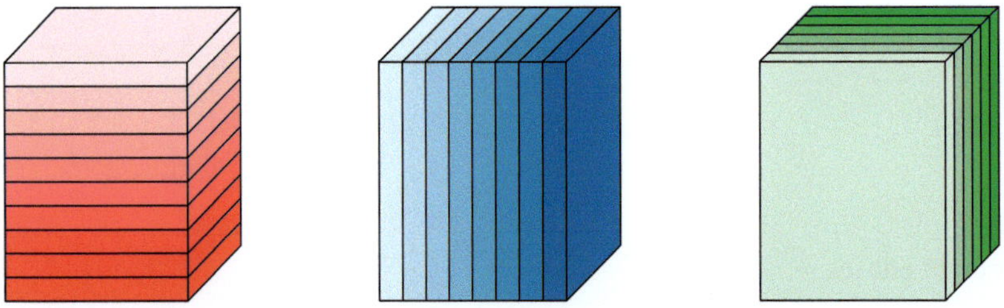

(a) Horizontal slices, $\mathbf{X}(i, :, :)$. (b) Lateral slices, $\mathbf{X}(:, j, :)$. (c) Frontal slices, $\mathbf{X}(:, :, k)$.

Figure 1.3 Two-way slices of $10 \times 8 \times 6$ tensor. Dark colors correspond to *higher* indices.

Example 1.2 (Three-way Tensor Slices) Consider the tensor $\mathcal{X}$ of size $3 \times 3 \times 2$ given by

$\mathcal{X} =$ 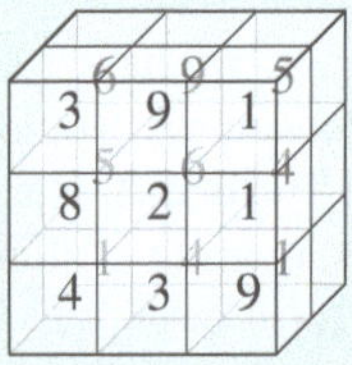

.

Since its third mode is size 2, it has two frontal slices, each of size 3×3, i.e., the size of the first two dimensions. So, we can specify $\mathcal{X}$ by listing its frontal slices:

$$\mathcal{X}(:, :, 1) = \begin{bmatrix} 3 & 9 & 1 \\ 8 & 2 & 1 \\ 4 & 3 & 9 \end{bmatrix} \quad \text{and} \quad \mathcal{X}(:, :, 2) = \begin{bmatrix} 6 & 9 & 5 \\ 5 & 6 & 4 \\ 1 & 4 & 1 \end{bmatrix}.$$

The middle horizontal and last lateral slices are

$$\mathcal{X}(2, :, :) = \begin{bmatrix} 8 & 5 \\ 2 & 6 \\ 1 & 4 \end{bmatrix} \quad \text{and} \quad \mathcal{X}(:, 3, :) = \begin{bmatrix} 1 & 5 \\ 1 & 4 \\ 9 & 1 \end{bmatrix}.$$

Exercise 1.3 For the tensor in Example 1.2: (a) What is $\mathcal{X}(1, :, :)$? (b) What is $\mathcal{X}(3, :, :)$? (c) What is $\mathcal{X}(:, 1, :)$? (d) What is $\mathcal{X}(:, 2, :)$?

Exercise 1.4 For the tensor in Example 1.1, list all the (a) horizontal, (b) lateral, and (c) frontal slices.

We can generalize the concept of frontal slices to a tensor of order d for $d > 3$ as follows: A **frontal slice** of a tensor holds every index fixed except the first two. This is convenient for display because the frontal slices are matrices.

Definition 1.4 (Frontal Slices of d-way Tensor) The frontal slices of a d-way tensor $\mathcal{X}$ of size $n_1 \times n_2 \times \cdots \times n_d$ are given by $\mathcal{X}(:,:,i_3,i_4,\ldots,i_d)$ for all $(i_3,i_4,\ldots,i_d)$ in $[n_3] \times [n_4] \times \cdots \times [n_d]$.

Example 1.3 (Frontal Slices) Consider the 4-way $3 \times 4 \times 3 \times 2$ tensor $\mathcal{Y}$ given by

$\mathcal{Y}(:,:,:,1) =$ 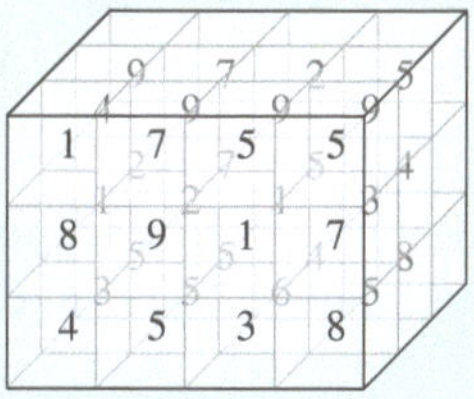

, $\mathcal{Y}(:,:,:,2) =$ 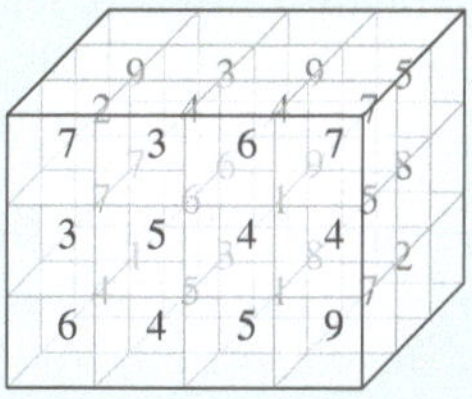

.

The tensor $\mathcal{Y}$ has six frontal slices as follows:

$$\mathcal{Y}(:,:,1,1) = \begin{bmatrix} 1 & 7 & 5 & 5 \\ 8 & 9 & 1 & 7 \\ 4 & 5 & 3 & 8 \end{bmatrix}, \quad \mathcal{Y}(:,:,1,2) = \begin{bmatrix} 7 & 3 & 6 & 7 \\ 3 & 5 & 4 & 4 \\ 6 & 4 & 5 & 9 \end{bmatrix},$$

$$\mathcal{Y}(:,:,2,1) = \begin{bmatrix} 4 & 9 & 9 & 9 \\ 1 & 2 & 1 & 3 \\ 3 & 5 & 6 & 5 \end{bmatrix}, \quad \mathcal{Y}(:,:,2,2) = \begin{bmatrix} 2 & 4 & 4 & 7 \\ 7 & 6 & 1 & 5 \\ 4 & 5 & 1 & 7 \end{bmatrix},$$

$$\mathcal{Y}(:,:,3,1) = \begin{bmatrix} 9 & 7 & 2 & 5 \\ 2 & 7 & 5 & 4 \\ 5 & 5 & 4 & 8 \end{bmatrix}, \quad \mathcal{Y}(:,:,3,2) = \begin{bmatrix} 9 & 3 & 9 & 5 \\ 7 & 6 & 9 & 8 \\ 1 & 3 & 8 & 2 \end{bmatrix}.$$

Exercise 1.5 Only frontal slices are defined for any order. (a) How many frontal slices does a tensor of size $m \times n \times p \times q$ have? (b) How about a tensor of size $n_1 \times n_2 \times \cdots \times n_d$?

More generally, fixing a single index in an arbitrary-order tensor yields a hyperslice. In other words, we define a **hyperslice** to be the subtensor defined by fixing a single index, and we call this a **mode-k hyperslice**. For example, if $\mathcal{X}$ is a 4-way tensor of size $m \times n \times p \times q$, then the mode-2 hyperslices are $\mathcal{X}(:,j,:,:)$ for all $j \in [n]$. For third-order tensors, mode-1 hyperslices are called horizontal, mode-2 hyperslices are called lateral, and mode-3 hyperslices are called frontal. However, we name the mode-k hyperslices only in the 3-way case.

Definition 1.5 (Mode-k Hyperslice) The mode-k hyperslice of a d-way tensor $\mathcal{X}$ of size $n_1 \times n_2 \times \cdots \times n_d$ is a $(d-1)$-way tensor of size $n_1 \times \cdots \times n_{k-1} \times n_{k+1} \times \cdots \times n_d$. The jth mode-k hyperslice is given by $\mathcal{X}(:,\ldots,:,j,:,\ldots,:)$.

Exercise 1.6 Let $\mathcal{Y}$ be the 4-way $3 \times 4 \times 3 \times 2$ tensor in Example 1.3. (a) What is the size of $\mathcal{Y}(1,:,:,:)$? (b) Write out $\mathcal{Y}(1,:,:,\ell)$ for each $\ell \in \{1,2\}$. (c) What is the size of $\mathcal{Y}(:,4,:,:)$? (d) Write out $\mathcal{Y}(:,4,:,\ell)$ for each $\ell \in \{1,2\}$. (e) What is the size of $\mathcal{Y}(:,:,2,:)$? (f) Write out $\mathcal{Y}(:,:,2,\ell)$ for each $\ell \in \{1,2\}$.

1.3 Tensor Fibers

> **Tensor fibers** are the generalization of matrix rows and columns.
> Tensor fibers are always oriented to be column vectors.

Tensor fibers are the analogs of matrix rows and columns. The main difference between matrix rows and columns and tensor fibers is that tensor fibers are always oriented as column vectors when used in calculations. For a 3-way tensor of size $m \times n \times p$, we have the following:

1. The **mode-1 fibers** of length m, also known as **column fibers**, range over all indices in the first mode, holding the second and third indices fixed. In other words, there are np column fibers of the form $\mathbf{x}_{:jk} \in \mathbb{R}^m$.

2. The **mode-2 fibers** of length n, also known as **row fibers**, range over all values in the second mode, holding the first and third indices fixed. In other words, there are mp row fibers of the form $\mathbf{x}_{i:k} \in \mathbb{R}^n$.

3. The **mode-3 fibers** of length p, also known as **tube fibers**, range over all values in the third mode, holding the first and second indices fixed. In other words, there are mn tube fibers of the form $\mathbf{x}_{ij:} \in \mathbb{R}^p$.

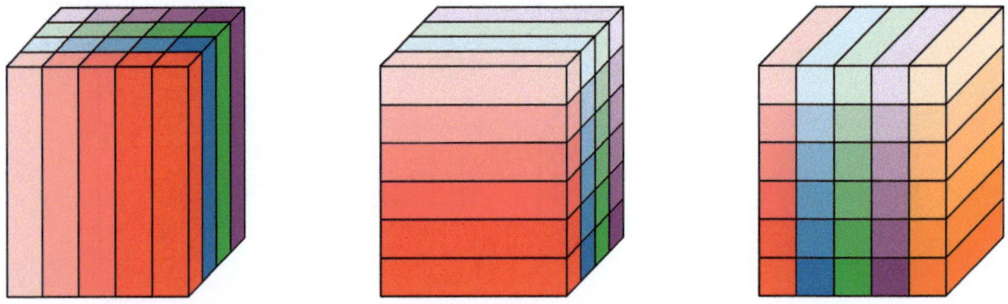

(a) Column fibers, $\mathbf{x}_{:jk}$. (b) Row fibers, $\mathbf{x}_{i:k}$. (c) Tube fibers, $\mathbf{x}_{ij:}$.

Figure 1.4 Fibers of a third-order tensor of size $6 \times 5 \times 4$.

Definition 1.6 (Fibers of a 3-way Tensor) Let $\mathcal{X}$ be a 3-way tensor of size $m \times n \times p$. The **column fibers** are vectors of length m given by $\mathcal{X}(:, j, k)$. The **row fibers** are vectors of length n given by $\mathcal{X}(i, :, k)$. The **tube fibers** are vectors of length p given by $\mathcal{X}(i, j, :)$.

The fibers for a third-order tensor are illustrated in Fig. 1.4. More generally, the mode-1 fibers of a third-order tensor $\mathcal{X}$ of size $m \times n \times p$ are given by

$$\mathbf{x}_{:jk} = \begin{bmatrix} x_{1jk} \\ x_{2jk} \\ \vdots \\ x_{mjk} \end{bmatrix} \in \mathbb{R}^m, \qquad \mathbf{x}_{i:k} = \begin{bmatrix} x_{i1k} \\ x_{i2k} \\ \vdots \\ x_{ink} \end{bmatrix} \in \mathbb{R}^n, \qquad \mathbf{x}_{ij:} = \begin{bmatrix} x_{ij1} \\ x_{ij2} \\ \vdots \\ x_{ijp} \end{bmatrix} \in \mathbb{R}^p.$$

Exercise 1.7 For an $m \times n \times p$ tensor: (a) How many column fibers are there? (b) How many row fibers? (c) How many tube fibers?

Example 1.4 (Three-way Tensor Fibers) Consider the 3-way tensor $\mathcal{X}$ defined in Example 1.2. Example mode-1, mode-2, and mode-3 fibers are, respectively,

$$\mathcal{X}(:,2,2) = \mathbf{x}_{:22} = \begin{bmatrix} 9 \\ 6 \\ 4 \end{bmatrix}, \quad \mathcal{X}(1,:,1) = \mathbf{x}_{1:1} = \begin{bmatrix} 3 \\ 9 \\ 1 \end{bmatrix}, \quad \text{and} \quad \mathcal{X}(3,2,:) = \mathbf{x}_{32:} = \begin{bmatrix} 3 \\ 4 \end{bmatrix}.$$

Exercise 1.8 For the $3 \times 4 \times 2$ tensor $\mathcal{X}$ given below, specify the following fibers: (a) $\mathcal{X}(2,:,2)$, (b) $\mathcal{X}(1,4,:)$, (c) $\mathcal{X}(2,3,:)$, (d) $\mathcal{X}(3,:,1)$, and (e) $\mathcal{X}(:,2,1)$.

$\mathcal{X} =$ 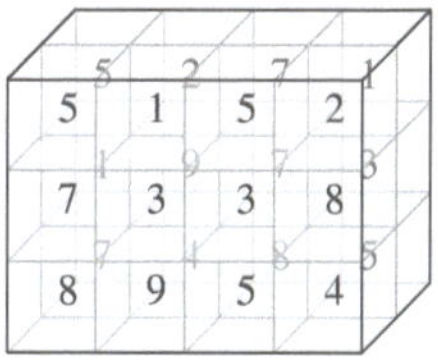

.

For a d-way tensor, a tensor fiber is a vector extracted from a d-way tensor by holding $d-1$ indices fixed. This is analogous to matrix rows and columns. Recall that each column in a matrix ranges over all values in the first dimension, holding the second dimension fixed, while each row in a matrix ranges over all values in the second dimension, holding the first dimension fixed. In general, we say a fiber is a mode-k fiber if all indices are fixed except the kth. For a general d-way tensor $\mathcal{X}$ of size $n_1 \times n_2 \times \cdots \times n_d$, its **mode-$k$ fibers** are vectors of length n_k.

Definition 1.7 (Mode-k Fiber) A **mode-k fiber** of a tensor is a vector produced by holding all indices but the kth fixed.

The concept is straightforward even though the notation is intricate:

$$\mathcal{X}(i_1,\ldots,i_{k-1},:,i_{k+1},\ldots,i_d) = \begin{bmatrix} \mathcal{X}(i_1,\ldots,i_{k-1},\ 1\ ,i_{k+1},\ldots,i_d) \\ \mathcal{X}(i_1,\ldots,i_{k-1},\ 2\ ,i_{k+1},\ldots,i_d) \\ \vdots \\ \mathcal{X}(i_1,\ldots,i_{k-1},n_k,i_{k+1},\ldots,i_d) \end{bmatrix} \in \mathbb{R}^{n_k}.$$

Example 1.5 (Four-way Tensor Fibers) Some example fibers from the 4-way tensor in Example 1.3 are as follows:

$$\text{Mode 1: } \mathcal{Y}(:,2,1,1) = \begin{bmatrix} 7 \\ 9 \\ 5 \end{bmatrix}, \qquad \text{Mode 2: } \mathcal{Y}(3,:,3,1) = \begin{bmatrix} 5 \\ 5 \\ 4 \\ 8 \end{bmatrix},$$

$$\text{Mode 3: } \mathcal{Y}(2,3,:,1) = \begin{bmatrix} 1 \\ 1 \\ 5 \end{bmatrix}, \qquad \text{Mode 4: } \mathcal{Y}(1,2,3,:) = \begin{bmatrix} 7 \\ 3 \end{bmatrix}.$$

Exercise 1.9 Let $\mathcal{Y}$ be the 4-way tensor in Example 1.3. Specify the following fibers: (a) $\mathcal{Y}(:, 1, 3, 2)$, (b) $\mathcal{Y}(1, :, 2, 1)$, (c) $\mathcal{Y}(3, 3, :, 1)$, and (d) $\mathcal{Y}(1, 2, 2, :)$.

Exercise 1.10 For an $m \times n \times p \times q$ tensor: (a) How many mode-1 fibers are there? (b) How many mode-2 fibers? (c) How many mode-3 fibers? (d) How many mode-4 fibers?

Exercise 1.11 For a tensor of size $n_1 \times n_2 \times \cdots \times n_d$, how many mode-$k$ fibers are there?

1.4 Tensor Mode-k Unfolding

The elements of a tensor can be rearranged to form various matrices in a procedure referred to as **unfolding**, also known as **matricization**. A particular unfolding of interest is the mode-k unfolding defined as follows.

Definition 1.8 (Informal Definition of Mode-k Unfolding) The **mode-k unfolding** of a tensor is a matrix whose columns are the mode-k fibers of that tensor, denoted as $\mathbf{X}_{(k)}$.

We defer the precise definitions (which explain how the columns are ordered) until Section 2.3. We illustrate the mode-k unfoldings of a 3-way tensor in Fig. 1.5.

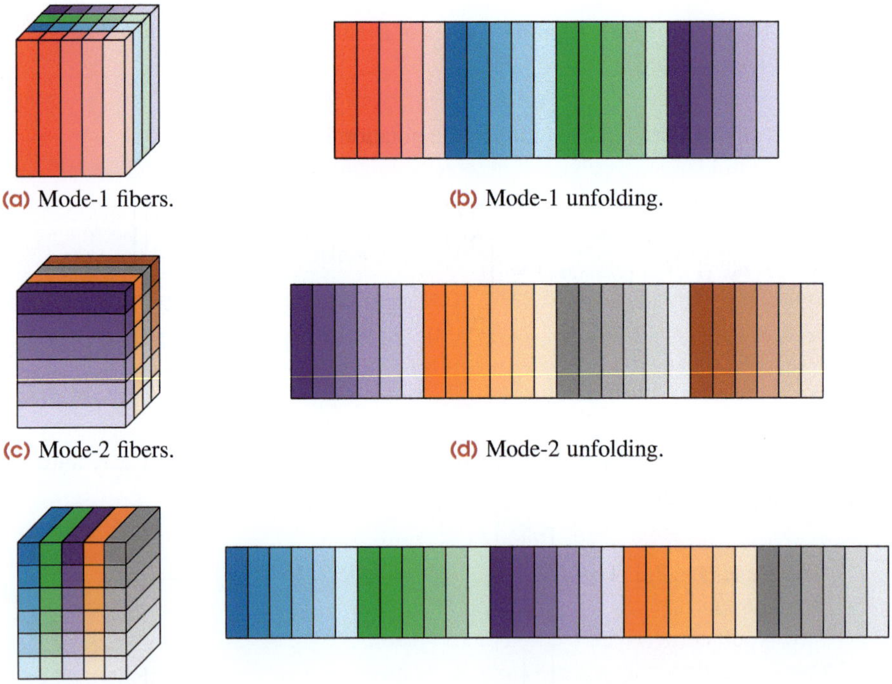

(a) Mode-1 fibers.

(b) Mode-1 unfolding.

(c) Mode-2 fibers.

(d) Mode-2 unfolding.

(e) Mode-3 fibers.

(f) Mode-3 unfolding.

Figure 1.5 Illustration of mode-k unfoldings of a 3-way tensor.

Example 1.6 (Tensor Unfolding) Consider the tensor $\mathcal{X}$ of size $3\times3\times2$ from Example 1.2:

$\mathcal{X} =$ 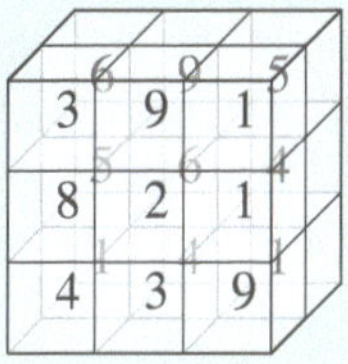

Its mode-1 and mode-2 unfoldings are

$$\mathbf{X}_{(1)} = \begin{bmatrix} 3 & 9 & 1 & 6 & 9 & 5 \\ 8 & 2 & 1 & 5 & 6 & 4 \\ 4 & 3 & 9 & 1 & 4 & 1 \end{bmatrix} \quad \text{and} \quad \mathbf{X}_{(2)} = \begin{bmatrix} 3 & 8 & 4 & 6 & 5 & 1 \\ 9 & 2 & 3 & 9 & 6 & 4 \\ 1 & 1 & 9 & 5 & 4 & 1 \end{bmatrix}.$$

Finally, its mode-3 unfolding is

$$\mathbf{X}_{(3)} = \begin{bmatrix} 3 & 8 & 4 & 9 & 2 & 3 & 1 & 1 & 9 \\ 6 & 5 & 1 & 9 & 6 & 4 & 5 & 4 & 1 \end{bmatrix}.$$

Exercise 1.12 Let $\mathcal{X}$ be a tensor of size $10 \times 8 \times 6$. What is the size of $\mathbf{X}_{(2)}$?

1.5 Example Tensors

We describe several tensors from real-world datasets to help us understand the prevalence of tensor-formatted data. These examples will be used throughout the book. As much as possible, we visualize the data in tensor format so that we can see the connection between the data and its representation as a tensor.

1.5.1 Miranda Scientific Simulation Data

Computational fluid dynamics uses numerical simulations to understand the flow of liquids or gases, with ubiquitous applications ranging from combustion engines to aerodynamics of aircraft wings to weather prediction. Mathematically, the problem can be solved using discretized partial differential equations. Direct numerical simulation is a technique that solves fluid flow problems on a uniform Cartesian grid, stepping through time. The datasets are massive since an $n \times n \times n$ Cartesian grid generates n^3 data for each timestep, resulting in terabytes of data from even modest sized simulations.

***Remark* 1.9** (Tensor versus Cartesian indexing)
Tensors are indexed starting in the front upper left corner, with the first index corresponding to the downward vertical direction, the second index corresponding to the horizontal direction, and the third index corresponding to the backward lateral direction. In contrast, Cartesian coordinates start in the back lower left corner, with the first index corresponding to the lateral direction, the second index corresponding to the horizontal direction, and the third index corresponding to the vertical direction.

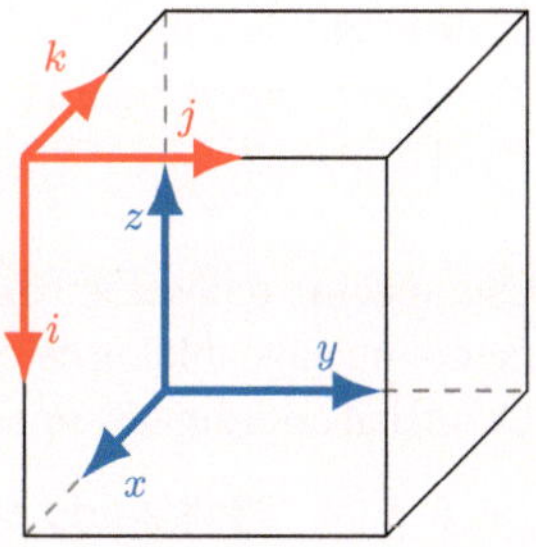

Our data comes originally from Cabot and Cook (2006) via the Scientific Data Reduction Benchmark (SDRBench) of Zhao et al. (2020). The simulation is a Rayleigh–Taylor instability direct numerical simulation of the mixing of two fluids of different densities. The calculation produces density measurements over time on a 3D uniform Cartesian spatial grid of size $3072 \times 3072 \times 3072$. In single precision, the density measurements from a single timestep requires more than 13 GB of storage.

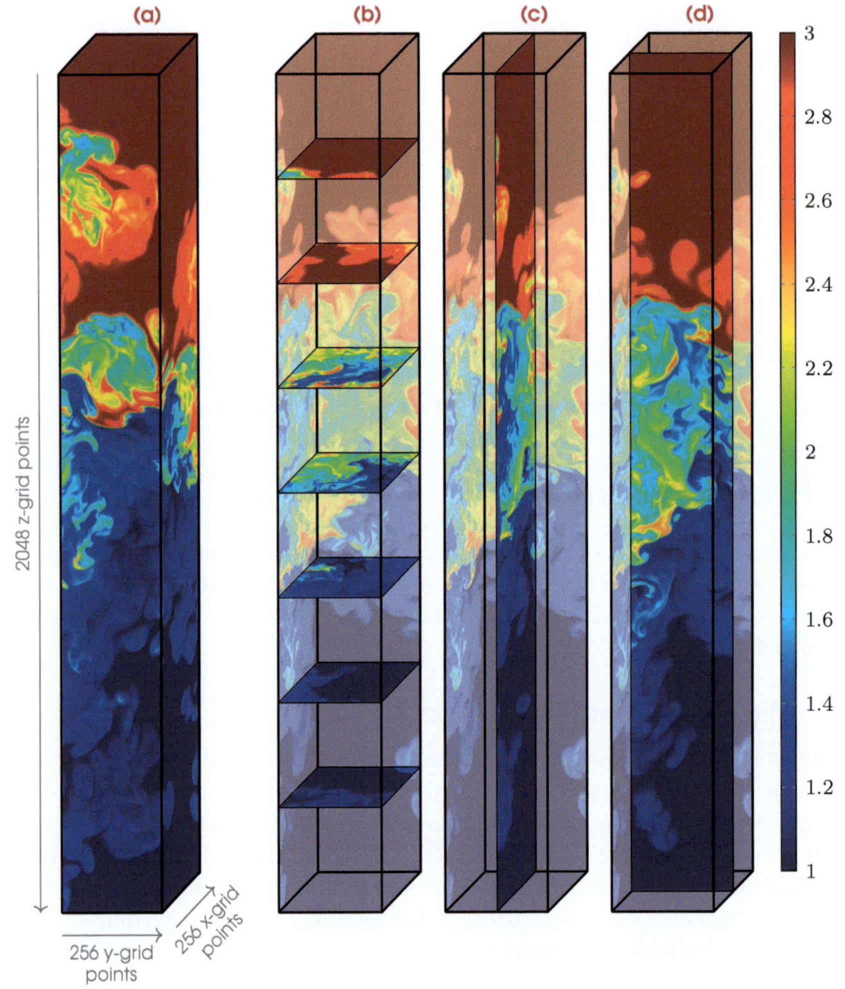

Figure 1.6 Miranda tensor of size $2048 \times 256 \times 256$, capturing the mixing of two fluids of different densities. Color indicates density. (a) Outermost slices: the horizontal slice at $i = 1$, the lateral slice at $j = 256$, and the frontal slice at $k = 1$. (b) Horizontal slices at $i = \{256, 512, \ldots, 1792\}$. (c) Lateral slice at $j = 128$. (d) Frontal slice at $k = 128$.

Our specific dataset is from a single time point and, in order to keep the memory requirements manageable, uses only a subset of the full spatial grid. Additionally, we remap the Cartesian coordinates to tensor coordinates per Remark 1.9. The resulting tensor is of size

$$2048 \text{ z-grid points} \quad \times \quad 256 \text{ y-grid points} \quad \times \quad 256 \text{ x-grid points.}$$

This tensor requires 1 GB of storage in double precision. The data is available for download (approximately 300 MB of lossless compressed storage) at https://gitlab.com/tensors/tensor_data_miranda_sim (Ballard et al., 2022).

> Simulation data on a regular grid can be represented as a tensor.

We visualize the Miranda tensor in Fig. 1.6. The top horizontal slice is purely the high-density fluid (density $= 3$) and the bottom horizontal slice is purely the low-density fluid (density $= 1$), and the mixing happens in between. We show middle slices in each mode.

Exercise 1.13 Using slice notation, what are the 2D matrices being visualized in Fig. 1.6?

1.5.2 EEM Fluorescence Spectroscopy Data

In fluorescence spectroscopy, a chemical sample is excited, and the light that is emitted is measured at several different wavelengths, resulting in an excitation–emission matrix (EEM) of fluorescence intensities. When EEM data is gathered for a number of samples, we obtain a 3-way tensor. This data can be used in analytical chemistry for estimating chemical compound concentrations and spectra from multiple mixtures. It has applications, for example, in environmental modeling. See Smilde et al. (2004, chapter 10.2) for further details.

Our specific EEM example data has been curated from a series of fluorescence spectroscopy experiments as reported by Acar et al. (2014). The data has been preprocessed to fill in missing data and replace negative entries as explained in the `README` file of the data repository. (We revisit the raw data in our discussion of handling missing data in Chapter 14.) All the entries are nonnegative. The data is available for download at https://gitlab.com/tensors/tensor_data_eem (Kolda, 2021a).

The data comprises EEM measurements on 18 samples, each of which is a mixture of three chemical compounds:

- valine–tyrosine–valine (Val-Tyr-Val), a peptide,
- tryptophan–glycine (Trp-Gly), a peptide,
- phenylalanine (Phe), an amino acid.

The intensities are measured at 251 emission wavelengths $(250, 251, \ldots, 500$ nm$)$ and 21 excitation wavelengths $(210, 215, \ldots, 310$ nm$)$. The 18 EEM profiles are shown in Fig. 1.8 as surface plots. The first three samples contain only a single compound, and each compound creates a peak (a bright spot) centered at a different point. (These samples can be removed to make the analysis more interesting.) Samples 4–18 are mixtures of the compounds, so their profiles are, in a sense, weighted combinations of the first three. For instance, the last mixture is a mixture of 3.75 parts Val-Tyr-Val and 5.00 parts Phe, so it can be viewed as a weighted combination of the first and third profiles.

Stacking the emission–excitation intensity profile matrices yields the 3-way EEM tensor of size

$$18 \text{ samples} \quad \times \quad 251 \text{ emissions} \quad \times \quad 21 \text{ excitations}.$$

It is illustrated in Fig. 1.7.

> Each sample produces an emission–excitation matrix, and the EEM data from multiple samples is combined to form the EEM tensor.

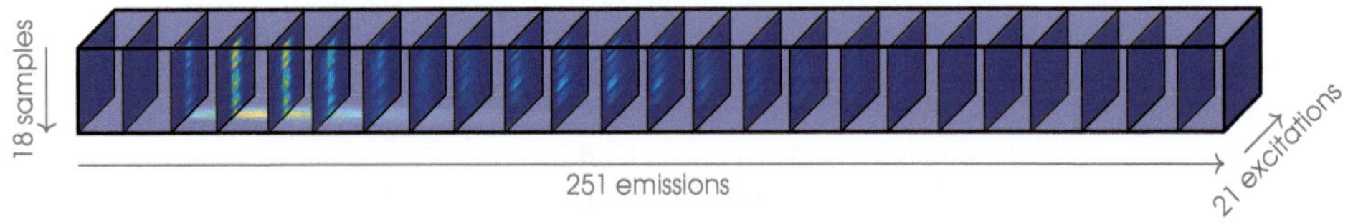

Figure 1.7 EEM tensor of size $18 \times 251 \times 21$, highlighting a selection of lateral slices.

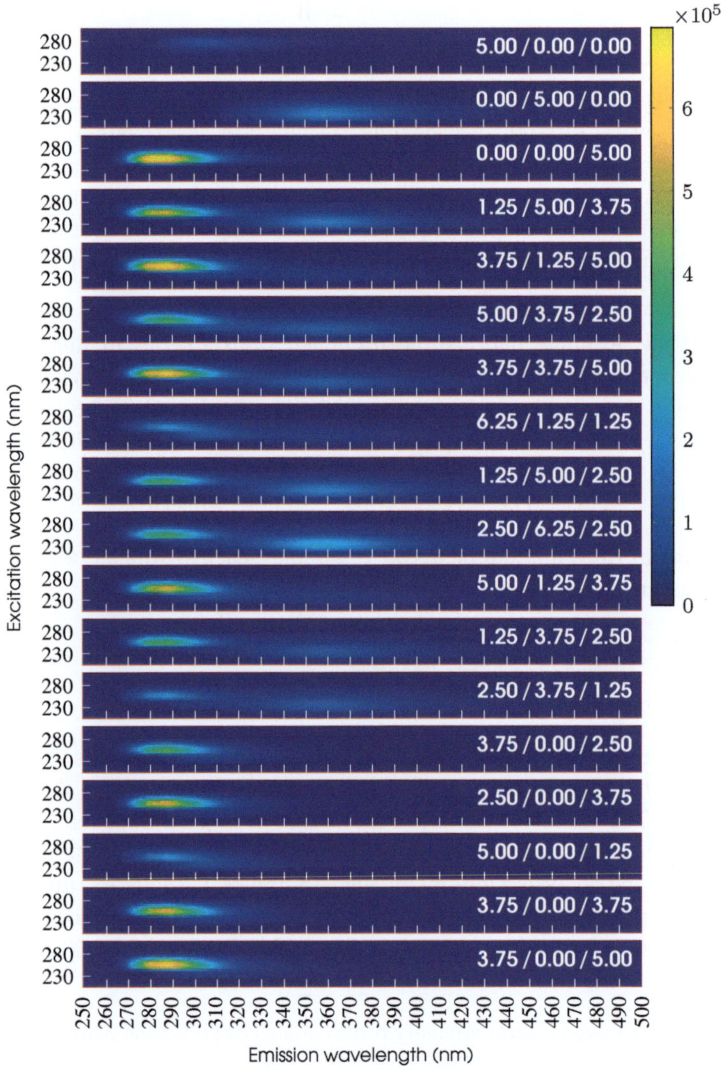

Figure 1.8 Emission–excitation intensity profiles of EEM tensor. The profiles correspond to horizontal slices of the EEM tensor, ordered from top ($\mathcal{X}(1, :, :)$) to bottom ($\mathcal{X}(18, :, :)$). Each profile is labeled at right with concentrations of three chemical compounds (Val-Tyr-Val / Trp-Gly / Phe). Each profile covers 21 excitation wavelengths (210, 215, ..., 310 nm) by 251 emission wavelengths (250, 251, ..., 500 nm).

1.5.3 Monkey BMI Neuronal Spike Data

We consider a dataset of monkey (Rhesus macaque) behavior using a brain–machine interface (BMI) in a series of trials. The monkey BMI tensor data has been curated from a series of experiments as reported in Vyas et al. (2018, 2020) and Williams et al. (2018) and is available for download at `https://gitlab.com/tensors/tensor_data_monkey_bmi` (Kolda, 2022a). In each of 88 experiments, a monkey moves a cursor to one of four targets (at 0, 90, 180, and 270 degrees) and holds it there for 500 ms using a BMI (Fig. 1.9).

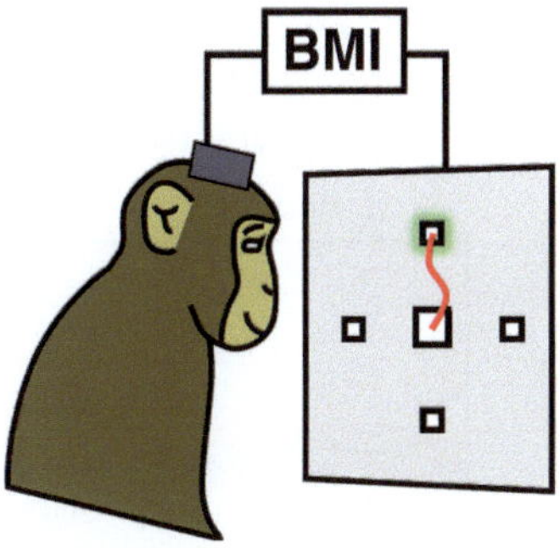

Figure 1.9 The BMI task is to move the cursor from the center to one of four targets.

During this task, neuron spike data is collected. The time per trial varies, but we have standardized every trial to 200 timesteps. Specifically, the data has been time-aligned so that $t = 0$ is the start, $t = 100$ is time of target acquisition, and $t = 200$ is the end after 500 ms of holding the cursor at the target. The data has been additionally preprocessed to smooth the spikes, remove trials for which target acquisition took more than 600 ms, and remove neurons with little to no activity. The neurons are sorted by level of activity, from greatest to least. The resulting tensor is

$$43 \text{ neurons} \quad \times \quad 200 \text{ timesteps} \quad \times \quad 88 \text{ trials}.$$

The tensor is shown in Fig. 1.10.

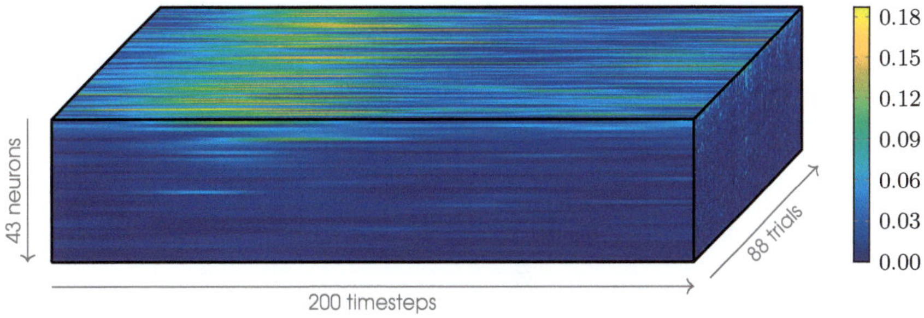

Figure 1.10 Monkey BMI tensor of size $43 \times 200 \times 88$.

The 88 trials are split among the four targets as shown in Table 1.2.

The activities of several neurons across the trials are shown in Fig. 1.11. Each subimage corresponds to a horizontal slice of the tensor, i.e., $\mathcal{X}(i, :, :)$ shows the activities of neuron i. Within each figure, the individual lines correspond to tensor row fibers, i.e., $\mathcal{X}(i, :, k)$ is

Table 1.2 Number of trials for each angle in the monkey BMI tensor

Angle	0	90	180	270
Count	20	28	21	19

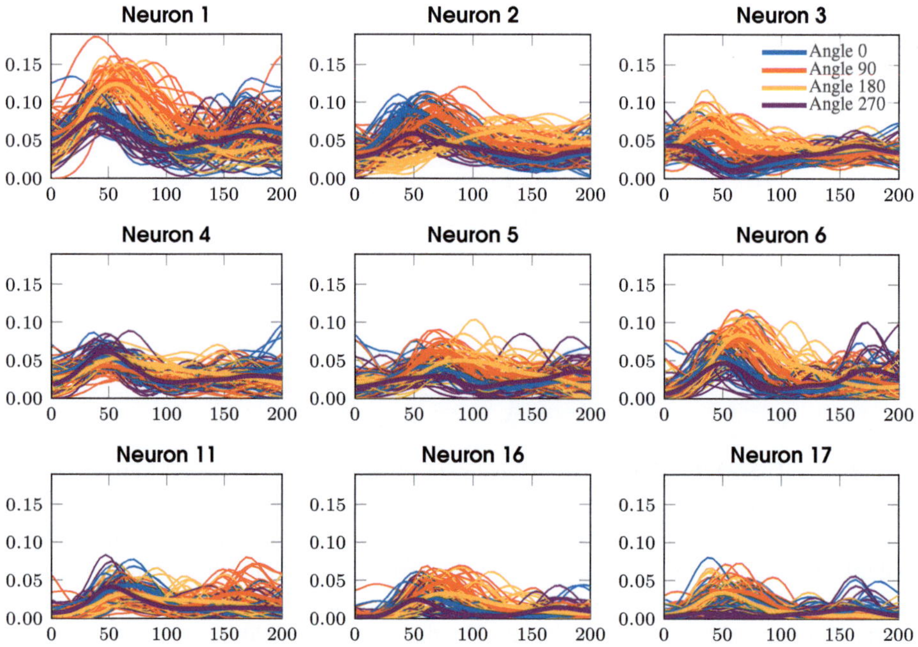

Figure 1.11 Activities of example neurons. For each neuron, thin lines correspond to activity in each of 88 trials, color-coded by the target angle. Thick lines are averages. Times 1–100 are target acquisition, and times 101–200 are holding the cursor at the target.

the activity of neuron i in trial k. The lines are color-coded according to the target. For each target, the average for all trials is shown as a thick line.

> The recording from a single neuron in a single trial is a vector of observations over time; the recordings of all neurons from a single trial forms a matrix; and the collection of all (time-normalized) trials forms the monkey BMI tensor.

Exercise 1.14 Which type of fiber (row, column, or tube) corresponds to the reading of an individual neuron from a single trial?

1.5.4 Chicago Crime Count Data

The Chicago crime data is statistics from public safety criminal activity reports in the city of Chicago. The data is available at www.cityofchicago.org, and we are using a 4-way tensor version corresponding to a single year of data, available at `https://gitlab.com/tensors/tensor_data_chicago_crime` in file `chicago_crime_2019.mat` (Kolda, 2022b).

The tensor modes correspond to 365 days (January 1 through December 31, 2019), 24

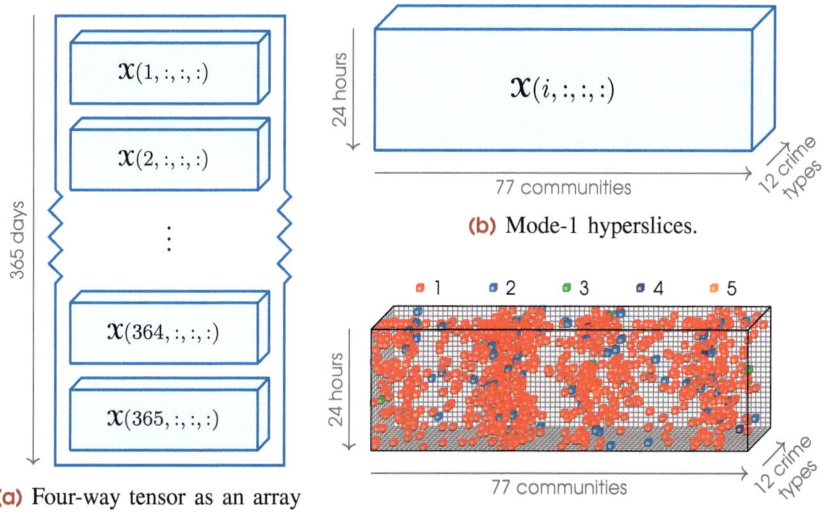

(a) Four-way tensor as an array of 3-way tensors.

(b) Mode-1 hyperslices.

(c) Sparsity pattern of $\mathcal{X}(1,:,:,:)$.

Figure 1.12 Chicago crime tensor of size $365 \times 24 \times 77 \times 12$.

hours, 77 communities, and 11 crime types. Entry $\mathcal{X}(i,j,k,\ell)$ is the number of times that crime ℓ happened in neighborhood k during hour j on day i. Hence, the tensor is formatted as

$$365 \text{ days} \quad \times \quad 24 \text{ hours} \quad \times \quad 77 \text{ communities} \quad \times \quad 12 \text{ crime-types}.$$

We have treated time as two-dimensional, splitting hours and days into two modes in order to expose daily patterns in addition to longer-term trends. We can visualize the 4-way tensor as an array of 3-way tensors as in Fig. 1.12a, and each 3-way subtensor is formatted as in Fig. 1.12b.

> Time can be multidimensional. For example, hourly data can be divided further into days, weeks, etc.

The tensor is **sparse** because it has only 230,591 nonzeros out of 8,094,240 entries; that is, only 2.85% of its entries are nonzero. Storing $\mathcal{X}$ as a sparse tensor (i.e., storing each nonzero and 4-tuple index) requires less than 15% of the storage of the dense tensor. To visualize the sparsity, consider the first mode-1 hyperslice, $\mathcal{X}(1,:,:,:)$, pictured in Fig. 1.12c. It has only 861 nonzeros out of 22,176 entries.

We compute some statistics on the Chicago crime tensor. The number of crime reports per day are shown in Fig. 1.13a. Crime reports are highest overall in the summer months, with a peak during August 1–4, which so happens to correspond to the Lollapalooza 2019 festival in Grant Park. The day with the most reports overall is January 1, 2019, keeping in mind that various factors affect the date of a crime report and the first of the year is presumably a popular day to choose when the exact date is uncertain.

Figure 1.13b shows the cumulative crimes per hour, with hour 0 corresponding to midnight to 12:59 a.m., and hour 23 corresponding to 11:00–11:59 p.m.. Crime reports are lowest in the hours 1:00–7:00 a.m. and peak at noon.

Totals crime reports per type are listed in Fig. 1.13c. The preprocessing of the data removed

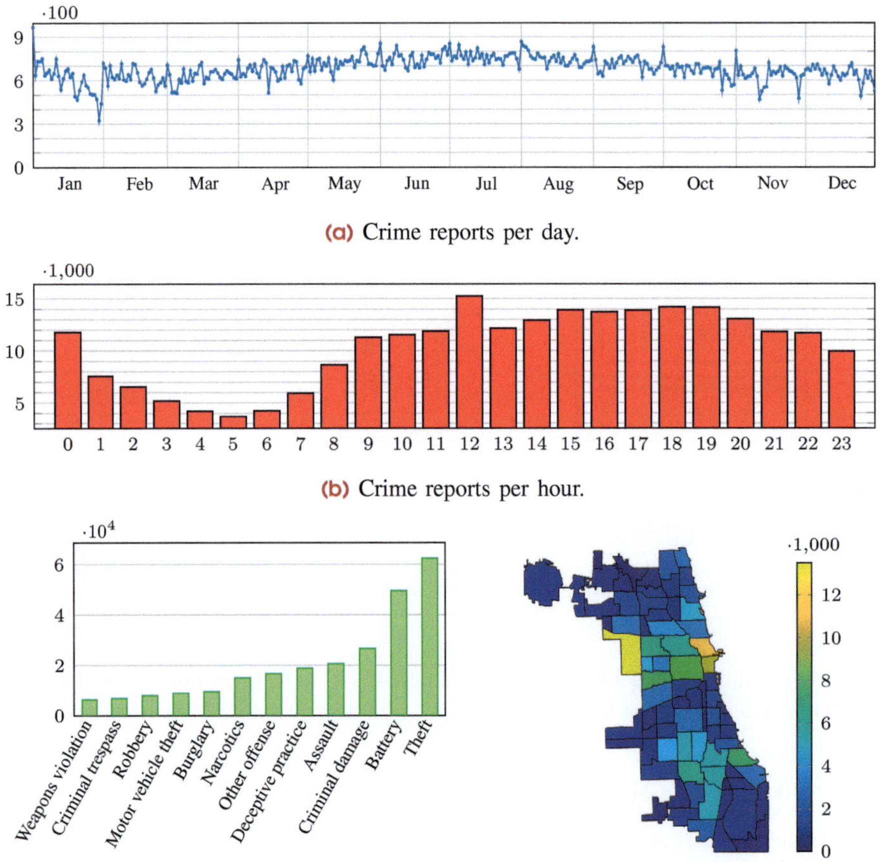

(a) Crime reports per day.

(b) Crime reports per hour.

(c) Crime reports by type. **(d)** Crime reports by neighborhood.

Figure 1.13 Chicago crime report counts from January 1, 2019 to December 31, 2019.

any crimes that occurred fewer than 5000 times in the time period of the data. The crimes are in order of overall prevalence, with theft corresponding to index 1, battery to index 2, and so on down to weapons violation corresponding to index 12.

A heatmap of the total crime frequency (over all crime types) per community is shown in Fig. 1.13d. This is not normalized by population. The majority of reports come from the community area known as Austin in the West Side region of Chicago.

Exercise 1.15 Load the tensor data and recreate Figs. 1.13a and 1.13b.

1.6 A First Look at Tensor Decompositions

The goal of this book is to learn how to **decompose** tensors into representations that might be smaller, more expressive, or some combination of these ideals. Like matrix decompositions, we seek a set of matrices/tensors that can be multiplied together appropriately to reconstruct the input. Unlike matrix decompositions, tensor decompositions are rarely exact representations and instead only approximations of the input. Most tensor decompositions can be viewed as generalizations of low-rank matrix approximations to higher-order data. We focus on two types of decompositions, Tucker and CP; we more briefly discuss other decompositions in Chapters 8 and 17.

1.6.1 A First Look at Tucker Decomposition

A **Tucker decomposition** *compresses* a tensor by decomposing into a smaller **core tensor** multiplied by a matrix in each mode.

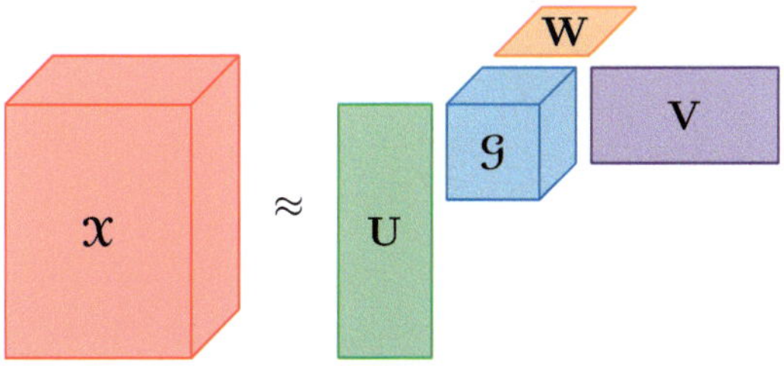

Figure 1.14 Tucker decomposition.

We visualize the 3-way case as in Fig. 1.14. Here $\mathcal{X}$ is the original 3-way tensor, $\mathcal{G}$ is the core 3-way tensor, and the matrices $\mathbf{U}$, $\mathbf{V}$, $\mathbf{W}$ are the matrices that are multiplied with $\mathcal{G}$ to approximate $\mathcal{X}$. The tensor $\mathcal{G}$ can be interpreted as a compressed version of $\mathcal{X}$, and the matrices $\mathbf{U}$, $\mathbf{V}$, $\mathbf{W}$ are bases for the subspaces onto which $\mathcal{X}$ is projected for compression.

In Tucker, it is possible to choose the size of the compressed tensor to ensure that the approximation error is below a user-specified error threshold. The challenge in the Tucker decomposition is identifying the optimal subspaces for compression.

1.6.2 A First Look at CP Decomposition

A **CP decomposition** expresses a tensor as a sum of vector outer products. The summands are called **components**. The vectors in the components are used for *interpretation*.

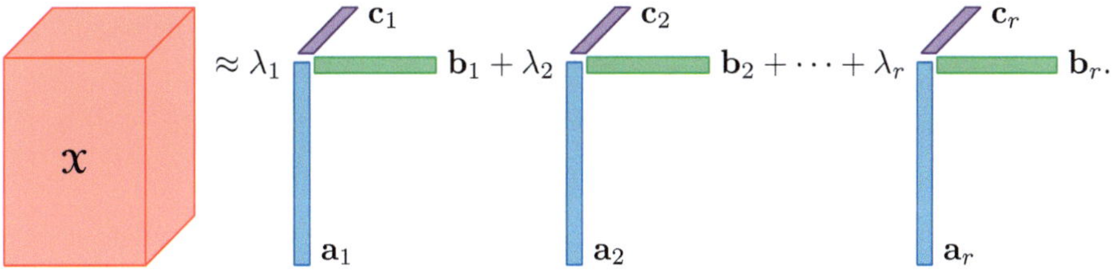

Figure 1.15 CP decomposition.

We visualize the 3-way CP decomposition in Fig. 1.15. Each component is the outer product of three vectors. The vectors constituting the components are usually explanatory as to the nature of the component.

In comparison to Tucker, CP decomposition is often viewed as more useful for interpretation. The challenges in CP decomposition are choosing an appropriate number of components and computing the optimal solution.

2 Indexing and Reshaping Tensors

Analyzing and computing with tensors involves repeatedly rearranging and reshaping the elements. To accomplish these tasks, we first need to understand how to map a **tuple index** of the form $(i, j, k) \in [m] \otimes [n] \otimes [p]$ to an equivalent **linear index** of the form $\ell \in [mnp]$. To do this, we show how to define a one-to-one and onto operator

$$\mathbb{L} : [m] \otimes [n] \otimes [p] \to [mnp]$$

that converts from a tuple to a linear index, along with its inverse

$$\mathbb{T} : [mnp] \to [m] \otimes [n] \otimes [p]$$

that maps a linear index back to a tuple. We explain the choices for these mappings and how they may be used in Section 2.1. With these operators for converting between tuple and linear indices, we are equipped to rearrange the elements of a tensor into useful vectors (Section 2.2) and matrices (Section 2.3). As certain matrix unfolding operations require a rearrangement of terms within the tensor, we further show how to permute a tensor and connect this with its vectorization via a tensor perfect shuffle operation in Section 2.4. Indexing and reshaping tensors are fundamental tools in tensor computations, and this chapter provides a detailed treatment of this topic.

2.1 Linear Indexing

A 3-way tensor $\mathcal{X} \in \mathbb{R}^{m \times n \times p}$ indexes its elements via a 3-tuple of the form $(i, j, k) \in [m] \otimes [n] \otimes [p]$. An alternative is **linear indexing**, whereby each element has an index $\ell \in [mnp]$.

For concreteness, consider a $2 \times 2 \times 2$ tensor with eight entries. The idea of linear indexing is to map every entry uniquely to a number in the range $\{ 1, 2, \ldots, 8 \}$. There are $8! = 40{,}320$ possible mappings in the $2 \times 2 \times 2$ case. However, not all these mappings are equally useful.

One desirable feature of a linear index is for certain fibers and slices to remain contiguous in the ordering. We can pick one mode's fibers to be contiguous, then the next, and so on. The result is that one set of slices will be contiguous in either column- or row-major order. For contiguous orders, the linearization function is based on mode **strides**, which means that the mapping from (i, j, k) to a linear index ℓ is of the form

$$\ell = 1 + s_1(i-1) + s_2(j-1) + s_3(k-1),$$

where s_1, s_2, and s_3 are the strides. Then the problem reduces to choosing the modes for contiguous fibers and slices. For the $2 \times 2 \times 2$ case, there are $3! = 6$ assignments of linear indices to the elements, as shown in Fig. 2.1. We refer to choice (a) as the **natural**

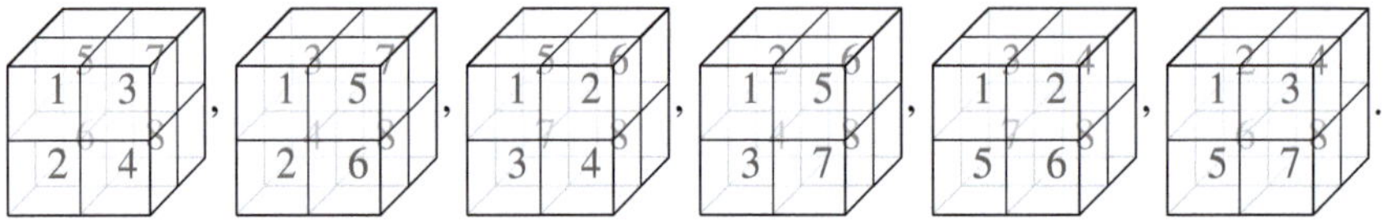

Figure 2.1 Six possible orderings of elements of a $2 \times 2 \times 2$ tensor.

ordering, which corresponds to the strides $s_1 = 1, s_2 = 2, s_3 = 4$, and by default use the natural ordering for linear indexing. Given an ordering, we can then refer to indices by their linear index $\ell \in [8]$ rather than a 3-tuple $(i, j, k) \in [2] \otimes [2] \otimes [2]$. This extends to d-way tensors as well.

> The **tuple** $(i, j, k) \in [m] \otimes [n] \otimes [p]$ is equivalent to its corresponding **linear index** $\ell = \mathbb{L}(i, j, k) \in [mnp]$.

The natural ordering shown in Fig. 2.1a corresponds to having the shortest stride in mode 1, the next shortest in mode 2, and so on, and is discussed in Section 2.1.1. A few special situations require other orderings. The **reverse ordering**, shown in Fig. 2.1f, corresponds to having the longest stride in mode 1, the next longest in mode 2, and so on, and is discussed in Section 2.1.2. Both the natural and reverse orderings are special cases of **general orderings** shown in Figs. 2.1a–2.1f and discussed in Section 2.1.3. Every ordering keeps different fibers and slices in order. For instance, Fig. 2.1b shows an ordering where the lateral slices are stored in column-major order, and Fig. 2.1c shows the frontal slices in row-major order.

Exercise 2.1 List the strides s_1, s_2, and s_3 for each of the six orderings in Fig. 2.1.

Although we focus here on stride-based linear indexing, there are many other options, such as blocked orderings. Any one-to-one and onto mapping $\mathbb{L}$ from tuple to linear index that can be efficiently described with $\mathcal{O}(d)$ parameters is potentially reasonable.

2.1.1 Natural Order Linear Indexing

Natural Ordering for 3-way Tensors

Consider a tensor of size $m \times n \times p$. We define the natural ordering to give the shortest strides to mode-1 fibers, the next shortest stride to mode-2 fibers, and the longest stride to mode-3 fibers. Specifically, the strides for each mode are

$$s_1 = 1, \quad s_2 = m, \quad \text{and} \quad s_3 = mn.$$

The **linear index** ℓ corresponding to (i, j, k) can then be computed as

$$\mathbb{L}(i, j, k) = 1 + s_1(i-1) + s_2(j-1) + s_3(k-1) = i + m(j-1) + mn(k-1). \tag{2.1}$$

This mapping is one-to-one and onto, which means that it can be inverted. The **tuple index** (i, j, k) can be computed from $\ell \in [mnp]$ as $(i, j, k) = \mathbb{T}(\ell)$, where

$$i = \mathbb{T}_1(\ell) = 1 + \lfloor((\ell - 1) \bmod ms_1)/s_1\rfloor = 1 + (\ell - 1) \bmod m, \tag{2.2a}$$
$$j = \mathbb{T}_2(\ell) = 1 + \lfloor((\ell - 1) \bmod ns_2)/s_2\rfloor = 1 + \lfloor((\ell - 1) \bmod nm)/m\rfloor, \tag{2.2b}$$
$$k = \mathbb{T}_3(\ell) = 1 + \lfloor((\ell - 1) \bmod ps_3)/s_3\rfloor = 1 + \lfloor(\ell - 1)/mn\rfloor. \tag{2.2c}$$

In Eqs. (2.2a)–(2.2c), $\lfloor x \rfloor$ is the *floor* operation, which means round x down to the nearest integer, and $x \bmod y$ means take the remainder of dividing x by y. The mod disappears in the equation for k because $\ell - 1 \leq ps_3 = mnp$.

The natural ordering corresponds to having the shortest stride in mode 1, the next shortest in mode 2, and so on.

Example 2.1 (Linear Indices with Natural Ordering) For a tensor of size $4 \times 3 \times 3$, the stride of the linear indices in the mode-1 direction (top-to-bottom) is $s_1 = 1$, the stride in the mode-2 direction (left-to-right) is $s_2 = m = 4$, and the stride in the mode-2 direction (front-to-back) is $s_3 = mn = 12$.

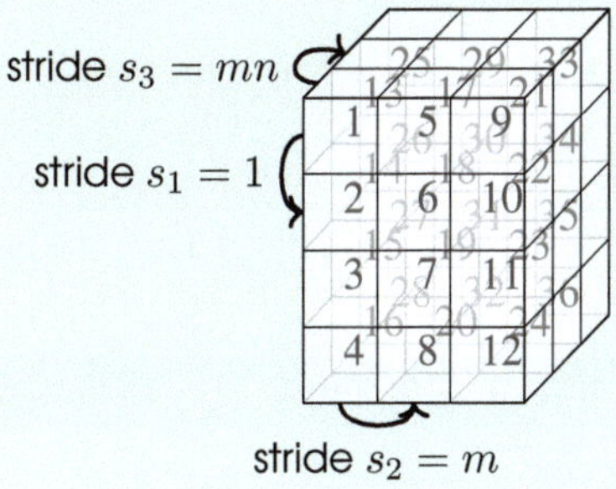

Using the strides, we can convert between tuples and linear indices.

For instance, given the tuple $(i, j, k) = (2, 1, 2)$, we can compute that $\mathbb{L}(2, 1, 2) = 2 + 0(4) + 1(12) = 14$.

Conversely, given linear index $\ell = 32$, we can compute $(i, j, k) = \mathbb{T}(\ell)$ via $i = 1 + (31 \bmod 4) = 4$, $j = 1 + \lfloor(31 \bmod 12)/4\rfloor = 2$, and $k = 1 + \lfloor 31/12 \rfloor = 3$.

Exercise 2.2 For a tensor of size $4 \times 3 \times 3$, list the linear indices of the following tuple indices: (a) $(3, 2, 3)$, (b) $(4, 3, 1)$, and (c) $(2, 2, 2)$. List the tuple indices for the following linear indices: (d) 16, (e) 7, and (f) 34.

Exercise 2.3 For a tensor of size $100 \times 80 \times 60$, list the linear indices of the following tuple indices: (a) $(70, 26, 58)$, (b) $(4, 36, 23)$, and (c) $(77, 64, 12)$. List the tuple indices for the following linear indices: (d) 235,087, (e) 213,882, and (f) 310,231.

It is possible to compose the linearization operation, as we show in the following proposition. In this proposition, we write $\mathbb{L}(i, j, k; m, n, p)$ to make the ambient sizes explicit. Further, the linear and tuple mappings can be defined for 2-tuples (the same formulas work with $p = 1$).

Proposition 2.1 (Composition of Linearization for 3-way) *Consider the conversion operators* $\mathbb{L}$ *and* $\mathbb{T}$ *defined in Eqs.* (2.1) *and* (2.2)*, respectively. If* $\hat{\ell} = \mathbb{L}(i, j; m, n)$ *and* $\ell = \mathbb{L}(\hat{\ell}, k; mn, p)$*, then* $\ell = \mathbb{L}(i, j, k; m, n, p)$ *and* $(i, j, k) = \mathbb{T}(\ell; m, n, p)$.

Proof. Assume $\hat{\ell} = \mathbb{L}(i, j; m, n)$ and $\ell = \mathbb{L}(\hat{\ell}, k; \hat{n}, p)$ for $\hat{n} = mn$. Then the linearization equivalence follows from

$$\ell = \hat{\ell} + mn(k-1) = i + m(j-1) + mn(k-1) = \mathbb{L}(i, j, k; m, n, p).$$

Conversely, converting from the linear indices $\hat{\ell}$ and ℓ to the tuples (i, j) and $(\hat{\ell}, k)$, respectively, yields

$$\begin{aligned} &\text{from } \hat{\ell}: \quad && i = 1 + (\hat{\ell} - 1) \bmod m, \quad && j = 1 + \lfloor (\hat{\ell} - 1)/m \rfloor, \text{ and} \\ &\text{from } \ell: \quad && \hat{\ell} = 1 + (\ell - 1) \bmod \hat{n}, \quad && k = 1 + \lfloor (\ell - 1)/\hat{n} \rfloor. \end{aligned}$$

We can combine these to see

$$\begin{aligned} i &= 1 + ((\ell - 1) \bmod mn) \bmod m = 1 + (\ell - 1) \bmod m, \\ j &= 1 + (\lfloor (\ell - 1) \bmod mn \rfloor / m), \text{ and} \\ k &= 1 + \lfloor (\ell - 1)/mn \rfloor. \end{aligned}$$

The simplification with respect to i comes from properties of modular arithmetic. Hence $(i, j, k) = \mathbb{T}(\ell; m, n, p)$. □

Exercise 2.4 Prove that if $\ell = \mathbb{L}(i, \mathbb{L}(j, k; n, p); m, np)$, then $\ell = \mathbb{L}(i, j, k; m, n, p)$.

Natural Ordering for d-way Tensors

For a general d-way tensor, the conversion between linear and tuple indices using the natural ordering is given as follows.

Definition 2.2: Linear/Tuple Index Conversion for Natural Ordering

The **strides** for the **natural ordering** are

$$s_1 = 1 \quad \text{and} \quad s_{k+1} = \prod_{\alpha=1}^{k} n_\alpha = s_k n_k \text{ for } k \in [d-1]. \tag{2.3a}$$

The **linear index** of the tuple $(i_1, i_2, \ldots, i_d) \in [n_1] \otimes [n_2] \otimes \cdots \otimes [n_d]$ is

$$\alpha = \mathbb{L}(i_1, i_2, \ldots, i_d) = 1 + \sum_{k=1}^{d} s_k(i_k - 1). \tag{2.3b}$$

The **tuple index** of $\alpha \in [N]$ with $N = \prod_{k=1}^{d} n_k$ is $(i_1, i_2, \ldots, i_d) = \mathbb{T}(\alpha)$, where

$$i_k = \mathbb{T}_k(i) = 1 + \Big\lfloor ((\alpha - 1) \bmod (n_k s_k))/s_k \Big\rfloor. \tag{2.3c}$$

The mappings $\mathbb{L}$ and $\mathbb{T}$ depend on the mode sizes, which we assume are generally clear by context. If not, the ambient dimensions can be made explicit as

$$\mathbb{L}(i_1, \ldots, i_d; n_1, \ldots, n_d) \quad \text{and} \quad \mathbb{T}(\alpha; n_1, \ldots, n_d).$$

Exercise 2.5 For a tensor of size $5 \times 4 \times 3 \times 4$, what are the strides (s_1, s_2, s_3, s_4) for the natural ordering?

Exercise 2.6 Write general d-way functions `lin2tup` and `tup2lin` to convert between linear and tuple indices and vice versa.

The composition property (Proposition 2.1) can be generalized to the d-way case as follows.

Proposition 2.3 (Composition of Linearization) *If we have two linear indices representing tuples from different domains as*

$$\alpha = \mathbb{L}(i_1, \ldots, i_{d'}; m_1, \ldots, m_{d'}) \quad \text{and} \quad \beta = \mathbb{L}(j_1, \ldots, j_d; n_1, \ldots, n_d),$$

then their linearization is equivalent to linearizing the original indices:

$$\mathbb{L}(\alpha, \beta; M, N) = \mathbb{L}(i_1, \ldots, i_{d'}, j_1, \ldots, j_d; m_1, \ldots, m_{d'}, n_1, \ldots, n_d),$$

where $M = \prod_{k=1}^{d'} m_k$ *and* $N = \prod_{k=1}^{d} n_k$.

Exercise 2.7 Prove Proposition 2.3. Hint: Use induction.

2.1.2 Reverse Ordering Linear Indexing

Reverse Ordering for 3-way Tensors

Consider a tensor of size $m \times n \times p$. We define the reverse ordering to be the opposite of the natural ordering giving the shortest strides to mode-3 fibers, the next shortest stride to mode-2 fibers, and the longest stride to mode-1 fibers. For the $2 \times 2 \times 2$ tensor, the reverse ordering corresponds to the ordering shown in Fig. 2.1f. Specifically, the strides for each mode are

$$s_1^* = np, \quad s_2^* = p, \quad \text{and} \quad s_3^* = 1.$$

The linear index $\ell = \mathbb{L}^*(i, j, k)$ corresponding to (i, j, k) in the reverse ordering can then be computed as

$$\mathbb{L}^*(i, j, k) = 1 + s_1^*(i-1) + s_2^*(j-1) + s_3^*(k-1) = np(i-1) + p(j-1) + k. \quad (2.4)$$

Here the asterisk denotes the reverse strides. This mapping is also one-to-one and onto, which means that it can be inverted. The tuple (i, j, k) can be computed from $\ell \in [mnp]$ as $(i, j, k) = \mathbb{T}^*(\ell)$, where

$$\begin{aligned}
i &= \mathbb{T}_1^*(\ell) = 1 + \lfloor ((\ell-1) \bmod m s_1^*)/s_1^* \rfloor = 1 + \lfloor (\ell-1)/np \rfloor, \\
j &= \mathbb{T}_2^*(\ell) = 1 + \lfloor ((\ell-1) \bmod n s_2^*)/s_2^* \rfloor = 1 + \lfloor ((\ell-1) \bmod np)/p \rfloor, \\
k &= \mathbb{T}_3^*(\ell) = 1 + \lfloor ((\ell-1) \bmod p s_3^*)/s_3^* \rfloor = 1 + (\ell-1) \bmod p.
\end{aligned}$$

The reverse ordering corresponds to having the longest stride in mode 1, the next longest in mode 2, and so on.

Exercise 2.8 Let $\ell = \mathbb{L}^*(i, j, k; m, n, p)$. Show $\ell = \mathbb{L}(k, j, i; p, n, m)$.

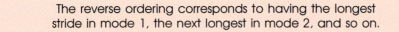

Example 2.2 (Linear Indices with Reverse Ordering) For a tensor of size $4 \times 3 \times 3$, the linear indices from the reverse ordering are as follows:

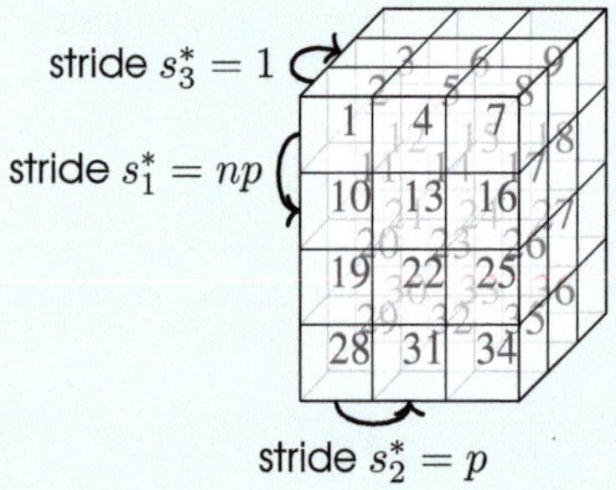

The strides are $s_1^* = 9$, $s_2^* = 3$, and $s_3^* = 1$.

For instance, given the tuple $(i, j, k) = (2, 1, 2)$, we can compute that $\mathbb{L}^*(2, 1, 2) = 1(9) + 0(3) + 2 = 11$.

Conversely, given linear index $\ell = 32$, we can compute $(i, j, k) = \mathbb{T}^*(\ell)$ via $i = 1 + \lfloor 31/9 \rfloor = 4$, $j = 1 + \lfloor (31 \bmod 9)/3 \rfloor = 2$, and $k = 1 + (31 \bmod 3) = 2$.

Example 2.3 (Comparison of Natural and Reverse Linear Indices) Consider the domain $4 \times 3 \times 2$. The linear indices corresponding to the natural and reverse orderings are as follows:

Tuple	$\mathbb{L}$	$\mathbb{L}^*$	Tuple	$\mathbb{L}$	$\mathbb{L}^*$	Tuple	$\mathbb{L}$	$\mathbb{L}^*$	Tuple	$\mathbb{L}$	$\mathbb{L}^*$
(1,1,1)	1	1	(2,1,1)	2	7	(3,1,1)	3	13	(4,1,1)	4	19
(1,2,1)	5	3	(2,2,1)	6	9	(3,2,1)	7	15	(4,2,1)	8	21
(1,3,1)	9	5	(2,3,1)	10	11	(3,3,1)	11	17	(4,3,1)	12	23
(1,1,2)	13	2	(2,1,2)	14	8	(3,1,2)	15	14	(4,1,2)	16	20
(1,2,2)	17	4	(2,2,2)	18	10	(3,2,2)	19	16	(4,2,2)	20	22
(1,3,2)	21	6	(2,3,2)	22	12	(3,3,2)	23	18	(4,3,2)	24	24

Reverse indexing is useful for Kronecker products. Recall the definition of the Kronecker product of two vectors from Definition A.20: for vectors $\mathbf{a} \in \mathbb{R}^m, \mathbf{b} \in \mathbb{R}^n$, the reverse linear index is exactly the index into the Kronecker product:

$$\mathbf{v} = \mathbf{a} \otimes \mathbf{b} \in \mathbb{R}^{mn} \quad \Leftrightarrow \quad v_\ell = a_i b_j, \text{ where } \ell = \mathbb{L}^*(i, j) = n(i-1) + j.$$

We generalize this to 3-way vector Kronecker products in Proposition 2.4.

Proposition 2.4 (Vector Kronecker Products and Reverse Linear Indexing) *Let* $\mathbf{a} \in \mathbb{R}^m$, $\mathbf{b} \in \mathbb{R}^n$, *and* $\mathbf{c} \in \mathbb{R}^p$, *and define* $\mathbf{v} = \mathbf{a} \otimes \mathbf{b} \otimes \mathbf{c} \in \mathbb{R}^{mnp}$. *Then* $v_\ell = a_i b_j c_k$, *where* $\ell = \mathbb{L}^*(i, j, k)$ *or* $(i, j, k) = \mathbb{T}^*(\ell)$.

Proof. Define $\mathbf{u} = \mathbf{a} \otimes \mathbf{b}$. By definition, $u_{\hat{\ell}} = a_i b_j$, where $\hat{\ell} = \mathbb{L}^*(i, j) = n(i-1) + j$ for all $\hat{\ell} \in [mn]$. Since the Kronecker product is associative, we have $\mathbf{v} = \mathbf{a} \otimes \mathbf{b} \otimes \mathbf{c} = \mathbf{u} \otimes \mathbf{c}$. By definition, $v_\ell = u_{\hat{\ell}} c_k$, where $\ell = \mathbb{L}^*(\hat{\ell}, k) = p(\hat{\ell} - 1) + k$. Expanding $u_{\hat{\ell}}$ and $\hat{\ell}$, we have $v_\ell = a_i b_j c_k$, where $\ell = p\big(n(i-1) + j - 1\big) + k = pn(i-1) + p(j-1) + k = \mathbb{L}^*(i, j, k)$. Hence, the claim. □

This idea extends directly to the 3-way Khatri–Rao product (see Definition A.21), as shown in Proposition 2.5.

Proposition 2.5 (Khatri–Rao Products and Reverse Linear Indexing) *Let* $\mathbf{A} \in \mathbb{R}^{m\times r}$, $\mathbf{B} \in \mathbb{R}^{n\times r}$, *and* $\mathbf{C} \in \mathbb{R}^{p\times r}$. *Consider their Khatri–Rao product, denoted by*

$$\mathbf{V} = \mathbf{A} \odot \mathbf{B} \odot \mathbf{C}.$$

Then, for all $(i, j, k, \ell) \in [m] \otimes [n] \otimes [p] \otimes [r]$, *we have*

$$v_{\alpha\ell} = a_{i\ell} b_{j\ell} c_{k\ell}, \quad \text{where} \quad \alpha = \mathbb{L}^*(i, j, k).$$

Exercise 2.9 Prove Proposition 2.5.

We can also consider the more general matrix Kronecker product (Definition A.17), which takes the products of all elements in two matrices, not necessarily of the same size.

Proposition 2.6 (Kronecker Products and Reverse Linear Indexing) *Let* $\mathbf{A} \in \mathbb{R}^{m\times q}$, $\mathbf{B} \in \mathbb{R}^{n\times r}$, $\mathbf{C} \in \mathbb{R}^{p\times s}$. *Then their Kronecker product*

$$\mathbf{X} = \mathbf{A} \otimes \mathbf{B} \otimes \mathbf{C}$$

is of size $mnp \times qrs$. *Further,*

$$x_{\alpha\beta} = a_{i_1 j_1} b_{i_2 j_2} c_{i_3 j_3}, \quad \text{where} \quad \alpha = \mathbb{L}^*(i_1, i_2, i_3; m, n, p), \; \beta = \mathbb{L}^*(j_1, j_2, j_3; q, r, s),$$

for all $(i_1, i_2, i_3, j_1, j_2, j_3) \in [m] \otimes [n] \otimes [p] \otimes [q] \otimes [r] \otimes [s]$.

Exercise 2.10 Prove Proposition 2.6.

We often express Kronecker products in reverse, i.e., $\mathbf{v} = \mathbf{c} \otimes \mathbf{b} \otimes \mathbf{a}$, so that the indices are computed using the natural linear index.

The Kronecker product seems to have been defined backwards! For this reason, we often work with the reverse Kronecker product so that the indexing uses $\mathbb{L}$ rather than $\mathbb{L}^*$, as we explore in Exercises 2.11–2.13.

Exercise 2.11 (Reverse Vector Kronecker Product) Let $\mathbf{a} \in \mathbb{R}^m$, $\mathbf{b} \in \mathbb{R}^n$, and $\mathbf{c} \in \mathbb{R}^p$, and define $\mathbf{v} = \mathbf{c} \otimes \mathbf{b} \otimes \mathbf{a} \in \mathbb{R}^{mnp}$. Show $v_\ell = a_i b_j c_k$, where $\ell = \mathbb{L}(i, j, k)$ or $(i, j, k) = \mathbb{T}(\ell)$.

Exercise 2.12 (Reverse Khatri–Rao Product) Let $\mathbf{A} \in \mathbb{R}^{m\times r}, \mathbf{B} \in \mathbb{R}^{n\times r}, \mathbf{C} \in \mathbb{R}^{p\times r}$, and define their *reverse* Khatri–Rao product

$$\mathbf{V} = \mathbf{C} \odot \mathbf{B} \odot \mathbf{A}.$$

Prove $v_{\alpha\ell} = a_{i\ell} b_{j\ell} c_{k\ell}$ for all $(i, j, k, \ell) \in [m] \otimes [n] \otimes [p] \otimes [r]$ and $\alpha = \mathbb{L}(i, j, k)$.

Exercise 2.13 (Reverse Kronecker Product) Let $\mathbf{A} \in \mathbb{R}^{m\times q}, \mathbf{B} \in \mathbb{R}^{n\times r}, \mathbf{C} \in \mathbb{R}^{p\times s}$, and define their *reverse* Kronecker product

$$\mathbf{V} = \mathbf{C} \otimes \mathbf{B} \otimes \mathbf{A}.$$

(a) What is the size of $\mathbf{V}$?

(b) What is the mapping such that $v_{\alpha\beta} = a_{i_1 j_1} b_{i_2 j_2} c_{i_3 j_3}$?

Reverse Ordering for d-way Tensors

For a general d-way tensor, the conversion between linear and tuple indices using the reverse ordering is the same as the definition for the natural ordering with the exception of the strides.

Definition 2.7 (Linear/Tuple Index Conversion for Reverse Ordering) The **strides** for the **reverse ordering** are

$$s_d^* = 1 \quad \text{and} \quad s_{k-1}^* = \prod_{\ell=k}^{d} n_\ell = s_k^* n_k \text{ for } k = d, \ldots, 2. \tag{2.5a}$$

The **(reverse) linear index** of $(i_1, i_2, \ldots, i_d) \in [n_1] \otimes [n_2] \otimes \cdots \otimes [n_d]$ is

$$\alpha = \mathbb{L}^*(i_1, i_2, \ldots, i_d) = 1 + \sum_{k=1}^{d} s_k^*(i_k - 1). \tag{2.5b}$$

The **(reverse) tuple index** of $\alpha \in [N]$ with $N = \prod_{k=1}^{d} n_k$ is $(i_1, i_2, \ldots, i_d) = \mathbb{T}^*(\alpha)$, where

$$i_k = \mathbb{T}_k^*(\alpha) = 1 + \lfloor((\alpha - 1) \bmod (n_k s_k^*))/s_k^* \rfloor. \tag{2.5c}$$

Exercise 2.14 Extend the functions `lin2tup` and `tup2lin` from Exercise 2.6 with an option to support reverse ordering.

Proposition 2.8 (Reverse/Natural Indexing Conversion) *We can convert from reverse indexing to natural indexing by reversing the indices and sizes:*

$$\alpha = \mathbb{L}^*(i_1, i_2, \ldots, i_d; n_1, n_2, \ldots, n_d) = \mathbb{L}(i_d, i_{d-1}, \ldots, i_1; n_d, n_{d-1}, \ldots, n_1).$$

Likewise,

$$i_k = \mathbb{T}_k^*(\alpha; n_1, n_2, \ldots, n_d) = \mathbb{T}_k(\alpha; n_d, n_{d-1}, \ldots, n_1).$$

The Kronecker product of d vectors can use reverse linear indexing for vectors in natural order *or* natural linear indexing for vectors in reverse order.

Proposition 2.9 (Vector Kronecker Products and Linear Indexing) *Let $\mathbf{a}_k \in \mathbb{R}^{n_k}$ for all $k \in [d]$, and define $N = \prod_{k=1}^{d} n_k$.*

(a) *If $\mathbf{u} = \mathbf{a}_1 \otimes \mathbf{a}_2 \otimes \cdots \otimes \mathbf{a}_d \in \mathbb{R}^N$, then $u_i = \prod_{k=1}^{d} \mathbf{a}_k(i_k)$, where $\alpha = \mathbb{L}^*(i_1, i_2, \ldots, i_d)$ or $(i_1, i_2, \ldots, i_d) = \mathbb{T}^*(\alpha)$.*

(b) *If $\mathbf{v} = \mathbf{a}_d \otimes \mathbf{a}_{d-1} \otimes \cdots \otimes \mathbf{a}_1 \in \mathbb{R}^N$, then $v_i = \prod_{k=1}^{d} \mathbf{a}_k(i_k)$, where $\alpha = \mathbb{L}(i_1, i_2, \ldots, i_d)$ or $(i_1, i_2, \ldots, i_d) = \mathbb{T}(\alpha)$.*

We can develop similar results for matrices; here we give the versions for the reverse Khatri–Rao and reverse Kronecker products.

Proposition 2.10 (Khatri–Rao Products and Linear Indexing) *Let $\mathbf{A}_k \in \mathbb{R}^{n_k \times r}$ for $k \in [d]$. Define $N = \prod_{k=1}^{d} n_k$. Then*

$$\mathbf{B} = \mathbf{A}_d \odot \mathbf{A}_{d-1} \odot \cdots \odot \mathbf{A}_1 \in \mathbb{R}^{N \times r}$$

is such that its elements satisfy

$$\mathbf{B}(\alpha, j) = \prod_{k=1}^{d} \mathbf{A}_k(i_k, j),$$

where $\alpha = \mathbb{L}(i_1, i_2, \ldots, i_d; n_1, n_2, \ldots, n_d)$ and $j \in [r]$.

Proposition 2.11 (Kronecker Products and Linear Indexing) *Let $\mathbf{A}_k \in \mathbb{R}^{m_k \times n_k}$ for $k \in [d]$. Define $M = \prod_{k=1}^{d} m_k$ and $N = \prod_{k=1}^{d} n_k$. Then*

$$\mathbf{B} = \mathbf{A}_d \otimes \mathbf{A}_{d-1} \otimes \cdots \otimes \mathbf{A}_1 \in \mathbb{R}^{M \times N}$$

is such that its elements satisfy

$$\mathbf{B}(\alpha, \beta) = \prod_{k=1}^{d} \mathbf{A}_k(i_k, j_k),$$

where $\alpha = \mathbb{L}(i_1, i_2, \ldots, i_d; m_1, m_2, \ldots, m_d)$ and $\beta = \mathbb{L}(j_1, j_2, \ldots, j_d; n_1, n_2, \ldots, n_d)$.

Exercise 2.15 Prove Proposition 2.11. We recommend using proof by induction and composition of linear indices.

2.1.3 General Ordering

General Ordering for 3-way Tensors

The natural ordering of the modes is $(1, 2, 3)$, and the reverse ordering is $(3, 2, 1)$. What if the ordering is something else, say $(2, 1, 3)$ or $(3, 1, 2)$? For the $2 \times 2 \times 2$ tensor in Fig. 2.1, the natural ordering corresponds to the ordering shown in Fig. 2.1a, the reverse ordering corresponds to the ordering shown in Fig. 2.1f, and the general ordering captures all possibilities.

For a tensor of size $m \times n \times p$, we can define the linear index using any mode ordering $\pi = (\pi_1, \pi_2, \pi_3)$ by using the strides

$$\bar{s}_{\pi_1} = 1, \quad \bar{s}_{\pi_2} = \begin{cases} m & \text{if } \pi_1 = 1 \\ n & \text{if } \pi_1 = 2 \\ p & \text{if } \pi_1 = 3 \end{cases}, \quad \bar{s}_{\pi_3} = \begin{cases} mn & \text{if } (\pi_1, \pi_2) = (1,2) \text{ or } (2,1) \\ mp & \text{if } (\pi_1, \pi_2) = (1,3) \text{ or } (3,1) \\ np & \text{if } (\pi_1, \pi_2) = (2,3) \text{ or } (3,2) \end{cases}.$$

Using these general strides, the linear index ℓ corresponding to (i, j, k) can then be computed as

$$\mathbb{L}^{(\pi)}(i, j, k) = 1 + \bar{s}_1(i-1) + \bar{s}_2(j-1) + \bar{s}_3(k-1),$$

where π denotes the specific permutation of the indices. The tuple (i, j, k) can be computed from $\ell \in [mnp]$ using the inverse function $(i, j, k) = \mathbb{T}^{(\pi)}(\ell)$, where

$$i = \mathbb{T}_1^{(\pi)}(\ell) = 1 + \lfloor ((\ell - 1) \bmod m\bar{s}_1)/\bar{s}_1 \rfloor,$$
$$j = \mathbb{T}_2^{(\pi)}(\ell) = 1 + \lfloor ((\ell - 1) \bmod n\bar{s}_2)/\bar{s}_2 \rfloor,$$
$$k = \mathbb{T}_3^{(\pi)}(\ell) = 1 + \lfloor ((\ell - 1) \bmod p\bar{s}_3)/\bar{s}_3 \rfloor.$$

Exercise 2.16 What is π for the natural ordering? For the reverse ordering?

Exercise 2.17 Consider the domain $[m] \otimes [n] \otimes [p]$ and the permuted ordering $\pi = (2, 1, 3)$. (a) What is the formula for the linear index ℓ of (i, j, k)? (b) Given the linear index ℓ, what is (i, j, k)?

General Ordering for d-way Tensors

We can then consider the general d-way case as follows.

Definition 2.12 (Linear/Tuple Index Conversion for General Ordering) The **strides** for the **general ordering** specified by $\pi = (\pi_1, \pi_2, \ldots, \pi_d)$ are

$$\bar{s}_{\pi_1} = 1 \quad \text{and} \quad \bar{s}_{\pi_{k+1}} = \prod_{\ell=1}^{k} n_{\pi_\ell} = \bar{s}_{\pi_k} n_{\pi_k} \text{ for } k \in [d-1].$$

The **(general) linear index** of $(i_1, i_2, \ldots, i_d) \in [n_1] \otimes [n_2] \otimes \cdots \otimes [n_d]$ is

$$\alpha = \mathbb{L}^{(\pi)}(i_1, i_2, \ldots, i_d) = 1 + \sum_{k=1}^{d} \bar{s}_k (i_k - 1). \tag{2.6a}$$

The **(general) tuple index** of $\alpha \in [N]$ with $N = \prod_{k=1}^{d} n_k$ is $(i_1, i_2, \ldots, i_d) = \mathbb{T}^{(\pi)}(\alpha)$, where

$$i_k = \mathbb{T}_k^{(\pi)}(\alpha) = 1 + \lfloor ((\alpha - 1) \bmod (n_k \bar{s}_k))/\bar{s}_k \rfloor. \tag{2.6b}$$

Exercise 2.18 How many different mode orderings are possible for a d-tuple?

We can always convert from an index using a general mode ordering to one using the natural ordering as follows.

Proposition 2.13 (From General to Natural Linear Ordering) *Let $i_1, \ldots, i_d \in [n_1] \otimes \cdots \otimes [n_d]$, then*

$$\mathbb{L}^{(\pi)}(i_1, \ldots, i_d; n_1, \ldots, n_d) = \mathbb{L}(i_{\pi_1}, \ldots, i_{\pi_d}, n_{\pi_1}, \ldots, n_{\pi_d}). \tag{2.7}$$

Conversely, for $\alpha \in \left[\prod_{k=1}^{d} n_k\right]$, we have

$$i_k = \mathbb{T}_k^{(\pi)}(\alpha; n_1, \ldots, n_d) = \mathbb{T}_k(\alpha; n_{\pi_1}, \ldots, n_{\pi_d}). \tag{2.8}$$

Exercise 2.19 (a) Extend the functions `lin2tup` and `tup2lin` from Exercise 2.6 with an option to support general ordering. (b) Validate the $2 \times 2 \times 2$ case using Fig. 2.1. (c) Numerically validate the equivalency in Proposition 2.13.

Exercise 2.20 Let $\mathbf{a}_k \in \mathbb{R}^{n_k}$ for $k \in [d]$ and define $\mathbf{v} = \mathbf{a}_{\pi(1)} \otimes \mathbf{a}_{\pi(2)} \otimes \cdots \otimes \mathbf{a}_{\pi(d)}$. (a) Given $(i_1, i_2, \ldots, i_d)$, for what value of α is it the case that $\mathbf{v}(\alpha) = \prod_{k=1}^{d} \mathbf{a}_k(i_k)$? (b) Conversely, given α, for what values of $(i_1, i_2, \ldots, i_d)$ does the statement hold?

2.2 Vectorization

The operation of **vectorization** converts a tensor to a vector. The elements are the same but simply arranged as a one-dimensional array. It is closely related to how the tensor is stored in computer memory, as we discuss further below. The ordering of the elements is controlled by the linear indexing discussed in the prior section. As a warm-up, we consider how linear indexing relates to vectorizing a matrix.

Example 2.4 (Vectorizing a Matrix) We briefly recall vectorization for matrices. Let $\mathbf{X}$ be a matrix of size $m \times n$. The operation $\text{vec}(\mathbf{X})$ stacks the columns of $\mathbf{X}$ to form a vector of length $p = mn$. Now we can ask: How are the entries in $\mathbf{y} = \text{vec}(\mathbf{X})$ related to the entries of $\mathbf{X}$? Given $(i, j) \in [m] \otimes [n]$, we can use the linear index so that

$$y_\ell = x_{ij}, \quad \text{where} \quad \ell = \mathbb{L}(i, j) = i + m(j-1).$$

Given $\ell \in [mn]$, we have $(i, j) = \mathbb{T}(\ell)$, so

$$x_{ij} = y_\ell, \quad \text{where} \quad \begin{aligned} i &= \mathbb{T}_1(\ell) = ((\ell - 1) \bmod m) + 1, \\ j &= \mathbb{T}_2(\ell) = \lfloor (\ell - 1)/m \rfloor + 1. \end{aligned}$$

2.2.1 Vectorizing 3-way Tensors

Consider a 3-way tensor $\mathcal{X}$ of size $m \times n \times p$; then $\text{vec}(\mathcal{X})$ is a column vector of size $q = mnp$. The entries of the tensor are ordered by their linear indices, per Eq. (2.3), as

$$\text{vec}(\mathcal{X}) = \underbrace{\begin{bmatrix} x_{111} \\ x_{211} \\ \vdots \\ x_{mnp} \end{bmatrix}}_{\textit{tuple indices}} = \underbrace{\begin{bmatrix} x_1 \\ x_2 \\ \vdots \\ x_q \end{bmatrix}}_{\textit{linear indices}} \Big\downarrow q = mnp. \tag{2.9}$$

Specifically, if $\mathbf{x} = \text{vec}(\mathcal{X})$, then $\mathbf{x}(\ell) = \mathcal{X}(i, j, k)$, where $\ell = \mathbb{L}(i, j, k) = i + m(j - 1) + mn(k - 1)$ or $(i, j, k) = \mathbb{T}(\ell)$. This ordering is the tensor analog of column-major ordering for matrices. See Fig. 2.2 for a visual illustration.

Exercise 2.21 Show that Eq. (2.9) is identical to matrix vectorization for an $m \times n \times p$ tensor with $p = 1$.

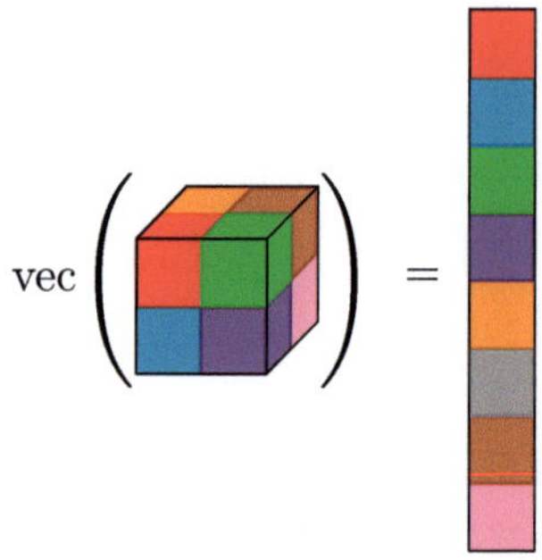

Figure 2.2 Vectorization of a $2 \times 2 \times 2$ tensor.

Example 2.5 (Vectorizing 3-way Tensor) Let $\mathcal{X}$ be defined as in Example 1.2. Its vectorization is

$$\text{vec}(\mathcal{X}) = [3\ 8\ 4\ 9\ 2\ 3\ 1\ 1\ 9\ 6\ 5\ 1\ 9\ 6\ 4\ 5\ 4\ 1]^{\mathsf{T}} \in \mathbb{R}^{18}.$$

Pictorially, this is illustrated as walking through the slices in order, traversing the columns in order within each slice:

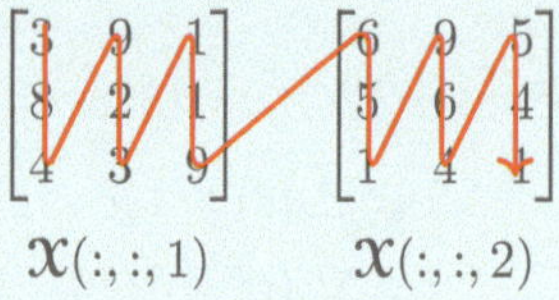

Each frontal slice is vectorized, and these are stacked to form the vectorization.

Exercise 2.22 Let the $2 \times 2 \times 2$ tensor $\mathcal{X}$ be given by

$$\mathcal{X}(:,:,1) = \begin{bmatrix} 8 & 7 \\ -3 & 9 \end{bmatrix} \quad \text{and} \quad \mathcal{X}(:,:,2) = \begin{bmatrix} -1 & 4 \\ 0 & 5 \end{bmatrix}.$$

What is $\text{vec}(\mathcal{X})$?

2.2.2 Vectorizing d-way Tensors

Now we consider vectorization for a general d-way array.

Definition 2.14: Vectorization of d-way Tensor

Let $\mathcal{X}$ be a tensor of size $n_1 \times n_2 \times \cdots \times n_d$. Its **vectorization**, $\text{vec}(\mathcal{X})$, is a column vector of length $N = \prod_{k=1}^{d} n_k$ such that entry $\alpha \in [N]$ is defined as $\alpha = \mathbb{L}(i_1, i_2, \ldots, i_d)$ and, conversely, $(i_1, i_2, \ldots, i_d) = \mathbb{T}(\alpha)$ (see Definition 2.2) so that

$$\text{vec}(\mathcal{X}) = \underbrace{\begin{bmatrix} x_{11\cdots1} \\ x_{21\cdots1} \\ \vdots \\ x_{n_1 n_2 \cdots n_d} \end{bmatrix}}_{\textit{tuple indices}} = \underbrace{\begin{bmatrix} x_1 \\ x_2 \\ \vdots \\ x_N \end{bmatrix}}_{\textit{linear indices}} \Bigg\downarrow N = \prod_{k=1}^{d} n_k. \tag{2.10}$$

Example 2.6 (Vectorizing d-way Tensor) Let $\mathcal{Y} \in \mathbb{R}^{3\times4\times3\times2}$ be as defined in Example 1.3:

$\mathcal{Y}(:,:,:,1) =$ 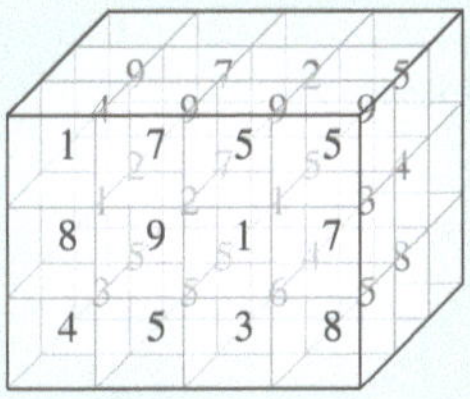

$, \mathcal{Y}(:,:,:,2) =$ 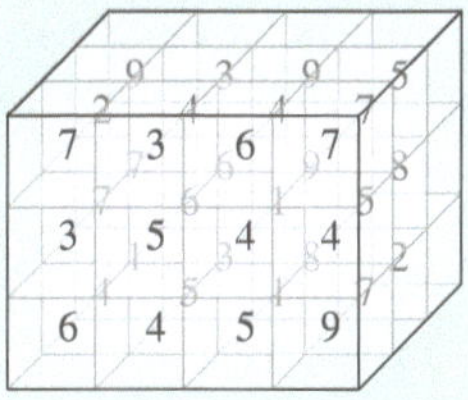

.

Then $\operatorname{vec}\mathcal{Y} \in \mathbb{R}^{72}$ with $\operatorname{vec}(\mathcal{Y}) =$

$$[1\,8\,4\,7\,9\,5\,5\,1\,3\,5\,7\,8\,4\,1\,3\,9\,2\,5\,9\,1\,6\,9\,3\,5\,9\,2\,5\,7\,7\,5\,2\,5\,4\,5\,4\,8 \ldots$$
$$7\,3\,6\,3\,5\,4\,6\,4\,5\,7\,4\,9\,2\,7\,4\,4\,6\,5\,4\,1\,1\,7\,5\,7\,9\,7\,1\,3\,6\,3\,9\,9\,8\,5\,8\,2]^{\intercal}.$$

2.2.3 Representing Tensors in Computer Memory

In a computer, a tensor $\mathcal{X}$ is stored internally as a vector.

A programming language may allow for multidimensional arrays to be stored as arrays of arrays of arrays or lists of lists of lists, but this is generally inefficient. Such a storage format means that locating element $(i_1, i_2, \ldots, i_d)$ requires navigating through a sequence of d memory references.

Instead, the most efficient way to store a tensor in computer memory is as a contiguous one-dimensional array, such as $\operatorname{vec}(\mathcal{X})$. This is efficient because computer memory is linear; hence, if we know the location of $\mathcal{X}(1, 1, \ldots, 1)$, we can find the location of element $(i_1, i_2, \ldots, i_d)$ by just looking $\big(\mathbb{L}(i_1, i_2, \ldots, i_d) - 1\big)$ spots ahead in memory. Additionally, storing the tensor as $\operatorname{vec}(\mathcal{X})$ allows for strided data access for tensor fibers. By keeping the entire multidimensional array in a contiguous block of memory, we improve spatial locality in various levels of the memory hierarchy.

The natural ordering for tensors is analogous to the column-major ordering of matrices, which is the default in MATLAB. In Python, the “F” (Fortran) ordering is recommended for NumPy multidimensional arrays to correspond with the descriptions here; the default “C” ordering corresponds to the reverse linear index.

The command **reshape** does not move any entries around but merely declares a new shape for an object. As an example, for $\mathcal{X} \in \mathbb{R}^{m\times n\times p}$ and $\mathbf{x} \in \mathbb{R}^{mnp}$, we have

$$\mathcal{X} = \operatorname{reshape}(\mathbf{x}, m \times n \times p) \quad \text{if and only if} \quad \mathbf{x} = \operatorname{vec}(\mathcal{X}).$$

This operation requires no memory movement or computation.

2.3 Unfolding or Matricization of a Tensor

Unfolding or **matricization** of a tensor rearranges its elements as a 2-way matrix. The total number of elements is unchanged. In other words, if a tensor $\mathcal{X}$ of size $n_1 \times n_2 \times \cdots \times n_d$ is unfolded to a matrix of size $M \times N$, then it must be the case that $MN = \prod_{k=1}^{d} n_k$.

2.3.1 Unfolding 3-way Tensors

Consider a 3-way tensor $\mathcal{X}$ of size $m \times n \times p$ which we can arrange as an $m \times np$ matrix, an $n \times mp$ matrix, or a $p \times mn$ matrix. Figure 2.3 provides an example illustration of the three different unfoldings alongside the vectorization.

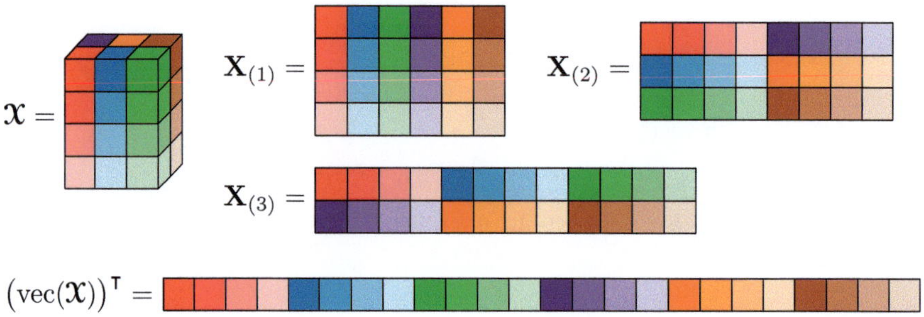

Figure 2.3 Unfoldings and vectorization of a $4 \times 3 \times 2$ tensor $\mathcal{X}$, using colors for each entry.

The mode-1 unfolding aligns the column fibers as the columns of the matrix.

Definition 2.15 (Mode-1 Unfolding of 3-way Tensor) For a tensor $\mathcal{X} \in \mathbb{R}^{m \times n \times p}$, the **mode-1 unfolding** is denoted as $\mathbf{X}_{(1)}$ and is a matrix of size $m \times np$ such that

$$\mathbf{X}_{(1)} = m \overbrace{\begin{bmatrix} x_{111} & x_{121} & \cdots & x_{1np} \\ x_{211} & x_{221} & \cdots & x_{2np} \\ \vdots & \vdots & \ddots & \vdots \\ x_{m11} & x_{m21} & \cdots & x_{mnp} \end{bmatrix}}^{np} \qquad \begin{gathered} \mathbf{X}_{(1)}(i,\ell) = \mathcal{X}(i,j,k) \\ \text{where} \\ \ell = (k-1)n + j. \end{gathered} \tag{2.11}$$

The mapping for the column index can also be expressed using the definitions of $\mathbb{L}$ and $\mathbb{T}$ from Eq. (2.3), i.e., the ℓ from Eq. (2.11) can be expressed as

$$\ell = \mathbb{L}(j,k) \quad \text{or, precisely,} \quad \ell = \mathbb{L}(j,k;n,p).$$

The ordering from the mode-1 unfolding has the benefit of preserving the same linear representations for $\mathcal{X}$ and for $\mathbf{X}_{(1)}$. This means that the computer representations in a column-major programming language such as MATLAB are equivalent, so it is only the interpretation that changes. The pseudocode is a single line as follows:

Mode-1 Unfolding of 3-way Tensor

$\{ \quad \mathbf{X}_{(1)} \leftarrow \text{reshape}(\mathcal{X}, m \times np)$

Exercise 2.23 Prove $\mathbf{X}_{(1)} = \text{reshape}(\mathcal{X}, m \times np)$.

The mode-2 unfolding arranges the row fibers as the columns of the matrix. This cannot be achieved by a reshape, but it does have a special structure, discussed in Section 2.3.3.

Definition 2.16 (Mode-2 Unfolding of 3-way Tensor) For a tensor $\mathcal{X} \in \mathbb{R}^{m \times n \times p}$, the **mode-2 unfolding**, denoted $\mathbf{X}_{(2)}$, is of size $n \times mp$ such that

$$\mathbf{X}_{(2)} = n \downarrow \overset{\xrightarrow{\quad mp \quad}}{\begin{bmatrix} x_{111} & x_{211} & \cdots & x_{m1p} \\ x_{121} & x_{221} & \cdots & x_{m2p} \\ \vdots & \vdots & \ddots & \vdots \\ x_{1n1} & x_{2n1} & \cdots & x_{mnp} \end{bmatrix}} \qquad \begin{gathered} \mathbf{X}_{(2)}(j, \ell) = \mathcal{X}(i, j, k) \\ \text{where} \\ \ell = (k-1)m + i = \mathbb{L}(i, k). \end{gathered} \tag{2.12}$$

The mode-3 unfolding arranges the tube fibers as the columns of the matrix. This cannot be achieved by a reshape either, but its transpose can; see Proposition 2.21.

Definition 2.17 (Mode-3 Unfolding of 3-way Tensor) For a tensor $\mathcal{X} \in \mathbb{R}^{m \times n \times p}$, the **mode-3 unfolding** denoted $\mathbf{X}_{(3)}$, is of size $p \times mn$ such that

$$\mathbf{X}_{(3)} = p \downarrow \overset{\xrightarrow{\quad mn \quad}}{\begin{bmatrix} x_{111} & x_{211} & \cdots & x_{mn1} \\ x_{112} & x_{212} & \cdots & x_{mn2} \\ \vdots & \vdots & \ddots & \vdots \\ x_{11p} & x_{21p} & \cdots & x_{mnp} \end{bmatrix}} \qquad \begin{gathered} \mathbf{X}_{(3)}(k, \ell) = \mathcal{X}(i, j, k) \\ \text{where} \\ \ell = (j-1)m + i = \mathbb{L}(i, j). \end{gathered} \tag{2.13}$$

Example 2.7 (Three-way Tensor Unfoldings) Let the tensor $\mathcal{X} \in \mathbb{R}^{3 \times 3 \times 2}$ be as defined in Example 1.2:

$\mathcal{X} =$ 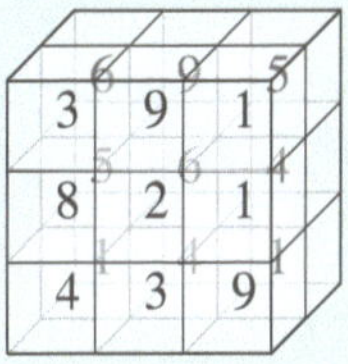

.

Then its three mode-k unfoldings are

$$\mathbf{X}_{(1)} = \begin{bmatrix} 3 & 9 & 1 & 6 & 9 & 5 \\ 8 & 2 & 1 & 5 & 6 & 4 \\ 4 & 3 & 9 & 1 & 4 & 1 \end{bmatrix} \in \mathbb{R}^{3 \times 6}, \quad \mathbf{X}_{(2)} = \begin{bmatrix} 3 & 8 & 4 & 6 & 5 & 1 \\ 9 & 2 & 3 & 9 & 6 & 4 \\ 1 & 1 & 9 & 5 & 4 & 1 \end{bmatrix} \in \mathbb{R}^{3 \times 6},$$

$$\text{and} \quad \mathbf{X}_{(3)} = \begin{bmatrix} 3 & 8 & 4 & 9 & 2 & 3 & 1 & 1 & 9 \\ 6 & 5 & 1 & 9 & 6 & 4 & 5 & 4 & 1 \end{bmatrix} \in \mathbb{R}^{2 \times 9}.$$

Exercise 2.24 Let the $2 \times 2 \times 2$ tensor $\mathcal{X}$ be given by

$$\mathcal{X}(:, :, 1) = \begin{bmatrix} 8 & 7 \\ -3 & 9 \end{bmatrix} \quad \text{and} \quad \mathcal{X}(:, :, 2) = \begin{bmatrix} -1 & 4 \\ 0 & 5 \end{bmatrix}.$$

What are $\mathbf{X}_{(1)}, \mathbf{X}_{(2)}, \mathbf{X}_{(3)}$?

Exercise 2.25 (Alternate Column Order in Unfolding) The natural ordering preserves the frontal slices and is generally the default. However, we could certainly change the ordering for the column indices. Consider:

$$\hat{\mathbf{X}}_{(1)}(i, \ell) = \mathcal{X}(i, j, k), \quad \text{where} \quad \ell = \mathbb{L}^*(j, k) \text{ and } (j, k) = \mathbb{T}^*(\ell).$$

What is $\hat{\mathbf{X}}_{(1)}$ for the tensor $\mathcal{X}$ in Example 1.2?

We consider here only the case of mapping a single tensor tuple index to each row and a pair of tensor tuple indices to each column. There are other possibilities, which we explore further in the general d-way case in the next subsection.

2.3.2 Unfolding d-way Tensors

We consider two types of unfolding. First, the mode-k unfolding of a d-way tensor (analogous to the 3-way case) maps one mode to the rows and the remainder to the columns in the natural ordering for the linearization. Second, the general unfolding can map any set of indices to the rows and the remainder to the columns, allowing for arbitrary permutations in the linearizations. We discuss each in turn.

Mode-k Unfolding of a d-way Tensor

The columns of the mode-k unfolding are the mode-k tensor fibers.

The mode-k unfolding organizes the mode-k fibers as the columns of the resulting matrix in natural order as follows.

Definition 2.18: Mode-k Unfolding

The **mode-k unfolding** of a tensor $\mathcal{X}$ of size $n_1 \times n_2 \times \cdots \times n_d$ is the matrix

$$\mathbf{X}_{(k)} \in \mathbb{R}^{n_k \times N_k}, \quad \text{where} \quad N_k = \prod_{\substack{\ell=1 \\ \ell \neq k}}^{d} n_\ell \quad \text{and} \tag{2.14a}$$

$$\mathbf{X}_{(k)}(i_k, \beta_k) = \mathcal{X}(i_1, \ldots, i_d) \quad \text{with} \quad \beta_k = \mathbb{L}(i_1, \ldots, i_{k-1}, i_{k+1}, \ldots, i_d). \tag{2.14b}$$

We have a special usage of $\mathbb{L}$ from Definition 2.2 because we are skipping mode k:

$$\mathbb{L}(i_1, \ldots, i_{k-1}, i_{k+1}, \ldots, i_d) = 1 + \sum_{\substack{\ell=1 \\ \ell \neq k}}^{d} s_\ell (i_\ell - 1), \quad \text{where} \quad s_\ell = \prod_{\substack{\alpha=1 \\ \alpha \neq k}}^{\ell-1} n_\alpha.$$

We use the convention that the first stride is 1 (since there is nothing to multiply); concretely, if $k > 1$, then the first stride is $s_1 = 1$; otherwise, we have $k = 1$ and the first stride is $s_2 = 1$.

Example 2.8 (Four-way Tensor Unfoldings) Consider the tensor $\mathcal{X}$ of size $2 \times 2 \times 2 \times 2$ given by

$\mathcal{X}(:,:,:,1) =$ 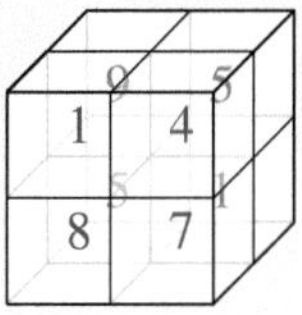

, $\mathcal{X}(:,:,:,2) =$ 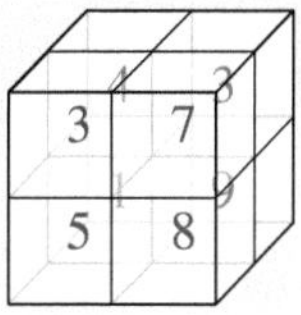

.

Its four mode-k unfoldings are

$$\mathbf{X}_{(1)} = \begin{bmatrix} 1 & 4 & 9 & 5 & 3 & 7 & 4 & 3 \\ 8 & 7 & 5 & 1 & 5 & 8 & 1 & 9 \end{bmatrix}, \quad \mathbf{X}_{(2)} = \begin{bmatrix} 1 & 8 & 9 & 5 & 3 & 5 & 4 & 1 \\ 4 & 7 & 5 & 1 & 7 & 8 & 3 & 9 \end{bmatrix},$$

$$\mathbf{X}_{(3)} = \begin{bmatrix} 1 & 8 & 4 & 7 & 3 & 5 & 7 & 8 \\ 9 & 5 & 5 & 1 & 4 & 1 & 3 & 9 \end{bmatrix}, \quad \mathbf{X}_{(4)} = \begin{bmatrix} 1 & 8 & 4 & 7 & 9 & 5 & 5 & 1 \\ 3 & 5 & 7 & 8 & 4 & 1 & 3 & 9 \end{bmatrix}.$$

Exercise 2.26 Prove that the mode-1 unfolding has the same linearization as the tensor, i.e., $\mathrm{vec}(\mathcal{X}) = \mathrm{vec}(\mathbf{X}_{(1)})$. Hint: Use the composition of linearization.

Example 2.9 (Four-way Tensor Unfolding) Let $\mathcal{Y} \in \mathbb{R}^{3 \times 4 \times 3 \times 2}$ be as defined in Example 1.3:

$\mathcal{Y}(:,:,:,1) =$ 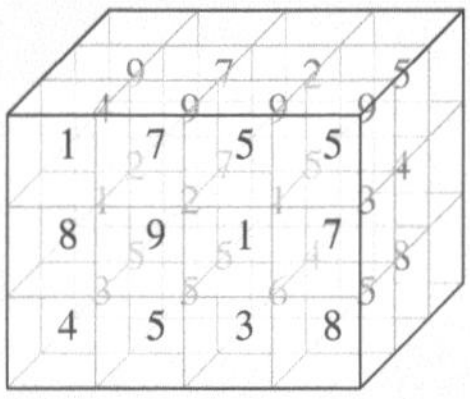

, $\mathcal{Y}(:,:,:,2) =$ 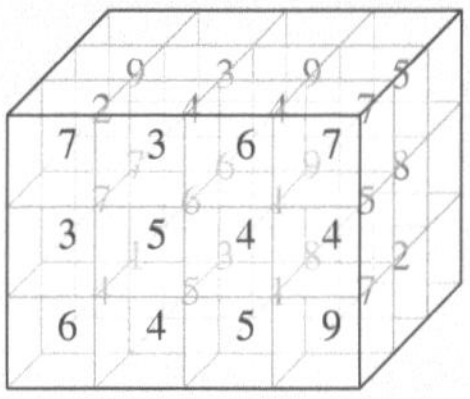

.

Then its mode-2 unfolding is

$$\mathbf{Y}_{(2)} = \begin{bmatrix} 1 & 8 & 4 & 4 & 1 & 3 & 9 & 2 & 5 & 7 & 3 & 6 & 2 & 7 & 4 & 9 & 7 & 1 \\ 7 & 9 & 5 & 9 & 2 & 5 & 7 & 7 & 5 & 3 & 5 & 4 & 4 & 6 & 5 & 3 & 6 & 3 \\ 5 & 1 & 3 & 9 & 1 & 6 & 2 & 5 & 4 & 6 & 4 & 5 & 4 & 1 & 1 & 9 & 9 & 8 \\ 5 & 7 & 8 & 9 & 3 & 5 & 5 & 4 & 8 & 7 & 4 & 9 & 7 & 5 & 7 & 5 & 8 & 2 \end{bmatrix}.$$

Exercise 2.27 For the tensor $\mathcal{Y}$ in Example 2.9, what is (a) $\mathbf{Y}_{(1)}$, (b) $\mathbf{Y}_{(3)}$, (c) $\mathbf{Y}_{(4)}$?

General Unfolding of a d-way Tensor

We can define more general matricizations where multiple modes map to the row and column modes of the matrix as follows. We use natural ordering for both row sets and columns sets of indices.

Definition 2.19: General Unfolding

Let the modes $\{1, \ldots, d\}$ be partitioned into two ordered sets:

$$\mathcal{R} = (r_1, r_2, \ldots, r_\delta) \quad \text{and} \quad \mathcal{C} = (c_1, c_2, \ldots, c_{d-\delta}). \tag{2.15a}$$

The **unfolding** of a tensor $\mathcal{X}$ of size $n_1 \times n_2 \times \cdots \times n_d$ with respect to row set $\mathcal{R}$ and column set $\mathcal{C}$ is the matrix

$$\mathbf{X}_{(\mathcal{R}\times\mathcal{C})} \in \mathbb{R}^{M\times N}, \quad \text{where} \quad M = \prod_{k\in\mathcal{R}} n_k \quad \text{and} \quad N = \prod_{k\in\mathcal{C}} n_k, \tag{2.15b}$$

and defined by $\mathbf{X}_{(\mathcal{R}\times\mathcal{C})}(\alpha, \beta) = \mathcal{X}(i_1, i_2, \ldots, i_d)$, where

$$\alpha = \mathbb{L}(i_{r_1}, \ldots, i_{r_\delta}) \in [M] \quad \text{and} \quad \beta = \mathbb{L}(i_{c_1}, \ldots, i_{c_{d-\delta}}) \in [N]. \tag{2.15c}$$

Exercise 2.28 For a 3-way tensor $\mathcal{X}$ of size $m \times n \times p$, prove the following: (a) The mode-2 unfolding is equivalent to general matricization with $\mathcal{R} = (2)$ and $\mathcal{C} = (1, 3)$. (b) The generalization matricization with $\mathcal{R} = (1, 2)$ and $\mathcal{C} = (3)$ is equal to $\mathbf{X}_{(3)}^{\mathsf{T}}$.

Exercise 2.29 Prove the following: (a) The mode-k unfolding is a special case of general matricization with $\mathcal{R} = (k)$ and $\mathcal{C} = (1, \ldots, k-1, k+1, \ldots, d)$. (b) Vectorization is a special case of general matricization with $\mathcal{R} = (1, \ldots, d)$ and $\mathcal{C} = \emptyset$.

Example 2.10 (General Unfolding) Consider $\mathcal{Y} \in \mathbb{R}^{3\times4\times3\times2}$ from Example 1.3:

$\mathcal{Y}(:,:,:,1) =$ 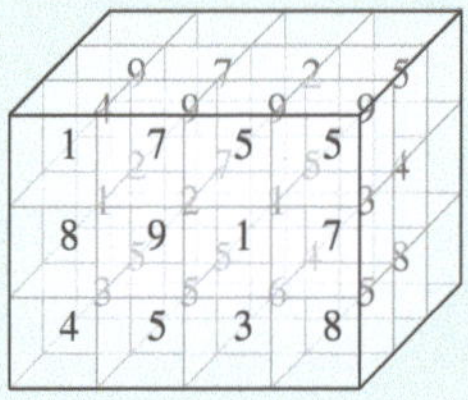

, $\mathcal{Y}(:,:,:,2) =$ 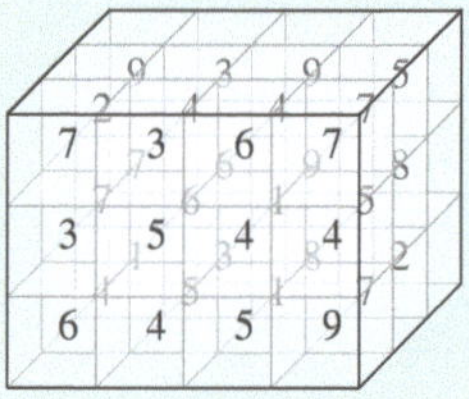

.

Then its unfolding with $\mathcal{R} = (1, 3)$ and $\mathcal{C} = (2, 4)$ is

$$\mathbf{Y}_{((1,3)\times(2,4))} = \begin{bmatrix} 1 & 7 & 5 & 5 & 7 & 3 & 6 & 7 \\ 8 & 9 & 1 & 7 & 3 & 5 & 4 & 4 \\ 4 & 5 & 3 & 8 & 6 & 4 & 5 & 9 \\ 4 & 9 & 9 & 9 & 2 & 4 & 4 & 7 \\ 1 & 2 & 1 & 3 & 7 & 6 & 1 & 5 \\ 3 & 5 & 6 & 5 & 4 & 5 & 1 & 7 \\ 9 & 7 & 2 & 5 & 9 & 3 & 9 & 5 \\ 2 & 7 & 5 & 4 & 7 & 6 & 9 & 8 \\ 5 & 5 & 4 & 8 & 1 & 3 & 8 & 2 \end{bmatrix} \in \mathbb{R}^{9\times8}.$$

Exercise 2.30 For the tensor in Example 2.10, what is its unfolding for $\mathcal{R} = (1, 4)$ and $\mathcal{C} = (2, 3)$?

Rearranging the elements of a tensor into an unfolded matrix in column-major order generally requires moving data around. However, no **memory movement** cost is incurred if the linearization of the tensor and its unfolding are identical.

We can characterize such an unfolding as follows.

Proposition 2.20 (No Memory Movement Unfolding) *For any $k \in [d]$, if $\mathcal{R} = (1, \ldots, k)$ and $\mathcal{C} = (k+1, \ldots, d)$, then for any d-way tensor, we have*

$$\text{vec}(\mathcal{X}) = \text{vec}\big(\mathbf{X}_{(\mathcal{R}\times\mathcal{C})}\big).$$

Exercise 2.31 Prove Proposition 2.20.

Example 2.11 (General Unfolding with No Memory Movement, 3-way) Let the tensor $\mathcal{X} \in \mathbb{R}^{3\times3\times2}$ be as defined in Example 1.2 and consider the unfolding using $\mathcal{R} = (1, 2)$ and $\mathcal{C} = (3)$:

$\mathcal{X} =$ 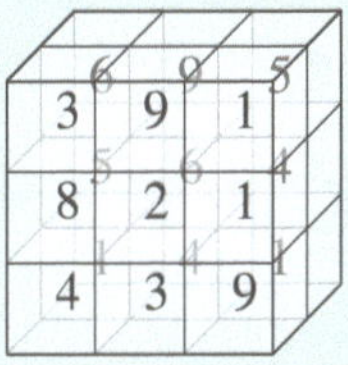

unfolds to

$$\mathbf{X}_{((1,2)\times3)} = \begin{bmatrix} 3 & 6 \\ 8 & 5 \\ 4 & 1 \\ 9 & 9 \\ 2 & 6 \\ 3 & 4 \\ 1 & 5 \\ 1 & 4 \\ 9 & 1 \end{bmatrix} \in \mathbb{R}^{9\times2},$$

which is the same vectorization as $\mathcal{X}$. In fact, $\mathbf{X}_{((1,2)\times3)} = \mathbf{X}^{\mathsf{T}}_{(3)}$.

Example 2.12 (General Unfolding with No Memory Movement, d-way) Let $\mathcal{Y} \in \mathbb{R}^{3\times4\times3\times2}$ be as defined in Example 1.3:

$\mathcal{Y}(:,:,:,1) =$ 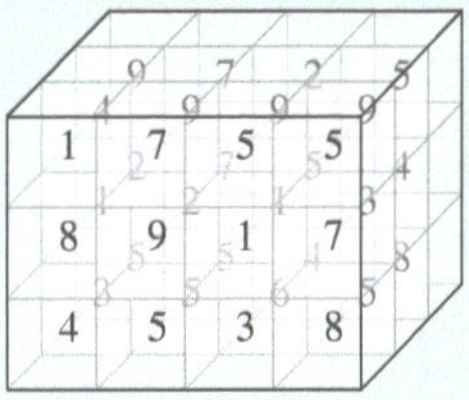

$, \mathcal{Y}(:,:,:,2) =$ 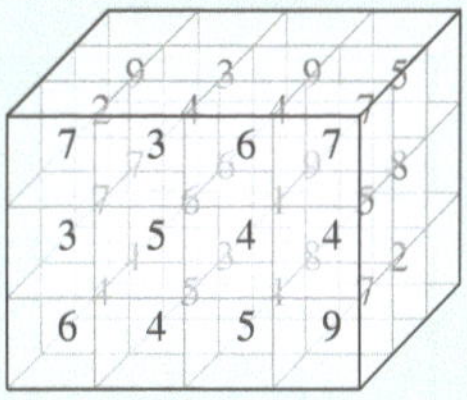

.

If $\mathcal{R} = (1, 2)$ and $\mathcal{C} = (3, 4)$, then

$$\mathbf{Y}_{((1,2)\times(3,4))} = \begin{bmatrix} 1 & 4 & 9 & 7 & 2 & 9 \\ 8 & 1 & 2 & 3 & 7 & 7 \\ 4 & 3 & 5 & 6 & 4 & 1 \\ 7 & 9 & 7 & 3 & 4 & 3 \\ 9 & 2 & 7 & 5 & 6 & 6 \\ 5 & 5 & 5 & 4 & 5 & 3 \\ 5 & 9 & 2 & 6 & 4 & 9 \\ 1 & 1 & 5 & 4 & 1 & 9 \\ 3 & 6 & 4 & 5 & 1 & 8 \\ 5 & 9 & 5 & 7 & 7 & 5 \\ 7 & 3 & 4 & 4 & 5 & 8 \\ 8 & 5 & 8 & 9 & 7 & 2 \end{bmatrix}.$$

We have again that $\text{vec}(\mathcal{Y}) = \text{vec}\big(\mathbf{Y}_{((1,2)\times(3,4))}\big)$.

Exercise 2.32 Let $\mathcal{X} \in \mathbb{R}^{n_1 \times n_2 \times \cdots \times n_d}$. Show

$$\mathbf{X}_{(d)}^{\mathsf{T}} = \begin{bmatrix} \operatorname{vec}(\mathcal{X}(:, \ldots, :, 1)) & \operatorname{vec}(\mathcal{X}(:, \ldots, :, 2)) & \cdots & \operatorname{vec}(\mathcal{X}(:, \ldots, :, n_k)) \end{bmatrix}.$$

Exercise 2.33 Let $\mathcal{X} \in \mathbb{R}^{n_1 \times n_2 \times \cdots \times n_d}$. Set $\mathcal{Y} = \mathcal{X}(:, \cdots, :, i_d) \in \mathbb{R}^{n_1 \times n_2 \times \cdots \times n_{d-1}}$ for some $i_d \in [n_d]$. For $k < d$, show that the unfolding ranks are related as $\operatorname{rank}(\mathbf{Y}_{(k)}) = 1$ if $\operatorname{rank}(\mathbf{X}_{(k)}) = 1$.

2.3.3 Structure of Mode-k Unfoldings

We saw in the previous subsection that the mode-1 unfolding has the same vectorization as $\mathcal{X}$, which means that there is no memory movement cost to perform matrix operations with the mode-1 unfolding. The other mode-k unfoldings are not in column-major order, so performing matrix operations with them requires reordering the elements in memory, which can be slow. However, the mode-k unfoldings do have structure that can be exploited when performing matrix operations without performing any explicit reordering (Austin et al., 2016; Ballard et al., 2020; Li et al., 2015).

Considering the mode-k unfolding defined in Eq. (2.14), define

$$M_k = \prod_{\ell=1}^{k-1} n_\ell \quad \text{and} \quad P_k = \prod_{\ell=k+1}^{d} n_\ell.$$

The mode-k unfolding has P_k column blocks, and each block is a row-major matrix of size $n_k \times M_k$. This is illustrated in Fig. 2.4.

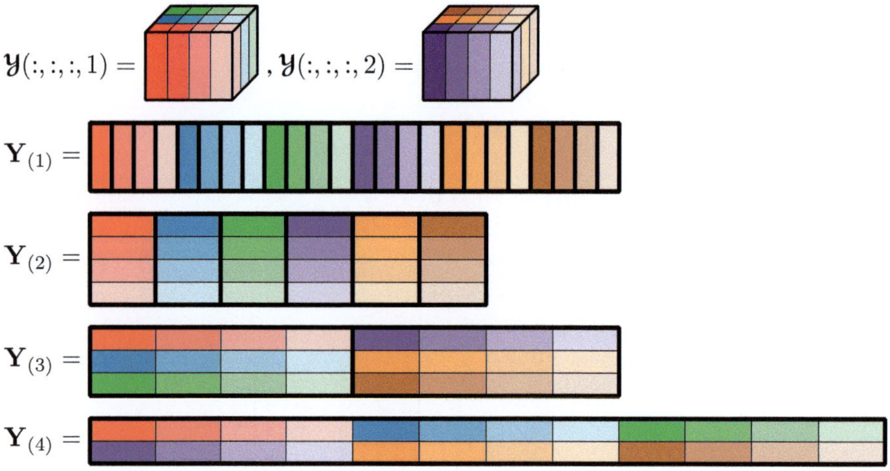

Figure 2.4 Block structure of mode-k unfoldings for a 4-way tensor of size $3 \times 4 \times 3 \times 2$ in terms of mode-1 fibers. Thick lines outline the blocks.

For ease of discussion, consider a tensor $\mathcal{Y}$ of size $3 \times 4 \times 3 \times 2$ such that $\operatorname{vec}(\mathcal{Y}) = \begin{bmatrix} 1 & 2 & 3 & \cdots & 72 \end{bmatrix}^{\mathsf{T}}$. In other words, each entry is the linear index of that entry.

For mode 1, there are $P_1 = 24$ blocks, each of which is of size $n_1 \times M_1 = 3 \times 1$:

$$\mathbf{Y}_{(1)} = \left[\begin{array}{c|c|c|c} 1 & 4 & \cdots & 70 \\ 2 & 5 & \cdots & 71 \\ 3 & 6 & \cdots & 72 \end{array}\right].$$

In this unfolding, as discussed in the prior subsection, $\mathbf{Y}_{(1)}$ naturally aligns with the natural ordering of $\mathcal{Y}$ so that $\operatorname{vec}(\mathbf{Y}_{(1)}) = \operatorname{vec}(\mathcal{Y})$. This means that $\mathbf{Y}_{(1)}$ is stored in column-major order in memory.

For mode 2, there are $P_2 = 6$ row-major blocks, each of which is of size $n_2 \times M_2 = 4 \times 3$:

$$\mathbf{Y}_{(2)} = \left[\begin{array}{ccc|ccc|c|ccc} 1 & 2 & 3 & 13 & 14 & 15 & \cdots & 61 & 62 & 63 \\ 4 & 5 & 6 & 16 & 17 & 18 & \cdots & 64 & 65 & 66 \\ 7 & 8 & 9 & 19 & 20 & 21 & \cdots & 67 & 68 & 69 \\ 10 & 11 & 12 & 22 & 23 & 24 & \cdots & 70 & 71 & 72 \end{array}\right].$$

For mode 3, there are $P_3 = 2$ row-major blocks, each of which is of size $n_3 \times M_3 = 3 \times 12$:

$$\mathbf{Y}_{(3)} = \left[\begin{array}{cccc|cccc} 1 & 2 & \cdots & 12 & 37 & 38 & \cdots & 48 \\ 13 & 14 & \cdots & 24 & 49 & 50 & \cdots & 60 \\ 25 & 26 & \cdots & 36 & 61 & 62 & \cdots & 72 \end{array}\right].$$

For mode 4, there is $P_4 = 1$ row-major block, which is of size $n_4 \times M_4 = 2 \times 36$:

$$\mathbf{Y}_{(4)} = \begin{bmatrix} 1 & 2 & \cdots & 36 \\ 37 & 38 & \cdots & 72 \end{bmatrix}.$$

Like mode-1, this aligns with the natural ordering of the tensor, except it is in terms of the transpose of the unfolding. In other words, $\operatorname{vec}(\mathbf{Y}_{(4)}^{\mathsf{T}}) = \operatorname{vec}(\mathcal{Y})$, so $\mathbf{Y}_{(4)}$ is stored in row-major order in memory. This can be generalized as follows.

Proposition 2.21 *For a d-way tensor $\mathcal{X}$, it holds that*

$$\operatorname{vec}\left(\mathbf{X}_{(1)}\right) = \operatorname{vec}\left(\mathbf{X}_{(d)}^{\mathsf{T}}\right) = \operatorname{vec}(\mathcal{X}).$$

Example 2.13 (Gram Computation with Unfolded Tensor) Consider a tensor $\mathcal{X}$ of size $4 \times 3 \times 5$. Suppose we want to compute $\mathbf{X}_{(2)}\mathbf{X}_{(2)}^{\mathsf{T}}$. Its mode-2 unfolding $\mathcal{X}$ is of size 3×20. We can write $\mathbf{X}_{(2)}$ as

$$\mathbf{X}_{(2)} = \begin{bmatrix} \mathbf{B}_1^{\mathsf{T}} & \mathbf{B}_2^{\mathsf{T}} & \mathbf{B}_3^{\mathsf{T}} & \mathbf{B}_4^{\mathsf{T}} & \mathbf{B}_5^{\mathsf{T}} \end{bmatrix},$$

where $\mathbf{B}_i$ corresponds to the ith chunk of 12 entries of $\operatorname{vec}(\mathcal{X})$ reshaped into a 4×3 matrix. Then we have

$$\mathbf{X}_{(2)}\mathbf{X}_{(2)}^{\mathsf{T}} = \sum_{i=1}^{5} \mathbf{B}_i^{\mathsf{T}}\mathbf{B}_i.$$

No rearrangement of data is required to form the $\mathbf{B}_i$ matrices.

2.4 Permuting a Tensor

Tensor **permutations** are the higher-order analog of matrix transposition. In fact, they are sometimes referred to as tensor transpositions (e.g., see Springer et al., 2017). If $\mathbf{Z}$ is the transpose of an $m \times n$ matrix $\mathbf{X}$, denoted as $\mathbf{Z} = \mathbf{X}^{\mathsf{T}}$, then we recall that

$$\mathbf{Z}(j, i) = \mathbf{X}(i, j) \quad \text{for all} \quad (i, j) \in [m] \otimes [n].$$

The size of $\mathbf{Z}$ is $n \times m$. There is only one nontrivial permutation on the two modes in a matrix. This means that $\mathbf{X}^{\mathsf{T}}$ is sufficient to indicate permutation of the two modes.

For an $m \times n \times p$ tensor $\mathcal{X}$, there are $3! = 6$ permutations (one is the identity), so it needs more substantial notation. We write

$$\mathcal{Z} = \mathbb{P}(\mathcal{X}, \pi),$$

where $\pi = (\pi_1, \pi_2, \pi_3)$ is a permutation of $(1, 2, 3)$. For example, every frontal slice of the 3-way tensor $\mathcal{X}$ is transposed if

$$\mathcal{Z} = \mathbb{P}\big(\mathcal{X}; (2,1,3)\big) \quad \Leftrightarrow \quad \mathcal{Z}(j,i,k) = \mathcal{X}(i,j,k) \text{ for all } (i,j,k) \in [m] \otimes [n] \otimes [p].$$

The resulting tensor $\mathcal{Z}$ is of size $n \times m \times p$.

Remark 2.22 (Avoiding tensor permutation) Tensor permutations are critical for understanding tensors but should be avoided in implementations due to the high costs of data movement in memory.

Example 2.14 (Tensor Permutation) Consider the $3 \times 3 \times 2$ tensor $\mathcal{X}$ in Example 1.2. Then $\mathcal{Z} = \mathbb{P}(\mathcal{X}, (3,2,1))$ is a tensor of size $2 \times 3 \times 3$ with

$\mathcal{Z} =$ 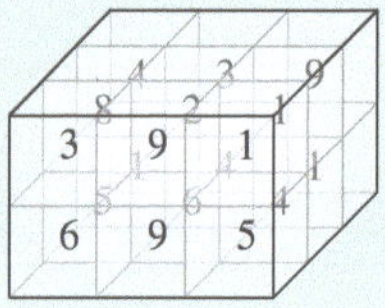 .

Its frontal slices are

$$\mathcal{Z}_1 = \begin{bmatrix} 3 & 9 & 1 \\ 6 & 9 & 5 \end{bmatrix}, \qquad \mathcal{Z}_2 = \begin{bmatrix} 8 & 2 & 1 \\ 5 & 6 & 4 \end{bmatrix}, \qquad \mathcal{Z}_3 = \begin{bmatrix} 4 & 3 & 9 \\ 1 & 4 & 1 \end{bmatrix}.$$

Exercise 2.34 Let $\mathcal{X}$ be the $2 \times 2 \times 2$ tensor in Example 1.1. (a) What is $\mathbb{P}(\mathcal{X}, (2,1,3))$? (b) What is $\mathbb{P}(\mathcal{X}, (3,1,2))$?

For an $n_1 \times n_2 \times \cdots \times n_d$ tensor, there are $d!$ permutations.

Definition 2.23 (Tensor Permutation) Let $\mathcal{X} \in n_1 \times n_2 \times \cdots \times n_d$ and let $\pi = (\pi_1, \pi_2, \ldots, \pi_d)$ be a permutation of $(1, \ldots, d)$. Then we define

$$\mathcal{Z} = \mathbb{P}(\mathcal{X}, \pi) \quad \text{if} \quad \mathcal{Z}(i_{\pi_1}, i_{\pi_2}, \ldots, i_{\pi_d}) = \mathcal{X}(i_1, i_2, \ldots, i_d).$$

The permuted tensor $\mathcal{Z}$ is of size $n_{\pi_1} \times n_{\pi_2} \times \cdots \times n_{\pi_d}$.

Exercise 2.35 Let $\mathcal{X}$ be the 4-way tensor of size $3 \times 2 \times 3 \times 2$ such that

$\mathcal{X}(:,:,:,1) =$

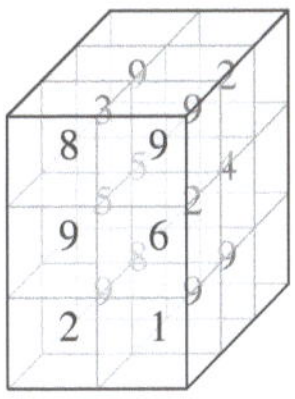

$, \quad \mathcal{X}(:,:,:,2) =$

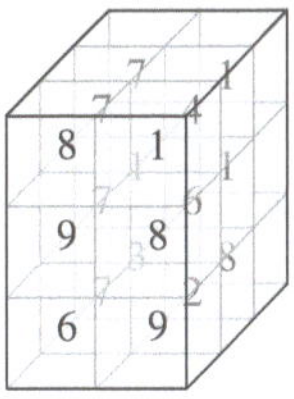

.

(a) What is $\mathbb{P}(\mathcal{X}, (3,2,1,4))$?
(b) What is $\mathbb{P}(\mathcal{X}, (4,3,1,2))$?

A permuted ordering can be specified as $\text{vec}_\pi(\mathcal{X}) \equiv \text{vec}(\mathbb{P}(\mathcal{X}, \pi))$ for the permutation $\pi = (\pi_1, \pi_2, \ldots, \pi_d)$.

Exercise 2.36 For the $\mathcal{X}$ for Example 2.5: (a) What is $\text{vec}_{(2,1,3)}(\mathcal{X})$? (b) What is $\text{vec}_{(3,2,1)}(\mathcal{X})$?

2.4.1 Permutations and Unfoldings

If we want to form an explicit tensor unfolding, the general computational approach is a permutation followed by a reshape. Per Remark 2.22, we generally want to avoid such an explicit computation! Nevertheless, we consider these algorithms from a mathematical point of view.

The mode-2 unfolding of a 3-way tensor, for instance, is accomplished via the following pseudocode:

Mode-2 Unfolding of 3-way Tensor

$\mathcal{Y} = \mathbb{P}(\mathcal{X}, (2,1,3))$
$\mathbf{X}_{(2)} = \text{reshape}(\mathcal{Y}, n \times mp)$

Exercise 2.37 For a 3-way tensor $\mathcal{X}$, prove $\mathbf{X}_{(2)} = \mathbf{Y}_{(1)}$, where $\mathcal{Y} = \mathbb{P}(\mathcal{X}, (2,1,3))$.

Exercise 2.38 What is the pseudocode for the mode-3 unfolding?

In the d-way case, a general unfolding can be implemented as follows. Recall that $\mathcal{R}$ and $\mathcal{C}$ are the sets of indices mapped to the rows and columns, respectively, per Definition 2.19.

General Unfolding of d-way Tensor

function UNFOLD($\mathcal{X} \in \mathbb{R}^{n_1 \times n_2 \times \cdots \times n_d}, \mathcal{R}, \mathcal{C}$)
 $M \leftarrow \prod_{k \in \mathcal{R}} n_k$, $N \leftarrow \prod_{k \in \mathcal{C}} n_k$
 $\mathcal{Y} \leftarrow \mathbb{P}(\mathcal{X}, (\mathcal{R}, \mathcal{C}))$
 $\mathbf{X}_{(\mathcal{R} \times \mathcal{C})} = \text{reshape}(\mathcal{Y}, M \times N)$
end function

Exercise 2.39 For a d-way tensor $\mathcal{X}$, prove $\mathbf{X}_{(\mathcal{R} \times \mathcal{C})} = \text{reshape}(\mathcal{Y}, M \times N)$, where $\mathcal{Y} = \mathbb{P}(\mathcal{X}, (\mathcal{R}, \mathcal{C}))$.

2.4.2 Tensor Perfect Shuffle Matrix

We can define a tensor perfect shuffle matrix that is analogous to the matrix perfect shuffle matrix (Definition A.10). As there are $d!$ possible permutations/transpositions for tensors, the tensor perfect shuffles require more substantial notation.

Definition 2.24 (Tensor Perfect Shuffle) The **perfect shuffle** for a mode permutation π is the permutation matrix $\mathbf{P}_\pi$, such that

$$\mathbf{P}_\pi \operatorname{vec}(\mathfrak{X}) = \operatorname{vec}\big(\mathbb{P}(\mathfrak{X}, \pi)\big)$$

for any tensor $\mathfrak{X}$ of size $n_1 \times n_2 \times \cdots \times n_d$. The size of $\mathbf{P}$ is $N \times N$, where $N = \prod_{k=1}^d n_k$. When $\pi = (k, 1, \ldots, k-1, k+1, \ldots, d)$, corresponding to a mode-k unfolding, we use the notation $\mathbf{P}_k$ such that

$$\mathbf{P}_k \operatorname{vec}(\mathfrak{X}) = \operatorname{vec}\big(\mathbf{X}_{(k)}\big).$$

The exact formula for $\mathbf{P}_\pi$ is given in the following proposition in terms of the permutation τ on $[N]$, i.e., $\mathbf{P}_\pi(j,:)$ is the $\tau(j)$-th row of the identity matrix.

Proposition 2.25 (Tensor Perfect Shuffle Permutation) *Let $\mathfrak{X}$ be a tensor of size $n_1 \times n_2 \times \cdots \times n_d$ and $\mathbf{x} = \operatorname{vec}(\mathfrak{X})$. Let $\pi = (\pi_1, \pi_2, \ldots, \pi_d)$ and $\mathfrak{Y} = \mathbb{P}(\mathfrak{X}, \pi)$. Define $\tau : [N] \to [N]$ by*

$$\tau(\alpha) \equiv 1 + \sum_{k=1}^{d} \Big\lfloor \big((\alpha - 1) \bmod n_k \bar{s}_k\big) / \bar{s}_k \Big\rfloor s_k \quad \textit{with} \tag{2.16}$$

$$s_1 = \bar{s}_{\pi_1} = 1 \quad \textit{and} \quad s_{k+1} = s_k n_k, \quad \bar{s}_{\pi_{k+1}} = \bar{s}_{\pi_k} n_{\pi_k} \quad \textit{for} \quad k \in [d-1]. \tag{2.17}$$

Then, if $\mathbf{y} = \operatorname{vec}(\mathfrak{Y})$, we have

$$\mathbf{y}(\alpha) = \mathbf{x}\big(\tau(\alpha)\big) \quad \textit{for all} \quad \alpha \in [N].$$

Proof. Let $\mathbf{y} = \operatorname{vec}(\mathfrak{Y})$. Then

$$\begin{aligned} \mathbf{y}(\beta) &= \mathfrak{X}(i_1, i_2, \ldots, i_d) && \text{where } (i_1, i_2, \ldots, i_d) = \mathbb{T}^{(\pi)}(\beta), \\ &= \mathbf{x}(\alpha) && \text{where } \alpha = \tau(\beta) = \mathbb{L}\big(\mathbb{T}^{(\pi)}(\beta)\big). \end{aligned}$$

□

Exercise 2.40 Write a function `tps` that uses the tensor perfect shuffle permutation in Eq. (2.16) to convert *directly* from $\mathbf{x} = \operatorname{vec}(\mathfrak{X})$ to $\mathbf{y} = \operatorname{vec}(\mathfrak{Y})$, where $\mathfrak{Y} = \mathbb{P}(\mathfrak{X}, \pi)$.

2.4.3 Linear Indexing and Permutations

There are connections between the different methods of tuple and linear indices, permutations, and the general index conversions, as we elucidate here and illustrate in Fig. 2.5.

For $\mathfrak{X} \in \mathbb{R}^{n_1 \times n_2 \times \cdots \times n_d}$, we can map between its tuple and linear indices using the basic mappings

$$\alpha = \mathbb{L}(i_1, i_2, \ldots, i_d; n_1, n_2, \ldots, n_d) \quad \text{and} \quad (i_1, i_2, \ldots, i_d) = \mathbb{T}(\alpha; n_1, n_2, \ldots, n_d).$$

In the above, we precisely specify the ambient dimensions so that there is no confusion.

If $\mathfrak{Y} = \mathbb{P}(\mathfrak{X}, \pi)$, then $\mathfrak{Y}$ is a permuted version of $\mathfrak{X}$. Thus, we have

$$\mathfrak{Y} \in \mathbb{R}^{m_1 \times m_2 \times \cdots \times m_d}, \quad \text{where} \quad m_k = n_{\pi_k} \text{ for all } k \in [d],$$

and the elements are related as

$$\mathfrak{Y}(j_1, j_2, \ldots, j_d) = \mathfrak{X}(i_1, i_2, \ldots, i_d), \quad \text{where} \quad j_k = i_{\pi_k} \text{ for all } k \in [d].$$

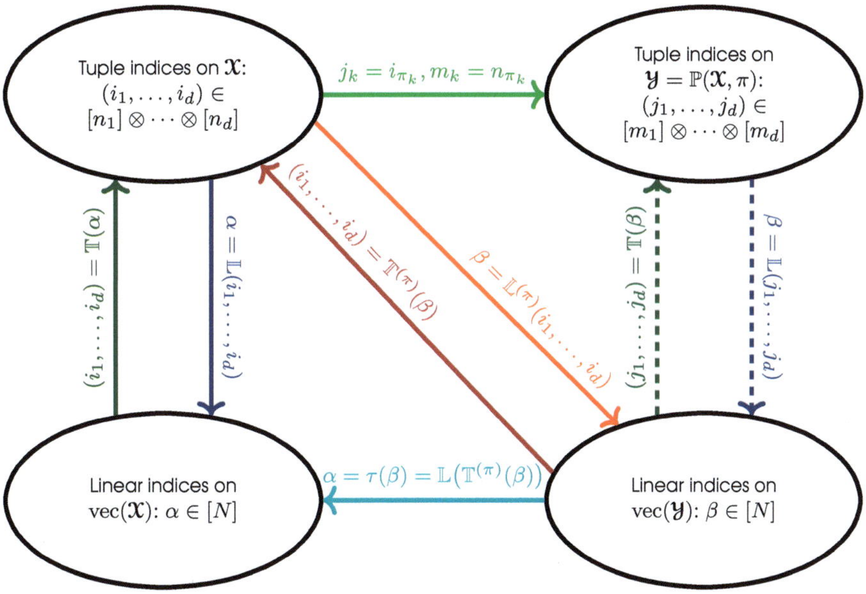

Figure 2.5 Key relationships for general tuple/linear index conversion and permuted tensors. Here $\mathcal{X}$ is a d-way tensor, π is a permutation of $\{1,2,\ldots,d\}$, $\mathcal{Y}$ is the permuted version of $\mathcal{X}$, and τ is the tensor perfect shuffle operator introduced in Proposition 2.25.

We can map between the tuple and linear indices of $\mathcal{Y}$ using

$$\beta = \mathbb{L}(j_1,j_2,\ldots,j_d;m_1,m_2,\ldots,m_d) \quad \text{and} \quad (j_1,j_2,\ldots,j_d) = \mathbb{T}(\beta;m_1,m_2,\ldots,m_d).$$

A key idea is that we can map directly from a tuple index of $\mathcal{X}$ to a linear index of $\mathcal{Y}$ using the general linear index:

$$\beta = \mathbb{L}^{(\pi)}(i_1,i_2,\ldots,i_d;n_1,n_2,\ldots,n_d).$$

Conversely, we can map from a linear index of $\mathcal{Y}$ to a tuple index of $\mathcal{X}$ via

$$(i_1,i_2,\ldots,i_d) = \mathbb{T}^{(\pi)}(\beta;n_1,n_2,\ldots,n_d).$$

> The general order linear index with π is equivalent to the natural order linear index on $\hat{\mathcal{X}} = \mathbb{P}(\mathcal{X};\pi)$.

Finally, we can consider mapping directly to the linear indices of $\mathcal{X}$ from those of $\mathcal{Y}$ using the tensor perfect shuffle:

$$\alpha = \tau(\beta) = \mathbb{L}\Big(\mathbb{T}^{(\pi)}(\beta;n_1,n_2,\ldots,n_d);n_1,n_2,\ldots,n_d\Big).$$

This means we can compute $\mathbf{y} = \mathrm{vec}(\mathcal{Y})$ directly from $\mathbf{x} = \mathrm{vec}(\mathcal{X})$ without ever explicitly computing the tuple indices:

$$\mathbf{y}(\beta) = \mathbf{x}\big(\tau(\beta)\big) \quad \text{for all} \quad \beta \in [N].$$

> We can map directly between the vectorized representations of a tensor $\mathcal{X}$ and a permutation $\mathcal{Y} = \mathbb{P}(\mathcal{X},\pi)$ using the tensor perfect shuffle.

3 Tensor Operations

Before we proceed to tensor decompositions, we discuss key kernels for tensors, including tensor times matrix (TTM), used extensively in Tucker decompositions, and the matricized tensor times Khatri–Rao product (MTTKRP), which is crucial for canonical polyadic (CP) decomposition. We provide mathematical definitions and properties as well as considerations for efficient implementations.

Most tensor operations are expressed in terms of unfoldings and matrix operations. Thus, we make heavy use of the concepts discussed in Chapter 2. While we may express tensor operations mathematically in terms of matrix operations, you will learn in this chapter that efficient implementations are generally not direct instantiations of these mathematical expressions. Indeed, it would be limiting to consider tensor operations as merely matrix operations in the same way it would be limiting to consider matrix operations as merely vector operations.

Efficient implementations minimize computations or floating pointing operations (flops) as well as data movement operations, such as tensor permutations. We assume throughout this chapter that the tensors are stored in memory using the *natural* ordering. This is important for the nuances of data layout and keeping the tensor data "in place" for computations. When possible, we want to cast our subroutines in terms of BLAS operations (see Section A.9.2), such as matrix–matrix multiplication. Details of the memory layout are crucial because BLAS requires that matrices be in row- or column-major order (contiguous in memory).

In concert with discussion of implementations, we establish mathematical properties of the various tensor operations. In subsequent chapters, we can use these tensor operations, their properties, and their implementations in our discussions of tensor decompositions.

3.1 Inner Products

The tensor inner product is the higher-order analog of the dot product.

3.1.1 Inner Products for 3-way Tensors

Analogously to vectors and matrices, the **inner product** of two 3-way tensors is the sum of the products of the corresponding entries. The tensors must be the same size, and the result is a scalar.

Definition 3.1: Inner Product (3-way)

The **inner product** of tensors $\mathcal{X}$ and $\mathcal{Y}$, both of size $m \times n \times p$, is

$$\langle \mathcal{X}, \mathcal{Y} \rangle = \sum_{i=1}^{m} \sum_{j=1}^{n} \sum_{k=1}^{p} x_{ijk} y_{ijk}. \tag{3.1}$$

The **norm** of a tensor is analogous to the matrix Frobenius or vector Euclidean norms, the square root of the inner product with itself.

Definition 3.2: Tensor Norm (3-way)

The **norm** of tensor $\mathcal{X}$ of size $m \times n \times p$ is

$$\|\mathcal{X}\| = \sqrt{\langle \mathcal{X}, \mathcal{X} \rangle} = \sqrt{\sum_{i=1}^{m} \sum_{j=1}^{n} \sum_{k=1}^{p} x_{ijk}^2}. \tag{3.2}$$

Exercise 3.1 Let $\mathcal{X}$ be a tensor of size $m \times n \times p$. Prove $\|\mathcal{X}\| = \| \operatorname{vec}(\mathcal{X}) \|_2$.

In the 3-way case, the computational complexity of computing the inner product of two tensors of size $m \times n \times p$ is $\mathcal{O}(mnp)$; likewise, the computational complexity of computing the norm of a tensor of size $m \times n \times p$ is $\mathcal{O}(mnp)$.

3.1.2 Inner Products for d-way Tensors

The definitions of inner product and norm for d-way tensors are straightforward extensions of those for 3-way tensors. For the inner product, the tensors must be the same size, and the result is a scalar.

Definition 3.3: Inner Product (d-way)

The **inner product** of tensors $\mathcal{X}$ and $\mathcal{Y}$, both of size $n_1 \times n_2 \times \cdots \times n_d$ is

$$\langle \mathcal{X}, \mathcal{Y} \rangle = \sum_{i_1=1}^{n_1} \sum_{i_2=1}^{n_2} \cdots \sum_{i_d=1}^{n_d} x_{i_1 i_2 \cdots i_d} \, y_{i_1 i_2 \cdots i_d}. \tag{3.3}$$

Definition 3.4: Tensor Norm (d-way)

The **norm** of tensor $\mathcal{X}$ of size $n_1 \times n_2 \times \cdots \times n_d$ is

$$\|\mathcal{X}\| = \sqrt{\langle \mathcal{X}, \mathcal{X} \rangle} = \sqrt{\sum_{i_1=1}^{n_1} \sum_{i_2=1}^{n_2} \cdots \sum_{i_d=1}^{n_d} x_{i_1 i_2 \cdots i_d}^2}. \tag{3.4}$$

In the d-way case, the computational complexity of computing the inner product of two tensors of size $n_1 \times n_2 \times \cdots \times n_d$ is $\mathcal{O}(N)$, where $N = \prod_{k=1}^{d} n_k$; likewise, the computational complexity of computing the norm of a tensor of size $n_1 \times n_2 \times \cdots \times n_d$ is $\mathcal{O}(N)$.

Exercise 3.2 Let $\mathcal{X}$ and $\mathcal{Y}$ be two tensors of size $n_1 \times n_2 \times \cdots \times n_d$. Prove $\langle \mathcal{X}, \mathcal{Y} \rangle = \mathbf{x}^\intercal \mathbf{y}$, where $\mathbf{x} = \operatorname{vec}(\mathcal{X})$ and $\mathbf{y} = \operatorname{vec}(\mathcal{Y})$.

3.2 Outer Products

In this section, we consider the outer product. The outer product of two vectors is a matrix (see Section A.3.4). In this section, we consider the outer products of three or more vectors, which produce higher-order tensors. We conclude with a brief discussion of how the notion of outer product applies to tensors of arbitrary order.

3.2.1 Outer Product of Three Vectors

The outer product of three vectors produces a 3-way tensor, as follows.

> **Definition 3.5: Outer Product of Three Vectors**
>
> The **outer product** of vectors $\mathbf{a} \in \mathbb{R}^m$, $\mathbf{b} \in \mathbb{R}^n$, $\mathbf{c} \in \mathbb{R}^p$ is denoted $\mathbf{a} \bigcirc \mathbf{b} \bigcirc \mathbf{c}$ and produces an $m \times n \times p$ tensor, such that element (i,j,k) equals $a_i b_j c_k$:
>
>The cost to compute the outer product of vectors of length m, n, and p is the product of the sizes: $\mathcal{O}(mnp)$.

Definition 3.6 (Rank-1 3-way Tensor) A 3-way tensor $\mathcal{X}$ is **rank 1** if it can be expressed as a vector outer product, i.e., there exist vectors $\mathbf{a}, \mathbf{b}, \mathbf{c}$ such that $\mathcal{X} = \mathbf{a} \bigcirc \mathbf{b} \bigcirc \mathbf{c}$.

Example 3.1 (Outer Product of Three Vectors) An example 3-way outer product is as follows. The darker numbers are the front slice and the lighter numbers are the back slice.

$$\begin{bmatrix} 2 \\ 1 \\ 4 \end{bmatrix} \bigcirc \begin{bmatrix} 5 \\ 3 \\ 1 \\ 2 \end{bmatrix} \bigcirc \begin{bmatrix} 1 \\ 2 \end{bmatrix} = \begin{array}{|cccc|} \hline 20 & 12 & 4 & 8 \\ 10 & 6 & 2 & 4 \\ 10 & 6 & 2 & 4 \\ 5 & 3 & 1 & 2 \\ 40 & 24 & 8 & 16 \\ 20 & 12 & 4 & 8 \\ \hline \end{array}$$

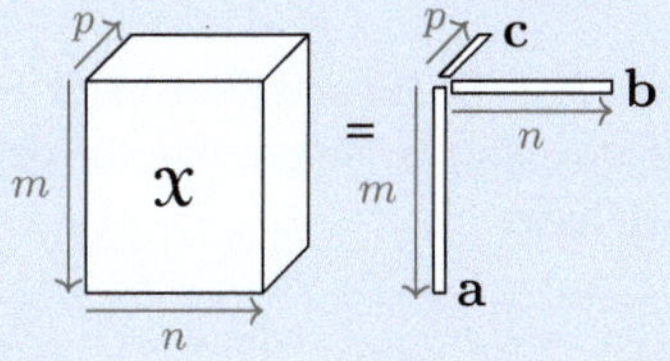

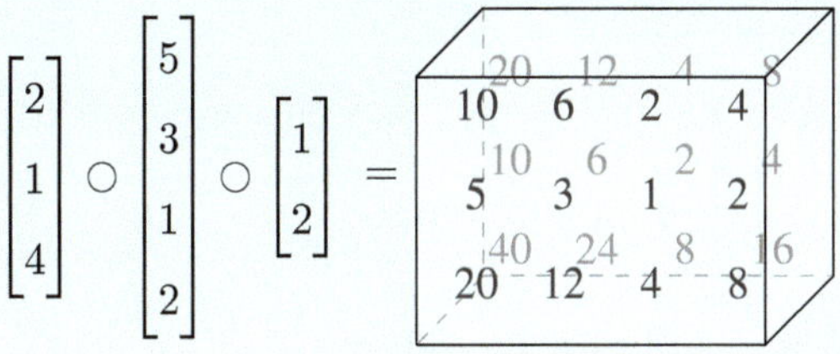

Exercise 3.3 Let $\mathbf{a} \in \mathbb{R}^m$, $\mathbf{b} \in \mathbb{R}^n$, $\mathbf{c} \in \mathbb{R}^p$. Define $\mathcal{X} = \mathbf{a} \bigcirc \mathbf{b} \bigcirc \mathbf{c}$ and $\mathbf{y} = \text{vec}(\mathcal{X})$. Prove $y_\ell = a_i b_j c_k$, where $\ell = \mathbb{L}(i,j,k)$ for all $(i,j,k) \in [m] \otimes [n] \otimes [p]$.

Exercise 3.4 Prove $\|\mathbf{a} \bigcirc \mathbf{b} \bigcirc \mathbf{c}\|^2 = \|\mathbf{a}\|_2^2 \|\mathbf{b}\|_2^2 \|\mathbf{c}\|_2^2$.

The outer product and reverse Kronecker product (Definition A.20) of vectors are identical except for the shape of the output. The Kronecker product produces a vector with reverse linearization (see Proposition 2.4 and Exercise 2.11), so this is why we need the reverse Kronecker product.

> The vector outer product and reverse vector Kronecker product are identical except for the shape of the output.

Proposition 3.7 spells out this relationship.

Proposition 3.7: Vector Kronecker and Outer Product Connections (3-way)

Let $\mathbf{a} \in \mathbb{R}^m$, $\mathbf{b} \in \mathbb{R}^n$, $\mathbf{c} \in \mathbb{R}^p$. *Then the following statements are equivalent:*

$$\mathcal{X} = \mathbf{a} \bigcirc \mathbf{b} \bigcirc \mathbf{c}, \tag{3.5a}$$

$$\operatorname{vec}(\mathcal{X}) = \mathbf{c} \otimes \mathbf{b} \otimes \mathbf{a}, \tag{3.5b}$$

$$\mathbf{X}_{(1)} = \mathbf{a}(\mathbf{c} \otimes \mathbf{b})^{\intercal}, \tag{3.5c}$$

$$\mathbf{X}_{(2)} = \mathbf{b}(\mathbf{c} \otimes \mathbf{a})^{\intercal}, \tag{3.5d}$$

$$\mathbf{X}_{(3)} = \mathbf{c}(\mathbf{b} \otimes \mathbf{a})^{\intercal}. \tag{3.5e}$$

Proof. We prove equivalence of Eqs. (3.5a) and (3.5b) and leave the remainder as an exercise. Define $\mathbf{u} = \operatorname{vec}(\mathcal{X})$ and $\mathbf{v} = \mathbf{c} \otimes \mathbf{b} \otimes \mathbf{a}$. Using the definition of vectorization from Eq. (2.9) and Exercise 2.11, we have

$$u_\ell = v_\ell \quad \Leftrightarrow \quad x_{ijk} = a_i b_j c_k, \quad \text{where} \quad (i,j,k) = \mathbb{T}(\ell; m, n, p)$$

for any $\ell \in [mnp]$ or $(i,j,k) \in [m] \otimes [n] \otimes [p]$. □

Exercise 3.5 Prove Eqs. (3.5c)–(3.5e) are each equivalent to Eq. (3.5a) in Proposition 3.7.

Example 3.2 (Vectorizing and Unfolding an Outer Product) Let $\mathbf{a} = \left[\begin{smallmatrix}2\\6\end{smallmatrix}\right]$, $\mathbf{b} = \left[\begin{smallmatrix}3\\4\end{smallmatrix}\right]$, and $\mathbf{c} = \left[\begin{smallmatrix}1\\5\end{smallmatrix}\right]$. Then $\mathcal{X} = \mathbf{a} \bigcirc \mathbf{b} \bigcirc \mathbf{c}$ is

$$\mathcal{X}(:,:,1) = \begin{bmatrix} 6 & 8 \\ 18 & 24 \end{bmatrix}, \quad \mathcal{X}(:,:,2) = \begin{bmatrix} 30 & 40 \\ 90 & 120 \end{bmatrix}.$$

Observe the following equivalencies:

$$\mathbf{c} \otimes \mathbf{b} \otimes \mathbf{a} = \begin{bmatrix} 6 & 18 & 8 & 24 & 30 & 90 & 40 & 120 \end{bmatrix}^{\intercal} = \operatorname{vec}(\mathcal{X}),$$

$$\mathbf{a}(\mathbf{c} \otimes \mathbf{b})^{\intercal} = \begin{bmatrix} 2 \\ 6 \end{bmatrix} \begin{bmatrix} 3 & 4 & 15 & 20 \end{bmatrix} = \begin{bmatrix} 6 & 8 & 30 & 40 \\ 18 & 24 & 90 & 120 \end{bmatrix} = \mathbf{X}_{(1)},$$

$$\mathbf{b}(\mathbf{c} \otimes \mathbf{a})^{\intercal} = \begin{bmatrix} 3 \\ 4 \end{bmatrix} \begin{bmatrix} 2 & 6 & 10 & 30 \end{bmatrix} = \begin{bmatrix} 6 & 18 & 30 & 90 \\ 8 & 24 & 40 & 120 \end{bmatrix} = \mathbf{X}_{(2)},$$

$$\mathbf{c}(\mathbf{b} \otimes \mathbf{a})^{\intercal} = \begin{bmatrix} 1 \\ 5 \end{bmatrix} \begin{bmatrix} 6 & 18 & 8 & 24 \end{bmatrix} = \begin{bmatrix} 6 & 18 & 8 & 24 \\ 30 & 90 & 40 & 120 \end{bmatrix} = \mathbf{X}_{(3)}.$$

Exercise 3.6 Let $\mathbf{a} \in \mathbb{R}^m$, $\mathbf{b} \in \mathbb{R}^n$, and $\mathbf{c} \in \mathbb{R}^p$. (a) If $\mathcal{X} = \mathbf{c} \bigcirc \mathbf{b} \bigcirc \mathbf{a}$, what is the size of $\mathcal{X}$? (b) What is $\operatorname{vec}(\mathcal{X})$ in terms of $\mathbf{a}, \mathbf{b}, \mathbf{c}$?

3.2.2 Outer Product of d Vectors

We can extend the definition of outer product in a straightforward way to the d-way case. The outer product of d vectors is a d-way tensor.

Definition 3.8: Outer Product of d Vectors

The **outer product** of d vectors $\mathbf{a}_k \in \mathbb{R}^{n_k}$ for all $k \in [d]$ is a d-way tensor denoted $\mathbf{a}_1 \bigcirc \mathbf{a}_2 \bigcirc \cdots \bigcirc \mathbf{a}_d$ of size $n_1 \times n_2 \times \cdots \times n_d$, such that element $(i_1, i_2, \ldots, i_d)$ is given by $\prod_{k=1}^{d} \mathbf{a}_k(i_k)$.

The cost to compute the outer product of d vectors is $\mathcal{O}(N)$ arithmetic operations, where $N = \prod_{k=1}^{d} n_k$. We discuss implementation in Section 3.2.3.

Definition 3.9 (Rank-1 d-way Tensor) A d-way tensor $\mathcal{X}$ is **rank 1** if it can be written as an outer product of d vectors. In other words, there exists vectors $\{\, \mathbf{a}_k \,\}_{k=1}^{d}$ such that $\mathcal{X} = \mathbf{a}_1 \bigcirc \mathbf{a}_2 \bigcirc \cdots \bigcirc \mathbf{a}_d$.

Exercise 3.7 Let $\{\, \mathbf{a}_k \,\}_{k=1}^{d}$ be a set of d vectors such that $\mathbf{a}_k \in \mathbb{R}^{n_k}$. Further, define $\mathcal{X} = \mathbf{a}_1 \bigcirc \mathbf{a}_2 \bigcirc \cdots \bigcirc \mathbf{a}_d$ and $\mathbf{y} = \operatorname{vec}(\mathcal{X})$. Prove $y_\alpha = \prod_{k=1}^{d} \mathbf{a}_k(i_k)$, where $\alpha = \mathbb{L}(i_1, i_2, \ldots, i_d)$.

As in the 3-way case (Proposition 3.7), the Kronecker product and outer product of d vectors are intimately related. The following proposition is the d-way analog of Proposition 3.7, with the addition of Eq. (3.6d), which relates general unfoldings of the vector outer product to an outer product of Kronecker products.

Proposition 3.10: Vector Kronecker and Outer Product Connections (d-way)

Let $\mathbf{a}_k \in \mathbb{R}^{n_k}$ for all $k \in [d]$. Then the following statements are equivalent.

$$\mathcal{X} = \mathbf{a}_1 \bigcirc \mathbf{a}_2 \bigcirc \cdots \bigcirc \mathbf{a}_d, \tag{3.6a}$$

$$\operatorname{vec}(\mathcal{X}) = \mathbf{a}_d \otimes \mathbf{a}_{d-1} \otimes \cdots \otimes \mathbf{a}_1, \tag{3.6b}$$

$$\mathbf{X}_{(k)} = \mathbf{a}_k (\mathbf{a}_d \otimes \cdots \otimes \mathbf{a}_{k+1} \otimes \mathbf{a}_{k-1} \otimes \cdots \otimes \mathbf{a}_1)^\intercal, \tag{3.6c}$$

$$\mathbf{X}_{(\mathcal{R} \times \mathcal{C})} = (\mathbf{a}_{r_\delta} \otimes \cdots \otimes \mathbf{a}_{r_1})(\mathbf{a}_{c_{d-\delta}} \otimes \cdots \otimes \mathbf{a}_{c_1})^\intercal, \tag{3.6d}$$

where $\mathcal{R} = (r_1, \ldots, r_\delta)$ and $\mathcal{C} = (c_1, \ldots, c_{d-\delta})$ is an ordered partitioning of $[d]$.

Exercise 3.8 Prove Proposition 3.10.

The vectorization of a vector outer product is the same as the Kronecker product of those vectors *in reverse order*, i.e., $\operatorname{vec}(\mathbf{a}_1 \bigcirc \mathbf{a}_2 \bigcirc \cdots \bigcirc \mathbf{a}_d) = \mathbf{a}_d \otimes \mathbf{a}_{d-1} \otimes \cdots \otimes \mathbf{a}_1$.

The following shorthand notation is common for Kronecker products of multiple vectors:

$$\bigotimes_{k=d}^{1} \mathbf{a}_k \equiv \mathbf{a}_d \otimes \mathbf{a}_{d-1} \otimes \cdots \otimes \mathbf{a}_1 \quad \text{or} \quad \bigotimes_{\substack{\ell=d \\ \ell \neq k}}^{1} \mathbf{a}_\ell \equiv \mathbf{a}_d \otimes \cdots \otimes \mathbf{a}_{k+1} \otimes \mathbf{a}_{k-1} \otimes \cdots \otimes \mathbf{a}_1.$$

Example 3.3 (Unfolding Outer Product of Four Vectors) Suppose that we have four vectors:

$$\mathbf{a} = \begin{bmatrix} 4 \\ 2 \end{bmatrix}, \quad \mathbf{b} = \begin{bmatrix} 3 \\ 1 \end{bmatrix}, \quad \mathbf{c} = \begin{bmatrix} 5 \\ 3 \end{bmatrix}, \quad \text{and} \quad \mathbf{d} = \begin{bmatrix} 3 \\ 5 \end{bmatrix}.$$

Then the frontal slices of $\mathcal{X} = \mathbf{a} \bigcirc \mathbf{b} \bigcirc \mathbf{c} \bigcirc \mathbf{d}$ are:

$$\mathcal{X}(:,:,1,1) = \begin{bmatrix} 180 & 60 \\ 90 & 30 \end{bmatrix}, \qquad \mathcal{X}(:,:,1,2) = \begin{bmatrix} 300 & 100 \\ 150 & 50 \end{bmatrix},$$

$$\mathcal{X}(:,:,2,1) = \begin{bmatrix} 108 & 36 \\ 54 & 18 \end{bmatrix}, \qquad \mathcal{X}(:,:,2,2) = \begin{bmatrix} 180 & 60 \\ 90 & 30 \end{bmatrix}.$$

Let $\mathcal{R} = (3, 1)$ and $\mathcal{C} = (2, 4)$. Then

$$(\mathbf{a} \otimes \mathbf{c})(\mathbf{d} \otimes \mathbf{b})^\intercal = \begin{bmatrix} 20 \\ 12 \\ 10 \\ 6 \end{bmatrix} \begin{bmatrix} 9 & 3 & 15 & 5 \end{bmatrix} = \begin{bmatrix} 180 & 60 & 300 & 100 \\ 108 & 36 & 180 & 60 \\ 90 & 30 & 150 & 50 \\ 54 & 18 & 90 & 30 \end{bmatrix} = \mathbf{X}_{(\mathcal{R} \times \mathcal{C})}.$$

3.2.3 General Outer Products

Outer products are not constrained to vectors, but the computation always reduces to computing outer products of vectors or, equivalently, Kronecker products of vectors.

Example 3.4 (Matrix and Vector Outer Product) The outer product of a vector $\mathbf{a} \in \mathbb{R}^m$ and a matrix $\mathbf{B} \in \mathbb{R}^{n \times p}$ is a tensor of size $m \times n \times p$. If $\mathcal{X} = \mathbf{a} \bigcirc \mathbf{B}$, then $x_{ijk} = a_i b_{jk}$ for all $(i, j, k) \in [m] \otimes [n] \otimes [p]$.

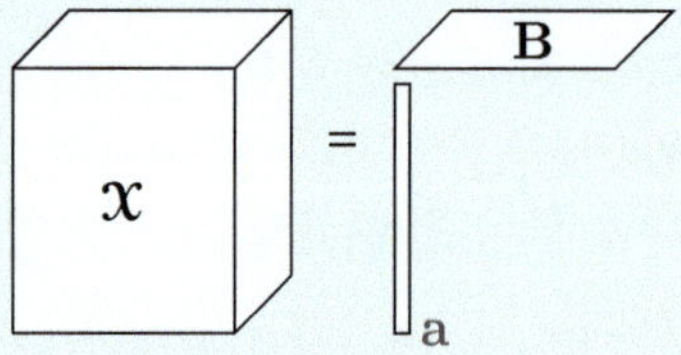

This can be computed as $\mathbf{a} \bigcirc \mathbf{B} = \text{reshape}(\mathbf{a} \bigcirc \text{vec}(\mathbf{B}), m \times n \times p)$.

We have already used this notion implicitly because the outer product is associative (i.e., the grouping of operations does not matter), and we generally compute a 3-way outer product by first computing a 2-way outer product and then an outer product of that matrix result and the remaining vector. This enables us to use efficient vector–vector operations and reduces the computational complexity from $2mnp$ operations to $mnp + \min\{mn, np\}$ compared to evaluating the definition directly.

Exercise 3.9 Using the definition of the outer product of two vectors (see Section A.3.4), prove $(\mathbf{a} \bigcirc \mathbf{b}) \bigcirc \mathbf{c} = \mathbf{a} \bigcirc (\mathbf{b} \bigcirc \mathbf{c}) = \mathbf{a} \bigcirc \mathbf{b} \bigcirc \mathbf{c}$.

The outer product between two 3-way tensors $\mathcal{X}$ and $\mathcal{Y}$ of size $m \times n \times p$ and $q \times r \times s$, respectively, reduces to

$$\mathcal{X} \circ \mathcal{Y} = \text{reshape}(\text{vec}(\mathcal{X}) \circ \text{vec}(\mathcal{Y}), m \times n \times p \times q \times r \times s).$$

The result is a 6-way tensor.

Most generally, the outer product between two arbitrary tensors $\mathcal{X}$ and $\mathcal{Y}$ of size $m_1 \times m_2 \times \cdots \times m_{d_1}$ and $n_1 \times n_2 \times \cdots \times n_{d_2}$, respectively, reduces to an outer product of two vectors followed by a reshape. In other words,

$$\mathcal{X} \circ \mathcal{Y} = \text{reshape}(\text{vec}(\mathcal{X}) \circ \text{vec}(\mathcal{Y}), m_1 \times \cdots \times m_{d_1} \times n_1 \times \cdots \times n_{d_2}).$$

The result is a $(d_1 + d_2)$-way tensor.

3.2.4 Tensor–Tensor Outer Products

We can now generalize from outer products of vectors to arbitrary tensors. As in the vector case, the outer product of two tensors computes all pairwise products between elements of the two objects.

Definition 3.11 (Tensor Outer Product) The **tensor outer product** of two tensors

$$\mathcal{X} \in \mathbb{R}^{m_1 \times m_2 \times \cdots \times m_d} \quad \text{and} \quad \mathcal{Y} \in \mathbb{R}^{n_1 \times n_2 \times \cdots \times n_{d'}}$$

is the tensor

$$\mathcal{Z} = \mathcal{X} \circ \mathcal{Y} \in \mathbb{R}^{m_1 \times m_2 \times \cdots \times m_d \times n_1 \times n_2 \times \cdots \times n_{d'}}$$

of order $(d + d')$, whose elements are given by

$$\mathcal{Z}(i_1, \ldots, i_d, j_1, \ldots, j_{d'}) = \mathcal{X}(i_1, \ldots, i_d)\, \mathcal{Y}(j_1, \ldots, j_{d'})$$

for all $(i_1, \ldots, i_d, j_1, \ldots, j_{d'}) \in [m_1] \otimes \cdots \otimes [m_d] \otimes [n_1] \otimes \cdots \otimes [n_{d'}]$.

The cost of the tensor–tensor outer product in Definition 3.11 is MN, where $M = \prod_{k=1}^{d} m_k$ and $N = \prod_{k=1}^{d} n_k$.

Thanks to the relationship between tensor and vector outer products, we can compute the tensor outer product using vector outer products or, equivalently, Kronecker products per the following theorem.

Proposition 3.12 (Tensor Outer Product Unfoldings) *For tensors $\mathcal{X}$, $\mathcal{Y}$, the following statements are equivalent:*

$$\mathcal{Z} = \mathcal{X} \circ \mathcal{Y}, \tag{3.7}$$

$$\text{vec}(\mathcal{Z}) = \text{vec}(\mathcal{X}) \circ \text{vec}(\mathcal{Y}), \quad \textit{and} \tag{3.8}$$

$$\text{vec}(\mathcal{Z}) = \text{vec}(\mathcal{Y}) \otimes \text{vec}(\mathcal{X}). \tag{3.9}$$

Example 3.5 (Tensor Outer Product as Kronecker Product) Let $\mathcal{X} \in \mathbb{R}^{m\times n\times p}$ and $\mathcal{Y} \in \mathbb{R}^{q\times r\times s}$. Their outer product $\mathcal{Z} = \mathcal{X} \circ \mathcal{Y}$ is of size $m \times n \times p \times q \times r \times s$. Its elements can be computed as

$$\mathbf{z} = \text{vec}(\mathcal{Y}) \otimes \text{vec}(\mathcal{X}),$$

and then rearranged into a tensor:

$$\mathcal{Z} = \text{reshape}(\mathbf{z}, m \times n \times p \times q \times r \times s).$$

The tensor outer product is an associative operation:

Proposition 3.13 (Outer Product Associativity) *Given any tensors $\mathcal{X}$, $\mathcal{Y}$, $\mathcal{Z}$, we have* $(\mathcal{X} \circ \mathcal{Y}) \circ \mathcal{Z} = \mathcal{X} \circ (\mathcal{Y} \circ \mathcal{Z})$.

Given the tensor outer product and Proposition 3.13, we see that we can compute the vector outer product of d vectors (Definition 3.8) as a sequence of $(d-1)$ binary tensor outer products in any order. This reduces the leading order arithmetic cost from $(d-1)N$ to N operations.

Exercise 3.10 Prove Proposition 3.13.

Exercise 3.11 For matrices $\mathbf{A} \in \mathbb{R}^{m\times n}$ and $\mathbf{B} \in \mathbb{R}^{p\times q}$, what is the connection between $\mathbf{A} \circ \mathbf{B}$, $\mathbf{B} \otimes \mathbf{A}$, and $\mathbf{A} \otimes \mathbf{B}$?

3.3 Tensor-Times-Matrix Products

The tensor-times-matrix (TTM) product is a mode-wise multiplication denoted as

$$\mathcal{X} \times_k \mathbf{U},$$

where $\mathcal{X}$ is a tensor, k is the mode for the TTM, and $\mathbf{U}$ is the matrix. It is a key operation for Tucker decomposition algorithms. We define it formally in terms of the mode-k unfolding.

Definition 3.14: Tensor-Times-Matrix Product

The mode-k **TTM product** of a tensor $\mathcal{X}$ with a matrix $\mathbf{U}$ is denoted as $\mathcal{Y} = \mathcal{X} \times_k \mathbf{U}$ and defined in terms of the matricized expression:

$$\mathbf{Y}_{(k)} = \mathbf{U}\mathbf{X}_{(k)}.$$

As the columns of a mode-k unfolding are the fibers of mode k, we can also interpret Definition 3.14 in terms of the matrix acting on the fibers.

The TTM $\mathcal{X} \times_k \mathbf{U}$ multiplies each mode-k fiber of $\mathcal{X}$ by $\mathbf{U}$.

If two successive TTMs are in the same mode, then we can combine the multiplicands as follows. The order of the TTMs matters.

Proposition 3.15 (TTM Grouping) *Let $\mathcal{X}$ be a tensor such that mode k is of size n. Then, for any $\mathbf{U} \in \mathbb{R}^{r \times n}$ and $\mathbf{V} \in \mathbb{R}^{q \times r}$, we have*

$$\mathcal{X} \times_k \mathbf{U} \times_k \mathbf{V} = \mathcal{X} \times_k (\mathbf{VU}).$$

Proof. Let $\mathcal{Y} = \mathcal{X} \times_k \mathbf{U}$. By Definition 3.14, $\mathbf{Y}_{(k)} = \mathbf{U}\mathbf{X}_{(k)}$. Let $\mathcal{Z} = \mathcal{X} \times_k \mathbf{U} \times_k \mathbf{V} = \mathcal{Y} \times_k \mathbf{V}$. Then

$$\mathbf{Z}_{(k)} = \mathbf{V}\mathbf{Y}_{(k)} = \mathbf{V}(\mathbf{U}\mathbf{X}_{(k)}) = (\mathbf{VU})\mathbf{X}_{(k)}.$$

Hence, $\mathcal{Z} = \mathcal{X} \times_k (\mathbf{VU})$. □

Exercise 3.12 (TTM and Permutation) Prove

$$\mathcal{Y} = \mathcal{X} \times_k \mathbf{U} \quad \text{if and only if} \quad \mathbb{P}(\mathcal{Y}, \pi) = \mathbb{P}(\mathcal{X}, \pi) \times_{\pi_k} \mathbf{U}.$$

3.3.1 TTM for 3-way Tensors

We give specialized definitions for the 3-way case, in an attempt to give some intuition for the concept, as well as efficient algorithms for computing a TTM in each mode.

Mode-1 TTM for 3-way Tensor

Definition 3.16 (TTM in Mode 1) The **TTM operation in mode 1** of $\mathcal{X} \in \mathbb{R}^{m \times n \times p}$ with a matrix $\mathbf{U} \in \mathbb{R}^{q \times m}$ is denoted as

$$\mathcal{Y} = \mathcal{X} \times_1 \mathbf{U}$$

and produces a $q \times n \times p$ tensor where the column (mode-1) fibers of $\mathcal{Y}$ are equal to the corresponding column fibers of $\mathcal{X}$ multiplied by $\mathbf{U}$. Specifically, $\mathbf{Y}_{(1)} = \mathbf{U}\mathbf{X}_{(1)}$, or

$$y_{\alpha jk} = \sum_{i=1}^{m} x_{ijk} u_{\alpha i} \quad \text{for all} \quad (\alpha, j, k) \in [q] \otimes [n] \otimes [p].$$

We can write the mode-1 TTM in terms of the column fibers as

$$\mathbf{y}_{:jk} = \mathbf{U}\mathbf{x}_{:jk} \quad \text{for all} \quad (j, k) \in [n] \otimes [p].$$

We visualize this in Fig. 3.1a where, for mode-1 multiplication, it is common to put the matrix to the left of the tensor so that the rows of $\mathbf{U}$ are perpendicular to the column fibers of $\mathcal{X}$. We draw arrows to show the first row of $\mathbf{U}$ and the first column fiber of $\mathcal{X}$. This example has $q < m$, so each column fiber gets shorter in the result. For the matrix form $\mathbf{Y}_{(1)} = \mathbf{U}\mathbf{X}_{(1)}$, see Fig. 3.1b.

We recall that $\mathcal{X}$ and $\mathbf{X}_{(1)}$ are stored identically in memory (see Exercise 2.26), which implies that $\mathbf{X}_{(1)}$ is in column-major layout. Hence, the mode-1 TTM computation can be computed in an efficient and straightforward way using a single matrix–matrix multiplication that follows the definition:

Mode-1 TTM for 3-way Tensor (Efficient)

1: $\mathbf{X} \leftarrow \text{reshape}(\mathcal{X}, m \times np)$ ▷ $\mathbf{X} = \mathbf{X}_{(1)}$
2: $\mathbf{Y} \leftarrow \mathbf{UX}$ ▷ Matrix–matrix multiply
3: $\mathcal{Y} \leftarrow \text{reshape}(\mathbf{Y}, q \times n \times p)$ ▷ $\mathbf{Y} = \mathbf{Y}_{(1)}$

The computational cost of the TTM in mode 1 is $\mathcal{O}(mnpq)$.

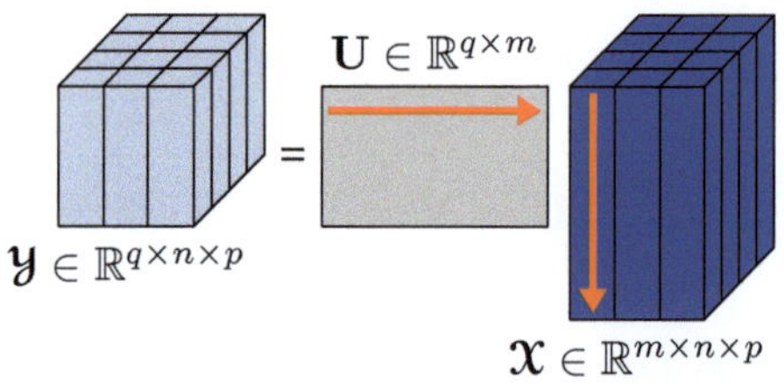

(a) Tensor form: the first row of $\mathbf{U}$ and first mode-1 fiber of $\mathcal{X}$ are emphasized with arrows.

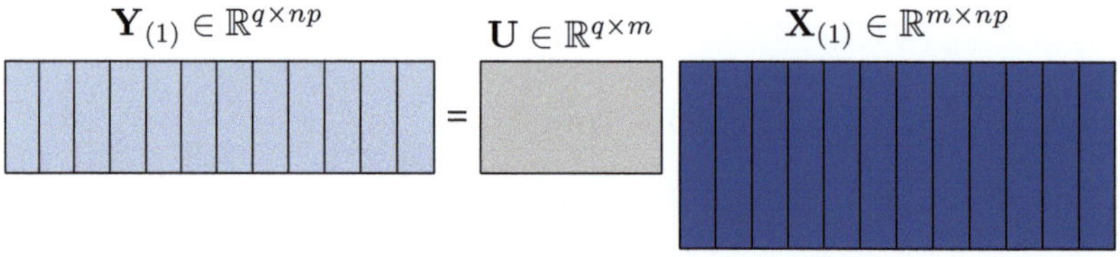

(b) Matrix form.

Figure 3.1 Mode-1 TTM (along column fibers).

Mode-2 TTM for 3-way Tensor

Definition 3.17 (TTM in Mode 2) The **TTM operation in mode 2** of $\mathcal{X} \in \mathbb{R}^{m \times n \times p}$ with a matrix $\mathbf{V} \in \mathbb{R}^{r \times n}$ is denoted as

$$\mathcal{Y} = \mathcal{X} \times_2 \mathbf{V}$$

and produces an $m \times r \times p$ tensor where the row (mode-2) fibers of $\mathcal{Y}$ are equal to the corresponding row fibers of $\mathcal{X}$ multiplied by $\mathbf{V}$. Specifically, $\mathbf{Y}_{(2)} = \mathbf{V}\mathbf{X}_{(2)}$, or

$$y_{i\beta k} = \sum_{j=1}^{n} x_{ijk} v_{\beta j} \quad \text{for all} \quad (i, \beta, k) \in [m] \otimes [r] \otimes [p].$$

Equivalently, we can write this in terms of the row fibers as

$$\mathbf{y}_{i:k} = \mathbf{V}\mathbf{x}_{i:k} \quad \text{for all} \quad (i, k) \in [m] \otimes [p].$$

The mode-2 TTM transforms the row fibers, and we picture mode-2 TTM with the matrix on the right of the tensor and shown in a transposed orientation as in Fig. 3.2. This orientation of $\mathbf{V}$ makes its rows perpendicular to the row fibers of $\mathcal{X}$. Here we have shown an example with $r > n$, so the second mode in the result tensor is enlarged in the result.

Efficient computation of mode-2 TTM is more complicated than mode-1 TTM because in order to perform a single high-performance matrix–matrix multiplication, the elements of $\mathcal{X}$ would have to be rearranged for the unfolding and likewise the result would have to be rearranged after reshaping. That is, we could compute $\mathcal{Y} = \mathcal{X} \times_2 \mathbf{V}$ as follows:

Mode-2 TTM for 3-way Tensor (Naive)

1: $\bar{\mathcal{X}} \leftarrow \mathbb{P}(\mathcal{X}, (2, 1, 3))$ ▷ Swap modes 1 and 2 to get $n \times m \times p$ tensor
2: $\mathbf{X} \leftarrow \text{reshape}(\bar{\mathcal{X}}, n \times mp)$ ▷ $\mathbf{X} = \bar{\mathbf{X}}_{(1)} = \mathbf{X}_{(2)}$
3: $\mathbf{Y} \leftarrow \mathbf{V}\mathbf{X}$ ▷ Matrix–matrix multiply
4: $\bar{\mathcal{Y}} \leftarrow \text{reshape}(\mathbf{Y}, r \times m \times p)$ ▷ $\mathbf{Y} = \bar{\mathbf{Y}}_{(1)} = \mathbf{Y}_{(2)}$
5: $\mathcal{Y} \leftarrow \mathbb{P}(\bar{\mathcal{Y}}, (2, 1, 3))$ ▷ Swap modes 1 and 2 back to get $m \times r \times p$ tensor

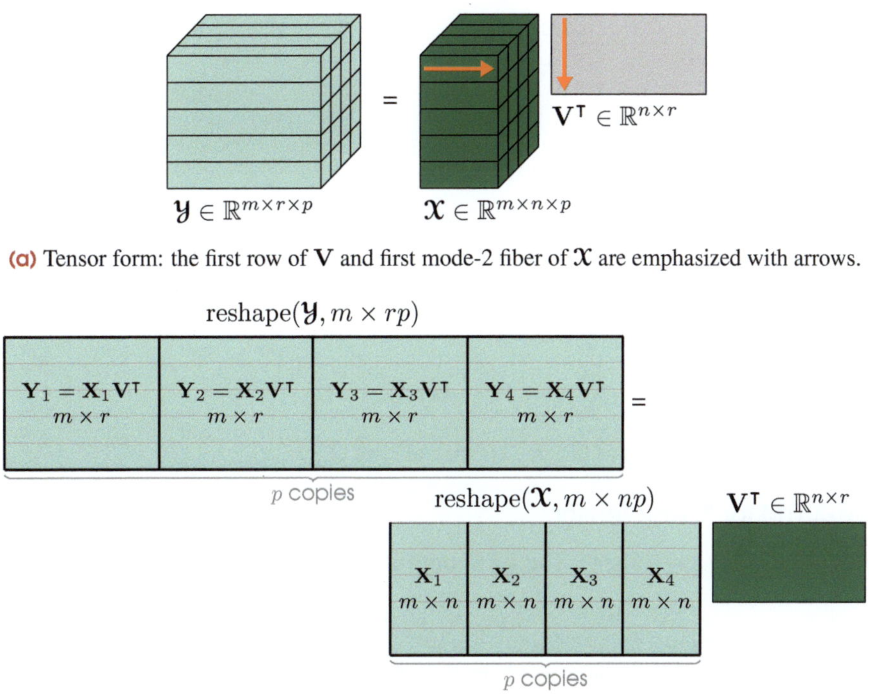

(a) Tensor form: the first row of $\mathbf{V}$ and first mode-2 fiber of $\mathcal{X}$ are emphasized with arrows.

(b) Special unfolding emphasizing block structure. Each block in matrix version of $\mathcal{X}$ is multiplied by $\mathbf{V}^\intercal$ to produce the corresponding block in matrix version of $\mathcal{Y}$.

Figure 3.2 Mode-2 TTM (along row fibers).

However, the above is a naive implementation because the permutations move elements around in memory, which is much slower than performing flops. Even though there are fewer moves in the permutation than flops in the matrix multiplication, the permutations often become efficiency bottlenecks.

Instead, we can compute TTM without performing any explicit permutations of the input or output tensors by considering the mode-2 unfolding **memory layout**. Recall from Section 2.3.3 that the internal ordering of the mode-2 unfolding has structure: If $\mathcal{X}$ is stored according to the natural ordering, then $\mathbf{X}_{(2)}$ has p contiguous blocks:

$$\mathbf{X}_{(2)} = \begin{bmatrix} \mathbf{B}_1^\intercal & \mathbf{B}_2^\intercal & \cdots & \mathbf{B}_p^\intercal \end{bmatrix}, \quad \text{where} \quad \mathbf{B}_k = \mathcal{X}(:,:,k) \text{ for } k \in [p].$$

Here each $\mathbf{B}_k$ corresponds to the $m \times n$ frontal slice $\mathcal{X}(:,:,k)$ (see Exercise 3.14) and *is stored contiguously in memory in column-major order*. The result tensor $\mathcal{Y}$ has an analogous structure:

$$\mathbf{Y}_{(2)} = \begin{bmatrix} \mathbf{C}_1^\intercal & \mathbf{C}_2^\intercal & \cdots & \mathbf{C}_p^\intercal \end{bmatrix},$$

where each $\mathbf{C}_k$ corresponds to the contiguous-in-memory, column-major $m \times r$ frontal slice $\mathcal{Y}(:,:,k)$ (see Fig. 3.2b). Hence, computing $\mathcal{Y} = \mathbf{V}\mathbf{X}_{(2)}$ is equivalent to computing $\mathbf{C}_k^\intercal = \mathbf{V}\mathbf{B}_k^\intercal$ for each $k \in [p]$. By transposing both sides of the equation, we can compute $\mathbf{C}_k = \mathbf{B}_k\mathbf{V}^\intercal$ for each $k \in [p]$ using a batch of matrix–matrix multiplications. Thus, the mode-2 TTM can be performed without explicit permutation as follows:

Mode-2 TTM for 3-way Tensor (Efficient)

1: **for** $k = 1$ to p **do**
2: $\quad \mathcal{Y}(:,:,k) \leftarrow \mathcal{X}(:,:,k)\mathbf{V}^{\mathsf{T}}$ ▷ Matrix–matrix multiply
3: **end for**

This can be cast as a batched BLAS operation, e.g., using the `pagemtimes` function in MATLAB.

Exercise 3.13 What is the arithmetic cost of $\mathcal{X} \times_2 \mathbf{V}$ with $\mathcal{X} \in \mathbb{R}^{m \times n \times p}$ and $\mathbf{V} \in r \times n$?

Exercise 3.14 Let $\mathcal{X} \in \mathbb{R}^{m \times n \times p}$. Using the definition of the mode-2 unfolding (Definition 2.16) and linear indexing, prove that

$$\mathbf{X}_{(2)} = \begin{bmatrix} \mathbf{B}_1^{\mathsf{T}} & \mathbf{B}_2^{\mathsf{T}} & \cdots & \mathbf{B}_p^{\mathsf{T}} \end{bmatrix},$$

where each $\mathbf{B}_k$ corresponds to the $m \times n$ frontal slice $\mathcal{X}(:,:,k)$.

Mode-3 TTM for 3-way Tensor

Definition 3.18 (TTM in Mode 3) The **TTM operation in mode 3** with a matrix $\mathbf{W} \in \mathbb{R}^{s \times p}$ is denoted as

$$\mathcal{Y} = \mathcal{X} \times_3 \mathbf{W}$$

and produces an $m \times n \times s$ tensor where the tube (mode-3) fibers of $\mathcal{Y}$ are equal to the corresponding tube fibers of $\mathcal{X}$ multiplied by $\mathbf{W}$. Specifically, $\mathbf{Y}_{(3)} = \mathbf{W}\mathbf{X}_{(3)}$, or

$$y_{ij\gamma} = \sum_{k=1}^{p} x_{ijk} w_{\gamma k} \quad \text{for all} \quad (i,j,\gamma) \in [m] \otimes [n] \otimes [s].$$

Equivalently, we can write this in terms of the tube fibers as

$$\mathbf{y}_{ij:} = \mathbf{W}\mathbf{x}_{ij:} \quad \text{for all} \quad (i,j) \in [m] \otimes [n].$$

The mode-3 TTM transforms the tube fibers, and we usually picture mode-3 TTM with the matrix above the tensor, as shown in Fig. 3.3a. The matrix is oriented so that its first row is at the bottom (since the numbering in mode-3 goes into the page) and perpendicular to the tube fibers.

Recall from Proposition 2.21 that for 3-way tensors, the mode-3 unfolding is stored rowwise in memory when the tensor is in natural ordering. We can instead use

$$\mathbf{Y}_{(3)}^{\mathsf{T}} = \mathbf{X}_{(3)}^{\mathsf{T}} \mathbf{W}^{\mathsf{T}}$$

to perform the multiplication, as shown in Fig. 3.3b, aligning the tube fibers to be the rows of the unfolded column-major matrices. This allows for a single matrix multiplication as follows:

Mode-3 TTM for 3-way Tensor (Efficient)

1: $\mathbf{X} \leftarrow \text{reshape}(\mathcal{X}, mn \times p)$ ▷ $\mathbf{X} = \mathbf{X}_{(3)}^{\mathsf{T}}$
2: $\mathbf{Y} \leftarrow \mathbf{X}\mathbf{W}^{\mathsf{T}}$ ▷ Matrix–matrix multiply
3: $\mathcal{Y} \leftarrow \text{reshape}(\mathbf{Y}, m \times n \times q)$ ▷ $\mathbf{Y} = \mathbf{Y}_{(3)}^{\mathsf{T}}$

Exercise 3.15 What is the computational cost of $\mathcal{X} \times_3 \mathbf{W}$ with $\mathcal{X} \in \mathbb{R}^{m \times n \times p}$ and $\mathbf{W} \in \mathbb{R}^{q \times p}$?

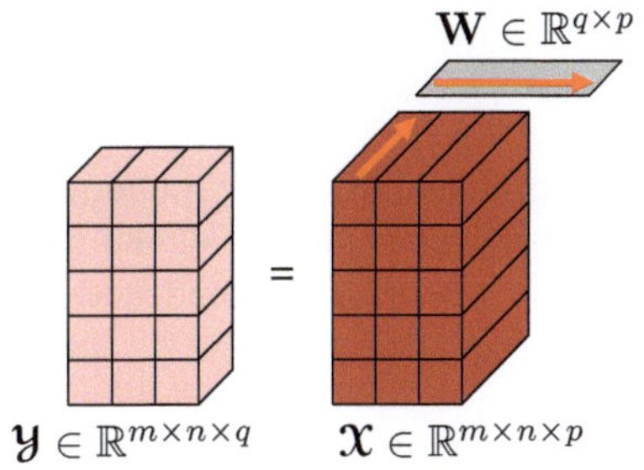

(a) Tensor form: the first row of $\mathbf{W}$ and first mode-3 fiber of $\mathcal{X}$ are emphasized with arrows.

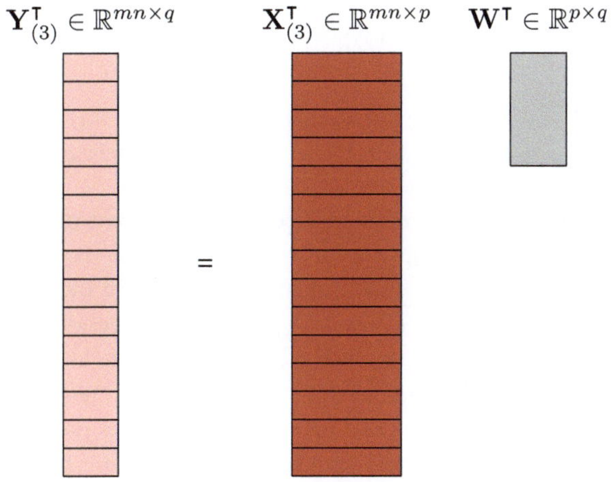

(b) Matrix form.

Figure 3.3 Mode-3 TTM (along tube fibers).

3.3.2 TTM for d-way Tensors

From Definition 3.14, for a general d-way tensor $\mathcal{X}$ of size $n_1 \times n_2 \times \cdots \times n_d$, the **mode-$k$ TTM** with a matrix $\mathbf{U} \in \mathbb{R}^{m \times n_k}$ is denoted as

$$\mathcal{Y} = \mathcal{X} \times_k \mathbf{U}$$

and satisfies

$$\mathbf{Y}_{(k)} = \mathbf{U}\mathbf{X}_{(k)},$$

where $\mathcal{Y}$ is a tensor of size $n_1 \times \cdots \times n_{k-1} \times m \times n_{k+1} \times \cdots \times n_d$. Expressed elementwise, we have

$$\mathcal{Y}(i_1, \ldots, i_{k-1}, j, i_{k+1}, \ldots, i_d) = \sum_{i_k=1}^{n_k} \mathcal{X}(i_1, i_2, \ldots, i_d)\mathbf{U}(j, i_k) \quad \text{for all} \quad j \in [m].$$

The cost of a TTM for inputs with these dimensions is $\mathcal{O}(Nm)$, where $N = \prod_{k=1}^{d} n_k$.

Mathematically, we can express a TTM computation as a single matrix multiplication: $\mathbf{Y}_{(k)} = \mathbf{U}\mathbf{X}_{(k)}$. However, in order to compute TTM using an efficient matrix multiplication subroutine, both input matrices must be stored in either row- or column-major order.

As shown in Section 2.3.3, for a d-way tensor $\mathcal{X}$ stored in natural order in memory, $\mathbf{X}_{(k)}$ is not in row- or column-major order unless $k = 1$ or $k = d$.

As in the 3-way case, one approach is to explicitly permute the entries of the input tensor unfolding, call the matrix multiplication subroutine, and perform the inverse permutation on the output to obtain the result tensor. The pseudocode for computing the TTM $\mathcal{Y} = \mathcal{X} \times_k \mathbf{U}$ with $\mathcal{X} \in \mathbb{R}^{n_1 \times n_2 \times \cdots \times n_d}$ and $\mathbf{U} \in \mathbb{R}^{r_k \times n_k}$ using explicit permutations is as follows:

Mode-k TTM for d-way Tensor (Naive)

$\bar{\mathcal{X}} \leftarrow \mathbb{P}(\mathcal{X}, (k, 1, \ldots, k-1, k+1, \ldots, d))$ ▷ Permute mode k to front
$\mathbf{X} \leftarrow \text{reshape}(\bar{\mathcal{X}}, n_k \times N_k)$ with $N_k = \prod_{\substack{\ell=1 \\ \ell \neq k}}^{d} n_\ell$ ▷ $\mathbf{X} = \bar{\mathbf{X}}_{(1)} = \mathbf{X}_{(k)}$
$\mathbf{Y} \leftarrow \mathbf{U}\mathbf{X}$ ▷ Matrix–matrix multiply
$\bar{\mathcal{Y}} \leftarrow \text{reshape}(\mathbf{Y}, r_k \times n_1 \times \cdots \times n_{k-1} \times n_{k+1} \times \cdots \times n_d)$ ▷ $\mathbf{Y} = \bar{\mathbf{Y}}_{(1)} = \mathbf{Y}_{(k)}$
$\mathcal{Y} \leftarrow \mathbb{P}(\bar{\mathcal{Y}}, (2, \ldots, k, 1, k+1, \ldots, d))$ ▷ Permute mode k back to original order

As in the 3-way case, this is not efficient because of the cost of rearranging the tensor entries. We can use the same approach as we did in the 3-way case. In fact, we can consider the d-way tensor as a 3-way tensor for the purpose of the mode-k multiplication. If we define $M_k = \prod_{j=1}^{k-1} n_j$ and $P_k = \prod_{j=k+1}^{d} n_j$ as in Section 2.3.3, we observe that the internal ordering of the d-way unfolding $\mathbf{X}_{(k)}$ is the same as the internal ordering of the mode-2 unfolding of a 3-way tensor $\bar{\mathcal{X}} \in \mathbb{R}^{M_k \times n_k \times P_k}$. Thus, we can reshape the d-way tensor into a 3-way tensor (no actual memory movement is performed), and the d-way pseudocode resembles the 3-way case using batched matrix multiplication:

Mode-k TTM for d-way Tensor (Efficient, except for $k = 1$)

$\bar{\mathcal{X}} \leftarrow \text{reshape}(\mathcal{X}, M_k \times n_k \times P_k)$ with $M_k = \prod_{j=1}^{k-1} n_j$ and $P_k = \prod_{j=k+1}^{d} n_j$
for $\ell = 1$ to P_k **do**
  $\bar{\mathcal{Y}}(:, :, \ell) \leftarrow \bar{\mathcal{X}}(:, :, \ell)\mathbf{U}^{\mathsf{T}}$ ▷ Batched matrix–matrix multiplies
end for
$\mathcal{Y} \leftarrow \text{reshape}(\bar{\mathcal{Y}}, n_1 \times \cdots \times n_{k-1} \times r \times n_{k+1} \times \cdots \times n_d)$

While this algorithm works for all modes, it is inefficient for $k = 1$. In that case, $M_k = M_1 = 1$, so the ℓth slice of $\bar{\mathcal{X}}$ is a single row vector, which implies that the TTM is computed via P_1 matrix–vector multiplications, which is generally less efficient than matrix–matrix operations. Because $\mathbf{X}_{(1)}$ is already in column-major order, we handle the first mode separately, computing $\mathbf{Y}_{(1)} = \mathbf{U}\mathbf{X}_{(1)}$ directly with a single matrix–matrix multiplication. In the case $k = d$, we have $P_k = P_d = 1$. There is only one loop iteration, which is efficient because it is again a single matrix–matrix multiplication operation. Algorithm 3.1 presents this approach with special handling of mode 1.

Exercise 3.16 Write two TTM functions `ttm_permute` and `ttm` for any mode of a d-way tensor. The `ttm_permute` function should perform an explicit permutation of the input tensor in order to perform the TTM with a single matrix multiplication (followed by an explicit permutation of the result). The `ttm` function should avoid explicit permutations and perform a sequence of matrix multiplications based on the internal structure of the input and output tensors, as in Algorithm 3.1.

(a) Compare timing results for TTMs in each mode of a tensor with dimension $500 \times 500 \times 500$ and a matrix of dimension 50×500.

Algorithm 3.1 Mode-k TTM for d-way Tensor

Require: tensor $\mathcal{X} \in \mathbb{R}^{n_1 \times n_2 \times \cdots \times n_d}$, matrix $\mathbf{U} \in \mathbb{R}^{r \times n_k}$, mode $k \in [d]$
Ensure: $\mathcal{Y} = \mathcal{X} \times_k \mathbf{U} \in \mathbb{R}^{n_1 \times \cdots \times n_{k-1} \times r \times n_{k+1} \times \cdots \times n_d}$

function TTM($\mathcal{X}, \mathbf{U}, k$)
    if $k = 1$ **then**
        $\mathbf{Y} \leftarrow \mathbf{U}\mathbf{X}_{(1)}$
        $\mathcal{Y} \leftarrow \text{reshape}(\mathbf{Y}, r \times n_2 \times \cdots \times n_d)$
    else
        $M_k \leftarrow \prod_{j=1}^{k-1} n_j$
        $P_k \leftarrow \prod_{j=k+1}^{d} n_j$
        $\bar{\mathcal{X}} \leftarrow \text{reshape}(\mathcal{X}, M_k \times n_k \times P_k)$
        for $\ell = 1$ to P_k **do**
            $\bar{\mathcal{Y}}(:,:,\ell) \leftarrow \bar{\mathcal{X}}(:,:,\ell)\mathbf{U}^{\mathsf{T}}$ ▷ Batched matrix–matrix multiplications
        end for
        $\mathcal{Y} \leftarrow \text{reshape}(\bar{\mathcal{Y}}, n_1 \times \cdots \times n_{k-1} \times r \times n_{k+1} \times \cdots \times n_d)$
    end if
    return $\mathcal{Y}$
end function

(b) Perform the same comparisons for a tensor with dimension $100 \times 100 \times 100 \times 100$ and matrix of dimension 10×100.

(c) Analyze your results and explain the performance you observe.

3.4 TTM in Multiple Modes

We often want to compute TTMs in multiple or all modes. For efficiency, we exploit the fact that the order of the multiplications does not matter, as captured in Proposition 3.19.

Proposition 3.19 (TTM Order) *Let $\mathcal{X}$ be a tensor such that mode k is of size m and mode ℓ is of size n. Then, for any $\mathbf{U} \in \mathbb{R}^{q \times m}$ and $\mathbf{V} \in \mathbb{R}^{r \times n}$ with $k \neq \ell$, we have*

$$(\mathcal{X} \times_k \mathbf{U}) \times_\ell \mathbf{V} = (\mathcal{X} \times_\ell \mathbf{V}) \times_k \mathbf{U}.$$

Exercise 3.17 Prove Proposition 3.19. As a hint, you can argue via Exercise 3.12 on permutations of the modes and TTMs, that it suffices to show $\mathcal{Y} \times_1 \mathbf{U} \times_2 \mathbf{V} = \mathcal{Y} \times_2 \mathbf{V} \times_1 \mathbf{U}$, where $\mathcal{Y} \in \mathbb{R}^{m \times n \times p}$ with p being the product of the remaining indices.

3.4.1 Multi-TTM for 3-way Tensors

For 3-way tensors, we consider TTMs in two or three modes. For example, for $\mathcal{X} \in \mathbb{R}^{m \times n \times p}$, the expression

$$\mathcal{Y} = \mathcal{X} \times_1 \mathbf{U} \times_2 \mathbf{V} \times_3 \mathbf{W} \tag{3.10}$$

multiplies $\mathcal{X}$ by $\mathbf{U} \in \mathbb{R}^{q \times m}$ in mode 1, by $\mathbf{V} \in \mathbb{R}^{r \times n}$ in mode 2, and by $\mathbf{W} \in \mathbb{R}^{s \times p}$ in mode 3. The size of $\mathcal{Y}$ is $q \times r \times s$. Applying the elementwise expressions from Definitions 3.16–3.18, we see that

$$y_{\alpha\beta\gamma} = \sum_{i=1}^{m}\sum_{j=1}^{n}\sum_{k=1}^{p} x_{ijk}u_{\alpha i}v_{\beta j}w_{\gamma k} \quad \text{for all} \quad (\alpha,\beta,\gamma) \in [q] \otimes [r] \otimes [s]. \tag{3.11}$$

The vectorization and unfoldings can be expressed using Kronecker products, as follows.

Proposition 3.20 (Multi-TTM Vectorization and Mode-k Unfolding, 3-way) *Let* $\mathcal{X} \in \mathbb{R}^{m \times n \times p}$, $\mathbf{U} \in \mathbb{R}^{q \times m}$, $\mathbf{V} \in \mathbb{R}^{r \times n}$, *and* $\mathbf{W} \in \mathbb{R}^{s \times p}$ *so that* $\mathcal{Y} \in \mathbb{R}^{q \times r \times s}$. *The following are equivalent:*

$$\mathcal{Y} = \mathcal{X} \times_1 \mathbf{U} \times_2 \mathbf{V} \times_3 \mathbf{W}, \tag{3.12}$$
$$\text{vec}(\mathcal{Y}) = (\mathbf{W} \otimes \mathbf{V} \otimes \mathbf{U})\,\text{vec}(\mathcal{X}), \tag{3.13}$$
$$\mathbf{Y}_{(1)} = \mathbf{U}\mathbf{X}_{(1)}(\mathbf{W} \otimes \mathbf{V})^{\intercal}, \tag{3.14}$$
$$\mathbf{Y}_{(2)} = \mathbf{V}\mathbf{X}_{(2)}(\mathbf{W} \otimes \mathbf{U})^{\intercal}, \tag{3.15}$$
$$\mathbf{Y}_{(3)} = \mathbf{W}\mathbf{X}_{(3)}(\mathbf{V} \otimes \mathbf{U})^{\intercal}. \tag{3.16}$$

Proof. We prove equivalence of Eqs. (3.13) and (3.15) and leave the remainder as an exercise. Define $\mathbf{M} = \mathbf{W} \otimes \mathbf{U}$. From the definition of matrix multiplication, Eq. (3.15) is equivalent to

$$\mathbf{Y}_{(2)}(\beta,\hat{\ell}) = \sum_{j=1}^{n}\sum_{\ell=1}^{mp} \mathbf{V}(\beta,j)\,\mathbf{X}_{(2)}(j,\ell)\,\mathbf{M}(\hat{\ell},\ell) \quad \text{for all} \quad (\beta,\hat{\ell}) \in [r] \otimes [qs]. \tag{3.17}$$

Let $(i,k) = \mathbb{T}(\ell; m, p)$ and $(\alpha,\gamma) = \mathbb{T}(\hat{\ell}; q, s)$. Then, from Definition 2.16,

$$\mathbf{X}_{(2)}(j,\ell) = \mathcal{X}(i,j,k) \quad \text{and} \quad \mathbf{Y}_{(2)}(\beta,\hat{\ell}) = \mathcal{Y}(\alpha,\beta,\gamma).$$

From the definition of Kronecker product (see Definition A.17 and Proposition 2.11), we also have that $\mathbf{M}(\hat{\ell},\ell) = \mathbf{U}(\alpha,i)\,\mathbf{W}(\gamma,k)$. Thus, Eq. (3.17) is equivalent to

$$\mathcal{Y}(\alpha,\beta,\gamma) = \sum_{i=1}^{m}\sum_{j=1}^{n}\sum_{k=1}^{p} \mathcal{X}(i,j,k)\,\mathbf{U}(\alpha,i)\,\mathbf{V}(\beta,j)\,\mathbf{W}(\gamma,k),$$

matching Eq. (3.11) and therefore equivalent to Eq. (3.13). □

These properties apply to TTMs in two modes as well. For example, if we have $\mathcal{Y} = \mathcal{X} \times_1 \mathbf{U} \times_3 \mathbf{W}$, then this can be written equivalently as $\mathcal{Y} = \mathcal{X} \times_1 \mathbf{U} \times_2 \mathbf{I}_n \times_3 \mathbf{W}$. Applying Proposition 3.20 to this expression, we find that $\mathcal{Y} = \mathcal{X} \times_1 \mathbf{U} \times_3 \mathbf{W}$ is equivalent to

$$\text{vec}(\mathcal{Y}) = (\mathbf{W} \otimes \mathbf{I}_n \otimes \mathbf{U})\,\text{vec}(\mathcal{X}),$$
$$\mathbf{Y}_{(1)} = \mathbf{U}\mathbf{X}_{(1)}(\mathbf{W} \otimes \mathbf{I}_n)^{\intercal},$$
$$\mathbf{Y}_{(2)} = \mathbf{X}_{(2)}(\mathbf{W} \otimes \mathbf{U})^{\intercal},$$
$$\mathbf{Y}_{(3)} = \mathbf{W}\mathbf{X}_{(3)}(\mathbf{I}_n \otimes \mathbf{U})^{\intercal}.$$

Equivalent expressions for multi-TTMs with other subsets of modes can be derived similarly.

Exercise 3.18 Complete the proof of Proposition 3.20 using the definitions, Proposition 2.6, and the properties of linearization and unfolding.

Exercise 3.19 Express the matrix SVD $\mathbf{X} = \mathbf{U}\mathbf{\Sigma}\mathbf{V}^\intercal$ using TTM notation.

As the following exercises explore, the cheapest method for computing multi-TTM is to perform a sequence of TTMs. The ordering of these operations can impact the cost, as explored further in Section 3.4.3.

Exercise 3.20 Suppose $\mathcal{X} \in \mathbb{R}^{n \times n \times n}$ and $\mathbf{U}, \mathbf{V}, \mathbf{W} \in \mathbb{R}^{n \times r}$. (a) What is the cost to compute $\text{vec}(\mathcal{Y}) = (\mathbf{W} \otimes (\mathbf{V} \otimes \mathbf{U}))\,\text{vec}(\mathcal{X})$? (b) What is the cost to compute $\mathbf{Y}_{(1)} = (\mathbf{U}\mathbf{X}_{(1)})(\mathbf{W} \otimes \mathbf{V})^\intercal$? (c) What is the cost to compute $\mathbf{Y}_{(1)} = \mathbf{U}\big(\mathbf{X}_{(1)}(\mathbf{W} \otimes \mathbf{V})^\intercal\big)$? (d) What is the cost to compute $\mathcal{Y} = \big((\mathcal{X} \times_1 \mathbf{U}) \times_2 \mathbf{V}\big) \times_3 \mathbf{W}$? (e) Which is the best approach if $r < n$? (f) Which is the best approach if $r > n$?

Exercise 3.21 Suppose $\mathcal{X} \in \mathbb{R}^{m \times n \times p}$, $\mathbf{U} \in \mathbb{R}^{q \times m}$, $\mathbf{V} \in \mathbb{R}^{r \times n}$, and $\mathbf{W} \in \mathbb{R}^{s \times p}$. We can compute $\mathcal{Y} = \mathcal{X} \times_1 \mathbf{U} \times_2 \mathbf{V} \times_3 \mathbf{W}$ using any of six possible orders on the TTMs. (a) What are the different costs? (b) If $s < r < q < p < n < m$, which is optimal?

3.4.2 TTM with Multiple Matrices for d-way Tensors

As in the 3-way case, it is often useful to compute the TTM in all modes, i.e., for a tensor $\mathcal{X} \in \mathbb{R}^{n_1 \times n_2 \times \cdots \times n_d}$ and matrices $\mathbf{U}_k \in \mathbb{R}^{m_k \times n_k}$ for all $k \in [d]$, we compute

$$\mathcal{Y} = \mathcal{X} \times_1 \mathbf{U}_1 \times_2 \mathbf{U}_2 \cdots \times_d \mathbf{U}_d. \tag{3.18}$$

Remark 3.21 (Covariant and contravariant notation) The multi-TTM operation is sometimes denoted using covariant or contravariant multiplication as, respectively,

$$\mathcal{Y} = (\mathbf{U}_1, \mathbf{U}_2, \ldots, \mathbf{U}_d)\,\mathcal{X} \quad \text{or} \quad \mathcal{Y} = \mathcal{X}\,(\mathbf{U}_1^\intercal, \mathbf{U}_2^\intercal, \ldots, \mathbf{U}_d^\intercal).$$

The analog of Proposition 3.20 on vectorization and unfolding is the following proposition for d-way tensors.

Proposition 3.22 (Multi-TTM Vectorization and Mode-k Unfolding) *The following are equivalent for* $\mathcal{X} \in \mathbb{R}^{n_1 \times n_2 \times \cdots \times n_d}$:

$$\mathcal{Y} = \mathcal{X} \times_1 \mathbf{U}_1 \times_2 \mathbf{U}_2 \cdots \times_d \mathbf{U}_d, \tag{3.19}$$

$$\text{vec}(\mathcal{Y}) = (\mathbf{U}_d \otimes \mathbf{U}_{d-1} \otimes \cdots \otimes \mathbf{U}_1)\,\text{vec}(\mathcal{X}), \tag{3.20}$$

$$\mathbf{Y}_{(k)} = \mathbf{U}_k \mathbf{X}_{(k)} (\mathbf{U}_d \otimes \cdots \otimes \mathbf{U}_{k+1} \otimes \mathbf{U}_{k-1} \otimes \cdots \otimes \mathbf{U}_1)^\intercal, \tag{3.21}$$

where Eq. (3.21) *holds for each* $k \in [d]$.

We have a more general result for arbitrary unfoldings as well, as discussed in Proposition 3.23.

Proposition 3.23 (Multi-TTM Unfolding) *Let $\mathcal{X} \in \mathbb{R}^{n_1 \times n_2 \times \cdots \times n_d}$, $\mathbf{U}_k \in \mathbb{R}^{m_k \times n_k}$ for all $k \in [d]$, and let the modes $\{1, \ldots, d\}$ be partitioned into two ordered sets:*

$$\mathcal{R} = (r_1, r_2, \ldots, r_\delta) \quad \textit{and} \quad \mathcal{C} = (c_1, c_2, \ldots, c_{d-\delta}).$$

Then

$$\mathcal{Y} = \mathcal{X} \times_1 \mathbf{U}_1 \times_2 \mathbf{U}_2 \cdots \times_d \mathbf{U}_d \in \mathbb{R}^{m_1 \times m_2 \times \cdots \times m_d}$$

if and only if

$$\mathbf{Y}_{(\mathcal{R} \times \mathcal{C})} = \big(\mathbf{U}_{r_\delta} \otimes \mathbf{U}_{r_{\delta-1}} \otimes \cdots \otimes \mathbf{U}_{r_1}\big) \mathbf{X}_{(\mathcal{R} \times \mathcal{C})} \big(\mathbf{U}_{c_{d-\delta}} \otimes \mathbf{U}_{c_{d-\delta-1}} \otimes \cdots \otimes \mathbf{U}_{c_1}\big)^{\mathsf{T}}.$$

Exercise 3.22 Prove Proposition 3.23.

In some cases, a multi-TTM may only involve a subset of the tensor modes. Propositions 3.22 and 3.23 apply in these cases by inserting identity matrices of appropriate dimensions to any modes that are not involved. In particular, if we wish to perform multi-TTM in all modes except mode k, then Proposition 3.22 implies the following are equivalent:

$$\begin{aligned}
\mathcal{Y} &= \mathcal{X} \times_1 \mathbf{U}_1 \cdots \times_{k-1} \mathbf{U}_{k-1} \times_{k+1} \mathbf{U}_{k+1} \cdots \times_d \mathbf{U}_d, \\
\operatorname{vec}(\mathcal{Y}) &= (\mathbf{U}_d \otimes \cdots \otimes \mathbf{U}_{k+1} \otimes \mathbf{I}_{n_k} \otimes \mathbf{U}_{k-1} \otimes \cdots \otimes \mathbf{U}_1) \operatorname{vec}(\mathcal{X}), \\
\mathbf{Y}_{(k)} &= \mathbf{X}_{(k)} (\mathbf{U}_d \otimes \cdots \otimes \mathbf{U}_{k+1} \otimes \mathbf{U}_{k-1} \otimes \cdots \otimes \mathbf{U}_1)^{\mathsf{T}}.
\end{aligned}$$

3.4.3 Efficient Multi-TTM Computation

Although we can compute a multi-TTM via an unfolding of the matrix and Kronecker products of the matrices to be multiplied, it is more efficient to perform a sequence of TTMs in individual modes; see Exercise 3.20.

The question is around the best order of the modes for the sequence of TTMs. First, we consider the case of two TTMs in the next proposition.

Proposition 3.24 (TTM Mode Ordering) *Let $\mathcal{X} \in \mathbb{R}^{n_1 \times n_2 \times \cdots \times n_d}$, $\mathbf{U}_k \in \mathbb{R}^{m_k \times n_k}$ and $\mathbf{U}_\ell \in \mathbb{R}^{m_\ell \times n_\ell}$ for $i, j \in [d]$, and consider $\mathcal{X} \times_k \mathbf{U}_k \times_\ell \mathbf{U}_\ell$. If*

$$\frac{1}{n_k} - \frac{1}{m_k} < \frac{1}{n_\ell} - \frac{1}{m_\ell}$$

then computing (a) $(\mathcal{X} \times_k \mathbf{U}_k) \times_\ell \mathbf{U}_\ell$ requires fewer computational operations than computing (b) $(\mathcal{X} \times_\ell \mathbf{U}_\ell) \times_k \mathbf{U}_k$.

Proof. Let $N = \prod_{j=1}^{d} n_j$. The cost to compute (a) is $N m_k + \frac{N m_k m_\ell}{n_k}$. Conversely, the cost to compute (b) is $N m_\ell + \frac{N m_k m_\ell}{n_\ell}$. We have

$$\begin{aligned}
\frac{1}{n_k} - \frac{1}{m_k} &< \frac{1}{n_j} - \frac{1}{m_j} \\
\frac{1}{m_j} + \frac{1}{n_k} &< \frac{1}{m_k} + \frac{1}{n_j} \\
N m_k + \frac{N m_k m_j}{n_k} &< N m_j + \frac{N m_k m_j}{n_j},
\end{aligned}$$

where the last step multiplies by Nm_km_j. Hence, the claim. □

This idea extends to a sequence of TTMs, where the cost depends on the order in which they are computed. Suppose we want to compute a multi-TTM with $p \le d$ matrices. A naive approach is to consider all $p!$ possible orderings, consider the computation cost, and then pick the best. Instead, we can order the modes according to the following proposition.

Proposition 3.25 (Multi-TTM Ordering, Fackler, 2019) *Given a tensor* $\mathcal{X} \in \mathbb{R}^{n_1 \times n_2 \times \cdots \times n_d}$ *and matrices* $\mathbf{U}_k \in \mathbb{R}^{m_k \times n_k}$ *for a set of* $p \le d$ *distinct modes, the multi-TTM ordering that minimizes computation cost is*

$$((\mathcal{X} \times_{\pi_1} \mathbf{U}_{\pi_1}) \times_{\pi_2} \mathbf{U}_{\pi_2}) \cdots \times_{\pi_p} \mathbf{U}_{\pi_p},$$

where

$$\beta_{\pi_1} \le \beta_{\pi_2} \le \cdots \le \beta_{\pi_p} \quad \text{with} \quad \beta_k = \frac{1}{n_k} - \frac{1}{m_k}. \tag{3.22}$$

Proof. Suppose the optimal order π is not in increasing order according to β. Then there exist two consecutive TTMs in modes π_i and π_{i+1} for some $i \in [\delta]$ such that the mode-π_i TTM is performed right before the mode-π_{i+1} TTM but $\beta_{\pi_i} > \beta_{\pi_{i+1}}$. We will argue that swapping these two TTMs will decrease the computational cost of the multi-TTM to arrive at a contradiction. That is, we consider an alternative order π' that is equal to π except that $\pi'_i = \pi_{i+1}$ and $\pi'_{i+1} = \pi_i$.

Because π and π' perform the same first $i-1$ TTMs, we ignore those matching costs. Likewise, the intermediate tensor that remains after the first $i+1$ TTMs is the same in both orderings, and they perform the same last $p-(i+1)$ TTMs, so we ignore those matching costs. Let

$$\mathcal{Y} = ((\mathcal{X} \times_{\pi_1} \mathbf{U}_{\pi_1}) \times_{\pi_2} \mathbf{U}_{\pi_2}) \cdots \times_{\pi_{i-1}} \mathbf{U}_{\pi_{i-1}}.$$

By Proposition 3.24, because $\beta_{\pi_i} > \beta_{\pi_{i+1}}$, $(\mathcal{Y} \times_{\pi_{i+1}} \mathbf{U}_{\pi_{i+1}}) \times_{\pi_i} \mathbf{U}_{\pi_i}$ is cheaper than $(\mathcal{Y} \times_{\pi_i} \mathbf{U}_{\pi_i}) \times_{\pi_{i+1}} \mathbf{U}_{\pi_{i+1}}$. Therefore, π' is a cheaper order than π, which is a contradiction. □

Efficient implementation of multi-TTM can be done via mode ordering according to Proposition 3.25 and then using the TTM algorithms for individual modes.

3.5 Matricized Tensor Times Khatri–Rao Product

The **matricized tensor times Khatri–Rao product (MTTKRP)** is the key computational kernel of most algorithms for computing the CP decomposition. Its name is a mouthful but comes directly from its structure, as we describe below.

3.5.1 MTTKRP for 3-way Tensors

Suppose $\mathcal{X} \in \mathbb{R}^{m \times n \times p}$. Let $\mathbf{B} \in \mathbb{R}^{n \times r}$ and $\mathbf{C} \in \mathbb{R}^{p \times r}$, which have row dimensions that each match a tensor dimension and column dimensions that match each other. Given these inputs, the MTTKRP is given by

$$\mathbf{U} = \mathbf{X}_{(1)}(\mathbf{C} \odot \mathbf{B}) \in \mathbb{R}^{m \times r},$$

which is a matricized tensor times a Khatri–Rao product, i.e., an MTTKRP.

If the Khatri–Rao product is formed explicitly, then the MTTKRP is matrix–matrix multiplication, which is typically a short and wide matrix times a tall and skinny matrix, as shown in Fig. 3.4. We will see later that we do not always want to form the Khatri–Rao product explicitly.

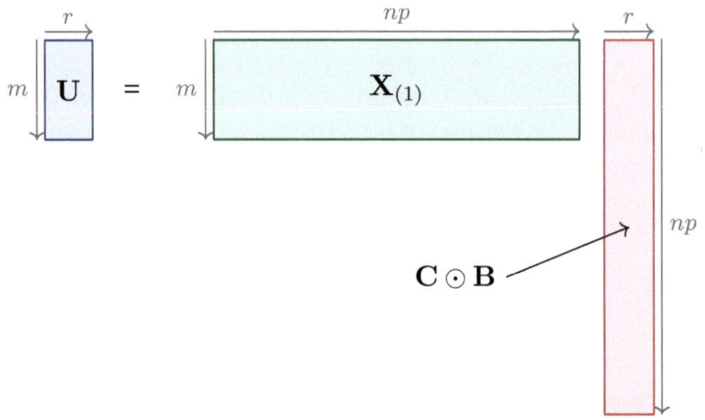

Figure 3.4 MTTKRP $\mathbf{V} = \mathbf{X}_{(1)}(\mathbf{C} \odot \mathbf{B})$.

We can define the MTTKRP for each mode as follows.

Definition 3.26 (TTM in Mode 3) Let $\mathcal{X} \in \mathbb{R}^{m \times n \times p}$, $\mathbf{A} \in \mathbb{R}^{m \times r}$, $\mathbf{B} \in \mathbb{R}^{n \times r}$, and $\mathbf{C} \in \mathbb{R}^{p \times r}$. The 3-way **MTTKRPs** are defined as follows:

$$\begin{aligned}
&\text{Mode-1 MTTKRP:} \quad \mathbf{U} = \mathbf{X}_{(1)}(\mathbf{C} \odot \mathbf{B}) \quad \in \mathbb{R}^{m \times r},\\
&\text{Mode-2 MTTKRP:} \quad \mathbf{V} = \mathbf{X}_{(2)}(\mathbf{C} \odot \mathbf{A}) \quad \in \mathbb{R}^{n \times r},\\
&\text{Mode-3 MTTKRP:} \quad \mathbf{W} = \mathbf{X}_{(3)}(\mathbf{B} \odot \mathbf{A}) \quad \in \mathbb{R}^{p \times r}.
\end{aligned}$$

Elementwise, we have

$$u_{i\ell} = \sum_{j=1}^{n} \sum_{k=1}^{p} x_{ijk} b_{j\ell} c_{k\ell} \quad \text{for all} \quad (i,\ell) \in [m] \otimes [r], \tag{3.23}$$

$$v_{j\ell} = \sum_{i=1}^{m} \sum_{k=1}^{p} x_{ijk} a_{i\ell} c_{k\ell} \quad \text{for all} \quad (j,\ell) \in [n] \otimes [r], \tag{3.24}$$

$$w_{k\ell} = \sum_{i=1}^{m} \sum_{j=1}^{n} x_{ijk} a_{i\ell} b_{j\ell} \quad \text{for all} \quad (k,\ell) \in [p] \otimes [r]. \tag{3.25}$$

Implementing an MTTKRP by matricizing the tensor, forming the Khatri–Rao product explicitly, and then performing matrix–matrix multiplication benefits from high performance of the final operation, which dominates the operation count. However, to use the matrix–matrix multiplication, the matricized tensor must be in row- or column-major order. For $k \in \{2, \ldots, d-1\}$, this means that matricizing the tensor requires explicitly permuting the entries of the tensor, which can be very slow because it runs at the speed of memory access. We focus on avoiding this computation while still casting the bulk of the computation of MTTKRP as matrix–matrix multiplication.

The cost to compute a 3-way MTTKRP is $\mathcal{O}(mnpr)$, regardless of mode.

Mode-1 MTTKRP for 3-way Tensor

Consider the computation of the mode-1 MTTKRP: $\mathbf{U} = \mathbf{X}_{(1)}(\mathbf{C} \odot \mathbf{B})$. In the first mode, we compute $\mathbf{C} \odot \mathbf{B}$ explicitly, and then, because $\text{vec}(\mathbf{X}_{(1)}) = \text{vec}(\mathcal{X})$, we can multiply by $\mathbf{X}_{(1)}$ without any memory movement in $\mathcal{X}$, performing

$$\mathbf{U} = \mathbf{X}_{(1)}(\mathbf{C} \odot \mathbf{B})$$

with a single matrix–matrix multiply:

Mode-1 MTTKRP for 3-way Tensor (Efficient)

$\mathbf{K} \leftarrow \mathbf{C} \odot \mathbf{B}$ ▷ Khatri–Rao product
$\mathbf{X} \leftarrow \text{reshape}(\mathcal{X}, m \times np)$ ▷ $\mathbf{X} = \mathbf{X}_{(1)}$
$\mathbf{U} \leftarrow \mathbf{X}\mathbf{K}$ ▷ Matrix–matrix multiply

The cost to compute the mode-1 MTTKRP this way is $npr + 2mnpr = \mathcal{O}(mnpr)$.

Mode-2 MTTKRP for 3-way Tensor

Consider the computation of the mode-2 MTTKRP: $\mathbf{V} = \mathbf{X}_{(2)}(\mathbf{C} \odot \mathbf{A})$. Unlike in mode 1, the matricized tensor in mode 2 is not stored column-major in memory. Thus, performing a single matrix multiplication requires forming the explicit Khatri–Rao product and explicitly permuting tensor elements to obtain $\mathbf{X}_{(2)}$ in column-major order. That is, we could compute $\mathbf{V} = \mathbf{X}_{(2)}(\mathbf{C} \odot \mathbf{A})$ as follows:

Mode-2 MTTKRP for 3-way Tensor (Naive)

1: $\mathbf{K} \leftarrow \mathbf{C} \odot \mathbf{A}$ ▷ Khatri–Rao product
2: $\bar{\mathcal{X}} \leftarrow \mathbb{P}(\mathcal{X}, (2, 1, 3))$ ▷ Swap modes 1 and 2 to get $n \times m \times p$ tensor
3: $\mathbf{X} \leftarrow \text{reshape}(\bar{\mathcal{X}}, n \times mp)$ ▷ $\mathbf{X} = \bar{\mathbf{X}}_{(1)} = \mathbf{X}_{(2)}$
4: $\mathbf{U} \leftarrow \mathbf{X}\mathbf{K}$ ▷ Matrix–matrix multiply

The above implementation is naive because the permutation requires memory movement, which is slower than performing flops. Instead, we can compute the mode-2 MTTKRP in two steps without forming the explicit Khatri–Rao product. From Eq. (3.24), we can write the expression elementwise as

$$v_{j\ell} = \sum_{i=1}^{m} \sum_{k=1}^{p} x_{ijk} a_{i\ell} c_{k\ell} = \sum_{i=1}^{m} a_{i\ell} \Bigg(\underbrace{\sum_{k=1}^{p} x_{ijk} c_{k\ell}}_{y_{ij\ell}} \Bigg).$$

This shows that there is a different temporary quantity we can compute instead of the explicit Khatri–Rao product of $\mathbf{C}$ and $\mathbf{A}$. In fact, we can express this temporary quantity in tensor notation as a TTM (see Section 3.3): $\mathcal{Y} = \mathcal{X} \times_3 \mathbf{C}^\intercal$. After $\mathcal{Y}$ is computed, the final result is computed as

$$v_{j\ell} = \sum_{i=1}^{m} y_{ij\ell} a_{i\ell}, \tag{3.26}$$

which is an instance of a batched tensor contraction (see Section 3.8.4). This computation can be performed as a sequence of independent matrix–vector products, e.g.,

$$\mathbf{V}(:, \ell) = \mathcal{Y}(:, :, \ell)^\intercal \mathbf{A}(:, \ell) \quad \text{for all} \quad \ell \in [r],$$

where $\mathcal{Y}(:, :, \ell)$ denotes the ℓth frontal slice of the tensor $\mathcal{Y}$, and these frontal slices have dimension $m \times n$ and are stored contiguously and column-major in memory, as discussed for the TTM in Section 3.3.1. Thus, the batched matrix–vector multiplies can be cast as a batched BLAS operation, e.g., using the `pagemtimes` function in MATLAB.

Mode-2 MTTKRP for 3-way Tensor (Efficient)

$\mathcal{Y} \leftarrow \mathcal{X} \times_3 \mathbf{C}^\intercal$ ▷ Mode-3 TTM; see Section 3.3.1
for $\ell = 1, \ldots, r$ **do**
  $\mathbf{V}(:, \ell) \leftarrow \mathcal{Y}(:, :, \ell)^\intercal \mathbf{A}(:, \ell)$ ▷ Batched matrix–vector multiplies
end for

The procedure is illustrated in Fig. 3.5.

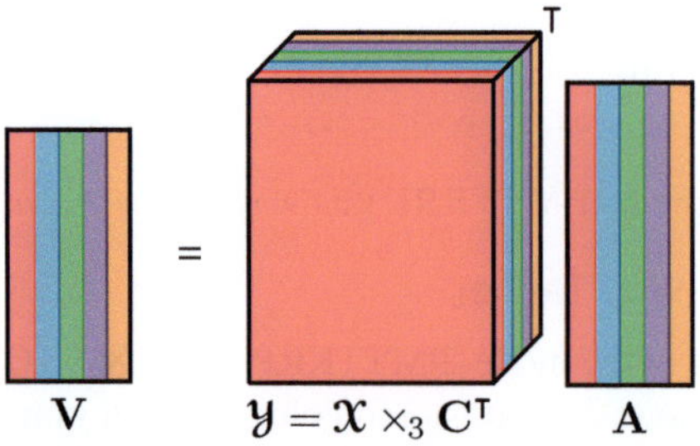

Figure 3.5 Mode-2 MTTKRP for a 3-way tensor: $\mathbf{V} = \mathbf{X}_{(2)}(\mathbf{C} \odot \mathbf{A})$. Tensor $\mathcal{Y} = \mathcal{X} \times_3 \mathbf{C}^\intercal \in \mathbb{R}^{m \times n \times r}$. Column ℓ of $\mathbf{V}$ is the ℓth frontal slice of $\mathcal{Y}$ transposed times column ℓ of $\mathbf{A}$.

The cost to compute the mode-2 MTTKRP this way is $2mnpr + 2mnr = \mathcal{O}(mnpr)$, the same leading order cost as in mode 1.

Mode-3 MTTKRP for 3-way Tensor

Consider the computation of the mode-3 MTTKRP: $\mathbf{W} = \mathbf{X}_{(3)}(\mathbf{B} \odot \mathbf{A})$. We recall that $\text{vec}\left((\mathbf{X}_{(3)})^\intercal\right) = \text{vec}(\mathcal{X})$, so we can work with the transpose of the mode-3 unfolding without data movement. So we can compute

$$\mathbf{W} = \left(\mathbf{X}_{(3)}^\intercal\right)^\intercal (\mathbf{B} \odot \mathbf{A})$$

with a single matrix–matrix multiply. Therefore, we first compute the Khatri–Rao product and then perform matrix multiplication as follows.

Mode-3 MTTKRP for 3-way Tensor (Efficient)

$\mathbf{K} \leftarrow \mathbf{B} \odot \mathbf{A}$ ▷ Khatri–Rao product
$\mathbf{X} \leftarrow \text{reshape}(\mathcal{X}, mn, p)$ ▷ $\mathbf{X} = \mathbf{X}_{(3)}^\intercal$
$\mathbf{U} \leftarrow \mathbf{X}^\intercal \mathbf{K}$ ▷ Matrix–matrix multiply

The cost to compute the mode-3 MTTKRP this way is $mnr + 2mnpr = \mathcal{O}(mnpr)$, the same leading order cost as in modes 1 and 2.

3.5.2 MTTKRP for d-way Tensors

Definition 3.27: MTTKRP

Let $\mathcal{X} \in \mathbb{R}^{n_1 \times n_2 \times \cdots \times n_d}$ and $\mathbf{A}_k \in \mathbb{R}^{n_k \times r}$ for all $k \in [d]$. Their mode-k MTTKRP is

$$\mathbf{B} = \mathbf{X}_{(k)}(\mathbf{A}_d \odot \cdots \odot \mathbf{A}_{k+1} \odot \mathbf{A}_{k-1} \odot \cdots \odot \mathbf{A}_1) \quad \in \mathbb{R}^{n_k \times r}. \tag{3.27}$$

Elementwise, the MTTKRP in mode k is given as

$$\mathbf{B}(i_k, j) = \sum_{i_1=1}^{n_1} \cdots \sum_{i_{k-1}=1}^{n_{k-1}} \sum_{i_{k+1}=1}^{n_{k+1}} \cdots \sum_{i_d=1}^{n_d} \mathcal{X}(i_1, i_2, \ldots, i_d) \prod_{\substack{\ell=1 \\ \ell \neq k}}^{d} \mathbf{A}_\ell(i_\ell, j), \tag{3.28}$$

for all $i_k \in [n_k]$ and $j \in [r]$. Pictorially, the MTTKRP is a short and wide matrix times a tall and skinny matrix, as depicted in Fig. 3.6. The straightforward approach to computing MTTKRP is to explicitly permute the entries of the input tensor unfolding, compute the Khatri–Rao product explicitly, and then call the efficient matrix multiplication subroutine, as follows:

Mode-k MTTKRP for d-way Tensor (Naive)

$\bar{\mathcal{X}} \leftarrow \mathbb{P}(\mathcal{X}, (k, 1, \ldots, k-1, k+1, \ldots, d))$ ▷ Permute mode k to front

$\mathbf{X} \leftarrow \text{reshape}(\bar{\mathcal{X}}, n_k \times N_k)$ with $N_k = \prod_{\substack{\ell=1 \\ \ell \neq k}}^{d} n_\ell$ ▷ $\mathbf{X} = \bar{\mathbf{X}}_{(1)} = \mathbf{X}_{(k)}$

$\mathbf{K} \leftarrow \mathbf{A}_d \odot \cdots \odot \mathbf{A}_{k+1} \odot \mathbf{A}_{k-1} \odot \cdots \odot \mathbf{A}_1$ ▷ Khatri–Rao product

$\mathbf{B} \leftarrow \mathbf{X}\mathbf{K}$ ▷ Matrix–matrix multiply

As in the 3-way case, we do not always want to form the Khatri–Rao product explicitly and instead prioritize avoiding explicit tensor permutation.

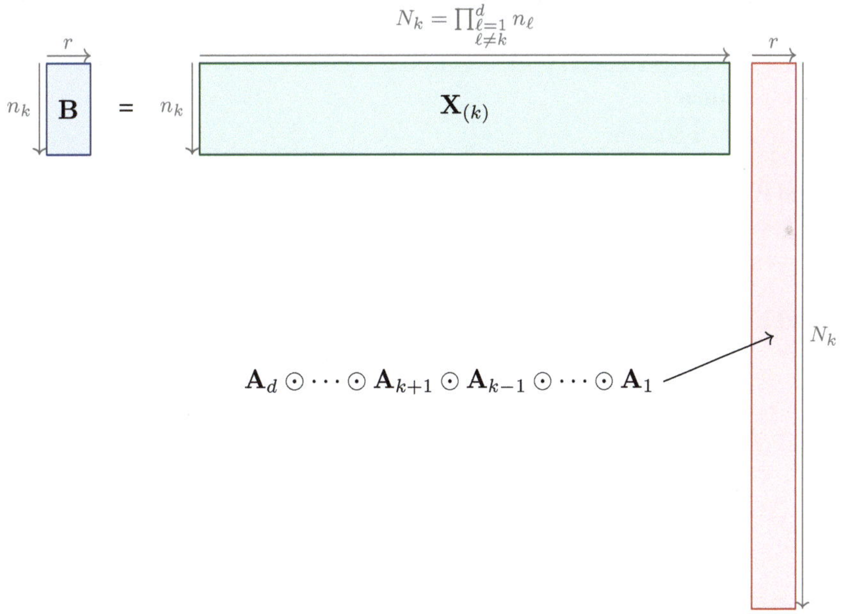

Figure 3.6 MTTKRP $\mathbf{B} = \mathbf{X}_{(k)}(\mathbf{A}_d \odot \cdots \odot \mathbf{A}_{k+1} \odot \mathbf{A}_{k-1} \odot \cdots \odot \mathbf{A}_1)$.

For modes 1 and d, we can compute the MTTKRP in a straightforward way, relying on the fact that $\text{vec}(\mathcal{X}) = \text{vec}(\mathbf{X}_{(1)}) = \text{vec}(\mathbf{X}_{(d)}^\intercal)$ so that there is no memory movement in forming $\mathbf{X}_{(k)}$. We then multiply that by the Khatri–Rao product for the result.

For $k \in \{2, \ldots, d-1\}$, the key idea is to simplify from the d-way case to the 3-way case by collapsing the lower modes (those smaller than k) and upper modes (those larger than k), and then using the method for the mode-2 MTTKRP of a 3-way tensor. We reshape the tensor from d-way to 3-way by linearizing the lower and upper modes and then form the Khatri–Rao products of the lower and the upper modes (see Exercise 3.24). Then the algorithm follows the strategy described for the mode-2 MTTKRP of a 3-way tensor as discussed in Section 3.5.1:

Mode-k MTTKRP for d-way Tensor for $1 < k < d$ (Efficient)

$\bar{\mathcal{X}} \leftarrow \text{reshape}(\mathcal{X}, M_k \times n_k \times P_k)$ with $M_k = \prod_{j=1}^{k-1} n_j$ and $P_k = \prod_{j=k+1}^{d} n_j$
$\mathbf{K}_L \leftarrow \mathbf{A}_{k-1} \odot \cdots \odot \mathbf{A}_1$ ▷ $M_k \times r$ Khatri–Rao product of "lower" modes
$\mathbf{K}_U \leftarrow \mathbf{A}_d \odot \cdots \odot \mathbf{A}_{k+1}$ ▷ $P_k \times r$ Khatri–Rao product of "upper" modes
$\mathcal{Y} \leftarrow \bar{\mathcal{X}} \times_3 \mathbf{K}_U^\mathsf{T}$ ▷ TTM (matrix–matrix multiply)
for $\ell = 1, \ldots, r$ **do**
$\quad \mathbf{B}(:, \ell) \leftarrow \mathcal{Y}(:, :, \ell)^\mathsf{T} \mathbf{K}_L(:, \ell)$ ▷ Batched matrix–vector multiplies
end for

The costs of this approach are dominated by $M_k r + P_k r$ to compute the Khatri–Rao products, $2Nr$ for the TTM, where $N = \prod_{\ell=1}^{d} n_\ell$, and $2 M_k n_k r$ for the batched matrix–vector multiplications, so the overall cost of MTTKRP is $\mathcal{O}(Nr)$ for every mode k. Nearly all of the MTTKRP computation is cast as matrix multiplication. We present the method for d-way mode-k MTTKRP in Algorithm 3.2.

Algorithm 3.2 Mode-k MTTKRP for d-way Tensor

Require: $\mathcal{X} \in \mathbb{R}^{n_1 \times n_2 \times \cdots \times n_d}$, $\{\mathbf{A}_\ell\}$ with $\mathbf{A}_\ell \in \mathbb{R}^{n_\ell \times r}$, $\ell \in [d]$
Ensure: $\mathbf{B} = \mathbf{X}_{(k)}(\mathbf{A}_d \odot \cdots \odot \mathbf{A}_{k+1} \odot \mathbf{A}_{k-1} \odot \cdots \odot \mathbf{A}_1)$
 1: **function** MTTKRP($\mathcal{X}, \{\mathbf{A}_\ell\}, k$)
 2: $\quad$ **if** $k > 1$ **then**
 3: $\quad\quad M_k \leftarrow \prod_{\ell=1}^{k-1} n_\ell$
 4: $\quad\quad \mathbf{K}_L \leftarrow \mathbf{A}_{k-1} \odot \cdots \odot \mathbf{A}_1$ ▷ KRP of "lower" modes
 5: $\quad$ **end if**
 6: $\quad$ **if** $k < d$ **then**
 7: $\quad\quad P_k \leftarrow \prod_{\ell=k+1}^{d} n_\ell$
 8: $\quad\quad \mathbf{K}_U \leftarrow \mathbf{A}_d \odot \cdots \odot \mathbf{A}_{k+1}$ ▷ KRP of "upper" modes
 9: $\quad$ **end if**
10: $\quad$ **if** $k = 1$ **then**
11: $\quad\quad \bar{\mathbf{X}} \leftarrow \text{reshape}(\mathcal{X}, n_1 \times P_d)$ ▷ Mode-1 unfolding
12: $\quad\quad \mathbf{B} \leftarrow \bar{\mathbf{X}} \mathbf{K}_U$ ▷ Matrix multiplication
13: $\quad$ **else if** $k = d$ **then**
14: $\quad\quad \bar{\mathbf{X}} \leftarrow \text{reshape}(\mathcal{X}, M_d \times n_d)$ ▷ Transpose of mode-d unfolding
15: $\quad\quad \mathbf{B} \leftarrow \bar{\mathbf{X}}^\mathsf{T} \mathbf{K}_L$ ▷ Matrix multiplication
16: $\quad$ **else**
17: $\quad\quad \bar{\mathcal{X}} \leftarrow \text{reshape}(\mathcal{X}, M_k \times n_k \times P_k)$ ▷ Reshape to 3-way tensor
18: $\quad\quad \mathcal{Y} \leftarrow \bar{\mathcal{X}} \times_3 \mathbf{K}_U^\mathsf{T}$ ▷ TTM (Algorithm 3.1)
19: $\quad\quad$ **for** $\ell = 1, \ldots, r$ **do**
20: $\quad\quad\quad \mathbf{B}(:, \ell) \leftarrow \mathcal{Y}(:, :, \ell)^\mathsf{T} \mathbf{K}_L(:, \ell)$ ▷ Batched matrix–vector multiplies
21: $\quad\quad$ **end for**
22: $\quad$ **end if**
23: $\quad$ **return** $\mathbf{B}$
24: **end function**

Exercise 3.23 In this exercise we will compare performance of two methods for MTTKRP.
(a) Implement a function `mttkrp` for MTTKRP for d-way tensors based on Algorithm 3.2.

(b) Implement a function `mttkrp_onemult` that uses the explicit tensor unfolding, computes the $(d-1)$-way Khatri–Rao product, and performs a single matrix multiplication.

(c) Generate two random tensors of dimensions $1000 \times 1000 \times 1000$ and $180 \times 180 \times 180 \times 180$, and generate random factor matrices with ranks 10 and 100, corresponding to four different input combinations. Compare the overall times for `mttkrp` and `mttkrp_onemult` in each mode. Explain your observations and how they correspond with your expectations.

(d) Determine where most of the time is spent in your function for each mode, and compare that with the theoretical analysis of the arithmetic cost of each step.

Exercise 3.24 Consider the mode-k MTTKRP for $k \in \{2, \dots, d-1\}$. Define $M_k = \prod_{\ell=1}^{k-1} n_\ell$ and $P_k = \prod_{\ell=k+1}^{d} n_\ell$. Then, let $\bar{\mathcal{X}} = \text{reshape}(\mathcal{X}, M_k \times n_k \times P_k)$ and define

$$\mathbf{K}_L = \mathbf{A}_{k-1} \odot \cdots \odot \mathbf{A}_1, \quad \text{and} \quad \mathbf{K}_U = \mathbf{A}_d \odot \cdots \odot \mathbf{A}_{k+1}.$$

Show

$$\mathbf{X}_{(k)}(\mathbf{A}_d \odot \cdots \odot \mathbf{A}_{k+1} \odot \mathbf{A}_{k-1} \odot \cdots \odot \mathbf{A}_1) = \bar{\mathbf{X}}_{(2)}(\mathbf{K}_U \odot \mathbf{K}_L).$$

3.6 Sequences of Multi-TTM and MTTKRP Operations

The multi-TTM computation is fundamental to Tucker decomposition, and the MTTKRP computation is fundamental to CP decomposition. In most of the algorithms we consider, there is a sequence of these computations involving repeated inputs and intermediate outputs. In this case, we can use **memoization** across modes, which means we store and reuse the intermediate values rather than recompute them. In the operations we consider here, memoization can reduce the overall computation by a factor of approximately $d/2$ for d-way tensors (Eswar et al., 2021; Kaya and Robert, 2019; Phan et al., 2013a).

3.6.1 Multi-TTM Sequence

A sequence of multi-TTM products in all modes but one is a computational kernel for some algorithms for Tucker decomposition, such as higher-order orthogonal iteration (Section 6.4). The sequence of multi-TTMs refers to computing:

$$\mathcal{Y}_k = \mathcal{X} \times_1 \mathbf{U}_1 \cdots \times_{k-1} \mathbf{U}_{k-1} \times_{k+1} \mathbf{U}_{k+1} \cdots \times_d \mathbf{U}_d \quad \text{for all} \quad k \in [d].$$

Each multi-TTM can be computed independently, but independent evaluation results in unnecessary recomputation since the sequence shares input data and intermediate computations.

Multi-TTM Sequence for 3-way Tensors

Consider a tensor $\mathcal{X} \in \mathbb{R}^{m \times n \times p}$ and matrices $\mathbf{U} \in \mathbb{R}^{q \times m}$, $\mathbf{V} \in \mathbb{R}^{r \times n}$, and $\mathbf{W} \in \mathbb{R}^{s \times p}$, with $q < m$, $r < n$ and $s < p$. Now suppose we want to compute

$$\begin{aligned} \mathcal{Y}_1 &= \mathcal{X} \times_2 \mathbf{V} \times_3 \mathbf{W}, \\ \mathcal{Y}_2 &= \mathcal{X} \times_1 \mathbf{U} \times_3 \mathbf{W}, \text{ and} \\ \mathcal{Y}_3 &= \mathcal{X} \times_1 \mathbf{U} \times_2 \mathbf{V}. \end{aligned}$$

If we assume $\beta_1 \leq \beta_2 \leq \beta_3$ according to the quantity given in Eq. (3.22), the most efficient TTM ordering for computing $\mathcal{Y}_1, \mathcal{Y}_2, \mathcal{Y}_3$ using independent multi-TTMs is $(\mathcal{X} \times_3 \mathbf{W}) \times_2$

$\mathbf{V}$, $(\mathcal{X} \times_3 \mathbf{W}) \times_1 \mathbf{U}$, and $(\mathcal{X} \times_2 \mathbf{V}) \times_1 \mathbf{U}$, respectively. The leading-order costs of these six TTMs is given by

$$2(mnps + mnrs + mnps + mnqs + mnpr + mpqr).$$

The term $mnps$ appears twice because $(\mathcal{X} \times_3 \mathbf{W})$ is computed twice.

Instead, we can first compute a memoization term $\mathcal{Y}_{12} = \mathcal{X} \times_3 \mathbf{W}$ and then use that to compute *both* $\mathcal{Y}_1$ and $\mathcal{Y}_2$ from $\mathcal{Y}_{12}$, as follows:

Multi-TTM for 3-way Tensor

$$\begin{aligned}
&\mathcal{Y}_{12} \leftarrow \mathcal{X} \times_3 \mathbf{W}\\
&\mathcal{Y}_1 \leftarrow \mathcal{Y}_{12} \times_2 \mathbf{V}\\
&\mathcal{Y}_2 \leftarrow \mathcal{Y}_{12} \times_1 \mathbf{U}\\
&\mathcal{Y}_3 \leftarrow \mathcal{X} \times_2 \mathbf{V} \times_1 \mathbf{U}
\end{aligned}$$

By storing and reusing the temporary tensor $\mathcal{Y}_{12} = \mathcal{X} \times_3 \mathbf{W}$, we avoid the double cost of computing $\mathcal{Y}_{12}$ and reduce the overall cost to

$$2(mnps + mnrs + mnqs + mnpr + mpqr).$$

If $m = n = p$ and $q = r = s$, then the cost of independent computation is approximately $6n^3r + 6n^2r^2$ versus the cost using memoization of $4n^3r + 6n^2r^2$. This provides an improvement of a factor of 1.5 in the leading-order term.

Multi-TTM Sequence for d-way Tensors

The benefits of memoization grow with the number of tensor modes d. Given a tensor $\mathcal{X} \in \mathbb{R}^{n_1 \times n_2 \times \cdots \times n_d}$ and matrices $\mathbf{U}_k \in \mathbb{R}^{r_k \times n_k}$ with $r_k < n_k$ for $k \in [d]$, we wish to compute

$$\mathcal{Y}_k = \mathcal{X} \times_1 \mathbf{U}_1 \cdots \times_{k-1} \mathbf{U}_{k-1} \times_{k+1} \mathbf{U}_{k+1} \cdots \times_d \mathbf{U}_d \quad \text{for all} \quad k \in [d].$$

We introduce a **dimension tree** to organize the memoization. The dimension tree has a root given by the original tensor $\mathcal{X}$, leaves given by the outputs $\{\, \mathcal{Y}_k \,\}$, and internal nodes $\{\, \mathcal{Y}_{\alpha:\beta} \,\}$ corresponding to temporary quantities defined as

$$\mathcal{Y}_{\alpha:\beta} = \mathcal{X} \times_1 \mathbf{U}_1 \cdots \times_{\alpha-1} \mathbf{U}_{\alpha-1} \times_{\beta+1} \mathbf{U}_{\beta+1} \cdots \times_d \mathbf{U}_d.$$

In other words, $\mathcal{Y}_{\alpha:\beta}$ is the result of TTMs in all modes *except* for α through β.

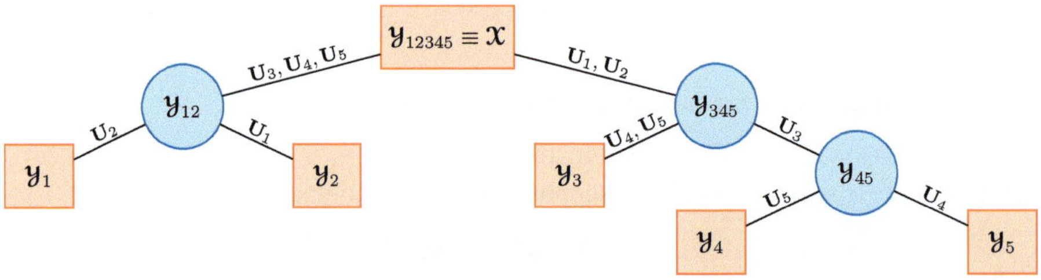

Figure 3.7 Dimension tree for computing $\mathcal{Y}_k = \mathcal{X} \times_1 \mathbf{U}_1 \cdots \times_{k-1} \mathbf{U}_{k-1} \times_{k+1} \mathbf{U}_{k+1} \cdots \times_d \mathbf{U}_d$ for all $k \in [d]$ for an order-5 tensor. Inputs and outputs are orange squares, and temporaries are blue circles. Each edge corresponds to one or more TTMs. Subscripts denote uncontracted modes.

An example dimension tree for a 5-way tensor is given in Fig. 3.7. The root node is the original tensor $\mathcal{X}$, which we can think of equivalently as $\mathcal{Y}_{12345}$. In the first level, we split the modes into $[1:2]$ and $[3:5]$. The left branch then computes the node

$$\mathcal{Y}_{12} = \mathcal{X} \times_3 \mathbf{U}_3 \times_4 \mathbf{U}_4 \times_5 \mathbf{U}_5.$$

These modes are split into 1 and 2, resulting in leaf nodes $\mathcal{Y}_1 = \mathcal{Y}_{12} \times_2 \mathbf{U}_2$ and $\mathcal{Y}_2 = \mathcal{Y}_{12} \times_1 \mathbf{U}_1$. After all its children are computed, $\mathcal{Y}_{12}$ can be discarded. The right branch from the root node computes

$$\mathcal{Y}_{345} = \mathcal{X} \times_1 \mathbf{U}_1 \times_2 \mathbf{U}_2.$$

These modes are split into 3 and $[4:5]$. On its left branch, we compute leaf node $\mathcal{Y}_3 = \mathcal{Y}_{345} \times_4 \mathbf{U}_4 \times_5 \mathbf{U}_5$. On its right branch, we compute node

$$\mathcal{Y}_{45} = \mathcal{Y}_{345} \times_3 \mathbf{U}_3.$$

These modes are split into 4 and 5, resulting in leaf nodes $\mathcal{Y}_4 = \mathcal{Y}_{45} \times_5 \mathbf{U}_5$ and $\mathcal{Y}_5 = \mathcal{Y}_{45} \times_4 \mathbf{U}_4$. The intermediates $\mathcal{Y}_{45}$ and $\mathcal{Y}_{345}$ can be discarded once their children have been computed.

The key observation is that only two TTMs involve the original tensor, and all other operations involve TTMs with temporary tensors, which require less computation when $r_k < n_k$ for each $k \in [d]$. So, rather than performing d TTMs with $\mathcal{X}$, we do only 2. If the costs are dominated by TTMs involving the original tensor, the overall reduction in leading-order computational cost by using memoization is by a factor of $d/2$. In the 5-way case, this equates to an improvement factor of approximately 2.5.

Algorithm 3.3 shows the pseudocode for recursively evaluating the dimension tree. The initial call is MULTI-TTM-SEQ($\mathcal{X}, \{\mathbf{U}_k\}, 1, d$). Every node in the tree involves a tensor with a contiguous set of modes $[\alpha : \beta] = \{\alpha, \alpha+1, \ldots, \beta\}$. This range is partitioned into $[\alpha : \ell]$ and $[\ell{+}1 : \beta]$, performing a sequence of TTMs to compute the temporary tensor associated with each part, and recursing on each temporary tensor. The partition mode is selected heuristically in Line 3. Determining an optimal choice is an NP-complete problem, but dynamic programming algorithms can obtain reasonable running time for small d (Kaya and Robert, 2019). Line 4 performs the multi-TTM for the left split, and Line 5 recurses on the left branch. Once that branch is finished, the leaf nodes are returned and the temporary $\mathcal{Y}_{\alpha:\beta}$ can be discarded. Similarly, Lines 6 and 7 handle the right branch. The base case occurs when $\alpha = \beta$ and all but one mode has been contracted (Line 2).

Exercise 3.25 Draw the dimension tree that Algorithm 3.3 would produce for a 7-way tensor of size $70 \times 60 \times 50 \times 40 \times 30 \times 20 \times 10$.

We have thus far assumed the inputs $\{\mathbf{U}_k\}$ are fixed throughout the computation. In the context of the higher-order orthogonal iteration algorithm (see Section 6.4), the matrix $\mathbf{U}_k$ is updated immediately after the tensor $\mathcal{Y}_k$ is computed and used in the subsequent computations. In this case, Algorithm 3.3 can be modified to return the updated matrices $\{\mathbf{U}_k\}$ and to perform the update of each $\mathbf{U}_k$ in the base case (when $\alpha = \beta = k$). Figure 3.8 shows an example computation sequence with numbers indicating the order of computation and differentiating the updated factors in green.

Algorithm 3.3 Multi-TTM Sequence (Recursive)

Require: $\mathcal{X} \in \mathbb{R}^{n_1 \times n_2 \times \cdots \times n_d}$, $\mathbf{U}_k \in \mathbb{R}^{r_k \times n_k}$ for all $k \in [d]$, $\alpha = 1$, $\beta = d$ (initial call)
Ensure: $\mathcal{Y}_k = \mathcal{X} \times_1 \mathbf{U}_1 \cdots \times_{k-1} \mathbf{U}_{k-1} \times_{k+1} \mathbf{U}_{k+1} \cdots \times_d \mathbf{U}_d$ for all $k \in [d]$ (final return)
function MULTI-TTM-SEQ($\mathcal{X}$, $\{\mathbf{U}_k\}$, α, β)
  if $\alpha = \beta$ **then return** $\{\mathcal{X}\}$ ▷ Return result in base case
  choose $\ell \in [\alpha : \beta]$ such that $\prod_{k=\alpha}^{\ell} r_k \approx \prod_{k=\ell+1}^{\beta} r_k$ ▷ Partition modes (heuristic)
  $\mathcal{Y}_{\alpha:\ell} \leftarrow \mathcal{X} \times_{\ell+1} \mathbf{U}_{\ell+1} \cdots \times_{\beta} \mathbf{U}_{\beta}$ ▷ Multi-TTM
  $\{\mathcal{Y}_{\alpha}, \cdots, \mathcal{Y}_{\ell}\} \leftarrow$ MULTI-TTM-SEQ($\mathcal{Y}_{\alpha:\ell}$, $\{\mathbf{U}_k\}$, α, ℓ)
  $\mathcal{Y}_{\ell+1:\beta} \leftarrow \mathcal{X} \times_{\alpha} \mathbf{U}_{\alpha} \cdots \times_{\ell} \mathbf{U}_{\ell}$ ▷ Multi-TTM
  $\{\mathcal{Y}_{\ell+1}, \ldots, \mathcal{Y}_{\beta}\} \leftarrow$ MULTI-TTM-SEQ($\mathcal{Y}_{\ell+1:\beta}$, $\{\mathbf{U}_k\}$, $\ell+1$, β)
  return $\{\mathcal{Y}_{\alpha}, \ldots, \mathcal{Y}_{\beta}\}$
end function

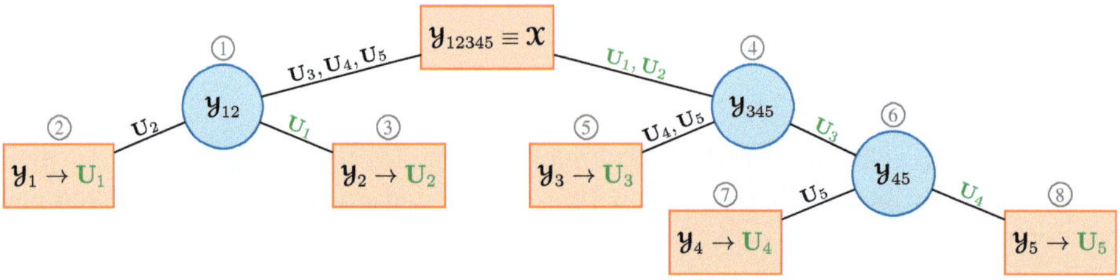

Figure 3.8 Repeat of Fig. 3.7 indicating the example order of computation for the updated factor $\mathbf{U}_k$ being created from $\mathcal{Y}_k$. Updated factors are indicated in green.

3.6.2 MTTKRP Sequence

Just like with TTM, most of the algorithms we consider for computing the CP decomposition require us to compute a sequence of MTTKRPs of the form

$$\mathbf{U}_k = \mathbf{X}_{(k)}(\mathbf{A}_d \odot \cdots \odot \mathbf{A}_{k+1} \odot \mathbf{A}_{k-1} \odot \cdots \odot \mathbf{A}_1) \quad \text{for all} \quad k \in [d].$$

In such cases, we can compute the sequence more cheaply if we memoize intermediate computations.

MTTKRP Sequence for 3-way Tensor

Consider a tensor $\mathcal{X} \in \mathbb{R}^{m \times n \times p}$, matrices $\mathbf{A} \in \mathbb{R}^{m \times r}$, $\mathbf{B} \in \mathbb{R}^{n \times r}$, and $\mathbf{C} \in \mathbb{R}^{p \times r}$, and the MTTKRPs:

$$\begin{aligned} \mathbf{U} &= \mathbf{X}_{(1)}(\mathbf{C} \odot \mathbf{B}), \\ \mathbf{V} &= \mathbf{X}_{(2)}(\mathbf{C} \odot \mathbf{A}), \quad \text{and} \\ \mathbf{W} &= \mathbf{X}_{(3)}(\mathbf{B} \odot \mathbf{A}). \end{aligned}$$

As described in Section 3.5, $\mathbf{V}$ can be computed by first computing an intermediate quantity $\mathcal{Y}_{12} = \mathcal{X} \times_3 \mathbf{C}^{\intercal}$ and then computing $\mathbf{V}$ as a batch of matrix–vector products between slices of $\mathcal{Y}_{12}$ and columns of $\mathbf{A}$. The computation of $\mathbf{U}$ can borrow $\mathcal{Y}_{12} = \mathcal{X} \times_3 \mathbf{C}^{\intercal}$, also in a batch of matrix–vector products between slices of $\mathcal{Y}$ and columns of $\mathbf{B}$, as follows:

MTTKRP Sequence for 3-way Tensor

$\mathcal{Y}_{12} \leftarrow \mathcal{X} \times_3 \mathbf{C}^\mathsf{T}$ ▷ Algorithm 3.1
for $\ell = 1, \ldots, r$ **do**
  $\mathbf{U}(:,\ell) \leftarrow \mathcal{Y}_{12}(:,:,\ell)\mathbf{B}(:,\ell)$ ▷ Batched matrix–vector multiplies
end for
for $\ell = 1, \ldots, r$ **do**
  $\mathbf{V}(:,\ell) \leftarrow \mathcal{Y}_{12}(:,:,\ell)^\mathsf{T}\mathbf{A}(:,\ell)$ ▷ Batched matrix–vector multiplies
end for
$\mathbf{W} \leftarrow \mathbf{X}_{(3)}(\mathbf{B} \odot \mathbf{A})$

The third output matrix $\mathbf{W}$ is computed as an independent MTTKRP and does not use any other computations. A visualization of the temporaries and dependencies in this pseudocode is given in Fig. 3.9.

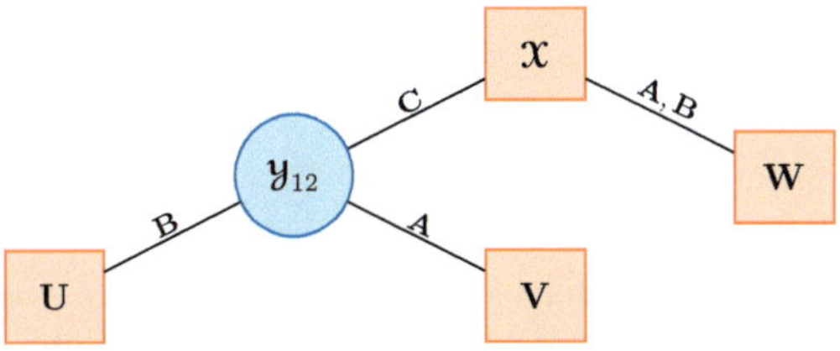

Figure 3.9 MTTKRP sequence using memoization for 3-way tensors. Temporaries are depicted as blue circles, and inputs/outputs are shown as orange squares.

Comparing the computational costs to those of performing three independent MTTKRPs, we see that we have avoided one of the three most expensive computations that involve the original tensor $\mathcal{X}$. If we store and reuse the tensor $\mathcal{Y}_{12}$, we have that the dominant cost of computing $\mathcal{Y}_{12}$ is $2mnpr$, and the dominant cost of computing $\mathbf{W}$ separately is also $2mnpr$. The dominant cost of computing the MTTKRPs independently is $6mnpr$, so using memoization provides a computational cost improvement of a factor of approximately 1.5 for 3-way tensors.

MTTKRP Sequence for d-way Tensors The benefits of memoization for an MTTKRP sequence grow with the number of tensor modes d. Given a tensor $\mathcal{X} \in \mathbb{R}^{n_1 \times n_2 \times \cdots \times n_d}$ and matrices $\mathbf{A}_k \in \mathbb{R}^{n_k \times r}$ for $k \in [d]$, we wish to compute

$$\mathbf{B}_k = \mathbf{X}_{(k)}(\mathbf{A}_d \odot \cdots \odot \mathbf{A}_{k+1} \odot \mathbf{A}_{k-1} \odot \cdots \odot \mathbf{A}_1) \quad \text{for all} \quad k \in [d].$$

Recall that

$$\mathbf{B}_k(i_k, j) = \sum_{i_1=1}^{n_1} \cdots \sum_{i_{k-1}=1}^{n_{k-1}} \sum_{i_{k+1}=1}^{n_{k+1}} \cdots \sum_{i_d=1}^{n_d} \mathcal{X}(i_1, i_2, \ldots, i_d) \prod_{\substack{\ell=1 \\ \ell \neq k}}^{d} \mathbf{A}_k(i_k, j)$$
$$\text{for all} \quad (i_k, j) \in [n_k] \otimes [r]. \quad (3.29)$$

Similar to the case of a multi-TTM sequence, we evaluate a dimension tree with a root given by the original tensor $\mathcal{X}$, leaves given by the MTTKRP results $\{\mathbf{B}_k\}$, and internal nodes corresponding to intermediate computations that are a partial computation of Eq. (3.29) stored as a tensor $\mathcal{Y}_{\alpha:\beta}$ of order $\beta - \alpha + 2$ and size $n_\alpha \times n_{\alpha+1} \times \cdots \times n_\beta \times r$ such that

$$\mathcal{Y}_{\alpha:\beta}(i_\alpha, \ldots, i_\beta, j) = \sum_{i_1=1}^{n_1} \cdots \sum_{i_{\alpha-1}=1}^{n_{\alpha-1}} \sum_{i_{\beta+1}=1}^{n_{\beta+1}} \cdots \sum_{i_d=1}^{n_d} \mathcal{X}(i_1, \ldots, i_d) \prod_{\substack{k=1 \\ k \notin [\alpha:\beta]}}^{d} \mathbf{A}_k(i_k, j).$$

This intermediate tensor has incorporated all the factor matrices *except* those in modes α through β and so can be reused in the computations for $\mathcal{Y}_\alpha = \mathbf{B}_\alpha$ through $\mathcal{Y}_\beta = \mathbf{B}_\beta$.

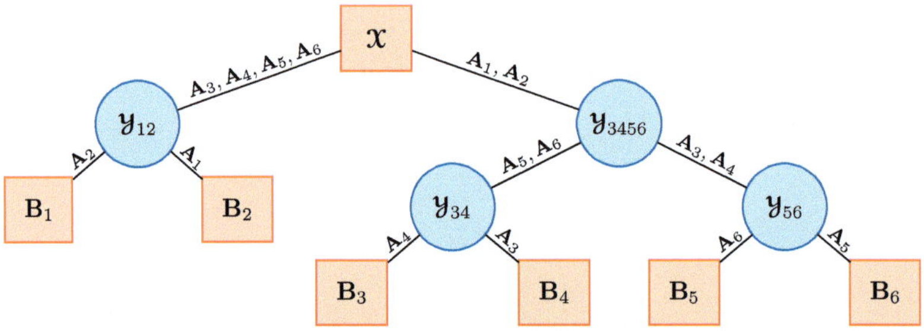

Figure 3.10 MTTKRP sequence using memoization for a 6-way tensor. Temporaries are depicted as blue circles, and inputs/outputs are orange squares. Subscripts indicate uncontracted modes.

An example dimension tree for a 6-way tensor is given in Fig. 3.10. Starting from the root node at $\mathcal{X}$, we split the modes into $[1 : 2]$ and $[3 : 6]$. The left branch computes $\mathcal{Y}_{12} \in \mathbb{R}^{n_1 \times n_2 \times r}$ using matrix–matrix multiplication with a reshaped version of $\mathcal{X}$ and a Khatri–Rao product of the factor matrices from the other subset of modes:

$$[\mathcal{Y}_{12}]_{\{1,2\}\times 3} = \mathbf{X}_{(\{1,2\}\times\{3,4,5,6\})}(\mathbf{A}_6 \odot \mathbf{A}_5 \odot \mathbf{A}_4 \odot \mathbf{A}_3).$$

The reshaped version of $\mathcal{X}$ has the same layout in memory (Proposition 2.20), so no memory movement is required. This intermediate quantity can be used to compute the leaf nodes $\mathbf{B}_1$ and $\mathbf{B}_2$ with batched matrix–vector multiplies via

$$\begin{aligned} \mathbf{B}_1(:,j) &= \mathbf{Y}_{12}(:,:,j)\mathbf{A}_2(:,j) \in \mathbb{R}^{n_1 \times r} \\ \mathbf{B}_2(:,j) &= \mathbf{Y}_{12}(:,:,j)^{\mathsf{T}}\mathbf{A}_1(:,j) \in \mathbb{R}^{n_2 \times r} \end{aligned} \quad \text{for all} \quad j \in [r].$$

After its children have been evaluated, $\mathcal{Y}_{12}$ can be discarded.

The right branch from the root node computes $\mathcal{Y}_{3456} \in \mathbb{R}^{n_1 \times n_2 \times n_3 \times n_4 \times r}$ (shaped as a matrix) using matrix–matrix multiplication with a reshaped and transposed version of $\mathcal{X}$ and a Khatri–Rao product of factor matrices from the other subset of modes:

$$[\mathcal{Y}_{3456}]_{\{1,2,3,4\}\times 5} = \mathbf{X}^{\mathsf{T}}_{(\{1,2\}\times\{3,4,5,6\})}(\mathbf{A}_2 \odot \mathbf{A}_1).$$

We branch by splitting the remaining modes into $[3 : 4]$ and $[5 : 6]$.

Along the left branch, the node $\mathcal{Y}_{34} \in \mathbb{R}^{n_3 \times n_4 \times r}$ is created via a Khatri–Rao product and batched matrix–vector multiplications along with some reshapes:

Example Left Branch of MTTKRP Sequence

$\mathcal{Z} \leftarrow \text{reshape}(\mathcal{Y}_{3456}, n_3 n_4 \times n_5 n_6 \times r)$
$\mathbf{K}_U \leftarrow \mathbf{A}_6 \odot \mathbf{A}_5$
for $j = 1, \ldots, r$ **do**
  $\mathbf{V}(:, j) \leftarrow \mathcal{Z}(:, :, j)\mathbf{K}_U(:, j)$
end for
$\mathcal{Y}_{34} \leftarrow \text{reshape}(\mathbf{V}, n_3 \times n_4 \times r)$

From $\mathcal{Y}_{34}$, we can compute leaf nodes $\mathbf{B}_3$ and $\mathbf{B}_4$ via

$$\begin{aligned} \mathbf{B}_3(:, j) &= \mathcal{Y}_{34}(:, :, j)\mathbf{A}_4(:, j) \\ \mathbf{B}_4(:, j) &= \mathcal{Y}_{34}(:, :, j)^\intercal \mathbf{A}_3(:, j) \end{aligned} \quad \text{for all} \quad j \in [r].$$

The intermediate quantity $\mathcal{Y}_{34}$ can be discarded after its children have all been computed.

Going back to $\mathcal{Y}_{3456}$ and following along the right branch, the node $\mathcal{Y}_{56} \in \mathbb{R}^{n_5 \times n_6 \times r}$ is created analogously to $\mathcal{Y}_{34}$ except that the frontal slices of $\mathcal{Z}$ are transposed:

Example Right Branch of MTTKRP Sequence

$\mathcal{Z} \leftarrow \text{reshape}(\mathcal{Y}_{3456}, n_3 n_4 \times n_5 n_6 \times r)$
$\mathbf{K}_U \leftarrow \mathbf{A}_4 \odot \mathbf{A}_3$
for $j = 1, \ldots, r$ **do**
  $\mathbf{V}(:, j) \leftarrow \mathcal{Z}(:, :, j)^\intercal \mathbf{K}_U(:, j)$
end for
$\mathcal{Y}_{56} \leftarrow \text{reshape}(\mathbf{V}, n_5 \times n_6 \times r)$

From $\mathcal{Y}_{56}$, we can compute the final leaf nodes $\mathbf{B}_5$ and $\mathbf{B}_6$ via

$$\begin{aligned} \mathbf{B}_5(:, j) &= \mathcal{Y}_{56}(:, :, j)\mathbf{A}_6(:, j) \\ \mathbf{B}_6(:, j) &= \mathcal{Y}_{56}(:, :, j)^\intercal \mathbf{A}_5(:, j) \end{aligned} \quad \text{for all} \quad j \in [r].$$

The key observation is that the entire tree can be evaluated with only two operations involving the original tensor, both of which are cast as matrix–matrix multiplication, and all other operations involve batched matrix–vector products with smaller intermediate tensors that require much less computation. The cost of each matrix–matrix multiplication is the same as the cost of a single MTTKRP (with no memoization), so the overall reduction factor in computation by using memoization for an MTTKRP sequence is approximately $d/2$.

Pseudocode for an MTTKRP sequence for the d-way case is provided in Algorithm 3.4. As with the multi-TTM sequence, we use recursion to implement the computations within the dimension tree. The division at the root node of the dimension tree is special, creating the quantities $\mathcal{Y}_{1:\ell}$ or $\mathcal{Y}_{\ell+1:d}$. These are computed via matrix–matrix multiplication with an appropriately reshaped tensor and Khatri–Rao product of the involved factor matrices. While the choice of ℓ does not affect the cost of the two MTTKRPs, we recommend choosing ℓ such that $n_1 \cdots n_\ell \approx n_{\ell+1} \cdots n_d$ in order to minimize the memory footprint and the computational cost of subsequent operations.

The rest of the tree is split recursively via the subfunction MTTKRP-SPLIT in Algorithm 3.4. At each node, we partition the remaining modes into two contiguous parts that balance the products of the dimensions. Given $\mathcal{Y}_{\alpha:\beta}$, we can create, for example, $\mathcal{Y}_{\ell:\beta}$ for some $\ell \in [\alpha : \beta]$ so that

$$\mathcal{Y}_{\ell:\beta}(i_\ell, \ldots, i_\beta, j) = \sum_{i_\alpha=1}^{n_\alpha} \cdots \sum_{i_{\ell-1}=1}^{n_{\ell-1}} \mathcal{Y}_{\alpha:\beta}(i_\alpha, \ldots, i_\beta, j) \prod_{k=\alpha}^{\ell-1} \mathbf{A}_k(i_k, j).$$

This can be computed by taking the Khatri–Rao product of the involved factor matrices, reshaping $\mathcal{Y}_{\alpha:\beta}$ into an appropriate 3-way tensor, and then doing batched matrix–vector multiplies. A similar logic allows transformation from $\mathcal{Y}_{\alpha:\beta}$ to $\mathcal{Y}_{\alpha:\ell}$. The quantity $\mathcal{Y}_{\alpha}$ is a 2-way tensor that is exactly $\mathbf{B}_{\alpha}$.

Algorithm 3.4 MTTKRP Sequence

Require: $\mathcal{X} \in \mathbb{R}^{n_1 \times n_2 \times \cdots \times n_d}$, $\mathbf{A}_k \in \mathbb{R}^{n_k \times r}$ for all $k \in [d]$
Ensure: $\mathbf{B}_k = \mathbf{X}_{(k)}(\mathbf{A}_d \odot \cdots \odot \mathbf{A}_{k+1} \odot \mathbf{A}_{k-1} \odot \cdots \odot \mathbf{A}_1)$ for all $k \in [d]$
function $\{\mathbf{B}_1, \mathbf{B}_2, \ldots, \mathbf{B}_d\} = \text{MTTKRP-SEQ}(\mathcal{X}, \{\mathbf{A}_k\})$
  choose split $\ell \in [d]$ such that $M_\ell = \prod_{k=1}^{\ell} n_k \approx P_\ell = \prod_{k=\ell+1}^{d} n_k$
  $\bar{\mathbf{X}} \leftarrow \text{reshape}(\mathcal{X}, M_\ell \times P_\ell)$
  $\mathbf{K}_U \leftarrow \mathbf{A}_d \odot \cdots \odot \mathbf{A}_{\ell+1}$ ▷ KRP of upper modes, $P_k \times r$
  $\mathcal{Y}_{1:\ell} \leftarrow \text{reshape}(\bar{\mathbf{X}}\mathbf{K}_U, n_1 \times \cdots \times n_\ell \times r)$ ▷ Matrix–matrix multiply
  $\{\mathbf{B}_1, \ldots, \mathbf{B}_\ell\} \leftarrow \text{MTTKRP-SPLIT}(\mathcal{Y}_{1:\ell}, \{\mathbf{A}_k\}, 1, \ell)$ ▷ Left branch
  $\mathbf{K}_L \leftarrow \mathbf{A}_\ell \odot \cdots \odot \mathbf{A}_1$ ▷ KRP of lower modes, $M_k \times r$
  $\mathcal{Y}_{\ell+1:d} = \text{reshape}(\bar{\mathbf{X}}^{\mathsf{T}}\mathbf{K}_L, n_{\ell+1} \times \cdots \times n_d \times r)$ ▷ Matrix–matrix multiply
  $\{\mathbf{B}_{\ell+1}, \ldots, \mathbf{B}_d\} \leftarrow \text{MTTKRP-SPLIT}(\mathcal{Y}_{\ell+1:d}, \{\mathbf{A}_k\}, \ell+1, d)$ ▷ Right branch
  return $\{\mathbf{B}_1, \mathbf{B}_2, \ldots, \mathbf{B}_d\}$
end function

function $\{\mathbf{B}_\alpha, \ldots, \mathbf{B}_\beta\} = \text{MTTKRP-SPLIT}(\mathcal{Y}_{\alpha:\beta}, \{\mathbf{A}_k\}, \alpha, \beta)$ ▷ Subfunction
  if $\alpha = \beta$ **then return** $\mathbf{B}_\alpha = \mathcal{Y}_\alpha$ ▷ Return result in base case
  choose split $\ell \in [\alpha : \beta]$ such that $M_\ell = \prod_{k=a}^{\ell} n_k \approx P_\ell = \prod_{k=\ell+1}^{b} n_k$
  $\mathcal{Z} \leftarrow \text{reshape}(\mathcal{Y}_{\alpha:\beta}, M_\ell \times P_\ell \times r)$
  $\mathbf{K}_U \leftarrow \mathbf{A}_\beta \odot \cdots \odot \mathbf{A}_{\ell+1}$ ▷ KRP of upper modes
  for $j = 1, \ldots, r$ **do**
    $\mathbf{V}(:, j) \leftarrow \mathcal{Z}(:, :, j)\mathbf{K}_U(:, j)$ ▷ Batched matrix–vector multiplies
  end for
  $\mathcal{Y}_{\alpha:\ell} \leftarrow \text{reshape}(\mathbf{V}, n_\alpha \times \cdots \times n_\ell \times r)$
  $\{\mathbf{B}_\alpha, \ldots, \mathbf{B}_\ell\} \leftarrow \text{MTTKRP-SPLIT}(\mathcal{Y}_{\alpha:\ell}, \{\mathbf{A}_k\}, \alpha, \ell)$ ▷ Left branch
  $\mathbf{K}_L \leftarrow \mathbf{A}_\ell \odot \cdots \odot \mathbf{A}_\alpha$ ▷ KRP of lower modes
  for $j = 1, \ldots, r$ **do**
    $\mathbf{W}(:, j) \leftarrow \mathcal{Z}(:, :, j)^{\mathsf{T}}\mathbf{K}_L(:, j)$ ▷ Batched matrix–vector multiplies
  end for
  $\mathcal{Y}_{\ell+1:\beta} \leftarrow \text{reshape}(\mathbf{W}, n_{\ell+1} \times \cdots \times n_\beta \times r)$
  $\{\mathbf{B}_{\ell+1}, \ldots, \mathbf{B}_\beta\} \leftarrow \text{MTTKRP-SPLIT}(\mathcal{Y}_{\ell+1:\beta}, \{\mathbf{A}_k\}, \ell+1, \beta)$ ▷ Right branch
  return $\{\mathbf{B}_\alpha, \ldots, \mathbf{B}_\beta\}$
end function

In the dimension tree visualization in Fig. 3.10, we can interpret each node in the tree as a function call: the root node corresponds to the single call to MTTKRP-SEQ, the internal nodes correspond to calls to the helper function MTTKRP-SPLIT, and the leaf nodes correspond to base cases of MTTKRP-SPLIT.

Exercise 3.26 Draw the dimension tree that Algorithm 3.4 would produce for a 6-way tensor of size $40 \times 40 \times 30 \times 30 \times 20 \times 20$.

As an example of the computational cost reduction, consider an input tensor of dimension $n \times n \times n \times n$ and factor matrices each of dimension $n \times r$. If we perform each of the four MTTKRPs using Algorithm 3.2, the total cost is approximately $8n^4r + 4n^3r + 4n^2r$. Using memoization (Algorithm 3.4), the cost is reduced to $4n^4r + 10n^2r$, an improvement by approximately a factor of 2.

Algorithm 3.4 assumes the inputs $\{\mathbf{A}_k\}$ are fixed throughout the computation. If $\mathbf{A}_k$ changes after computation of $\mathbf{B}_k$ as in the alternating least squares algorithm (see Chapter 11), Algorithm 3.4 can be modified to return the updated matrices $\{\mathbf{A}_k\}$ instead of the leaf matrices $\{\mathbf{B}_k\}$ and to perform the update of each $\mathbf{A}_k$ in the base case of MTTKRP-SPLIT (when $\alpha = \beta = k$).

Exercise 3.27 Update the dimension tree in Fig. 3.10 in the case where $\mathbf{A}_k$ is recomputed from $\mathbf{Y}_k$ and should be used for all subsequent computations. Indicate the updated factor matrices and order of computation in a way analogous to the multi-TTM sequence given in Fig. 3.8.

3.7 Sparse Tensors and Operation Efficiencies

We say that a tensor is **sparse** if the vast majority of its elements are 0. In such cases, storing only the nonzeros and their indices requires less memory than storing every element. The key property of sparse tensors is that they can be stored using less memory than dense tensors and operations with 0s can be avoided to save computation. The **number of nonzeros** in the tensor is denoted as $\text{nnz}(\mathcal{X})$. In this section, we show how to store and operate with sparse tensors efficiently.

We focus primarily on **coordinate format** (sometimes abbreviated as COO format), introduced in Section 3.7.1. This format stores nonzero values and corresponding indices in such a way that we can iterate through them, and it does not assume any particular ordering to the indices. The storage required is proportional to the number of nonzeros. We discuss other sparse formats in Section 3.7.5.

3.7.1 Coordinate Format for Sparse Tensors

The COO format was formalized by Bader and Kolda (2007), and is used by the Tensor Toolbox for MATLAB (Bader et al., 2023), Python Tensor Toolbox (Dunlavy et al., 2022), TensorLab for MATLAB (Vervliet et al., 2017), and TensorFlow (TensorFlow Team, 2022).

Coordinate Format for 3-way Sparse Tensors

Let $\mathcal{X}$ be a 3-way tensor of size $m \times n \times p$. Storing $\mathcal{X}$ as a dense tensor requires $\mathcal{O}(mnp)$ storage. We say $\mathcal{X}$ is sparse if $q \equiv \text{nnz}(\mathcal{X}) \ll mnp$. The key property of sparse tensors is that they can be stored using many fewer values than the dense tensor, and operations with 0s can be avoided to save computation.

Definition 3.28 (Coordinate Format for 3-way Tensor) Let $\mathcal{X}$ in $m \times n \times p$ be a sparse tensor with $q \equiv \text{nnz}(\mathcal{X})$ nonzeros. Its **coordinate format** representation stores $\mathcal{X}$ as $[\![\mathbf{\Omega}, \mathbf{v}]\!]$, where

- $\mathbf{\Omega} \in \mathbb{N}^{q \times 3}$ stores the (i, j, k) tuples of the nonzeros, one tuple per row, and
- $\mathbf{v} \in \mathbb{R}^q$ stores the corresponding nonzero values.

The ℓth nonzero has value given by entry ℓ in $\mathbf{v}$ and coordinates given by row ℓ of $\mathbf{\Omega}$; in other words,

$$v_\ell = \mathcal{X}(\omega_{1\ell}, \omega_{2\ell}, \omega_{3\ell}).$$

Remark 3.29 (How much storage does a sparse tensor require?) The total storage for a 3-way sparse tensor $\mathcal{X}$ stored in coordinate format is three natural number indices and one real value per nonzero. We can potentially be more efficient in the storage of the tuple indices. For instance, each (i, j, k) can be packed into $\lceil \log_2 m \rceil + \lceil \log_2 n \rceil + \lceil \log_2 p \rceil$ bits or (with a bit more computation) converted to a linear index requiring $\lceil \log_2(mnp) \rceil$ bits. How much these details matter depends on the dimensions and number of nonzeros in the problem. We generally say simply that the storage is proportional to the number of nonzeros.

Example 3.6 (Coordinate Format) Consider the tensor $\mathcal{X} \in \mathbb{R}^{5\times 5\times 3}$ and its sparse representation $[\![\boldsymbol{\Omega}, \mathbf{v}]\!]$. It needs to store $3q = 12$ indices and $q = 4$ values versus $N = \prod_{k=1}^{d} n_k = 75$ values for the full tensor:

$\mathcal{X} =$

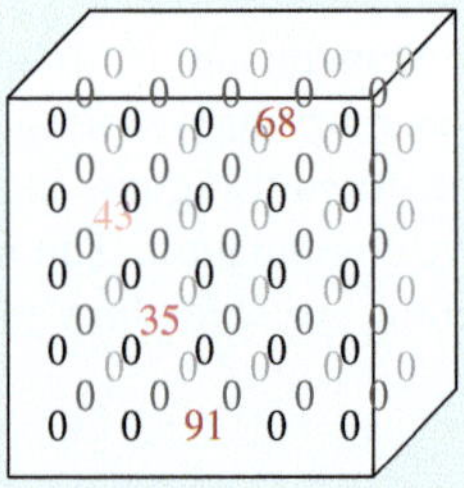

$$, \quad \boldsymbol{\Omega} = \begin{bmatrix} 1 & 4 & 1 \\ 3 & 1 & 3 \\ 4 & 2 & 2 \\ 5 & 3 & 1 \end{bmatrix} \in \mathbb{N}^{q\times d} \text{ and } \mathbf{v} = \begin{bmatrix} 68 \\ 43 \\ 35 \\ 91 \end{bmatrix} \in \mathbb{R}^q.$$

Exercise 3.28 Consider the tensor $\mathcal{X}$ of size $3 \times 3 \times 3$ whose frontal slices are

$$\mathbf{X}_1 = \begin{bmatrix} 0 & 0 & 0 \\ 0 & 0 & 0 \\ 9 & 0 & 0 \end{bmatrix}, \quad \mathbf{X}_2 = \begin{bmatrix} 0 & 0 & 0 \\ 0 & 0 & 0 \\ 0 & 0 & 9 \end{bmatrix}, \quad \text{and} \quad \mathbf{X}_3 = \begin{bmatrix} 0 & 2 & 0 \\ 0 & 0 & 4 \\ 8 & 0 & 0 \end{bmatrix}.$$

(a) What is $\text{nnz}(\mathcal{X})$? (b) What are $\boldsymbol{\Omega}$ and $\mathbf{v}$?

Exercise 3.29 (Permutation of Sparse Tensor) Let $\mathcal{X}$ be a sparse tensor of size $m \times n \times p$ represented by $\boldsymbol{\Omega} \in \mathbb{R}^{q\times 3}$ and $\mathbf{v} \in \mathbb{R}^q$. If $\mathcal{Y} = \mathbb{P}(\mathcal{X}, [3, 1, 2])$, what is $\mathcal{Y}$'s sparse representation?

Remark 3.30 (Arbitrary nonzero order in coordinate format) Coordinate format storage does not prescribe a particular order on the nonzeros.

Coordinate Format for d-way Sparse Tensors

The idea of coordinate format is easily extended to d-way tensors as follows.

Definition 3.31 (Coordinate Format for d-way Tensor) Let $\mathcal{X}$ in $n_1 \times n_2 \times \cdots \times n_d$ be a sparse tensor with $q \equiv \text{nnz}(\mathcal{X})$ nonzeros. Its **coordinate format** representation stores $\mathcal{X}$ as $[\![\boldsymbol{\Omega}, \mathbf{v}]\!]$, where

- $\boldsymbol{\Omega} \in \mathbb{N}^{q\times d}$ stores the $(i_1, i_2, \ldots, i_d)$ tuples of the nonzeros, one per row, and
- $\mathbf{v} \in \mathbb{R}^q$ stores the corresponding nonzero values.

The ℓth nonzero has coordinates given by row ℓ of $\boldsymbol{\Omega}$ and value given by entry ℓ in $\mathbf{v}$; in other words,

$$v_\ell = \mathcal{X}(\omega_{1\ell}, \omega_{2\ell}, \cdots, \omega_{d\ell}).$$

Exercise 3.30 Make the simple assumption that each mode index and nonzero value requires the same amount of storage. (a) What is the storage requirement for a d-way dense tensor $\mathcal{X}$ of size $n_1 \times n_2 \times \cdots \times n_d$? (b) What is the storage requirement if $\mathcal{X}$ is instead a sparse tensor with q nonzeros? (c) Define ρ to be the proportion of nonzeros in $\mathcal{X}$, i.e., $\rho = \text{nnz}(\mathcal{X})/N$ for $N = \prod_{k=1}^{d} n_k$. For what range of ρ values is sparse storage more efficient than dense storage?

Assembling a Sparse Tensor in Coordinate Format

To assemble a sparse tensor, we need paired lists of subscripts and values. The only potential issue is resolving duplicates in the subscripts, in which case we would sum the values associated with any repeated subscript, as shown in Example 3.7.

Example 3.7 (Assembling a Sparse Tensor) We have to sum up values corresponding to any duplicate coordinate tuples:

$$\boldsymbol{\Omega} = \begin{bmatrix} 1 & 1 & 1 \\ 2 & 1 & 1 \\ 2 & 2 & 2 \\ 1 & 1 & 1 \\ 1 & 2 & 2 \end{bmatrix}, \mathbf{v} = \begin{bmatrix} 1 \\ 1 \\ 1 \\ 1 \\ 1 \end{bmatrix} \quad \Rightarrow \quad \boldsymbol{\Omega} = \begin{bmatrix} 1 & 1 & 1 \\ 2 & 1 & 1 \\ 2 & 2 & 2 \\ 1 & 2 & 2 \end{bmatrix}, \mathbf{v} = \begin{bmatrix} 2 \\ 1 \\ 1 \\ 1 \end{bmatrix}.$$

Duplicate indices → (fourth row of the first $\boldsymbol{\Omega}$)

Finding duplicate entries generally involves sorting the tuples, for a cost of $\mathcal{O}(q \log q)$, where $q = \text{nnz}(\mathcal{X})$. This could potentially be completed in $\mathcal{O}(q)$ time using a hash table.

Exercise 3.31 Let $\mathcal{X}$ and $\mathcal{Y}$ be sparse tensors of size $m \times n \times p$, and let $\mathcal{Z} = \mathcal{X} + \mathcal{Y}$. (a) Prove $\text{nnz}(\mathcal{Z}) \leq \text{nnz}(\mathcal{X}) + \text{nnz}(\mathcal{Y})$. (b) Under what conditions on $\mathcal{X}$ and $\mathcal{Y}$ do we have $\text{nnz}(\mathcal{Z}) = \text{nnz}(\mathcal{X}) + \text{nnz}(\mathcal{Y})$?

3.7.2 Norm of a Sparse Tensor

The norm of a 3-way sparse tensor $\mathcal{X} = [\![\boldsymbol{\Omega}, \mathbf{v}]\!]$ can be computed by considering only the nonzero entries of the tensor. Recall from Definition 3.31 that $\boldsymbol{\Omega} \in \mathbb{N}^{q \times 3}$ contains the indices of the nonzeros, and $\mathbf{v} \in \mathbb{R}^q$ contains the corresponding values, where $q = \text{nnz}(\mathcal{X})$. Then we can omit 0 entries from the sum, yielding

$$\|\mathcal{X}\| = \|\mathbf{v}\|_2 = \sqrt{\sum_{\alpha=1}^{q} v_\alpha^2}.$$

The cost to compute the norm of a sparse tensor is $\mathcal{O}(\text{nnz}(\mathcal{X}))$.

Exercise 3.32 (a) What is the formula to compute the norm of a sparse d-way tensor? (b) What is the computational cost? (c) What is the difference compared to the norm of a sparse 3-way tensor?

3.7.3 MTTKRP for 3-way Sparse Tensors

Let $\mathcal{X}$ be a sparse tensor of size $m \times n \times p$, $\mathbf{B} \in \mathbb{R}^{n \times r}$, and $\mathbf{C} \in \mathbb{R}^{p \times r}$. Consider the problem of computing

$$\mathbf{U} = \mathbf{X}_{(1)}(\mathbf{C} \odot \mathbf{B}),$$

which is written elementwise (see Eq. (3.23)) as

$$u_{i\ell} = \sum_{j=1}^{n} \sum_{k=1}^{p} x_{ijk} b_{j\ell} c_{k\ell} \quad \text{for all} \quad (i,\ell) \in [m] \otimes [r].$$

The dense calculation costs $\mathcal{O}(mnpr)$ operations.

Using the sparse structure of $\mathcal{X} = [\![\boldsymbol{\Omega}, \mathbf{v}]\!]$, we can be more efficient, as only nonzero tensor values contribute to the output. Each nonzero contributes to only a single row of $\mathbf{U}$; in other words, nonzero α multiplied with row $\omega_{\alpha 2}$ of $\mathbf{B}$ and row $\omega_{\alpha 3}$ of $\mathbf{C}$, contributes to row $\omega_{\alpha 1}$ of $\mathbf{U}$. Thus, we can rewrite the above equation as

$$u_{i\ell} = \sum_{\substack{\alpha=1 \\ \omega_{\alpha 1}=i}}^{q} v_\alpha \, \mathbf{B}(\omega_{\alpha 2}, \ell) \, \mathbf{C}(\omega_{\alpha 3}, \ell) \quad \text{for all} \quad (i,\ell) \in [m] \otimes [r]. \tag{3.30}$$

In practice, we typically iterate contiguously through the nonzeros of $\mathcal{X}$, as follows.

Sparse Mode-1 MTTKRP for 3-way Tensor

$\mathbf{U} \leftarrow \mathbf{0}$
for $\alpha \in [q]$ **do** $\quad \triangleright\, q = \text{nnz}(\mathcal{X})$
  for $\ell \in [r]$ **do**
    $\mathbf{U}(\omega_{\alpha 1}, \ell) \leftarrow \mathbf{U}(\omega_{\alpha 1}, \ell) + v_\alpha \, \mathbf{B}(\omega_{\alpha 2}, \ell) \, \mathbf{C}(\omega_{\alpha 3}, \ell)$
  end for
end for

If we iterate contiguously through the nonzeros, then the access pattern into the rows of matrices $\mathbf{U}$, $\mathbf{B}$, and $\mathbf{C}$ is generally irregular. We do have flexibility in the structure of the loops over the nonzeros and the columns of the matrices, which is important for high-performance implementations.

The total computational work is $\mathcal{O}(qr)$, where $q = \text{nnz}(\mathcal{X})$. If $q \ll mnp$, then the work is greatly reduced compared to the usual calculation with a dense $\mathcal{X}$.

Exercise 3.33 Write an algorithm to compute $\mathbf{W} = \mathbf{X}_{(3)}(\mathbf{B} \odot \mathbf{A})$ for sparse $\mathcal{X} = [\![\boldsymbol{\Omega}, \mathbf{v}]\!]$.

3.7.4 MTTKRP for d-way Sparse Tensors

In the d-way case, consider the mode-k MTTKRP:

$$\mathbf{B} = \mathbf{X}_{(k)}(\mathbf{A}_d \odot \cdots \odot \mathbf{A}_{k+1} \odot \mathbf{A}_{k-1} \odot \cdots \odot \mathbf{A}_1).$$

If the tensor is sparse with $\mathcal{X} = [\![\boldsymbol{\Omega}, \mathbf{v}]\!]$, we can do summations over the nonzeros:

$$\begin{aligned}
\mathbf{B}(i_k, j) &= \sum_{i_1=1}^{n_1} \cdots \sum_{i_{k-1}=1}^{n_{k-1}} \sum_{i_{k+1}=1}^{n_{k+1}} \cdots \sum_{i_d=1}^{n_d} \left(\mathcal{X}(i_1, i_2, \ldots, i_d) \prod_{\substack{\ell=1 \\ \ell \neq k}}^{d} \mathbf{A}_\ell(i_\ell, j) \right) \\
&= \sum_{\substack{\alpha=1 \\ \omega_{\alpha k}=i_k}}^{q} \left(v_\alpha \prod_{\substack{\ell=1 \\ \ell \neq k}}^{d} \mathbf{A}_\ell(\omega_{\alpha \ell}, j) \right).
\end{aligned}$$

As shown in Algorithm 3.5, we can implement the operation by iterating contiguously through the nonzeros and accessing the rows of the factor matrices that correspond to the coordinates of the nonzero. If we iterate contiguously through the nonzeros, then the access pattern into the matrices is random. The temporary variable z can be an array to enable flexibility in structuring the loops over the nonzeros (indexed by α) and the columns of the matrices (indexed by j). However, we want to stress that the variable z should never be instantiated as a $q \times r$ matrix since that much memory is prohibitive. The instantiation should depend on how the loops are structured. For instance, it is common to process an entire row in parallel, in which case the z variable should be a vector of length r. The computational cost to compute the MTTKRP with a sparse tensor with q nonzeros is $\mathcal{O}(qrd)$.

Algorithm 3.5 Mode-k MTTKRP for Sparse d-way Tensor

Require: $\mathcal{X} = [\![\mathbf{\Omega}, \mathbf{v}]\!] \in \mathbb{R}^{n_1 \times \cdots \times n_d}$, $\mathbf{\Omega} \in \mathbb{N}^{q \times d}$, $\mathbf{v} \in \mathbb{R}^q$, $\{\, \mathbf{A}_\ell \in \mathbb{R}^{n_\ell \times r} \,\}_{\ell \in [d], \ell \neq k}$, $k \in [d]$

Ensure: $\mathbf{B} = \mathbf{X}_{(k)}(\mathbf{A}_d \odot \cdots \odot \mathbf{A}_{k+1} \odot \mathbf{A}_{k-1} \odot \cdots \odot \mathbf{A}_1)$

function MTTKRP($\mathbf{\Omega}, \mathbf{v}, \{\mathbf{A}_\ell\}, k$)
  $\mathbf{B} \leftarrow \mathbf{0}$ ▷ Zero matrix of size $n_k \times r$
  for $\alpha \in [q]$ **do** ▷ $\mathcal{X}(\omega_{\alpha 1}, \ldots, \omega_{\alpha d}) = v_\alpha, \quad q = \text{nnz}(\mathcal{X})$
    for $j \in [r]$ **do**
      $z \leftarrow v_\alpha$ ▷ Temporary variable depending on (α, j)
      for $\ell \in \{1, \ldots, k-1, k+1, \ldots, d\}$ **do**
        $z \leftarrow z \; \mathbf{A}_\ell(\omega_{\alpha\ell}, j)$
      end for
      $\mathbf{B}(\omega_{\alpha k}, j) \leftarrow \mathbf{B}(\omega_{\alpha k}, j) + z$
    end for
  end for
  return $\mathbf{B}$
end function

Since MTTKRP is a key computational kernel, many papers have studied the efficiency of this operation for sparse tensors, including Bader and Kolda (2007), Helal et al. (2021), Kaya and Uçar (2015), Kolda et al. (2005), Li et al. (2017, 2018), Phipps and Kolda (2019), and Smith and Karypis (2015).

3.7.5 Other Data Structures for Sparse Tensors

The data structure for a sparse tensor impacts both storage and computational efficiency. Generally, the preference is to access data in contiguous blocks and reuse these blocks as much as possible before moving on. Sparse computations, however, necessitate some amount of jumping around in memory. The optimal choice of data structure depends on the specific computational architecture and nature of the data tensor.

A hierarchical variation of COO called HiCOO (Li et al., 2018) stores the tensor as a sparse tensor of small dense blocks, potentially reducing the storage and increasing locality. Similar ideas have been proposed for hypersparse matrices (Buluç and Gilbert, 2008).

There are several storage formats that are mode specific. For example, compressed sparse fiber (Smith and Karypis, 2015) represents the tensor using a tree structure terminating in compressed mode fibers. This is akin to compressed sparse row or column format for matrices, and the representation is specific to a mode ordering. Typically, multiple copies of the tensor are stored with different compression orders for MTTKRP efficiency in each mode.

Even for coordinate format, many variations can be considered. For instance, Phipps and Kolda (2019) extended the COO format to include permutations that sort the nonzeros according to the indices in mode k to improve data locality, adding some extra storage to the COO format. Helal et al. (2021) use a linearized version of COO format to gain more compression and optimize the conversions between linear and tuple indices.

3.8 Tensor Contraction

A **tensor contraction** combines two tensors by summing, or *contracting*, across a subset of matched modes that have the same size, and the result is a tensor whose size is the union of the sizes of the non-contracted modes, potentially in some specified order. The inner product is a tensor contraction that contracts along all modes. A mode-k TTM is a tensor contraction: It contracts mode-k of the tensor with mode-2 of the matrix and arranges the order of the output modes in a particular way.

3.8.1 Tensor Contraction for 3-way Tensors

Consider two tensors:

$$\mathcal{X} \in \mathbb{R}^{m \times n \times p} \quad \text{and} \quad \mathcal{Y} \in \mathbb{R}^{p \times q \times r}.$$

The last mode of $\mathcal{X}$ and the first mode of $\mathcal{Y}$ have the same size, so we can contract along these modes. The result is a tensor $\mathcal{Z}$ of size $m \times n \times q \times r$ and defined by

$$\mathcal{Z}(i_1, i_2, j_1, j_2) = \sum_{k=1}^{p} \mathcal{X}(i_1, i_2, k)\mathcal{Y}(k, j_1, j_2), \tag{3.31}$$

for all $(i_1, i_2, j_1, j_2) \in [m] \otimes [n] \otimes [q] \otimes [r]$. In this elementwise expression, we specify an ordering on the modes that are not contracted. While a mode ordering is required of an implementation, we can express tensor contractions without specifying orders using tensor network diagrams (see Section 3.8.3).

The tensor contraction in Eq. (3.31) can be computed very efficiently using matrix–matrix multiplication as follows. The result is a matrix of size $mn \times qr$ and is computed as $\mathbf{Z} = \mathbf{X}_{(3)}^{\intercal}\mathbf{Y}_{(1)}$. Recalling that $\mathbf{X}_{(3)}^{\intercal}$ and $\mathbf{Y}_{(1)}$ require no reorganization of entries, this translates to the following algorithm:

Example Tensor Contraction as Matrix Multiplication

$\mathbf{X} \leftarrow \text{reshape}(\mathcal{X}, mn \times p)$
$\mathbf{Y} \leftarrow \text{reshape}(\mathcal{Y}, p \times qr)$
$\mathbf{Z} \leftarrow \mathbf{XY}$
$\mathcal{Z} \leftarrow \text{reshape}(\mathbf{Z}, m \times n \times q \times r)$

Contracting the last mode of the first tensor with the first mode of the second tensor is one of the easiest scenarios to convert to matrix–matrix multiplication. More generally, matching end modes can be done without data movement. Matching general pairs of modes requires more care to achieve efficient computations. However, tensor contraction can always be implemented as matrix–matrix multiplication.

Exercise 3.34 Consider two tensors, $\mathcal{X} \in \mathbb{R}^{m \times n \times p}$ and $\mathcal{Y} \in \mathbb{R}^{m \times q \times r}$. Consider the tensor contraction:

$$\mathcal{Z}(i_1, i_2, j_1, j_2) = \sum_{k=1}^{p} \mathcal{X}(k, i_1, i_2) \mathcal{Y}(k, j_1, j_2), \tag{3.32}$$

for all $(i_1, i_2, j_1, j_2) \in [n] \otimes [p] \otimes [q] \otimes [r]$. Write an algorithm to compute this using only reshape and matrix–matrix multiplication.

3.8.2 Tensor Contraction for d-way Tensors

Tensor contraction can be challenging to understand because the simplicity of the idea is quickly overwhelmed by notation. Einstein notation (discussed in Section 3.8.5) is one of many mathematical formulations for expressing tensor contractions.

To make things a little easier to digest, our first definition assumes that modes of the input and output tensors have been permuted to a convenient order.

Definition 3.32: Tensor Contraction with Ordered Modes

Let $\mathcal{X}$ be a tensor of order $(\alpha + \mu)$ and size $m_1 \times m_2 \times \cdots \times m_\alpha \times p_1 \times p_2 \times \cdots \times p_\mu$, and let $\mathcal{Y}$ be a tensor of order $(\beta + \mu)$ and size $n_1 \times n_2 \times \cdots \times n_\beta \times p_1 \times p_2 \times \cdots \times p_\mu$. The **tensor contraction** along the last μ modes yields a tensor $\mathcal{Z}$ of order $(\alpha + \beta)$ and of size $m_1 \times m_2 \times \cdots \times m_\alpha \times n_1 \times n_2 \times \cdots \times n_\beta$, where entries of $\mathcal{Z}$ are given by

$$\mathcal{Z}(i_1, i_2, \ldots, i_\alpha, j_1, j_2, \ldots, j_\beta) =$$
$$\sum_{k_1=1}^{p_1} \sum_{k_2=1}^{p_2} \cdots \sum_{k_\mu=1}^{p_\mu} \mathcal{X}(i_1, i_2, \ldots, i_\alpha, k_1, k_2, \ldots, k_\mu) \mathcal{Y}(j_1, j_2, \ldots, j_\beta, k_1, k_2, \ldots, k_\mu),$$

for all $(i_1, i_2, \ldots, i_\alpha, j_1, j_2, \ldots, j_\beta) \in [m_1] \otimes [m_2] \otimes \cdots \otimes [m_\alpha] \times [n_1] \otimes [n_2] \otimes \cdots \otimes [n_\beta]$.

The cost of the tensor contraction in Definition 3.32 is $\mathcal{O}(MNP)$, where $M = \prod_{k=1}^{\alpha} m_k$, $N = \prod_{k=1}^{\beta} n_k$, and $P = \prod_{k=1}^{\mu} p_k$.

Tensor contractions can be computed using matrix–matrix multiplication as elucidated in Proposition 3.33.

Proposition 3.33 (Tensor Contraction as Matrix–Matrix Multiplication) *Let $\mathcal{X}$ be a tensor of order $(\alpha + \mu)$ and size $m_1 \times \cdots \times m_\alpha \times p_1 \times \cdots \times p_\mu$, and let $\mathcal{Y}$ be a tensor of order $(\beta + \mu)$ and size $n_1 \times \cdots \times n_\beta \times p_1 \times \cdots \times p_\mu$. Let $\mathcal{A} = (\alpha + 1, \ldots, \alpha + \mu)$ and $\mathcal{B} = (\beta + 1, \ldots, \beta + \mu)$ specify the last μ modes that are to be contracted. Then the contraction $\mathcal{Z}$ in Definition 3.32 is equivalent to*

$$\mathbf{Z}_{(\mathcal{R} \times \mathcal{C})} = \mathbf{X}_{(\mathcal{A}^c \times \mathcal{A})} \mathbf{Y}_{(\mathcal{B} \times \mathcal{B}^c)},$$

where $\mathcal{R} = (1, \ldots, \alpha)$, $\mathcal{C} = (\alpha + 1, \ldots, \alpha + \beta)$, $\mathcal{A}^c = (1, \ldots, \alpha)$, and $\mathcal{B}^c = (1, \ldots, \beta)$.

The tensors are not always arranged with the modes ordered so that the last μ modes are matching. This is a matter of indexing and can easily be remedied with a permutation that has no impact on the mathematical formula.

3.8.3 Tensor Network Diagrams

Sometimes it is useful to visualize tensor contraction using **tensor network diagrams**, as shown in Fig. 3.11. In a tensor network diagram, each tensor is represented by a node, and each mode is represented by an edge. Contraction along a mode is indicated when edges from two different nodes connect. (This is only possible if both modes are the same dimension.) The contraction binds the two tensors together, and the output is a single tensor with the union of the non-connected edges. We often indicate the size of the dimension by labeling the edges. Tensor network diagrams do not indicate the order of the modes, so this removes some of the notational complication. However, any implementation of the tensor contraction needs to take the mode order into account.

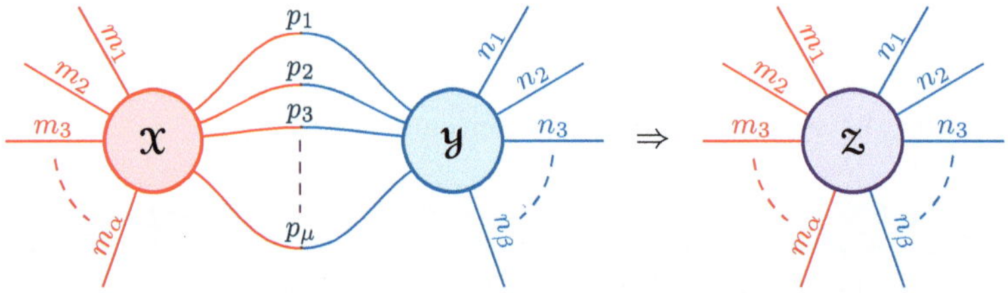

Figure 3.11 Tensor network diagram of tensor contraction of $\mathcal{X}$ of size $m_1 \times m_2 \times \cdots \times m_\alpha \times p_1 \times p_2 \times \cdots \times p_\mu$ and $\mathcal{Y}$ of size $n_1 \times n_2 \times \cdots \times n_\beta \times p_1 \times p_2 \times \cdots \times p_\mu$, contracting along the last μ modes, to form $\mathcal{Z}$ of size $m_1 \times m_2 \times \cdots \times m_\alpha \times n_1 \times n_2 \times \cdots \times n_\beta$.

We can express, for example, matrix–vector products using tensor network diagrams, as we show in Example 3.8.

Example 3.8 (Tensor Network Diagram for Matrix–Vector Product)

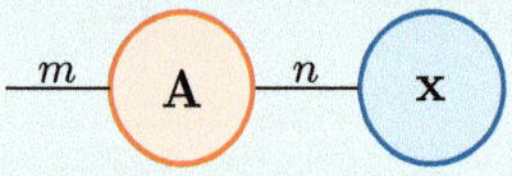

Let $\mathbf{A} \in \mathbb{R}^{m \times n}$ and $\mathbf{x} \in \mathbb{R}^n$. The tensor network diagram to the left shows how $\mathbf{Ax}$ can be shown as a tensor network.

The TTM product can be illustrated as a tensor network. The tensor network view does not distinguish the mode index on the tensor or the matrix.

Example 3.9 (Tensor Network Diagram for TTM)

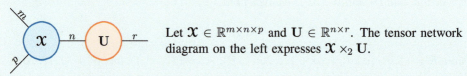

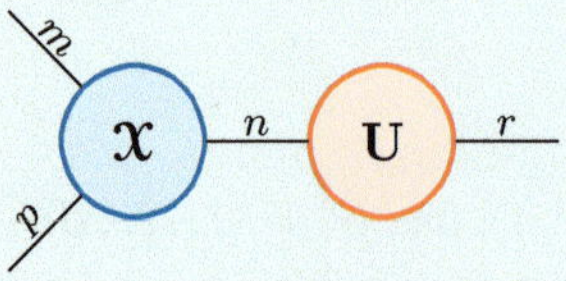

Let $\mathcal{X} \in \mathbb{R}^{m \times n \times p}$ and $\mathbf{U} \in \mathbb{R}^{n \times r}$. The tensor network diagram on the left expresses $\mathcal{X} \times_2 \mathbf{U}$.

One utility of tensor networks is the ability to draw a collection of tensor contractions. In Example 3.10, we show two TTMs.

Example 3.10 (Tensor Network Diagram for Two TTMs)

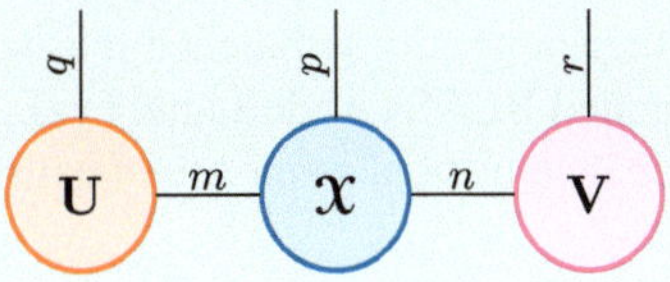

Let $\mathcal{X} \in \mathbb{R}^{m \times n \times p}$, $\mathbf{U} \in \mathbb{R}^{m \times r}$, and $\mathbf{V} \in \mathbb{R}^{n \times r}$. The tensor network diagram on the left expresses $\mathcal{X} \times_1 \mathbf{U} \times_2 \mathbf{V}$.

Exercise 3.35 Draw the tensor network diagram for $\mathcal{X} \times_1 \mathbf{U} \times_2 \mathbf{V} \times_3 \mathbf{W}$, where $\mathcal{X}$ is a 3-way tensor and $\mathbf{U}, \mathbf{V}, \mathbf{W}$ are appropriately sized matrices.

The tensor contraction in Eq. (3.31) is illustrated in Example 3.11.

Example 3.11 (Tensor Network Diagram for Tensor Contraction of 3-way Tensors)

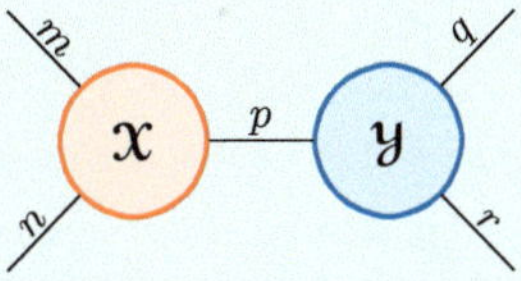

For tensors, $\mathcal{X} \in \mathbb{R}^{m \times n \times p}$ and $\mathcal{Y} \in \mathbb{R}^{p \times q \times r}$, consider the tensor contraction defined by

$$\mathcal{Z}(i_1, i_2, j_1, j_2) = \sum_{k=1}^{p} \mathcal{X}(i_1, i_2, k)\mathcal{Y}(k, j_1, j_2).$$

Its tensor network diagram is shown on the left.

Exercise 3.36 Let $\mathcal{X} \in \mathbb{R}^{m \times n \times p}, \mathcal{Y} \in \mathbb{R}^{q \times m \times r}$. Define the tensor $\mathcal{Z} \in \mathbb{R}^{n \times p \times q \times r}$ as

$$\mathcal{Z}(i_1, i_2, j_1, j_2) = \sum_{k=1}^{m} \mathcal{X}(k, i_1, i_2)\mathcal{Y}(j_1, k, j_2).$$

Draw the tensor network diagram of the tensor contraction.

3.8.4 Batched Tensor Contractions

Tensor contractions may also include **batched** modes. In this case, the batched modes are neither inner (contracted) or outer (uncontracted) modes; instead, they correspond to common modes across the input and output tensors. We can view batched contractions as a set of independent contractions performed on corresponding subtensors, one for each configuration of batched mode indices.

The simplest batched operation is the Hadamard (elementwise) product of vectors $\mathbf{z} = \mathbf{x} * \mathbf{y}$, with elements specified by $z_i = x_i y_i$. Another batched operation is scaling the columns of a matrix each by a different value, i.e., if $\mathbf{X} \in \mathbb{R}^{m \times n}$ and $\mathbf{y} \in \mathbb{R}^n$, we have $z_{ij} = x_{ij} y_j$ for all $(i, j) \in [m] \otimes [n]$.

A Khatri–Rao product of two matrices (see Section A.4.4) is a batched contraction of two matrices with no inner mode, and with the output reshaped into a matrix. If $\mathbf{K} = \mathbf{A} \odot \mathbf{B}$, then $\mathbf{K}_{\ell r} = \mathbf{A}_{ir}\mathbf{B}_{jr}$ with $\ell = \mathbb{L}(i, j)$.

In Sections 3.5 and 3.6.2, we use batched matrix–vector multiplications during efficient computation of (sequences of) MTTKRPs. In this case, we have a 3-way tensor and a matrix as inputs, and slices of the tensor are multiplied with columns of the matrix. Expressed elementwise, the batched contraction is given by (see Eq. (3.26)): $v_{j\ell} = \sum_{i=1}^{m} y_{ij\ell} a_{i\ell}$ for all $(j, \ell) \in [n] \otimes [r]$. In this case, there is one inner mode indexed by i, one outer mode indexed by j, and one batched mode indexed by ℓ.

General batched tensor contractions need specification of the inner modes of each input tensor as well as specification of the batched modes of each input tensor. Pairs of inner modes and pairs of batched modes must have matching dimensions. Some batched tensor contractions can be implemented using the interface for batched BLAS (Abdelfattah et al., 2021), which has the potential to deliver higher performance than using a sequence of calls to BLAS.

3.8.5 Einstein Notation

As noted in Section 3.8.2, notation for tensor contractions can be unwieldy. In **Einstein notation**, tensor contractions are expressed elementwise and summation symbols are omitted. Contracted modes are indicated by indices that appear in both inputs and not in the output. Some versions separate the indices into subscripts and superscripts, indicating covariant (e.g., row vector) and contravariant (e.g., column vector) orientations, respectively. Einstein notation can express tensor contractions as defined in Definition 3.32 as well as the more general batched tensor contractions discussed in Section 3.8.4.

Some examples of Einstein notation are as follows:

- vector outer product $\mathcal{X} = \mathbf{a} \bigcirc \mathbf{b} \bigcirc \mathbf{c}$: $x_{ijk} = a_i b_j c_k$,
- tensor inner product $u = \langle \mathcal{X}, \mathcal{Y} \rangle$: $u = x_{ijk} y_{ijk}$,
- matrix–vector multiplication $\mathbf{y} = \mathbf{A}\mathbf{x}$: $y_i = a_{ij} x_j$,
- tensor contraction $\mathcal{Z}(j,k,\ell,h) = \sum_i \mathcal{X}(i,j,k)\mathcal{Y}(\ell,i,h)$: $z_{jk\ell h} = x_{ijk} y_{\ell ih}$,
- Hadamard product $\mathbf{z} = \mathbf{x} * \mathbf{y}$: $z_i = x_i y_i$,
- batched matrix–vector products $\mathbf{V}(j,\ell) = \sum_i \mathcal{Y}(i,j,\ell)\mathbf{A}(i,\ell)$: $v_{j\ell} = y_{ij\ell} a_{i\ell}$.

We can differentiate among inner, outer, and batched modes when a batched tensor contraction is specified in Einstein notation: Inner modes correspond to indices that appear in both inputs but not the output, outer modes correspond to indices that appear in one input and the output, and batched modes correspond to indices that appear in both inputs and the output.

Part II

Tucker Decomposition

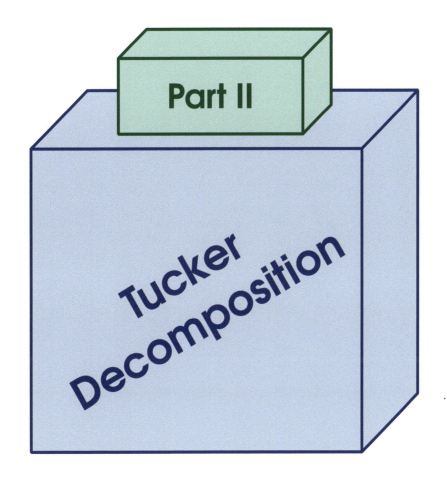

4 Tucker Decomposition

The Tucker decomposition (Hitchcock, 1927; Tucker, 1966) deconstructs a tensor into a **core tensor** and **factor matrices**. It is most often useful in the context of compression, in which case there is some trade-off between the accuracy of the approximation and the level of compression. The Tucker decomposition chooses the factor matrices such that the range of factor matrix k captures most of the span of the mode-k fibers of the tensor. These factor matrices are used to compress the original tensor to a smaller core tensor (Fig. 4.1).

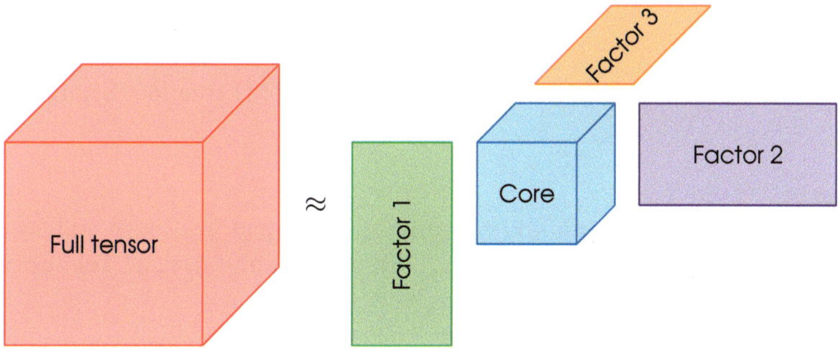

Figure 4.1 Tucker decomposition.

Tucker decompositions can yield significant compression with minimal loss in accuracy. For scientific combustion simulation datasets, Ballard et al. (2020) showed compression ratios of 100 to 200,000 times, which equates to 99–99.999% compression. The size of the core tensor determines the degree of compression.

This chapter provides a high-level overview of the Tucker decomposition. Section 4.1 describes the Tucker decomposition and the compression ratio. We discuss how to choose the core size in Section 4.2 and algorithms in Section 4.3. Reconstruction from a compressed Tucker representation is discussed in Section 4.4; in particular, partial reconstruction does not require an intermediate full reconstruction. Finally, Section 4.5 demonstrates the effectiveness of Tucker compression on the $2048 \times 256 \times 256$ Miranda scientific simulation data tensor. We see that we can generate a Tucker approximation that is 148 times smaller than the original tensor and has less than 1% error.

4.1 Formulation of Tucker Decomposition

Before we delve into the decomposition, we first define the **multilinear rank** or **multirank** of a tensor. This captures the ranks of all mode-k unfoldings.

Definition 4.1 (Multirank) The **multilinear rank** or **multirank** of a 3-way tensor $\mathcal{X}$ is

$$\text{multirank}(\mathcal{X}) = (q, r, s), \quad \text{where} \quad q = \text{rank}(\mathbf{X}_{(1)}), \quad r = \text{rank}(\mathbf{X}_{(2)}), \text{ and } s = \text{rank}(\mathbf{X}_{(3)}).$$

More generally, for a d-way tensor $\mathcal{X}$, it is

$$\text{multirank}(\mathcal{X}) = (r_1, r_2, \ldots, r_d), \quad \text{where} \quad r_k = \text{rank}\big(\mathbf{X}_{(k)}\big) \quad \text{for all} \quad k \in [d].$$

4.1.1 Tucker Decomposition for 3-way Tensors

In the 3-way case, given a tensor $\mathcal{X} \in \mathbb{R}^{m \times n \times p}$ and target core size $q \times r \times s$, we want to find a core tensor $\mathcal{G} \in \mathbb{R}^{q \times r \times s}$ and factor matrices $\mathbf{U} \in \mathbb{R}^{m \times q}$, $\mathbf{V} \in \mathbb{R}^{n \times r}$, and $\mathbf{W} \in \mathbb{R}^{p \times s}$ such that

$$x_{ijk} \approx \sum_{\alpha=1}^{q} \sum_{\beta=1}^{r} \sum_{\gamma=1}^{s} g_{\alpha\beta\gamma} u_{i\alpha} v_{j\beta} w_{k\gamma} \quad \text{for all} \quad (i, j, k) \in [m] \otimes [n] \otimes [p]. \tag{4.1}$$

The shorthand expression is

$$\mathcal{X} \approx [\![\mathcal{G}; \mathbf{U}, \mathbf{V}, \mathbf{W}]\!].$$

Another way to express this using tensor times matrix (TTM) notation (Section 3.3) is

$$\mathcal{X} \approx \mathcal{G} \times_1 \mathbf{U} \times_2 \mathbf{V} \times_3 \mathbf{W}. \tag{4.2}$$

We generally assume that the multilinear rank of $\mathcal{G}$ is equal to its size and so refer to a Tucker decomposition with a core of size $q \times r \times s$ as a **rank-(q, r, s) Tucker decomposition**

This is pictured visually in Fig. 4.2. This figure shows the orientation of each tensor and matrix with directional arrows. For instance, the $(1, 1)$ element of $\mathbf{W}$ is in the lower left corner since numbering for mode 3 goes into the page. We orient each factor so that it is perpendicular to the mode it multiplies.

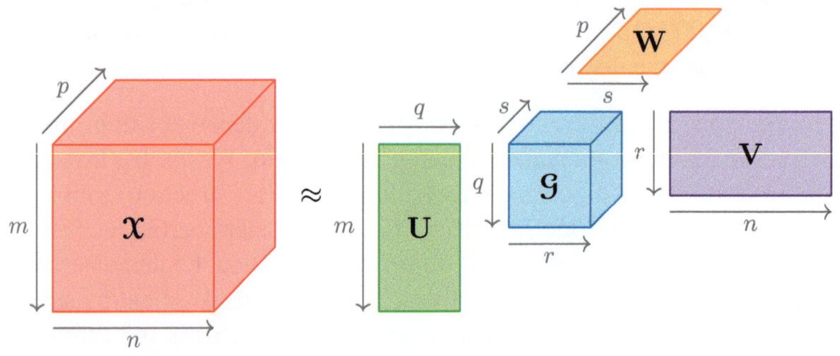

Figure 4.2 Tucker decomposition $\mathcal{X} \approx [\![\mathcal{G}; \mathbf{U}, \mathbf{V}, \mathbf{W}]\!]$.

We say the decomposition is **exact** if $\mathcal{X} = [\![\mathcal{G}; \mathbf{U}, \mathbf{V}, \mathbf{W}]\!]$. An example of an exact decomposition is shown in Example 4.1. The Tucker decomposition is not unique, and we show an alternative exact decomposition of the tensor from Example 4.1 in Example 4.4. A detailed discussion of nonuniqueness can be found in Section 5.3.

Example 4.1 (Tucker Decomposition) Consider the $3 \times 3 \times 3$ tensor $\mathcal{X}$ defined by

$$\mathbf{X}_1 = \begin{bmatrix} 1 & 1 & 0 \\ 1 & -1 & -1 \\ 0 & 2 & 1 \end{bmatrix}, \quad \mathbf{X}_2 = \begin{bmatrix} 2 & 2 & 0 \\ 1 & -3 & -2 \\ 1 & 5 & 2 \end{bmatrix}, \quad \text{and} \quad \mathbf{X}_3 = \begin{bmatrix} 1 & 1 & 0 \\ 0 & -2 & -1 \\ 1 & 3 & 1 \end{bmatrix}.$$

It has an exact rank-$(2, 2, 2)$ Tucker decomposition given by $[\![\mathcal{G}; \mathbf{U}, \mathbf{V}, \mathbf{W}]\!]$ with

$$\mathbf{G}_1 = \begin{bmatrix} 1 & 0 \\ 1 & 1 \end{bmatrix}, \mathbf{G}_2 = \begin{bmatrix} 1 & 0 \\ 0 & 1 \end{bmatrix}, \mathbf{U} = \begin{bmatrix} 1 & 0 \\ 0 & -1 \\ 1 & 1 \end{bmatrix}, \mathbf{V} = \begin{bmatrix} 1 & -1 \\ 1 & 1 \\ 0 & 1 \end{bmatrix}, \text{ and } \mathbf{W} = \begin{bmatrix} 0 & 1 \\ 1 & 1 \\ 1 & 0 \end{bmatrix}.$$

Visually, we can depict this as:

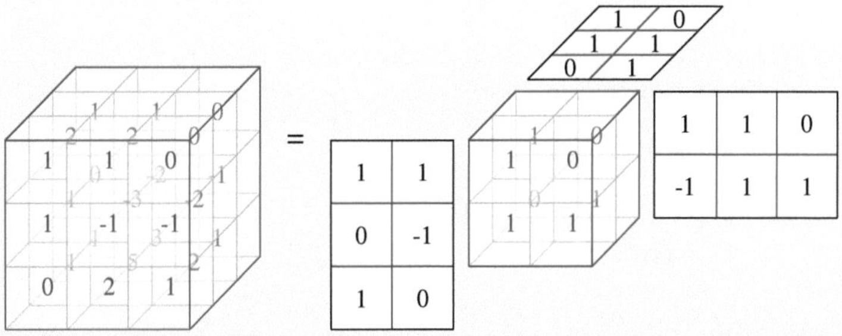

The orientations of the $\mathbf{V}$ and $\mathbf{W}$ matrices are shown to conform to the orientation of the core tensor so that the first row of $\mathbf{V}$ is vertical, and the first row of $\mathbf{W}$ is closest to the core tensor.

Exercise 4.1 For the tensor in Example 4.1, verify $\mathcal{X} = [\![\mathcal{G}; \mathbf{U}, \mathbf{V}, \mathbf{W}]\!]$ using Eq. (4.1) for elements (a) x_{111}, (b) x_{322}, and (c) x_{213}.

When the Tucker decomposition is approximate, we measure the **approximation error** as the relative error:

$$\begin{matrix}\text{approximation} \\ \text{error}\end{matrix} = \frac{\|\mathcal{X} - [\![\mathcal{G}; \mathbf{U}, \mathbf{V}, \mathbf{W}]\!]\|}{\|\mathcal{X}\|}.$$

The **compression ratio** is the size of the original tensor versus the total size of the Tucker tensor (the size of the core plus the size of the factor matrices), yielding

$$\begin{matrix}\text{compression} \\ \text{ratio}\end{matrix} = \frac{mnp}{qrs + mq + nr + ps} \approx \frac{mnp}{qrs}. \tag{4.3}$$

Example 4.2 (Compression Ratio, 3-way) If $\mathcal{X}$ is of size $100 \times 100 \times 100$ and $\mathcal{G}$ is of size $25 \times 25 \times 25$, then

$$\begin{matrix}\text{compression} \\ \text{ratio}\end{matrix} = \frac{100^3}{25^3 + 3(100)(25)} = 43.24 \quad \approx \quad \frac{100^3}{25^3} = 64.$$

4.1.2 Tucker Decomposition for d-way Tensors

In the d-way case, given $\mathcal{X} \in \mathbb{R}^{n_1 \times n_2 \times \cdots \times n_d}$ and target core size $r_1 \times r_2 \times \cdots \times r_d$, we want to find a core tensor $\mathcal{G} \in \mathbb{R}^{r_1 \times r_2 \times \cdots \times r_d}$ and factor matrices $\mathbf{U}_k \in \mathbb{R}^{r_k \times n_k}$ such that

$$\mathcal{X}(i_1, i_2, \ldots, i_d) \approx \sum_{j_1=1}^{r_1} \sum_{j_2=1}^{r_2} \cdots \sum_{j_d=1}^{r_d} \mathcal{G}(j_1, j_2, \ldots, j_d) \mathbf{U}_1(i_1, j_1) \mathbf{U}_2(i_2, j_2) \cdots \mathbf{U}_d(i_d, j_d)$$

for all $(i_1, i_2, \ldots, i_d) \in [n_1] \otimes [n_2] \otimes \cdots \otimes [n_d]$. The shorthand expression is

$$\mathcal{X} \approx [\![\mathcal{G}; \mathbf{U}_1, \mathbf{U}_2, \ldots, \mathbf{U}_d]\!].$$

Another way of expressing this using TTM notation is

$$\mathcal{X} \approx \mathcal{G} \times_1 \mathbf{U}_1 \times_2 \mathbf{U}_2 \cdots \times_d \mathbf{U}_d. \tag{4.4}$$

We refer to a Tucker decomposition with a core of size $r_1 \times r_2 \times \cdots \times r_d$ as a **rank-$(r_1, r_2, \ldots, r_d)$ Tucker decomposition**.

The **approximation error** is the relative error:

$$\text{approximation error} = \frac{\|\mathcal{X} - [\![\mathcal{G}; \mathbf{U}_1, \mathbf{U}_2, \ldots, \mathbf{U}_d]\!]\|}{\|\mathcal{X}\|}.$$

The **compression ratio** is the size of the original tensor versus the total size of the Tucker tensor (the size of the core plus the size of the factor matrices), yielding

$$\text{compression ratio} = \frac{\prod_{k=1}^{d} n_k}{\prod_{k=1}^{d} r_k + \sum_{k=1}^{d} r_k n_k} \approx \frac{\prod_{k=1}^{d} n_k}{\prod_{k=1}^{d} r_k}.$$

Example 4.3 (Compression Ratio, 4-way) If $\mathcal{X}$ is of size $100 \times 100 \times 100 \times 100$ and $\mathcal{G}$ is of size $25 \times 25 \times 25 \times 25$, then

$$\text{compression ratio} = \frac{100^4}{25^4 + 4(100)(25)} = 249.6 \approx \frac{100^4}{25^4} = 256.$$

Exercise 4.2 If a tensor of size $384 \times 384 \times 256 \times 7$ has an approximate Tucker decomposition with a core of size $83 \times 81 \times 23 \times 6$, what is the compression ratio?

4.2 Choosing the Tucker Decomposition Rank

The rank of a Tucker decomposition, given by the size of $\mathcal{G}$, directly impacts the amount of compression, so the choice of rank is consequential.

There are two formulations for the approximate Tucker decomposition optimization problem. We can pick whether to prioritize compression (i.e., by using a fixed compression ratio) or accuracy (i.e., by specifying an error bound).

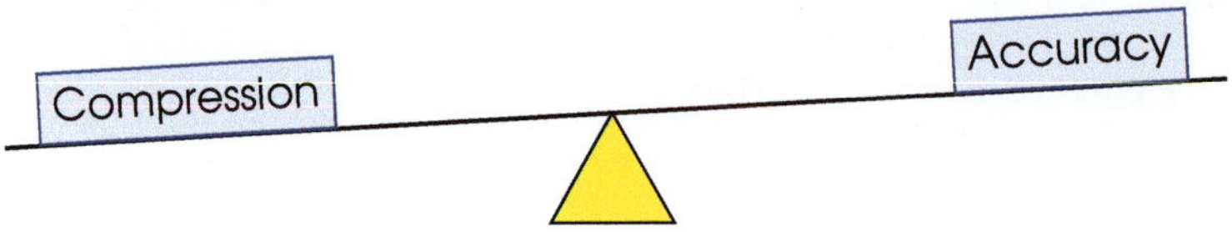

4.2.1 Specified Multirank

The first option in finding a Tucker decomposition is to fix the Tucker core size, which fixes the compression ratio. Then the goal is to find the Tucker approximation with the lowest error for that given core size.

Consider the 3-way case with $\mathcal{X} \in \mathbb{R}^{m\times n\times p}$. We specify that the core will be of size $q \times r \times s$, so the goal is to find a rank-(q, r, s) Tucker decomposition that minimizes the error:

$$\begin{aligned} &\min_{\mathcal{G},\mathbf{U},\mathbf{V},\mathbf{W}} \quad \big\|\mathcal{X} - [\![\mathcal{G}; \mathbf{U}, \mathbf{V}, \mathbf{W}]\!]\big\| \\ &\text{subject to} \quad \mathcal{G} \in \mathbb{R}^{q\times r\times s}, \mathbf{U} \in \mathbb{R}^{m\times q}, \mathbf{V} \in \mathbb{R}^{n\times r}, \mathbf{W} \in \mathbb{R}^{p\times s}. \end{aligned} \tag{4.5}$$

In the rank-specified formulation, we know what the compression ratio will be but cannot say in advance what the error will be.

Finding a minimizer of Eq. (4.5) that yields an optimal Tucker decomposition is a nonlinear nonconvex optimization problem without a closed form solution, but we can find approximations that are within $\sqrt{d}$ of optimal for a d-way tensor using the HOSVD or ST-HOSVD algorithms described in Sections 4.3.1 and 4.3.2.

4.2.2 Specified Accuracy

The second option in finding a Tucker decomposition is to specify the accuracy in terms of a maximum relative error, ε. Consider a 3-way tensor $\mathcal{X} \in \mathbb{R}^{m\times n\times p}$. We seek sizes q, r, and s such that a rank-(q, r, s) Tucker decomposition maximizes the compression ratio in Eq. (4.3) while satisfying

$$\big\|\mathcal{X} - [\![\mathcal{G}; \mathbf{U}, \mathbf{V}, \mathbf{W}]\!]\big\| \leq \varepsilon\big\|\mathcal{X}\big\|.$$

Achieving the error bound is always possible, as we can obtain 0 error by taking $\mathcal{G} = \mathcal{X}$ and identity matrices for each factor.

Consider the case of 0 error ($\varepsilon = 0$), which we refer to as an **exact Tucker decomposition**. If we choose (q, r, s) to be the multilinear rank of $\mathcal{X}$, then we can find a rank-(q, r, s) Tucker decomposition with 0 error. We defer further details of why this works and how to choose the ranks for other values of ε until Chapter 7.

In the error-specified formulation, we cannot guarantee in advance what the Tucker ranks and resulting compression ratio will be.

> For Tucker decomposition, we can specify core rank *or* error tolerance.

4.3 Methods for Computing Tucker Decomposition

Direct or iterative methods can be used for computing Tucker decompositions. Computational algorithms are covered in depth in Chapter 6, but we provide brief overviews of the main methods here. All the methods that we discuss depend on two key functions, as follows.

- **Leading left singular vectors:** LLSV$(\mathbf{X}, r)$ takes as input an $m \times n$ matrix $\mathbf{X}$ and rank $r \leq \min\{m, n\}$ and returns an orthonormal left factor matrix ($\mathbf{U}$) in the solution of the low-rank matrix factorization problem

$$\min_{\mathbf{U},\mathbf{Z}} \|\mathbf{X} - \mathbf{U}\mathbf{Z}\|_F^2 \quad \text{subject to} \quad \mathbf{U} \in \mathbb{O}^{m\times r},\ \mathbf{Z} \in \mathbb{R}^{r\times n}.$$

An optimal solution is given by a matrix $\mathbf{U}$ whose columns are the r leading left singular vectors of $\mathbf{X}$ and $\mathbf{Z} = \mathbf{U}^\intercal\mathbf{X}$ (see Section A.8). This can also work with a specified error tolerance on the matrix approximation problem rather than a specified rank. If $m \leq n$, the cost is $\mathcal{O}(m^2 n)$.

- **Tensor compression:** The TTM operation denoted $\mathcal{X} \times_k \mathbf{U}^\intercal$ compresses the tensor $\mathcal{X}$ in mode k using orthonormal $\mathbf{U}$. If $\mathcal{X}$ is of size $n_1 \times n_2 \times \cdots \times n_d$ and $\mathbf{U}$ is of size $n_k \times r$, the cost to apply this operation is $\prod_{k=1}^{d} n_k r$, and the size of the compressed result is $n_1 \times \cdots \times n_{k-1} \times r \times n_{k+1} \times \cdots \times n_d$. Compression can be applied in different modes in *any* order without changing the result.

4.3.1 Higher-Order SVD

The **higher-order SVD (HOSVD)** algorithm is probably the best-known method for computing a Tucker decomposition. It was first proposed by Tucker (1966) as the Tucker1 method and later popularized as HOSVD by De Lathauwer et al. (2000a). It is sometimes also referred to as the multilinear SVD (MLSVD).

The HOSVD can work with a specified rank or use a specified accuracy to determine an appropriate rank. (The HOSVD inherits from the SVD the ability to work with either a fixed error or fixed rank; see Section A.8.) The HOSVD solves the problem for each mode *independently*, using LLSV of each mode-wise unfolding. For a 3-way tensor $\mathcal{X}$, the pseudocode to compute a rank-(q, r, s) Tucker decomposition $\mathcal{T} = [\![\mathcal{G}; \mathbf{U}, \mathbf{V}, \mathbf{W}]\!]$ is as follows.

HOSVD

```
U ← LLSV(X_(1), q)
V ← LLSV(X_(2), r)
W ← LLSV(X_(3), s)
G ← X ×_1 Uᵀ ×_2 Vᵀ ×_3 Wᵀ        ▷ Compress to size q × r × s
```

If we specify the accuracy ε of the Tucker decomposition, we would solve each LLSV to an accuracy of $\varepsilon/\sqrt{3}$. We defer the detailed explanation of this algorithm to Chapter 6 and touch here on just a few salient points. The HOSVD is a direct algorithm, not iterative. The HOSVD computes only an approximate solution to the Tucker minimization problem in Eq. (4.5). However, that solution is within $\sqrt{3}$ of optimal, meaning that

$$\|\mathcal{X} - \mathcal{T}\| \leq \sqrt{3}\|\mathcal{X} - \mathcal{T}^*\|,$$

where $\mathcal{T}$ is the solution computed by the HOSVD and $\mathcal{T}^*$ is the optimal rank-(q, r, s) Tucker approximation. For this reason, we say that the HOSVD is **quasi-optimal**; see Chapter 7 for further discussion.

Exercise 4.3 What is the computational complexity of the HOSVD to compute a rank-(r, r, r) Tucker decomposition for an $n \times n \times n$ tensor?

If $(q, r, s) = \text{multirank}(\mathcal{X})$, then the HOSVD produces an *exact* decomposition, such that $[\![\mathcal{G}; \mathbf{U}, \mathbf{V}, \mathbf{W}]\!] = \mathcal{T}$.

Example 4.4 (Exact HOSVD) Consider the $3 \times 3 \times 3$ tensor used in Example 4.1. Computing the rank-$(2, 2, 2)$ Tucker decomposition of that tensor using the HOSVD yields the following decomposition:

$$\mathbf{U} = \begin{bmatrix} 0.3017 & 0.7587 \\ -0.5062 & 0.6406 \\ 0.8079 & 0.1181 \end{bmatrix}, \ \mathbf{V} = \begin{bmatrix} 0.1529 & 0.9000 \\ 0.9124 & 0.0302 \\ 0.3797 & -0.4349 \end{bmatrix}, \ \mathbf{W} = \begin{bmatrix} 0.3429 & -0.7410 \\ 0.8132 & -0.0735 \\ 0.4703 & 0.6675 \end{bmatrix},$$

$$\mathcal{G}(:,:,1) = \begin{bmatrix} 8.3325 & -0.0960 \\ 0.1117 & 3.0290 \end{bmatrix}, \quad \text{and} \quad \mathcal{G}(:,:,2) = \begin{bmatrix} 0.2405 & 0.8765 \\ -0.4054 & -0.6190 \end{bmatrix}.$$

This decomposition is different than that in Example 4.1 even though both are exact.

The situation in the d-way case is similar. Suppose $\mathcal{X}$ is a d-way tensor of size $n_1 \times n_2 \times \cdots \times n_d$ and we want to compute a rank-$(r_1, r_2, \ldots, r_d)$ Tucker decomposition. Then, for each mode $k \in [d]$, HOSVD computes a factor matrix that best approximates the span of the mode-k fibers of $\mathcal{X}$ in the sense of minimizing the error of the mode-k fibers projected onto this basis. Each factor matrix is computed via the SVD of the mode-k unfolding (the matrix whose columns are the mode-k fibers of $\mathcal{X}$). If we specify the accuracy ε of the Tucker decomposition instead of the ranks, we would solve each LLSV to an accuracy of $\varepsilon/\sqrt{d}$. In the d-way case, the quasi-optimality result is

$$\|\mathcal{X} - \mathcal{T}\| \leq \sqrt{d}\|\mathcal{X} - \mathcal{T}^*\|,$$

where $\mathcal{T}$ is the solution computed by the HOSVD and $\mathcal{T}^*$ is the optimal approximation for the given rank.

We delay a detailed complexity discussion until Section 6.2 and discuss a basic scenario here. For a d-way tensor of size $n \times \cdots \times n$ and a rank-$(r, \ldots, r)$ approximation with $r \leq n$, the computational cost of HOSVD is

$$\mathcal{O}(dn^{d+1}).$$

4.3.2 Sequentially Truncated HOSVD

ST-HOSVD has the same quasi-optimality as HOSVD, but the computational complexity is lower.

Vannieuwenhoven et al. (2012) and Hackbusch (2019) introduced a variant of HOSVD called **sequentially truncated HOSVD (ST-HOSVD)** that is more computationally efficient than HOSVD and generally preferred. It also uses the SVD of the mode-k unfolding but differs from HOSVD in that it compresses mode k as soon as it computes the mode-k factor matrix, before computing the mode-$(k+1)$ factor matrix. ST-HOSVD can also work with a fixed error or fixed rank.

ST-HOSVD

1: $\mathbf{U} \leftarrow \text{LLSV}(\mathbf{X}_{(1)}, q)$
2: $\mathcal{G} \leftarrow \mathcal{X} \times_1 \mathbf{U}^\intercal$ ▷ Compress to size $q \times n \times p$
3: $\mathbf{V} \leftarrow \text{LLSV}(\mathbf{G}_{(2)}, r)$
4: $\mathcal{G} \leftarrow \mathcal{G} \times_2 \mathbf{V}^\intercal$ ▷ Compress to size $q \times r \times p$
5: $\mathbf{W} \leftarrow \text{LLSV}(\mathbf{G}_{(3)}, s)$
6: $\mathcal{G} \leftarrow \mathcal{G} \times_3 \mathbf{W}^\intercal$ ▷ Compress to size $q \times r \times s$

Like HOSVD, the ST-HOSVD method is not iterative and has fixed computational cost given the dimensions and rank.

Exercise 4.4 What is the computational complexity of the ST-HOSVD to compute a rank-(r, r, r) Tucker decomposition for an $n \times n \times n$ tensor?

The quasi-optimality guarantees are the same for HOSVD and ST-HOSVD. In practice, ST-HOSVD often yields lower error than HOSVD, but there is no guarantee.

We delay a detailed complexity discussion until Section 6.3, but for a d-way tensor of size $n \times \cdots \times n$ and a rank-$(r, \ldots, r)$ approximation with $r \leq n$, the computational cost of ST-HOSVD is

$$\mathcal{O}(n^{d+1}).$$

Compared to the cost of HOSVD, ST-HOSVD is about $\mathcal{O}(d)$ times cheaper, ignoring the lower-order terms of the computational cost.

4.3.3 Higher-Order Orthogonal Iteration

The **higher-order orthogonal iteration (HOOI)** algorithm is an iterative method for solving the rank-specified formulation. The 3-way method was originally known as Tucker ALS or TUCKALS3, as proposed by Kroonenberg and De Leeuw (1980), and the d-way extension is from Kapteyn et al. (1986). The HOOI name was popularized by De Lathauwer et al. (2000b).

The HOOI algorithm starts with initial guesses for the factor matrices, uses those to partially compress the tensor in all modes but one, and uses that compressed version to solve for the remaining factor matrix. This algorithm is iterative, so initial guesses for the factor matrices are needed by the algorithm. Its solution will always be at least as good as its initial guess, but it has no guarantees of quasi-optimality on its own.

HOOI

while not converged **do**
  $\mathcal{Y} \leftarrow \mathcal{X} \times_2 \mathbf{V}^\intercal \times_3 \mathbf{W}^\intercal$ ▷ Compress to size $m \times r \times s$
  $\mathbf{U} \leftarrow \text{LLSV}(\mathbf{Y}_{(1)}, q)$
  $\mathcal{Y} \leftarrow \mathcal{X} \times_1 \mathbf{U}^\intercal \times_3 \mathbf{W}^\intercal$ ▷ Compress to size $q \times n \times s$
  $\mathbf{V} \leftarrow \text{LLSV}(\mathbf{Y}_{(2)}, r)$
  $\mathcal{Y} \leftarrow \mathcal{X} \times_1 \mathbf{U}^\intercal \times_2 \mathbf{V}^\intercal$ ▷ Compress to size $q \times r \times p$
  $\mathbf{W} \leftarrow \text{LLSV}(\mathbf{Y}_{(3)}, s)$
end while
$\mathcal{G} \leftarrow \mathcal{Y} \times_3 \mathbf{W}^\intercal$ ▷ Compress to size $q \times r \times s$

HOOI can be initialized with the solutions produced by HOSVD or ST-HOSVD, but there is not much room for improvement because these are quasi-optimal already. HOOI is highly effective with a random initialization and quickly converges in practice.

For a d-way tensor of size $n \times \cdots \times n$ and a rank-$(r, \ldots, r)$ approximation with $r \leq n$, the computational cost of a single iteration of HOOI is

$$\mathcal{O}(n^d r).$$

A single iteration of HOOI is less than the total cost of ST-HOSVD by a factor of $\mathcal{O}(n/r)$; on the other hand, HOOI requires multiple iterations. If HOOI needs fewer then $\mathcal{O}(n/r)$ iterations, it might be faster. We provide a detailed algorithm and general complexity discussion in Section 6.4.

4.3.4 Choice of Method

Given the same target rank, there is empirically little difference in the relative errors obtained by HOSVD, ST-HOSVD, and HOOI, as all three methods provide close to optimal solutions for the specified rank. In fact, HOSVD and ST-HOSVD are **quasi-optimal** methods; specifically, the Tucker decomposition produced by either method has error within a factor of $\sqrt{d}$ of optimal for a d-way tensor; see Chapter 7.

> For a fixed multilinear rank, both HOSVD and ST-HOSVD produce approximation Tucker decompositions that are within $\sqrt{d}$ of optimal for a d-way tensor.

In the case of specified rank, then, the choice of method depends on speed. By comparing the computational costs of the direct methods, we can conclude that ST-HOSVD is faster than HOSVD and generally preferable. Each iteration of HOOI is cheaper than ST-HOSVD, but which method is faster depends on how much cheaper each HOOI iteration is and how many iterations HOOI requires. The relative cost of each iteration depends on the target ranks: greater compression ratios favor HOOI and smaller compression ratios favor ST-HOSVD. While HOOI does not have the same quasi-optimality guarantees as ST-HOSVD, it can achieve comparable approximation error to ST-HOSVD in as few as two iterations when initialized randomly.

In the case of specified approximation error, both HOSVD and ST-HOSVD can adaptively select the ranks to satisfy the error tolerance. Because ST-HOSVD is cheaper than HOSVD, it is preferred in this case. The HOOI algorithm depends on a specification of the ranks, so it cannot adapt ranks subject to the error tolerance without further modification.

For truly massive tensors, a main challenge is storing the original tensor before compression. This has motivated the development of parallel (Ballard et al., 2020) and streaming algorithms (Sun et al., 2020).

4.4 Reconstruction from Tucker Decomposition

Tucker decomposition compresses the input tensor. In many cases, we eventually want to **reconstruct** the compressed tensor. A particular advantage of Tucker decomposition is that we can do partial reconstruction efficiently, in time and space proportional to the reconstructed part. We give a high-level overview of reconstruction here. A more complete discussion is provided in Sections 5.5 and 5.6.

4.4.1 Full Reconstruction

It order to completely decompress a Tucker approximation, we reconstruct the full tensor from the Tucker format by evaluating Eq. (4.2) or Eq. (4.4). This means multiplying the core tensor with the factor matrices in their respective modes. (This operation is known as multi-TTM, as described in Sections 3.4.1 and 3.4.2.)

For a 3-way tensor of size $m \times n \times p$ and a rank-(q, r, s) approximation, the computational cost of full reconstruction is

$$\mathcal{O}(mqrs + mnrs + mnps),$$

assuming the TTMs are performed in the order $\{1, 2, 3\}$.

For a d-way tensor of size $n_1 \times n_2 \times \cdots \times n_d$ and a rank-$(r_1, r_2, \ldots, r_d)$ approximation, the cost is

$$\mathcal{O}\left(\sum_{k=1}^{d}\left(\prod_{i=1}^{k} n_i\right)\left(\prod_{j=k}^{d} r_j\right)\right),$$

assuming we reconstruct the modes in the order $\{1, 2, \ldots, d\}$. The cost of full reconstruction is less than the cost of methods for computing the Tucker decomposition.

These costs are detailed in Section 5.5.

4.4.2 Partial Reconstruction

> Given a Tucker-format tensor, we can partially reconstruct a subtensor of the full-format tensor without first forming the full tensor, saving both computation and memory footprint.

If we want to reconstruct only a *part* of the Tucker approximation, we could perform a full reconstruction and then extract the desired subtensor. A particular advantage of using Tucker compression is that we can perform partial reconstruction more cheaply by exploiting the structure of Tucker decomposition. If we want to reconstruct only a subset of the indices of a particular mode, we can first extract the corresponding rows of the factor matrix in that mode before combining it with everything else. This makes the computational cost of reconstruction much cheaper and reduces the memory footprint to only the size of the subtensor we are reconstructing.

If the subtensor corresponds to subsets of indices in all modes, we extract the rows of each factor matrix first, reducing the dimensions in every mode before performing the computation. For example, the cost to reconstruct a subtensor of size $\bar{m} \times \bar{n} \times \bar{p}$ from a rank-(q, r, s) approximation of a tensor with full dimensions $m \times n \times p$ reduces to

$$\mathcal{O}(\bar{m}qrs + \bar{m}\bar{n}rs + \bar{m}\bar{n}\bar{p}s),$$

assuming the natural TTM order, which is significantly cheaper than the cost of full reconstruction.

We can perform other mode-wise computations besides selection as well. For example, we can downsample a particular mode by taking averages of consecutive indices. Because this operation is a linear operation applied to the fibers of that mode, the operation can be applied to the factor matrix rather than the fully reconstructed tensor.

4.5 Example: Tucker Compression of Miranda Scientific Simulation Tensor

The Miranda scientific simulation tensor (Ballard et al., 2022) is of size $2048 \times 256 \times 256$ and represents density at a snapshot in time from a 3D fluid flow simulation of mixing fluids of different densities. The dataset is described in detail in Section 1.5.1.

Exercise 4.5 Load the Miranda scientific simulation tensor. (a) How many entries does the Miranda tensor have? (b) What is the range of values?

We can compress the Miranda scientific simulation tensor using low-rank Tucker decompositions. In Table 4.1 we summarize the results of compression with four different error tolerances. For instance, using an error tolerance of $\varepsilon = 10^{-2}$ yields a Tucker decomposition of rank $232 \times 43 \times 41$, with relative error 0.00983. This is 148 times smaller than the original dataset.

Table 4.1 Tucker compression of $2048 \times 256 \times 256$ Miranda scientific simulation tensor

Tolerance (ε)	Relative error	Core size	Compression ratio	% of original size
10^{-1}	$8.73 \cdot 10^{-2}$	$13 \times 3 \times 2$	4,775	0.02
10^{-2}	$9.83 \cdot 10^{-3}$	$232 \times 43 \times 41$	148	0.67
10^{-3}	$9.88 \cdot 10^{-4}$	$583 \times 102 \times 99$	19	5.31
10^{-4}	$9.85 \cdot 10^{-5}$	$934 \times 161 \times 158$	5	19.19

Exercise 4.6 Load the Miranda dataset. (a) Compress the Miranda scientific simulation tensor using $\varepsilon = 10^{-3}$. (b) What is the relative error? (c) What is the range of values in the reconstruction? (d) What is the largest entrywise error?

To get a sense of the errors introduced, we inspect a subset of the data at different compression levels in Fig. 4.3. We visualize a set of partial lateral slices for different j values. In these images, gravity is pulling the denser fluid downward. There is no discernible visual difference up to a compression level of 19 times (5% of the original data size). At 148 times compression (<1% of the original data size), we see slight ghosting artifacts. At 4775 times compression (<0.05% of the original data), the picture becomes entirely blurry, giving only a very approximate sense of the densities of the mixing fluids.

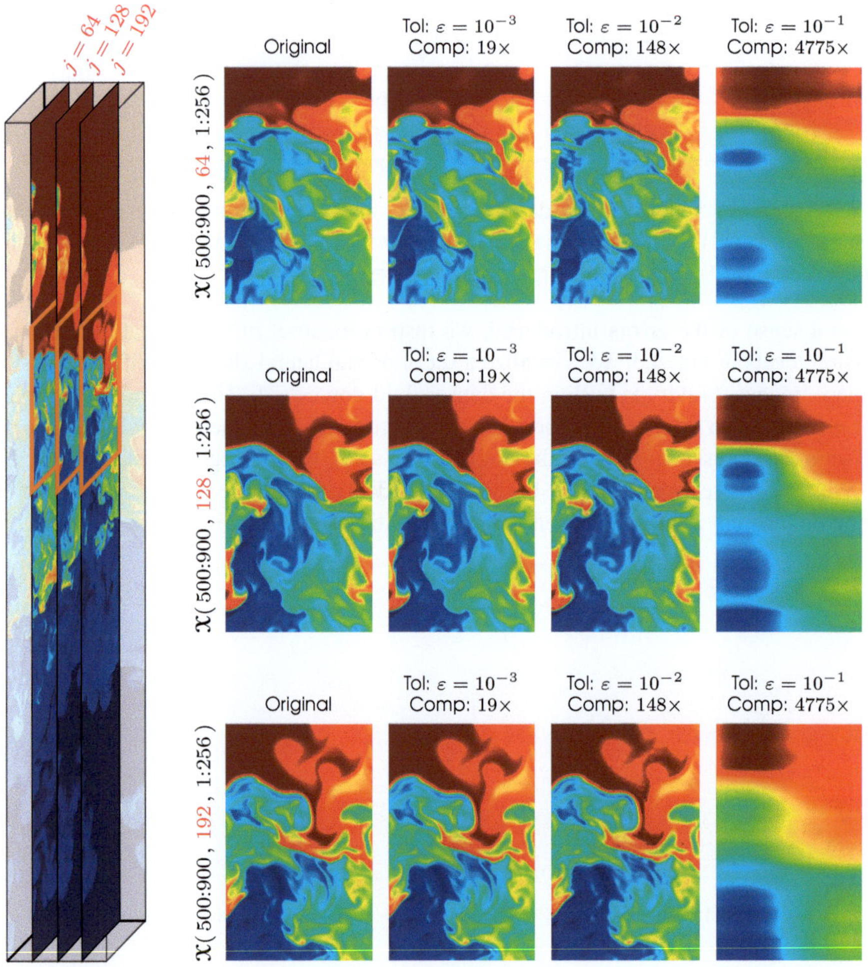

Figure 4.3 Original versus compressed Miranda scientific simulation dataset. On the left is the Miranda tensor of size $2048 \times 256 \times 256$, with orange boxes around the regions shown on the right. On the right are example regions $\mathcal{X}(500{:}900, j, 1{:}256)$ for $j \in \{ 64, 128, 192 \}$ for the original tensor and three reconstructions.

5 Tucker Tensor Structure

Before we talk about algorithms for computing the Tucker decomposition in Chapter 6, we delve into the special properties of a **Tucker tensor**. A Tucker tensor is a tensor that is stored as the product of a core tensor with a set of factor matrices (decomposed format) rather that the full version (a dense tensor). In this chapter, we explain its structure, its lack of uniqueness, how that enables us to impose orthonormality on the factors, and how to express its vectorization and unfoldings in terms of its constituent parts. This knowledge is useful in the algorithm discussions that follow. Computationally, its structure makes many computations (e.g., computing the norm) less expensive than with the full tensor.

5.1 Tucker Tensor Format

A **Tucker tensor** is a tensor that is expressed as the TTM product (see Section 3.3) of a core tensor and factor matrices.

5.1.1 Tucker Format for 3-way Tensors

For a 3-way tensor, the Tucker format is as follows.

Definition 5.1: Tucker Tensor (3-way)

A 3-way **Tucker tensor** $\mathcal{T} = [\![\mathcal{G}; \mathbf{U}, \mathbf{V}, \mathbf{W}]\!]$ is defined to be the multi-TTM product of a **core tensor** $\mathcal{G} \in \mathbb{R}^{q \times r \times s}$ with **factor matrices** $\mathbf{U} \in \mathbb{R}^{m \times q}$, $\mathbf{V} \in \mathbb{R}^{n \times r}$, $\mathbf{W} \in \mathbb{R}^{p \times s}$. In other words,

$$\mathcal{T} = [\![\mathcal{G}; \mathbf{U}, \mathbf{V}, \mathbf{W}]\!] \equiv \mathcal{G} \times_1 \mathbf{U} \times_2 \mathbf{V} \times_3 \mathbf{W} \in \mathbb{R}^{m \times n \times p}. \tag{5.1}$$

We often say the Tucker tensor is **rank-(q, r, s)** because that is the size of the core.

Using the properties of TTM, the (i, j, k) element of $\mathcal{T}$ from Eq. (5.1) can be expressed as

$$t_{ijk} = \sum_{\alpha=1}^{q} \sum_{\beta=1}^{r} \sum_{\gamma=1}^{s} g_{\alpha\beta\gamma}\, u_{i\alpha} v_{j\beta} w_{k\gamma}. \tag{5.2}$$

Exercise 5.1 Using the definition of TTM (Section 3.3.1), prove the elementwise expression Eq. (5.2) for $\mathcal{T} = \mathcal{G} \times_1 \mathbf{U} \times_2 \mathbf{V} \times_3 \mathbf{W}$.

A 3-way Tucker tensor is depicted in Fig. 5.1. We show factor matrices in orientations that "match up" so that the row dimension is in line with the corresponding mode of $\mathcal{T}$ and the column dimension is perpendicular to the corresponding mode of $\mathcal{G}$. This means that $\mathbf{V}$

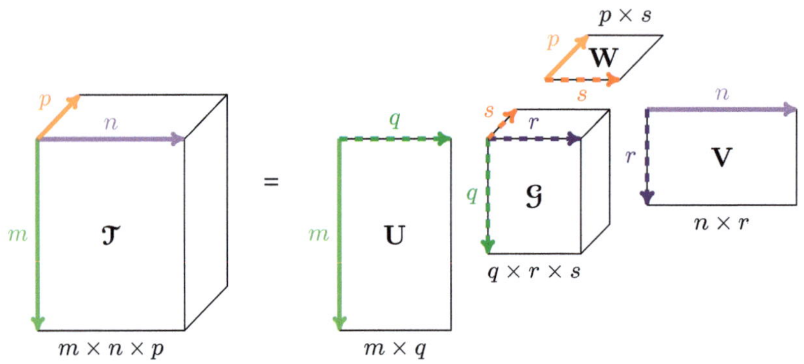

Figure 5.1 3-way Tucker tensor.

looks transposed and $\mathbf{W}$ looks flipped. The rows in $\mathbf{U}, \mathbf{V}, \mathbf{W}$ and matching dimensions of $\mathcal{T}$ are shown with light colors, The columns in the matrices and matching dimension of $\mathcal{G}$ are shown with corresponding dark colors. The arrows show the directions of each mode.

A major motivation for the Tucker tensor format is its storage efficiency. Consider the simplified case of a tensor of size $n \times n \times n$ stored as a Tucker tensor with a core of size $r \times r \times r$. The storage for the Tucker core and three factor matrices is $r^3 + 3nr$; in comparison, the storage for the full tensor is n^3. If $n = 100$ and $r = 10$, the Tucker tensor is 250 times smaller than the equivalent full tensor.

Exercise 5.2 (Three-way Tucker Tensor Storage) What is the storage for a 3-way Tucker tensor of size $m \times n \times p$ with a core of size $q \times r \times s$?

Exercise 5.3 Let $\mathcal{X} = [\![\mathcal{G}_1; \mathbf{U}_1, \mathbf{V}_1, \mathbf{W}_1]\!]$ and let $\mathcal{Y} = [\![\mathcal{G}_2; \mathbf{U}_2, \mathbf{V}_2, \mathbf{W}_2]\!]$ be Tucker tensors of size $m \times n \times p$. Further, assume $\mathcal{G}_1$ is of size $q_1 \times r_1 \times s_1$ and $\mathcal{G}_2$ is of size $q_2 \times r_2 \times s_2$. Express $\mathcal{Z} = \mathcal{X} + \mathcal{Y}$ as a Tucker tensor with a core of size $(q_1 + q_2) \times (p_1 + p_2) \times (q_1 + q_2)$.

5.1.2 Tucker Format for d-way Tensors

Definition 5.2: Tucker tensor (d-way)

A d-way **Tucker tensor** $\mathcal{T} = [\![\mathcal{G}; \mathbf{U}_1, \mathbf{U}_2, \dots, \mathbf{U}_d]\!]$ is defined to be the multi-TTM product of a **core tensor** $\mathcal{G} \in \mathbb{R}^{r_1 \times r_2 \times \cdots \times r_d}$ with **factor matrices** $\mathbf{U}_k \in \mathbb{R}^{n_k \times r_k}$ for all $k \in [d]$. In other words,

$$\mathcal{T} = [\![\mathcal{G}; \mathbf{U}_1, \mathbf{U}_2, \dots, \mathbf{U}_d]\!] = \mathcal{G} \times_1 \mathbf{U}_1 \times_2 \mathbf{U}_2 \cdots \times_d \mathbf{U}_d \in \mathbb{R}^{n_1 \times n_2 \times \cdots \times n_d}. \quad (5.3)$$

We say the Tucker tensor is **rank-$(r_1, r_2, \dots, r_d)$**.

The $(i_1, i_2, \dots, i_d)$ element of $\mathcal{T}$ from Eq. (5.3) can be expressed as

$$\mathcal{T}(i_1, i_2, \dots, i_d) = \sum_{j_1=1}^{r_1} \sum_{j_2=1}^{r_2} \cdots \sum_{j_d=1}^{r_d} \mathcal{G}(j_1, j_2, \dots, j_d) \prod_{k=1}^{d} \mathbf{U}_k(i_k, j_k). \quad (5.4)$$

The storage differentials become more extreme for higher-order tensors. The cost to store the Tucker tensor is $\prod_{k=1}^{d} r_k + \sum_{k=1}^{d} r_k n_k$ versus $\prod_{k=1}^{d} n_k$. The size of the Tucker tensor is still exponential in d, but the savings can be substantial. If $r_k = \frac{1}{2}n_k$ for all $k \in [d]$, then the storage reduction is 2^d.

> A d-way tensor of size $n \times n \times \cdots \times n$ requires n^d storage. If it can be represented as a rank-$(r, r, \ldots, r)$ Tucker tensor, the storage reduces to $r^d + dnr$. The difference is approximately $(n/r)^d$, an exponential reduction!

If $n = n_1 = \cdots = n_d$, then the storage is $drn + r^d$ in factored form versus n^d for the full tensor. An example of the difference this can make is shown in Fig. 5.2.

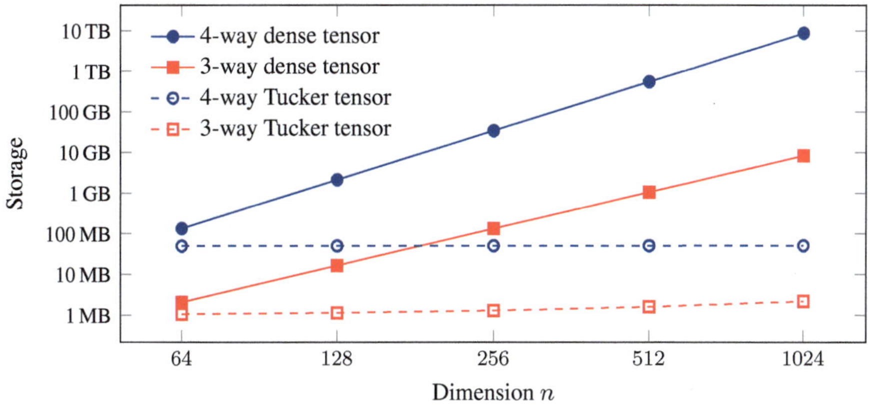

Figure 5.2 Tucker tensor storage for 3-way $n \times n \times n$ or 4-way $n \times n \times n \times n$ tensor with cores of size $50 \times 50 \times 50$ and $50 \times 50 \times 50 \times 50$, respectively, versus the storage for the full tensor.

> **Remark 5.3** (Tucker tensor with huge core) For the operations we discuss in this chapter, there is not necessarily a requirement that $\mathcal{G}$ be smaller than $\mathcal{T}$. To the contrary, it could be the case that $\mathcal{G}$ is a large sparse tensor such that $\text{nnz}(\mathcal{G}) \ll \prod_{k=1}^{d} r_k$ and then the total size of the Tucker tensor is
>
> $$\text{nnz}(\mathcal{G}) + \sum_{k=1}^{d} r_k n_k,$$
>
> which may still be much smaller than the equivalent full tensor, which has size $\prod_{k=1}^{d} n_k$, even when $r_k > n_k$.

5.2 Unfolding a Tucker Tensor

5.2.1 Vectorizing or Unfolding 3-way Tucker Tensors

Consider a 3-way tensor of the form

$$\mathcal{T} = [\![\mathcal{G}; \mathbf{U}, \mathbf{V}, \mathbf{W}]\!] \quad \text{with} \quad \mathcal{G} \in \mathbb{R}^{q \times r \times s}, \mathbf{U} \in \mathbb{R}^{m \times q}, \mathbf{V} \in \mathbb{R}^{n \times r}, \mathbf{W} \in \mathbb{R}^{p \times s}.$$

Recall that the vectorization of a tensor rearranges its elements into a vector (see Definition 2.14). The vectorization of a Tucker tensor has the following form.

Proposition 5.4 (Tucker Tensor Vectorization, 3-way) *The vectorization of the Tucker tensor* $\mathcal{T} = [\![\mathcal{G}; \mathbf{U}, \mathbf{V}, \mathbf{W}]\!]$ *is*

$$\mathrm{vec}(\mathcal{T}) = (\mathbf{W} \otimes \mathbf{V} \otimes \mathbf{U})\,\mathrm{vec}(\mathcal{G}).$$

Exercise 5.4 Prove Proposition 5.4 using Proposition 3.20.

The illustration for a $3 \times 3 \times 3$ Tucker tensor $\mathcal{T}$ with a core $\mathcal{G}$ of size $2 \times 2 \times 2$ can be visualized as in Fig. 5.3. The scaling here is accurate, providing a sense of the sizes of the objects. The Kronecker product is very large if multiplied out, and we would generally not do this in practice.

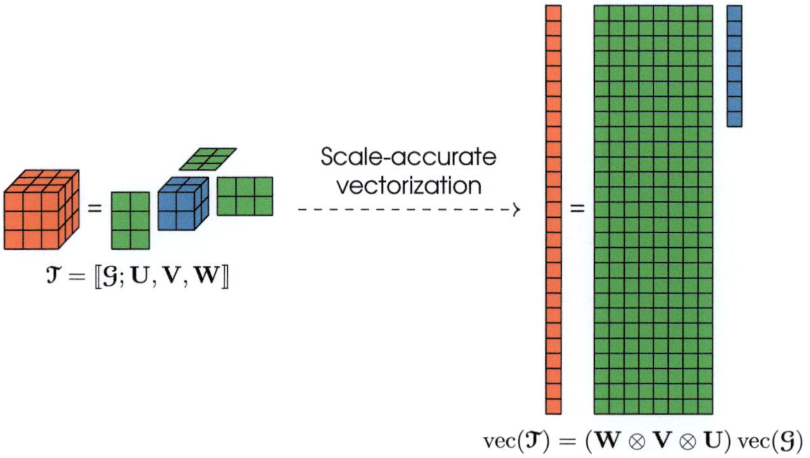

Figure 5.3 Vectorization of a rank-$(2, 2, 2)$ Tucker tensor of size $3 \times 3 \times 3$.

Recall that the mode-k unfolding of an $m \times n \times p$ tensor rearranges its mode-k fibers as columns; see Definitions 2.15–2.17. The unfoldings of a Tucker tensor has the following forms.

Proposition 5.5 (Tucker Tensor Mode-k Unfolding, 3-way) *The mode-k unfoldings of the Tucker tensor* $\mathcal{T} = [\![\mathcal{G}; \mathbf{U}, \mathbf{V}, \mathbf{W}]\!]$ *are*

$$\begin{aligned} \mathbf{T}_{(1)} &= \mathbf{U}\mathbf{G}_{(1)}(\mathbf{W} \otimes \mathbf{V})^{\intercal}, \\ \mathbf{T}_{(2)} &= \mathbf{V}\mathbf{G}_{(2)}(\mathbf{W} \otimes \mathbf{U})^{\intercal}, \quad \textit{and} \\ \mathbf{T}_{(3)} &= \mathbf{W}\mathbf{G}_{(3)}(\mathbf{V} \otimes \mathbf{U})^{\intercal}. \end{aligned}$$

Exercise 5.5 Prove Proposition 5.5 using Proposition 3.20.

Exercise 5.6 If $\mathcal{T} = [\![\mathcal{G}; \mathbf{U}, \mathbf{V}, \mathbf{W}]\!]$ is of size $n \times n \times n$, $\mathcal{G}$ is of size $r \times r \times r$ with $r < n$, and $\mathbf{U}$, $\mathbf{V}$, and $\mathbf{W}$ have full column rank, show $\mathrm{multirank}(\mathcal{T}) = \mathrm{multirank}(\mathcal{G})$. Hint: Use Proposition A.6c.

We can visualize the mode-2 unfolding in Fig. 5.4 for a tensor $\mathcal{T}$ of size $3 \times 3 \times 3$ with a Tucker core of size $2 \times 2 \times 2$. The intermediate matrices are smaller than in the vectorization case.

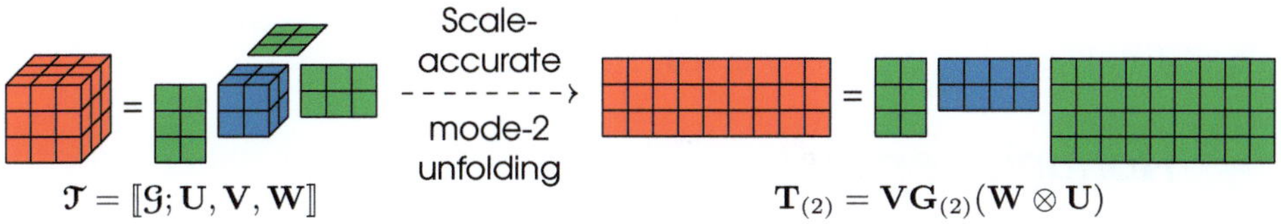

Figure 5.4 Mode-1 unfolding of rank-$(2, 2, 2)$ Tucker tensor of size $3 \times 3 \times 3$.

5.2.2 Vectorizing or Unfolding d-way Tucker Tensors

Suppose $\mathcal{T}$ is a d-way Tucker tensor of the form:

$$\mathcal{T} = [\![\mathcal{G}; \mathbf{U}_1, \mathbf{U}_2, \ldots, \mathbf{U}_d]\!] \in \mathbb{R}^{n_1 \times n_2 \times \cdots \times n_d} \quad \text{with} \quad \mathcal{G} \in \mathbb{R}^{r_1 \times r_2 \times \cdots \times r_d}$$
$$\text{and} \quad \mathbf{U} \in \mathbb{R}^{n_k \times r_k} \quad \text{for all} \quad k \in [d].$$

The following propositions specify the vectorization and mode-wise unfoldings of $\mathcal{T}$.

Proposition 5.6 (Tucker Tensor Vectorization, d-way) *The vectorization of the Tucker tensor $\mathcal{T} = [\![\mathcal{G}; \mathbf{U}_1, \mathbf{U}_2, \ldots, \mathbf{U}_d]\!]$ is*

$$\operatorname{vec}(\mathcal{T}) = (\mathbf{U}_d \otimes \mathbf{U}_{d-1} \otimes \cdots \otimes \mathbf{U}_1) \operatorname{vec}(\mathcal{G}).$$

Proof. Let $\mathbf{B} = \mathbf{U}_d \otimes \mathbf{U}_{d-1} \otimes \cdots \otimes \mathbf{U}_1$, $\mathbf{g} = \operatorname{vec}(\mathcal{G})$, $N = \prod_{k=1}^{d} n_k$, and $R = \prod_{k=1}^{d} r_k$. Consider an arbitrary index $i \in [N]$. By Proposition 2.11 and Definition 2.14, the ith entry of $\mathbf{Bg}$ is given by

$$\sum_{j=1}^{R} \mathbf{B}(i,j)\, \mathbf{g}(j) = \sum_{j_1=1}^{r_1} \cdots \sum_{j_d=1}^{r_d} \mathbf{U}_1(i_1, j_1) \cdots \mathbf{U}_d(i_d, j_d)\, \mathcal{G}(j_1, \ldots, j_d),$$

for $i = \mathbb{L}(i_1, \ldots, i_d)$ and $j = \mathbb{L}(j_1, \ldots, j_d)$. By Eq. (5.4) and Definition 2.14, this is exactly the ith element of $\operatorname{vec}(\mathcal{T})$. □

Proposition 5.7 (Tucker Tensor Mode-k Unfolding, d-way) *The mode-k unfolding of the Tucker tensor $\mathcal{T} = [\![\mathcal{G}; \mathbf{U}_1, \mathbf{U}_2, \ldots, \mathbf{U}_d]\!]$ is*

$$\mathbf{T}_{(k)} = \mathbf{U}_k \mathbf{G}_{(k)} (\mathbf{U}_d \otimes \cdots \otimes \mathbf{U}_{k+1} \otimes \mathbf{U}_{k-1} \otimes \cdots \otimes \mathbf{U}_1)^{\intercal}.$$

Proof. Let $\mathbf{B} = \mathbf{U}_d \otimes \cdots \otimes \mathbf{U}_{k+1} \otimes \mathbf{U}_{k-1} \otimes \cdots \otimes \mathbf{U}_1$, $N_k = \prod_{\substack{\ell=1 \\ \ell \neq k}}^{d} n_\ell$, and $R_k = \prod_{\substack{\ell=1 \\ \ell \neq k}}^{d} r_\ell$. Consider an arbitrary index $(i_k, j_k) \in [n_k] \times [N_k]$. By Proposition 2.11 and Definition 2.18, entry (i_k, j_k) of $\mathbf{U}_k \mathbf{G}_{(k)} \mathbf{B}^{\intercal}$ is given by

$$\sum_{\alpha_k=1}^{r_k} \sum_{\beta_k=1}^{R_k} \mathbf{U}_k(i_k, \alpha_k) \mathbf{G}_{(k)}(\alpha_k, \beta_k) \mathbf{B}(j_k, \beta_k) =$$
$$\sum_{\alpha_1=1}^{r_1} \sum_{\alpha_2=1}^{r_2} \cdots \sum_{\alpha_d=1}^{r_d} \mathbf{U}_k(i_k, \alpha_k) \mathcal{G}(\alpha_1, \ldots, \alpha_d) \prod_{\substack{\ell=1 \\ \ell \neq k}}^{d} \mathbf{U}_\ell(i_\ell, \alpha_\ell),$$

for $j_k = \mathbb{L}(i_1, \ldots, i_{k-1}, i_{k+1}, \ldots, i_d)$ and $\beta_k = \mathbb{L}(\alpha_1, \ldots, \alpha_{k-1}, \alpha_{k+1}, \ldots, \alpha_d)$. By Eq. (5.4) and Definition 2.18, this is exactly entry (i_k, j) of $\mathbf{T}_{(k)}$. □

5.3 Nonuniqueness

The Tucker tensor representation is not unique.

The Tucker representation of a tensor is not unique. Consider a 3-way Tucker tensor given by Eq. (5.1). Given a nonsingular matrix $\mathbf{A} \in \mathbb{R}^{q \times q}$, we have

$$\mathcal{G} \times_1 \mathbf{U} \times_2 \mathbf{V} \times_3 \mathbf{W} = (\mathcal{G} \times_1 \mathbf{A}^{-1}) \times_1 (\mathbf{UA}) \times_2 \mathbf{V} \times_3 \mathbf{W},$$

by the TTM grouping property (see Proposition 3.15). This is illustrated in Fig. 5.5.

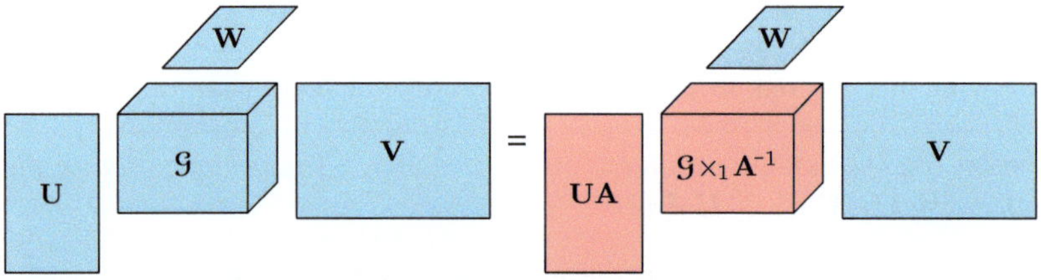

Figure 5.5 A Tucker tensor is nonunique because the core and a factor matrix can be multiplied by a nonsingular matrix and its inverse.

Further, we can transform all modes. Given nonsingular matrices $\mathbf{A} \in \mathbb{R}^{q \times q}$, $\mathbf{B} \in \mathbb{R}^{r \times r}$, and $\mathbf{C} \in \mathbb{R}^{s \times s}$, we have

$$[\![\mathcal{G}; \mathbf{U}, \mathbf{V}, \mathbf{W}]\!] = \left[\!\left[(\mathcal{G} \times_1 \mathbf{A}^{-1} \times_2 \mathbf{B}^{-1} \times_3 \mathbf{C}^{-1}); \mathbf{UA}, \mathbf{VB}, \mathbf{WC}\right]\!\right].$$

More generally, consider the d-way case as in Eq. (5.3), where each factor matrix is $\mathbf{U}_k \in \mathbb{R}^{n_k \times r_k}$. If we choose $\mathbf{V}_k$ to be an $r_k \times r_k$ *invertible* matrix for each $k \in [d]$, then

$$[\![\mathcal{G}; \mathbf{U}_1, \mathbf{U}_2, \ldots, \mathbf{U}_d]\!] = \left[\!\left[(\mathcal{G} \times_1 \mathbf{V}_1^{-1} \times_2 \mathbf{V}_2^{-1} \cdots \times_d \mathbf{V}_d^{-1}); \mathbf{U}_1\mathbf{V}_1, \mathbf{U}_2\mathbf{V}_2, \ldots, \mathbf{U}_d\mathbf{V}_d\right]\!\right].$$

The nonuniqueness of the Tucker format means that a particular Tucker representation is *not* interpretable. In contrast to the CP decomposition (see Chapter 9), we cannot assign meaning to the values in a particular vector of a factor matrix. Instead, the columns of the factor matrix form a basis of the subspace that captures the fibers of that mode. While the subspace is unique, the basis vectors that span it are not, and we can think of the post-multiplication by a nonsingular matrix as a change of basis that does not change the underlying subspace.

5.4 Imposing Orthonormal Factor Matrices

Assuming the core is smaller than the full tensor, we can *always* transform a Tucker tensor to have orthonormal factor matrices.

While the nonuniqueness of Tucker prevents us from interpreting a particular representation, we can use it to our advantage both mathematically and computationally. Given any

Tucker tensor where the core is smaller than the full tensor, we can **impose orthonormality** on its factor matrices. Consider the 3-way Tucker tensor representation,

$$[\![\bar{\mathcal{G}}; \mathbf{U}, \mathbf{V}, \bar{\mathbf{W}}]\!] \in \mathbb{R}^{m \times n \times p},$$

where $\bar{\mathcal{G}}$ is of size $q \times r \times s$ with $s < p$. Suppose $\bar{\mathbf{W}} \in \mathbb{R}^{p \times s}$ is not orthonormal. We can decompose $\bar{\mathbf{W}}$ into a product of two matrices where the first is orthonormal:

$$\bar{\mathbf{W}} = \mathbf{W}\mathbf{Z}, \quad \text{where} \quad \mathbf{W} \in \mathbb{R}^{p \times s} \quad \text{is orthonormal and} \quad \mathbf{Z} \in \mathbb{R}^{s \times s}.$$

We can use, for instance, the (economy) QR factorization with $\bar{\mathbf{W}} = \mathbf{Q}\mathbf{R}$, setting $\mathbf{W} = \mathbf{Q}$ and $\mathbf{Z} = \mathbf{R}$; alternatively, we can use the (economy) SVD, with $\bar{\mathbf{W}} = \mathbf{U}\mathbf{\Sigma}\mathbf{V}^\intercal$, setting $\mathbf{W} = \mathbf{U}$ and $\mathbf{Z} = \mathbf{\Sigma}\mathbf{V}^\intercal$. Now, using Propositions 3.15 and 3.19, we can write

$$\begin{aligned}
[\![\bar{\mathcal{G}}; \mathbf{U}, \mathbf{V}, \bar{\mathbf{W}}]\!] &= \bar{\mathcal{G}} \times_1 \mathbf{U} \times_2 \mathbf{V} \times_3 (\mathbf{W}\mathbf{Z}) \\
&= (\bar{\mathcal{G}} \times_3 \mathbf{Z}) \times_1 \mathbf{U} \times_2 \mathbf{V} \times_3 \mathbf{W} \\
&= [\![\mathcal{G}; \mathbf{U}, \mathbf{V}, \mathbf{W}]\!] \quad \text{with} \quad \mathcal{G} \equiv \bar{\mathcal{G}} \times_3 \mathbf{Z}.
\end{aligned}$$

At this point, $\mathbf{W}$ is orthonormal and $\mathcal{G}$ may be smaller if the economy SVD is used and $\operatorname{rank}(\bar{\mathbf{W}}) < p$. If needed, we can use a similar procedure to make the other factor matrices orthonormal. Thus, without loss of generality, we generally assume that a Tucker tensor's factor matrices are all orthonormal.

Formally, we can state the following results.

Proposition 5.8 (Orthonormal Tucker for 3-way) *Let $\mathbf{U} \in \mathbb{R}^{m \times q}$, $\mathbf{V} \in \mathbb{R}^{n \times r}$, $\mathbf{W} \in \mathbb{R}^{p \times s}$, and $\mathcal{G} \in \mathbb{R}^{q \times r \times z}$. If $q \leq m$, $r \leq n$, and $s \leq p$, then there exists orthonormal factor matrices $\bar{\mathbf{U}} \in \mathbb{O}^{m \times q}$, $\bar{\mathbf{V}} \in \mathbb{O}^{n \times r}$, $\bar{\mathbf{W}} \in \mathbb{O}^{p \times s}$, and modified core $\bar{\mathcal{G}} \in \mathbb{R}^{q \times r \times z}$ such that $[\![\mathcal{G}; \mathbf{U}, \mathbf{V}, \mathbf{W}]\!] = [\![\bar{\mathcal{G}}; \bar{\mathbf{U}}, \bar{\mathbf{V}}, \bar{\mathbf{W}}]\!]$.*

Proposition 5.9 (Orthonormal Tucker for d-way) *Let $\mathbf{U}_k \in \mathbb{R}^{n_k \times r_k}$ for all $k \in [d]$ and $\mathcal{G} \in \mathbb{R}^{\mathbf{r}}$. If $r_k \leq n_k$ for all $k \in [d]$, then there exists a set of orthonormal factor matrices $\left\{ \bar{\mathbf{U}}_k \in \mathbb{O}^{n_k \times r_k} \right\}_{k=1}^{d}$ and modified core $\bar{\mathcal{G}} \in \mathbb{R}^{\mathbf{r}}$ such that $[\![\mathcal{G}; \mathbf{U}_1, \mathbf{U}_2, \dots, \mathbf{U}_d]\!] = [\![\bar{\mathcal{G}}; \bar{\mathbf{U}}_1, \bar{\mathbf{U}}_2, \dots, \bar{\mathbf{U}}_d]\!]$.*

As we will see in Section 5.7 and Chapter 6, many computations involving Tucker tensors and algorithms for computing Tucker decompositions become simpler and cheaper when the factor matrices are orthonormal.

Exercise 5.7 Let $\mathcal{T} = \mathcal{G} \times_1 \mathbf{U} \times_2 \mathbf{V} \times_3 \mathbf{W}$ with $\mathbf{U}, \mathbf{V}, \mathbf{W}$ orthonormal. Prove $\|\mathcal{T}\| = \|\mathcal{G}\|$.

Exercise 5.8 Derive the cost to convert a Tucker tensor to a Tucker tensor with orthonormal factor matrices using a QR factorization for each mode.

5.5 Full Reconstruction

We generally work with a Tucker tensor in factored from. However, we may eventually need to reconstruct it. We discuss here the methodology for reconstructing the entire tensor. See also the discussion of efficient partial reconstruction in Section 5.6.

5.5.1 Full Reconstruction for 3-way Tucker Tensors

Suppose we want to reconstruct an $m \times n \times p$ full tensor $\mathcal{X}$ from a 3-way Tucker tensor $[\![\mathcal{G}; \mathbf{U}, \mathbf{V}, \mathbf{W}]\!]$ of rank (q, r, s). We must compute

$$\mathcal{X} = \mathcal{G} \times_1 \mathbf{U} \times_2 \mathbf{V} \times_3 \mathbf{W}.$$

We can compute it in multiple steps by performing a TTM with each factor matrix and the core in turn: first $\mathbf{U}$, then $\mathbf{V}$, and then $\mathbf{W}$ to produce the full reconstruction: $\mathcal{X} = ((\mathcal{G} \times_1 \mathbf{U}) \times_2 \mathbf{V}) \times_3 \mathbf{W}$. This process is illustrated in Fig. 5.6.

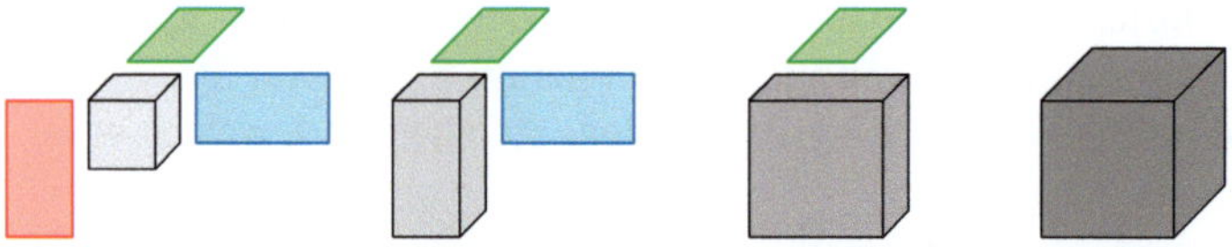

Figure 5.6 Reconstruction from a 3-way Tucker tensor.

The total cost of full reconstruction performed in this mode order is

$$\mathcal{O}(mqrs + mnrs + mnps).$$

Multiplying with the factor matrices in a different order, e.g.,

$$(((\mathcal{G} \times_2 \mathbf{V}) \times_3 \mathbf{W}) \times_1 \mathbf{U}),$$

can change and potentially reduce the total number of operations.

Exercise 5.9 (a) Illustrate the steps of full reconstruction as in Fig. 5.6, starting with mode 2, then mode 3, and then mode 1, i.e., $(((\mathcal{G} \times_2 \mathbf{V}) \times_3 \mathbf{W}) \times_1 \mathbf{U})$. (b) What is the computational cost?

5.5.2 Full Reconstruction for d-way Tucker Tensors

Suppose we want to reconstruct an $n_1 \times n_2 \times \cdots \times n_d$ full tensor from a d-way Tucker tensor of rank $(r_1, r_2, \ldots, r_d)$. We must compute

$$\mathcal{X} = \mathcal{G} \times_1 \mathbf{U}_1 \times_2 \mathbf{U}_2 \cdots \times_d \mathbf{U}_d.$$

If we multiply the factor matrices in the order shown, $(\cdots((\mathcal{G} \times_1 \mathbf{U}_1) \times_2 \mathbf{U}_2) \cdots \times_3 \mathbf{U}_d)$, then the total cost of reconstruction is

$$\mathcal{O}\left(\sum_{k=1}^{d}\left(\prod_{i=1}^{k} n_i\right)\left(\prod_{j=k}^{d} r_j\right)\right).$$

Example 5.1 (Tucker Reconstruction Cost, d-way) For a d-way Tucker tensor of size $n \times n \times \cdots \times n$ and rank $r \times r \times \cdots \times r$ with $r < n$, the cost of full reconstruction is $\mathcal{O}(nr^d + n^2r^{d-1} + \cdots + n^dr) = \mathcal{O}(n^dr)$.

5.6 Partial Reconstruction

Section 5.5 describes how to reconstruct the full tensor from its Tucker format. In many situations, we do not need to reconstruct the entire tensor. A major advantage of Tucker decomposition for compression is that it supports efficient partial reconstruction.

5.6.1 Partial Reconstruction of 3-way Tucker Tensors

Suppose we only need a subset of the reconstruction, such as only horizontal slices 5–9. We can express this via a selection matrix $\mathbf{S}$ that picks out indices 5–9:

$$\mathbf{S} = \begin{bmatrix} 0 & 0 & 0 & 0 & 1 & 0 & 0 & 0 & 0 & 0 & \dots & 0 \\ 0 & 0 & 0 & 0 & 0 & 1 & 0 & 0 & 0 & 0 & \dots & 0 \\ 0 & 0 & 0 & 0 & 0 & 0 & 1 & 0 & 0 & 0 & \dots & 0 \\ 0 & 0 & 0 & 0 & 0 & 0 & 0 & 1 & 0 & 0 & \dots & 0 \\ 0 & 0 & 0 & 0 & 0 & 0 & 0 & 0 & 1 & 0 & \dots & 0 \end{bmatrix}.$$

Then the partially reconstructed tensor can be expressed mathematically as $\bar{\mathcal{X}} = \hat{\mathcal{X}} \times_1 \mathbf{S}$. However, we can avoid explicitly constructing $\hat{\mathcal{X}}$ at all by observing that

$$\hat{\mathcal{X}} \times_1 \mathbf{S} = \mathcal{G} \times_1 (\mathbf{SU}) \times_2 \mathbf{V} \times_3 \mathbf{W}.$$

By first computing $\bar{\mathbf{U}} = \mathbf{SU}$, we can more efficiently construct $\bar{\mathcal{X}}$ using a sequence of smaller TTMs, as illustrated in Fig. 5.7.

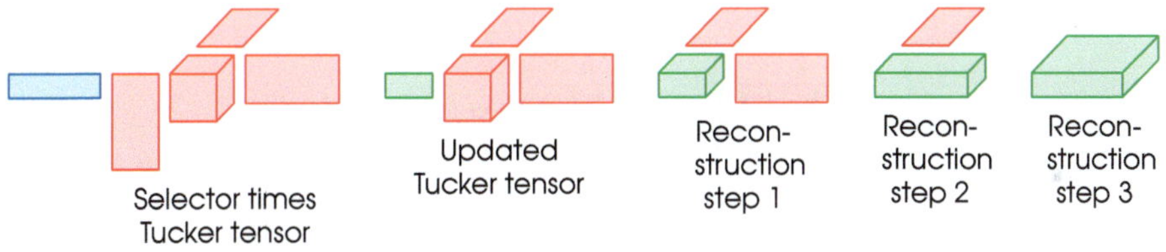

Figure 5.7 Partial reconstruction from a 3-way Tucker tensor. The blue part represents a selector matrix that pulls out a subset of rows of the first factor matrix. Green parts represent realized savings from the partial reconstruction.

If $\mathbf{S}$ is $\bar{m} \times m$, the memory cost reduces to $\bar{m}np$ and the computational cost reduces to

$$\mathcal{O}(\bar{m}qrs + \bar{m}nrs + \bar{m}nps).$$

No computation is required to form $\bar{\mathbf{U}} = \mathbf{SU}$, as it is simply a subset of the rows of $\mathbf{U}$. We need not form $\mathbf{S}$ explicitly in this case.

Exercise 5.10 Suppose we only need to reconstruct a single frontal slice of a rank-(q, r, s) Tucker tensor of total size $m \times n \times p$.

(a) Which mode does the selector matrix impact? What is the size of the selector matrix?

(b) Write down the sequence of operations.

(c) Illustrate the sequence of operation as in Fig. 5.7.

Downsampling

In some cases, the resolution of the fully reconstructed data is higher than we need for downstream analysis. In these cases, we can downsample by using matrices that average elements. For instance, we can create a matrix of size $m/2 \times m$ that averages every consecutive pair of horizontal slices.

$$\mathbf{S} = \begin{bmatrix} 1/2 & 1/2 & 0 & 0 & 0 & \cdots & 0 & 0 \\ 0 & 0 & 1/2 & 1/2 & 0 & \cdots & 0 & 0 \\ \vdots & \vdots & \vdots & \vdots & \vdots & \ddots & \vdots & \vdots \\ 0 & 0 & 0 & 0 & 0 & \cdots & 1/2 & 1/2 \end{bmatrix}.$$

This would reduce the overall size of the reconstruction by a factor of 2. If we made similar downsampling matrices for each of the three modes, the overall size of the reconstruction would be smaller by a factor of 8. Each element in the result would be the average of a $2 \times 2 \times 2$ block of eight entries.

5.6.2 Partial Reconstruction of d-way Tucker Tensors

As in the 3-way case, we can realize substantial computational savings with partial or downsampled computations. Suppose each mode k is sub- or downsampled to size $m_k \leq n_k$. We can express this by multiplying mode k by a subsampling matrix $\mathbf{S}_k \in \mathbb{R}^{m_n \times n_k}$, so the partial reconstruction is computed as

$$\mathcal{G} \times_1 \mathbf{S}_1\mathbf{U}_1 \times_2 \mathbf{S}_2\mathbf{U}_2 \cdots \times_d \mathbf{S}_d\mathbf{U}_d.$$

Then the total reconstruction cost is reduced to at most

$$\mathcal{O}\left(\sum_{k=1}^{d}\left(\prod_{i=1}^{k} m_i\right)\left(\prod_{j=k}^{d} r_j\right) + m_k n_k r_k\right).$$

Example 5.2 (Partial Reconstruction of d-way Tucker Tensor) Consider a d-way Tucker tensor of size $n \times n \times \cdots \times n$ and rank $r \times r \times \cdots \times r$. To create a downsampled reconstruction of size $m \times m \times \cdots \times m$, the cost is $\mathcal{O}(mr^d + m^2r^{d-1} + \cdots + m^dr + dmnr)$. In most cases, the term $\mathcal{O}(m^dr)$ dominates.

Exercise 5.11 Implement a function for efficient *partial* reconstruction for d-way Tucker tensors. Your function should take as input a Tucker tensor of the form $[\![\mathcal{G}; \mathbf{A}_1, \mathbf{A}_2, \ldots, \mathbf{A}_d]\!]$ and d sets of indices $\mathcal{I}_d \subseteq [n_d]$, and it should return an explicit subtensor corresponding to the Cartesian product of those indices. Your function should avoid the full reconstruction of the Tucker tensor and use a more efficient method. (You may use an existing TTM function.) (a) Implement a partial reconstruction function that processes the modes in order (1 to d). (b) Implement a helper function that determines the best ordering for the multi-TTM using Proposition 3.25. (c) To improve your partial reconstruction function, process modes in the optimal order as given by your helper function.

5.7 Operations on Tucker Tensors

Tensors in Tucker format can require less space than their full format representations, and operations on Tucker tensors can require much less computation as well.

5.7.1 Inner Products and Norms of Tucker Tensors

Inner Product for 3-way Tucker Tensors

Consider the problem of computing an inner product of two Tucker tensors of the forms:

$$\begin{aligned}
\mathcal{X} &= [\![\mathcal{G}; \mathbf{U}_1, \mathbf{U}_2, \mathbf{U}_3]\!], \qquad & \mathcal{G} &\in \mathbb{R}^{r\times r\times r}, \qquad & \mathbf{U}_1, \mathbf{U}_2, \mathbf{U}_3 &\in \mathbb{R}^{n\times r},\\
\mathcal{Y} &= [\![\mathcal{H}; \mathbf{V}_1, \mathbf{V}_2, \mathbf{V}_3]\!], & \mathcal{H} &\in \mathbb{R}^{q\times q\times q}, & \mathbf{V}_1, \mathbf{V}_2, \mathbf{V}_3 &\in \mathbb{R}^{n\times q}.
\end{aligned}$$

To compute the inner product of full tensors would cost $\mathcal{O}(n^3)$, and forming the full tensors from their Tucker representations would cost $\mathcal{O}(rn^3 + qn^3)$. If we assume $r < q < n$, then we can find some computational advantages working with the tensors implicitly as

$$\begin{aligned}
\langle \mathcal{X}, \mathcal{Y} \rangle &= \langle \mathcal{G} \times_1 \mathbf{U}_1 \times_2 \mathbf{U}_2 \times_3 \mathbf{U}_3, \mathcal{Y} \rangle\\
&= \langle \mathcal{G}, \mathcal{Y} \times_1 \mathbf{U}_1^{\intercal} \times_2 \mathbf{U}_2^{\intercal} \times_3 \mathbf{U}_3^{\intercal} \rangle\\
&= \langle \mathcal{G}, \mathcal{H} \times_1 \mathbf{U}_1^{\intercal}\mathbf{V}_1 \times_2 \mathbf{U}_2^{\intercal}\mathbf{V}_2 \times_3 \mathbf{U}_3^{\intercal}\mathbf{V}_3 \rangle.
\end{aligned}$$

Computing $\mathbf{W}_1 \equiv \mathbf{U}_1^{\intercal}\mathbf{V}_1$ costs $\mathcal{O}(rqn)$, and likewise for $\mathbf{W}_2 \equiv \mathbf{U}_2^{\intercal}\mathbf{V}_2$ and $\mathbf{W}_3 = \mathbf{U}_3^{\intercal}\mathbf{V}_3$. Computing $\mathcal{F} \equiv \mathcal{H} \times_1 \mathbf{W}_1 \times_2 \mathbf{W}_2 \times_3 \mathbf{W}_3$ costs $\mathcal{O}(rq^3)$. Finally, computing $\langle \mathcal{G}, \mathcal{F} \rangle$ costs $\mathcal{O}(r^3)$. The dominant costs are $\mathcal{O}(rqn + rq^3)$. So, we have reduced the cost from

$$\mathcal{O}(qn^3) \quad \text{to} \quad \mathcal{O}(qrn + rq^3).$$

We can generalize efficient computation of inner products to noncubical Tucker tensors (with noncubical cores) – see Exercise 5.12.

Exercise 5.12 Give an efficient algorithm for computing the inner product of two Tucker tensors $\langle \mathcal{X}_1, \mathcal{X}_2 \rangle$ and derive the computational cost. Assume that the tensors have common full dimensions $m \times n \times p$, $\mathcal{X}_1$ has core dimensions $q_1 \times r_1 \times s_1$ and $\mathcal{X}_2$ has core dimensions $q_2 \times r_2 \times s_2$.

Inner Product for d-way Tucker Tensors

Consider the d-way case with

$$\begin{aligned}
\mathcal{X} &= [\![\mathcal{G}; \mathbf{U}_1, \mathbf{U}_2, \dots, \mathbf{U}_d]\!], \qquad & \mathcal{G} &\in \mathbb{R}^{r\times r\times \cdots \times r}, \qquad & \mathbf{U}_1, \mathbf{U}_2, \dots, \mathbf{U}_d &\in \mathbb{R}^{n\times r},\\
\mathcal{Y} &= [\![\mathcal{H}; \mathbf{V}_1, \mathbf{V}_2, \dots, \mathbf{V}_d]\!], & \mathcal{H} &\in \mathbb{R}^{q\times q\times \cdots \times q}, & \mathbf{V}_1, \mathbf{V}_2, \dots, \mathbf{V}_d &\in \mathbb{R}^{n\times q}.
\end{aligned}$$

To compute the inner product of full tensors would cost $\mathcal{O}(n^d)$, and forming the full tensors from the Tucker format would cost $\mathcal{O}(rn^d + qn^d)$. If we assume $r < q < n$, then we can find some computational advantages working with the tensors implicitly as

$$\begin{aligned}
\langle \mathcal{X}, \mathcal{Y} \rangle &= \langle \mathcal{G} \times_1 \mathbf{U}_1 \times_2 \mathbf{U}_2 \cdots \times_d \mathbf{U}_d, \mathcal{Y} \rangle\\
&= \langle \mathcal{G}, \mathcal{Y} \times_1 \mathbf{U}_1^{\intercal} \times_2 \mathbf{U}_2^{\intercal} \cdots \times_d \mathbf{U}_d^{\intercal} \rangle\\
&= \langle \mathcal{G}, \mathcal{H} \times_1 \mathbf{U}_1^{\intercal}\mathbf{V}_1 \times_2 \mathbf{U}_2^{\intercal}\mathbf{V}_2 \cdots \times_d \mathbf{U}_d^{\intercal}\mathbf{V}_d \rangle.
\end{aligned}$$

Computing $\mathbf{W}_k \equiv \mathbf{V}_k\mathbf{U}_k^{\intercal}$ for all $k \in [d]$ costs $\mathcal{O}(drqn)$. Computing $\mathcal{F} \equiv \mathcal{H} \times_1 \mathbf{W}_1 \times_2 \mathbf{W}_2 \cdots \times_d \mathbf{W}_d$ costs $\mathcal{O}(rq^d)$. Finally, computing $\langle \mathcal{G}, \mathcal{F} \rangle$ costs $\mathcal{O}(r^d)$. The dominant cost is $\mathcal{O}(rqn)$. So, we have reduced the cost from

$$\mathcal{O}(qn^d) \quad \text{to} \quad \mathcal{O}(drqn + rq^d).$$

If $r < q < n$, these cost savings can be substantial. We can generalize this efficient computation of inner products to noncubical tensors – see Exercise 5.13.

Exercise 5.13 What is the computational complexity of computing $\langle \mathcal{X}, \mathcal{Y} \rangle$ for

$$\mathcal{X} = [\![\mathcal{G}; \mathbf{U}_1, \mathbf{U}_2, \ldots, \mathbf{U}_d]\!], \quad \mathcal{G} \in \mathbb{R}^{r_1 \times r_2 \times \cdots \times r_d}, \quad \mathbf{U}_k \in \mathbb{R}^{n_k \times r_k} \text{ for all } k \in [d],$$
$$\mathcal{Y} = [\![\mathcal{H}; \mathbf{V}_1, \mathbf{V}_2, \ldots, \mathbf{V}_d]\!], \quad \mathcal{H} \in \mathbb{R}^{q_1 \times q_2 \times \cdots \times q_d}, \quad \mathbf{V}_k \in \mathbb{R}^{n_k \times q_k} \text{ for all } k \in [d].$$

Norm of 3-way Tucker Tensor

In order to compute the norm of a Tucker tensor $\mathcal{T} = [\![\mathcal{G}, \mathbf{U}, \mathbf{V}, \mathbf{W}]\!]$, we can reduce the problem to tensors of the size of the core $\mathcal{G}$. Applying the same argument as in the inner product, we have

$$\|\mathcal{T}\|^2 = \langle \mathcal{T}, \mathcal{T} \rangle = \langle \mathcal{G} \times_1 (\mathbf{U}^\intercal \mathbf{U}) \times_2 (\mathbf{V}^\intercal \mathbf{V}) \times_3 (\mathbf{W}^\intercal \mathbf{W}), \mathcal{G} \rangle. \tag{5.5}$$

Pictorially, we can visualize this as shown in Fig. 5.8.

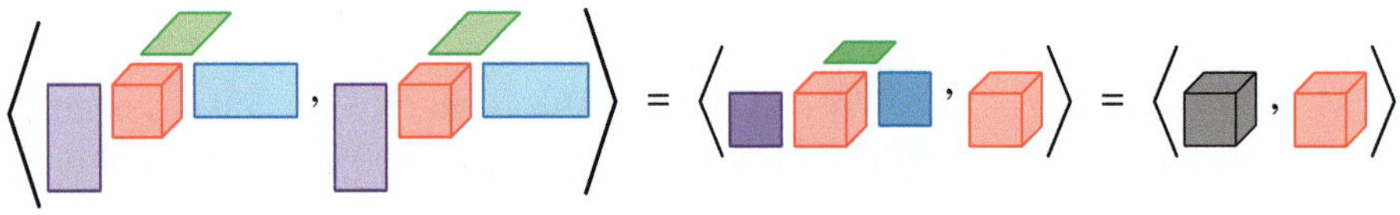

Figure 5.8 A Tucker tensor norm calculation without forming the full tensor.

Computing the norm of a full $m \times n \times p$ tensor requires $\mathcal{O}(mnp)$ operations, which is proportional to the *product* of the full tensor dimensions. When a tensor is in Tucker format, the computation increases with the *sum* of the full tensor dimensions and is typically dominated by a cost proportional to the product of the reduced dimensions: $\mathcal{O}(qrs)$. Evaluating the reduced expression requires computing the Gram matrix of each factor matrix using $\mathcal{O}(mq^2 + nr^2 + ps^2)$ operations, performing the multi-TTM operation with the core with $\mathcal{O}(q^2rs + qr^2s + qrs^2)$ operations, and finally the standard tensor inner product requiring $\mathcal{O}(qrs)$ operations.

Computing the norm of a Tucker tensor whose factor matrices are orthonormal is even easier. Because the Gram matrix of each factor matrix is an identity, Eq. (5.5) simplifies to

$$\langle \mathcal{T}, \mathcal{T} \rangle = \langle \mathcal{G}, \mathcal{G} \rangle. \tag{5.6}$$

In fact, an efficient alternative algorithm to compute the norm of a Tucker tensor is to first orthogonalize the factor matrices and then compute the norm of the transformed core – see Exercise 5.8.

Norm of d-way Tucker Tensor

The norm for the general d-way tensor $\mathcal{T} = [\![\mathcal{G}; \mathbf{U}_1, \mathbf{U}_2, \ldots, \mathbf{U}_d]\!]$ is

$$\|\mathcal{T}\|^2 = \langle \mathcal{T}, \mathcal{T} \rangle = \langle \mathcal{G} \times_1 \mathbf{U}_1^\intercal \mathbf{U}_1 \times_2 \mathbf{U}_2^\intercal \mathbf{U}_2 \cdots \times_d \mathbf{U}_d^\intercal \mathbf{U}_d, \mathcal{G} \rangle.$$

Analogous to the 3-way case, the cost to form the full tensor and compute its norm directly versus computing the norm by exploiting the Tucker format is

$$\mathcal{O}\left(r_d \prod_{k=1}^{d} n_k \right) \quad \text{versus} \quad \mathcal{O}\left(\sum_{k=1}^{d} n_k r_k^2 + r_d \prod_{k=1}^{d} r_k \right).$$

Here we have assumed that the TTMs are performed in the natural order. If the full tensor and core are both cubical, then the difference is

$$\mathcal{O}(rn^d) \quad \text{versus} \quad \mathcal{O}(nr^2 + r^{d+1}).$$

As in the 3-way case, orthonormal factor matrices mean that $\mathbf{U}_k^\intercal \mathbf{U}_k = \mathbf{I}$ for all $k \in [d]$, so the computation simplifies as stated in the proposition below.

Proposition 5.10: Norm Equivalence for Tucker Tensor and its Core

If $\mathcal{T} = [\![\mathcal{G}; \mathbf{U}_1, \dots, \mathbf{U}_d]\!]$ *with* $\mathbf{U}_k$ *orthonormal for all* $k \in [d]$*, then* $\|\mathcal{T}\| = \|\mathcal{G}\|$.

5.7.2 TTM for Tucker Tensors

The Tucker tensor involves TTMs, but we may also compute a TTM with a Tucker tensor. As shown in Section 5.6, this can be done without affecting the core. The key is that we maintain Tucker structure of the output tensor. The computation involves only the factor matrix in the mode of the TTM; the core and other factor matrices are not even accessed.

TTM for 3-way Tucker Tensors

Proposition 5.11 (TTM for 3-way Tucker Tensor) *Consider the Tucker tensor*

$$\mathcal{X} = [\![\mathcal{G}; \mathbf{U}, \mathbf{V}, \mathbf{W}]\!] \quad \textit{with} \quad \mathcal{G} \in \mathbb{R}^{q \times r \times s}, \mathbf{U} \in \mathbb{R}^{m \times q}, \mathbf{V} \in \mathbb{R}^{n \times r}, \mathbf{W} \in \mathbb{R}^{p \times s}.$$

Let $\bar{\mathbf{U}} \in \mathbb{R}^{\bar{q} \times m}$, $\bar{\mathbf{V}} \in \mathbb{R}^{\bar{r} \times n}$, *and* $\bar{\mathbf{W}} \in \mathbb{R}^{\bar{s} \times p}$*. Then*

$$\begin{aligned} \mathcal{X} \times_1 \bar{\mathbf{U}} &= [\![\mathcal{G}; \bar{\mathbf{U}}\mathbf{U}, \mathbf{V}, \mathbf{W}]\!], \\ \mathcal{X} \times_2 \bar{\mathbf{V}} &= [\![\mathcal{G}; \mathbf{U}, \bar{\mathbf{V}}\mathbf{V}, \mathbf{W}]\!], \quad \textit{and} \\ \mathcal{X} \times_3 \bar{\mathbf{W}} &= [\![\mathcal{G}; \mathbf{U}, \mathbf{V}, \bar{\mathbf{W}}\mathbf{W}]\!]. \end{aligned}$$

Exercise 5.14 Prove Proposition 5.11.

The cost of a TTM for a Tucker tensor is only that of the multiplication between the input matrix and the factor matrix in the mode of the TTM. In the notation of Proposition 5.11, the costs are $\mathcal{O}(mq\bar{q})$, $\mathcal{O}(nr\bar{r})$, and $\mathcal{O}(ps\bar{s})$ for each respective mode.

Given matrices $\bar{\mathbf{U}}$, $\bar{\mathbf{V}}$, and $\bar{\mathbf{W}}$ as in Proposition 5.11, we can also consider a multi-TTM computation:

$$\mathcal{X} \times_1 \bar{\mathbf{U}} \times_2 \bar{\mathbf{V}} \times_3 \bar{\mathbf{W}} = [\![\mathcal{G}; \bar{\mathbf{U}}\mathbf{U}, \bar{\mathbf{V}}\mathbf{V}, \bar{\mathbf{W}}\mathbf{W}]\!].$$

This cost of this computation is $\mathcal{O}(mq\bar{q} + nr\bar{r} + ps\bar{s})$. The multi-TTM with a Tucker tensor is illustrated in Fig. 5.9.

TTM for d-way Tucker Tensors

A TTM for a d-way Tucker tensor has the same properties for the 3-way case, as a TTM in mode k is computed independently of the other $d-1$ modes. Given $\mathcal{X} = [\![\mathcal{G}; \mathbf{U}_1, \dots, \mathbf{U}_d]\!]$ and a matrix $\bar{\mathbf{U}}_k \in \mathbb{R}^{\bar{r}_k \times n_k}$, for example, we have

$$\mathcal{X} \times_k \bar{\mathbf{U}}_k = [\![\mathcal{G}; \mathbf{U}_1, \dots, \bar{\mathbf{U}}_k \mathbf{U}_k, \dots, \mathbf{U}_d]\!].$$

5.7.3 MTTKRP with Tucker Tensors

We consider MTTKRP of a Tucker tensor, utilizing its factored form.

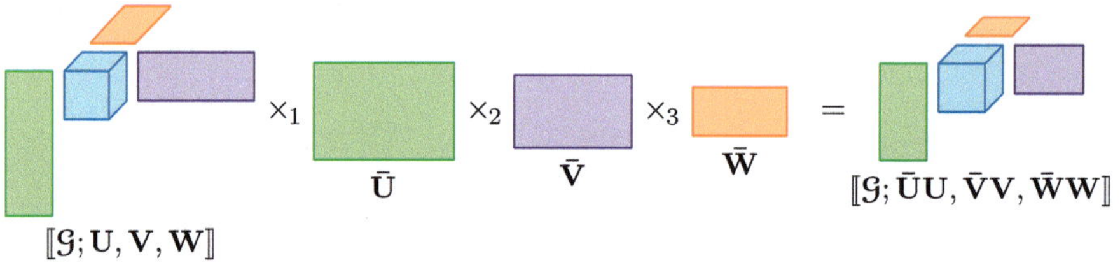

Figure 5.9 Multi-TTM with a Tucker tensor.

MTTKRP with 3-way Tucker Tensors

Consider the MTTKRP of a 3-way Tucker tensor.

Proposition 5.12 (MTTKRP for 3-way Tucker Tensors) *Let* $\mathcal{X} = [\![\mathcal{G}; \mathbf{U}, \mathbf{V}, \mathbf{W}]\!] \in \mathbb{R}^{m \times n \times p}$ *be a Tucker tensor and let* $\mathbf{A} \in \mathbb{R}^{m \times r}$, $\mathbf{B} \in \mathbb{R}^{n \times r}$, *and* $\mathbf{C} \in \mathbb{R}^{p \times r}$. *Then*

$$\mathbf{X}_{(1)}(\mathbf{C} \odot \mathbf{B}) = \mathbf{U}\mathbf{G}_{(1)}\big((\mathbf{W}^\intercal\mathbf{C}) \odot (\mathbf{V}^\intercal\mathbf{B})\big),$$
$$\mathbf{X}_{(2)}(\mathbf{C} \odot \mathbf{A}) = \mathbf{V}\mathbf{G}_{(2)}\big((\mathbf{W}^\intercal\mathbf{C}) \odot (\mathbf{U}^\intercal\mathbf{A})\big), \text{ and}$$
$$\mathbf{X}_{(3)}(\mathbf{B} \odot \mathbf{A}) = \mathbf{W}\mathbf{G}_{(3)}\big((\mathbf{V}^\intercal\mathbf{C}) \odot (\mathbf{U}^\intercal\mathbf{A})\big).$$

Exercise 5.15 Prove Proposition 5.12.

Thus, we can convert the MTTKRP of the Tucker tensor to an MTTKRP with the core. If we assume that $\mathcal{X}$ is of size $n \times n \times n$, $\mathcal{G}$ is of size $q \times q \times q$, and $\mathbf{C}, \mathbf{B}$ are of size $n \times r$, then the work reduces from $\mathcal{O}(rn^3)$ to $\mathcal{O}(rnq + rq^3)$.

Exercise 5.16 For a 3-way Tucker tensor, derive the expressions and costs for the MTTKRP with respect to modes 2 and 3.

MTTKRP with d-way Tucker Tensors

A similar result holds in the d-way case.

Proposition 5.13 (MTTKRP for d-way Tucker Tensors) *Let* $\mathcal{X} = [\![\mathcal{G}; \mathbf{A}_1, \mathbf{A}_2, \ldots, \mathbf{A}_d]\!] \in \mathbb{R}^{n_1 \times n_2 \times \cdots \times n_d}$ *and let* $\mathbf{A}_k \in \mathbb{R}^{n_k \times r}$ *for all* $k \in [d]$. *Then*

$$\begin{aligned}\mathbf{X}_{(k)}&(\mathbf{A}_d \odot \cdots \odot \mathbf{A}_{k+1} \odot \mathbf{A}_{k-1} \odot \cdots \odot \mathbf{A}_1)\\ &= \mathbf{U}_k\mathbf{G}_{(k)}(\mathbf{B}_d \odot \cdots \odot \mathbf{B}_{k+1} \odot \mathbf{B}_{k-1} \odot \cdots \odot \mathbf{B}_1),\\ &\qquad \text{where} \quad \mathbf{B}_k \equiv \mathbf{U}_k^\intercal\mathbf{A}_k \quad \text{for all} \quad k \in [d].\end{aligned}$$

Exercise 5.17 Prove Proposition 5.13.

Exercise 5.18 Compare the computational costs of evaluating the MTTKRP as in Proposition 5.13 with those of forming the full tensor and performing a MTTKRP with an explicit $\mathcal{X}$.

6 Tucker Algorithms

Computing a Tucker decomposition (Tucker, 1966) involves finding factor matrices that define the bases for compression. The low-rank matrix decomposition problem has a well-defined solution given by the SVD. The difficulty for Tucker decomposition is that we cannot easily solve for all the factor matrices simultaneously. Instead, we solve for one at a time. In this chapter, we present three different algorithms that use this tactic in slightly different ways: higher-order singular value decomposition (HOSVD), sequentially truncated HOSVD (ST-HOSVD), and higher-order orthogonal iteration (HOOI). We focus on the algorithms and defer discussion of the error bounds to Chapter 7.

6.1 Optimization Formulation

6.1.1 Tucker Optimization Problem for 3-way Tensors

For $\mathcal{X} \in \mathbb{R}^{m \times n \times p}$, the problem of computing the optimal rank-(q, r, s) Tucker decomposition, $\mathcal{X} \approx [\![\mathcal{G}; \mathbf{U}, \mathbf{V}, \mathbf{W}]\!]$, is a nonlinear, nonconvex, least squares optimization problem. Specifically, it is the solution to

$$\begin{aligned} \min \quad & \left\| \mathcal{X} - \mathcal{G} \times_1 \mathbf{U} \times_2 \mathbf{V} \times_3 \mathbf{W} \right\| \\ \text{subject to} \quad & \mathcal{G} \in \mathbb{R}^{q \times r \times s}, \mathbf{U} \in \mathbb{R}^{m \times q}, \mathbf{V} \in \mathbb{R}^{n \times r}, \mathbf{W} \in \mathbb{R}^{p \times s}. \end{aligned} \tag{6.1}$$

In general, this formulation is the most natural way to express the optimization problem because it explicitly compares $\mathcal{X}$ to its Tucker approximation. The objective function value is the absolute error, which we denote using ERR. In the remainder of this subsection, we will derive a simplified formulation that eliminates $\mathcal{G}$; the new formulation will be more amenable to the solution methods we discuss in the remainder of the chapter.

Elimination of the Core

We can simplify the Tucker optimization problem by eliminating the core $\mathcal{G}$ from the optimization. As explained in Section 5.4, we can impose orthonormality on all the factor matrices without any loss of generality. Thus, Eq. (6.1) is equivalent to the constrained problem:

$$\begin{aligned} \min \quad & \left\| \mathcal{X} - \mathcal{G} \times_1 \mathbf{U} \times_2 \mathbf{V} \times_3 \mathbf{W} \right\| \\ \text{subject to} \quad & \mathcal{G} \in \mathbb{R}^{q \times r \times s}, \mathbf{U} \in \mathbb{O}^{m \times q}, \mathbf{V} \in \mathbb{O}^{n \times r}, \mathbf{W} \in \mathbb{O}^{p \times s}. \end{aligned} \tag{6.2}$$

Now consider the problem of solving for $\mathcal{G}$ if $\mathbf{U}$, $\mathbf{V}$, and $\mathbf{W}$ were known. If we express the problem in vectorized form (using Proposition 5.4), we have a linear least squares problem:

$$\begin{aligned} \min \quad & \left\| \operatorname{vec}(\mathcal{X}) - (\mathbf{W} \otimes \mathbf{V} \otimes \mathbf{U}) \operatorname{vec}(\mathcal{G}) \right\|_2 \\ \text{subject to} \quad & \mathcal{G} \in \mathbb{R}^{q \times r \times s}. \end{aligned}$$

The coefficient matrix $(\mathbf{W} \otimes \mathbf{V} \otimes \mathbf{U})$ is orthonormal (see Exercise A.27), so the solution for $\mathcal{G}$ is $\text{vec}(\mathcal{G}) = (\mathbf{W} \otimes \mathbf{V} \otimes \mathbf{U})^\intercal \text{vec}(\mathcal{X})$. In tensor notation, this equates to

$$\mathcal{G} = \mathcal{X} \times_1 \mathbf{U}^\intercal \times_2 \mathbf{V}^\intercal \times_3 \mathbf{W}^\intercal. \tag{6.3}$$

Thus, any optimal solution of Eq. (6.2) has a $\mathcal{G}$ that satisfies Eq. (6.3).

Substituting this expression for $\mathcal{G}$ into Eq. (6.1) and using Proposition 3.15, we have

$$\begin{aligned} \mathcal{X} - \mathcal{G} \times_1 \mathbf{U} \times_2 \mathbf{V} \times_3 \mathbf{W} &= \mathcal{X} - (\mathcal{X} \times_1 \mathbf{U}^\intercal \times_2 \mathbf{V}^\intercal \times_3 \mathbf{W}^\intercal) \times_1 \mathbf{U} \times_2 \mathbf{V} \times_3 \mathbf{W} \\ &= \mathcal{X} - \mathcal{X} \times_1 \mathbf{U}\mathbf{U}^\intercal \times_2 \mathbf{V}\mathbf{V}^\intercal \times_3 \mathbf{W}\mathbf{W}^\intercal. \end{aligned} \tag{6.4}$$

Thus, we obtain an optimization problem equivalent to Eq. (6.1), but it is now in terms of only the three factor matrices and with no dependency of the core $\mathcal{G}$:

$$\begin{aligned} \min \quad & \|\mathcal{X} - \mathcal{X} \times_1 \mathbf{U}\mathbf{U}^\intercal \times_2 \mathbf{V}\mathbf{V}^\intercal \times_3 \mathbf{W}\mathbf{W}^\intercal\| \\ \text{subject to} \quad & \mathbf{U} \in \mathbb{O}^{m \times q}, \mathbf{V} \in \mathbb{O}^{n \times r}, \mathbf{W} \in \mathbb{O}^{p \times s}. \end{aligned} \tag{6.5}$$

Equivalence to Maximization

We can use the elimination of $\mathcal{G}$ to rewrite the objective function as a maximization problem, as elucidated in Proposition 6.1.

Proposition 6.1 (Alternative 3-way Tucker Optimization Problem) *Let $\mathcal{X}$ be a 3-way tensor of size $m \times n \times p$. Let $\mathbf{U} \in \mathbb{O}^{m \times q}$, $\mathbf{V} \in \mathbb{O}^{n \times r}$, and $\mathbf{W} \in \mathbb{O}^{p \times s}$ be orthonormal matrices. If $\mathcal{G} = \mathcal{X} \times_1 \mathbf{U}^\intercal \times_2 \mathbf{V}^\intercal \times_3 \mathbf{W}^\intercal$ and $\mathcal{T} = [\![\mathcal{G}; \mathbf{U}, \mathbf{V}, \mathbf{W}]\!]$, then*

$$\|\mathcal{X} - \mathcal{T}\|^2 = \|\mathcal{X}\|^2 - \|\mathcal{G}\|^2 = \|\mathcal{X}\|^2 - \|\mathcal{X} \times_1 \mathbf{U}^\intercal \times_2 \mathbf{V}^\intercal \times_3 \mathbf{W}^\intercal\|^2.$$

Proof. Let the conditions of the proposition hold. Then we have

$$\begin{aligned} \|\mathcal{X} - \mathcal{T}\|^2 &= \|\text{vec}(\mathcal{X})\|_2^2 - 2\langle \text{vec}(\mathcal{X}), \text{vec}(\mathcal{T}) \rangle + \|\text{vec}(\mathcal{T})\|_2^2 && \text{by Proposition A.1} \\ &= \|\mathcal{X}\|^2 - 2\langle \text{vec}(\mathcal{X}), \text{vec}(\mathcal{T}) \rangle + \|\mathcal{G}\|^2 && \text{by Exercise 5.7} \\ &= \|\mathcal{X}\|^2 - 2\langle \text{vec}(\mathcal{X}), (\mathbf{W} \otimes \mathbf{V} \otimes \mathbf{U}) \,\text{vec}(\mathcal{G}) \rangle + \|\mathcal{G}\|^2 && \text{by Proposition 5.6} \\ &= \|\mathcal{X}\|^2 - 2\langle (\mathbf{W}^\intercal \otimes \mathbf{V}^\intercal \otimes \mathbf{U}^\intercal) \,\text{vec}(\mathcal{X}), \text{vec}(\mathcal{G}) \rangle + \|\mathcal{G}\|^2 && \text{by Proposition A.4} \\ &= \|\mathcal{X}\|^2 - 2\langle \mathcal{X} \times_1 \mathbf{U}^\intercal \times_2 \mathbf{V}^\intercal \times_3 \mathbf{W}^\intercal, \mathcal{G} \rangle + \|\mathcal{G}\|^2 && \text{by Proposition 5.6} \\ &= \|\mathcal{X}\|^2 - \|\mathcal{G}\|^2 && \text{by Eq. (6.3).} \end{aligned}$$

Hence, the claim. □

Proposition 6.1 shows that the squared objective function in Eq. (6.1), equivalently Eq. (6.5), can be expressed instead as

$$\|\mathcal{X}\|^2 - \|\mathcal{X} \times_1 \mathbf{U}^\intercal \times_2 \mathbf{V}^\intercal \times_3 \mathbf{W}^\intercal\|^2.$$

In the context of optimization, the first term can be ignored, since it is constant. Thus, an optimal rank-(q, r, s) Tucker approximation of $\mathcal{X} \in \mathbb{R}^{m \times n \times p}$, i.e., a minimizer of Eq. (6.5), is the solution to

$$\max \|\mathcal{X} \times_1 \mathbf{U}^\intercal \times_2 \mathbf{V}^\intercal \times_3 \mathbf{W}^\intercal\| \quad \text{subject to} \quad \mathbf{U} \in \mathbb{O}^{m \times q}, \mathbf{V} \in \mathbb{O}^{n \times r}, \mathbf{W} \in \mathbb{O}^{p \times s}. \tag{6.6}$$

This is also a solution of the original optimization problem in Eq. (6.1) with the optimal core given by Eq. (6.3).

The idea is that we want to find the optimal combination of modewise subspaces (defined by the ranges of the factor matrices) to produce a compressed representation,

$$\mathcal{G} = \mathcal{X} \times_1 \mathbf{U}^\intercal \times_2 \mathbf{V}^\intercal \times_3 \mathbf{W}^\intercal,$$

with maximal norm, as pictured in Fig. 6.1. The larger that norm is, the closer the approximation is to $\mathcal{X}$.

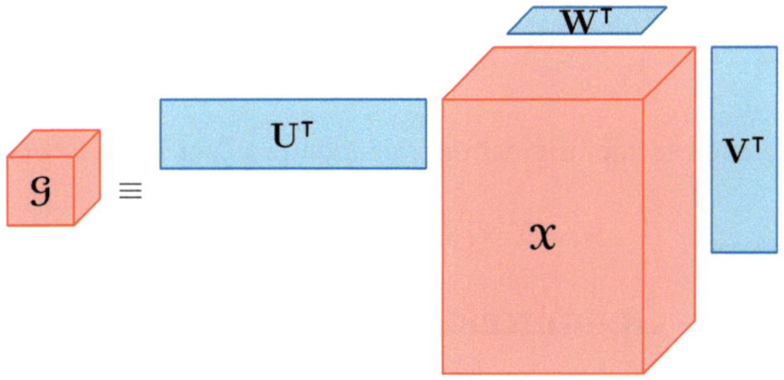

Figure 6.1 Compressing $\mathcal{X}$ to Tucker format $\mathcal{G} \equiv \mathcal{X} \times_1 \mathbf{U}^\intercal \times_2 \mathbf{V}^\intercal \times_3 \mathbf{W}^\intercal$.

> ***Remark 6.2*** (Norm of tucker core) If the Tucker decomposition is exact, then $\|\mathcal{G}\|^2 = \|\mathcal{X}\|^2$. This means that $\mathcal{G}$ has captured the entirety of $\mathcal{X}$ and the compression is lossless. Otherwise, we have lossy compression, with $\|\mathcal{G}\|^2/\|\mathcal{X}\|^2 \in [0,1]$ indicating how well $\mathcal{G}$ represents $\mathcal{X}$.

6.1.2 Tucker Optimization Problem for d-way Tensors

The d-way Tucker optimization problem is analogous to the 3-way case. It is still a nonlinear, nonconvex, least squares optimization problem. The optimal rank-$(r_1, r_2, \ldots, r_d)$ Tucker decomposition of $\mathcal{X} \in \mathbb{R}^{n_1 \times n_2 \times \cdots \times n_d}$ is a solution to

$$\begin{aligned} \min \quad & \|\mathcal{X} - \mathcal{G} \times_1 \mathbf{U}_1 \times_2 \mathbf{U}_2 \cdots \times_d \mathbf{U}_d\| \\ \text{subject to} \quad & \mathcal{G} \in \mathbb{R}^{r_1 \times r_2 \times \cdots \times r_d} \quad \text{and} \quad \mathbf{U}_k \in \mathbb{R}^{n_k \times r_k} \quad \text{for all} \quad k \in [d]. \end{aligned} \tag{6.7}$$

Exercise 6.1 (Optimal Core for d-way Tucker Decomposition) If orthonormal $\mathbf{U}_k$ matrices are fixed for all $k \in [d]$, show that $\mathcal{G} = \mathcal{X} \times_1 \mathbf{U}_1^\intercal \times_2 \mathbf{U}_2^\intercal \cdots \times_d \mathbf{U}_d^\intercal$ optimizes Eq. (6.7).

Imposing orthonormality on the factor matrices, we can eliminate the core tensor to obtain the formulation:

$$\begin{aligned} \min \quad & \|\mathcal{X} - \mathcal{X} \times_1 \mathbf{U}_1\mathbf{U}_1^\intercal \cdots \times_d \mathbf{U}_d\mathbf{U}_d^\intercal\| \\ \text{subject to} \quad & \mathbf{U}_k \in \mathbb{O}^{n_k \times r_k} \quad \text{for all} \quad k \in [d]. \end{aligned} \tag{6.8}$$

We can also derive a d-way version of Proposition 6.1, as follows.

Proposition 6.3 (Alternative d-way Tucker Optimization Problem) *Let $\mathcal{X}$ be a d-way tensor of size $n_1 \times n_2 \times \cdots \times n_d$. Let $\mathbf{U}_k \in \mathbb{O}^{n_k \times r_k}$ for all $k \in [d]$ be orthonormal matrices. If $\mathcal{G} = \mathcal{X} \times_1 \mathbf{U}_1^\intercal \times_2 \mathbf{U}_2^\intercal \cdots \times_d \mathbf{U}_d^\intercal$ and $\mathcal{T} = [\![\mathcal{G}; \mathbf{U}_1, \mathbf{U}_2, \ldots, \mathbf{U}_d]\!]$, then*

$$\|\mathcal{X} - \mathcal{T}\|^2 = \|\mathcal{X}\|^2 - \|\mathcal{G}\|^2 = \|\mathcal{X}\|^2 - \|\mathcal{X} \times_1 \mathbf{U}_1^\intercal \times_2 \mathbf{U}_2^\intercal \cdots \times_d \mathbf{U}_d^\intercal\|^2.$$

Exercise 6.2 Prove Proposition 6.3.

Finally, an optimal rank-$(r_1, r_2, \ldots, r_d)$ Tucker decomposition of $\mathcal{X} \in \mathbb{R}^{n_1 \times n_2 \times \cdots \times n_d}$, i.e., a minimizer of Eq. (6.8), is a solution to

$$\max \left\|\mathcal{X} \times_1 \mathbf{U}_1^\intercal \times_2 \mathbf{U}_2^\intercal \cdots \times_d \mathbf{U}_d^\intercal\right\| \quad \text{subject to} \quad \mathbf{U}_k \in \mathbb{O}^{n_k \times r_k} \text{ for all } k \in [d]. \tag{6.9}$$

This is also a solution to the original optimization problem in Eq. (6.7) with the optimal core given by

$$\mathcal{G} = \mathcal{X} \times_1 \mathbf{U}_1^\intercal \times_2 \mathbf{U}_2^\intercal \cdots \times_d \mathbf{U}_d^\intercal. \tag{6.10}$$

6.1.3 Modewise Optimization

The Tucker optimization problem as given in Eqs. (6.6) and (6.9) maximizes over all factor matrices simultaneously. If we restrict our attention to a single mode's factor matrices, keeping all others fixed, then the problem simplifies. For example, if we fix $\mathbf{U}$ and $\mathbf{V}$ and solve for $\mathbf{W}$, then Eq. (6.6) becomes

$$\max \left\|\mathcal{X} \times_1 \mathbf{U}^\intercal \times_2 \mathbf{V}^\intercal \times_3 \mathbf{W}^\intercal\right\| \quad \text{subject to} \quad \mathbf{W} \in \mathbb{O}^{p \times s},$$

or equivalently unfolded in the third mode (see Proposition 5.5),

$$\max \left\|\mathbf{W}^\intercal \mathbf{X}_{(3)}(\mathbf{V} \otimes \mathbf{U})\right\|_F \quad \text{subject to} \quad \mathbf{W} \in \mathbb{O}^{p \times s}. \tag{6.11}$$

The matrix $\mathbf{X}_{(3)}(\mathbf{V} \otimes \mathbf{U})$ is fixed, so Eq. (6.11) can be expressed as

$$\max \|\mathbf{W}^\intercal \mathbf{Y}\|_F \quad \text{subject to} \quad \mathbf{W} \in \mathbb{O}^{p \times s},$$

where $\mathbf{Y} = \mathbf{X}_{(3)}(\mathbf{V} \otimes \mathbf{U})$. This maximization problem is an alternative formulation of the low-rank matrix approximation problem, and it is discussed in detail in Section A.8. By Theorem A.26, the optimal $\mathbf{W} \in \mathbb{O}^{s \times p}$ is given by the leading s left singular vectors of the SVD of $\mathbf{Y}$ and satisfies

$$\|\mathbf{Y}\|_F^2 - \|\mathbf{W}^\intercal \mathbf{Y}\|_F^2 = \|(\mathbf{I} - \mathbf{W}\mathbf{W}^\intercal)\mathbf{Y}\|_F^2 = \sum_{i=s+1}^{p} \sigma_i(\mathbf{Y})^2,$$

where $\sigma_i(\mathbf{Y})$ denotes the ith singular value of $\mathbf{Y}$. Instead of specifying s, it is also possible to specify an absolute error tolerance ε and choose the minimum s such that $\|(\mathbf{I} - \mathbf{W}\mathbf{W}^\intercal)\mathbf{Y}\|_F \leq \varepsilon$. The latter is useful in choosing the rank to satisfy a specified error threshold.

Each of our Tucker decomposition algorithms will use this modewise optimization, so we provide the **leading left singular vectors (LLSV)** subroutine in Algorithm 6.1 for this procedure. It computes the r leading left singular vectors of a given input matrix, and it determines the appropriate r if the algorithm is given an error threshold, ε, rather than r.

Algorithm 6.1 Leading Left Singular Vectors (LLSV)

Require: $\mathbf{Y} \in \mathbb{R}^{m \times n}$, target rank $r \leq \min\{m, n\}$ or absolute error tolerance $\varepsilon \geq 0$
Ensure: $\mathbf{W} \in \mathbb{O}^{m \times r}$ and $\textsc{Err} \equiv \|(\mathbf{I} - \mathbf{W}\mathbf{W}^\intercal)\mathbf{Y}\|_F$, where $\|\mathbf{W}^\intercal\mathbf{Y}\|_F$ is maximal and, if ε is given, r is selected such that $\textsc{Err} \leq \varepsilon$

1: **function** LLSV($\mathbf{Y}, r$ or ε)
2: $\{\mathbf{U}, \mathbf{\Sigma}, \mathbf{V}\} \leftarrow \text{SVD}(\mathbf{Y})$ ▷ Use economy SVD, $\mathbf{\Sigma} = \text{diag}\{\sigma_1, \sigma_2, \ldots, \sigma_m\}$
3: **if** ε specified **then**
4: $r \leftarrow \min\{ r \in [m] \mid \sum_{i=r+1}^{m} \sigma_i^2 \leq \varepsilon^2 \}$ ▷ Determine rank
5: **end if**
6: $\mathbf{W} \leftarrow \mathbf{U}(:, 1{:}r)$ ▷ r leading left singular vectors of $\mathbf{Y}$
7: $\textsc{Err} \leftarrow (\sum_{i=r+1}^{m} \sigma_i^2)^{1/2}$
8: **return** $\{\mathbf{W}, \textsc{Err}\}$
9: **end function**

For simplicity, the algorithm calls an SVD routine which returns left and right singular vectors, and the complexity is $\mathcal{O}(\min\{m^2n, mn^2\})$. See Section A.5.3 for a discussion of the SVD. In practice, we do not need to compute the right singular vectors, which can save computational cost; see Section A.5.5.

Exercise 6.3 Implement Algorithm 6.1 using a standard SVD routine.

If $m < n$, as will often be the case for Tucker decomposition, we can compute things differently. Let the eigendecomposition of the $m \times m$ symmetric Gram matrix $\mathbf{Y}\mathbf{Y}^\intercal$ be

$$\mathbf{U}\mathbf{\Lambda}\mathbf{U}^\intercal = \mathbf{Y}\mathbf{Y}^\intercal,$$

where $\mathbf{U}$ is orthogonal and $\mathbf{\Lambda} = \text{diag}\{\lambda_1, \lambda_2, \ldots, \lambda_d\}$ sorted so that $\lambda_1 \geq \lambda_2 \geq \cdots \geq \lambda_m$. The left singular vectors of $\mathbf{Y}$ are given by $\mathbf{U}$ and its singular values are $\sigma_i^2 = \lambda_i$ for all $i \in [m]$ (see Eq. (A.15)). Forming $\mathbf{Y}\mathbf{Y}^\intercal$ is a symmetric matrix–matrix multiply for a cost of $\mathcal{O}(m^2n)$ and the complexity of the eigenvalue problem is $\mathcal{O}(m^3)$; see Section A.5.4. Because the constants are better, this is generally more efficient than computing the SVD using standard techniques, though it is not as numerically accurate.

If $m > n$, then computing the eigendecomposition of $\mathbf{Y}\mathbf{Y}^\intercal$ is more expensive than standard approaches. It is possible to compute the eigendecomposition of $\mathbf{Y}^\intercal\mathbf{Y}$, which is a smaller matrix in this case, but its eigenvectors are the *right* singular vectors $\mathbf{V}$ of $\mathbf{Y}$. We can recover the left singular vectors using $\mathbf{U} = \mathbf{Y}\mathbf{V}\mathbf{\Sigma}^{-1}$. While this reduces the computational cost by a constant factor compared to using standard techniques, it is also not as numerically accurate.

Exercise 6.4 (LLSV with Gram Matrix and Eigendecomposition) Implement Algorithm 6.1 using the eigendecomposition of the Gram matrix approach we just described instead of a standard SVD routine when $m < n$. Verify that the codes produce the same results. Compare the timing of the two variations for (a) $m = 500$ and $n = 500$, (b) $m = 500$ and $n = 5000$, and (c) $m = 500$ and $n = 50{,}000$.

If $\mathbf{Y}$ is a mode-k unfolding of a tensor, as will be the case for the Tucker decomposition, it is possible to compute the Gram matrix $\mathbf{Y}\mathbf{Y}^\intercal$ without any permutation of the original tensor, saving memory movement cost; see Example 2.13.

If the rank is relatively small, then an iterative method is also an option for computing the SVD. In this case, only the largest singular values are computed. Then Line 4 can be replaced with

$$r = \min\left\{ r \in [m] \;\middle|\; \sum_{i=1}^{r} \sigma_i^2 \geq (1-\varepsilon^2)\|\mathbf{Y}\|_F^2 \right\}, \tag{6.12}$$

and Line 7 can be replaced with $\text{ERR} = (\|\mathbf{Y}\|_F^2 - \sum_{i=1}^{r} \sigma_i^2)^{1/2}$.

Exercise 6.5 Prove Eq. (6.12) and Line 4 of Algorithm 6.1 are mathematically equivalent.

6.2 Higher-Order SVD

The (truncated) **higher-order SVD (HOSVD)** is the simplest Tucker decomposition algorithm. The idea is to perform the modewise optimization in each mode independently, ignoring the factor matrices in the other modes. HOSVD was proposed by Tucker (1966) as the Tucker1 method and popularized under its current name by De Lathauwer et al. (2000a). It is sometimes also referred to as the multilinear SVD (MLSVD).

Even though HOSVD optimizes each mode independently, it produces a quasi-optimal decomposition, with an approximation error within a factor of $\sqrt{d}$ of the optimal solution. We present the algorithm and its computational cost in this section, and prove the quasi-optimality in Chapter 7.

6.2.1 HOSVD for 3-way Tensors

Algorithm 6.3 gives the HOSVD algorithm to compute a rank-(q, r, s) Tucker decomposition. It computes each factor matrix independently as the leading left singular vectors of the corresponding modewise unfolding. Finally, it computes the core and the absolute error of the approximation. Note that the error computation uses Proposition 6.1, making it cheap to compute.

If $\varepsilon \geq 0$ is specified rather than rank (q, r, s), we choose the mode ranks using a key property of HOSVD (shown later in Theorem 7.3):

$$\|\mathcal{X} - \mathcal{T}\|^2 \leq \|(\mathbf{I} - \mathbf{U}\mathbf{U}^\intercal)\mathbf{X}_{(1)}\|_F^2 + \|(\mathbf{I} - \mathbf{V}\mathbf{V}^\intercal)\mathbf{X}_{(2)}\|_F^2 + \|(\mathbf{I} - \mathbf{W}\mathbf{W}^\intercal)\mathbf{X}_{(3)}\|_F^2.$$

Hence, if LLSV chooses the mode ranks such that the relative errors $\varepsilon_1, \varepsilon_2, \varepsilon_3$ are all no greater than $(\varepsilon/\sqrt{3})\|\mathcal{X}\|$, then the final solution is guaranteed to satisfy $\|\mathcal{X} - \mathcal{T}\| \leq \varepsilon\|\mathcal{X}\|$. Note that the LLSV input tolerance is for absolute error while the HOSVD input tolerance is for relative error. We can also adjust the error tolerance specified for later modes based on the actual errors in previous modes; e.g., if $\varepsilon_1 \ll (\varepsilon/\sqrt{3})\|\mathcal{X}\|$ due to a large gap in singular values, then ε_2 and ε_3 can be larger.

Complexity Analysis

The complexity analysis of Algorithm 6.2 depends on that of the LLSV function. For an $m \times n$ matrix, we assume the complexity is $\mathcal{O}(\min\{m, n\}mn)$. However, we note that the hidden constant and the accuracy depends on the underlying SVD algorithm used, and sometimes the complexity can be greatly reduced for lower accuracy guarantees by, e.g., using iterative methods if the matrix is sparse.

The overall cost of the LLSVs in Lines 4–6 can be written as

$$\mathcal{O}\big((\min\{m, np\} + \min\{n, mp\} + \min\{p, mn\})\, mnp\big). \tag{6.13}$$

Algorithm 6.2 Higher-Order SVD (HOSVD) for 3-way Tensor

Require: $\mathcal{X} \in \mathbb{R}^{m \times n \times p}$, rank $(q, r, s) \in [m] \otimes [n] \otimes [p]$ or relative error tolerance $\varepsilon \geq 0$
Ensure: Tucker tensor $\mathcal{T}$ of rank (q, r, s) with $\mathcal{T} \approx \mathcal{X}$ or $\text{ERR} \equiv \|\mathcal{X} - \mathcal{T}\| \leq \varepsilon \|\mathcal{X}\|$
1: **function** HOSVD($\mathcal{X}$, (q, r, s) or ε)
2: $\quad \chi \leftarrow \|\mathcal{X}\|$
3: $\quad$ **if** ε defined **then** $\bar{\varepsilon} \leftarrow (\varepsilon/\sqrt{3})\chi$
4: $\quad [\mathbf{U}, \varepsilon_1] \leftarrow \text{LLSV}(\mathbf{X}_{(1)}, q \text{ or } \bar{\varepsilon})$ $\quad \triangleright$ q leading left sing. vectors of $\mathbf{X}_{(1)}$
5: $\quad [\mathbf{V}, \varepsilon_2] \leftarrow \text{LLSV}(\mathbf{X}_{(2)}, r \text{ or } \bar{\varepsilon})$ $\quad \triangleright$ r leading left sing. vectors of $\mathbf{X}_{(2)}$
6: $\quad [\mathbf{W}, \varepsilon_3] \leftarrow \text{LLSV}(\mathbf{X}_{(3)}, s \text{ or } \bar{\varepsilon})$ $\quad \triangleright$ s leading left sing. vectors of $\mathbf{X}_{(3)}$
7: $\quad \mathcal{G} \leftarrow \mathcal{X} \times_1 \mathbf{U}^\intercal \times_2 \mathbf{V}^\intercal \times_3 \mathbf{W}^\intercal$ $\quad \triangleright$ Compress in all modes
8: $\quad \text{ERR} \leftarrow (\chi^2 - \|\mathcal{G}\|^2)^{1/2}$ $\quad \triangleright$ Equivalent to $\|\mathcal{X} - \mathcal{T}\|$
9: $\quad$ **return** $\{\mathcal{G}, \mathbf{U}, \mathbf{V}, \mathbf{W}, \text{ERR}\}$ $\quad \triangleright$ $\mathcal{T} \equiv [\![\mathcal{G}; \mathbf{U}, \mathbf{V}, \mathbf{W}]\!]$
10: **end function**

If $m \leq np$, $n \leq mp$, and $p \leq mn$, then this simplifies to

$$\mathcal{O}(m^2np + mn^2p + mnp^2).$$

Next, consider the cost of the multi-TTM operation in Line 7 to compute $\mathcal{G}$. As shown in Section 3.3, TTM is an associative operation across modes, so we can choose the order of operations. If we order the multi-TTM as $(1, 2, 3)$, the cost is

$$\mathcal{O}(mnpq + npqr + pqrs). \tag{6.14}$$

The first term corresponds to computing $\mathcal{X} \times_1 \mathbf{U}^\intercal$, the second term corresponds to that result times $\mathbf{V}^\intercal$ in mode 2, and the third term corresponds to that result times $\mathbf{W}^\intercal$ in mode 3. Thus, the multi-TTM cost is usually dominated by the first TTM. In the 3-way case, it is straightforward to enumerate the cost of all six orderings and choose the most efficient; see Section 3.4.

Comparing Eq. (6.13) with Eq. (6.14), we see that the overall cost of HOSVD is dominated by the cost of the LLSVs, since it must be the case that $q \leq \min\{m, np\}$, $r \leq \min\{n, mp\}$ and $s \leq \min\{p, mn\}$.

Exercise 6.6 Consider the Miranda tensor of size $2048 \times 256 \times 256$.

(a) Compute the ratio of computational complexity of each line of Lines 4–7 in Algorithm 6.3 for $(q, s, r) = (600, 100, 100)$ versus $(q, s, r) = (300, 50, 50)$.
(b) Use HOSVD to compute a rank-$(600, 100, 100)$ Tucker decomposition. How long did it take? What is the error?
(c) Use HOSVD to compute a rank-$(300, 50, 50)$ Tucker decomposition. How long did it take? What is the error?
(d) What is the ratio of computation times for each step for the two ranks? How does it compare to the ratios estimated based on the computational complexity?

6.2.2 HOSVD for d-way Tensors

The HOSVD algorithm to compute a rank-$(r_1, r_2, \ldots, r_d)$ Tucker decomposition of a d-way tensor $\mathcal{X}$ is presented in Algorithm 6.3. The kth factor matrix is the r_k leading singular vectors of the mode-k unfolding of $\mathcal{X}$. The algorithm's last steps compute the core and absolute error of the approximation. The error computation uses Proposition 6.3 to compute the error implicitly and inexpensively.

If $\varepsilon \geq 0$ is specified rather than rank $(r_1, r_2, \ldots, r_d)$, then we want to compute a solution such that $\|\mathcal{X} - \mathcal{T}\| \leq \varepsilon\|\mathcal{X}\|$. We use the following property of HOSVD (looking ahead to Theorem 7.4):

$$\|\mathcal{X} - \mathcal{T}\|^2 \leq \sum_{k=1}^{d} \|\mathcal{X} \times_k (\mathbf{I} - \mathbf{U}_k\mathbf{U}_k^{\intercal})\|_F^2.$$

Hence, if each factor matrix satisfies $\|(\mathbf{I} - \mathbf{U}_k\mathbf{U}_k^{\intercal})\mathbf{X}_{(k)}\|_F \leq (\varepsilon/\sqrt{d})\|\mathbf{X}_{(k)}\|_F$, then the final solution is guaranteed to satisfy $\|\mathcal{X} - \mathcal{T}\| \leq \varepsilon\|\mathcal{X}\|$. As in the 3-way case, we can use any division of the errors among the modes, including adaptive techniques, but here we opt for the same error in each mode.

Algorithm 6.3 Higher-Order SVD (HOSVD) for d-way Tensor

Require: $\mathcal{X} \in \mathbb{R}^{n_1 \times n_2 \times \cdots \times n_d}$, rank $(r_1, r_2, \ldots, r_d)$ or relative error tolerance $\varepsilon \geq 0$
Ensure: Tucker tensor $\mathcal{T}$ of rank $(r_1, r_2, \ldots, r_d)$ with $\mathcal{T} \approx \mathcal{X}$ or $\text{ERR} \equiv \|\mathcal{X} - \mathcal{T}\| \leq \varepsilon\|\mathcal{X}\|$

1: **function** HOSVD($\mathcal{X}$, $(r_1, r_2, \ldots, r_d)$ or ε)
2: $\quad \chi \leftarrow \|\mathcal{X}\|$
3: $\quad$ **if** ε defined **then** $\bar{\varepsilon} \leftarrow (\varepsilon/\sqrt{d})\chi$
4: $\quad$ **for** $k = 1, \ldots, d$ **do**
5: $\quad\quad [\mathbf{U}_k, \varepsilon_k] \leftarrow \text{LLSV}(\mathbf{X}_{(k)}, r_k \text{ or } \bar{\varepsilon})$ $\quad \triangleright$ r_k leading left sing. vectors of $\mathbf{X}_{(k)}$
6: $\quad$ **end for**
7: $\quad \mathcal{G} \leftarrow \mathcal{X} \times_1 \mathbf{U}_1^{\intercal} \times_2 \mathbf{U}_2^{\intercal} \cdots \times_d \mathbf{U}_d^{\intercal}$ $\quad \triangleright$ Compress in all modes
8: $\quad \text{ERR} \leftarrow (\chi^2 - \|\mathcal{G}\|^2)^{1/2}$ $\quad \triangleright$ Equivalent to $\|\mathcal{X} - \mathcal{T}\|$
9: $\quad$ **return** $\{\mathcal{G}, \mathbf{U}_1, \mathbf{U}_2, \ldots, \mathbf{U}_d, \text{ERR}\}$ $\quad \triangleright$ $\mathcal{T} \equiv [\![\mathcal{G}; \mathbf{U}_1, \mathbf{U}_2, \ldots, \mathbf{U}_d]\!]$
10: **end function**

Complexity Analysis

Defining $N = \prod_{k=1}^{d} n_k$ and $N_k = \prod_{\ell \neq k} n_\ell$, the total cost of the LLSVs in Lines 4–6 is

$$\mathcal{O}\left(N \sum_{k=1}^{d} \min\{n_k, N_k\}\right).$$

If we assume $n_k \leq N_k$, this simplifies to $\mathcal{O}(N \sum_{k=1}^{d} n_k)$. The cost for the multi-TTM in Line 7 to compute $\mathcal{G}$ is

$$\mathcal{O}\left(\sum_{k=1}^{d}\left(\prod_{\ell=1}^{k} r_\ell\right)\left(\prod_{\ell=k}^{d} n_\ell\right)\right) = \mathcal{O}\Big(r_1 N + r_1 r_2 n_2 n_3 \cdots n_d + \cdots + r_1 r_2 \cdots r_d n_d\Big).$$

As in the 3-way case, we can change the order of the TTMs (per Proposition 3.19) to minimize the computational complexity. No matter the order of the TTMs, the cost of the LLSVs dominate the overall complexity of HOSVD because $r_k \leq n_k$ for all k.

Exercise 6.7 (a) Implement HOSVD. (b) With the Miranda scientific simulation tensor, compute the HOSVD for a rank of $232 \times 43 \times 41$, timing each call to LLSV and the TTM compression step. (c) How do the timings compare?

Exercise 6.8 With the Miranda scientific simulation tensor, denoted $\mathcal{X}$, compute an approximation that maximizes compression subject to satisfying a relative error tolerance $\varepsilon = 10^{-2}$ in the following ways.

(a) Compute a low-rank matrix approximation of $\mathbf{X}_{(1)}$.
(b) Compute a low-rank matrix approximation of $\mathbf{X}_{(2)}$.
(c) Compute a low-rank matrix approximation of $\mathbf{X}_{(3)}$.
(d) Compute a Tucker approximation using HOSVD.
(e) Compare and analyze your results in terms of computation time, final accuracy, and storage requirements.
(f) What method gives the greatest compression?

6.3 Sequentially Truncated HOSVD

We can improve the efficiency of HOSVD using a technique called sequential truncation. The HOSVD computes all the factor matrices and *then* computes the core. In contrast, the **sequentially truncated higher-order SVD (ST-HOSVD)** computes a factor matrix in a mode and then compresses the tensor in that mode *before* computing the next factor matrix. Vannieuwenhoven et al. (2012) introduced this approach and coined the name *sequentially truncated HOSVD*; Hackbusch (2019) simultaneously developed the same idea under the name *successive HOSVD projection*. ST-HOSVD differs from HOSVD in that it selects each factor matrix in turn, taking into account the effects of the prior selections. As a result, it is more computationally efficient than HOSVD and often (but not always) yields a better solution. The order of computation impacts the computational cost and the result, and different orders produce different Tucker representations with different approximation errors. Like HOSVD, ST-HOSVD produces a quasi-optimal decomposition for any order, with an approximation error within a factor of $\sqrt{d}$ of the optimal solution. We present the algorithm and its computational cost in this section, and we prove the error decomposition and quasi-optimality in Chapter 7.

6.3.1 ST-HOSVD for 3-way Tensors

ST-HOSVD for a 3-way tensor is given in Algorithm 6.4, which can take the target rank (p, q, r) as input. After each factor matrix is computed, the tensor is truncated in that mode so that the size of the tensor is successively reduced, and the truncation in the last mode produces the core tensor of the Tucker representation.

If we are instead given an error tolerance ε as input to Algorithm 6.4, then we use the following error decomposition of ST-HOSVD (detailed later in Theorem 7.5):

$$\|\mathcal{X} - \mathcal{T}\|^2 = \|(\mathbf{I} - \mathbf{U}\mathbf{U}^\intercal)\mathbf{X}_{(1)}\|_F^2 + \|(\mathbf{I} - \mathbf{V}\mathbf{V}^\intercal)\mathbf{Y}_{(2)}\|_F^2 + \|(\mathbf{I} - \mathbf{W}\mathbf{W}^\intercal)\mathbf{Z}_{(3)}\|_F^2, \quad (6.15)$$

where $\mathcal{Y} = \mathcal{X} \times_1 \mathbf{U}^\intercal$ and $\mathcal{Z} = \mathcal{X} \times_1 \mathbf{U}^\intercal \times_2 \mathbf{V}^\intercal$. Hence, if each summand has error less than or equal to $(\varepsilon/\sqrt{3})\|\mathcal{X}\|$, the final solution satisfies $\|\mathcal{X} - \mathcal{T}\| \leq \varepsilon\|\mathcal{X}\|$ with $\|\mathcal{X} - \mathcal{T}\|^2 = \varepsilon_1^2 + \varepsilon_2^2 + \varepsilon_3^2$.

As with HOSVD, we can adjust the error tolerance specified for later modes based on the actual errors in previous modes. In the case of ST-HOSVD, we have computed the error exactly (rather than only an upper bound), so the adjustments can be more precise.

The decomposition of the error in Eq. (6.15) also implies that the absolute error of the approximation can be computed directly from the errors returned by LLSV, as given in Line 9.

Algorithm 6.4 Sequentially Truncated HOSVD (ST-HOSVD) for 3-way Tensor

Require: $\mathcal{X} \in \mathbb{R}^{m \times n \times p}$, rank (q, r, s) or relative error tolerance $\varepsilon \geq 0$
Ensure: Tucker tensor $\mathcal{T}$ of rank (q, r, s) with $\mathcal{T} \approx \mathcal{X}$ or $\text{ERR} \equiv \|\mathcal{X} - \mathcal{T}\| \leq \varepsilon \|\mathcal{X}\|$

1: **function** ST-HOSVD($\mathcal{X}$, (q, r, s) or ε)
2:     **if** ε defined **then** $\bar{\varepsilon} \leftarrow (\varepsilon/\sqrt{3})\|\mathcal{X}\|$
3:     $[\mathbf{U}, \varepsilon_1] \leftarrow \text{LLSV}(\mathbf{X}_{(1)}, q \text{ or } \bar{\varepsilon})$ ▷ q leading left sing. vectors of $\mathbf{X}_{(1)}$
4:     $\mathcal{Y} \leftarrow \mathcal{X} \times_1 \mathbf{U}^\intercal$ ▷ Compress mode 1
5:     $[\mathbf{V}, \varepsilon_2] \leftarrow \text{LLSV}(\mathbf{Y}_{(2)}, r \text{ or } \bar{\varepsilon})$ ▷ r leading left sing. vectors of $\mathbf{Y}_{(2)}$
6:     $\mathcal{Z} \leftarrow \mathcal{Y} \times_2 \mathbf{V}^\intercal$ ▷ Compress mode 2
7:     $[\mathbf{W}, \varepsilon_3] \leftarrow \text{LLSV}(\mathbf{Z}_{(3)}, s \text{ or } \bar{\varepsilon})$ ▷ s leading left sing. vectors of $\mathbf{Z}_{(3)}$
8:     $\mathcal{G} \leftarrow \mathcal{Z} \times_3 \mathbf{W}^\intercal$ ▷ Compress mode 3
9:     $\text{ERR} \leftarrow (\varepsilon_1^2 + \varepsilon_2^2 + \varepsilon_3^2)^{1/2}$ ▷ Equivalent to $\|\mathcal{X} - \mathcal{T}\|$
10:     **return** $\{\, \mathcal{G}, \mathbf{U}, \mathbf{V}, \mathbf{W}, \text{ERR} \,\}$ ▷ $\mathcal{T} \equiv [\![\mathcal{G}; \mathbf{U}, \mathbf{V}, \mathbf{W}]\!]$
11: **end function**

Complexity Analysis

The complexity of each line is as follows:

- Line 3 – $\mathcal{O}(\min\{m, np\}\, mnp)$ for LLSV of $m \times np$ matrix,
- Line 4 – $\mathcal{O}(qmnp)$ for TTM,
- Line 5 – $\mathcal{O}(\min\{n, qp\}\, qnp)$ for LLSV of $n \times qp$ matrix,
- Line 6 – $\mathcal{O}(qrnp)$ for TTM,
- Line 7 – $\mathcal{O}(\min\{p, qr\}\, qrp)$ for LLSV of $p \times qr$ matrix,
- Line 8 – $\mathcal{O}(qrsp)$ for TTM.

Then the total cost of the three LLSVs is

$$\mathcal{O}(\min\{m, np\}\, mnp + \min\{n, qp\}\, qnp + \min\{p, qr\}\, qrp). \tag{6.16}$$

If we have $m \leq np$, $n \leq qp$, and $p \leq qr$, the cost of the LLSVs simplifies to

$$\mathcal{O}(m^2 np + qn^2 p + qrp^2).$$

The total cost of the three TTM truncations is

$$\mathcal{O}(mnpq + npqr + pqrs). \tag{6.17}$$

Comparing the LLSV costs of HOSVD in Eq. (6.13) and ST-HOSVD in Eq. (6.16), we see that the first terms match and that the second and third terms are smaller for ST-HOSVD by factors of at least $\frac{m}{q}$ and $\frac{mn}{qr}$, respectively, since we must have $\min\{n, qp\} \leq \min\{n, mp\}$ and $\min\{p, qr\} \leq \min\{p, mn\}$. Comparing the TTM costs of HOSVD in Eq. (6.14) and ST-HOSVD in Eq. (6.17), we see that they are equivalent, assuming the same mode order is used in both algorithms. Because the LLSV costs of HOSVD dominate those of the TTMs, the reduction in LLSV costs by ST-HOSVD is significant and leads to noticeable speedups in practice.

The intuition for the better efficiency of ST-HOSVD is that for each matrix LLSV, the number of columns involved is reduced when compared to the corresponding matrix LLSV for HOSVD. When the truncation ranks are specified in advance, the mode order can be chosen to minimize computational complexity as in the case of multi-TTM.

Exercise 6.9 Consider the Miranda scientific simulation tensor of size $2048 \times 256 \times 256$.

(a) With mode order $(1, 2, 3)$, compute the ratio of computational complexity of each of Lines 3–8 in Algorithm 6.4 for $(q, s, r) = (600, 100, 100)$ versus $(q, s, r) = (300, 50, 50)$.

(b) Use ST-HOSVD to compute a rank-$(600, 100, 100)$ Tucker decomposition of the data. How long did it take? What is the error? How does this compare to HOSVD?

(c) Use ST-HOSVD to compute a rank-$(300, 50, 50)$ Tucker decomposition. How long did it take? What is the error? How does this compare to HOSVD?

(d) What is the ratio of computation times for each step for the two ranks? How does it compare to the ratios estimated based on the computational complexity?

6.3.2 ST-HOSVD for d-way Tensors

The ST-HOSVD for a d-way tensor that takes specified rank or error as input is provided in Algorithm 6.5. The error formulation is based on the ST-HOSVD error decomposition (looking ahead to Theorem 7.6):

$$\|\mathcal{X} - \mathcal{T}\|^2 = \sum_{k=1}^{d} \|\mathcal{G}^{(k)} \times_k (\mathbf{I} - \mathbf{U}_k \mathbf{U}_k^\intercal)\|_F^2,$$

where $\mathcal{G}^{(k)} = \mathcal{X} \times_1 \mathbf{U}_1^\intercal \cdots \times_{k-1} \mathbf{U}_{k-1}^\intercal$ is the *residual tensor* at the start of iteration k. Hence, if each factor matrix satisfies

$$\left\|(\mathbf{I} - \mathbf{U}_k \mathbf{U}_k^\intercal)\mathbf{G}_{(k)}^{(k)}\right\|_F \leq (\varepsilon/\sqrt{d})\|\mathcal{X}\|,$$

the final solution satisfies $\|\mathcal{X} - \mathcal{T}\| \leq \varepsilon\|\mathcal{X}\|$ with $\|\mathcal{X} - \mathcal{T}\|^2 = \varepsilon_1^2 + \cdots + \varepsilon_d^2$ because LLSV guarantees $\varepsilon_k \leq (\varepsilon/\sqrt{d})\|\mathcal{X}\|$ for each k.

Algorithm 6.5 Sequentially Truncated HOSVD (ST-HOSVD) for d-way Tensor

Require: $\mathcal{X} \in \mathbb{R}^{n_1 \times n_2 \times \cdots \times n_d}$, rank $(r_1, r_2, \ldots, r_d)$ or relative error tolerance $\varepsilon \geq 0$
Ensure: Tucker tensor $\mathcal{T}$ of rank $(r_1, r_2, \ldots, r_d)$ with $\mathcal{T} \approx \mathcal{X}$ or $\text{ERR} \equiv \|\mathcal{X} - \mathcal{T}\| \leq \varepsilon\|\mathcal{X}\|$

```
1:  function ST-HOSVD(𝒳, (r_1, r_2, ..., r_d) or ε)
2:      if ε defined then ε̄ ← (ε/√d)‖𝒳‖
3:      𝒢 ← 𝒳
4:      for k = 1, ..., d do
5:          [U_k, ε_k] ← LLSV(G_(k), r_k or ε̄)    ▷ r_k leading left sing. vectors of residual
6:          𝒢 ← 𝒢 ×_k U_k^T                        ▷ Compress in mode k
7:      end for
8:      ERR ← (Σ_{k=1}^d ε_k^2)^{1/2}              ▷ Equivalent to ‖𝒳 − 𝒯‖
9:      return {𝒢, U_1, U_2, ..., U_d, ERR}         ▷ 𝒯 ≡ ⟦𝒢; U_1, U_2, ..., U_d⟧
10: end function
```

Complexity Analysis

Define $Q_k \equiv \prod_{\ell<k} r_\ell$ and $P_k \equiv \prod_{\ell>k} n_\ell$. Then the total cost of the LLSVs in Line 5 is

$$\mathcal{O}\left(\sum_{k=1}^{d} n_k Q_k P_k \min\{n_k, Q_k P_k\}\right).$$

If we have $n_k \le Q_k P_k$ for all $k \in [d]$, this simplifies to $\mathcal{O}(\sum_{k=1}^d n_k^2 Q_k P_k)$. The cost for the TTMs in Line 6 is the same as for Algorithm 6.3:

$$\mathcal{O}\left(\sum_{k=1}^{d}\left(\prod_{\ell=1}^{k} r_\ell\right)\left(\prod_{\ell=k}^{d} n_\ell\right)\right) = \mathcal{O}\left(\sum_{k=1}^{d} r_k n_k Q_k P_k\right).$$

Comparing to HOSVD, we see that the cost of LLSVs is reduced (except for the first one) and the cost of the TTMs matches exactly, assuming the same mode order is used. Thus, HOSVD performs more computation than ST-HOSVD, and the difference is more pronounced when the truncation ranks are small relative to the input dimensions. As in the 3-way case, when the ranks are specified in advance, we can change the mode order of the algorithm to minimize the computational complexity.

Exercise 6.10 (a) Implement ST-HOSVD. Your implementation should accept the mode order as an input parameter. (b) Repeat Exercise 6.9 with mode order $(3, 2, 1)$.

6.4 Higher-Order Orthogonal Iteration

An alternative to HOSVD and ST-HOSVD is **higher-order orthogonal iteration (HOOI)**. It is a block coordinate descent method (see Section B.3.7) that starts off with initial guesses for all the factor matrices and improves then repeatedly cycles through optimizing each factor matrix individually. It maintains orthonormality of the factor matrices at each step. This is an alternating least squares approach to solving the Tucker minimization problem as given in Eq. (6.5) for 3-way and Eq. (6.8) for d-way. It is analogous to the CP-ALS algorithm for computing CP decompositions (see Chapter 11).

In the 3-way case, this method was originally called Tucker ALS or TUCKALS3, as proposed by Kroonenberg and De Leeuw (1980). It was extended to d-way by Kapteyn et al. (1986) and now goes by the name HOOI, as popularized by De Lathauwer et al. (2000b).

Unlike HOSVD and ST-HOSVD, HOOI is an iterative algorithm, so its computational cost and approximation error depend on the number of iterations. Each iteration of HOOI is cheaper than ST-HOSVD, and the relative cost of HOOI decreases as the truncation ranks decrease. HOOI often converges quickly and can achieve an approximation error on par with HOSVD or ST-HOSVD in as few as two iterations.

While HOSVD and ST-HOSVD can be applied with specified ranks or specified error tolerance, HOOI can only be used with specified ranks.

6.4.1 HOOI for 3-way Tensors

The HOOI algorithm, given in Algorithm 6.6, starts with an initial guess for the factor matrices as input. It alternates among the factors matrices, solving for one using LLSV while holding the others fixed. This is repeated until the relative change in the error is below the threshold τ or the maximum number of iterations (MAXITERS) is exceeded.

For two factor matrices fixed, the third factor matrix can be computed via a modewise optimization, as described in Section 6.1.3. For instance, to update the second mode factor matrix $\mathbf{V}$ as in Eq. (6.11), we compute the leading left singular vectors of the mode-2 unfolding of $\mathcal{X} \times_1 \mathbf{U}^\intercal \times_3 \mathbf{W}^\intercal$, i.e., $\mathbf{X}_{(2)}(\mathbf{W} \otimes \mathbf{U})^\intercal$. The number of columns of this matrix is qs, which is generally much smaller than the number of columns of $\mathbf{X}_{(2)}$, mp. Since we are solving each subproblem exactly, the objective function value is nondecreasing.

Algorithm 6.6 Higher-Order Orthogonal Iteration (HOOI) for 3-way Tensor

Require: $\mathcal{X} \in \mathbb{R}^{m\times n\times p}$, initial matrices $\mathbf{U} \in \mathbb{R}^{q\times r}$, $\mathbf{V} \in \mathbb{R}^{n\times r}$, $\mathbf{W} \in \mathbb{R}^{p\times s}$, convergence tolerance $\tau > 0$, maximum iterations $\text{MAXITERS} \in \mathbb{N}$

Ensure: rank-(q, r, s) Tucker tensor $[\![\mathcal{G}; \mathbf{U}, \mathbf{V}, \mathbf{W}]\!] \approx \mathcal{X}$

1: **function** HOOI($\mathcal{X}, \mathbf{U}, \mathbf{V}, \mathbf{W}, \tau, \text{MAXITERS}$)
2: $\quad \chi \leftarrow \|\mathcal{X}\|$
3: $\quad$ **for** $t = 1, 2, \ldots, \text{MAXITERS}$ **do**
4: $\quad\quad \mathcal{Y} \leftarrow \mathcal{X} \times_2 \mathbf{V}^\intercal \times_3 \mathbf{W}^\intercal$
5: $\quad\quad \mathbf{U} \leftarrow \text{LLSV}(\mathbf{Y}_{(1)}, q)$ ▷ Update first factor matrix
6: $\quad\quad \mathcal{Y} \leftarrow \mathcal{X} \times_1 \mathbf{U}^\intercal \times_3 \mathbf{W}^\intercal$
7: $\quad\quad \mathbf{V} \leftarrow \text{LLSV}(\mathbf{Y}_{(2)}, r)$ ▷ Update second factor matrix
8: $\quad\quad \mathcal{Y} \leftarrow \mathcal{X} \times_1 \mathbf{U}^\intercal \times_2 \mathbf{V}^\intercal$
9: $\quad\quad \mathbf{W} \leftarrow \text{LLSV}(\mathbf{Y}_{(3)}, s)$ ▷ Update third factor matrix
10: $\quad\quad \mathcal{G} \leftarrow \mathcal{Y} \times_3 \mathbf{W}^\intercal$ ▷ Compute core
11: $\quad\quad \text{ERR}_t \leftarrow (\chi^2 - \|\mathcal{G}\|^2)^{1/2}$ ▷ Equivalent to $\|\mathcal{X} - [\![\mathcal{G}; \mathbf{U}, \mathbf{V}, \mathbf{W}]\!]\|$
12: $\quad\quad$ **if** $(t > 1)$ and $(\text{ERR}_t - \text{ERR}_{t-1} < \tau\chi)$ **then**
13: $\quad\quad\quad$ **break** ▷ Change in relative error $< \tau$
14: $\quad\quad$ **end if**
15: $\quad$ **end for**
16: $\quad$ **return** $\{\mathcal{G}, \mathbf{U}, \mathbf{V}, \mathbf{W}, \text{ERR}_t\}$ ▷ Tucker tensor is $[\![\mathcal{G}; \mathbf{U}, \mathbf{V}, \mathbf{W}]\!]$
17: **end function**

Within an iteration, for each mode, the primary operations are to compute a reduced tensor via multi-TTM and to compute the leading left singular vectors of its unfolding. The reduced tensors are much smaller than the data tensor because all but one of the modes has been reduced from the original size to the low-rank dimension.

Complexity Analysis

The cost of a HOOI iteration, assuming the multi-TTMs are computed in order, is as follows:

- Line 4 – $\mathcal{O}(mnpr + mprs)$ for multi-TTM,
- Line 5 – $\mathcal{O}(mrs\ \min\{m, rs\})$ for LLSV of $m \times rs$ matrix,
- Line 6 – $\mathcal{O}(mnpq + npqs)$ for multi-TTM,
- Line 7 – $\mathcal{O}(nqs\ \min\{n, qs\})$ for LLSV of $n \times qs$ matrix,
- Line 8 – $\mathcal{O}(mnpq + nprs)$ for multi-TTM,
- Line 9 – $\mathcal{O}(pqr\ \min\{p, qr\})$ for LLSV of $p \times qr$ matrix,
- Line 10 – $\mathcal{O}(pqrs)$ for TTM.

Observe that the multi-TTMs share some computation: Lines 6 and 8 both compute $\mathcal{X} \times_1 \mathbf{U}^\intercal$ first, and $\mathbf{U}$ doesn't change between those two lines. Thus, we can avoid the cost of recomputing that quantity (see also Section 3.6.1).

For comparison with previous algorithms, we can write the LLSV costs as

$$\mathcal{O}\big(mrs\ \min\{m, rs\} + nqs\ \min\{n, qs\} + pqr\ \min\{p, qr\}\big), \tag{6.18}$$

and the costs of the TTM truncations together are

$$\mathcal{O}(mnpq + mnpr + mprs + npqs + nprs + pqrs). \tag{6.19}$$

Compared to HOSVD and ST-HOSVD, the LLSVs are much cheaper and the TTM costs are comparable. As HOSVD and ST-HOSVD are typically dominated by LLSVs, a single iteration of HOOI is cheaper than HOSVD or ST-HOSVD, and the difference is more pronounced for smaller ranks.

Exercise 6.11 Consider the Miranda tensor of size $2048 \times 256 \times 256$.

(a) Compute the ratio of computational complexity of each of Lines 4–9 in Algorithm 6.6 for $(q, s, r) = (600, 100, 100)$ versus $(q, s, r) = (300, 50, 50)$.

(b) Use HOOI to compute a rank-$(600, 100, 100)$ Tucker decomposition. How many iterations does it take? How long did it take? What is the error?

(c) Use HOOI to compute a rank-$(60, 10, 10)$ Tucker decomposition. How many iterations does it take? How long did it take? What is the error?

(d) What is the ratio of computation times for each step for the two ranks? How does it compare to the ratios estimated based on the computational complexity?

(e) How does HOOI compare to HOSVD and ST-HOSVD in terms of accuracy and running time?

6.4.2 HOOI for d-way Tensor

As in the 3-way case, HOOI for a d-way tensor (see Algorithm 6.7) computes a solution iteratively, starting with the data tensor and initial guesses for the factor matrices. Checking for convergence can be done by tracking the norm of the core, as it determines the approximation error (see Proposition 6.1). When the error ceases to improve by a sufficient amount, the iterations can cease. When initialized randomly, HOOI can converge to an approximation error comparable to HOSVD or ST-HOSVD in as few as two iterations.

Algorithm 6.7 Higher-Order Orthogonal Iteration (HOOI) for d-way Tensors

Require: $\mathcal{X} \in \mathbb{R}^{n_1 \times n_2 \times \cdots \times n_d}$, initial matrices $\mathbf{U}_k \in \mathbb{R}^{n_k \times r_k}$ for $k \in [d]$, convergence tolerance $\tau > 0$, maximum iterations MAXITERS $\in \mathbb{N}$

Ensure: rank-$(r_1, r_2, \ldots, r_d)$ Tucker tensor $[\![\mathcal{G}; \mathbf{U}_1, \mathbf{U}_2, \ldots, \mathbf{U}_d]\!] \approx \mathcal{X}$

1: **function** HOOI($\mathcal{X}, \mathbf{U}_1, \mathbf{U}_2, \ldots, \mathbf{U}_d, \tau,$ MAXITERS)
2: $\quad \chi = \|\mathcal{X}\|$
3: $\quad$ **for** $t = 1, 2, \ldots,$ MAXITERS **do**
4: $\quad\quad$ **for** $k = 1, 2, \ldots, d$ **do**
5: $\quad\quad\quad \mathcal{Y} \leftarrow \mathcal{X} \times_1 \mathbf{U}_1^\intercal \cdots \times_{k-1} \mathbf{U}_{k-1}^\intercal \times_{k+1} \mathbf{U}_{k+1}^\intercal \cdots \times_d \mathbf{U}_d^\intercal$
6: $\quad\quad\quad \mathbf{U}_k \leftarrow \text{LLSV}(\mathbf{Y}_{(k)}, r_k)$ ▷ Update kth factor matrix
7: $\quad\quad$ **end for**
8: $\quad\quad \mathcal{G} \leftarrow \mathcal{Y} \times_d \mathbf{U}_d^\intercal$ ▷ Compute core
9: $\quad\quad \text{ERR}_t \leftarrow (\chi^2 - \|\mathcal{G}\|^2)^{1/2}$ ▷ Equivalent to $\|\mathcal{X} - [\![\mathcal{G}; \mathbf{U}_1, \mathbf{U}_2, \ldots, \mathbf{U}_d]\!]\|$
10: $\quad\quad$ **if** $(t > 1)$ and $(\text{ERR}_t - \text{ERR}_{t-1} < \tau\chi)$ **then**
11: $\quad\quad\quad$ **break** ▷ Change in relative error $< \tau$
12: $\quad\quad$ **end if**
13: $\quad$ **end for**
14: $\quad$ **return** $\{\mathcal{G}, \mathbf{U}_1, \mathbf{U}_2, \ldots, \mathbf{U}_d, \text{ERR}_t\}$ ▷ Tucker tensor is $[\![\mathcal{G}; \mathbf{U}_1, \mathbf{U}_2, \ldots, \mathbf{U}_d]\!]$
15: **end function**

Complexity Analysis

The cost of the multi-TTMs in Line 5 depends on the order they are evaluated. Assuming the TTMs are done in increasing mode order, the total TTM cost for an iteration of HOOI is given by

$$\mathcal{O}\left(\sum_{k=1}^{d} n_k \sum_{\substack{\ell=1\\ \ell\neq k}}^{d} \left(\prod_{\substack{m=1\\ m\neq k}}^{\ell} r_m\right)\left(\prod_{\substack{m=\ell\\ m\neq k}}^{d} n_m\right)\right).$$

The most expensive operation of each of the d multi-TTMs is typically the first TTM involving the full tensor $\mathcal{X}$ since its complexity involves $N = \prod_{k=1}^{d} n_k$.

To reduce the computational cost of the multi-TTMs, we can reuse partial computations per the discussion of memoization in Section 3.6.1. While the exact complexity depends on the structure of the dimension tree used, memoization typically reduces the total number of TTMs from $d^2 - d$ down to $\mathcal{O}(d \log d)$. More importantly, it reduces the number of TTMs involving the full tensor $\mathcal{X}$ (and a complexity factor of N) from d down to 2.

For $R_k \equiv \prod_{\ell\neq k} r_\ell$ for all $k \in [d]$, the cost of the LLSVs in Line 6 in a single iteration of HOOI is

$$\mathcal{O}\left(\sum_{k=1}^{d} n_k R_k \min\{n_k, R_k\}\right).$$

The cost of the final TTM to compute the core in Line 10 is $n_d \prod_{k=1}^{d} r_k$, which is typically negligible.

Thus, the cost per iteration of HOOI is dominated by TTMs, and in particular the two TTMs involving the input tensor (assuming memoization is used). Comparing the costs of HOOI to ST-HOSVD and HOSVD, we observe that a single iteration of HOOI is cheaper than the other two methods. For the rank-specified problem, whether HOOI is more efficient depends on the number of HOOI iterations performed as well as the input dimensions and truncation ranks.

Exercise 6.12 Consider the computation of a rank-$r \times r \times \cdots \times r$ approximation of a d-way tensor of size $n \times n \times \cdots \times n$. Assume $r \ll n$. (a) Compare the costs of HOOI and ST-HOSVD. (b) Approximately how many iterations of HOOI would you expect to be able to perform in the time it takes to run ST-HOSVD?

Exercise 6.13 Using the Miranda scientific simulation tensor, compare HOOI (initialized randomly) and ST-HOSVD in terms of the computation time and final error. Do five runs each to get some measure of the variance (the solution should not change for ST-HOSVD, but the runtimes may vary somewhat). Do this for each of the following core sizes:

(a) $13 \times 3 \times 2$

(b) $232 \times 43 \times 41$

(c) $583 \times 102 \times 99$

(d) $934 \times 161 \times 158$.

6.5 Other Methods

Tucker decomposition is useful as a compression method, but the tensors may be so large that they do not fit into memory. Parallel algorithms for Tucker decomposition have been developed by Austin et al. (2016) and Ballard et al. (2020). Another option is randomized methods, though these may lose the optimality guarantees (Ahmadi-Asl et al., 2021; Malik and Becker, 2018; Sun et al., 2020), or a combination of parallelization and randomization (Minster et al., 2024).

The Tucker optimization methods discussed thus far are alternating methods. It is possible to solve this directly using optimization methods, but the factor matrices are generally constrained to lie on a Grassmanian manifold; see Eldén and Savas (2009) and Uschmajew (2010).

Sparse tensors present a special challenge for Tucker decomposition because the sparsity is typically destroyed in the intermediate computations needed to compute the Tucker decomposition. Thus, Kaya and Uçar (2016) and Kolda and Sun (2008) take special care to avoid the so-called "intermediate blow-up problem."

We have not considered the problem of nonnegative Tucker factorizations, which usually constrains both the factors and the core to be nonnegative. This substantially modifies the optimization problem and solutions; see Mørup et al. (2008) and Phan and Cichocki (2008, 2011).

7 Tucker Approximation Error

A nice property of Tucker decomposition is that we can determine the exact approximation error for ST-HOSVD and tight bounds for HOSVD. With this information, we can choose the ranks of the decomposition to satisfy a given error threshold. Additionally, for the specified-rank formulation, we can prove that both HOSVD and ST-HOSVD are quasi-optimal, meaning that their relative approximation error is within $\sqrt{d}$ of optimal for a d-way tensor. In this chapter, we derive the approximation errors for Tucker decompositions computed via HOSVD and ST-HOSVD. From this analysis, we show how to choose the ranks in the course of the algorithm to satisfy a given error tolerance as presented in Chapter 6. We conclude with a proof of the quasi-optimality of HOSVD and ST-HOSVD. This chapter derives primarily from the work of De Lathauwer et al. (2000a), Hackbusch (2019), and Vannieuwenhoven et al. (2012).

7.1 Decomposing the Approximation Error

Our goal in this section is to decompose the Tucker approximation error across the modes of the tensor. This is the key insight into establishing the quasi-optimality of HOSVD and ST-HOSVD, and it also guides the algorithms in choosing ranks to satisfy a prescribed approximation error.

Theorem 7.1: Tucker Decomposition Error for 3-way Tensors (Vannieuwenhoven et al., 2012)

If $\mathcal{T} = \mathcal{G} \times_1 \mathbf{U} \times_2 \mathbf{V} \times_3 \mathbf{W}$ *is a Tucker approximation of a tensor* $\mathcal{X}$ *with* $\mathbf{U}$, $\mathbf{V}$, *and* $\mathbf{W}$ *orthonormal and* $\mathcal{G} = \mathcal{X} \times_1 \mathbf{U}^\intercal \times_2 \mathbf{V}^\intercal \times_3 \mathbf{W}^\intercal$, *then*

$$\begin{aligned}\|\mathcal{X} - \mathcal{T}\|^2 = \|\mathcal{X} \times_1 (\mathbf{I} - \mathbf{U}\mathbf{U}^\intercal)\|^2 & \\ + \|\mathcal{X} \times_1 \mathbf{U}\mathbf{U}^\intercal \times_2 (\mathbf{I} - \mathbf{V}\mathbf{V}^\intercal)\|^2 & \\ + \|\mathcal{X} \times_1 \mathbf{U}\mathbf{U}^\intercal \times_2 \mathbf{V}\mathbf{V}^\intercal \times_3 (\mathbf{I} - \mathbf{W}\mathbf{W}^\intercal)\|^2 &.\end{aligned}$$

Proof. Given $\mathcal{G} = \mathcal{X} \times_1 \mathbf{U}^\intercal \times_2 \mathbf{V}^\intercal \times_3 \mathbf{W}^\intercal$, we can eliminate it from the expression of the residual tensor $\mathcal{X} - \mathcal{T}$ as in Eq. (6.4). Then, we decompose the residual tensor using a telescoping sum and then combine terms to write it as a sum of three tensors corresponding to the approximation error of each mode:

$$
\begin{aligned}
\mathcal{X} - \mathcal{T} &= \mathcal{X} - \mathcal{X} \times_1 \mathbf{U}\mathbf{U}^\intercal \times_2 \mathbf{V}\mathbf{V}^\intercal \times_3 \mathbf{W}\mathbf{W}^\intercal \\
&= \mathcal{X} - \mathcal{X} \times_1 \mathbf{U}\mathbf{U}^\intercal + \mathcal{X} \times_1 \mathbf{U}\mathbf{U}^\intercal - \mathcal{X} \times_1 \mathbf{U}\mathbf{U}^\intercal \times_2 \mathbf{V}\mathbf{V}^\intercal \qquad (7.1)\\
&\qquad + \mathcal{X} \times_1 \mathbf{U}\mathbf{U}^\intercal \times_2 \mathbf{V}\mathbf{V}^\intercal - \mathcal{X} \times_1 \mathbf{U}\mathbf{U}^\intercal \times_2 \mathbf{V}\mathbf{V}^\intercal \times_3 \mathbf{W}\mathbf{W}^\intercal \\
&= \underbrace{\mathcal{X} \times_1 (\mathbf{I} - \mathbf{U}\mathbf{U}^\intercal)}_{\mathcal{A}} + \underbrace{\mathcal{X} \times_1 \mathbf{U}\mathbf{U}^\intercal \times_2 (\mathbf{I} - \mathbf{V}\mathbf{V}^\intercal)}_{\mathcal{B}} \qquad (7.2)\\
&\qquad + \underbrace{\mathcal{X} \times_1 \mathbf{U}\mathbf{U}^\intercal \times_2 \mathbf{V}\mathbf{V}^\intercal \times_3 (\mathbf{I} - \mathbf{W}\mathbf{W}^\intercal)}_{\mathcal{C}}.
\end{aligned}
$$

Observe, by Proposition A.9, that for any tensors $\mathcal{Y}, \mathcal{Z}$ and orthonormal matrix $\mathbf{Q}$ with compatible dimensions in mode k, $\langle \mathcal{Y} \times_k \mathbf{Q}\mathbf{Q}^\intercal, \mathcal{Z} \times_k (\mathbf{I} - \mathbf{Q}\mathbf{Q}^\intercal) \rangle = 0$.

Thus,

$$
\begin{aligned}
\langle \mathcal{A}, \mathcal{B} \rangle &= \left\langle \mathcal{X} \times_1 (\mathbf{I} - \mathbf{U}\mathbf{U}^\intercal), (\mathcal{X} \times_2 (\mathbf{I} - \mathbf{V}\mathbf{V}^\intercal)) \times_1 \mathbf{U}\mathbf{U}^\intercal \right\rangle = 0,\\
\langle \mathcal{A}, \mathcal{C} \rangle &= \left\langle \mathcal{X} \times_1 (\mathbf{I} - \mathbf{U}\mathbf{U}^\intercal), (\mathcal{X} \times_2 \mathbf{V}\mathbf{V}^\intercal \times_3 (\mathbf{I} - \mathbf{W}\mathbf{W}^\intercal)) \times_1 \mathbf{U}\mathbf{U}^\intercal \right\rangle = 0,\\
\langle \mathcal{B}, \mathcal{C} \rangle &= \left\langle (\mathcal{X} \times_1 \mathbf{U}\mathbf{U}^\intercal) \times_2 (\mathbf{I} - \mathbf{V}\mathbf{V}^\intercal), (\mathcal{X} \times_1 \mathbf{U}\mathbf{U}^\intercal \times_3 (\mathbf{I} - \mathbf{W}\mathbf{W}^\intercal)) \times_2 \mathbf{V}\mathbf{V}^\intercal \right\rangle = 0.
\end{aligned}
$$

Then we have

$$
\begin{aligned}
\|\mathcal{X} - \mathcal{T}\|^2 = \|\mathcal{A} + \mathcal{B} + \mathcal{C}\|^2 &= \langle \mathcal{A} + \mathcal{B} + \mathcal{C}, \mathcal{A} + \mathcal{B} + \mathcal{C} \rangle\\
&= \|\mathcal{A}\|^2 + \|\mathcal{B}\|^2 + \|\mathcal{C}\|^2 + 2\langle \mathcal{A}, \mathcal{B} \rangle + 2\langle \mathcal{A}, \mathcal{C} \rangle + 2\langle \mathcal{B}, \mathcal{C} \rangle\\
&= \|\mathcal{A}\|^2 + \|\mathcal{B}\|^2 + \|\mathcal{C}\|^2.
\end{aligned}
$$

□

The approximation error in the second mode per Eq. (7.2), given by $\mathcal{B}$, is based on $\mathbf{I} - \mathbf{V}\mathbf{V}^\intercal$ applied to the tensor $\mathcal{X} \times_1 \mathbf{U}\mathbf{U}^\intercal$ and not the original tensor $\mathcal{X}$. That is, the error in the later modes depends on the projections in the previous modes. However, the telescoping sum uses an arbitrary ordering on the modes. Any permutation of the modes works, yielding six distinct decompositions of the residual for 3-way tensors.

The result can be extended to d-way tensors.

Theorem 7.2: Tucker Decomposition Error for d-way Tensors (Vannieuwenhoven et al., 2012)

If $\mathcal{T} = \mathcal{G} \times_1 \mathbf{U}_1 \times_2 \mathbf{U}_2 \cdots \times_d \mathbf{U}_d$ is a Tucker approximation of a tensor $\mathcal{X}$ with $\mathbf{U}_1, \mathbf{U}_2, \dots, \mathbf{U}_d$ orthonormal and $\mathcal{G} = \mathcal{X} \times_1 \mathbf{U}_1^\intercal \times_2 \mathbf{U}_2^\intercal \cdots \times_d \mathbf{U}_d^\intercal$, then

$$
\begin{aligned}
\|\mathcal{X} - \mathcal{T}\|^2 &= \|\mathcal{X} \times_1 (\mathbf{I} - \mathbf{U}_1\mathbf{U}_1^\intercal)\|^2 + \|\mathcal{X} \times_1 \mathbf{U}_1\mathbf{U}_1^\intercal \times_2 (\mathbf{I} - \mathbf{U}_2\mathbf{U}_2^\intercal)\|^2 + \cdots\\
&\quad + \left\|\mathcal{X} \times_1 \mathbf{U}_1\mathbf{U}_1^\intercal \cdots \times_{d-1} \mathbf{U}_{d-1}\mathbf{U}_{d-1}^\intercal \times_d (\mathbf{I} - \mathbf{U}_d\mathbf{U}_d^\intercal)\right\|^2.
\end{aligned}
$$

Exercise 7.1 Prove Theorem 7.2.

7.2 HOSVD Error

We can use the decomposition of the approximation error to obtain an upper bound on the error from HOSVD. Recall that HOSVD computes the leading left singular vectors of each modewise unfolding of the original tensor using the matrix SVD.

7.2.1 HOSVD Error for 3-way Tensors

Theorem 7.3: HOSVD Error for 3-way Tensors (De Lathauwer et al., 2000a)

Let $\mathcal{T} = [\![\mathcal{G}; \mathbf{U}, \mathbf{V}, \mathbf{W}]\!]$ be the rank-(q, r, s) Tucker decomposition of $\mathcal{X}$ computed by the HOSVD algorithm (Algorithm 6.2). Then

$$\begin{aligned}\|\mathcal{X} - \mathcal{T}\|^2 &\leq \|\mathcal{X} \times_1 (\mathbf{I} - \mathbf{U}\mathbf{U}^\intercal)\|^2 + \|\mathcal{X} \times_2 (\mathbf{I} - \mathbf{V}\mathbf{V}^\intercal)\|^2 + \|\mathcal{X} \times_3 (\mathbf{I} - \mathbf{W}\mathbf{W}^\intercal)\|^2 \\ &= \sum_{i=q+1}^{m} \sigma_i(\mathbf{X}_{(1)})^2 + \sum_{j=r+1}^{n} \sigma_j(\mathbf{X}_{(2)})^2 + \sum_{k=s+1}^{p} \sigma_k(\mathbf{X}_{(3)})^2,\end{aligned}$$

where $\sigma_i(\mathbf{A})$ denotes the ith singular value of a matrix $\mathbf{A}$.

Proof. By Proposition A.9, applying an orthogonal projection via TTM to any mode of a tensor can only decrease its norm. That is, for any tensor $\mathcal{Y}$ and orthonormal matrix $\mathbf{Q}$ with compatible dimensions in mode k, $\|\mathcal{Y} \times_k \mathbf{Q}\mathbf{Q}^\intercal\| \leq \|\mathcal{Y}\|$.

Then, from Theorem 7.1, we have

$$\begin{aligned}\|\mathcal{X} - \mathcal{T}\|^2 &= \|\mathcal{X} \times_1 (\mathbf{I} - \mathbf{U}\mathbf{U}^\intercal)\|^2 + \|\mathcal{X} \times_1 \mathbf{U}\mathbf{U}^\intercal \times_2 (\mathbf{I} - \mathbf{V}\mathbf{V}^\intercal)\|^2 \\ &\qquad + \|\mathcal{X} \times_1 \mathbf{U}\mathbf{U}^\intercal \times_2 \mathbf{V}\mathbf{V}^\intercal \times_3 (\mathbf{I} - \mathbf{W}\mathbf{W}^\intercal)\|^2 \\ &\leq \|\mathcal{X} \times_1 (\mathbf{I} - \mathbf{U}\mathbf{U}^\intercal)\|^2 + \|\mathcal{X} \times_2 (\mathbf{I} - \mathbf{V}\mathbf{V}^\intercal)\|^2 + \|\mathcal{X} \times_3 (\mathbf{I} - \mathbf{W}\mathbf{W}^\intercal)\|^2 \\ &= \|(\mathbf{I} - \mathbf{U}\mathbf{U}^\intercal)\mathbf{X}_{(1)}\|_F^2 + \|(\mathbf{I} - \mathbf{V}\mathbf{V}^\intercal)\mathbf{X}_{(2)}\|_F^2 + \|(\mathbf{I} - \mathbf{W}\mathbf{W}^\intercal)\mathbf{X}_{(3)}\|_F^2.\end{aligned}$$

As $\mathbf{U}$, $\mathbf{V}$, and $\mathbf{W}$ are the leading left singular vectors of the respective modewise unfoldings, the result follows from Theorem A.26. □

The bound from Theorem 7.3 motivates HOSVD (Algorithm 6.2) with specified error ε. By definition of LLSV, we have that $\mathbf{U}$ satisfies $\|(\mathbf{I} - \mathbf{U}\mathbf{U}^\intercal)\mathbf{X}_{(1)}\|_F^2 \leq \frac{\varepsilon^2}{3}\|\mathcal{X}\|^2$, $\mathbf{V}$ satisfies $\|(\mathbf{I} - \mathbf{V}\mathbf{V}^\intercal)\mathbf{X}_{(2)}\|_F^2 \leq \frac{\varepsilon^2}{3}\|\mathcal{X}\|^2$, and $\mathbf{W}$ satisfies $\|(\mathbf{I} - \mathbf{W}\mathbf{W}^\intercal)\mathbf{X}_{(3)}\|_F^2 \leq \frac{\varepsilon^2}{3}\|\mathcal{X}\|^2$. Thus, $\|\mathcal{X} - \mathcal{T}\| \leq \varepsilon\|\mathcal{X}\|$.

7.2.2 HOSVD Error for d-way Tensors

We can generalize the error bound for HOSVD to d-way tensors as follows.

Theorem 7.4: HOSVD Error for d-way Tensors (De Lathauwer et al., 2000a)

Let $\mathcal{T} = [\![\mathcal{G}; \mathbf{U}_1, \mathbf{U}_2, \ldots, \mathbf{U}_d]\!]$ by the rank-$(r_1, r_2, \ldots, r_d)$ Tucker decomposition of $\mathcal{X}$ computed by the HOSVD algorithm (Algorithm 6.3). Then

$$\|\mathcal{X} - \mathcal{T}\|^2 \leq \sum_{k=1}^{d} \|\mathcal{X} \times_k (\mathbf{I} - \mathbf{U}_k\mathbf{U}_k^\intercal)\|^2 = \sum_{k=1}^{d} \sum_{i=r_k+1}^{n_k} \sigma_i(\mathbf{X}_{(k)})^2,$$

where $\sigma_i(\mathbf{A})$ denotes the ith singular value of a matrix $\mathbf{A}$.

Exercise 7.2 Prove Theorem 7.4.

As in the 3-way case, this motivates HOSVD (Algorithm 6.3) with specified error ε.

7.3 ST-HOSVD Error

We can again use the decomposition of the approximation error. In the previous section, we used the error decomposition to upper bound the HOSVD error. In the case of ST-HOSVD, the error decomposition yields exactly the ST-HOSVD error.

7.3.1 ST-HOSVD Error for 3-way Tensors

Theorem 7.5: ST-HOSVD Error (3-way) (Hackbusch, 2019; Vannieuwenhoven et al., 2012)

Let $\mathcal{T} = [\![\mathcal{G}; \mathbf{U}, \mathbf{V}, \mathbf{W}]\!]$ *by the rank-*(q, r, s) *Tucker decomposition of* $\mathcal{X}$ *computed by the ST-HOSVD algorithm (Algorithm 6.4). Then*

$$\begin{aligned}\|\mathcal{X} - \mathcal{T}\|^2 &= \|\mathcal{X} \times_1 (\mathbf{I} - \mathbf{U}\mathbf{U}^\intercal)\|^2 + \|\mathcal{Y} \times_2 (\mathbf{I} - \mathbf{V}\mathbf{V}^\intercal)\|^2 + \|\mathcal{Z} \times_3 (\mathbf{I} - \mathbf{W}\mathbf{W}^\intercal)\|^2 \\ &= \sum_{i=q+1}^{m} \sigma_i(\mathbf{X}_{(1)})^2 + \sum_{j=r+1}^{n} \sigma_j(\mathbf{Y}_{(2)})^2 + \sum_{k=s+1}^{p} \sigma_k(\mathbf{Z}_{(3)})^2,\end{aligned}$$

where $\mathcal{Y} = \mathcal{X} \times_1 \mathbf{U}^\intercal$, $\mathcal{Z} = \mathcal{X} \times_1 \mathbf{U}^\intercal \times_2 \mathbf{V}^\intercal$, *and* $\sigma_i(\mathbf{A})$ *denotes the ith singular value of a matrix* $\mathbf{A}$.

Proof. We consider each of three terms on the right-hand side in turn, showing that each is equivalent to the corresponding term in Theorem 7.1. The first mode terms match exactly.

For the second mode, recall from Proposition A.7 that applying a column orthonormal matrix to any mode of a tensor maintains its norm. That is, for a tensor $\mathcal{W}$ and orthonormal matrix $\mathbf{Q}$ with compatible dimensions in mode k, we have $\|\mathcal{W} \times_k \mathbf{Q}\| = \|\mathcal{W}\|$. Then

$$\|\mathcal{Y} \times_2 (\mathbf{I} - \mathbf{V}\mathbf{V}^\intercal)\|^2 = \|\mathcal{X} \times_1 \mathbf{U}^\intercal \times_2 (\mathbf{I} - \mathbf{V}\mathbf{V}^\intercal)\|^2 = \|\mathcal{X} \times_1 \mathbf{U}\mathbf{U}^\intercal \times_2 (\mathbf{I} - \mathbf{V}\mathbf{V}^\intercal)\|^2.$$

Similarly, for the third mode, we have

$$\begin{aligned}\|\mathcal{Z} \times_3 (\mathbf{I} - \mathbf{W}\mathbf{W}^\intercal)\|^2 &= \|\mathcal{X} \times_1 \mathbf{U}^\intercal \times_2 \mathbf{V}^\intercal \times_3 (\mathbf{I} - \mathbf{W}\mathbf{W}^\intercal)\|^2 \\ &= \|\mathcal{X} \times_1 \mathbf{U}\mathbf{U}^\intercal \times_2 \mathbf{V}\mathbf{V}^\intercal \times_3 (\mathbf{I} - \mathbf{W}\mathbf{W}^\intercal)\|^2.\end{aligned}$$

As $\mathbf{U}$, $\mathbf{V}$, and $\mathbf{W}$ are the leading left singular vectors of the respective modewise unfoldings of $\mathcal{X}$, $\mathcal{Y}$, and $\mathcal{Z}$, the final equality follows from Theorem A.26. □

As with HOSVD, Theorem 7.5 justifies Algorithm 6.5 with specified error tolerance. Algorithm 6.5 sets the modewise absolute error tolerance to be $(\varepsilon/\sqrt{3})\|\mathcal{X}\|$ for each mode. From Theorem 7.5 and the guarantees of Algorithm 6.1, we have that

$$\text{ERR} = \sqrt{\varepsilon_1^2 + \varepsilon_2^2 + \varepsilon_3^2} \leq \sqrt{(\varepsilon^2/3)\|\mathcal{X}\|^2 + (\varepsilon^2/3)\|\mathcal{X}\|^2 + (\varepsilon^2/3)\|\mathcal{X}\|^2} = \varepsilon\|\mathcal{X}\|.$$

7.3.2 ST-HOSVD Error for d-way Tensors

Similar results to Theorem 7.5 can be achieved in the d-way case.

Theorem 7.6: ST-HOSVD Error (d-way) (Hackbusch, 2019; Vannieuwenhoven et al., 2012)

Let $\mathcal{T} = [\![\mathcal{G}; \mathbf{U}_1, \mathbf{U}_2, \ldots, \mathbf{U}_d]\!]$ by the rank-$(r_1, r_2, \ldots, r_d)$ Tucker decomposition of $\mathcal{X}$ computed by the ST-HOSVD algorithm. Then

$$\begin{aligned}\|\mathcal{X} - \mathcal{T}\|^2 &= \sum_{k=1}^{d} \|\mathcal{G}^{(k)} \times_k (\mathbf{I} - \mathbf{U}_k\mathbf{U}_k^\intercal)\|^2 \\ &= \sum_{k=1}^{d} \sum_{i=r_k+1}^{n_k} \sigma_i\left(\mathbf{G}_{(k)}^{(k)}\right)^2,\end{aligned}$$

where $\mathcal{G}^{(k)} = \mathcal{X} \times_1 \mathbf{U}_1^\intercal \cdots \times_{k-1} \mathbf{U}_{k-1}^\intercal$ and $\sigma_i(\mathbf{A})$ is the ith singular value of the matrix $\mathbf{A}$.

Proof. We consider the kth of d terms in the outer summation of the right-hand side and show that it is equivalent to the kth term in Theorem 7.2. We have

$$\begin{aligned}\|\mathcal{G}^{(k)} \times_k (\mathbf{I} - \mathbf{U}_k\mathbf{U}_k^\intercal)\|^2 &= \|\mathcal{X} \times_1 \mathbf{U}_1^\intercal \cdots \times_{k-1} \mathbf{U}_{k-1}^\intercal \times_k (\mathbf{I} - \mathbf{U}_k\mathbf{U}_k^\intercal)\|^2 \\ &= \|\mathcal{X} \times_1 \mathbf{U}_1\mathbf{U}_1^\intercal \cdots \times_{k-1} \mathbf{U}_{k-1}\mathbf{U}_{k-1}^\intercal \times_k (\mathbf{I} - \mathbf{U}_k\mathbf{U}_k^\intercal)\|^2,\end{aligned}$$

where the last equality is a result of Proposition A.7 and the fact that a TTM in any mode with a column orthonormal matrix maintains the norm of the tensor. ST-HOSVD computes $\mathbf{U}_k$ to be the leading left singular vectors of the mode-k unfolding of $\mathcal{G}^{(k)}$, so

$$\|\mathcal{G}^{(k)} \times_k (\mathbf{I} - \mathbf{U}_k\mathbf{U}_k^\intercal)\|^2 = \sum_{i=r_k+1}^{n_k} \sigma_i\left(\mathbf{G}_{(k)}^{(k)}\right)^2$$

follows from Theorem A.26. □

Using this result, we can justify the variation of the d-way ST-HOSVD algorithm, Algorithm 6.5, using a user-specified error. We can partition the error tolerance in any way so long as $\sum_{k=1}^{d} \varepsilon_k^2 \leq \varepsilon^2\|\mathcal{X}\|^2$.

Exercise 7.3 Consider the ST-HOSVD algorithm in Algorithm 6.5. Let ε_k denote the relative error of the LLSV: $\varepsilon_k = \|(\mathbf{I} - \mathbf{U}_k\mathbf{U}_k^\intercal)\mathbf{G}_{(k)}\|_F / \|\mathbf{G}_{(k)}\|_F$. Prove that replacing the modewise error tolerance in Line 5 with

$$\sqrt{\left(\varepsilon^2\|\mathcal{X}\|^2 - \sum_{i=1}^{k-1} \varepsilon_i^2\right) / (d - k + 1)}$$

still ensures the Tucker decomposition error tolerance is satisfied.

7.4 Quasi-optimality

We show in this section that both HOSVD and ST-HOSVD produce quasi-optimal solutions. That is, the Tucker decompositions returned by these algorithms are within a factor $\sqrt{d}$ of the optimal Tucker decomposition for a given rank. This relies on the fact that each algorithm uses the SVD to solve the modewise problems, and the SVD computes the optimal solution for each matrix case. We prove the quasi-optimality for 3-way tensors in Theorems 7.7 and 7.9 and leave the proofs of the results for d-way tensors (Theorems 7.8 and 7.10) as exercises.

Theorem 7.7: Quasi-optimality of HOSVD for 3-way Tensors (Hackbusch, 2019; Vannieuwenhoven et al., 2012)

Let $\mathcal{T}$ be the rank-(q,r,s) Tucker decomposition computed by the HOSVD algorithm for the 3-way tensor $\mathcal{X}$. Then $\mathcal{T}$ is within a factor $\sqrt{3}$ of optimal:

$$\|\mathcal{X} - \mathcal{T}\| \leq \sqrt{3}\, \|\mathcal{X} - \mathcal{T}^*\|,$$

where $\mathcal{T}^*$ is an optimal rank-(q,r,s) decomposition.

Proof. Given a tensor $\mathcal{X}$, let $\mathcal{T} = [\![\mathcal{G}; \mathbf{U}, \mathbf{V}, \mathbf{W}]\!]$ be the Tucker decomposition computed by the HOSVD algorithm, and let $\mathcal{T}^* = [\![\mathcal{G}^*; \mathbf{U}^*, \mathbf{V}^*, \mathbf{W}^*]\!]$ be an optimal Tucker decomposition. From Theorem 7.3, we have

$$\|\mathcal{X} - \mathcal{T}\|^2 \leq \|\mathcal{X} \times_1 (\mathbf{I} - \mathbf{U}\mathbf{U}^\intercal)\|^2 + \|\mathcal{X} \times_2 (\mathbf{I} - \mathbf{V}\mathbf{V}^\intercal)\|^2 + \|\mathcal{X} \times_3 (\mathbf{I} - \mathbf{W}\mathbf{W}^\intercal)\|^2.$$

Consider the first term on the right-hand side. HOSVD computes $\mathbf{U}$ to be the leading left singular vectors of $\mathbf{X}_{(1)}$. From Theorem A.26, $\mathbf{U}\mathbf{U}^\intercal\mathbf{X}_{(1)}$ is the *best* rank-q approximation of $\mathbf{X}_{(1)}$. In particular, it has a smaller approximation error than the rank-q approximation given by $\mathbf{T}^*_{(1)} = \mathbf{U}^*\mathbf{G}^*_{(1)}(\mathbf{W}^* \otimes \mathbf{V}^*)^\intercal$. That is, while $\mathcal{T}^*$ is an optimal Tucker decomposition of $\mathcal{X}$, its mode-1 unfolding is not necessarily an optimal low-rank approximation of $\mathbf{X}_{(1)}$. Thus,

$$\|\mathcal{X} \times_1 (\mathbf{I} - \mathbf{U}\mathbf{U}^\intercal)\| = \|\mathbf{X}_{(1)} - \mathbf{U}\mathbf{U}^\intercal\mathbf{X}_{(1)}\|_F \leq \|\mathbf{X}_{(1)} - \mathbf{T}^*_{(1)}\|_F = \|\mathcal{X} - \mathcal{T}^*\|.$$

Similar arguments for the second and third terms give $\|\mathcal{X} - \mathcal{T}\|^2 \leq 3\|\mathcal{X} - \mathcal{T}^*\|^2$, and the result follows. □

Theorem 7.8: Quasi-optimality of HOSVD for d-way Tensors (Hackbusch, 2019; Vannieuwenhoven et al., 2012)

Let $\mathcal{T}$ be the rank-$(r_1, r_2, \ldots, r_d)$ Tucker decomposition computed by the HOSVD algorithm (Algorithm 6.3) for the d-way tensor $\mathcal{X}$. Then $\mathcal{T}$ is within a factor $\sqrt{d}$ of optimal:

$$\|\mathcal{X} - \mathcal{T}\| \leq \sqrt{d}\, \|\mathcal{X} - \mathcal{T}^*\|,$$

where $\mathcal{T}^*$ is the optimal rank-$(r_1, r_2, \ldots, r_d)$ approximation.

Exercise 7.4 Prove Theorem 7.8.

Theorem 7.9: Quasi-optimality of ST-HOSVD for 3-way Tensors (Hackbusch, 2019; Vannieuwenhoven et al., 2012)

Let $\mathcal{T}$ be the rank-(q, r, s) Tucker approximation computed by the ST-HOSVD algorithm (Algorithm 6.4) for the 3-way tensor $\mathcal{X}$. Then $\mathcal{T}$ is within a factor $\sqrt{3}$ of optimal:

$$\|\mathcal{X} - \mathcal{T}\| \leq \sqrt{3}\, \|\mathcal{X} - \mathcal{T}^*\|,$$

where $\mathcal{T}^*$ is the optimal rank-(q, r, s) approximation.

Proof. Given a tensor $\mathcal{X}$, let $\mathcal{T} = [\![\mathcal{G}; \mathbf{U}, \mathbf{V}, \mathbf{W}]\!]$ be the Tucker decomposition computed by the ST-HOSVD algorithm, and let $\mathcal{T}^* = [\![\mathcal{G}^*; \mathbf{U}^*, \mathbf{V}^*, \mathbf{W}^*]\!]$ be an optimal Tucker decomposition. From Theorem 7.5, we have

$$\|\mathcal{X} - \mathcal{T}\|^2 = \|\mathcal{X} \times_1 (\mathbf{I} - \mathbf{U}\mathbf{U}^\intercal)\|^2 + \|\mathcal{Y} \times_2 (\mathbf{I} - \mathbf{V}\mathbf{V}^\intercal)\|^2 + \|\mathcal{Z} \times_3 (\mathbf{I} - \mathbf{W}\mathbf{W}^\intercal)\|^2,$$

where $\mathcal{Y} = \mathcal{X} \times_1 \mathbf{U}^\intercal$ and $\mathcal{Z} = \mathcal{X} \times_1 \mathbf{U}^\intercal \times_2 \mathbf{V}^\intercal$.

Consider the first term on the right-hand side. ST-HOSVD computes $\mathbf{U}$ to be the leading left singular vectors of $\mathbf{X}_{(1)}$. From Theorem A.26, this is the best rank-q approximation of $\mathbf{X}_{(1)}$. In particular, it has a smaller approximation error than that of the rank-q approximation given by $\mathbf{T}^*_{(1)} = \mathbf{U}^*\mathbf{G}^*_{(1)}(\mathbf{W}^* \otimes \mathbf{V}^*)^\intercal$. That is, while $\mathcal{T}^*$ is an optimal Tucker decomposition of $\mathcal{X}$, its mode-1 unfolding is not necessarily an optimal low-rank approximation of $\mathbf{X}_{(1)}$. Thus,

$$\|\mathcal{X} \times_1 (\mathbf{I} - \mathbf{U}\mathbf{U}^\intercal)\| = \|\mathbf{X}_{(1)} - \mathbf{U}\mathbf{U}^\intercal\mathbf{X}_{(1)}\|_F \leq \|\mathbf{X}_{(1)} - \mathbf{T}^*_{(1)}\|_F = \|\mathcal{X} - \mathcal{T}^*\|.$$

Consider the second term. Again from Theorem A.26, ST-HOSVD computes the best rank-r approximation to $\mathbf{Y}_{(2)}$. In particular, it is smaller than the squared error of the rank-r approximation given by the mode-2 unfolding of $\mathcal{T}^* \times_1 \mathbf{U}^\intercal$, which is $\mathbf{V}^*\mathbf{G}^*_{(2)}(\mathbf{W}^* \otimes \mathbf{U}^\intercal\mathbf{U}^*)^\intercal$. Thus,

$$\begin{aligned}
\|\mathcal{Y} \times_2 (\mathbf{I} - \mathbf{V}\mathbf{V}^\intercal)\| &= \|\mathbf{Y}_{(2)} - \mathbf{V}\mathbf{V}^\intercal\mathbf{Y}_{(2)}\|_F \\
&\leq \|\mathbf{Y}_{(2)} - \mathbf{V}^*\mathbf{G}^*_{(2)}(\mathbf{W}^* \otimes \mathbf{U}^\intercal\mathbf{U}^*)^\intercal\|_F \\
&= \|\mathcal{Y} - \mathcal{T}^* \times_1 \mathbf{U}^\intercal\| \\
&= \|\mathcal{X} \times_1 \mathbf{U}^\intercal - \mathcal{T}^* \times_1 \mathbf{U}^\intercal\| \\
&= \|(\mathcal{X} - \mathcal{T}^*) \times_1 \mathbf{U}^\intercal\| \\
&\leq \|\mathcal{X} - \mathcal{T}^*\|,
\end{aligned}$$

where the last inequality is due to Proposition A.7 and the fact that a TTM with a row orthonormal matrix can only decrease the norm of a tensor.

The argument for the third term is similar. ST-HOSVD computes the best rank-s approximation to $\mathbf{Z}_{(3)}$, and therefore it is smaller than the squared error of the mode-3 unfolding of $\mathcal{T}^* \times_1 \mathbf{U}^\intercal \times_2 \mathbf{V}^\intercal$, another rank-$s$ approximation. Thus,

$$\begin{aligned}
\|\mathcal{Z} \times_3 (\mathbf{I} - \mathbf{W}\mathbf{W}^\intercal)\| &= \|\mathbf{Z}_{(3)} - \mathbf{W}\mathbf{W}^\intercal \mathbf{Z}_{(3)}\|_F \\
&\leq \|\mathbf{Z}_{(3)} - \mathbf{W}^* \mathbf{G}^*_{(3)} (\mathbf{V}^\intercal \mathbf{V}^* \otimes \mathbf{U}^\intercal \mathbf{U}^*)^\intercal\|_F \\
&= \|\mathcal{Z} - \mathcal{T}^* \times_1 \mathbf{U}^\intercal \times_2 \mathbf{V}^\intercal\| \\
&= \|\mathcal{X} \times_1 \mathbf{U}^\intercal \times_2 \mathbf{V}^\intercal - \mathcal{T}^* \times_1 \mathbf{U}^\intercal \times_2 \mathbf{V}^\intercal\| \\
&= \|(\mathcal{X} - \mathcal{T}^*) \times_1 \mathbf{U}^\intercal \times_2 \mathbf{V}^\intercal\| \\
&\leq \|\mathcal{X} - \mathcal{T}^*\|.
\end{aligned}$$

Combining terms, we have $\|\mathcal{X} - \mathcal{T}\|^2 \leq 3\|\mathcal{X} - \mathcal{T}^*\|^2$, and the result follows. □

Theorem 7.10: Quasi-optimality of ST-HOSVD for d-way Tensors (Hackbusch, 2019; Vannieuwenhoven et al., 2012)

Let $\mathcal{T}$ be the rank-$(r_1, r_2, \ldots, r_d)$ Tucker approximation computed by the ST-HOSVD algorithm (Algorithm 6.5) for the d-way tensor $\mathcal{X}$. Then $\mathcal{T}$ is within a factor $\sqrt{d}$ of optimal:

$$\|\mathcal{X} - \mathcal{T}\| \leq \sqrt{d}\, \|\mathcal{X} - \mathcal{T}^*\|,$$

where $\mathcal{T}^*$ is the optimal rank-$(r_1, r_2, \ldots, r_d)$ approximation.

Exercise 7.5 Prove Theorem 7.10.

8 Tensor Train Decomposition

The **tensor train (TT) decomposition** compresses a tensor $\mathcal{X}$ of *any* order into a series of products of 3-way (or lower-order) tensors. Figure 8.1 provides a conceptual illustration of the tensor decomposition for a d-way tensor. For a tensor of size $n_1 \times n_2 \times \cdots \times n_d$, train car $\mathcal{G}_k$ is of size $r_{k-1} \times n_k \times r_k$, with $r_0 = r_d = 1$ (so that the engine and caboose are matrices). We explain the details in the sections that follow.

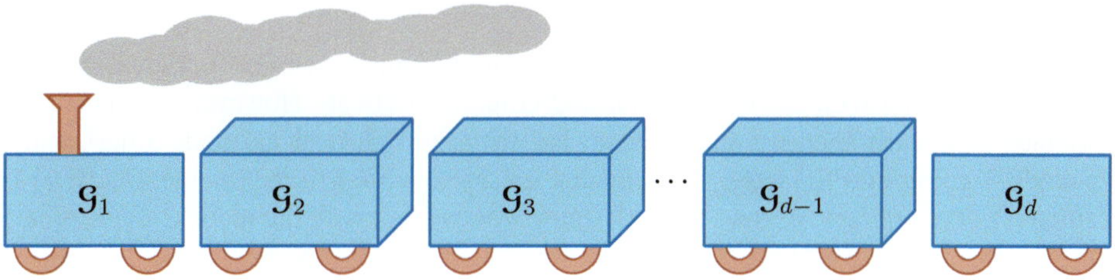

Figure 8.1 A conceptual tensor train decomposition. The engine and caboose are matrices, and the remaining train cars are 3-way tensors.

The TT decomposition aims to avoid the **curse of dimensionality** in the Tucker decomposition. As an illustration, consider a d-way tensor of size $n \times n \times \cdots \times n$, which requires n^d storage. The storage is exponential in d, so we say this is the curse of dimensionality. A Tucker decomposition of the tensor has a core of size $r \times r \times \cdots \times r$ and d factor matrices of size $n \times r$, which requires $r^d + dnr$ storage. The storage is still exponential in d, even though the base is lower, so Tucker still suffers from the curse of dimensionality. If we make the same simplifying assumption of a tensor of size $n \times n \times \cdots \times n$ and all interior ranks being equal (i.e., $r_1 = \cdots = r_{d-1} = r$), then a TT decomposition requires $(d-2)nr^2 + 2nr$ storage. There is no direct exponential dependence on d, so the TT decomposition appears to be free from the curse of dimensionality. However, it is not quite as simple as that, as we must still consider the accuracy of the decomposition. The Tucker decomposition of equivalent rank will yield a better approximation.

The tensor train decomposition was developed by Oseledets (2011) and Oseledets and Tyrtyshnikov (2009), but it was later observed to be a rediscovery of an older method in quantum chemistry known as **matrix product states (MPS)**; see Grasedyck et al. (2013) and Hackbusch (2014) and references therein. Additionally, this is a special case of a more general method known as hierarchical tensor decomposition; see Section 17.4.2.

In this chapter, we discuss the TT decomposition, an SVD-based algorithm for fitting it, the quasi-optimality of the resulting solution, and a comparison of TT with Tucker on example datasets.

8.1 Formulation of the TT Decomposition

We consider the formulation of the TT decomposition for 3-way, 4-way, and d-way tensors. The case for 3-way tensors is almost identical to Tucker, but we include it for completeness.

8.1.1 TT Decomposition of 3-way Tensors

For a 3-way tensor $\mathcal{X}$ of size $m \times n \times p$, the TT decomposition is the product of:

- a tensor $\mathcal{G}_1$ of size $1 \times m \times r$ (a matrix),
- a tensor $\mathcal{G}_2$ of size $r \times n \times s$, and
- a tensor $\mathcal{G}_3$ of size $s \times p \times 1$ (a matrix).

As with Tucker, the size parameters (r, s) have to be specified by the user or determined by algorithm to achieve a specified error tolerance. Elementwise, the approximation is

$$\mathcal{X}(i,j,k) \approx \sum_{\alpha=1}^{r} \sum_{\beta=1}^{s} \mathcal{G}_1(i,\alpha)\, \mathcal{G}_2(\alpha,j,\beta)\, \mathcal{G}_3(\beta,k). \tag{8.1}$$

We can visualize what is happening in Fig. 8.2. The two-mode tensors (i.e., matrices) $\mathcal{G}_1$ and $\mathcal{G}_3$ are oriented with rows horizontal and columns vertical. However, the tensor $\mathcal{G}_2$ is oriented differently than we have seen so far, with mode 1 vertical, mode 3 horizontal, and mode 2 going into the page. This makes it easy to visualize that element (i, j, k) is calculated as the product of row i from $\mathcal{G}_1$ (an r row vector) with the mode-2 hyperslice j from $\mathcal{G}_2$ (an $r \times s$ matrix) times column k from $\mathcal{G}_3$ (an s column vector).

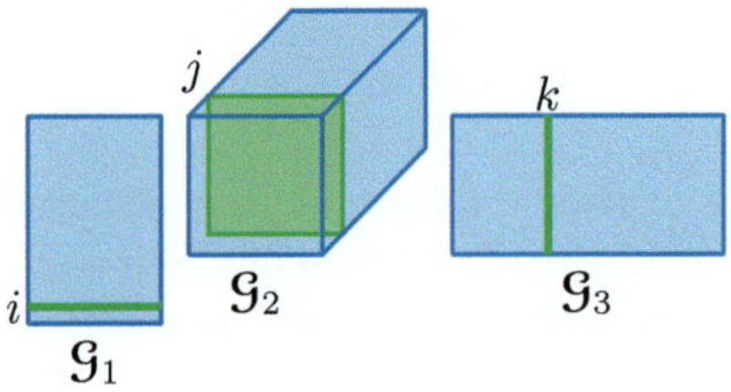

Figure 8.2 Calculating element (i, j, k) from TT decomposition of a 3-way tensor.

The tensor network diagram is shown in Fig. 8.3. Recall from Section 3.8.3 that the degree of the node is the order of the tensor, and connection between two nodes indicates contraction in that dimension. The 3-way tensor $\mathcal{X}$ is the product of a 2-way tensor $\mathcal{G}_1$, a 3-way tensor $\mathcal{G}_2$, and a 2-way tensor $\mathcal{G}_3$. The TT decomposition is a train with three cars.

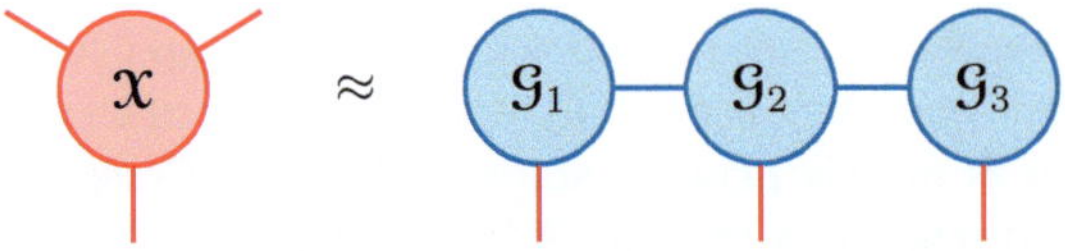

Figure 8.3 Tensor network diagram of TT decomposition of a 3-way tensor.

In the 3-way case, the TT decomposition is identical to Tucker, except that it only compresses in two of the three modes. Hence, there is no advantage to TT decomposition in the 3-way case.

For illustrative purposes, consider the problem of computing a tensor from a given TT decomposition: $\hat{\mathcal{X}} = [\![\mathcal{G}_1, \mathcal{G}_2, \mathcal{G}_3]\!]$, where we use the $[\![\cdot]\!]$ notation to denote the tensor train constructed from the constituent parts. There are a few different ways to do the reconstruction, but we will give an example of going from right to left in Fig. 8.4. In Step 1, we create a tensor $\mathcal{Y}$ of size $r \times n \times p$ that combines $\mathcal{G}_2$ and $\mathcal{G}_3$ via matrix–matrix multiply of reshapings:

$$\mathbf{Y}_{(\{1,2\}\times 3)} = \underbrace{[\mathcal{G}_2]_{(\{1,2\}\times 3)}}_{rn\times s} \underbrace{\mathcal{G}_3}_{s\times p}.$$

Then we can compute $\hat{\mathcal{X}}$ of size $m \times n \times p$ via matrix–matrix multiply of reshapings:

$$\hat{\mathbf{X}}_{(1\times\{2,3\})} = \underbrace{\mathcal{G}_1}_{m\times r} \underbrace{\mathbf{Y}_{(1\times\{2,3\})}}_{r\times np}.$$

While it is mathematically difficult to express the shifts in the expressions from matrices to tensors and vice versa, the computations do not require any rearrangement in memory.

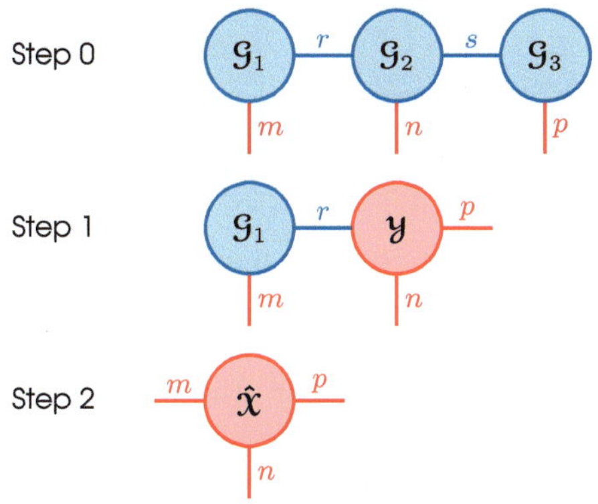

Figure 8.4 Reconstruction of a 3-way tensor from TT decomposition $\hat{\mathcal{X}} = [\![\mathcal{G}_1, \mathcal{G}_2, \mathcal{G}_3]\!]$.

Exercise 8.1 What is the cost for each step of the reconstruction illustrated in Fig. 8.4?

Exercise 8.2 Consider the case of reconstructing only $\hat{\mathcal{X}}(:, j, :)$ of size $m \times p$. Explain how to do that in two steps, with a cost of $\mathcal{O}(rsp)$ for the first step and $\mathcal{O}(mrp)$ for the second step.

8.1.2 TT Decomposition of 4-way Tensors

If $\mathcal{X}$ is a 4-way tensor of size $n_1 \times n_2 \times n_3 \times n_4$, we would compress it to the product of

- a tensor $\mathcal{G}_1$ of size $1 \times n_1 \times r_1$,
- a tensor $\mathcal{G}_2$ of size $r_1 \times n_2 \times r_2$,
- a tensor $\mathcal{G}_3$ of size $r_2 \times n_3 \times r_3$, and
- a tensor $\mathcal{G}_4$ of size $r_3 \times n_4 \times 1$.

Elementwise, this means

$$\mathcal{X}(i_1, i_2, i_3, i_4) \approx \sum_{j_1=1}^{r_1} \sum_{j_2=1}^{r_2} \sum_{j_3=1}^{r_3} \mathcal{G}_1(i_1, j_1)\, \mathcal{G}_2(j_1, i_2, j_2)\, \mathcal{G}_3(j_2, i_3, j_3)\, \mathcal{G}_4(j_3, i_4). \quad (8.2)$$

Figure 8.5 explains this formula: It is the product of row i_1 from $\mathcal{G}_1$, mode-2 hyperslice i_2 from $\mathcal{G}_2$, mode-2 hyperslice i_3 from $\mathcal{G}_3$, and column i_4 from $\mathcal{G}_4$.

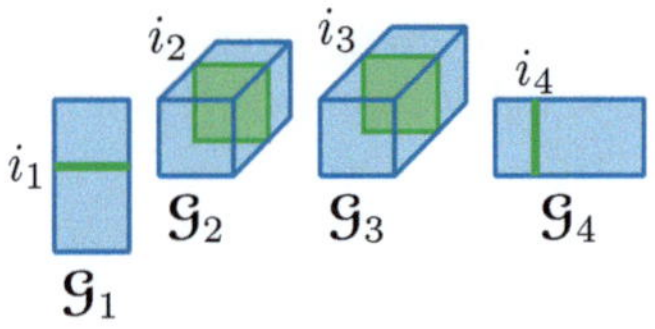

Figure 8.5 Calculating element (i_1, i_2, i_3, i_4) from a TT decomposition of a 4-way tensor.

In the TT decomposition, there is generally no guarantee that small values of r_k will yield an accurate approximation. In fact, it can be the case that r_k is relatively large with $r_k > n_k$ for some k, as shown in Fig. 8.6. We describe how large each r_k can grow in Remark 8.1.

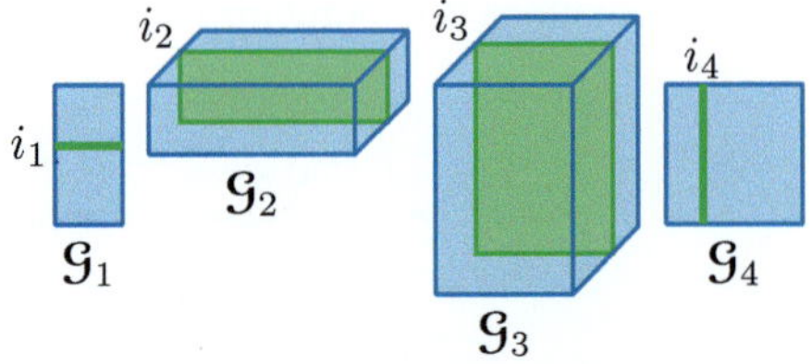

Figure 8.6 Calculating element (i_1, i_2, i_3, i_4) from a TT decomposition of a 4-way tensor.

The tensor network diagram of a 4-way tensor is shown in Fig. 8.7. Now node $\mathcal{X}$ has four edges emanating to show it is a 4-way tensor. The TT decomposition is a train with four cars.

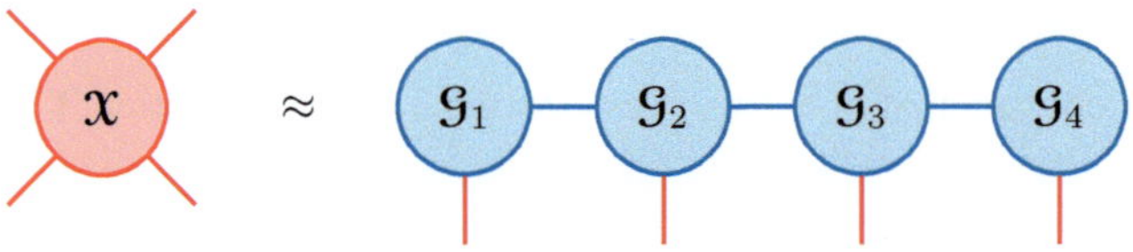

Figure 8.7 Tensor network diagram of a TT decomposition of a 4-way tensor.

To reconstruct a tensor from a 4-way TT decomposition ($\hat{\mathcal{X}} = [\![\mathcal{G}_1, \mathcal{G}_2, \mathcal{G}_3, \mathcal{G}_4]\!]$), we can compute the reconstruction as pictured in Fig. 8.8. We have a choice in the order of operations and can contract along the connected edges in any order. In the first step, we contract $\mathcal{G}_3$ and $\mathcal{G}_4$ to get a tensor $\mathcal{Y}$ of size $r_2 \times n_3 \times n_4$. In the second step, we contract $\mathcal{G}_1$ and $\mathcal{G}_2$ to get a tensor $\mathcal{Z}$ of size $n_1 \times n_2 \times r_2$. Finally, in the third step, we contract $\mathcal{Z}$ and $\mathcal{Y}$ to get the final result, $\hat{\mathcal{X}}$.

Exercise 8.3 In Fig. 8.8, explicitly state the reshaping for the matrix–matrix multiplication needed to compute $\mathcal{Y}$, $\mathcal{Z}$, and $\hat{\mathcal{X}}$.

8.1.3 TT Decomposition of d-way Tensors

If $\mathcal{X}$ is a d-way tensor of size $n_1 \times n_2 \times \cdots \times n_d$, the TT decomposition compresses it to the product of two matrices and $(d-2)$ tensors of order three, as shown in Fig. 8.9. The matrix $\mathcal{G}_1$ is of size $n_1 \times r_1$, the matrix $\mathcal{G}_d$ is of size $r_{d-1} \times n_d$, and the tensors $\mathcal{G}_k$ for $k \in \{2, \ldots, d-1\}$ are of size $r_{k-1} \times n_k \times r_k$.

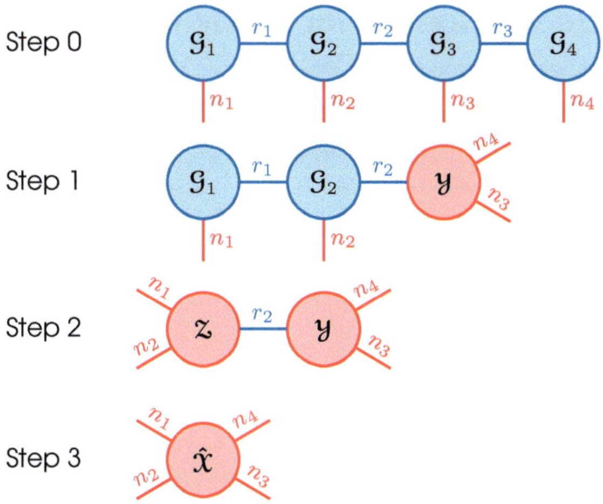

Figure 8.8 Reconstruction of a 4-way tensor from TT decomposition.

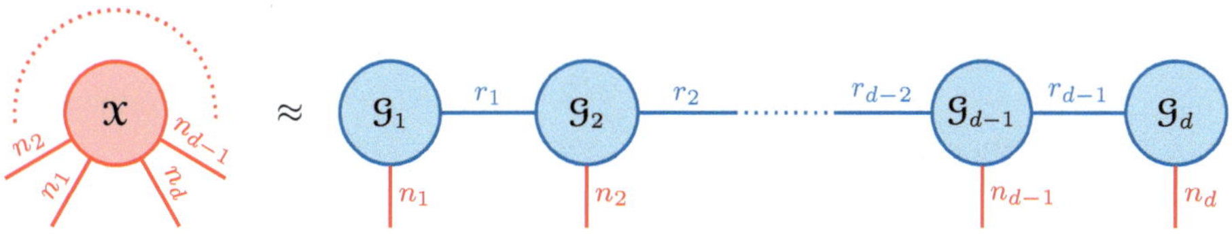

Figure 8.9 TT decomposition of a d-way tensor.

Elementwise, for all $(i_1, i_2, \ldots, i_d) \in [n_1] \otimes [n_2] \otimes \cdots \otimes [n_d]$, we have

$$\mathcal{X}(i_1, i_2, \ldots, i_d) \approx \sum_{j_1=1}^{r_1} \sum_{j_2=1}^{r_2} \cdots \sum_{j_{d-1}=1}^{r_{d-1}} \mathcal{G}_1(i_1, j_1) \left(\prod_{k=2}^{d-1} \mathcal{G}_k(j_{k-1}, i_k, j_k) \right) \mathcal{G}_d(j_d, i_d).$$

8.2 Algorithm and Error Analysis

There is a variety of TT decomposition methods, and here we cover a basic algorithm with controllable error. The algorithm computes a series of SVDs and can choose the size of each component of the decomposition to preserve a specified error.

For the algorithms, recall that the function LLSV refers to Algorithm 6.1 and calculates the leading left singular vectors for a specified rank or error and returns the subspace error. In other words,

$$[\mathbf{U}, \varepsilon] = \text{LLSV}(\mathbf{Y}, r \text{ or } \bar{\varepsilon})$$

returns the matrix $\mathbf{U} \in \mathbb{O}^{n \times r}$ (the set of $n \times r$ orthonormal matrices) that minimizes the subspace error:

$$\varepsilon = \|(\mathbf{I} - \mathbf{U}\mathbf{U}^\intercal)\mathbf{Y}\|_F = \min_{\mathbf{V} \in \mathbb{O}^{n \times r}} \|(\mathbf{I} - \mathbf{V}\mathbf{V}^\intercal)\mathbf{Y}\|_F.$$

Equivalently, the best rank-r approximation is given by $\mathbf{Y} \approx \mathbf{U}(\mathbf{U}^\intercal \mathbf{Y})$ (see Theorem A.26). If ε is specified, then r is chosen to be the dimension of the smallest subspace such that the subspace error satisfies $\varepsilon \le \bar{\varepsilon}$.

8.2.1 TT-SVD Decomposition for 4-way Tensors

The algorithm for 4-way TT decomposition is shown in Algorithm 8.1 and illustrated in Fig. 8.10. The user can specify (r_1, r_2, r_3) or select these ranks automatically to guarantee ε error, as explained in the analysis that follows.

Algorithm 8.1 TT-SVD for 4-way Tensors

Require: $\mathcal{X} \in \mathbb{R}^{n_1 \times n_2 \times n_3 \times n_4}$, ranks (r_1, r_2, r_3) or relative error tolerance $\varepsilon \geq 0$
Ensure: TT decomposition $\hat{\mathcal{X}}$ of rank (r_1, r_2, r_3) or $\text{ERR} = \|\mathcal{X} - \hat{\mathcal{X}}\| \leq \varepsilon \|\mathcal{X}\|$

function TTSVD($\mathcal{X}$, (r_1, r_2, r_3) or ε)
  $\bar{\varepsilon} \leftarrow (\varepsilon/\sqrt{3})\|\mathcal{X}\|$
  $[\mathbf{G}_1, \varepsilon_1] \leftarrow \text{LLSV}(\mathbf{X}_{(1)}, r_1 \text{ or } \bar{\varepsilon})$ ▷ $n_1 \times r_1$ orthonormal
  $\mathcal{G}_1 \leftarrow \mathbf{G}_1$
  $\mathbf{Y}_2 \leftarrow \mathbf{G}_1^\intercal \mathbf{X}_{(1)}$ ▷ Reduced to size $r_1 \times n_2 n_3 n_4$
  $\bar{\mathbf{Y}}_2 \leftarrow \text{reshape}(\mathbf{Y}_2, r_1 n_2 \times n_3 n_4)$
  $[\mathbf{G}_2, \varepsilon_2] \leftarrow \text{LLSV}(\bar{\mathbf{Y}}_2, r_2 \text{ or } \bar{\varepsilon})$ ▷ $r_1 n_2 \times r_2$ orthonormal
  $\mathcal{G}_2 \leftarrow \text{reshape}(\mathbf{G}_2, r_1 \times n_2 \times r_2)$
  $\mathbf{Y}_3 \leftarrow \mathbf{G}_2^\intercal \bar{\mathbf{Y}}_2$ ▷ Reduced to size $r_2 \times n_3 n_4$
  $\bar{\mathbf{Y}}_3 \leftarrow \text{reshape}(\mathbf{Y}_3, r_2 n_3 \times n_4)$
  $[\mathbf{G}_3, \varepsilon_3] \leftarrow \text{LLSV}(\bar{\mathbf{Y}}_3, r_3 \text{ or } \bar{\varepsilon})$ ▷ $r_2 n_3 \times r_3$ orthonormal
  $\mathcal{G}_3 \leftarrow \text{reshape}(\mathbf{G}_3, r_2 \times n_3 \times r_3)$
  $\mathbf{Y}_4 \leftarrow \mathbf{G}_3^\intercal \bar{\mathbf{Y}}_3$ ▷ Reduced to size $r_3 \times n_4$
  $\mathcal{G}_4 \leftarrow \mathbf{Y}_4$
  $\text{ERR} \leftarrow \sqrt{\varepsilon_1^2 + \varepsilon_2^2 + \varepsilon_3^2}$ ▷ $\text{ERR} = \|\mathcal{X} - \hat{\mathcal{X}}\|$
  return $\{\mathcal{G}_1, \mathcal{G}_2, \mathcal{G}_3, \mathcal{G}_4, \text{ERR}\}$ ▷ $\hat{\mathcal{X}} \equiv [\![\mathcal{G}_1, \mathcal{G}_2, \mathcal{G}_3, \mathcal{G}_4]\!]$
end function

We compute the tensor trains, $\mathcal{G}_k$, in order. To compute $\mathcal{G}_1$, we compute a matrix $\mathbf{G}_1$ that is the LLSV of $\mathcal{X}$ unfolded to $\mathbf{X}_{(1)}$. Then, we set $\mathbf{Y}_2 = \mathbf{G}_1^\intercal \mathbf{X}_{(1)}$ so that

$$\mathbf{X}_{(1)} \approx \mathbf{G}_1 \mathbf{Y}_2.$$

The matrix $\mathbf{G}_1$ is $\mathcal{G}_1$. The matrix $\mathbf{Y}_2$ of size $r_1 \times n_2 n_3 n_4$ is the projection of $\mathbf{X}_{(1)}$ down to the subspace spanned by the columns of $\mathbf{G}_1$. We can envision $\mathbf{Y}_2$ as a *remainder tensor* $\mathcal{Y}_2$ of size $r_1 \times n_2 \times n_3 \times n_4$; this is what remains to be factored.

To compute $\mathcal{G}_2$, we reshape $\mathcal{Y}_2$ to $\bar{\mathbf{Y}}_2$ of size $r_1 n_2 \times n_3 n_4$ and compute its LLSV to get $\mathbf{G}_2$. Then, we set $\mathbf{Y}_3 = \mathbf{G}_2^\intercal \bar{\mathbf{Y}}_2$ so that

$$\bar{\mathbf{Y}}_2 \approx \mathbf{G}_2 \mathbf{Y}_3.$$

The tensor $\mathcal{G}_2$ comes from $\mathbf{G}_2$ reshaped to size $r_1 \times n_2 \times r_2$. The matrix $\mathbf{Y}_3$ of size $r_2 \times n_3 n_4$ is the projection of $\bar{\mathbf{Y}}_2$ down to the subspace spanned by the columns of $\mathbf{G}_2$. We can envision $\mathbf{Y}_2$ as a tensor $\mathcal{Y}_2$ of size $r_2 \times n_3 \times n_4$.

Finally, to compute $\mathcal{G}_3$ and $\mathcal{G}_4$, we reshape $\mathbf{Y}_3$ to $\bar{\mathbf{Y}}_3$ of size $r_2 n_3 \times n_4$ and compute its LLSV $\mathbf{G}_3$ and set $\mathbf{Y}_4 = \mathbf{G}_3^\intercal \bar{\mathbf{Y}}_3$ so that

$$\bar{\mathbf{Y}}_3 \approx \mathbf{G}_3 \mathbf{Y}_4.$$

Then $\mathcal{G}_3$ is $\mathbf{G}_3$ reshaped to size $r_2 \times n_3 \times r_3$ and $\mathcal{G}_4$ is $\mathbf{Y}_4$ (the remainder, which is now just a matrix) of size $r_3 \times n_4$.

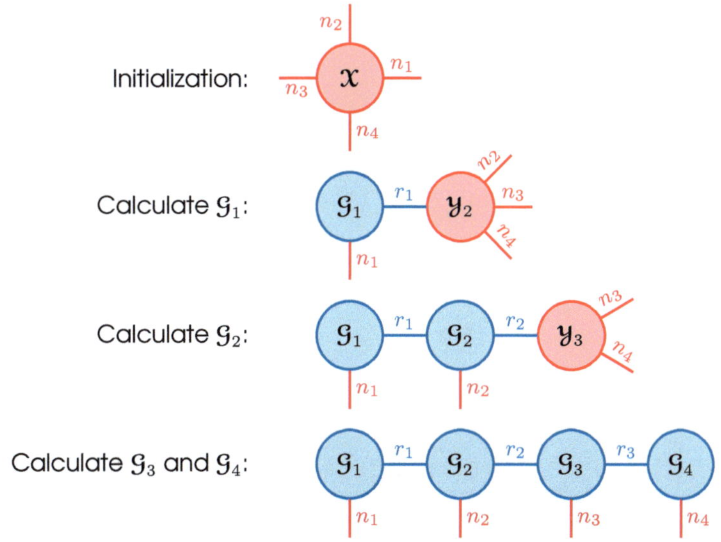

Figure 8.10 Illustration of TT decomposition of a 4-way tensor.

Remark 8.1 (How large can TT ranks grow?) Let us consider how big the dimensions of each $\mathcal{G}_k$ can be. For simplicity, assume $\mathcal{X}$ is of size $n\times n\times n\times n$. In Step 1, we have $r_1 \leq n$. In Step 2, we have $r_2 \leq \min\{r_1 n, n^2\} \leq n^2$. In Step 3, we have $r_3 \leq \min\{r_2 n, n\} \leq n$. So, it can be the case that $\mathcal{G}_2$ is as large as $n \times n \times n^2$, the size of $\mathcal{X}$!

Error Analysis of 4-way TT Decomposition

Algorithm 8.1 sequentially projects $\mathcal{X}$ down onto reduced subspaces. However, the methodology may not make this obvious. Here we express the projections as linear transformations on $\text{vec}(\mathcal{X})$.

In the first step, we create an approximation of $\mathcal{X}$ as

$$\begin{aligned}
\text{vec}(\mathcal{X}) &\approx \text{vec}(\mathbf{G}_1\mathbf{Y}_2) = \text{vec}(\mathbf{G}_1\mathbf{G}_1^{\intercal}\mathbf{X}_{(1)}) \\
&= (\mathbf{I}_{n_2n_3n_4} \otimes \mathbf{G}_1\mathbf{G}_1^{\intercal})\,\text{vec}(\mathcal{X}) \\
&= (\mathbf{I}_{n_2n_3n_4} \otimes \mathbf{G}_1)(\mathbf{I}_{n_2n_3n_4} \otimes \mathbf{G}_1)^{\intercal}\,\text{vec}(\mathcal{X}) \\
&= \mathbf{U}_1 \underbrace{\mathbf{U}_1^{\intercal}\,\text{vec}(\mathcal{X})}_{\text{vec}(\mathbf{Y}_2)}, \qquad \text{where} \quad \mathbf{U}_1 = \mathbf{I}_{n_2n_3n_4} \otimes \mathbf{G}_1.
\end{aligned}$$

Observe that the Kronecker product $\mathbf{U}_1 = \mathbf{I}_{n_2n_3n_4} \otimes \mathbf{G}_1$ is orthonormal by Exercise A.27. Next, we proceed to build an approximation of $\mathbf{Y}_2$ and $\mathbf{Y}_3$, using similar arguments to deduce that

$$\begin{aligned}
\text{vec}(\mathbf{Y}_2) &\approx \mathbf{U}_2\mathbf{U}_2^{\intercal}\,\text{vec}(\mathbf{Y}_2), \qquad \text{where} \quad \mathbf{U}_2 = \mathbf{I}_{n_3n_4} \otimes \mathbf{G}_2, \\
\text{vec}(\mathbf{Y}_3) &\approx \mathbf{U}_3\mathbf{U}_3^{\intercal}\,\text{vec}(\mathbf{Y}_3), \qquad \text{where} \quad \mathbf{U}_3 = \mathbf{I}_{n_4} \otimes \mathbf{G}_3.
\end{aligned}$$

Here $\mathbf{U}_2$ and $\mathbf{U}_3$ are also orthonormal by Exercise A.27. Putting this sequence of approximations together, we have that overall TT approximation to $\mathcal{X}$ is given by

$$\text{vec}(\mathcal{X}) \approx \text{vec}(\hat{\mathcal{X}}) \equiv \mathbf{U}_1\mathbf{U}_2\mathbf{U}_3\mathbf{U}_3^{\intercal}\mathbf{U}_2^{\intercal}\mathbf{U}_1^{\intercal}\,\text{vec}(\mathcal{X}).$$

Thus, we can use a telescoping sum to see

$$\begin{aligned}
&\operatorname{vec}(\mathcal{X}) - \operatorname{vec}(\hat{\mathcal{X}}) \\
&= \operatorname{vec}(\mathcal{X}) - \mathbf{U}_1\mathbf{U}_1^\intercal \operatorname{vec}(\mathcal{X}) \\
&\qquad + \mathbf{U}_1\mathbf{U}_1^\intercal \operatorname{vec}(\mathcal{X}) - \mathbf{U}_1\mathbf{U}_2\mathbf{U}_2^\intercal\mathbf{U}_1^\intercal \operatorname{vec}(\mathcal{X}) \\
&\qquad\qquad + \mathbf{U}_1\mathbf{U}_2\mathbf{U}_2^\intercal\mathbf{U}_1^\intercal \operatorname{vec}(\mathcal{X}) - \underbrace{\mathbf{U}_1\mathbf{U}_2\mathbf{U}_3\mathbf{U}_3^\intercal\mathbf{U}_2^\intercal\mathbf{U}_1^\intercal \operatorname{vec}(\mathcal{X})}_{\operatorname{vec}(\hat{\mathcal{X}})} \\
&= (\mathbf{I} - \mathbf{U}_1\mathbf{U}_1^\intercal) \operatorname{vec}(\mathcal{X}) \\
&\qquad + \mathbf{U}_1(\mathbf{I} - \mathbf{U}_2\mathbf{U}_2^\intercal) \underbrace{\mathbf{U}_1^\intercal \operatorname{vec}(\mathcal{X})}_{\operatorname{vec}(\mathbf{Y}_2)} \\
&\qquad\qquad + \mathbf{U}_1\mathbf{U}_2(\mathbf{I} - \mathbf{U}_3\mathbf{U}_3^\intercal) \underbrace{\mathbf{U}_2^\intercal\mathbf{U}_1^\intercal \operatorname{vec}(\mathcal{X})}_{\operatorname{vec}(\mathbf{Y}_3)} \\
&= (\mathbf{I} - \mathbf{U}_1\mathbf{U}_1^\intercal) \operatorname{vec}(\mathcal{X}) + \mathbf{U}_1(\mathbf{I} - \mathbf{U}_2\mathbf{U}_2^\intercal) \operatorname{vec}(\mathbf{Y}_2) + \mathbf{U}_1\mathbf{U}_2(\mathbf{I} - \mathbf{U}_3\mathbf{U}_3^\intercal) \operatorname{vec}(\mathbf{Y}_3).
\end{aligned}$$

By Proposition A.9, we can obtain the following proposition.

Proposition 8.2 (Norm Decomposition) *For any orthonormal matrix* $\mathbf{U} \in \mathbb{R}^{n \times p}$ *with* $n \geq p$ *and vectors* $\mathbf{a} \in \mathbb{R}^n$ *and* $\mathbf{b} \in \mathbb{R}^p$*, we can split the norm*

$$\|(\mathbf{I} - \mathbf{U}\mathbf{U}^\intercal)\mathbf{a} + \mathbf{U}\mathbf{b}\|_2^2 = \|(\mathbf{I} - \mathbf{U}\mathbf{U}^\intercal)\mathbf{a}\|_2^2 + \|\mathbf{b}\|_2^2.$$

Proof. We have

$$\begin{aligned}
&\|(\mathbf{I} - \mathbf{U}\mathbf{U}^\intercal)\mathbf{a} + \mathbf{U}\mathbf{b}\|_2^2 \\
&\qquad = \|(\mathbf{I} - \mathbf{U}\mathbf{U}^\intercal)\left[(\mathbf{I} - \mathbf{U}\mathbf{U}^\intercal)\mathbf{a} + \mathbf{U}\mathbf{b}\right]\|_2^2 + \|\mathbf{U}\mathbf{U}^\intercal\left[(\mathbf{I} - \mathbf{U}\mathbf{U}^\intercal)\mathbf{a} + \mathbf{U}\mathbf{b}\right]\|_2^2 \\
&\qquad = \|(\mathbf{I} - \mathbf{U}\mathbf{U}^\intercal)\mathbf{a}\|_2^2 + \|\mathbf{U}\mathbf{b}\|_2^2 \\
&\qquad = \|(\mathbf{I} - \mathbf{U}\mathbf{U}^\intercal)\mathbf{a}\|_2^2 + \|\mathbf{b}\|_2^2 \quad \text{by Proposition A.7.} \qquad \square
\end{aligned}$$

Therefore, using Proposition 8.2 repeatedly, we can decompose the error as

$$\begin{aligned}
&\|\mathcal{X} - \hat{\mathcal{X}}\|^2 \\
&= \|(\mathbf{I} - \mathbf{U}_1\mathbf{U}_1^\intercal) \operatorname{vec}(\mathcal{X}) + \mathbf{U}_1[(\mathbf{I} - \mathbf{U}_2\mathbf{U}_2^\intercal) \operatorname{vec}(\mathbf{Y}_2) + \mathbf{U}_2(\mathbf{I} - \mathbf{U}_3\mathbf{U}_3^\intercal) \operatorname{vec}(\mathbf{Y}_3)]\|_2^2 \\
&= \|(\mathbf{I} - \mathbf{U}_1\mathbf{U}_1^\intercal) \operatorname{vec}(\mathcal{X})\|_2^2 + \|(\mathbf{I} - \mathbf{U}_2\mathbf{U}_2^\intercal) \operatorname{vec}(\mathbf{Y}_2) + \mathbf{U}_2(\mathbf{I} - \mathbf{U}_3\mathbf{U}_3^\intercal) \operatorname{vec}(\mathbf{Y}_3)\|_2^2 \\
&= \|(\mathbf{I} - \mathbf{U}_1\mathbf{U}_1^\intercal) \operatorname{vec}(\mathcal{X})\|_2^2 + \|(\mathbf{I} - \mathbf{U}_2\mathbf{U}_2^\intercal) \operatorname{vec}(\mathbf{Y}_2)\|_2^2 + \|(\mathbf{I} - \mathbf{U}_3\mathbf{U}_3^\intercal) \operatorname{vec}(\mathbf{Y}_3)\|_2^2 \\
&= \|(\mathbf{I} - \mathbf{G}_1\mathbf{G}_1^\intercal)\mathbf{X}_{(1)}\|_F^2 + \|(\mathbf{I} - \mathbf{G}_2\mathbf{G}_2^\intercal)\bar{\mathbf{Y}}_2\|_F^2 + \|(\mathbf{I} - \mathbf{G}_3\mathbf{G}_3^\intercal)\bar{\mathbf{Y}}_3\|_F^2.
\end{aligned}$$

The TT squared error is exactly the sum of the approximation errors from each of the LLSV steps. This means that we can compute the ranks for a TT decomposition that achieves a desired error. We formalize this in the next result.

Theorem 8.3 (Error of 4-way TT Decomposition) *Let* $\mathcal{X} \in n_1 \times n_2 \times n_3 \times n_4$ *and let* $\hat{\mathcal{X}} = [\![\mathcal{G}_1, \mathcal{G}_2, \mathcal{G}_3, \mathcal{G}_4]\!]$ *be its TT decomposition calculated by Algorithm 8.1. Then*

$$\|\mathcal{X} - \hat{\mathcal{X}}\|^2 = \varepsilon_1^2 + \varepsilon_2^2 + \varepsilon_3^2,$$

where ε_k *are the LLSV errors from Lines 3, 7, and 11.*

8.2.2 TT-SVD for d-way Tensors

The algorithm for an arbitrary order-d tensor $\mathcal{X}$ is given in Algorithm 8.2. This is analogous to the algorithm for the 4-way tensor.

In the start of each iteration, we have residual tensor $\mathcal{Y}_k$ of size $r_{k-1} \times n_k \times \cdots \times n_d$ of order $(d-k+2)$ that still has $(d-k)$ modes left to be reduced in size. In the first iteration, $\mathcal{Y}_1 = \mathcal{X}$ with $r_0 = 1$; in the remaining iterations, the matrix $\bar{\mathbf{Y}}_k$ is the tensor $\mathcal{Y}_k$ reshaped to size $(r_{k-1}n_k) \times (n_{k+1} \cdots n_d)$. We never explicitly reference the tensor $\mathcal{Y}$, only different unfoldings of it.

In Line 10, we compute the LLSV of $\bar{\mathbf{Y}}_k$ so that $\mathbf{G}_k$ is given by the leading left singular vectors and is of size $r_{k-1}n_k \times r_k$ (an orthonormal matrix) and

$$\bar{\mathbf{Y}}_k \approx \mathbf{G}_k \mathbf{Y}_{k+1} = \mathbf{G}_k \mathbf{G}_k^\intercal \bar{\mathbf{Y}}_k.$$

The matrix $\mathbf{Y}_{k+1}$ of size $r_k \times (n_{k+1} \cdots n_d)$ is the projection of $\bar{\mathbf{Y}}_k$ onto the subspace spanned by the columns of $\mathbf{G}_k$. The error in the low-rank factorization is

$$\varepsilon_k = \|\bar{\mathbf{Y}}_k - \mathbf{G}_k \mathbf{G}_k^\intercal \bar{\mathbf{Y}}_k\|_F \leq \min_{\operatorname{rank}(\mathbf{W})=r_k} \|\bar{\mathbf{Y}}_k - \mathbf{W}\|_F.$$

In order that the train cars link together for the tensor contraction operation, $\mathbf{G}_k$ is reshaped to $\mathcal{G}_k$ of size $r_{k-1} \times n_k \times r_k$.

The caboose is given by the final remainder, $\mathcal{G}_d = \mathbf{Y}_d$, and this completes the decomposition. The value $\textsc{Err} = \|\mathcal{X} - \hat{\mathcal{X}}\|$ can be computed from the LLSV errors, as we will show in Theorem 8.6.

Algorithm 8.2 TT-SVD for d-way Tensors

Require: $\mathcal{X} \in \mathbb{R}^{n_1 \times n_2 \times \cdots \times n_d}$, ranks $(r_1, r_2, \ldots, r_{d-1})$ or error tolerance $\varepsilon \geq 0$
Ensure: TT decomposition $\hat{\mathcal{X}}$ of rank $(r_1, r_2, \ldots, r_{d-1})$ or $\textsc{Err} = \|\mathcal{X} - \hat{\mathcal{X}}\| \leq \varepsilon\|\mathcal{X}\|$
1: **function** TTSVD($\mathcal{X}$, $(r_1, r_2, \ldots, r_{d-1})$ or ε)
2: $\quad \bar{\varepsilon} \leftarrow (\varepsilon/\sqrt{d-1})\|\mathcal{X}\|$
3: $\quad r_0 \leftarrow 1$
4: $\quad$ **for** $k = 1, \ldots, d-1$ **do**
5: $\qquad$ **if** $k = 1$ **then**
6: $\qquad\quad \bar{\mathbf{Y}}_1 \leftarrow \mathbf{X}_{(1)}$
7: $\qquad$ **else**
8: $\qquad\quad \bar{\mathbf{Y}}_k \leftarrow \operatorname{reshape}\big(\mathbf{Y}_k, (r_{k-1}n_k) \times (n_{k+1} \cdots n_d)\big)$
9: $\qquad$ **end if**
10: $\qquad [\mathbf{G}_k, \varepsilon_k] \leftarrow \operatorname{LLSV}(\bar{\mathbf{Y}}_k, r_k \text{ or } \bar{\varepsilon})$ $\quad \triangleright$ $r_{k-1}n_k \times r_k$ orthonormal
11: $\qquad \mathbf{Y}_{k+1} \leftarrow \mathbf{G}_k^\intercal \bar{\mathbf{Y}}_k$ $\quad \triangleright$ Remainder of size $r_k \times (n_{k+1} \cdots n_d)$
12: $\qquad \mathcal{G}_k \leftarrow \operatorname{reshape}(\mathbf{G}_k, r_{k-1} \times n_k \times r_k)$ $\quad \triangleright$ Reshape result to 3-way tensor
13: $\quad$ **end for**
14: $\quad \mathcal{G}_d \leftarrow \mathbf{Y}_d$
15: $\quad \textsc{Err} \leftarrow \sqrt{\sum_{k=1}^{d-1} \varepsilon_k^2}$
16: $\quad$ **return** $\{\mathcal{G}_1, \mathcal{G}_2, \ldots, \mathcal{G}_d, \textsc{Err}\}$ $\quad \triangleright$ $\hat{\mathcal{X}} \equiv [\![\mathcal{G}_1, \mathcal{G}_2, \ldots, \mathcal{G}_d]\!]$
17: **end function**

Remark 8.4 (How large can TT ranks grow?) Let us consider how big the dimensions of each $\mathcal{G}_k$ can be. For simplicity, assume $\mathcal{X}$ is a d-way tensor of size $n \times n \times \cdots \times n$. Let $\bar{r}_k$ denote the maximum possible rank at step k. In iteration k, we have

$$\bar{r}_k = \min\{\, \bar{r}_{k-1}n, n^{d-k} \,\}.$$

We can conclude,

$$\bar{r}_k = \begin{cases} n^k & \text{if } k \leq \lfloor d/2 \rfloor \\ n^{d-k} & \text{otherwise} \end{cases}.$$

In particular, if d is even and $k = d/2$, then $\mathcal{G}_k$ could be of size $n^{k-1} \times n \times n^k$, meaning its total size is n^d, the same as $\mathcal{X}$!

Complexity of TT-SVD

At step k, the TT-SVD calculates the LLSV for the matrix $\bar{\mathbf{Y}}_k$ of size $(r_{k-1}n_k) \times (n_{k+1} \cdots n_d)$. Define $P_k \equiv \prod_{\ell > k} n_\ell$ for all $k \in [d-1]$. At iteration k, the cost of the LLSV in Line 10 is

$$\mathcal{O}(r_{k-1}n_k P_k \min\{r_{k-1}n_k, P_k\}),$$

and the cost of the matrix–matrix multiplication in Line 11 is

$$\mathcal{O}(r_k r_{k-1} n_k P_k).$$

Since $r_k \leq \min\{r_{k-1}n_k, P_k\}$, the LLSV cost dominates. Hence, the total cost is

$$\sum_{k=1}^{d-1} \mathcal{O}(r_{k-1}n_k P_k \min\{r_{k-1}n_k, P_k\}).$$

Letting $N = \prod_{k=1}^{d} n_k$ and recalling that $r_0 = 1$, the first step has cost $\mathcal{O}(n_1 N)$, which is the same as for ST-HOSVD.

Error Analysis of d-way TT Decomposition

Just as in the 4-way case, Algorithm 8.2 sequentially projects $\mathcal{X}$ down onto reduced subspaces. We provide a more general analysis for the d-way case, requiring more extensive definitions. For consistency, we treat the first and last matrices in the TT decomposition as 3-way tensors $\mathcal{G}_0 \in \mathbb{R}^{r_0 \times n_1 \times r_1}$ and $\mathcal{G}_d \in \mathbb{R}^{r_{d-1} \times n_d \times r_d}$ with $r_0 = r_d = 1$.

At iteration k of the algorithm, the *residual tensor* $\mathcal{Y}_k$ is of order $d - k + 2$ and size $r_{k-1} \times n_k \times \cdots \times n_d$. For $k = 1$, the tensor $\mathcal{Y}_1$ is of size $1 \times n_1 \times n_2 \times \cdots \times n_d$. In Algorithm 8.2, the matrix $\mathbf{Y}_k$ in the algorithm is $\mathcal{Y}_k$ reshaped to size $r_{k-1} \times (n_k \cdots n_d)$, and the matrix $\bar{\mathbf{Y}}_k$ is $\mathcal{Y}_k$ reshaped to size $r_{k-1}n_k \times (n_{k+1} \cdots n_d)$.

Using the $\mathbf{G}_k$ orthonormal matrices of size $r_{k-1}n_k \times r_k$ from Line 10 (the TT components), we define

$$\mathbf{U}_k = \mathbf{I}_{n_{k+1}\cdots n_d} \otimes \mathbf{G}_k \in \mathbb{R}^{r_{k-1}n_k\cdots n_d \times r_k n_{k+1}\cdots n_d} \quad \text{for all} \quad k \in [d-1]. \tag{8.3}$$

Exercise 8.4 Let $k \in [d-1]$. Prove that $\mathbf{U}_1 \cdots \mathbf{U}_{k-2}\mathbf{U}_{k-1} = \mathbf{I}_{n_{k+1}\cdots n_d} \otimes \mathbf{W}_k$, where $\mathbf{W}_k$ is an orthonormal matrix with

$$\mathbf{W}_k = (\mathbf{I}_{n_2\cdots n_k} \otimes \mathbf{G}_1) \cdots (\mathbf{I}_{n_{k-1}n_k} \otimes \mathbf{G}_{k-2})(\mathbf{I}_{n_k} \otimes \mathbf{G}_{k-1}) \in \mathbb{R}^{n_1\cdots n_k \times n_k r_{k-1}}.$$

By Exercise A.27, the matrices $\mathbf{U}_k$ are orthonormal. Using these matrices instead of the $\mathbf{G}_k$ enables us to avoid the notation awkwardness of reshaping from $\mathbf{Y}_k$ to $\bar{\mathbf{Y}}_k$ at each step and instead reason with respect to $\mathbf{y}_k \equiv \text{vec}(\mathcal{Y}_k)$. Specifically, from Line 11, we can relate subsequent $\mathbf{y}_k$ recursively via

$$\mathbf{y}_{k+1} = \text{vec}(\mathbf{G}_k^\intercal \bar{\mathbf{Y}}_k) = (\mathbf{I}_{n_{k+1}\cdots n_d} \otimes \mathbf{G}_k^\intercal)\,\text{vec}(\bar{\mathbf{Y}}_k) = \mathbf{U}_k^\intercal \mathbf{y}_k, \tag{8.4}$$

with $\mathbf{y}_1 = \text{vec}(\mathcal{X})$. With this formulation, we can elicit the following relationship:

$$\mathbf{y}_{k+1} = \mathbf{U}_k^\intercal \cdots \mathbf{U}_1^\intercal\,\text{vec}(\mathcal{X}). \tag{8.5}$$

Exercise 8.5 Show $\|(\mathbf{I} - \mathbf{U}_k\mathbf{U}_k^\intercal)\mathbf{y}_k\|_2 = \|(\mathbf{I} - \mathbf{G}_k\mathbf{G}_k^\intercal)\bar{\mathbf{Y}}_k\|_F$.

Let us define $\mathcal{X}_k$ to be the TT model that has been built by the start of iteration k of the algorithm. In other words, $\mathcal{X}_k$ is the tensor contraction of $\mathcal{G}_1$ to $\mathcal{G}_{k-1}$ and $\mathcal{Y}_k$; see Fig. 8.11. This means that $\mathcal{X}_1 = \mathcal{X}$ and $\mathcal{X}_d = \hat{\mathcal{X}} = [\![\mathcal{G}_1, \mathcal{G}_2, \cdots, \mathcal{G}_{d-1}, \mathcal{G}_d]\!]$ (since $\mathcal{G}_d = \mathcal{Y}_d$).

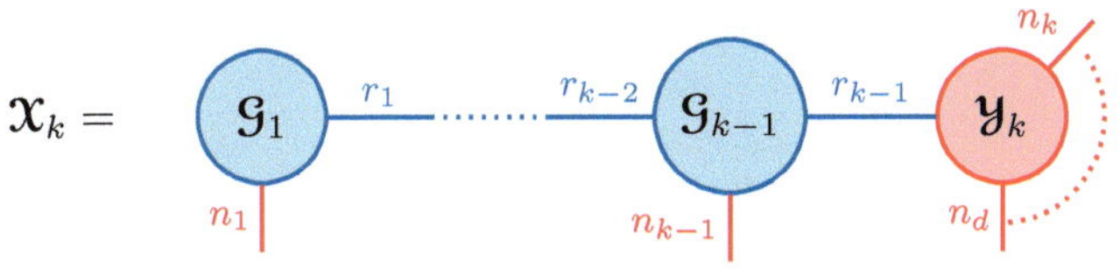

Figure 8.11 TT decomposition model of a d-way tensor before step k of the algorithm.

If we define $\mathbf{x}_k \equiv \text{vec}(\mathcal{X}_k)$, then that series of $k-1$ tensor contractions can be expressed in vectorized notation as

$$\begin{aligned} \mathbf{x}_k &= \text{vec}(\mathcal{X}_k) \\ &= \mathbf{U}_1 \cdots \mathbf{U}_{k-1}\mathbf{y}_k \\ &= \mathbf{U}_1 \cdots \mathbf{U}_{k-1}\mathbf{U}_{k-1}^\intercal \cdots \mathbf{U}_1^\intercal\,\text{vec}(\mathcal{X}). \end{aligned} \tag{8.6}$$

The second step uses Eq. (8.5). At the initial step, we have $\mathbf{x}_1 = \mathbf{y}_1 = \text{vec}(\mathcal{X})$; and, after the final step, we have $\mathbf{x}_d = \text{vec}(\hat{\mathcal{X}})$.

Exercise 8.6 Show $\mathbf{x}_{k+1} = \mathbf{U}_k\mathbf{U}_k^\intercal\mathbf{x}_k$.

Proposition 8.5 (TT Error Recursion) *Let $\mathcal{X} \in n_1 \times n_2 \times \cdots \times n_d$ and let $\mathcal{X}_k$ be the tensor contraction of $\mathcal{G}_1$ through $\mathcal{G}_{k-1}$ and $\mathcal{Y}_d$ as illustrated in Fig. 8.11. That is, $\mathcal{X}_k$ is the TT model that has been built by the beginning of iteration k in Algorithm 8.2. Then, for any $k \in [d-1]$, we have*

$$\|\mathbf{x}_k - \mathbf{x}_d\|_2^2 = \varepsilon_k^2 + \|\mathbf{x}_{k+1} - \mathbf{x}_d\|_2^2,$$

where ε_k is the LLSV error from Line 10.

Proof. Recall two useful facts from Proposition A.7. First, the product of orthonormal matrices is orthonormal. Second, $\|\mathbf{U}\mathbf{x}\|_2 = \|\mathbf{x}\|_2$ for orthonormal $\mathbf{U}$ and any $\mathbf{x}$.

For $k \in [d-1]$, we have

$$\begin{aligned}
&\|\mathbf{x}_k - \mathbf{x}_d\|_2^2 \\
&\quad = \|\mathbf{U}_1 \cdots \mathbf{U}_{k-1}(\mathbf{y}_k - \mathbf{U}_k \cdots \mathbf{U}_{d-1}\mathbf{y}_d)\|_2^2 && \text{by Eq. (8.6)} \\
&\quad = \|\mathbf{y}_k - \mathbf{U}_k \cdots \mathbf{U}_{d-1}\mathbf{y}_d\|_2^2 \\
&\quad = \|\mathbf{y}_k - \mathbf{U}_k\mathbf{U}_k^\intercal\mathbf{y}_k + \mathbf{U}_k\mathbf{U}_k^\intercal\mathbf{y}_k - \mathbf{U}_k \cdots \mathbf{U}_{d-1}\mathbf{y}_d\|_2^2 \\
&\quad = \|(\mathbf{I} - \mathbf{U}_k\mathbf{U}_k^\intercal)\mathbf{y}_k + \mathbf{U}_k(\mathbf{y}_{k+1} - \mathbf{U}_{k+1} \cdots \mathbf{U}_{d-1}\mathbf{y}_d)\|_2^2 && \text{by Eq. (8.4)} \\
&\quad = \|(\mathbf{I} - \mathbf{U}_k\mathbf{U}_k^\intercal)\mathbf{y}_k\|_2 + \|\mathbf{y}_{k+1} - \mathbf{U}_{k+1} \cdots \mathbf{U}_{d-1}\mathbf{y}_d\|_2^2 && \text{by Prop. 8.2} \\
&\quad = \|(\mathbf{I} - \mathbf{U}_k\mathbf{U}_k^\intercal)\mathbf{y}_k\|_2 + \|\mathbf{U}_1 \cdots \mathbf{U}_k\mathbf{y}_{k+1} - \mathbf{U}_1 \cdots \mathbf{U}_{d-1}\mathbf{y}_d\|_2^2 \\
&\quad = \|(\mathbf{I} - \mathbf{U}_k\mathbf{U}_k^\intercal)\mathbf{y}_k\|_2 + \|\mathbf{x}_{k+1} - \mathbf{x}_d\|_2^2
\end{aligned}$$

Exercise 8.5 completes the proof. □

The following theorem states that the squared error of the TT-SVD decomposition is *exactly* the sum of the squared errors from the SVD computations. An inequality version of this result appeared in Oseledets and Tyrtyshnikov (2010), though this result appears again with a different proof in Oseledets (2011). Theorem 8.6 is the d-way analog of Theorem 8.3 for 4-way tensors.

Theorem 8.6 (Error of d-way TT Decomposition) *Let $\mathcal{X} \in n_1 \times n_2 \times \cdots \times n_d$ and let $\hat{\mathcal{X}} = [\![\mathcal{G}_1, \mathcal{G}_2, \cdots, \mathcal{G}_{d-1}, \mathcal{G}_d]\!]$ be its TT decomposition calculated by Algorithm 8.2. Then*

$$\|\mathcal{X} - \hat{\mathcal{X}}\|^2 = \sum_{k=1}^{d-1} \varepsilon_k^2,$$

where ε_k is the LLSV error in Line 10 of Algorithm 8.2.

Proof. Using Proposition 8.2, we have

$$\begin{aligned}
\|\mathcal{X} - \hat{\mathcal{X}}\|^2 &= \|\operatorname{vec}(\mathcal{X}) - \operatorname{vec}(\hat{\mathcal{X}})\|_2^2 = \|\mathbf{x}_1 - \mathbf{x}_d\|_2^2 \\
&= \varepsilon_1^2 + \|\mathbf{x}_2 - \mathbf{x}_d\|_2^2 \\
&= \varepsilon_1^2 + \varepsilon_2^2 + \|\mathbf{x}_3 - \mathbf{x}_d\|_2^2 \\
&\ \ \vdots \\
&= \varepsilon_1^2 + \varepsilon_2^2 + \cdots + \varepsilon_{d-1}^2 + \|\mathbf{x}_d - \mathbf{x}_d\|_2^2.
\end{aligned}$$

□

We can further establish the quasi-optimality of the TT decomposition.

Theorem 8.7 (Quasi-optimality of d-way TT Decomposition) *Let $\mathcal{X} \in n_1 \times n_2 \times \cdots \times n_d$ and let $\hat{\mathcal{X}} = [\![\mathcal{G}_1, \mathcal{G}_2, \cdots, \mathcal{G}_{d-1}, \mathcal{G}_d]\!]$ be its TT decomposition of rank $(r_1, r_2, \ldots, r_{d-1})$ calculated by Algorithm 8.2. Then $\hat{\mathcal{X}}$ is within a factor of $\sqrt{d-1}$ of optimal:*

$$\|\mathcal{X} - \hat{\mathcal{X}}\| \leq \sqrt{d-1}\, \|\mathcal{X} - \mathcal{X}^*\|,$$

where $\mathcal{X}^*$ is the optimal rank $(r_1, r_2, \ldots, r_{d-1})$ TT decomposition.

Proof. Let $\mathcal{X}^* = [\![\mathcal{G}_1^*, \cdots, \mathcal{G}_d^*]\!]$ be the optimal rank-$(r_1, \ldots, r_{d-1})$ TT decomposition of $\mathcal{X}$. Let $\mathbf{x} = \text{vec}(\mathcal{X})$ and $\mathbf{x}^* = \text{vec}(\mathcal{X}^*)$.

For any $k \in [d]$, define $\mathcal{A}_k$ to be the tensor contraction of $\mathcal{G}_1^*$ through $\mathcal{G}_k^*$ and $\mathcal{B}_k$ to be the tensor contraction of $\mathcal{G}_{k+1}^*$ through $\mathcal{G}_d^*$:

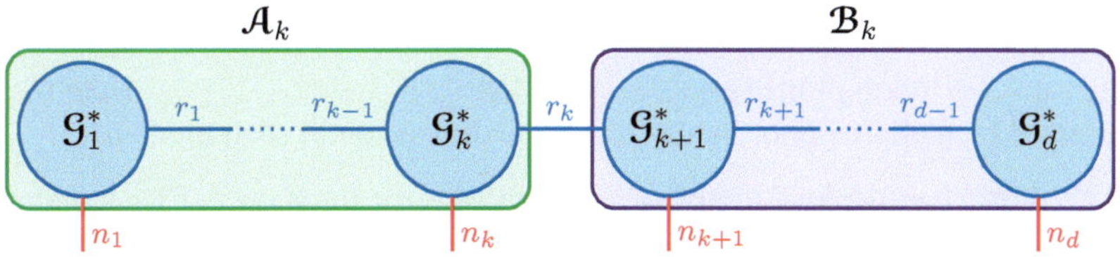

Then we can say $\mathbf{x}^* = \text{vec}(\mathbf{A}_k\mathbf{B}_k)$, where

$$\mathbf{A}_k = \text{reshape}(\mathcal{A}_k, (n_1 \ldots n_k) \times r_k) \quad \text{and} \quad \mathbf{B}_k = \text{reshape}(\mathcal{B}_k, r_k \times (n_{k+1} \ldots n_d)).$$

Let the orthonormal matrices $\{ \mathbf{U}_k \}$ associated with the TT decomposition tensor $\{ \mathcal{G}_k \}$ be as defined in Eq. (8.3). Since the product or orthonormal matrices is orthonormal, the matrix $\mathbf{U}_1 \cdots \mathbf{U}_{k-1}$ is orthonormal. Since $\|\mathbf{U}^\intercal\mathbf{x}\|_2 \leq \|\mathbf{x}\|_2$ for any orthonormal $\mathbf{U}$ (Proposition A.7), we have

$$\|\mathcal{X} - \mathcal{X}^*\| = \|\mathbf{x} - \mathbf{x}^*\|_2 \geq \|\mathbf{U}_{k-1}^\intercal \cdots \mathbf{U}_1^\intercal(\mathbf{x} - \mathbf{x}^*)\|_2.$$

By Eq. (8.5), $\mathbf{U}_{k-1}^\intercal \cdots \mathbf{U}_1^\intercal\mathbf{x} = \mathbf{y}_k$. By Exercise 8.4, we can write

$$\mathbf{U}_{k-1}^\intercal \cdots \mathbf{U}_1^\intercal = \mathbf{I}_{n_{k+1}\cdots n_d} \otimes \mathbf{W}_k^\intercal,$$

where $\mathbf{W}_k$ is of size $n_1 \cdots n_k \times n_k r_{k-1}$. Hence,

$$\mathbf{U}_{k-1}^\intercal \cdots \mathbf{U}_1^\intercal\mathbf{x}^* = \left(\mathbf{I}_{n_{k+1}\cdots n_d} \otimes \mathbf{W}_k^\intercal\right) \text{vec}(\mathbf{A}_k\mathbf{B}_k) = \text{vec}(\underbrace{\mathbf{W}_k^\intercal\mathbf{A}_k}_{\mathbf{C}_k}\mathbf{B}_k),$$

where the last step is by Eq. (A.11e) and we define $\mathbf{C}_k = \mathbf{W}_k^\intercal\mathbf{A}_k$ of size $n_k r_{k-1} \times r_k$. Putting this all together, we have

$$\begin{aligned}
\|\mathcal{X} - \mathcal{X}^*\| &\geq \|\mathbf{U}_{k-1}^\intercal \cdots \mathbf{U}_1^\intercal(\mathbf{x} - \mathbf{x}^*)\|_2 \\
&= \|\mathbf{y}_k - \text{vec}(\mathbf{C}_k\mathbf{B}_k)\|_2 \\
&= \|\bar{\mathbf{Y}}_k - \mathbf{C}_k\mathbf{B}_k\|_F \geq \varepsilon_k.
\end{aligned}$$

The last step is because $\mathbf{C}_k\mathbf{B}_k$ is a rank-k matrix, and we know ε_k is the best possible residual for a rank-k factorization of $\bar{\mathbf{Y}}_k$.

Finally, combining the last statement with Theorem 8.6, we have

$$\|\mathcal{X} - \hat{\mathcal{X}}\|^2 = \sum_{k=1}^{d-1} \varepsilon_k^2 \leq \sum_{k=1}^{d-1} \|\mathcal{X} - \mathcal{X}^*\|^2 = (d-1)\|\mathcal{X} - \mathcal{X}^*\|^2. \qquad \square$$

8.3 Example: TT of Discretized Function Tensor

We consider an example tensor known to have small TT ranks (Tobler, 2012, example 3.9). The tensor is a discretization of a multivariate function with elements given by the formula

$$x_{i_1 i_2 \cdots i_d} = \frac{1}{t_{i_1} + t_{i_2} + \cdots t_{i_d}} \quad \text{for} \quad (i_1, i_2, \ldots, i_d) \in [n] \otimes [n] \otimes \cdots \otimes [n], \tag{8.7}$$

where $\mathbf{t}$ is a discretization of the range $[1, 10]$ so that $t_i = 1 + (i-1)\frac{9}{n-1}$. Here the tensor is parametrized by the number of modes d and the dimension in each mode n.

Figure 8.12 shows the memory footprint and relative error for several TT decompositions of two instantiations of the input tensor, one for $d = 5$ and $n = 40$ and one for $d = 8$ and $n = 10$. These sizes are chosen so that the two tensors have approximately the same number of entries. The decompositions are computed using Algorithm 8.2 with specified relative tolerances ranging from 10^{-1} to 10^{-6}.

For comparison, we also compute Tucker decompositions using the same tolerances. We observe that for the smaller value of $d = 5$, there is little difference between TT and Tucker in navigating the trade-off between memory and error. However, for the larger value of $d = 8$ and smaller value of $n = 10$, TT is much more memory-efficient than Tucker for the same approximation error. This is because the TT ranks and Tucker ranks are comparable for this tensor, so the 3-way TT cores require much less memory than the 8-way Tucker core. In general, the TT ranks grow larger than the Tucker ranks, particularly in the middle modes, so which format provides more efficient decompositions is problem-dependent.

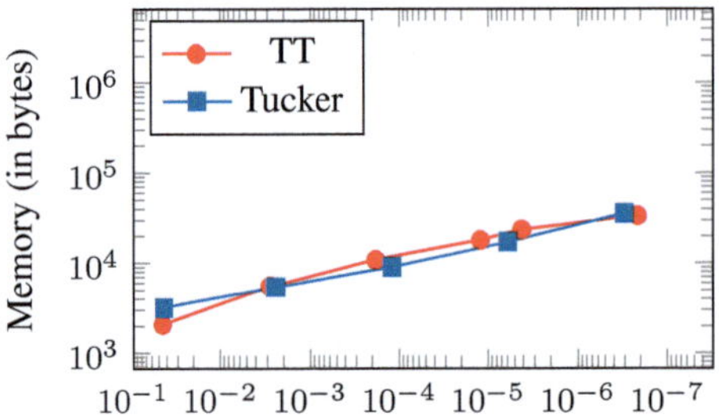

(a) Tucker versus TT decomposition of a 5-way tensor of size $40 \times \cdots \times 40$.

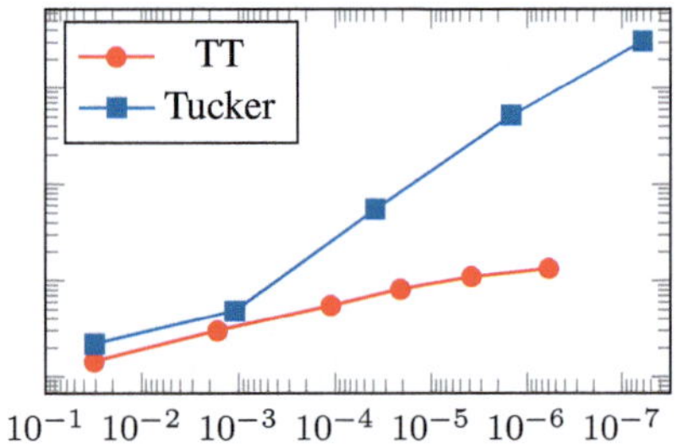

(b) Tucker versus TT decomposition of an 8-way tensor of size $10 \times \cdots \times 10$.

(c) Corresponding ranks.

Rel.	$d=5, n=40$		$d=8, n=10$	
error	TT	Tucker	TT	Tucker
10^{-1}	$(1,1,1,1)$	$(1,1,1,1,1)$	$(1,1,1,1,1,1,1)$	$(1,1,1,1,1,1,1,1)$
10^{-2}	$(2,2,2,2)$	$(2,2,2,2,2)$	$(2,2,2,2,2,2,2)$	$(2,2,2,2,2,2,2,2)$
10^{-3}	$(3,3,3,3)$	$(3,3,3,3,3)$	$(3,3,3,3,3,3,3)$	$(3,3,3,3,3,3,3,3)$
10^{-4}	$(4,4,4,4)$	$(4,4,4,4,4)$	$(3,4,4,4,4,4,3)$	$(3,3,3,3,3,3,3,3)$
10^{-5}	$(4,5,5,4)$	$(4,4,4,4,4)$	$(4,4,5,5,5,4,4)$	$(4,4,4,4,4,4,4,4)$
10^{-6}	$(5,6,6,5)$	$(5,5,5,5,5)$	$(5,5,5,5,5,5,5)$	$(5,5,5,5,5,5,5,5)$

Figure 8.12 Memory–error trade-off for TT and Tucker decompositions of tensor defined by Eq. (8.7). Explicit representation of the two tensors requires approximately 800 MB ($\approx 10^9$ bytes) in both cases.

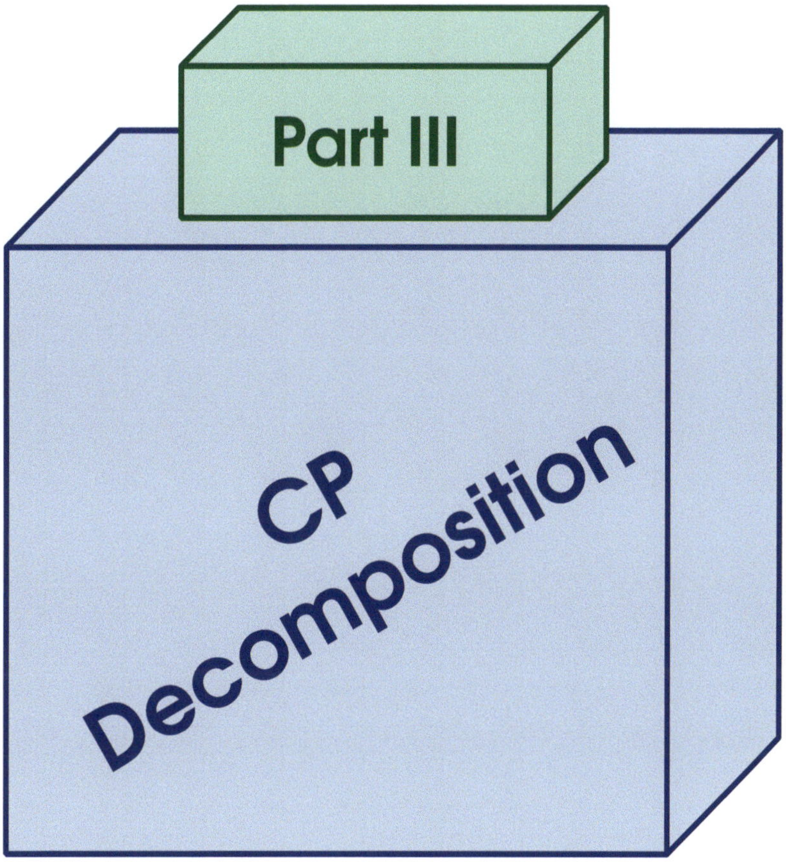
Part III
CP Decomposition

9 Canonical Polyadic Decomposition

The **CP decomposition** of a tensor refers to its expression as a sum of r rank-1 components (Carroll and Chang, 1970; Harshman, 1970; Hitchcock, 1927). Each **component** is a vector outer product. We refer to r colloquially as the **rank** of the decomposition, though this is technically only precise if r is minimal. Each vector is called a **factor**, and the set of factors of a mode is called a **factor matrix**. We can visualize this in the case of a 3-way tensor as shown in Fig. 9.1.

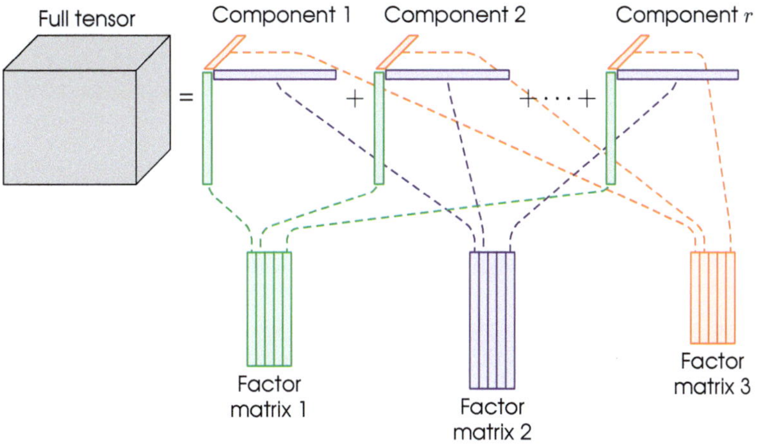

Figure 9.1 CP tensor factorization for a 3-way tensor, illustrating how columns of factor matrices are used to construct components of the decomposition.

In the 3-way case, each component is the outer product of three factors. Specifically, component j is the outer product of column j of factor matrix 1, column j of factor matrix 2, and column j of factor matrix 3. The factors are *matched* and not interchangeable. We provide detailed mathematical formulas in what follows, but the main idea here is that CP reduces a 3-way tensor to three factor matrices, each containing r factor vectors. The factors are useful for interpretation of the data, and the rows of the factor matrices map to latent representations.

The CP decomposition goes by a variety of names, including CANDECOMP (canonical decomposition), PARAFAC (parallel factors), or canonical polyadic (CP) decomposition. See Section 9.9 for further discussion on the origins of the nomenclature.

> The canonical polyadic (CP) decomposition is also known as CANDECOMP (canonical decomposition) or PARAFAC (parallel factors).

This chapter covers some basics about the CP decomposition, including its formulation and utility for interpretation, its expression as an optimization problem, computational methods, and example applications.

9.1 Formulation of CP Decomposition

The CP decomposition is a method for unsupervised learning because it finds patterns in multiway data. As we show using applications in Sections 9.6–9.8, the resulting vectors reveal inherent structures within the data. A typical use case is analyzing data measurements formatted as

object × feature × scenario .

This is visualized in Fig. 9.2. This is just a prototypical scenario and should not be limiting.

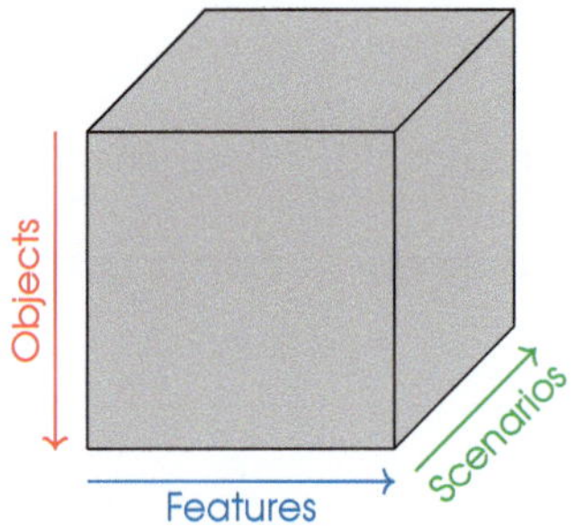

Figure 9.2 Prototypical format of a tensor in data analysis.

For example, we discuss an example in Section 9.6 of looking at different emission × excitation matrices for samples with different compositions, which might be better interpreted as feature × feature × scenario. Further, CP decomposition is not limited to 3-way tensors; see Section 9.1.2.

9.1.1 CP Decomposition for 3-way Tensors

We provide the mathematical formulation of CP for 3-way tensors. Given a tensor $\mathcal{X} \in \mathbb{R}^{m \times n \times p}$ and decomposition rank $r \in \mathbb{N}$, the goal is to find factor matrices $\mathbf{A} \in \mathbb{R}^{m \times r}$, $\mathbf{B} \in \mathbb{R}^{n \times r}$, and $\mathbf{C} \in \mathbb{R}^{p \times r}$, such that

$$x_{ijk} \approx \sum_{\ell=1}^{r} a_{i\ell}\, b_{j\ell}\, c_{k\ell} \quad \text{for all} \quad (i,j,k) \in [m] \otimes [n] \otimes [p].$$

We write this in shorthand as

$$\mathcal{X} \approx [\![\mathbf{A}, \mathbf{B}, \mathbf{C}]\!].$$

Definition 9.1 (Tensor Rank) Given a tensor $\mathcal{X} \in \mathbb{R}^{m \times n \times p}$, its **rank** is the smallest r such that there exists $\mathbf{A} \in \mathbb{R}^{m \times r}$, $\mathbf{B} \in \mathbb{R}^{n \times r}$, and $\mathbf{C} \in \mathbb{R}^{p \times r}$ with $\mathcal{X} = [\![\mathbf{A}, \mathbf{B}, \mathbf{C}]\!]$.

If $\mathcal{X} = [\![\mathbf{A}, \mathbf{B}, \mathbf{C}]\!]$, then we say that the decomposition is **exact**. The **rank** of a tensor $\mathcal{X}$ is the smallest r for which it has an exact CP decomposition. The rank of a tensor may be larger than the largest of its dimensions; see Chapter 16 for a detailed discussion on typical and maximal ranks. Computing the exact rank of a tensor is NP-hard (Håstad, 1990; Hillar and Lim, 2013), but as most data tensors are noisy, we typically seek approximate rather than exact decompositions. As mentioned previously, the term "rank" is used colloquially to refer to the number of components in the CP decomposition, but this is technically only an upper bound on the rank of the decomposition. Finally, we note that the rank depends on the field and that the rank over $\mathbb{C}$, the complex numbers, may be less than the rank over $\mathbb{R}$, the reals.

Remark 9.2 (Tensor rank and tensor size) The rank of a tensor can be larger than any of its dimensions. For a tensor $\mathcal{X}$ of size $m \times n \times p$, it is typically the case that $\text{rank}(\mathcal{X}) > \max\{m, n, p\}$. This contrasts with the matrix case, where $\text{rank}(\mathbf{X}) \leq \min\{m, n\}$ for any matrix $\mathbf{X}$ of size $m \times n$.

If we denote the columns of the factor matrices as

$$\mathbf{A} = [\mathbf{a}_1\, \mathbf{a}_2 \cdots \mathbf{a}_r], \quad \mathbf{B} = [\mathbf{b}_1\, \mathbf{b}_2 \cdots \mathbf{b}_r], \quad \text{and} \quad \mathbf{C} = [\mathbf{c}_1\, \mathbf{c}_2 \cdots \mathbf{c}_r],$$

then we can visualize the 3-way CP decomposition as in Fig. 9.3.

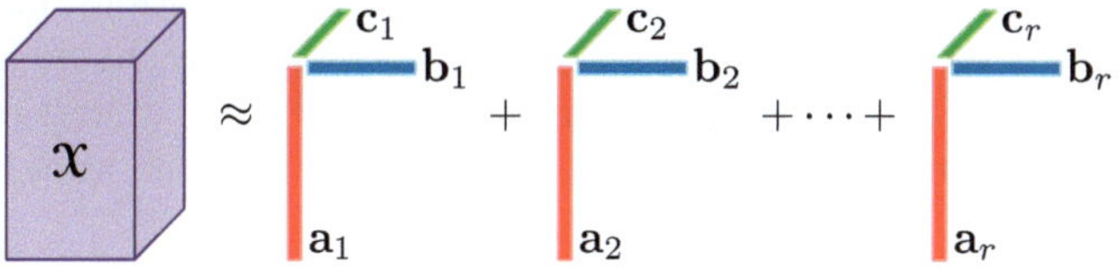

Figure 9.3 CP decomposition of a 3-way tensor.

This is sometimes written using **vector outer products** (Section 3.2) as

$$\mathcal{X} \approx \sum_{\ell=1}^{r} \mathbf{a}_\ell \circ \mathbf{b}_\ell \circ \mathbf{c}_\ell.$$

The (i, j, k) entry of an outer product $\mathbf{a} \circ \mathbf{b} \circ \mathbf{c}$ is $a_i b_j c_k$. (Sometimes the notation $\otimes$ is used for outer product rather than $\circ$, but we reserve the former symbol for the matrix Kronecker product.)

Example 9.1 ($2 \times 2 \times 2$ Tensor of Rank 3, Kruskal, 1983) Consider the $2 \times 2 \times 2$ tensor $\mathcal{X}$ given by

$$\mathcal{X}(:,:,1) = \begin{bmatrix} 1 & 0 \\ 0 & 1 \end{bmatrix} \quad \text{and} \quad \mathcal{X}(:,:,1) = \begin{bmatrix} 0 & 1 \\ -1 & 0 \end{bmatrix}.$$

A rank decomposition is $\mathcal{X} = [\![\mathbf{A}, \mathbf{B}, \mathbf{C}]\!]$, with

$$\mathbf{A} = \begin{bmatrix} 1 & 0 & 1 \\ 0 & 1 & -1 \end{bmatrix}, \quad \mathbf{B} = \begin{bmatrix} 1 & 0 & 1 \\ 0 & 1 & 1 \end{bmatrix}, \quad \text{and} \quad \mathbf{C} = \begin{bmatrix} 1 & 1 & 0 \\ -1 & 1 & 1 \end{bmatrix}.$$

This means $\text{rank}(\mathcal{X}) = 3$, larger than any single dimension of $\mathcal{X}$. (We defer the details of proving this is a rank decomposition to Section 16.8.2.)

Exercise 9.1 Validate $\mathcal{X} = [\![\mathbf{A}, \mathbf{B}, \mathbf{C}]\!]$ for quantities defined in Example 9.1.

Explicit weights for the CP components are optional.

There is also a variation of CP that uses explicit **components weights**, $\boldsymbol{\lambda} \in \mathbb{R}^r$:

$$x_{ijk} \approx \sum_{\ell=1}^{r} \lambda_\ell \, a_{i\ell} \, b_{j\ell} \, c_{k\ell} \quad \text{for all} \quad (i,j,k) \in [m] \otimes [n] \otimes [p].$$

This is useful if we want to scale the factors to length 1 (i.e., $\|\mathbf{a}_\ell\|_2 = \|\mathbf{b}_\ell\|_2 = \|\mathbf{c}_\ell\|_2 = 1$ for all $\ell \in [r]$). We write this in shorthand as

$$\mathcal{X} \approx [\![\boldsymbol{\lambda}; \mathbf{A}, \mathbf{B}, \mathbf{C}]\!].$$

In this format, we can easily sort the components from largest to smallest using the λ_ℓ values. The weights are optional and generally not used in fitting the model; their significance is in interpretation because components with a smaller λ_ℓ are less important than those with a larger λ_ℓ.

Exercise 9.2 Rewrite the factorization $[\![\mathbf{A}, \mathbf{B}, \mathbf{C}]\!]$ in Example 9.1 using weights and normalizing the factors to unit length.

The storage required for the CP factorization is linear in the dimensions, i.e., $r(m+n+p)$ storage, making it potentially orders of magnitude smaller than the original tensor of size mnp. This would seem to make CP an ideal method for compression, except for the problem that we cannot easily determine the rank for a specified error threshold; see Section 9.2.2.

9.1.2 CP Decomposition for d-way Tensors

CP can be extended naturally to d-way tensors. Consider a d-way tensor $\mathcal{X} \in \mathbb{R}^{n_1 \times n_2 \times \cdots \times n_d}$. Its CP factorization of rank $r \in \mathbb{N}$ involves factor matrices $\mathbf{A}_k \in \mathbb{R}^{n_k \times r}$ for $k \in [d]$, such that

$$\mathcal{X}(i_1, i_2, \ldots, i_d) \approx \sum_{j=1}^{r} \mathbf{A}_1(i_1, j) \, \mathbf{A}_2(i_2, j) \cdots \mathbf{A}_r(i_r, j)$$
$$\text{for all} \quad (i_1, i_2, \ldots, i_d) \in [n_1] \otimes [n_2] \otimes \cdots \otimes [n_d].$$

We express this in shorthand as

$$\mathcal{X} \approx [\![\mathbf{A}_1, \mathbf{A}_2, \ldots, \mathbf{A}_d]\!].$$

Exercise 9.3 What is the storage requirement for the d-way CP factorization of rank r?

9.1.3 Connection to Matrix Low-Rank Approximation

The CP decomposition can be considered a higher-order analog of PCA (see Section C.4), and PCA is an application of the SVD. PCA decomposes a matrix into the sum of outer products of pairs of vectors, known as components and loadings. Other methods such as independent component analysis (ICA) and nonnegative matrix factorization (NMF) are similar because they are also sums of vector outer products. The PCA component and loading vectors can be used for interpretation in ways analogous to interpretation using the CP factors. However, PCA requires that the component and loading vectors be orthogonal, whereas an advantage of CP decomposition is that it does not require orthogonality of the factors.

In fact, an issue with matrix low-rank approximation is that it lacks uniqueness, unless there are additional constraints, such as orthogonality or independence. Cattell (1944) was an early proponent of tensor factorizations who asked, "What set of factors will be most parsimonious at once with respect to this and other matrices considered together?" CP tensor decomposition addresses this question because it can be viewed as factorizing multiple matrices simultaneously. Further, factorizing multiple matrices simultaneously can ensure uniqueness of the factors without additional constraints and yield better interpretability (see Section 9.2.3).

9.2 Properties of CP Decompositions

9.2.1 Inherent Ambiguities

CP has two fundamental ambiguities: scaling and permutation. If it is unique except for those ambiguities, it is called **essentially unique**.

Any CP decomposition has two inherent ambiguities: permutation and scaling. The **permutation ambiguity** means that we can reorder the components of the decomposition without changing the sum. (This is discussed in detail in Section 10.4.1.)

Exercise 9.4 Which of the following two expressions is equivalent to the factorization in Example 9.1? Why?

$$\text{Choice 1:} \quad \mathbf{A} = \begin{bmatrix} 0 & 1 & -1 \\ 1 & 0 & 1 \end{bmatrix}, \quad \mathbf{B} = \begin{bmatrix} 0 & 1 & 1 \\ 1 & 0 & 1 \end{bmatrix}, \quad \text{and} \quad \mathbf{C} = \begin{bmatrix} -1 & 1 & 1 \\ 1 & 1 & 0 \end{bmatrix}.$$

$$\text{Choice 2:} \quad \mathbf{A} = \begin{bmatrix} 1 & 1 & 0 \\ -1 & 0 & 1 \end{bmatrix}, \quad \mathbf{B} = \begin{bmatrix} 1 & 1 & 0 \\ 1 & 0 & 1 \end{bmatrix}, \quad \text{and} \quad \mathbf{C} = \begin{bmatrix} 0 & 1 & 1 \\ 1 & -1 & 1 \end{bmatrix}.$$

The **scaling ambiguity** is a bit more complex and has to do with the optional weight term in the CP decomposition. We can, for example, scale $\mathbf{a}_1$ by 4 and $\mathbf{b}_1$ by $\frac{1}{2}$ and $\mathbf{c}_1$ by $\frac{1}{2}$ without changing their outer product. Thus, the scaling is ambiguous. (This is discussed in detail in Section 10.4.2.) The scaling ambiguity means that there is a manifold of equivalent solutions, which can be challenging for optimization methods.

9.2.2 Fundamental Challenges

There are several fundamental challenges to computing CP decompositions, which we briefly touch upon here and discuss in more detail in subsequent chapters.

Determining the rank of a tensor is NP-hard (Håstad, 1990; Hillar and Lim, 2013). For example, there is a famous $9 \times 9 \times 9$ problem for which the rank is bounded between 19 and 23, but the exact rank is still unknown (Bläser, 2003; Laderman, 1976). This tensor, given later in Eq. (16.10), has attracted particular attention because it corresponds to identifying a fast algorithm for matrix multiplication, which can be formulated as a CP tensor decomposition problem. We discuss the connection between tensor rank and fast matrix multiplication in Section 16.6.

Luckily, for most applications we do not need to find an exact rank decomposition and can instead use a rank-k approximation. Some heuristics for choosing an approximate rank are discussed in Section 9.4.1. However, there is still a problem in that the best rank-k

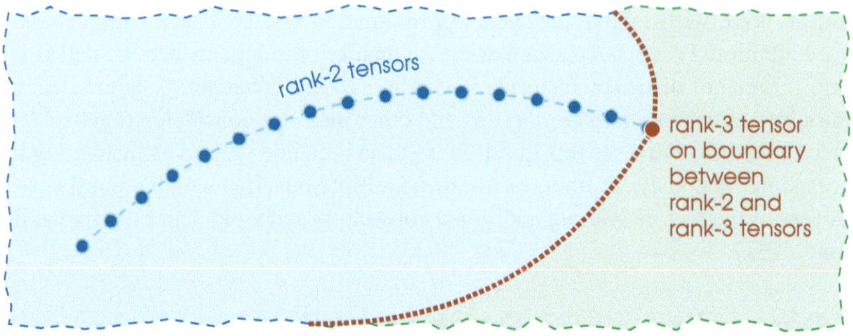

Figure 9.4 In space of $2 \times 2 \times 2$ tensors, a sequence of rank-2 tensors converges to a rank-3 tensor because the set of rank-2 tensors is not closed. The measure-zero boundary between rank-2 (blue) and rank-3 (green) tensors contains tensors of rank 0, 1, 2 and 3.

approximation of a tensor may not exist. The set of tensors of a given rank is not necessarily a closed set and can converge to a tensor of higher rank. Consequently, a tensor of rank r may be the limit of a sequence of tensors of rank less than r. Thus, the problem of finding a best rank-k approximation may be ill-posed (de Silva and Lim, 2008; Paatero, 2000), as illustrated in Fig. 9.4. Ill-posedness is discussed further in Chapter 16, including Example 16.2, which is an explicit sequence of rank-2 tensors that converge to a tensor of rank 3. Pragmatically, however, this problem appears to be uncommon in practice and can be mitigated with regularization on the factors; see Section 9.4.2.

9.2.3 Uniqueness

> A sufficient condition for a 3-way CP decomposition $[\![\mathbf{A}, \mathbf{B}, \mathbf{C}]\!]$ to be **essentially unique** is that $\operatorname{rank}(\mathbf{A}) = \operatorname{rank}(\mathbf{B}) = r$ and every pair of columns in $\mathbf{C}$ is linearly independent.

One important benefit of the CP decomposition, assuming we can compute it, is that it is unique under mild conditions. For example, an exact 3-way CP decomposition $\mathcal{X} = [\![\mathbf{A}, \mathbf{B}, \mathbf{C}]\!]$ is unique up to permutation and scaling if $\operatorname{rank}(\mathbf{A}) = \operatorname{rank}(\mathbf{B}) = r$ and every pair of columns of $\mathbf{C}$ is linearly independent (Kruskal, 1989); see Sections 10.5 and 16.7 for further details. Not every tensor meets the conditions for uniqueness, as we see in Example 9.2.

Example 9.2 (Nonuniqueness) Consider the $2 \times 2 \times 2$ tensor $\mathcal{X}$ from Example 9.1 given by

$$\mathcal{X}(:,:,1) = \begin{bmatrix} 1 & 0 \\ 0 & 1 \end{bmatrix} \quad \text{and} \quad \mathcal{X}(:,:,1) = \begin{bmatrix} 0 & 1 \\ -1 & 0 \end{bmatrix}.$$

An alternate rank decomposition of $\mathcal{X}$ is $\mathcal{X} = [\![\hat{\mathbf{A}}, \hat{\mathbf{B}}, \hat{\mathbf{C}}]\!]$ with

$$\hat{\mathbf{A}} = \begin{bmatrix} 2 & 1 & 1 \\ 0 & 1 & -1 \end{bmatrix}, \quad \hat{\mathbf{B}} = \begin{bmatrix} 0 & 1 & 1 \\ 1 & 1 & -1 \end{bmatrix}, \quad \text{and} \quad \hat{\mathbf{C}} = \begin{bmatrix} 0 & 1/2 & 1/2 \\ 1 & -1/2 & 1/2 \end{bmatrix}.$$

Observe that this is not a scaling or permutation of the other rank decomposition in Example 9.1. Hence, the decomposition of $\mathcal{X}$ is *not* unique.

Exercise 9.5 Show $\mathcal{X} = [\![\hat{\mathbf{A}}, \hat{\mathbf{B}}, \hat{\mathbf{C}}]\!]$ for the quantities in Example 9.2.

9.3 Overview of Methods for Computing CP

Fitting the CP decomposition is a rich topic of study. In this section, we give a high-level overview of some methods for computing CP, with pointers to extensive discussions in the chapters that follow. For the purposes of this discussion, we assume that the rank r is already specified; see Section 9.4.1 for discussion on choosing r.

To compute the CP model, we want to minimize the sum of squares error. We focus on the situation of a 3-way tensor $\mathcal{X} \in \mathbb{R}^{m \times n \times p}$ for this overview. In this case, the least squares error is

$$\left\| \mathcal{X} - [\![\mathbf{A}, \mathbf{B}, \mathbf{C}]\!] \right\|^2 \equiv \sum_{i=1}^{m} \sum_{j=1}^{n} \sum_{k=1}^{p} \left(x_{ijk} - \sum_{\ell=1}^{r} a_{i\ell}\, b_{j\ell}\, c_{k\ell} \right)^2. \tag{9.1}$$

Thus, the CP optimization problem for given $r \in \mathbb{N}$ is

$$\min_{\mathbf{A},\mathbf{B},\mathbf{C}} \left\| \mathcal{X} - [\![\mathbf{A}, \mathbf{B}, \mathbf{C}]\!] \right\|^2 \quad \text{subject to} \quad \mathbf{A} \in \mathbb{R}^{m \times r}, \mathbf{B} \in \mathbb{R}^{n \times r}, \mathbf{C} \in \mathbb{R}^{p \times r}. \tag{9.2}$$

This problem is a nonconvex nonlinear least-squares problem. It may be ill-posed unless we impose bound constraints or regularization, though this may not be a problem in practice.

The usual way to solve the CP optimization problem in Eq. (9.2) is using *iterative* optimization methods. We give a brief overview of these methods in the context of 3-way tensors in Sections 9.3.1 and 9.3.2. Detailed derivations and discussions of the algorithms for both 3-way and d-way tensors are provided in Chapters 11–13.

In general, it is not possible to compute CP using direct methods except in special circumstances that are primarily interesting for theoretical analysis; see Section 9.3.3 and Section 16.8.

Additionally, it is not possible to use a greedy approach where, for example, we compute the best rank-1 factorization and assume this is the first component of the best rank-2 factorization. See Section 16.9 for further discussion and examples.

9.3.1 Alternating Least Squares (CP-ALS)

The workhorse method for solving the CP optimization problem is **alternating least squares (CP-ALS)**, proposed simultaneously by Carroll and Chang (1970) and Harshman (1970). In optimization nomenclature, this is a form of block coordinate descent (see Section B.3.7). The main idea is that we cycle through the factor matrices, optimizing with respect to each single factor matrix while holding the others fixed, and repeating this cycle until convergence.

In the 3-way case, the CP-ALS algorithm is as follows.

Prototype CP-ALS, 3-way

while not converged **do**
  $\mathbf{A} \leftarrow \arg\min_{\mathbf{A}} \left\| \mathcal{X} - [\![\mathbf{A}, \mathbf{B}, \mathbf{C}]\!] \right\|^2$
  $\mathbf{B} \leftarrow \arg\min_{\mathbf{B}} \left\| \mathcal{X} - [\![\mathbf{A}, \mathbf{B}, \mathbf{C}]\!] \right\|^2$
  $\mathbf{C} \leftarrow \arg\min_{\mathbf{C}} \left\| \mathcal{X} - [\![\mathbf{A}, \mathbf{B}, \mathbf{C}]\!] \right\|^2$
end while

We defer details of the method until Chapter 11. Briefly, each subproblem is a linear least squares problem. The cost to solve the subproblem is $\mathcal{O}(mnpr)$.

Exercise 9.6 Consider solving for $\mathbf{A} \in \mathbb{R}^{m \times r}$ as in the first subproblem. (a) Show how this is a linear least squares problem. (b) Show that the computational complexity is $\mathcal{O}(mnpr)$, where we assume $r < \min\{m, n, p\}$.

The reduction to linear least squares problems means that each subproblem can be solved exactly and efficiently, making CP-ALS a standard for comparison in the development of new algorithms.

There are numerous extensions on this idea, including CP-ALS with nonnegativity constraints (Bro and De Jong, 1997), streaming versions of CP-ALS (Zhou et al., 2016), and randomized methods focused on efficiently solving the least squares subproblems (Battaglino et al., 2018; Cheng et al., 2016; Larsen and Kolda, 2022; Vervliet and De Lathauwer, 2016), to name a few.

9.3.2 All-at-Once Optimization (CP-OPT and CP-NLS)

Another approach to solve the CP optimization problem in Eq. (9.2) is to use standard **optimization** methods that operate on all unknowns simultaneously. In other words, we group the factor matrices into a single vector of unknowns,

$$\min_{\mathbf{v}} f(\mathbf{v}), \quad \text{where} \quad \mathbf{v} \equiv \begin{bmatrix} \operatorname{vec}(\mathbf{A}) \\ \operatorname{vec}(\mathbf{B}) \\ \operatorname{vec}(\mathbf{C}) \end{bmatrix} \in \mathbb{R}^{r(m+n+p)} \quad \text{and} \quad f(\mathbf{v}) \equiv \left\| \mathcal{X} - [\![\mathbf{A}, \mathbf{B}, \mathbf{C}]\!] \right\|^2.$$

In Chapter 12, we show how to use gradient-based optimization methods (CP-OPT) to solve Eq. (9.2) (Acar et al., 2011a). Gradient-based optimization methods include gradient descent (see Section B.3.2) and quasi-Newton methods such as L-BFGS (see Section B.3.5). Each iteration of a gradient-based optimization method involves computing $\nabla f(\mathbf{v}_k)$, the gradient at the current iterate, and its cost is the same cost as one iteration of CP-ALS: $\mathcal{O}(mnpr)$.

In Chapter 13, we discuss **nonlinear least squares** optimization (CP-NLS) methods for Eq. (9.2) (Paatero, 1997, 1999; Phan et al., 2013b; Tomasi and Bro, 2005, 2006). These methods depend on the Jacobian of $\phi(\mathbf{v}) \equiv \operatorname{vec}(\mathcal{X} - [\![\mathbf{A}, \mathbf{B}, \mathbf{C}]\!])$ as well as the gradient. Since it is a nonlinear least-squares problem, we can solve it using specialized methods such as **damped Gauss–Newton** (see Section B.3.6). At each iteration, a CP-NLS method solves a linear system of the form

$$(\mathbf{J}^\intercal \mathbf{J} + \lambda \mathbf{I})\mathbf{d}_k = -\nabla f(\mathbf{v}_k), \tag{9.3}$$

where $\mathbf{J} \in \mathbb{R}^{r(m+n+p) \times mnp}$ is the Jacobian of ϕ at $\mathbf{v}_k$ and λ is a damping parameter. In general, NLS methods are only competitive with gradient-based methods if the linear system in Eq. (9.3) is solved using a preconditioned conjugate gradient method that never forms $\mathbf{J}^\intercal \mathbf{J}$ explicitly (Vervliet and De Lathauwer, 2019), and we focus primarily on this approach.

9.3.3 Direct Computation via Simultaneous Diagonalization

In general, CP cannot be computed *directly*. There is an exception in a very specific scenario: a 3-way tensor of size $m \times n \times p$ of exact rank $r \leq \min\{m, n, p\}$. In this case,

CP may be able to be computed directly using an approach known as **simultaneous diagonalization** (Domanov and De Lathauwer, 2014; Harshman, 1972; Leurgans et al., 1993; Sanchez and Kowalski, 1990; ten Berge and Tendeiro, 2009).[1] We describe a simple version of this approach in Section 16.8.4. The rank condition is a specific and unusual circumstance since a generic tensor of size $m \times n \times p$ would not have rank sufficiently small to satisfy the conditions because a randomly generated $m \times n \times p$ tensor will have rank $r > \min\{m, n, p\}$ for most choices of (m, n, p); see Section 16.4. Furthermore, because a small perturbation may change the rank, the simultaneous diagonalization approach is sensitive to noise in the data. Thus, the practical utility of simultaneous diagonalization is limited.

9.4 Practical Considerations

There are several computational considerations that are common to all methods. These considerations may even be more important than the choice of solution method.

9.4.1 Choosing the CP Rank

> There is no general method for determining the rank of a tensor, so heuristics are used in practice.

Before we discuss computational methods for CP, we have the problem of choosing an appropriate rank for the decomposition. As mentioned in Section 9.2.2, there is no general methodology for determining the rank of a tensor. For this reason, most users employ heuristics.

Until we achieve an error of 0, increasing the rank always enables an improved fit. Ideally, we want the smallest rank that fits the *signal* but not the *noise* in the measurements. So, one common practice is to choose the smallest rank r that significantly reduces the relative error compared to rank $r - 1$. For a 3-way tensor, the relative error is

$$\text{relative error} = \frac{\|\mathcal{X} - [\![\mathbf{A}, \mathbf{B}, \mathbf{C}]\!]\|}{\|\mathcal{X}\|} = \frac{\left(\sum_{i=1}^{m}\sum_{j=1}^{n}\sum_{k=1}^{p}\left(x_{ijk} - \sum_{\ell=1}^{r} a_{i\ell}\, b_{j\ell}\, c_{k\ell}\right)^2\right)^{\frac{1}{2}}}{\left(\sum_{i=1}^{m}\sum_{j=1}^{n}\sum_{k=1}^{p} x_{ijk}^2\right)^{\frac{1}{2}}}.$$

Figure 9.5 shows an example of the plot we might get with the relative error decreasing as the value of the CP rank, r, increases. In this case, we see a major difference between $r = 1$ and $r = 2$ and again between $r = 2$ and $r = 3$. Going from $r = 3$ to $r = 4$, however, the change is only 0.39%, so this is a reason to consider $r = 3$ as the "best" rank. What qualifies as a significant enough change as the rank changes may vary by application.

One caveat, as we discuss in more detail in the next section, is that we cannot compute the best rank-r factorization because the optimization methods may converge to only a local minimum. For this reason, we recommend a methodology such as using multiple random starts and then selecting the best relative error for each rank. Figure 9.5 uses the lowest relative error of five runs for each choice of rank r.

[1] The simultaneous diagonalization approach is sometimes mistakenly referred to as Jennrich's Algorithm, but this is an incorrect attribution. See `www.mathsci.ai/post/jennrich/` for further details.

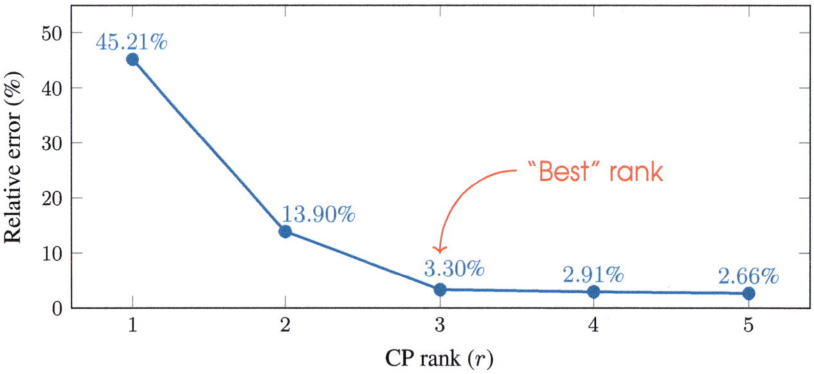

Figure 9.5 Choosing the smallest rank that significantly improves the error for EEM tensor.

There are many other heuristics for choosing the rank. One of the most popular is the core consistency diagnostic, also known as CORCONDIA, that considers all combinations of the existing factors in a Tucker model (Bro and Kiers, 2003). Another option is to choose a rank that yields stable components (Williams et al., 2018).

9.4.2 Regularization

It may be desirable to add a regularization term to the least squares problem, e.g., replace Eq. (11.2) with

$$\left\| \mathcal{X} - [\![\mathbf{A}, \mathbf{B}, \mathbf{C}]\!] \right\|^2 + \rho\left(\|\mathbf{A}\|_F^2 + \|\mathbf{B}\|_F^2 + \|\mathbf{C}\|_F^2 \right), \tag{9.4}$$

where $\rho > 0$ is the regularization term. When the rank is uncertain, regularization may encourage zeroing out of extra factors. Additionally, regularization addresses any issues with the low-rank factorization problem being ill-posed. The main challenge in regularization is choosing a suitable regularization parameter.

9.4.3 Initialization and Multiple Runs

Because the CP optimization problem in Eq. (9.2) is nonconvex, there is no guarantee that any optimization method will converge to a global minimizer. For this reason, standard practice is to run the optimization multiple times using different random guesses, and then to select the best answer according to criteria such as the relative error.

> The CP optimization problem is nonconvex, so **multiple runs** of the optimization with different starting points are strongly recommended to increase the likelihood of converging to a global minimizer.

There are several methods for randomly initializing CP-ALS. In the 3-way case, we need to make initial guesses for $\mathbf{A} \in \mathbb{R}^{m \times r}$, $\mathbf{B} \in \mathbb{R}^{n \times r}$, and $\mathbf{C} \in \mathbb{R}^{p \times r}$.

- **Random.** Using random factor matrices, for example, entries drawn from the standard normal distribution, is usually effective. In other words,

$$a_{i\ell}, b_{j\ell}, c_{k\ell} \sim \mathcal{N}(0,1) \quad \text{for all} \quad i \in [m], j \in [n], k \in [p], \ell \in [r].$$

- **Random fiber combination.** The initial factor matrix is a random linear combination of the mode-k fibers, ensuring that the initial guess is within the range of the column space of the matrix of mode-k fibers; see Sherman and Kolda (2020). In this case, we use

$$\begin{aligned} \mathbf{A} &= \mathbf{X}_{(1)}\boldsymbol{\Omega} \quad \text{where} \quad \Omega \in \mathbb{R}^{np \times r} \text{ is random}, \\ \mathbf{B} &= \mathbf{X}_{(2)}\boldsymbol{\Omega} \quad \text{where} \quad \Omega \in \mathbb{R}^{mp \times r} \text{ is random}, \\ \mathbf{C} &= \mathbf{X}_{(3)}\boldsymbol{\Omega} \quad \text{where} \quad \Omega \in \mathbb{R}^{mn \times r} \text{ is random}. \end{aligned}$$

The main computational cost is the matrix–matrix multiplies: $\mathcal{O}(mnpr)$.

- **HOSVD.** The HOSVD (see Section 6.2) has the advantage of ensuring that the initial factors for mode k are the leading left singular vectors of the matrix of mode-k fibers. In this case, we use

$$\begin{aligned} \mathbf{A} &= r \text{ leading left singular vectors of } \mathbf{X}_{(1)}, \\ \mathbf{B} &= r \text{ leading left singular vectors of } \mathbf{X}_{(2)}, \\ \mathbf{C} &= r \text{ leading left singular vectors of } \mathbf{X}_{(3)}. \end{aligned}$$

  This initialization is only available if $r \leq \min\{m, n, p\}$. The main advantage of the HOSVD is that the initial guesses are within the "leading subspace" of each mode. Otherwise, the primary disadvantage of the HOSVD is the cost of computing the SVD of the unfolded tensor. Assuming each dimension is smaller than the product of the other two, the cost is $\mathcal{O}(mnp(m + n + p))$.

- **HOSVD with random projection.** We can combine the previous two ideas so that we need only take the SVD of a smaller matrix; see the randomized range finder in Halko et al. (2011). In this case, we use

$$\begin{aligned} \mathbf{A} &= r \text{ leading left singular vectors of } \mathbf{X}_{(1)}\boldsymbol{\Omega} \quad \text{where} \quad \Omega \in \mathbb{R}^{np \times q} \text{ is random}, \\ \mathbf{B} &= r \text{ leading left singular vectors of } \mathbf{X}_{(2)}\boldsymbol{\Omega} \quad \text{where} \quad \Omega \in \mathbb{R}^{mp \times q} \text{ is random}, \\ \mathbf{C} &= r \text{ leading left singular vectors of } \mathbf{X}_{(3)}\boldsymbol{\Omega} \quad \text{where} \quad \Omega \in \mathbb{R}^{mn \times q} \text{ is random}. \end{aligned}$$

  Like HOSVD, this initialization is only available if $r \leq \min\{m, n, p\}$. If $q = r + \mathcal{O}(1) < \min\{m, n, p\}$, the computational cost is $\mathcal{O}(mnpq + q^2(m + n + p))$.

9.4.4 Preprocessing

Since the CP model is optimizing the sum of squared errors, as in Eq. (9.1), we have to consider the scaling of the data. If the data is measuring quantities on different scales, which may happen when fusing data of different types or from multiple sources, then these values may not contribute equally to the sum of squared errors measure. For instance, if we measure the weight of newborn babies in kilograms and the height in centimeters, the average weight may be something like 3 kg whereas the height will be around 50 cm. A 10% error in the height will contribute much more to the sum of squares error than a 10% error in the weight, which may skew the results. One normalization option is to center and scale each set of variables, i.e., subtract the mean and divide by the standard deviation. Another normalization option is to rescale the data to the $[0, 1]$ interval.

9.4.5 Postprocessing

The inherent scaling and permutation ambiguities discussed in Section 9.2.1 can potentially hinder consistent interpretation of results and comparison of solutions from different starting points. Hence, it is useful to postprocess any solution as follows:

1. **Normalization of components.** Normalize the factors in a consistent way, such as normalizing all the factors to unit length and using an explicit component weight.
2. **Reorder the components in order of decreasing weight.** There is no prescribed order for components, but ordering by weight is often useful since then the most significant components are first.
3. **Resolve sign ambiguity as best as possible.** While the scaling ambiguity can be addressed via normalization, there is no clear resolution for sign ambiguity. Several methods have been proposed in the literature (Bro et al., 2008, 2013). A simple solution is to set the largest magnitude entry to be positive in each factor, assuming that this flips the sign for an *even* number of factors.[2]

9.4.6 Comparison of Methods

Comparing different methods for computing CP must be done with some care. The following are caveats to bear in mind:

- Problems with different qualities (tensor order and size, decomposition rank, component correlations, sparsity, constraints, etc.) could change the comparison results.
- Stopping conditions should be consistent, if possible. Additionally, solutions should be validated to ensure that all the methods converge to the same solution or at least a solution of equivalent quality (e.g., same relative error).
- Optimization methods vary in the cost per iteration. Therefore, the number of iterations is not necessarily an ideal metric.
- The time to converge is an alternative to number of iterations, but this can vary according to the implementation and computer architecture. Therefore, the total time is not necessarily an ideal metric.
- The computational complexity per iteration can be a useful metric but does not reflect total number of iterations required nor the nuances of the implementation.

In general, there is no perfectly consistent way to compare methods. Most importantly, different methods may be appropriate in different contexts.

9.5 Extensions of CP

In this section, we present extensions to CP for incorporating constraints, handling missing data, changing the objective function, and imposing symmetry. We provide in-depth coverage for incomplete data (Chapter 14) and alternative objective functions (Chapter 15) in their own chapters.

9.5.1 Nonnegativity and Other Constraints

Nonnegative tensor factorizations constrain the factor matrices to be positive. This often leads to more interpretable components. The formulation in the 3-way case would be:

$$\begin{aligned} &\min \quad \left\| \mathcal{X} - [\![\mathbf{A}, \mathbf{B}, \mathbf{C}]\!] \right\|^2 \\ &\text{subject to} \quad \mathbf{A} \geq \mathbf{0}, \quad \mathbf{B} \geq \mathbf{0}, \quad \text{and} \quad \mathbf{C} \geq \mathbf{0}. \end{aligned}$$

[2] A reference implementation can be found in the Tensor Toolbox for MATLAB in the function `@ktensor/fixsigns.m`.

These constraints are elementwise. The idea was proposed in matrix factorization by Paatero and Tapper (1994) and later by Lee and Seung (1999, 2001). For tensor factorization, Bro and De Jong (1997) proposed nonnegative CP and used an alternating approach to solve a specially adapted nonnegative least squares (NNLS) solver for each subproblem. Paatero (1997, 1999) simultaneously proposed nonnegative CP for tensors using a Gauss–Newton method with a logarithmic barrier function to enforce the nonnegativity constraint.

An advantage of the all-at-once optimization approach is that we can choose an optimization methods that can handle constraints. For example, we can solve the CP optimization problem with bound constraints by using the bound-constrained L-BFGS (L-BFGS-B) method of Zhu et al. (1997).

> *Remark* 9.3 (Constraints) One potential advantage of using standard optimization methods is that many already have support for constraints.

Other constraints are also possible. For example, Friedlander and Hatz (2008) impose sparseness constraints on the factors (using an $\ell 1$-norm penalty function) as well as nonnegativity.

One constraint that is popular but *not recommended* is requiring the factor matrices to be orthogonal. A tensor that has a decomposition where all of its factor matrices are orthogonal is called an **orthogonally decomposable (ODECO)** tensor. We stress that the space of ODECO tensors is measure 0, meaning that the probability of a randomly generated tensor having a decomposition with factor matrices that are orthogonal is 0. Therefore, constraining factor matrices to be orthogonal (even just a subset of the matrices) is not recommended. See, e.g., Kolda (2001, 2003) and also Section 17.1.8.

> The space of orthogonally decomposable (ODECO) tensors is measure 0.

9.5.2 Methods for Incomplete Data (EM and CP-WOPT)

A special case arises when $\mathcal{X}$ is only partly known, in which case we say that $\mathcal{X}$ is incomplete because it has missing data. We discuss computing CP for problems with incomplete data in Chapter 14. These methods can be used for **tensor completion**, but its main goal is the decomposition itself. Here we give a high-level overview.

Consider a 3-way tensor $\mathcal{X} \in \mathbb{R}^{m \times n \times p}$ where some entries are unknown. It useful to define the **weight tensor** $\mathcal{W} \in \mathbb{R}^{m \times n \times p}$, such that

$$w_{ijk} = \begin{cases} 1 & \text{if } x_{ijk} \text{ is known} \\ 0 & \text{otherwise} \end{cases}.$$

If the proportion of known values is very small, we refer to $\mathcal{X}$ as a **scarce tensor**, which can benefit from special handling akin to what we do for sparse tensors and result in computational and memory efficiencies.

Expectation Maximization for CP (CP-EM)

One approach for a small amount of missing data is **expectation maximization**; see Kiers (1997) for discussion of EM in the context of tensor factorization. A guess is made for the missing data using the current model (expectation step) and then the model is updated to best fit the data (maximization step). The algorithm proceeds as follows.

EM for Missing Data

while not converged **do**
  $\hat{\mathcal{X}} \leftarrow \mathcal{W} * \mathcal{X} + (1 - \mathcal{W}) * [\![\mathbf{A}, \mathbf{B}, \mathbf{C}]\!]$
  $(\mathbf{A}, \mathbf{B}, \mathbf{C}) \leftarrow$ factor matrices of CP decomposition of $\hat{\mathcal{X}}$
end while

The notation $*$ represents elementwise multiplication. The advantage of this approach is that existing solvers for CP can be used. The disadvantage is that it involves computing the CP decomposition multiple times.

Exercise 9.7 Suppose only a few entries of $\mathcal{X}$ are missing so that $(1 - \mathcal{W})$ is extremely sparse. (a) How would you compute $\hat{\mathcal{X}} \leftarrow \mathcal{W} * \mathcal{X} + (1 - \mathcal{W}) * [\![\mathbf{A}, \mathbf{B}, \mathbf{C}]\!]$ efficiently? (b) What is the computational complexity?

Weighted Optimization for CP (CP-WOPT)

An alternate approach to EM is to optimize with respect to only the known values. Tomasi and Bro (2005) have considered damped Gauss–Newton (nonlinear least squares) methods, and Acar et al. (2010, 2011b) propose using gradient-based methods. The optimization can be formulated as a **weighted optimization** problem:

$$\min_{\mathbf{A},\mathbf{B},\mathbf{C}} \left\| \mathcal{W} * (\mathcal{X} - [\![\mathbf{A}, \mathbf{B}, \mathbf{C}]\!]) \right\|^2 = \sum_{i=1}^{m} \sum_{j=1}^{n} \sum_{k=1}^{p} w_{ijk} \Big(x_{ijk} - \sum_{\ell=1}^{r} a_{i\ell}\, b_{j\ell}\, c_{k\ell} \Big)^2. \tag{9.5}$$

Equation (9.5) can also be solved using weighted alternating least squares (CP-WALS). See Chapter 14 for further details.

9.5.3 Other Loss Functions with Generalized CP

The generalized CP framework allows for objection functions other than sum of squared errors, such as KL divergence for count data.

The de facto loss function for CP decomposition is the sum of squared errors as in Eq. (9.2), but alternative loss functions are possible and can provide superior interpretation for integer count data, binary data, nonnegative data, etc.

For example, KL divergence has been made famous in matrix factorization by Lee and Seung (1999, 2001) and extended to CP tensor factorization by Welling and Weber (2001); see also Chi and Kolda (2012), Hansen et al. (2015), and Shashua and Hazan (2005). For a 3-way tensor of nonnegative integers, the KL divergence objective function is

$$\sum_{i=1}^{m} \sum_{j=1}^{n} \sum_{k=1}^{p} m_{ijk} - x_{ijk} \log m_{ijk}, \quad \text{where} \quad \mathcal{M} = [\![\mathbf{A}, \mathbf{B}, \mathbf{C}]\!].$$

The **generalized CP (GCP) decomposition** framework was designed for alternative loss functions, such as KL divergence. We describe GCP and options for loss functions in Chapter 15.

9.5.4 Methods for Symmetric Tensors

If a tensor is symmetric, then it is natural to desire a symmetric factorization in which all factor matrices are equal. If a tensor is partially symmetric, then we would likewise desire that the corresponding factors be equal. When two or more factor matrices are equal, the problem is no longer linear with respect to the individual factor matrices. For this reason, there is no way to enforce symmetry in the standard CP-ALS approach. One technique is to ignore the symmetry and then make corrections (e.g., averaging the factors) in postprocessing (Carroll and Chang, 1970; Kolda, 2015a; ten Berge et al., 1988, 2004). This works surprisingly well, but it has few theory guarantees.

The more standard approach is direct optimization, in which we compute the gradients and apply an optimization method (Kolda, 2015a). If the symmetric tensor has special structure, such as being an empirical moment tensor, the CP model can be calculated without forming the tensor at all (Sherman and Kolda, 2020). See Section 17.3 for further discussion.

9.6 Example: CP on EEM Tensor

We consider the EEM tensor from fluorescence spectroscopy (Acar et al., 2014; Kolda, 2021a), as described in Section 1.5.2. The EEM tensor, denoted here by $\mathcal{X}$, is of size $18 \times 251 \times 21$, corresponding to 18 samples generating 251×21 excitation–emission matrices. The norm of the tensor is $\|\mathcal{X}\| = 2.17 \times 10^7$. Figure 9.6 shows some lateral slices on this tensor.

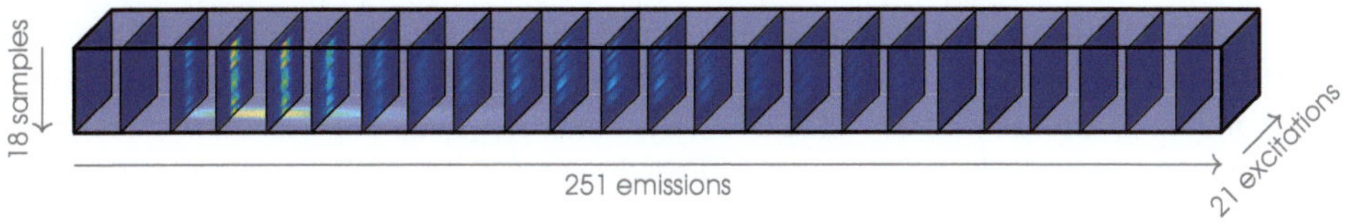

Figure 9.6 EEM tensor.

Exercise 9.8 (a) Using an existing code for computing CP, compute the CP model of the EEM tensor for ranks $r \in \{1, 2, 3, 4, 5\}$, using five different initial guesses for each r. (b) Plot the lowest relative error for each rank. (c) Which rank seems best and why?

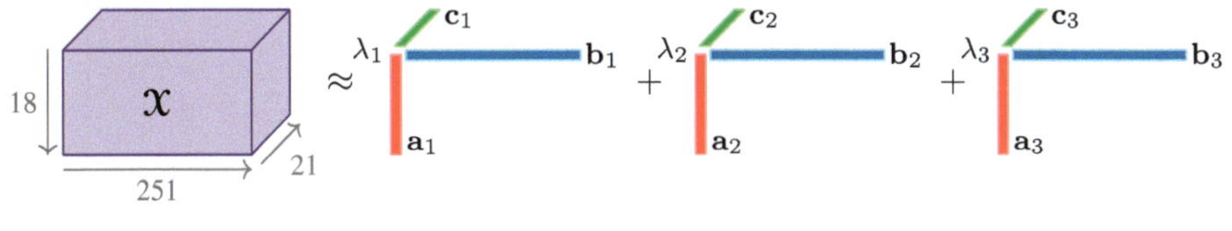

Figure 9.7 Rank-3 CP decomposition of EEM tensor.

Consider a rank-3 CP factorization of $\mathcal{X} \approx [\![\boldsymbol{\lambda}; \mathbf{A}, \mathbf{B}, \mathbf{C}]\!]$, with $\boldsymbol{\lambda} \in \mathbb{R}^3$, $\mathbf{A} \in \mathbb{R}^{18\times 3}$, $\mathbf{B} \in \mathbb{R}^{251\times 3}$, and $\mathbf{C} \in \mathbb{R}^{21\times 3}$, whose form is illustrated (not to scale) as in Fig. 9.7. We can calculate an approximate CP decomposition with $r = 3$, such that the relative error is

$$\|\mathcal{X} - [\![\boldsymbol{\lambda}; \mathbf{A}, \mathbf{B}, \mathbf{C}]\!]\| \;/\; \|\mathcal{X}\| = 3.30\%.$$

With the factors normalized, such that

$$\|\mathbf{a}_j\|_2 = \|\mathbf{b}_j\|_2 = \|\mathbf{c}_j\|_2 = 1 \quad \text{for all} \quad j \in \{1, 2, 3\},$$

we have **component weights** of

$$\lambda_1 = 1.77 \times 10^7, \quad \lambda_2 = 9.49 \times 10^6, \quad \text{and} \quad \lambda_3 = 4.29 \times 10^6.$$

Exercise 9.9 What are the λ values for the best rank-3 tensor computed in Exercise 9.8?

9.6.1 Comparing to EEM Ground Truth

Ideally, the three components in the CP model correspond to the three analytes in the mixtures. Recall from the description of the EEM tensor in Section 1.5.2 that we happen to know the true mixture matrix, which we denote here as $\mathbf{A}_{\text{true}}$ along with its column-normalized version $\hat{\mathbf{A}}_{\text{true}}$:

$$\mathbf{A}_{\text{true}} = \begin{bmatrix} 5.00 & 0.00 & 0.00 \\ 0.00 & 5.00 & 0.00 \\ 0.00 & 0.00 & 5.00 \\ 1.25 & 5.00 & 3.75 \\ 3.75 & 1.25 & 5.00 \\ 5.00 & 3.75 & 2.50 \\ 3.75 & 3.75 & 5.00 \\ 6.25 & 1.25 & 1.25 \\ 1.25 & 5.00 & 2.50 \\ 2.50 & 6.25 & 2.50 \\ 5.00 & 1.25 & 3.75 \\ 1.25 & 3.75 & 2.50 \\ 2.50 & 3.75 & 1.25 \\ 3.75 & 0.00 & 2.50 \\ 2.50 & 0.00 & 3.75 \\ 5.00 & 0.00 & 1.25 \\ 3.75 & 0.00 & 3.75 \\ 3.75 & 0.00 & 5.00 \end{bmatrix} \quad \text{and} \quad \hat{\mathbf{A}}_{\text{true}} = \begin{bmatrix} 0.33 & 0.00 & 0.00 \\ 0.00 & 0.38 & 0.00 \\ 0.00 & 0.00 & 0.36 \\ 0.08 & 0.38 & 0.27 \\ 0.25 & 0.09 & 0.36 \\ 0.33 & 0.28 & 0.18 \\ 0.25 & 0.28 & 0.36 \\ 0.41 & 0.09 & 0.09 \\ 0.08 & 0.38 & 0.18 \\ 0.16 & 0.47 & 0.18 \\ 0.33 & 0.09 & 0.27 \\ 0.08 & 0.28 & 0.18 \\ 0.16 & 0.28 & 0.09 \\ 0.25 & 0.00 & 0.18 \\ 0.16 & 0.00 & 0.27 \\ 0.33 & 0.00 & 0.09 \\ 0.25 & 0.00 & 0.27 \\ 0.25 & 0.00 & 0.36 \end{bmatrix}.$$

The $\mathbf{A}$ matrix in the factorization should ideally match $\hat{\mathbf{A}}_{\text{true}}$, up to permutation. Compare the $\mathbf{A}$ that was computed versus a permuted version of $\hat{\mathbf{A}}_{\text{true}}$:

$$\mathbf{A} = \begin{bmatrix} -0.00 & 0.00 & 0.31 \\ 0.00 & 0.39 & 0.03 \\ 0.35 & 0.01 & 0.01 \\ 0.28 & 0.36 & 0.11 \\ 0.33 & 0.10 & 0.26 \\ 0.20 & 0.29 & 0.33 \\ 0.32 & 0.28 & 0.26 \\ 0.11 & 0.11 & 0.39 \\ 0.21 & 0.38 & 0.10 \\ 0.21 & 0.46 & 0.19 \\ 0.27 & 0.10 & 0.33 \\ 0.21 & 0.28 & 0.09 \\ 0.12 & 0.29 & 0.17 \\ 0.21 & 0.00 & 0.24 \\ 0.28 & 0.00 & 0.16 \\ 0.11 & 0.00 & 0.31 \\ 0.28 & 0.01 & 0.24 \\ 0.32 & 0.01 & 0.25 \end{bmatrix} \quad \text{versus} \quad \hat{\mathbf{A}}_{\text{true}} \begin{bmatrix} 0 & 0 & 1 \\ 0 & 1 & 0 \\ 1 & 0 & 0 \end{bmatrix} = \begin{bmatrix} 0.00 & 0.00 & 0.33 \\ 0.00 & 0.38 & 0.00 \\ 0.36 & 0.00 & 0.00 \\ 0.27 & 0.38 & 0.08 \\ 0.36 & 0.09 & 0.25 \\ 0.18 & 0.28 & 0.33 \\ 0.36 & 0.28 & 0.25 \\ 0.09 & 0.09 & 0.41 \\ 0.18 & 0.38 & 0.08 \\ 0.18 & 0.47 & 0.16 \\ 0.27 & 0.09 & 0.33 \\ 0.18 & 0.28 & 0.08 \\ 0.09 & 0.28 & 0.16 \\ 0.18 & 0.00 & 0.25 \\ 0.27 & 0.00 & 0.16 \\ 0.09 & 0.00 & 0.33 \\ 0.27 & 0.00 & 0.25 \\ 0.36 & 0.00 & 0.25 \end{bmatrix}.$$

These are very close, especially given that some inaccuracies are expected due to the inexactness of the mixture preparations and instrumentation of the experiment. Since we know the columns of $\mathbf{A}_{\text{true}}$ correspond to the chemicals Val-Tyr-Val, Try-Gly, and Phe, we can infer that the components of the computed CP model refer to these same chemicals in permuted order, i.e., Phe, Try-Gly, and Val-Tyr-Val, respectively.

Exercise 9.10 (a) What permutation best matches $\mathbf{A}_{\text{true}}$ to the $\mathbf{A}$ in the best rank-3 tensor computed in Exercise 9.8? (b) What are the cosines of the angles between the matched vectors?

9.6.2 Interpreting CP Factors for EEM Tensor

We can visualize the components of $[\![\mathbf{A}, \mathbf{B}, \mathbf{C}]\!]$ as shown in Fig. 9.8. Recall that the tensor is organized as sample (18) $\times$ emission (251) $\times$ excitation (21). In the visualization, we plot the vectors corresponding to the factors of the CP decomposition. The first mode factor of the first component, $\mathbf{a}_1$, is in the upper left location. It is normalized to the norm of the component. It has 18 entries, which we plot as a bar chart. Note that this factor is 0 for the first two elements of $\mathbf{a}_1$, meaning that this component does not contribute to the first two samples. The second mode factor of the first component, $\mathbf{b}_1$, is in the top middle plot. This is normalized to length 1, and here we just plot it in a line plot. We denote the individual data points, of which there are 251, as dots. The third mode factor of the first component, $\mathbf{c}_1$, is in the top right plot. This is also normalized to length 1. This factor has only 21 data points, and is also plotted as a line plot with dots for the individual points. From the discussion of the true mixtures in the prior subsection, we can deduce that the combination of $\mathbf{b}_1$ and $\mathbf{c}_1$ yield the emission–excitation profile for the compound Phe, which we label in the background of that row of plots. The second and third components are in the middle and bottom sets of plots, respectively, corresponding to the other compounds as labeled.

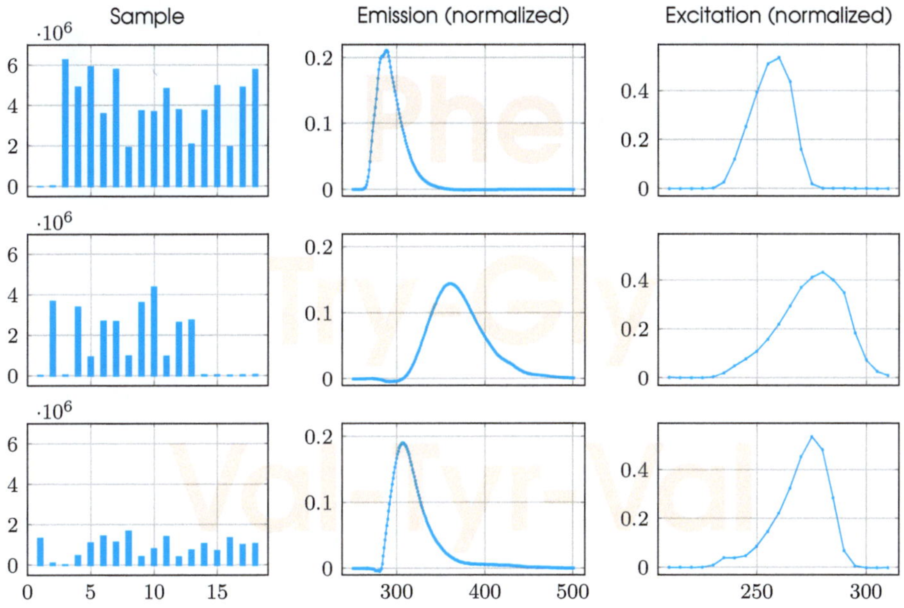

Figure 9.8 CP factors for EEM tensor computed by CP-ALS with $r = 3$.

> ***Remark 9.4*** (Stopping conditions for CP-ALS) The stopping condition used for CP-ALS in computing Fig. 9.8 was that the change in the relative error in subsequent iterations was less than 10^{-4}.

Exercise 9.11 (a) In Fig. 9.8, what does it mean that several of the values of $\mathbf{a}_2$ are at or near zero? (b) How does this relate to the ground truth? (c) Does it "make sense"?

Exercise 9.12 (a) Plot the factors for all rank-3 CPs computed in Exercise 9.8. (b) Are they all the same? (c) How does the best compare to Fig. 9.8? (d) Plot the factors for all rank-4 and 5 solutions. (e) How do they compare to the best rank-3 factorization?

Exercise 9.13 (a) With 50 random initializations, compute rank-3 CP decompositions of the EEM tensor. (b) What is the range of relative errors? (c) How often is it with 0.01 of the lowest relative error?

9.7 Example: CP on Monkey BMI Tensor

Recall the monkey BMI neuron activation data from Section 1.5.3 (Kolda, 2022a; Vyas et al., 2018, 2020) and pictured in Fig. 9.9. In this experiment, a monkey uses a brain–machine interface to move a cursor to a target location at an angle of 0, 90, 180, or 270 degrees relative to the starting point. After achieving the target, the monkey must hold the cursor at the target location for 500 ms. The data is normalized so that the first half of each trial is target acquisition and the second half is holding the cursor at the target. Data are recorded from 88 neurons over 88 trials. The number of trials for each target is documented in Table 1.2. The tensor is arranged as 55 neurons $\times$ 200 timesteps $\times$ 88 trials.

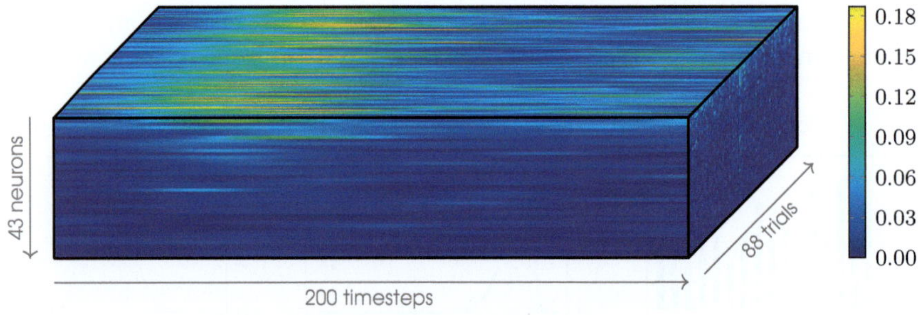

Figure 9.9 Monkey BMI tensor.

9.7.1 Nonnegative CP on Monkey BMI Tensor

We illustrate a rank-10 factorization in Fig. 9.10. This data is nonnegative, so for this example we compute a nonnegative tensor factorization. The 10-component factorization

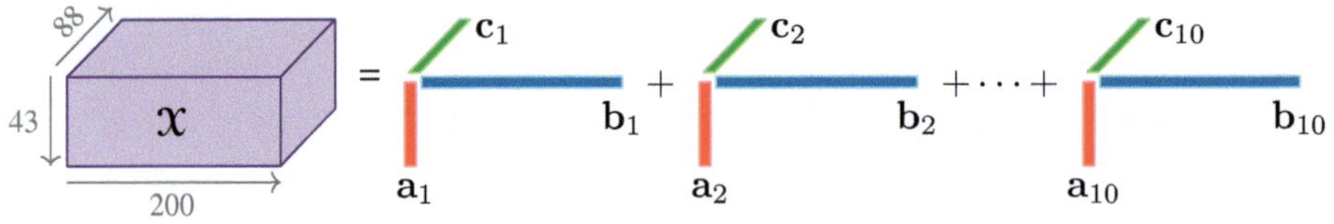

Figure 9.10 Rank-10 nonnegative CP decomposition of monkey BMI tensor.

yields a relative error of

$$\frac{\|\mathcal{X} - [\![\boldsymbol{\lambda}; \mathbf{A}, \mathbf{B}, \mathbf{C}]\!]\|}{\|\mathcal{X}\|} = 35.08\%.$$

This may seem large, but many real-world datasets have larger errors. This does not necessarily mean that the factorization is not useful, as we see below.

An illustration of a 10-component nonnegative factorization is shown in Fig. 9.11. We plot each component as a row in the figure. The component numbers are plotted along the left side. The first plot is a bar chart plotting the neuron activity levels, normalized to the norm of the component. The neurons are sorted according to total activity across all trials, from most to least active. In the middle is a plot of the time mode. It is interesting that the curves are smooth since we did nothing explicitly to enforce smoothness. Recall that the first 100 timesteps correspond to obtaining the target and the second 100 timesteps correspond to maintaining the cursor at the target. Finally, on the right is the plot of the different trials, as a scatter chart. Each is colored by the target angle, even though the tensor decomposition does not have access to that information.

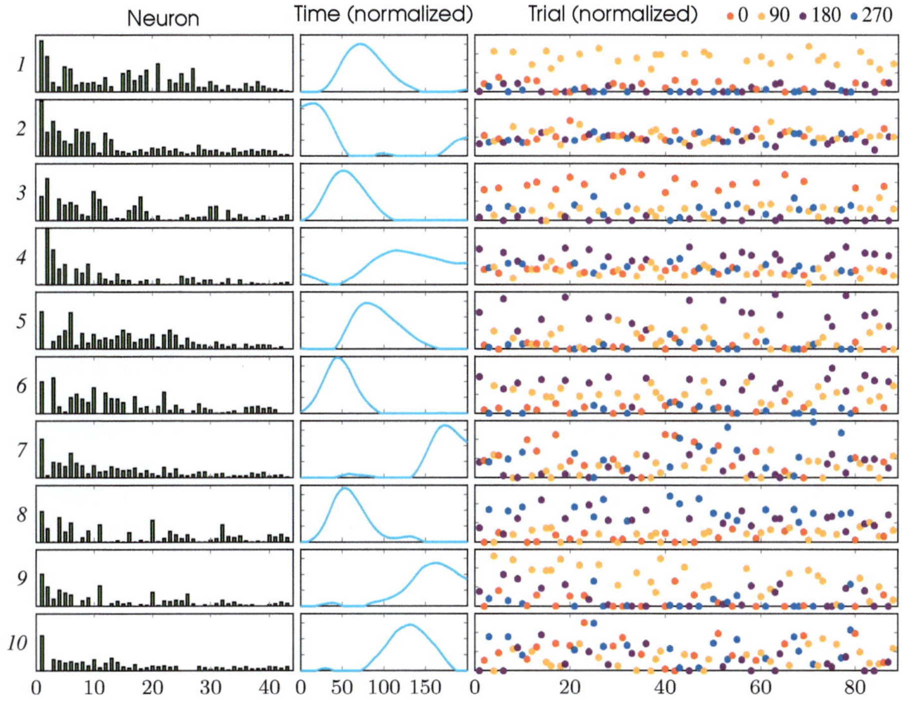

Figure 9.11 CP factorization of monkey BMI tensor data with 10 components, constrained to be nonnegative. Each component is displayed as a row, with neuron activation level in the first column as bar charts (scaled to component magnitude), time in the second column as line plots (scaled to unit norm), and trials color-coded in scatter plots in the third column (scaled to unit norm).

We can make some interpretation of the components:

- Component 1 corresponds to the 90-degree target (yellow).
- Components 2 is fairly consistent across all trials and seems to correspond to activity at the onset of each trial.
- Component 3 corresponds to the 0-degree target (red).
- Component 4 seems to be active mostly toward the end of each trial and has weak correlation with 180 degrees (purple).
- Component 5 corresponds fairly well to the 180-degree target (purple), but the lowest scoring 180-degree trials and not well separated from the highest scoring 90-degree targets (yellow).
- Component 6 corresponds to 90- or 180-degree targets (yellow and purple).
- Component 7 corresponds to activity at the end of each trial.

- Component 8 corresponds to 180- and 270-degree targets (blue and purple), somewhat mixed together.
- Component 9 is correlated mainly with the 90-degree target (yellow).
- Component 10 corresponds mainly to the second half of the trial, where the cursor is held at the target location.

This factorization does not have components that clearly associate with the targets; however, the results can still be useful, as we demonstrate in the clustering demonstration in the next subsection. Additionally, we have an alternative and more interpretable factorization using GCP in Section 15.6.

Remark 9.5 (Computational methodology) The results in Fig. 9.11 were computed using the CP-OPT methodology, as described in Chapter 12, using the objective function $\|\mathcal{X} - [\![\mathbf{A}, \mathbf{B}, \mathbf{C}]\!]\| / \|\mathcal{X}\|$. (Dividing by $\|\mathcal{X}\|$ impacts the scaling of the problem.) We use a lower bound of 0 on all optimization variables. The optimization method is bound-constrained limited-memory BFGS (L-BFGS-B) with the following settings per Zhu et al. (1997). The memory parameter (`m`) is 5. The method stopped after 209 iterations (423 total iterations) because the gradient was below the projected gradient tolerance (`pgtol`) of `1e-5`. The other stopping conditions (not triggered) were set as follows: maximum number of iterations (`maxIts`) was 1000, maximum number of total iterations including inner iterations for the line search (`maxTotalIts`) was 10,000, and the function tolerance divided by machine epsilon (`factr`) was `1e-10/eps` or `4.5e5`.

Exercise 9.14 (a) Using an existing code for computing nonnegative CP, decompose the monkey BMI tensor with ranks 5 through 15, using at least three starting points per run. (b) Plot the best relative error versus CP rank and consider how to choose the rank.

9.7.2 Clustering Monkey BMI Trials

Recall that the tensor has no explicit information about the differences between the trials. If we did not already know that differences between the trials, could we separate them based on the tensor analysis of the neuron signals? To answer this question, we consider each row in the $\mathbf{C}$ matrix, of size 88×10, to be a set of features describing the trial and apply the k-means clustering algorithm to the data (using five replicates and correlation as the distance measure). The resulting clustering perfectly partitions the trials according to the angles as shown in the confusion matrix in Table 9.1.

Table 9.1 Cluster confusion matrix comparing experiment angle and cluster using factor matrix $\mathbf{C}$ from rank-10 CP factorization of monkey BMI tensor

Cluster	0	90	180	270
1	0	28	0	0
2	0	0	0	19
3	20	0	0	0
4	0	0	21	0

Exercise 9.15 (a) Using the results of Exercise 9.14, cluster the data as described above. (b) Produce the confusion matrix for each rank. (c) How does the clustering performance vary with the rank?

9.8 Example: GCP on Chicago 2019 Crime Tensor

We consider the **Chicago crime tensor** (Kolda, 2022b), as described in Section 1.5.4. The Chicago crime tensor, denoted here by $\mathcal{X}$, is a 4-way tensor of size $365 \times 24 \times 77 \times 12$, where each entry denotes the count for a particular day, hour, community, and crime type. The values are integers in the range $\{0, 1, 2, \ldots, 23\}$.

The factorization will have four factor matrices, so we have a model of the form

$$\mathcal{M} \equiv [\![\mathbf{A}_1, \mathbf{A}_2, \mathbf{A}_3, \mathbf{A}_4]\!].$$

9.8.1 Choosing the Objective Function

The difference between CP and GCP is that GCP allows for other objective functions. In many applications, using different objective functions leads to more meaningful interpretations of the factors. Since $\mathcal{X}$ contains count data, it is appropriate to minimize the KL divergence loss function:

$$\sum_{i=1}^{365} \sum_{j=1}^{24} \sum_{k=1}^{77} \sum_{\ell=1}^{12} m_{ijk\ell} - x_{ijk\ell} \log(m_{ijk\ell}), \tag{9.6}$$

which has discarded constant terms. This corresponds to assuming that the tensor entries are Poisson distributed, and the value $m_{ijk\ell}$ corresponds to the mean value of the Poisson distribution for entry (i, j, k, ℓ).

9.8.2 Choosing the Model Rank

The first question is the choice of rank, so we run an experiment to see how loss function varies as we increase the rank. Additionally, we run each experiment three times to see how much variation there is per run. The results are shown in Fig. 9.12. The three runs yield nearly identical loss values in all cases. The decrease in the function value continues to improve as the rank increase, so there is not necessarily a clear choice for the "best" rank. Nevertheless, we focus on the rank-7 solution in the remainder of our discussion and leave investigation of other ranks as exercises.

9.8.3 Interpreting the Decomposition

The rank-7 decomposition is shown in Fig. 9.13. The components are presented in order of overall magnitude, and the components have been normalized to unit norm *except* the day component, which reflects the weight of the component overall. The first component corresponds to the day and is of length 365, and the beginning of each month is indicated by a vertical gridline. The second component corresponds to the hour, with hour 0 corresponding to midnight to 12:59 a.m., hour 1 corresponding to 1:00–1:59 a.m., and so on. The third component corresponds to community area. Map visualizations are provided in Fig. 9.14. The fourth component corresponds to crime type.

We can make a few observations about the components:

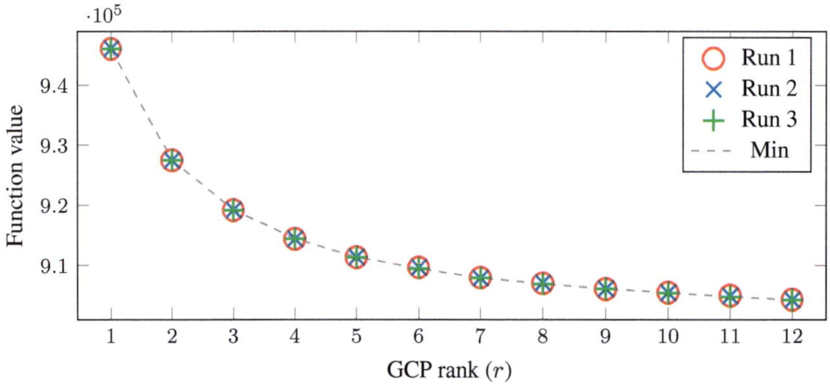

Figure 9.12 GCP rank versus KL divergence loss metric for Chicago crime tensor.

- Component 1 is most active in the areas known as "Near North" and "Loop," which are heavily populated by tourists. We see a pattern of crime reports peaking during afternoon hours (roughly noon to 6 p.m.). The main crime type is theft. These crimes are active throughout the entire year. There is a peak in early August, and the timing and location indicate that this peak may be connected with the Lollapalooza festival, which took place in Grant Park (Loop area) on August 1–4.

- Component 2 peaks in the area known as Austin (in the West Side) but involves many other parts of the city as well. The most prevalent crime types are battery and assault. This is consistent throughout the year and drops off in the overnight hours.

- Component 3 is consistent throughout the year. It is mainly during the daytime with peaks around 10 a.m. and 8 p.m. The neighborhoods correspond to the region known as West Side. The main crime is narcotics.

- Component 4 has mild peaks approximately every weekend, with more activity in the warmer months. These are mainly in the middle of the night, peaking around midnight. The primary area is again Austin in the West Side. The primary crime type is battery.

- Component 5 has strong peaks every weekend and also is in the middle of the night. The main areas for this one, however, are Near North and Lakeview. Both theft and battery are prevalent.

- Component 6 is fairly consistent across the days, hours, and communities. The main crime types are theft and criminal damage.

- Component 7 is interesting because it has a large peak on January 1 and peaks at the beginning of each month. The top times are noon, midnight, and 9 a.m. The communities are throughout the city. The top crime is deceptive practice. One interpretation is that the crimes identified by this component are those that do not have an easily identified start time, so the reports just provide an approximation that is the first day of the year or month and an arbitrary hour.

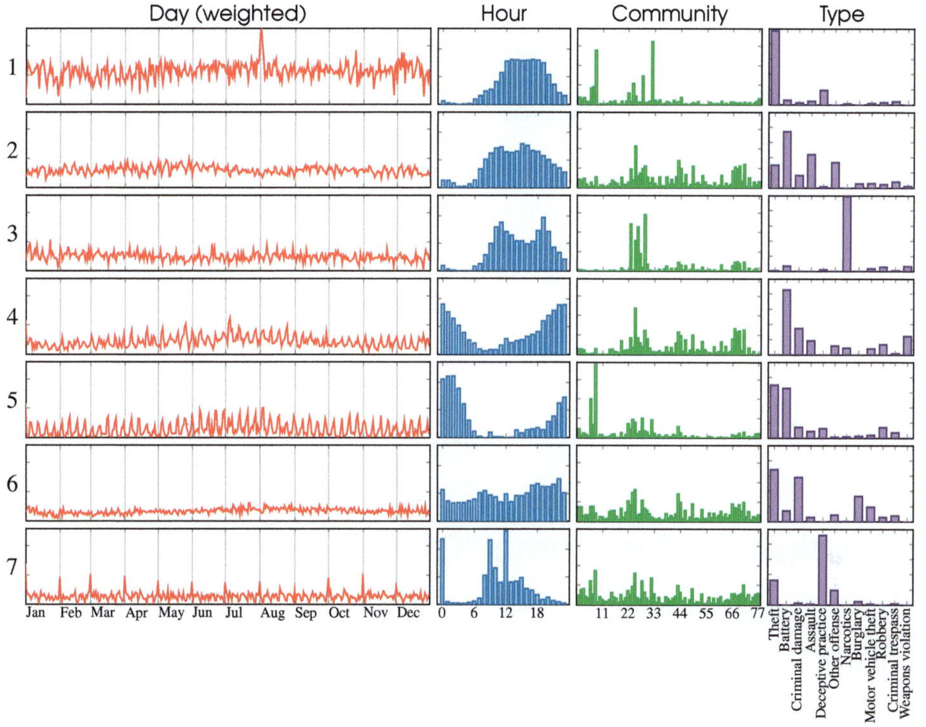

Figure 9.13 Chicago crime tensor rank-7 GCP (KL divergence for count data) factors. Each row represents one component, sorted from largest to smallest magnitude. Factors for hour, community, and (crime) type normalized to length 1. Factors for day hold the weight of the component.

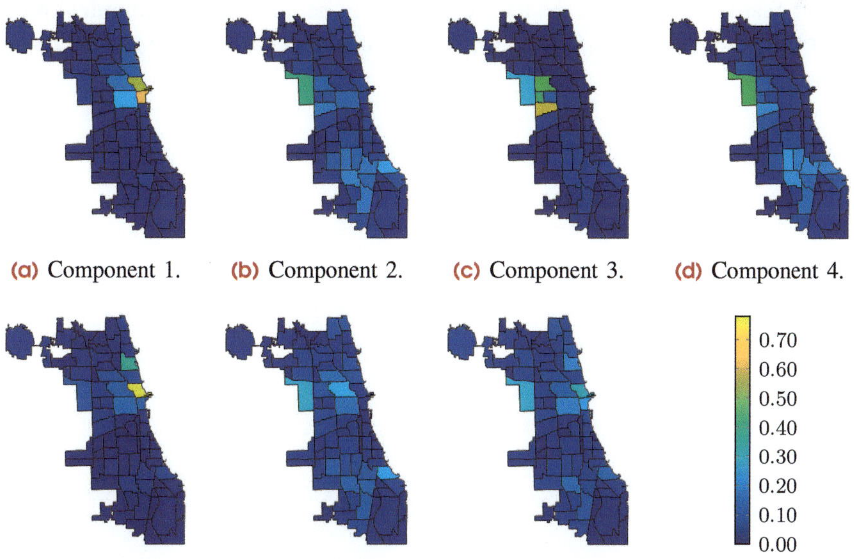

(a) Component 1. (b) Component 2. (c) Component 3. (d) Component 4.

(e) Component 5. (f) Component 6. (g) Component 7.

Figure 9.14 Map visualization for factor 3 (community) of Fig. 9.13.

Remark 9.6 (Computational methodology) These results in Figs. 9.12–9.14 were computed using the GCP-OPT methodology as described in Chapter 15. We use the objective function in Eq. (9.6) (but add 10^{-10} to the quantity inside the log) and impose a lower bound of 0 on all optimization variables. The optimization method is bound-constrained limited-memory BFGS (L-BFGS-B) with the following settings per Zhu et al. (1997). The method stopped after 430 iterations (915 total iterations) because the change in the relative change function value was less than the tolerance of 2.22×10^{-9} (corresponding to `factr` equal to 10^7). The other stopping conditions (not triggered) were set as follows: maximum number of iterations (`maxIts`) was 500, maximum number of total iterations including inner iterations for the line search (`maxTotalIts`) was 5000, and the projected gradient tolerance was 0.8094, which is 10^{-7} times the total size of the tensor (8,094,240).

Exercise 9.16 (a) Compute a decomposition using any method that produces a nonnegative decomposition of rank 7. (b) Do the components have any interpretation similar to the above?

9.9 Origins of the Name "CP"

A natural first question is what does "CP" mean? The name comes to us via an interesting evolution. The original idea of CP is attributed to Hitchcock (1927), whose algebraic treatment referred to CP as a **polyadic** expression. (We also attribute the Tucker decomposition to the same work.) In 1970, two different groups proposed 3-way CP independently. Carroll and Chang (1970) proposed the canonical decomposition of 3-way tensors, abbreviated as **CANDECOMP**. Simultaneously, Harshman (1970) proposed the same idea under the name of parallel factors, abbreviated as **PARAFAC**. Several other groups came up with the idea of CP as well (see, e.g., Möcks, 1988). The multitude of names made the topic somewhat confusing in literature searches, so Kiers (2000) proposed a compromise name of "CP," short for CANDECOMP/PARAFAC, which were the two primary names in use at the time. Starting circa 2010, the term CP started to be expanded as **canonical polyadic**; see, for example, Phan et al. (2011), Royer et al. (2011), and Sorensen and De Lathauwer (2010).

10 Kruskal Tensor Structure

Before we talk about how to compute the CP decomposition in subsequent chapters, we focus on the special properties of a **Kruskal tensor**, which forms the approximation to the data tensor in a CP decomposition. A Kruskal tensor is a tensor that can be expressed as the sum of vector outer products. We say a tensor is a Kruskal tensor when we store the vectors to form the outer products (a decomposed format) rather than the full version (a dense tensor). Working with Kruskal tensors makes many computations, such as computing the norm, less expensive than with the equivalent full tensor.

10.1 Rank-1 Tensors

Rank-1 tensors are the building blocks of Kruskal tensors, so we begin with these.

10.1.1 Rank-1 3-way Tensors

Definition 10.1 (Rank-1 3-way Tensor) In the 3-way case, a **rank-1 tensor** is a tensor that can be written as the outer product of three vectors. In other words, a tensor $\mathcal{X} \in \mathbb{R}^{m \times n \times p}$ is rank 1 if there exist vectors $\mathbf{a} \in \mathbb{R}^m$, $\mathbf{b} \in \mathbb{R}^n$, and $\mathbf{c} \in \mathbb{R}^p$ such that $\mathcal{X} = \mathbf{a} \bigcirc \mathbf{b} \bigcirc \mathbf{c}$ or, elementwise,

$$x_{ijk} = a_i b_j c_k \quad \text{for all} \quad (i,j,k) \in [m] \otimes [n] \otimes [p].$$

We visualize a rank-1 tensor in Fig. 10.1.

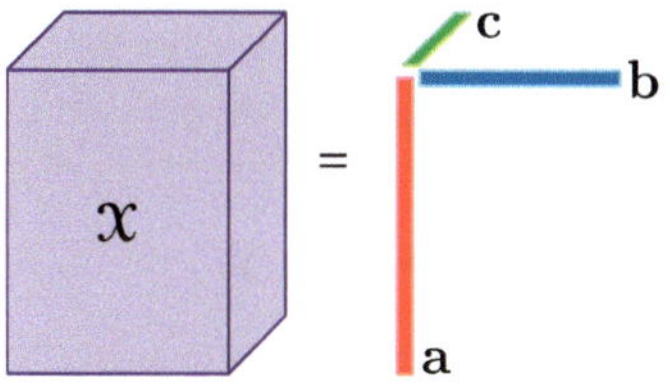

Figure 10.1 Rank-1 3-way tensor.

It is more efficient to store a 3-way rank-1 tensor as a set of vectors rather than as a full tensor; the storage is $m + n + p$ for the vectors versus mnp for the full tensor.

Example 10.1 (Rank-1 Tensor) Let $\mathbf{a} = \left[\begin{smallmatrix}1\\0\end{smallmatrix}\right]$, $\mathbf{b} = \left[\begin{smallmatrix}1\\0\end{smallmatrix}\right]$, and $\mathbf{c} = \left[\begin{smallmatrix}1\\-1\end{smallmatrix}\right]$. Then $\mathcal{X} = \mathbf{a} \circ \mathbf{b} \circ \mathbf{c}$ means

$$\mathcal{X}(:,:,1) = \begin{bmatrix} 1 & 0 \\ 0 & 0 \end{bmatrix} \quad \text{and} \quad \mathcal{X}(:,:,2) = \begin{bmatrix} -1 & 0 \\ 0 & 0 \end{bmatrix}.$$

Exercise 10.1 Show that the norm of $\mathcal{X} = \mathbf{a} \circ \mathbf{b} \circ \mathbf{c}$ can be computed as $\|\mathcal{X}\| = \|\mathbf{a}\|_2 \|\mathbf{b}\|_2 \|\mathbf{c}\|_2$ for a cost of only $\mathcal{O}(m + n + p)$ versus $\mathcal{O}(mnp)$ for the full tensor.

Exercise 10.2 Prove the following. A tensor $\mathcal{X} \in \mathbb{R}^{m \times n \times p}$ is rank 1 if and only if $\text{rank}(\mathbf{X}_{(1)}) = \text{rank}(\mathbf{X}_{(2)}) = \text{rank}(\mathbf{X}_{(3)}) = 1$.

10.1.2 Rank-1 d-way Tensors

The d-way case is analogous to the 3-way case.

Definition 10.2 (Rank-1 d-way Tensor) A **rank-1 tensor** of order d is a tensor that can be written as the outer product of d vectors. In other words, $\mathcal{X} \in \mathbb{R}^{n_1 \times n_2 \times \cdots \times n_d}$ is rank 1 if there exist vectors $\{ \mathbf{a}_k \}_{k=1}^{d}$ with $\mathbf{a}_k \in \mathbb{R}^{n_k}$ for all $k \in [d]$ such that

$$\mathcal{X} = \mathbf{a}_1 \circ \cdots \circ \mathbf{a}_d. \tag{10.1}$$

Equivalently, each element of $\mathcal{X}$ can be written as the product of elements of the vectors so that

$$x_{i_1 \cdots i_d} = \prod_{k=1}^{d} \mathbf{a}_k(i_k) \quad \text{for all} \quad (i_1, \ldots, i_d) \in [n_1] \otimes \cdots \otimes [n_d]. \tag{10.2}$$

The storage efficiencies become even more pronounced for d-way rank-1 tensors. The storage for the vectors is $\sum_{k=1}^{d} n_k$ versus the storage for the full tensor of $\prod_{k=1}^{d} n_k$.

Exercise 10.3 Let $\mathbf{a}_k \in \mathbb{R}^n$ for all $k \in [d]$. (a) What is the storage for a rank-1 tensor $\mathcal{X} = \mathbf{a}_1 \circ \cdots \circ \mathbf{a}_d$? (b) What would the storage be for a dense tensor of size $n \times n \times \cdots \times n$? (c) How do these compare?

10.2 Kruskal Tensor Format

The storage for a Kruskal tensor in factored form (storing only the factor matrices) is proportional in the *sum* of its dimensions versus storage that is the *product* of the dimensions for the full tensor.

10.2.1 Kruskal 3-way Tensor Format

A **Kruskal tensor** is a tensor that is expressed as the sum of rank-1 tensors.

Definition 10.3: Kruskal Tensor (3-way)

A 3-way **Kruskal tensor** $\mathcal{K} = [\![\mathbf{A}, \mathbf{B}, \mathbf{C}]\!]$ is defined by **factor matrices** $\mathbf{A} \in \mathbb{R}^{m \times r}$, $\mathbf{B} \in \mathbb{R}^{n \times r}$, and $\mathbf{C} \in \mathbb{R}^{p \times r}$. Specifically, it is the sum of the outer products of the matching matrix columns:

$$\mathcal{K} = \sum_{\ell=1}^{r} \mathbf{a}_\ell \circ \mathbf{b}_\ell \circ \mathbf{c}_\ell \quad \in \mathbb{R}^{m \times n \times p},$$

where $\mathbf{a}_\ell$, $\mathbf{b}_\ell$, and $\mathbf{c}_\ell$ represent column ℓ of $\mathbf{A}$, $\mathbf{B}$, and $\mathbf{C}$, respectively. Each outer product $\mathbf{a}_\ell \circ \mathbf{b}_\ell \circ \mathbf{c}_\ell$ is referred to as a **component**, and each vector is referred to as a **factor**. We refer to r as the **number of components** or, colloquially, the **rank**.

The factor matrices can have different numbers of rows but must each have the same number of columns, depicted visually (with columns labeled) as shown in Fig. 10.2a. The jth column of each factor matrix is used in the jth component of the Kruskal tensor. A 3-way Kruskal tensor is defined completely by three matrices; thus, we use the shorthand $\mathcal{K} = [\![\mathbf{A}, \mathbf{B}, \mathbf{C}]\!]$. Visually, a 3-way Kruskal tensor is depicted as shown in Fig. 10.2b. The name and notation $[\![\mathbf{A}, \mathbf{B}, \mathbf{C}]\!]$ follows Bader and Kolda (2007) and is in tribute to the pioneering work of Kruskal (1977, 1989).

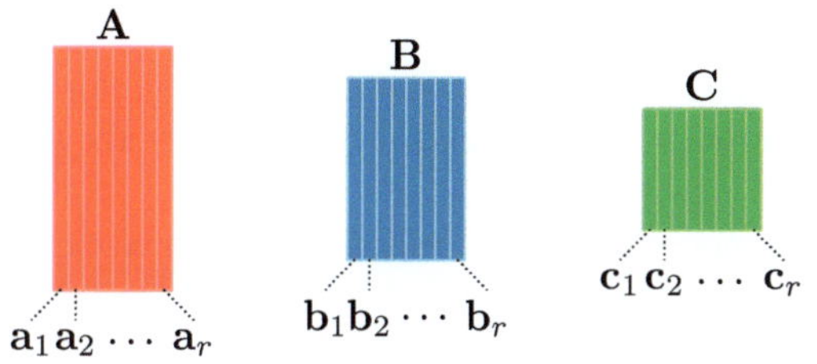

(a) Factor matrices with columns labeled.

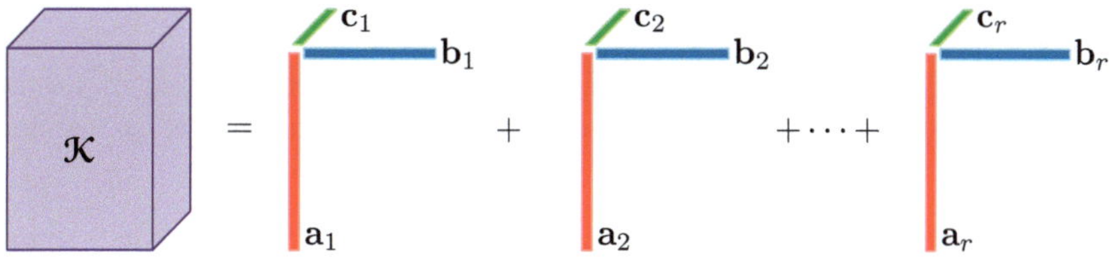

(b) 3-way Kruskal tensor $\mathcal{K} = [\![\mathbf{A}, \mathbf{B}, \mathbf{C}]\!]$.

Figure 10.2 Conversion of factor matrices to 3-way Kruskal tensor.

The (i, j, k) element of $\mathcal{K} = [\![\mathbf{A}, \mathbf{B}, \mathbf{C}]\!]$ can be expressed as

$$\mathcal{K}(i, j, k) = \sum_{\ell=1}^{r} a_{i\ell} b_{j\ell} c_{k\ell}. \tag{10.3}$$

A tensor is stored in Kruskal tensor form by storing *only* its factor matrices. This means that the storage for a Kruskal tensor is $r(m + n + p)$. In comparison, the storage for a full tensor is mnp.

Example 10.2 (Rank-2 Kruskal Tensor) Let

$$\mathbf{A} = \begin{bmatrix} -1 & 2 \\ 2 & 0 \\ -1 & 1 \end{bmatrix}, \quad \mathbf{B} = \begin{bmatrix} 1 & -2 \\ 0 & -2 \\ -1 & 1 \end{bmatrix}, \quad \text{and} \quad \mathbf{C} = \begin{bmatrix} 0 & 2 \\ -2 & -1 \end{bmatrix}.$$

Then $\mathcal{X} = [\![\mathbf{A}, \mathbf{B}, \mathbf{C}]\!]$ means

$$\mathcal{X}(:,:,1) = \begin{bmatrix} -8 & -8 & 4 \\ 0 & 0 & 0 \\ -4 & -4 & 2 \end{bmatrix} \quad \text{and} \quad \mathcal{X}(:,:,2) = \begin{bmatrix} 6 & 4 & -4 \\ -4 & 0 & 4 \\ 4 & 2 & -3 \end{bmatrix}.$$

10.2.2 Kruskal d-way Tensor Format

Definition 10.4: Kruskal Tensor (d-way)

A d-way **Kruskal tensor** $\mathcal{K} = [\![\mathbf{A}_1, \mathbf{A}_2, \ldots, \mathbf{A}_d]\!]$ is defined by d **factor matrices** $\mathbf{A}_k \in \mathbb{R}^{n_k \times r}$ to be the sum of the outer products of the matching matrix columns:

$$\mathcal{K} = \sum_{j=1}^{r} \mathbf{A}_1(:,j) \circ \mathbf{A}_2(:,j) \circ \cdots \circ \mathbf{A}_d(:,j) \quad \in \mathbb{R}^{n_1 \times n_2 \times \cdots \times n_d}.$$

Each outer product is referred to as a **component**, and each vector is referred to as a **factor**. We refer to r as the **number of components** or, colloquially, the **rank**.

The $(i_1, i_2, \ldots, i_d)$ element of $\mathcal{K} = [\![\mathbf{A}_1, \mathbf{A}_2, \ldots, \mathbf{A}_d]\!]$ can be expressed as

$$\mathcal{K}(i_1, i_2, \ldots, i_d) = \sum_{j=1}^{r} \prod_{k=1}^{d} \mathbf{A}_k(i_k, j). \tag{10.4}$$

If $n = n_1 = \cdots = n_k$, then the storage is drn in factored format versus n^d for the full tensor, which correspond to a many orders of magnitude difference in storage, as shown in Fig. 10.3.

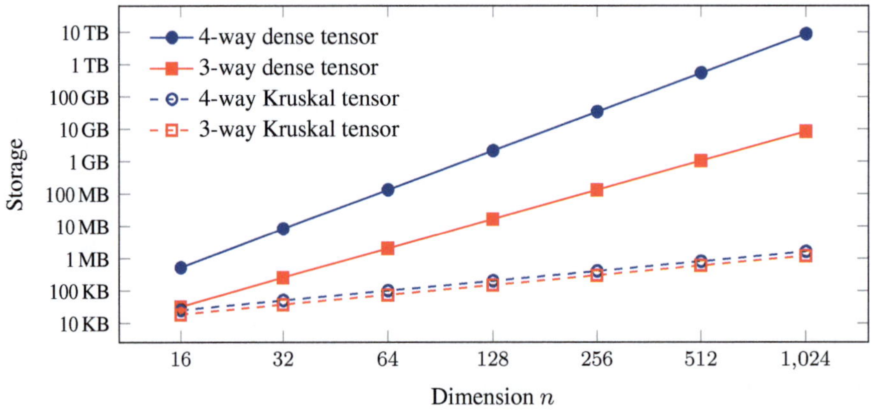

Figure 10.3 Kruskal tensor storage for 3-way $n \times n \times n$ or 4-way $n \times n \times n \times n$ tensor with $r = 50$ versus the full tensor.

10.2.3 Kruskal 3-way Tensor Format with Component Weights

Normalizing the factors and weights makes the magnitude of each component explicit. It is then also typical to reorder the components so that $\lambda_1 \geq \lambda_2 \geq \cdots \geq \lambda_r$.

A Kruskal tensor may also have **component weights**. We can compute the norm of each component of a Kruskal tensor using Exercise 10.1. It may be convenient to express the Kruskal tensor with explicit weights that represent the norms. For example, given a rank-1 tensor $\mathcal{K} = \mathbf{a} \circ \mathbf{b} \circ \mathbf{c}$, we define $\lambda = \|\mathbf{a}\|_2 \|\mathbf{b}\|_2 \|\mathbf{c}\|_2$. Then we have $\mathcal{K} = \lambda\, \bar{\mathbf{a}} \circ \bar{\mathbf{b}} \circ \bar{\mathbf{c}}$, where $\bar{\mathbf{a}} = \mathbf{a}/\|\mathbf{a}\|_2$, $\bar{\mathbf{b}} = \mathbf{b}/\|\mathbf{b}\|_2$, and $\bar{\mathbf{c}} = \mathbf{c}/\|\mathbf{c}\|_2$ all have unit norm.

To this end, it is useful to define the Kruskal tensor with an optional weight vector. The weights need not be restricted to component norms. In the 3-way case, we have the following.

Definition 10.5: Kruskal Tensor with Weights (3-way)

A 3-way **Kruskal tensor** $\mathcal{K} = [\![\boldsymbol{\lambda}; \mathbf{A}, \mathbf{B}, \mathbf{C}]\!]$ is defined by **factor matrices** $\mathbf{A} \in \mathbb{R}^{m \times r}$, $\mathbf{B} \in \mathbb{R}^{n \times r}$, and $\mathbf{C} \in \mathbb{R}^{p \times r}$, and a **weight vector** $\boldsymbol{\lambda} \in \mathbb{R}^r$. Specifically, it is the sum of the outer products of the matching matrix columns:

$$\mathcal{K} = \sum_{\ell=1}^{r} \lambda_\ell \, \mathbf{a}_\ell \circ \mathbf{b}_\ell \circ \mathbf{c}_\ell \quad \in \mathbb{R}^{m \times n \times p}.$$

Each outer product $\lambda_\ell \, \mathbf{a}_\ell \circ \mathbf{b}_\ell \circ \mathbf{c}_\ell$ is referred to as a **component**, each λ_ℓ is a **component weight**, and each vector is referred to as a **factor**. We refer to r as the **number of components**.

If $\lambda_1 = \cdots = \lambda_r = 1$, then Definition 10.5 is equivalent to Definition 10.3.

Exercise 10.4 If $\mathcal{K} = [\![\boldsymbol{\lambda}; \mathbf{A}, \mathbf{B}, \mathbf{C}]\!]$, what is $\mathcal{K}(i, j, k)$?

Exercise 10.5 Consider the rank-1 tensor $\mathbf{a} \circ \mathbf{b} \circ \mathbf{c}$. Let $\hat{\mathbf{a}} = \alpha \mathbf{a}$, $\hat{\mathbf{b}} = \beta \mathbf{b}$, and $\hat{\mathbf{c}} = \gamma \mathbf{c}$, where $\alpha\beta\gamma = 1$. Show that $\|\mathbf{a} \circ \mathbf{b} \circ \mathbf{c}\| = \|\hat{\mathbf{a}} \circ \hat{\mathbf{b}} \circ \hat{\mathbf{c}}\|$.

10.2.4 Kruskal d-way Tensor Format with Component Weights

The extension to d-way is analogous, as we formalize in Definition 10.6.

Definition 10.6: Kruskal Tensor with Weights (d-way)

A d-way **Kruskal tensor** $\mathcal{K} = [\![\boldsymbol{\lambda}; \mathbf{A}_1, \mathbf{A}_2, \ldots, \mathbf{A}_d]\!]$ is defined by d **factor matrices** $\mathbf{A}_k \in \mathbb{R}^{n_k \times r}$ and a **weight vector** $\boldsymbol{\lambda} \in \mathbb{R}^r$ to be the sum of the weighted outer products of the matching matrix columns:

$$\mathcal{K} = \sum_{j=1}^{r} \lambda_j \; \mathbf{A}_1(:, j) \circ \mathbf{A}_2(:, j) \circ \cdots \circ \mathbf{A}_d(:, j) \quad \in \mathbb{R}^{n_1 \times n_2 \times \cdots \times n_d}.$$

Each outer product $\lambda_j \, \mathbf{a}_j \circ \mathbf{b}_j \circ \mathbf{c}_j$ is referred to as a **component**, each λ_j is referred to as a **component weight**, and each vector is referred to as a **factor**. We refer to r as the **number of components**.

This definition is equivalent to Definition 10.4 if $\lambda_1 = \cdots \lambda_r = 1$. Strictly speaking, the weights are redundant in the definition of a Kruskal tensor.

The $(i_1, i_2, \ldots, i_d)$ element of $\mathcal{K} = [\![\boldsymbol{\lambda}; \mathbf{A}_1, \mathbf{A}_2, \ldots, \mathbf{A}_d]\!]$ can be expressed as

$$\mathcal{K}(i_1, i_2, \ldots, i_d) = \sum_{j=1}^{r} \lambda_j \prod_{k=1}^{d} \mathbf{A}_k(i_k, j). \tag{10.5}$$

For a given Kruskal tensor, a normalized version with weights can be computed as shown in the following algorithm.

Kruskal Tensor Renormalization

> **given** $\{\mathbf{A}_1, \mathbf{A}_2, \ldots, \mathbf{A}_d\}$
> **for** $j = 1, \ldots, r$ **do**
> $\lambda_j \leftarrow 1$
>   **for** $k = 1, \ldots, d$ **do**
> $\eta_{kj} \leftarrow \|\mathbf{A}_k(:,j)\|_2$
> $\lambda_j \leftarrow \lambda_j \eta_{kj}$
> $\mathbf{B}_k(:,j) \leftarrow \mathbf{A}_k(:,j)/\eta_{kj}$
>   **end for**
> **end for**
> **return** $\{\boldsymbol{\lambda}, \mathbf{B}_1, \mathbf{B}_2, \ldots, \mathbf{B}_d\}$ $\triangleright$ $[\![\mathbf{A}_1, \mathbf{A}_2, \ldots, \mathbf{A}_d]\!] = [\![\boldsymbol{\lambda}; \mathbf{B}_1, \mathbf{B}_2, \ldots, \mathbf{B}_d]\!]$

If the tensor already has weights, then λ_j need not be initialized to one. The value η_{jk} can be any nonzero value, such as the 1-norm or infinity norm of column j. The key is that it is balanced by being multiplied into the weight and divided out of the factor.

Example 10.3 (Renormalizing Rank-2 Kruskal Tensor) Let

$$\mathbf{A}_1 = \begin{bmatrix} -1 & 2 \\ 2 & 0 \\ -1 & 1 \end{bmatrix}, \quad \mathbf{A}_2 = \begin{bmatrix} 1 & -2 \\ 0 & -2 \\ -1 & 1 \end{bmatrix}, \quad \mathbf{A}_3 = \begin{bmatrix} 0 & 2 \\ -2 & -1 \end{bmatrix}.$$

We can renormalize the columns of each factor so that the component weights are the products of the column norms:

$$\boldsymbol{\lambda} = \begin{bmatrix} (\sqrt{6})(\sqrt{2})(\sqrt{4}) \\ (\sqrt{5})(\sqrt{5})(\sqrt{9}) \end{bmatrix} = \begin{bmatrix} 6.93 \\ 15.00 \end{bmatrix}.$$

Then $[\![\mathbf{A}_1, \mathbf{A}_2, \mathbf{A}_3]\!] = [\![\boldsymbol{\lambda}; \mathbf{B}_1, \mathbf{B}_2, \mathbf{B}_3]\!]$, where all the columns for the factor matrices have been rescaled to norm 1:

$$\mathbf{B}_1 = \begin{bmatrix} -0.41 & 0.89 \\ 0.82 & 0.00 \\ -0.41 & 0.45 \end{bmatrix}, \quad \mathbf{B}_2 = \begin{bmatrix} 0.71 & -0.67 \\ 0.00 & -0.67 \\ -0.71 & 0.33 \end{bmatrix}, \quad \text{and} \quad \mathbf{B}_3 = \begin{bmatrix} 0.00 & 0.89 \\ -1.00 & -0.45 \end{bmatrix}.$$

10.3 Unfolding a Kruskal Tensor

10.3.1 Vectorizing or Unfolding a 3-way Kruskal Tensor

Recall that a vectorization of a tensor rearranges its elements into a vector; see Eq. (2.9). For a rank-1 tensor, the vectorization is a Kronecker product of its factor vectors, as given in Eq. (3.5b) of Proposition 3.7. To vectorize a Kruskal tensor, we can think of summing the vectorizations of the components, which we can express via matrix–vector multiplication with the Khatri–Rao product of factor matrices.

Proposition 10.7 (Kruskal Tensor Vectorization, 3-way) *The vectorization of the Kruskal tensor* $\mathcal{K} = [\![\boldsymbol{\lambda}; \mathbf{A}, \mathbf{B}, \mathbf{C}]\!]$ *with* $\boldsymbol{\lambda} \in \mathbb{R}^r$, $\mathbf{A} \in \mathbb{R}^{m \times r}$, $\mathbf{B} \in \mathbb{R}^{m \times r}$, $\mathbf{C} \in \mathbb{R}^{m \times r}$ *is*

$$\operatorname{vec}(\mathcal{K}) = (\mathbf{C} \odot \mathbf{B} \odot \mathbf{A})\boldsymbol{\lambda}.$$

An illustration of the vectorization is shown in Fig. 10.4.

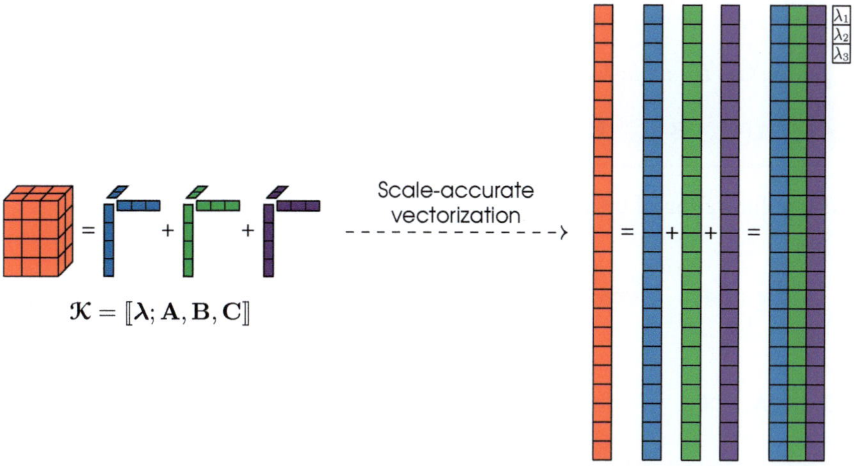

$$\text{vec}(\mathcal{K}) = \sum_{\ell=1}^{3} \lambda_\ell \, \mathbf{c}_\ell \otimes \mathbf{b}_\ell \otimes \mathbf{a}_\ell = (\mathbf{C} \odot \mathbf{B} \odot \mathbf{A})\boldsymbol{\lambda}$$

Figure 10.4 Vectorization of $4 \times 3 \times 2$ Kruskal tensor with 3 components.

Example 10.4 (Kruskal Tensor Vectorization, 3-way) We revisit the $2 \times 2 \times 2$ tensor of rank 3 from Example 9.1. We have

$$\mathcal{X}(:,:,1) = \begin{bmatrix} 1 & 0 \\ 0 & 1 \end{bmatrix} \quad \text{and} \quad \mathcal{X}(:,:,1) = \begin{bmatrix} 0 & 1 \\ -1 & 0 \end{bmatrix},$$

and $\mathcal{X} = [\![\mathbf{A}, \mathbf{B}, \mathbf{C}]\!]$, with

$$\mathbf{A} = \begin{bmatrix} 1 & 0 & 1 \\ 0 & 1 & -1 \end{bmatrix}, \quad \mathbf{B} = \begin{bmatrix} 1 & 0 & 1 \\ 0 & 1 & 1 \end{bmatrix}, \quad \text{and} \quad \mathbf{C} = \begin{bmatrix} 1 & 1 & 0 \\ -1 & 1 & 1 \end{bmatrix}.$$

Then Proposition 10.7 says

$$(\mathbf{C} \odot \mathbf{B} \odot \mathbf{A})\mathbf{1}_3 = \begin{bmatrix} 1 & 0 & 0 \\ 0 & 0 & -0 \\ 0 & 0 & 0 \\ 0 & 1 & -0 \\ -1 & 0 & 1 \\ 0 & 0 & -1 \\ 0 & 0 & 1 \\ 0 & 1 & -1 \end{bmatrix} \begin{bmatrix} 1 \\ 1 \\ 1 \end{bmatrix} = \begin{bmatrix} 1 \\ 0 \\ 0 \\ 1 \\ 0 \\ -1 \\ 1 \\ 0 \end{bmatrix} = \text{vec}(\mathcal{X}).$$

Exercise 10.6 Prove Proposition 10.7. Hint: Use Proposition 3.7.

The mode-k unfolding of Kruskal tensors is used repeatedly in developing algorithms for computing CP decompositions.

Proposition 10.8: Mode-k Unfolding of Kruskal Tensor (3-way)

Let $\mathcal{K} = [\![\mathbf{A}, \mathbf{B}, \mathbf{C}]\!]$. *Its mode-$k$ unfoldings are*

$$\mathbf{K}_{(1)} = \mathbf{A}(\mathbf{C} \odot \mathbf{B})^{\intercal}, \quad \mathbf{K}_{(2)} = \mathbf{B}(\mathbf{C} \odot \mathbf{A})^{\intercal}, \quad \textit{and} \quad \mathbf{K}_{(3)} = \mathbf{C}(\mathbf{B} \odot \mathbf{A})^{\intercal}.$$

We provide an illustration of the mode-1 unfolding in Fig. 10.5.

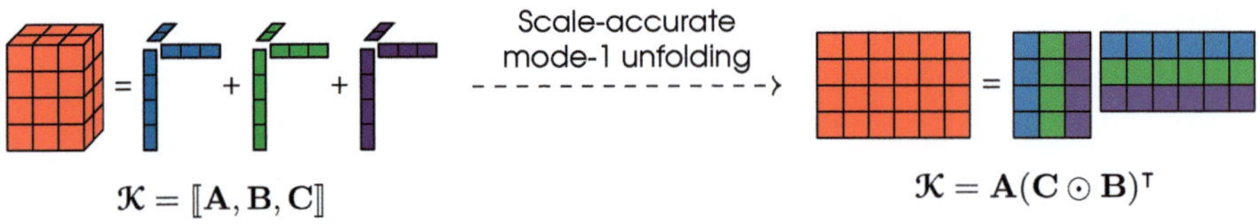

Figure 10.5 Mode-1 unfolding of $4 \times 3 \times 2$ Kruskal tensor with 3 components.

Example 10.5 (Kruskal Tensor Unfolding, 3-way) Using the same setup as Example 10.4, observe the equivalencies of the unfoldings per Proposition 10.8.

$$\mathbf{A}(\mathbf{C} \odot \mathbf{B})^{\intercal} = \begin{bmatrix} 1 & 0 & 1 \\ 0 & 1 & -1 \end{bmatrix} \begin{bmatrix} 1 & 0 & 0 \\ 0 & 1 & 0 \\ -1 & 0 & 1 \\ 0 & 1 & 1 \end{bmatrix} = \begin{bmatrix} 1 & 0 & 0 & 1 \\ 0 & 1 & -1 & 0 \end{bmatrix} = \mathbf{X}_{(1)},$$

$$\mathbf{B}(\mathbf{C} \odot \mathbf{A})^{\intercal} = \begin{bmatrix} 1 & 0 & 1 \\ 0 & 1 & 1 \end{bmatrix} \begin{bmatrix} 1 & 0 & 0 \\ 0 & 1 & -0 \\ -1 & 0 & 1 \\ 0 & 1 & -1 \end{bmatrix} = \begin{bmatrix} 1 & 0 & 0 & -1 \\ 0 & 1 & 1 & 0 \end{bmatrix} = \mathbf{X}_{(2)},$$

$$\mathbf{C}(\mathbf{B} \odot \mathbf{A})^{\intercal} = \begin{bmatrix} 1 & 1 & 0 \\ -1 & 1 & 1 \end{bmatrix} \begin{bmatrix} 1 & 0 & 1 \\ 0 & 0 & -1 \\ 0 & 0 & 1 \\ 0 & 1 & -1 \end{bmatrix} = \begin{bmatrix} 1 & 0 & 0 & 1 \\ 0 & -1 & 1 & 0 \end{bmatrix} = \mathbf{X}_{(3)}.$$

Exercise 10.7 Prove Proposition 10.8. Hint: Use Proposition 3.7.

Exercise 10.8 How many computational operations are required to compute the unfolding of a Kruskal tensor?

Exercise 10.9 What are the mode-k unfoldings for $\mathcal{K} = [\![\boldsymbol{\lambda}; \mathbf{A}, \mathbf{B}, \mathbf{C}]\!]$?

10.3.2 Vectorizing or Unfolding a d-way Kruskal Tensor

For the d-way case, recall that the vectorization of a tensor of size $n_1 \times n_2 \times \cdots \times n_d$ rearranges its elements into a vector of length $N = \prod_{k=1}^{d} n_k$ (see Definition 2.14).

Proposition 10.9 (Kruskal Tensor Vectorization, d-way) *The vectorization of the Kruskal tensor* $\mathcal{K} = [\![\boldsymbol{\lambda}; \mathbf{A}_1, \mathbf{A}_2, \ldots, \mathbf{A}_d]\!]$ *is*

$$\text{vec}(\mathcal{K}) = (\mathbf{A}_d \odot \mathbf{A}_{d-1} \odot \cdots \odot \mathbf{A}_1)\boldsymbol{\lambda}.$$

Proof. Let $N = \prod_{k=1}^{d} n_k$. Then we have

$$
\begin{aligned}
\operatorname{vec}(\mathcal{K}) &= \operatorname{vec}\Big(\sum_{j=1}^{r} \lambda_j \mathbf{A}_1(:,j) \circ \cdots \circ \mathbf{A}_d(:,j)\Big) && \text{via Definition 10.6} \\
&= \sum_{j=1}^{r} \lambda_j \operatorname{vec}\big(\mathbf{A}_1(:,j) \circ \cdots \circ \mathbf{A}_d(:,j)\big) && \text{via linearity of vec operation} \\
&= \sum_{j=1}^{r} \lambda_j \underbrace{\mathbf{A}_d(:,j) \otimes \cdots \otimes \mathbf{A}_1(:,j)}_{j\text{th column of } (\mathbf{A}_d \odot \mathbf{A}_{d-1} \odot \cdots \odot \mathbf{A}_1)} && \text{via Proposition 3.10} \\
&= (\mathbf{A}_d \odot \mathbf{A}_{d-1} \odot \cdots \odot \mathbf{A}_1)\boldsymbol{\lambda}.
\end{aligned}
$$

Hence, the claim. □

In the d-way case, recall that the mode-k unfolding of a tensor of size $n_1 \times n_2 \times \cdots \times n_d$ rearranges its entries into a matrix of size $n_k \times N_k$, where $N_k = \prod_{\substack{\ell=1 \\ \ell \neq k}}^{d} n_k$ (see Definition 2.18).

> **Proposition 10.10** (Mode-k Unfolding of Kruskal Tensor, d-way) *The mode-k unfolding of the Kruskal tensor $\mathcal{K} = [\![\boldsymbol{\lambda}; \mathbf{A}_1, \mathbf{A}_2, \ldots, \mathbf{A}_d]\!]$ is*
>
> $$\mathbf{K}_{(k)} = \mathbf{A}_k \boldsymbol{\Lambda} \big(\mathbf{A}_d \odot \cdots \odot \mathbf{A}_{k+1} \odot \mathbf{A}_{k-1} \odot \cdots \odot \mathbf{A}_1\big)^{\intercal},$$
>
> *where $\boldsymbol{\Lambda} \equiv \operatorname{diag}(\boldsymbol{\lambda})$. (If there are no weights, then $\boldsymbol{\Lambda} = \mathbf{I}$).*

This can be proved directly by rearranging terms in the elementwise expression as we did for vectorization.

Exercise 10.10 Prove Proposition 10.10.

The general unfolding of a tensor of size $n_1 \times n_2 \times \cdots \times n_d$ rearranges the elements into a matrix of size $M \times N$, where $MN = \prod_{k=1}^{d} n_k$ (see Definition 2.19).

> **Proposition 10.11** (Unfolding of a Kruskal Tensor, d-way) *Let the modes $\{1, \ldots, d\}$ be partitioned into two ordered sets:*
>
> $$\mathcal{R} = (r_1, r_2, \ldots, r_\delta) \quad \textit{and} \quad \mathcal{C} = (c_1, c_2, \ldots, c_{d-\delta}).$$
>
> *The unfolding of the Kruskal tensor $\mathcal{K} = [\![\boldsymbol{\lambda}; \mathbf{A}_1, \mathbf{A}_2, \ldots, \mathbf{A}_d]\!]$ with respect to row set $\mathcal{R}$ and column set $\mathcal{C}$ is*
>
> $$\mathbf{K}_{(\mathcal{R} \times \mathcal{C})} = \big(\mathbf{A}_{r_\delta} \odot \mathbf{A}_{r_{\delta-1}} \odot \cdots \odot \mathbf{A}_{r_1}\big) \boldsymbol{\Lambda} \big(\mathbf{A}_{c_{d-\delta}} \odot \mathbf{A}_{c_{d-\delta-1}} \odot \cdots \odot \mathbf{A}_{c_1}\big)^{\intercal}.$$

Exercise 10.11 Prove Proposition 10.11.

10.4 Kruskal Tensor Ambiguities

A Kruskal tensor has inherent permutation and scaling ambiguities.

10.4.1 Permutation Ambiguity

Consider the 3-way Kruskal tensor

$$\mathcal{K} = \mathbf{a}_1 \circ \mathbf{b}_1 \circ \mathbf{c}_1 + \mathbf{a}_2 \circ \mathbf{b}_2 \circ \mathbf{c}_2 + \mathbf{a}_3 \circ \mathbf{b}_3 \circ \mathbf{c}_3.$$

We can write this as $\mathcal{K} = [\![\mathbf{A}, \mathbf{B}, \mathbf{C}]\!]$, where

$$\begin{aligned} \mathbf{A} &= [\ \mathbf{a}_1\ \mathbf{a}_2\ \mathbf{a}_3\ ] \in \mathbb{R}^{m \times 3}, \\ \mathbf{B} &= [\ \mathbf{b}_1\ \mathbf{b}_2\ \mathbf{b}_3\ ] \in \mathbb{R}^{n \times 3}, \text{ and} \\ \mathbf{C} &= [\ \mathbf{c}_1\ \mathbf{c}_2\ \mathbf{c}_3\ ] \in \mathbb{R}^{p \times 3}. \end{aligned}$$

However, the order of the rank-1 components does not matter. Hence, we can equivalently write $\mathcal{K}$ as

$$\mathcal{K} = \mathbf{a}_2 \circ \mathbf{b}_2 \circ \mathbf{c}_2 + \mathbf{a}_3 \circ \mathbf{b}_3 \circ \mathbf{c}_3 + \mathbf{a}_1 \circ \mathbf{b}_1 \circ \mathbf{c}_1.$$

So, we can express this equivalently with *permuted* factor matrices, so long as every matrix is permuted in the same way. We have $\mathcal{K} = [\![\hat{\mathbf{A}}, \hat{\mathbf{B}}, \hat{\mathbf{C}}]\!]$, where

$$\begin{aligned} \hat{\mathbf{A}} &= [\ \mathbf{a}_2\ \mathbf{a}_3\ \mathbf{a}_1\ ] \in \mathbb{R}^{m \times 3}, \\ \hat{\mathbf{B}} &= [\ \mathbf{b}_2\ \mathbf{b}_3\ \mathbf{b}_1\ ] \in \mathbb{R}^{n \times 3}, \text{ and} \\ \hat{\mathbf{C}} &= [\ \mathbf{c}_2\ \mathbf{c}_3\ \mathbf{c}_1\ ] \in \mathbb{R}^{p \times 3}. \end{aligned}$$

Exercise 10.12 Let $\mathbf{A} = [\![\mathbf{a}_1\ \mathbf{a}_2\ \mathbf{a}_3]\!]$ and $\hat{\mathbf{A}} = [\![\mathbf{a}_2\ \mathbf{a}_3\ \mathbf{a}_1]\!]$. Find the permutation matrix $\mathbf{P} \in \mathbb{R}^{3 \times 3}$ such that $\hat{\mathbf{A}} = \mathbf{AP}$.

Definition 10.12 (Permutation Ambiguity for Kruskal Tensors) Let $\mathbf{P}$ be an $r \times r$ permutation matrix. Given a 3-way Kruskal tensor $[\![\mathbf{A}, \mathbf{B}, \mathbf{C}]\!]$ with r components, we have

$$[\![\mathbf{A}, \mathbf{B}, \mathbf{C}]\!] = [\![\mathbf{AP}, \mathbf{BP}, \mathbf{CP}]\!].$$

More generally, given a d-way Kruskal tensor $[\![\mathbf{A}_1, \mathbf{A}_2, \dots, \mathbf{A}_d]\!]$ with r components, we have

$$[\![\mathbf{A}_1, \mathbf{A}_2, \dots, \mathbf{A}_d]\!] = [\![\mathbf{A}_1\mathbf{P}, \mathbf{A}_2\mathbf{P}, \dots, \mathbf{A}_d\mathbf{P}]\!].$$

Thus, there is no inherent order to the columns of the factor matrices. We refer to this as the **permutation ambiguity**.

Exercise 10.13 Let $\mathbf{P}$ be an $r \times r$ permutation matrix and let $[\![\mathbf{A}_1, \mathbf{A}_2, \dots, \mathbf{A}_d]\!]$ be a Kruskal tensor with r components. Prove $[\![\mathbf{A}_1, \mathbf{A}_2, \dots, \mathbf{A}_d]\!] = [\![\mathbf{A}_1\mathbf{P}, \mathbf{A}_2\mathbf{P}, \dots, \mathbf{A}_d\mathbf{P}]\!]$.

10.4.2 Scaling Ambiguity

Consider a rank-1 3-way tensor

$$\mathcal{K} = \mathbf{a} \circ \mathbf{b} \circ \mathbf{c}.$$

Let scalars $\alpha, \beta, \gamma \in \mathbb{R}$ be such that their product is 1: $\alpha\beta\gamma = 1$. Define the new vectors

$$\hat{\mathbf{a}} = \alpha\mathbf{a}, \quad \hat{\mathbf{b}} = \beta\mathbf{b}, \quad \text{and} \quad \hat{\mathbf{c}} = \gamma\mathbf{c},$$

and the new tensor

$$\hat{\mathcal{K}} = \hat{\mathbf{a}} \circ \hat{\mathbf{b}} \circ \hat{\mathbf{c}}.$$

It is easy to see that $\hat{\mathcal{K}} = \mathcal{K}$ because

$$\hat{\mathcal{K}}(i,j,k) = \hat{a}_i\,\hat{b}_j\,\hat{c}_k = (\alpha a_i)\,(\beta b_j)\,(\gamma c_k) = (\alpha\beta\gamma)a_i b_j c_k = a_i b_j c_k = \mathcal{K}(i,j,k)$$

for any $(i,j,k) \in [m] \otimes [n] \otimes [p]$. Given a Kruskal tensor with r components, the factors of each individual component can be rescaled independently. We refer to this as **scaling ambiguity** because any scaling works so long as the product of the scaling factors is 1.

Definition 10.13 (Scaling Ambiguity for Kruskal Tensors) In the 3-way case, let $\mathbf{D_A}, \mathbf{D_B}, \mathbf{D_C} \in \mathbb{R}^{r \times r}$ be diagonal matrices such that $\mathbf{D_A D_B D_C} = \mathbf{I}$. If $[\![\mathbf{A}, \mathbf{B}, \mathbf{C}]\!]$ is a Kruskal tensor with r components, then

$$[\![\mathbf{A}, \mathbf{B}, \mathbf{C}]\!] = [\![\mathbf{A D_A}, \mathbf{B D_B}, \mathbf{C D_C}]\!].$$

Likewise, in the d-way case, let $\{\mathbf{D}_k\}_{k=1}^{d}$ be $r \times r$ diagonal matrices such that $\mathbf{D}_1\mathbf{D}_2 \cdots \mathbf{D}_d = \mathbf{I}$. If $[\![\mathbf{A}_1, \mathbf{A}_2, \ldots, \mathbf{A}_d]\!]$ is a Kruskal tensor with r components, then

$$[\![\mathbf{A}_1, \mathbf{A}_2, \ldots, \mathbf{A}_d]\!] = [\![\mathbf{A}_1\mathbf{D}_1, \mathbf{A}_2\mathbf{D}_2, \ldots, \mathbf{A}_d\mathbf{D}_d]\!].$$

Thus, there is no inherent scaling to the factors. We refer to this as the **scaling ambiguity**.

Sign Ambiguity A special case of the scaling ambiguity is the **sign ambiguity**. That is, we can flip the signs of any *pair* of vectors without changing the full tensor and without changing the norms of the factors. Sometimes this is exploited to improve interpretation; for example, we can flip the signs so that the largest entry of each vector is positive, provided that the signs can be flipped in *pairs*.

***Remark* 10.14** (Ambiguity mitigation) We can largely mitigate permutation and scaling ambiguities by normalizing the components and sorting them by weight. However, the sign ambiguity is more challenging to cleanly resolve.

Figure 10.6 shows an example of the scaling and sign ambiguity for a rank-1 tensor. Each column depicts one of the three factors of the 3-way, rank-1 tensor, where in each plot the x-axis corresponds to the vector index and the y-axis corresponds to the value of the vector entry. The first two rows show different scalings of the factors, and the final row shows how it might be normalized, with all the largest entries positive (we were able to flip the signs of the last two components compared to the top row) and an explicit component weight:

$$\lambda = \|\mathbf{a}\|_2\|\mathbf{b}\|_2\|\mathbf{c}\|_2, \qquad \bar{\mathbf{a}} = \mathbf{a}/\|\mathbf{a}\|_2, \qquad \bar{\mathbf{b}} = -\mathbf{b}/\|\mathbf{b}\|_2, \qquad \bar{\mathbf{c}} = -\mathbf{c}/\|\mathbf{c}\|_2.$$

10.5 Kruskal Tensor Uniqueness

An important property of higher-order Kruskal tensors is that they are *often* unique, up to the inherent permutation and scaling ambiguities described in Section 10.4. In such a case, we say the Kruskal tensor is **essentially unique**. Uniqueness is very helpful in interpreting the factors of a CP decomposition, like those shown in Sections 9.6–9.8. We can normalize and reorder the factors so that the permutation and scaling ambiguities have a minimal impact on interpretation of an essentially unique factorization. The main ambiguity that can be challenging to resolve is the sign ambiguity, as discussed in Section 10.4.2.

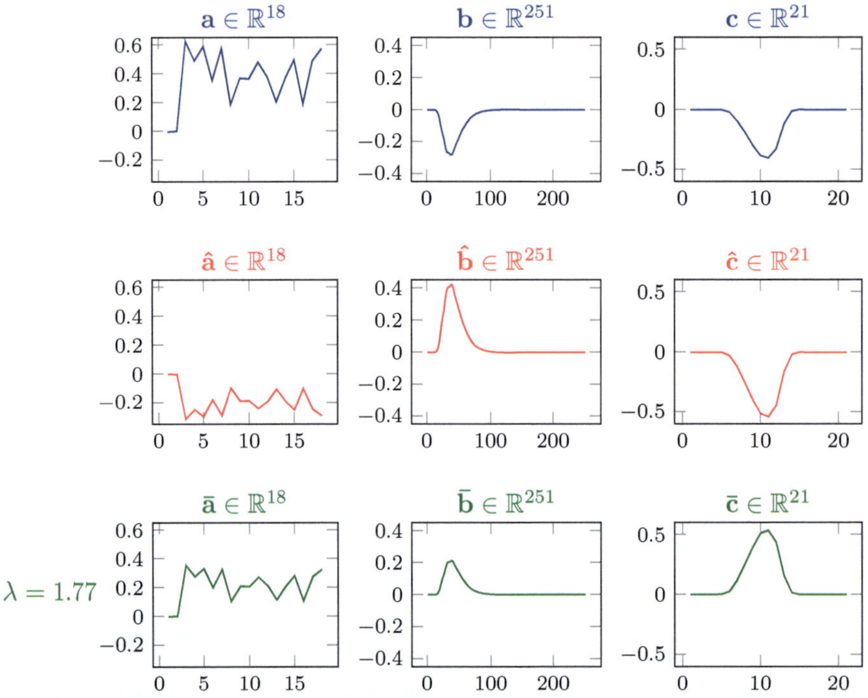

Figure 10.6 Scaling and sign ambiguity for rank-1 tensor. Each row illustrates factors of the *same* rank-1 tensor: $\mathbf{a} \bigcirc \mathbf{b} \bigcirc \mathbf{c} = \hat{\mathbf{a}} \bigcirc \hat{\mathbf{b}} \bigcirc \hat{\mathbf{c}} = \lambda\, \bar{\mathbf{a}} \bigcirc \bar{\mathbf{b}} \bigcirc \bar{\mathbf{c}}$. The bottom row has each component normalized and sign-flipped, with the weight of the component listed to the left.

We first formalize the concept of essential uniqueness for 3-way tensors.

Definition 10.15: Essential Uniqueness (3-way)

We say a Kruskal tensor $\mathcal{K} = [\![\mathbf{A}, \mathbf{B}, \mathbf{C}]\!]$ is **essentially unique** if it is unique up to permutation and scaling ambiguity. That is, if $\mathcal{K}$ is essentially unique then, for any other factorization $\hat{\mathcal{K}} = [\![\hat{\mathbf{A}}, \hat{\mathbf{B}}, \hat{\mathbf{C}}]\!]$ such that $\hat{\mathcal{K}} = \mathcal{K}$, there exists an $r \times r$ permutation matrix $\mathbf{P}$ and $r \times r$ diagonal scaling matrices $\{ \mathbf{D}_1, \mathbf{D}_2, \mathbf{D}_3 \}$ with $\mathbf{D}_{\mathbf{A}}\mathbf{D}_{\mathbf{B}}\mathbf{D}_{\mathbf{C}} = \mathbf{I}$ such that $\mathbf{A} = \hat{\mathbf{A}}\mathbf{D}_{\mathbf{A}}\mathbf{P}, \mathbf{B} = \hat{\mathbf{B}}\mathbf{D}_{\mathbf{B}}\mathbf{P}, \mathbf{C} = \hat{\mathbf{C}}\mathbf{D}_{\mathbf{C}}\mathbf{P}$.

A key property of Kruskal tensors is their essential uniqueness, achieved under mild conditions, such as having full rank factor matrices, per the following corollary of Kruskal's famous uniqueness theorem (Theorem 16.14).

Corollary 10.16 (Sufficient Conditions for Uniqueness, 3-way) *A Kruskal tensor* $\mathcal{K} = [\![\mathbf{A}, \mathbf{B}, \mathbf{C}]\!]$ *is essentially unique if* $\operatorname{rank}(\mathbf{A}) = \operatorname{rank}(\mathbf{B}) = \operatorname{rank}(\mathbf{C}) = r$.

Uniqueness results with less stringent conditions are discussed in Section 16.7. For example, if $\operatorname{rank}(\mathbf{A}) = \operatorname{rank}(\mathbf{B}) = r$ and every pair of columns from $\mathbf{C}$ is linearly independent, then $\mathcal{K} = [\![\mathbf{A}, \mathbf{B}, \mathbf{C}]\!]$ is still essentially unique.

Remark 10.17 (What does uniqueness mean for approximate decompositions?) If we compute an inexact CP decomposition of a tensor $\mathcal{X}$:

$$\mathcal{X} \approx [\![\mathbf{A}, \mathbf{B}, \mathbf{C}]\!],$$

then we can only say that $\mathcal{Y} = [\![\mathbf{A}, \mathbf{B}, \mathbf{C}]\!]$ is essentially unique. Although this uniqueness may be useful, it does not necessarily prohibit existence of a completely different approximation,

$$\mathcal{X} \approx [\![\hat{\mathbf{A}}, \hat{\mathbf{B}}, \hat{\mathbf{C}}]\!]$$

such that $[\![\mathbf{A}, \mathbf{B}, \mathbf{C}]\!] \neq [\![\hat{\mathbf{A}}, \hat{\mathbf{B}}, \hat{\mathbf{C}}]\!]$.

Kruskal tensors are not always essentially unique. If $d = 2$, for example (the matrix case), then $\mathbf{K} = [\![\mathbf{A}, \mathbf{B}]\!] = \mathbf{A}\mathbf{B}^\intercal = (\mathbf{A}\mathbf{M})(\mathbf{M}^{-1}\mathbf{B}^\intercal)$ for *any* nonsingular matrix $\mathbf{M}$, so $\mathbf{K}$ is not essentially unique. Example 9.2 shows that there is a 3-way tensor that has multiple Kruskal representations and is not essentially unique.

We can extend the ideas to d-way tensors as follows.

Definition 10.18: Essential Uniqueness (d-way)

We say a Kruskal tensor $\mathcal{K} = [\![\mathbf{A}_1, \mathbf{A}_2, \dots, \mathbf{A}_d]\!]$ is **essentially unique** if it is unique up to permutation and scaling ambiguity. That is, if $\mathcal{K}$ is essentially unique then, for any other factorization $\hat{\mathcal{K}} = [\![\mathbf{B}_1, \mathbf{B}_2, \dots, \mathbf{B}_d]\!]$ such that $\hat{\mathcal{K}} = \mathcal{K}$, there exists an $r \times r$ permutation matrix $\mathbf{P}$ and $r \times r$ diagonal scaling matrices $\{\, \mathbf{D}_1, \mathbf{D}_2, \dots, \mathbf{D}_d \,\}$ with $\mathbf{D}_1\mathbf{D}_2 \cdots \mathbf{D}_d = \mathbf{I}$ such that $\mathbf{A}_k = \mathbf{B}_k\mathbf{D}_k\mathbf{P}$ for all $k \in [d]$.

The following is a corollary of Theorem 16.15, the generalization of Kruskal's uniqueness theorem by Sidiropoulos and Bro (2000). The full result has less stringent requirements; see Section 16.7.

Theorem 10.19: Sufficient Conditions for Kruskal Tensor Uniqueness (d-way)

A Kruskal tensor $\mathcal{K} = [\![\mathbf{A}_1, \mathbf{A}_2, \dots, \mathbf{A}_d]\!]$ with r components and $d \geq 3$ is essentially unique if its factor matrices all have rank r.

Theorem 10.19 only applies if $r \leq \min \{\, n_k \mid k \in [d] \,\}$.

10.6 Full Construction from Kruskal Tensors

This section discusses the full construction of a dense tensor from a Kruskal factored tensor. We generally want to work with a Kruskal tensor in factored form, since computing its full form is expensive in time and memory. However, in situations where we need to compute the full form, we want to do so efficiently.

10.6.1 Full Construction from 3-way Kruskal Tensors

Consider the 3-way Kruskal tensor $\mathcal{K} = [\![\mathbf{A}, \mathbf{B}, \mathbf{C}]\!]$. A straightforward computation of $\mathcal{X} = \text{full}([\![\mathbf{A}, \mathbf{B}, \mathbf{C}]\!])$ uses Proposition 10.9 as follows.

Full 3-way Kruskal Tensor (Naive)

1: $\mathbf{L} \leftarrow \mathbf{C} \odot \mathbf{B} \odot \mathbf{A}$
2: $\mathbf{v} \leftarrow \mathbf{L}\mathbf{1}_r$
3: $\mathcal{X} \leftarrow \text{reshape}(\mathbf{v}, m \times n \times p)$

This method computes the Khatri–Rao product in the first step. In the second step, it multiplies the result of the first step times the all-1s vector of length r, producing a vectorized version of the final result. A problem with the above method is that it creates the intermediate $\mathbf{L}$ matrix of size $mnp \times r$, requiring r times more storage than the final result.

Instead, it is more efficient to compute the mode-1 matrix unfolding of the final result from Proposition 10.8:

Full 3-way Kruskal Tensor (Efficient)

1: $\mathbf{R} \leftarrow \mathbf{C} \odot \mathbf{B}$
2: $\mathbf{Y} \leftarrow \mathbf{A}\mathbf{R}^\intercal$
3: $\mathcal{X} \leftarrow \text{reshape}(\mathbf{Y}, m \times n \times p)$

In this case, the first step computes the Khatri–Rao product of just two of the three matrices. In the second step, this result is multiplied times the remaining matrix. We use the mode-1 unfolding because the result is already in the correct order to be reshaped into the final result without any permutation. The intermediate $\mathbf{R}$ matrix is of size $np \times r$ and will generally be smaller than the final result. Additionally, the matrix–matrix multiply in the second step is generally more efficient than matrix–vector multiply as in the second step of the naive version.

Exercise 10.14 Write down an analogous efficient method for $\mathcal{X} = \text{full}(⟦\boldsymbol{\lambda}; \mathbf{A}, \mathbf{B}, \mathbf{C}⟧)$.

10.6.2 Full Construction from d-way Kruskal Tensors

Now consider the general d-way problem. We want to compute a general unfolding such that $\text{vec}(\mathbf{X}_{(\mathcal{R}\times\mathcal{C})}) = \text{vec}(\mathcal{X})$, i.e., the entries are in the same order. This restricts us to partitions of the form

$$\mathcal{R} = \{1, \ldots, k\} \quad \text{and} \quad \mathcal{C} = \{k+1, \ldots, d\}.$$

The algorithm to compute $\mathcal{X} = \text{full}(⟦\mathbf{A}_1, \mathbf{A}_2, \ldots, \mathbf{A}_d⟧)$ is as follows:

Full d-way Kruskal Tensor

1: $k \leftarrow$ "split point"
2: $\mathbf{L} \leftarrow \mathbf{A}_k \odot \mathbf{A}_{k-1} \odot \cdots \odot \mathbf{A}_1$
3: $\mathbf{R} \leftarrow \mathbf{A}_d \odot \mathbf{A}_{d-1} \odot \cdots \odot \mathbf{A}_{k+1}$
4: $\mathbf{Y} \leftarrow \mathbf{L}\mathbf{R}^\intercal$
5: $\mathcal{X} \leftarrow \text{reshape}(\mathbf{Y}, n_1 \times n_2 \times \cdots \times n_d)$

We explain how to determine the split point below, after we consider the storage and computation time for each step. For all $k \in [d]$, define

$$M_k = \prod_{\ell \leq k} n_\ell \quad \text{and} \quad N_k = \prod_{\ell > k} n_\ell. \tag{10.6}$$

To compute $\mathbf{L}$, the computation and storage are both $M_k r$. To compute $\mathbf{R}$, the computation and storage are both $N_k r$. Finally, to compute $\mathbf{Y}$, the computation is $M_k N_k r$ and the storage is $M_k N_k$. The choice split point impacts the computation and storage costs for

$\mathbf{L}$ and $\mathbf{R}$, so we want to find the k that minimizes $M_k + N_k$. Thus, the "split point" minimization problem is

$$\min_k M_k + N_k. \tag{10.7}$$

If we want to compute $\mathcal{X} = \text{full}(\llbracket \boldsymbol{\lambda}; \mathbf{A}_1, \mathbf{A}_2, \ldots, \mathbf{A}_d \rrbracket)$, then we could change line 4 to be $\mathbf{Y} \leftarrow \mathbf{L}\,\text{diag}(\boldsymbol{\lambda})\mathbf{R}^\intercal$. However, it is more efficient to absorb $\boldsymbol{\lambda}$ into the smallest factor before the full reconstruction. In other words, absorbing into the last factor, we have

$$\text{full}\Big(\llbracket \boldsymbol{\lambda}; \mathbf{A}_1, \mathbf{A}_2, \ldots, \mathbf{A}_d \rrbracket\Big) = \text{full}\Big(\llbracket \mathbf{A}_1, \mathbf{A}_2, \ldots, \mathbf{A}_{d-1}, (\mathbf{A}_d\,\text{diag}(\boldsymbol{\lambda})) \rrbracket\Big).$$

Exercise 10.15 Suppose we have a tensor of size $100 \times 40 \times 80 \times 200$. What is the optimal split point per Eq. (10.7)?

10.6.3 Masked Full Construction from a Kruskal Tensor

In some situations, we need only reconstruct a *subset* of the entries of a Kruskal tensor. For example, this happens in the case of computing a CP decomposition for incomplete tensors, as discussed in Chapter 14. If the subset of entries is relatively few, computing the full reconstruction and then extracting only the masked entries may be inefficient. Instead, we can compute the masked entries directly.

Masked Full from 3-way Kruskal Tensors

Consider a 3-way Kruskal tensor $\llbracket \mathbf{A}, \mathbf{B}, \mathbf{C} \rrbracket$ of size $m \times n \times p$ and rank r. The masked reconstruction creates a sparse tensor $\hat{\mathcal{K}}$ of size $m \times n \times p$, such that

$$\hat{\mathcal{K}} = \mathcal{M} * \llbracket \mathbf{A}, \mathbf{B}, \mathbf{C} \rrbracket,$$

where the mask $\mathcal{M}$ is a sparse tensor of size $m \times n \times p$ with 0s for masked entries and 1s for unmasked entries. Assuming $\mathcal{M}$ has q 1 values, we can express it as a sparse tensor $\mathcal{M} = \llbracket \boldsymbol{\Omega}, \mathbf{1} \rrbracket$, where

$$\boldsymbol{\Omega} \in \mathbb{N}^{q \times 3}$$

are the indices of the unmasked entries. See Section 3.7 for details on sparse tensors.

The masked reconstruction will have the same generic sparsity pattern as $\mathcal{M}$, so we just need to compute the array of values as shown in the following pseudocode.

Masked Full from 3-way Kruskal Tensor

```
v ← 0                                        ▷ Zero vector of length q
for α ∈ [q] do
    for ℓ ∈ [r] do
        v_q ← v_q + A(ω_1q, ℓ) B(ω_2q, ℓ) C(ω_3q, ℓ)
    end for
end for
return v                                     ▷ K̂ = ⟦Ω, v⟧
```

Then we have $\hat{\mathcal{K}} = \llbracket \boldsymbol{\Omega}, \mathbf{v} \rrbracket$; there is a trivial possibility that some of the reconstructed entries may be zero, but these would simply be ignored or removed in the sparse representation. The time for a full reconstruction of $\llbracket \mathbf{A}, \mathbf{B}, \mathbf{C} \rrbracket$ and then applying the mask $\mathcal{M}$ would be proportional to $\mathcal{O}(mnpr)$, whereas the time for masked reconstruction is proportional to $\mathcal{O}(qr)$.

Masked Reconstruction for d-way Kruskal Tensors

The situation for d-way tensors is analogous to the 3-way case. Given a Kruskal tensor and mask, we can construct a sparse tensor using the elementwise expression Eq. (10.4). This method is formalized in Algorithm 10.1. The computational cost of masked reconstruction for a d-way, rank-r Kruskal tensor with q entries is $\mathcal{O}(qrd)$. The temporary variable z can be an array to enable flexibility in structuring the loops over the nonzeros (indexed by α) and the columns of the factor matrices (indexed by j).

Algorithm 10.1 Masked Full from d-way Kruskal Tensor

Require: Sparse mask $\mathcal{M} = [\![\boldsymbol{\Omega}, \mathbf{1}]\!] \in \mathbb{R}^{n_1 \times \cdots \times n_d}$ with $\boldsymbol{\Omega} \in \mathbb{N}^{q \times d}$, $\{\, \mathbf{A}_j \in \mathbb{R}^{n_j \times r} \,\}_{j \in [d]}$

Ensure: Vector $\mathbf{v}$ yielding the sparse representation $[\![\boldsymbol{\Omega}, \mathbf{v}]\!] = \mathcal{M} * [\![\mathbf{A}_1, \mathbf{A}_2, \ldots, \mathbf{A}_d]\!]$

function MASKEDFULL($\boldsymbol{\Omega}, \mathbf{A}_1, \mathbf{A}_2, \ldots, \mathbf{A}_d$)
    $\mathbf{v} \leftarrow \mathbf{0}$ ▷ Zero vector of length q
    for $\alpha = 1$ to q **do**
        for $j = 1$ to r **do**
            $z \leftarrow 1$ ▷ Temporary variable depending on (α, j)
            for $\ell = 1$ to d **do**
                $z \leftarrow z \, \mathbf{A}_\ell(\omega_{\alpha\ell}, j)$
            end for
            $v_\alpha \leftarrow v_\alpha + z$
        end for
    end for
    return $\mathbf{v}$ ▷ $[\![\boldsymbol{\Omega}, \mathbf{v}]\!] = \mathcal{M} * [\![\mathbf{A}_1, \mathbf{A}_2, \ldots, \mathbf{A}_d]\!]$
end function

***Remark* 10.20** (Similarity of masked reconstruction and sparse MTTKRP) The computational structure of this approach mirrors that of MTTKRP for sparse tensors (Algorithm 3.5 in Section 3.7.4). In an MTTKRP for a sparse tensor, the inputs are a sparse tensor and $d-1$ factor matrices (usually from a Kruskal tensor), and the output is a matrix. In a masked reconstruction, the inputs are a sparse mask tensor and a Kruskal tensor (i.e., d factor matrices), and the output is a sparse tensor. Nevertheless, the loops are similar, so optimizations applied to one can be useful for the other.

10.7 Operations with Kruskal Tensors

Many operations with Kruskal tensors are more computationally and memory efficient than with the equivalent full tensor. We assume throughout this section that any specified Kruskal tensor has conforming factor matrices, i.e., this means that all the factor matrices have the same number of columns and the weight vector has that number of entries. In the 3-way case, for instance,

$$\mathcal{K} = [\![\boldsymbol{\lambda}; \mathbf{A}, \mathbf{B}, \mathbf{C}]\!] \quad \text{with} \quad \boldsymbol{\lambda} \in \mathbb{R}^r, \mathbf{A} \in \mathbb{R}^{m \times r}, \mathbf{B} \in \mathbb{R}^{m \times r}, \mathbf{C} \in \mathbb{R}^{m \times r}. \tag{10.8}$$

In the d-way case, the analog is

$$\mathcal{K} = [\![\boldsymbol{\lambda}; \mathbf{A}_1, \mathbf{A}_2, \ldots, \mathbf{A}_d]\!] \quad \text{with} \quad \boldsymbol{\lambda} \in \mathbb{R}^r, \mathbf{A}_k \in \mathbb{R}^{n_k \times r} \text{ for all } k \in [d]. \tag{10.9}$$

Additionally, all the results apply to a Kruskal tensor without weights by setting $\boldsymbol{\lambda}$ equal to the all-1s vector. We use the notation $\boldsymbol{\Lambda} \equiv \text{diag}(\boldsymbol{\lambda})$.

10.7.1 Inner Products and Norms of Kruskal Tensors

Inner Products and Norms of 3-way Kruskal Tensors

Computing the inner product of two Kruskal tensors is very efficient, as we show below. We consider first the 3-way case.

Proposition 10.21 (Kruskal Tensor Inner Product, 3-way) *Consider the 3-way Kruskal tensors $\mathcal{K} = [\![\mathbf{A}, \mathbf{B}, \mathbf{C}]\!]$ and $\bar{\mathcal{K}} = [\![\bar{\mathbf{A}}, \bar{\mathbf{B}}, \bar{\mathbf{C}}]\!]$ of size $m \times n \times p$ with r and $\bar{r}$ components, respectively. Their inner product is*

$$\langle \mathcal{K}, \bar{\mathcal{K}} \rangle = \mathbf{1}_r^{\mathsf{T}} (\mathbf{A}^{\mathsf{T}} \bar{\mathbf{A}} * \mathbf{B}^{\mathsf{T}} \bar{\mathbf{B}} * \mathbf{C}^{\mathsf{T}} \bar{\mathbf{C}}) \mathbf{1}_{\bar{r}},$$

where $\mathbf{1}_r$ and $\mathbf{1}_{\bar{r}}$ are vectors of all 1s of lengths r and $\bar{r}$, respectively

Proof. We have

$$\begin{aligned}
\langle \mathcal{K}, \bar{\mathcal{K}} \rangle &= \big\langle \operatorname{vec}(\mathcal{K}), \operatorname{vec}(\bar{\mathcal{K}}) \big\rangle, \\
&= \big\langle (\mathbf{C} \odot \mathbf{B} \odot \mathbf{A}) \mathbf{1}_r, (\bar{\mathbf{C}} \odot \bar{\mathbf{B}} \odot \bar{\mathbf{A}}) \mathbf{1}_{\bar{r}} \big\rangle && \text{per Proposition 10.8,} \\
&= \mathbf{1}_r^{\mathsf{T}} (\mathbf{C} \odot \mathbf{B} \odot \mathbf{A})^{\mathsf{T}} (\bar{\mathbf{C}} \odot \bar{\mathbf{B}} \odot \bar{\mathbf{A}}) \mathbf{1}_{\bar{r}}, \\
&= \mathbf{1}_r^{\mathsf{T}} (\mathbf{A}^{\mathsf{T}} \bar{\mathbf{A}} * \mathbf{B}^{\mathsf{T}} \bar{\mathbf{B}} * \mathbf{C}^{\mathsf{T}} \bar{\mathbf{C}}) \mathbf{1}_{\bar{r}} && \text{per Proposition A.23.}
\end{aligned}$$
□

Exercise 10.16 (a) What is the computational and storage complexity of $\langle \mathcal{K}, \bar{\mathcal{K}} \rangle$ in Proposition 10.21? (b) How does this compare to computing the inner product of two full tensors?

Exercise 10.17 (a) What is $\langle \mathcal{K}, \bar{\mathcal{K}} \rangle$ for $\mathcal{K} = [\![\boldsymbol{\lambda}, \mathbf{A}, \mathbf{B}, \mathbf{C}]\!]$ and $\bar{\mathcal{K}} = [\![\bar{\boldsymbol{\lambda}}, \bar{\mathbf{A}}, \bar{\mathbf{B}}, \bar{\mathbf{C}}]\!]$, both of size $m \times n \times p$ with r and $\bar{r}$ components, respectively? (b) What is the computational and storage complexity?

The norm of a 3-way tensor is then a corollary.

Corollary 10.22 (Kruskal Tensor Norm, 3-way) *Consider the 3-way Kruskal tensors $\mathcal{K} = [\![\boldsymbol{\lambda}; \mathbf{A}, \mathbf{B}, \mathbf{C}]\!]$. Its norm is*

$$\|\mathcal{K}\|^2 = \boldsymbol{\lambda}^{\mathsf{T}} (\mathbf{A}^{\mathsf{T}} \mathbf{A} * \mathbf{B}^{\mathsf{T}} \mathbf{B} * \mathbf{C}^{\mathsf{T}} \mathbf{C}) \boldsymbol{\lambda}.$$

Exercise 10.18 What is the computational and storage complexity for computing $\|\mathcal{K}\|$ for $\mathcal{K} = [\![\boldsymbol{\lambda}; \mathbf{A}, \mathbf{B}, \mathbf{C}]\!]$ of size $m \times n \times p$ with r components.

Inner Products and Norms of d-way Kruskal Tensors

The situation is analogous for the d-way case.

Proposition 10.23 (Kruskal Tensor Inner Product, d-way) *Consider the d-way Kruskal tensors $\mathcal{K}_{\mathbf{A}}$ and $\mathcal{K}_{\mathbf{B}}$ of size $n_1 \times n_2 \times \cdots \times n_d$ defined as $\mathcal{K}_{\mathbf{A}} = [\![\boldsymbol{\lambda}; \mathbf{A}_1, \mathbf{A}_2, \ldots, \mathbf{A}_d]\!]$ and $\mathcal{K}_{\mathbf{B}} = [\![\boldsymbol{\gamma}; \mathbf{B}_1, \mathbf{B}_2, \ldots, \mathbf{B}_d]\!]$. Then*

$$\langle \mathcal{K}_{\mathbf{A}}, \mathcal{K}_{\mathbf{B}} \rangle = \boldsymbol{\lambda}^{\mathsf{T}} (\mathbf{A}_d^{\mathsf{T}} \mathbf{B}_d * \mathbf{A}_{d-1}^{\mathsf{T}} \mathbf{B}_{d-1} * \cdots * \mathbf{A}_1^{\mathsf{T}} \mathbf{B}_1) \boldsymbol{\gamma}.$$

If $\mathcal{K}_{\mathbf{A}}$ has r components and $\mathcal{K}_{\mathbf{B}}$ has s components, then the computational cost is $\mathcal{O}(rs \sum_{k=1}^{d} n_k)$.

In the above result, we do not assume that $\mathcal{K}_{\mathbf{A}}$ and $\mathcal{K}_{\mathbf{B}}$ have the same number of components. We prove only the first part of the result and leave the second part as an exercise.

Proof. We have

$$\begin{aligned}
\langle \mathcal{K}_{\mathbf{A}}, \mathcal{K}_{\mathbf{B}} \rangle &= \langle \mathrm{vec}(\mathcal{K}_{\mathbf{A}}), \mathrm{vec}(\mathcal{K}_{\mathbf{B}}) \rangle && \text{per Exercise 3.2} \\
&= \langle (\mathbf{A}_d \odot \cdots \odot \mathbf{A}_1)\boldsymbol{\lambda}, (\mathbf{B}_d \odot \cdots \odot \mathbf{B}_1)\boldsymbol{\gamma} \rangle && \text{per Proposition 10.9} \\
&= \boldsymbol{\lambda}^{\mathsf{T}} (\mathbf{A}_d \odot \cdots \odot \mathbf{A}_1)^{\mathsf{T}} (\mathbf{B}_d \odot \cdots \odot \mathbf{B}_1)\boldsymbol{\gamma} \\
&= \boldsymbol{\lambda}^{\mathsf{T}} \left(\mathbf{A}_d^{\mathsf{T}} \mathbf{B}_d * \cdots * \mathbf{A}_1^{\mathsf{T}} \mathbf{B}_1 \right) \boldsymbol{\gamma} && \text{per Proposition A.23.}
\end{aligned}$$

Hence, the claim. □

Exercise 10.19 (a) Prove the statement about total work in Proposition 10.23. (b) How does the work compare to the cost for two full tensors? (c) How does the storage compare?

An immediate corollary is the norm of a Kruskal tensor.

Corollary 10.24 (Kruskal Tensor Norm, d-way) *Consider the d-way Kruskal tensor* $\mathcal{K} = [\![\boldsymbol{\lambda}; \mathbf{A}_1, \mathbf{A}_2, \ldots, \mathbf{A}_d]\!]$ *of size* $n_1 \times n_2 \times \cdots \times n_d$ *with r components. Then*

$$\|\mathcal{K}\|^2 = \boldsymbol{\lambda}^{\mathsf{T}} (\mathbf{A}_d^{\mathsf{T}} \mathbf{A}_d * \mathbf{A}_{d-1}^{\mathsf{T}} \mathbf{A}_{d-1} * \cdots * \mathbf{A}_1^{\mathsf{T}} \mathbf{A}_1) \boldsymbol{\lambda}.$$

Further, the total work is $\mathcal{O}(r^2 \sum_{k=1}^{d} n_k)$.

10.7.2 Approximation Error

Since Kruskal tensors are often used to provide approximations to data tensors, we may wish to compute

$$\textsc{Err} = \|\mathcal{X} - [\![\mathbf{A}, \mathbf{B}, \mathbf{C}]\!]\|^2,$$

where $\mathcal{X} \in \mathbb{R}^{m \times n \times p}$ is a data tensor and $[\![\mathbf{A}, \mathbf{B}, \mathbf{C}]\!]$ is a rank-r approximation of $\mathcal{X}$.

The most obvious way to compute this is to first compute the full tensor $\mathcal{Y} = \mathrm{full}([\![\mathbf{A}, \mathbf{B}, \mathbf{C}]\!])$, as discussed in Section 10.6, and then calculate the norm of the difference, $\|\mathcal{X} - \mathcal{Y}\|^2$. The complexity is dominated by the computation of $\mathcal{Y}$ and so is $\mathcal{O}(mnpr)$. In general, this is the best we can do for dense $\mathcal{X}$.

However, there are some scenarios where we may want to avoid forming $\mathrm{full}([\![\mathbf{A}, \mathbf{B}, \mathbf{C}]\!])$ explicitly. For instance, if $\mathcal{X}$ is sparse, the memory requirement for $\mathrm{full}([\![\mathbf{A}, \mathbf{B}, \mathbf{C}]\!])$ may be prohibitive.

Approximation Error, 3-way

Consider an alternate way to compute the error:

$$\|\mathcal{X} - [\![\mathbf{A}, \mathbf{B}, \mathbf{C}]\!]\|^2 = \|\mathcal{X}\|^2 + \|[\![\mathbf{A}, \mathbf{B}, \mathbf{C}]\!]\|^2 - 2\langle \mathcal{X}, [\![\mathbf{A}, \mathbf{B}, \mathbf{C}]\!] \rangle. \tag{10.10}$$

Let us assume that the norm of $\mathcal{X}$ is precomputed. From Proposition 10.21, the second term can be computed efficiently for a computational cost of $\mathcal{O}((m+n+p)r)$:

$$\|[\![\mathbf{A}, \mathbf{B}, \mathbf{C}]\!]\|^2 = \mathbf{1}_r^{\mathsf{T}} (\mathbf{A}^{\mathsf{T}}\mathbf{A} * \mathbf{B}^{\mathsf{T}}\mathbf{B} * \mathbf{C}^{\mathsf{T}}\mathbf{C}) \mathbf{1}_r.$$

So, the problem reduces to when the last term can be computed efficiently. Rewriting in terms of matrices, the third term can be expressed as:

$$\langle \mathcal{X}, [\![\mathbf{A}, \mathbf{B}, \mathbf{C}]\!] \rangle = \langle \mathbf{X}_{(3)}, \mathbf{C}(\mathbf{B} \odot \mathbf{A})^\intercal \rangle = \langle \mathbf{X}_{(3)}(\mathbf{B} \odot \mathbf{A}), \mathbf{C} \rangle.$$

The first term in the resulting dot product is an MTTKRP.

Sparse Tensor If $\mathcal{X}$ is sparse, then computing the MTTKRP $\mathbf{X}_{(3)}(\mathbf{B} \odot \mathbf{A})$ costs $\mathcal{O}(\text{nnz}(\mathcal{X})r)$. So the dot product with $\mathbf{C}$ can be computed for an additional cost of pr^2. More importantly, we avoid the storage cost of mnp for $\mathcal{Y} = \text{full}([\![\mathbf{A}, \mathbf{B}, \mathbf{C}]\!])$.

Exercise 10.20 Let $\mathcal{X}$ be sparse. Write an efficient algorithm to compute $\langle \mathcal{X}, [\![\mathbf{A}, \mathbf{B}, \mathbf{C}]\!] \rangle$ directly, without computing any MTTKRPs.

Extra Information In the midst of algorithms to compute a CP decomposition of the form $[\![\mathbf{A}, \mathbf{B}, \mathbf{C}]\!]$, it is not unusual that we have already computed the MTTKRP $\mathbf{X}_{(3)}(\mathbf{B} \odot \mathbf{A})$. So the dot product with $\mathbf{C}$ can be computed for an additional cost of pr^2.

Exercise 10.21 Consider the computation of $\text{ERR} = \|\mathcal{X} - [\![\boldsymbol{\lambda}; \mathbf{A}, \mathbf{B}, \mathbf{C}]\!]\|^2$ (with explicit weights). Let $\chi = \|\mathcal{X}\|$, $\mathbf{U} = \mathbf{X}_{(3)}(\mathbf{B} \odot \mathbf{A})$, and $\mathbf{V} = (\mathbf{B}^\intercal\mathbf{B}) * (\mathbf{A}^\intercal\mathbf{A})$.

(a) Show $\left\|\mathcal{X} - [\![\boldsymbol{\lambda}; \mathbf{A}, \mathbf{B}, \mathbf{C}]\!]\right\|^2 = \left\|\mathcal{X}\right\|^2 + \left\|[\![\boldsymbol{\lambda}; \mathbf{A}, \mathbf{B}, \mathbf{C}]\!]\right\|^2 - 2\langle \mathcal{X}, [\![\boldsymbol{\lambda}; \mathbf{A}, \mathbf{B}, \mathbf{C}]\!] \rangle$.
Hint: Convert to equivalent vectorized expression.

(b) Show $\alpha \equiv \boldsymbol{\lambda}^\intercal(\mathbf{C}^\intercal\mathbf{C} * \mathbf{V})\boldsymbol{\lambda} = \left\|[\![\boldsymbol{\lambda}; \mathbf{A}, \mathbf{B}, \mathbf{C}]\!]\right\|^2$.

(c) Show $\beta \equiv \mathbf{1}_r^\intercal\mathbf{C}^\intercal\mathbf{U}\boldsymbol{\lambda} = \langle \mathcal{X}, [\![\boldsymbol{\lambda}; \mathbf{A}, \mathbf{B}, \mathbf{C}]\!] \rangle$.

(d) Show $\text{ERR} = \chi^2 + \beta - 2\alpha$.

Approximation Error, d-way

In the d-way case, we may want to compute

$$\text{ERR} = \left\|\mathcal{X} - [\![\mathbf{A}_1, \mathbf{A}_2, \ldots, \mathbf{A}_d]\!]\right\|^2,$$

where $\mathcal{X} \in \mathbb{R}^{n_1 \times n_2 \times \cdots \times n_d}$ and $[\![\mathbf{A}_1, \mathbf{A}_2, \ldots, \mathbf{A}_d]\!]$ is a rank-r approximation of $\mathcal{X}$. Computing $\mathcal{Y} = \text{full}([\![\mathbf{A}_1, \mathbf{A}_2, \ldots, \mathbf{A}_d]\!])$ costs $\mathcal{O}(Nr)$, where $N = \prod_{k=1}^d n_k$ and that dominates the cost of computing the error. In general, this is the best we can do for dense $\mathcal{X}$.

As discussed above, however, it is not unusual that we already know some quantities of interest, such as

$$\begin{aligned} \chi = \|\mathcal{X}\|^2, \quad \mathbf{U} &= \mathbf{X}_{(k)}(\mathbf{A}_d \odot \cdots \odot \mathbf{A}_{k+1} \odot \mathbf{A}_{k-1} \odot \cdots \odot \mathbf{A}_1), \quad \text{and} \\ \mathbf{V} &= \mathbf{A}_d^\intercal\mathbf{A}_d * \cdots * \mathbf{A}_{k+1}^\intercal\mathbf{A}_{k+1} * \mathbf{A}_{k-1}^\intercal\mathbf{A}_{k-1} * \cdots * \mathbf{A}_1^\intercal\mathbf{A}_1. \end{aligned}$$

In such a scenario, we can compute the approximate error more efficiently. We can rewrite

$$\|\mathcal{X} - [\![\mathbf{A}_1, \mathbf{A}_2, \ldots, \mathbf{A}_d]\!]\|^2 = \|\mathcal{X}\|^2 + \|[\![\mathbf{A}_1, \mathbf{A}_2, \ldots, \mathbf{A}_d]\!]\|^2 - 2\langle \mathcal{X}, [\![\mathbf{A}_1, \mathbf{A}_2, \ldots, \mathbf{A}_d]\!] \rangle.$$

The first term is already calculated as χ. From Proposition 10.23, the second computation is $\mathcal{O}(r^2)$:

$$\|[\![\mathbf{A}_1, \mathbf{A}_2, \ldots, \mathbf{A}_d]\!]\|^2 = \mathbf{1}_r^\intercal(\mathbf{V} * \mathbf{A}_k^\intercal\mathbf{A}_k)\mathbf{1}_r.$$

Rewriting in terms of matrices, the third computation is $\mathcal{O}(r^3)$:

$$\begin{aligned} \langle \mathcal{X}, [\![\mathbf{A}_1, \mathbf{A}_2, \ldots, \mathbf{A}_d]\!] \rangle &= \langle \mathbf{X}_{(k)}, \mathbf{A}_k(\mathbf{A}_d \odot \cdots \odot \mathbf{A}_{k+1} \odot \mathbf{A}_{k-1} \odot \cdots \odot \mathbf{A}_1)^\intercal \rangle \\ &= \langle \mathbf{X}_{(k)}(\mathbf{A}_d \odot \cdots \odot \mathbf{A}_{k+1} \odot \mathbf{A}_{k-1} \odot \cdots \odot \mathbf{A}_1), \mathbf{A}_k \rangle \\ &= \langle \mathbf{U}, \mathbf{A}_k \rangle. \end{aligned}$$

Exercise 10.22 Let $\mathcal{X} \in \mathbb{R}^{n_1 \times n_2 \times \cdots \times n_d}$ and let $[\![\boldsymbol{\lambda}; \mathbf{A}_1, \mathbf{A}_2, \ldots, \mathbf{A}_d]\!]$ be a rank-r approximation of $\mathcal{X}$. Assume we have computed

$$\mathbf{U}_d = \mathbf{X}_{(d)}(\mathbf{A}_{d-1} \odot \cdots \odot \mathbf{A}_1) \quad \text{and} \quad \mathbf{V}_d = (\mathbf{A}_{d-1}^{\mathsf{T}}\mathbf{A}_{d-1}) * \cdots * (\mathbf{A}_1^{\mathsf{T}}\mathbf{A}_1).$$

(a) How can we efficiently calculate $\|\mathcal{X} - [\![\boldsymbol{\lambda}; \mathbf{A}_1, \mathbf{A}_2, \ldots, \mathbf{A}_d]\!]\|^2$? (b) What is the computational complexity?

***Remark* 10.25** (Accuracy of efficient error evaluation) This efficient method for computing the relative error does sacrifice some accuracy compared to the direct method of computation. We typically care only about the order of magnitude of relative error, so some loss of accuracy is not a problem. The efficient method cannot compute relative error values smaller than the square root of machine precision (around 10^{-8} in double precision). This is because the expression in Eq. (10.10) relies on cancellation to compute small values, and the roundoff error due to subtraction is of size $\mathcal{O}(\varepsilon_{\text{m}}\|\mathcal{X}\|^2)$, where ε_{m} is machine precision. After taking a square root and dividing by $\|\mathcal{X}\|$ to compute the relative error value, the error in the computed relative error value becomes $\mathcal{O}(\sqrt{\varepsilon_{\text{m}}})$. To accurately compute relative error values smaller than $\mathcal{O}(\sqrt{\varepsilon_{\text{m}}})$, we must use the more expensive, direct evaluation of the error.

10.7.3 MTTKRP with Kruskal Tensors

MTTKRP with 3-way Kruskal Tensors

Let $\mathcal{K} = [\![\mathbf{A}, \mathbf{B}, \mathbf{C}]\!]$ be a Kruskal tensor of size $m \times n \times p$ with r components. Consider the MTTKRP of $\mathcal{K}$ with $\bar{\mathbf{B}} \in \mathbb{R}^{n \times s}$ and $\bar{\mathbf{C}} \in \mathbb{R}^{p \times s}$. The special structure of $\mathcal{K}$ can yield computational savings. For instance, consider the following mode-1 MTTKRP: $\mathbf{K}_{(1)}(\bar{\mathbf{C}} \odot \bar{\mathbf{B}})$. If $\mathcal{K}$ were a full tensor, that computation would cost $\mathcal{O}(mnps)$ operations. Its structure means that

$$\mathbf{K}_{(1)}(\bar{\mathbf{C}} \odot \bar{\mathbf{B}}) = \mathbf{A}(\mathbf{C} \odot \mathbf{B})^{\mathsf{T}}(\bar{\mathbf{C}} \odot \bar{\mathbf{B}}) = \mathbf{A}(\mathbf{C}^{\mathsf{T}}\bar{\mathbf{C}} * \mathbf{B}^{\mathsf{T}}\bar{\mathbf{B}}).$$

The cost of this operation is $\mathcal{O}((m+n+p)rs)$, and the full version of $\mathcal{K}$ is never formed.

Exercise 10.23 Let $\mathcal{K} = [\![\boldsymbol{\lambda}; \mathbf{A}, \mathbf{B}, \mathbf{C}]\!]$ (with weights) be a Kruskal tensor, and let $\bar{\mathbf{A}} \in \mathbb{R}^{m \times s}$ and $\bar{\mathbf{C}} \in \mathbb{R}^{p \times s}$. How can $\mathbf{K}_{(2)}(\bar{\mathbf{C}} \odot \bar{\mathbf{A}})$ be computed in fewer than $\mathcal{O}(mnps)$ operations?

MTTKRP with d-way Kruskal Tensors

Consider the d-way MTTKRP (see Definition 3.27) where the tensor is a Kruskal tensor. The special structure means the MTTKRP can be computed implicitly.

Proposition 10.26 (Kruskal Tensor MTTKRP) *Let $\mathcal{K} = [\![\boldsymbol{\lambda}; \mathbf{A}_1, \mathbf{A}_2, \ldots, \mathbf{A}_d]\!]$ be a Kruskal tensor of size $n_1 \times n_2 \times \cdots \times n_d$ with r components, and let $\mathbf{B}_k \in \mathbb{R}^{n_k \times s}$ for all $k \in [d]$. Then the mode-k MTTKRP can be computed as*

$$\begin{aligned}
&\mathbf{K}_{(k)}(\mathbf{B}_d \odot \cdots \odot \mathbf{B}_{k+1} \odot \mathbf{B}_{k-1} \odot \cdots \odot \mathbf{B}_1) = \\
&\quad \mathbf{A}_k \boldsymbol{\Lambda}(\mathbf{A}_d^{\mathsf{T}}\mathbf{B}_d * \cdots * \mathbf{A}_{k+1}^{\mathsf{T}}\mathbf{B}_{k+1} * \mathbf{A}_{k-1}^{\mathsf{T}}\mathbf{B}_{k-1} * \cdots * \mathbf{A}_1^{\mathsf{T}}\mathbf{B}_1) \in \mathbb{R}^{n_k \times s}. \quad (10.11)
\end{aligned}$$

The total work is $\mathcal{O}(rs\sum_{k=1}^{d} n_k)$.

Exercise 10.24 Prove Proposition 10.26 and compare to the total work for a full tensor.

Exercise 10.25 (Mode-k Gramian of a Kruskal Tensor) For the Kruskal tensor $\mathcal{K} = [\![\boldsymbol{\lambda}; \mathbf{A}_1, \mathbf{A}_2, \ldots, \mathbf{A}_d]\!]$ of size $n_1 \times n_2 \times \cdots \times n_d$ and r components: (a) How can we efficiently compute $\mathbf{K}_{(k)}\mathbf{K}_{(k)}^{\mathsf{T}}$? (b) What is the total cost?

10.7.4 TTM with Kruskal Tensors

Recall from Section 3.3 that the mode-k TTM modifies all the mode-k fibers of a tensor by multiplying them by the specified matrix. We generally do not directly need TTM for any CP computations, but this does have application in the case of computing CP on a Tucker-structured tensor core; see Section 17.2.

TTM with 3-way Kruskal Tensors

In the 3-way case, the TTM with a Kruskal tensor has a special structure, as follows.

Proposition 10.27 (Kruskal TTM, 3-way) *Let $\mathcal{K} = [\![\boldsymbol{\lambda}; \mathbf{A}, \mathbf{B}, \mathbf{C}]\!]$ be an $m \times n \times p$ Kruskal tensor with r components. Let $\mathbf{U} \in \mathbb{R}^{\bar{m} \times m}$, $\mathbf{V} \in \mathbb{R}^{\bar{n} \times n}$, $\mathbf{W} \in \mathbb{R}^{\bar{p} \times p}$. Then we have*

$$\begin{aligned}
\mathcal{K} \times_1 \mathbf{U} &= [\![\boldsymbol{\lambda}; \mathbf{UA}, \mathbf{B}, \mathbf{C}]\!] \in \mathbb{R}^{\bar{m} \times n \times p}, \\
\mathcal{K} \times_2 \mathbf{V} &= [\![\boldsymbol{\lambda}; \mathbf{A}, \mathbf{VB}, \mathbf{C}]\!] \in \mathbb{R}^{m \times \bar{n} \times p}, \\
\mathcal{K} \times_3 \mathbf{W} &= [\![\boldsymbol{\lambda}; \mathbf{A}, \mathbf{B}, \mathbf{WC}]\!] \in \mathbb{R}^{m \times n \times \bar{p}}, \\
\mathcal{K} \times_1 \mathbf{U} \times_2 \mathbf{V} \times_3 \mathbf{W} &= [\![\boldsymbol{\lambda}; \mathbf{UA}, \mathbf{VB}, \mathbf{WC}]\!] \in \mathbb{R}^{\bar{m} \times \bar{n} \times \bar{p}}.
\end{aligned}$$

Exercise 10.26 Prove Proposition 10.27.

Exercise 10.27 What is the cost of updating a Kruskal tensor *implicitly* via a TTM versus the standard cost of a TTM?

TTM with d-way Kruskal Tensors

Proposition 10.28 (Kruskal TTM, d-way) *Let $\mathcal{K} = [\![\boldsymbol{\lambda}; \mathbf{A}_1, \mathbf{A}_2, \ldots, \mathbf{A}_d]\!]$ be a Kruskal tensor and let $\mathbf{V}$ be a matrix of size $n_k \times m$, where n_k is the size of mode k of $\mathcal{X}$. Then*

$$\mathcal{K} \times_k \mathbf{V} = [\![\boldsymbol{\lambda}; \mathbf{A}_1, \ldots, \mathbf{A}_{k-1}, \mathbf{VA}_k, \mathbf{A}_{k+1}, \ldots, \mathbf{A}_d]\!].$$

Proof. Define $\mathcal{Y} = \mathcal{K} \times_k \mathbf{V}$. Then

$$\begin{aligned}
\mathbf{Y}_{(k)} &= \mathbf{VK}_{(k)} && \text{per Definition 3.14} \\
&= \mathbf{V}\big(\mathbf{A}_k \boldsymbol{\Lambda} (\mathbf{A}_d \odot \cdots \odot \mathbf{A}_{k+1} \odot \mathbf{A}_{k-1} \odot \cdots \odot \mathbf{A}_1)\big) && \text{per Proposition 10.10} \\
&= (\mathbf{VA}_k) \boldsymbol{\Lambda} (\mathbf{A}_d \odot \cdots \odot \mathbf{A}_{k+1} \odot \mathbf{A}_{k-1} \odot \cdots \odot \mathbf{A}_1).
\end{aligned}$$

Plugging $\mathbf{VA}_k$ in as factor matrix k for $\mathcal{Y}$ in Proposition 10.10 completes the proof. □

Thus, a Kruskal tensor can be updated via a TTM *implicitly* at a cost of a small matrix multiplication: $\mathcal{O}(mn_k r)$. Compare this to the standard cost of a TTM, which is $\mathcal{O}(m \prod_{k=1}^{d} n_k)$.

10.8 Measuring Similarity of Kruskal Tensors

As we have discussed, Kruskal tensors have inherent permutation and scaling ambiguities. This means that measuring the *similarity* of two Kruskal tensors can be challenging. There are many ways this can be done, and here we present just one idea that will open the door to other options.

10.8.1 Measuring Similarity of 3-way Kruskal Tensors

Consider first the simple case of two *rank-1* 3-way Kruskal tensors with normalized factors. Let

$$\begin{aligned} \mathcal{K} &= \lambda\, \mathbf{a} \circ \mathbf{b} \circ \mathbf{c} && \text{with } \|\mathbf{a}\|_2 = \|\mathbf{b}\|_2 = \|\mathbf{c}\|_2 = 1, \quad \text{and} \\ \bar{\mathcal{K}} &= \bar{\lambda}\, \bar{\mathbf{a}} \circ \bar{\mathbf{b}} \circ \bar{\mathbf{c}} && \text{with } \|\bar{\mathbf{a}}\|_2 = \|\bar{\mathbf{b}}\|_2 = \|\bar{\mathbf{c}}\|_2 = 1. \end{aligned}$$

One measure that we can use for comparison is the cosine of that angle between them, $\langle \text{vec}(\mathcal{K}), \text{vec}(\bar{\mathcal{K}}) \rangle$, which is 1 if the vectors are perfectly aligned. This works out to

$$\text{score}(\mathcal{K}, \bar{\mathcal{K}}) = \langle \mathbf{a}, \bar{\mathbf{a}} \rangle \, \langle \mathbf{b}, \bar{\mathbf{b}} \rangle \, \langle \mathbf{c}, \bar{\mathbf{c}} \rangle \in [-1, 1].$$

This is sometimes referred to as **congruence** (Tomasi and Bro, 2006).

We usually are only comparing the factors for tensors that are identical in norm or close to it, which would imply that $\lambda \approx \bar{\lambda}$. However, if we want to also account explicitly for the weights, we can add some sort of penalty for the difference in the weights, such as

$$\psi(\lambda, \bar{\lambda}) \equiv 1 - \frac{|\lambda - \bar{\lambda}|}{\max\{\, \lambda, \bar{\lambda} \,\}} \in [0, 1]. \tag{10.12}$$

Then we could score the similarity as a weighted congruence:

$$\text{score}(\mathcal{K}, \bar{\mathcal{K}}) = \psi(\lambda, \bar{\lambda}) \, \langle \mathbf{a}, \bar{\mathbf{a}} \rangle \, \langle \mathbf{b}, \bar{\mathbf{b}} \rangle \, \langle \mathbf{c}, \bar{\mathbf{c}} \rangle \in [-1, 1].$$

So, we understand now how to compare two rank-1 3-way components.

Next, consider the problem of comparing two 3-way tensors with normalized factors. Let

$$\begin{aligned} \mathcal{K} &= [\![\boldsymbol{\lambda}; \mathbf{A}, \mathbf{B}, \mathbf{C}]\!] && \text{with } \|\bar{\mathbf{a}}_j\|_2 = \|\bar{\mathbf{b}}_j\|_2 = \|\bar{\mathbf{c}}_j\|_2 = 1 \text{ for all } j \in [r], \quad \text{and} \\ \bar{\mathcal{K}} &= [\![\bar{\boldsymbol{\lambda}}; \bar{\mathbf{A}}, \bar{\mathbf{B}}, \bar{\mathbf{C}}]\!] && \text{with } \|\mathbf{a}_j\|_2 = \|\mathbf{b}_j\|_2 = \|\mathbf{c}_j\|_2 = 1 \text{ for all } j \in [r]. \end{aligned}$$

We can take the average of all the matched-pair component scores, but we must consider the permutation ambiguity. This means we should ideally find the permutation of components that maximizes the average of the r matched-pair component scores:

$$\text{score}(\mathcal{K}, \bar{\mathcal{K}}) = \max \left\{ \tfrac{1}{r} \textstyle\sum_{j=1}^{r} \text{score}(\mathcal{K}_j, \bar{\mathcal{K}}_{\pi_j}) \;\middle|\; \pi \in \Pi(r) \right\}, \tag{10.13}$$

where the $\mathcal{K}_j$ and $\bar{\mathcal{K}}_j$ pick out the jth component. In other words,

$$\mathcal{K}_j \equiv \lambda_j \mathbf{a}_j \circ \mathbf{b}_j \circ \mathbf{c}_j \quad \text{and} \quad \bar{\mathcal{K}}_j = \bar{\lambda}_j \bar{\mathbf{a}}_j \circ \bar{\mathbf{b}}_j \circ \bar{\mathbf{c}}_j.$$

Here $\Pi(r)$ is the set of all r-permutations. This is a *weighted bipartite matching* problem, also known as an *assignment* problem. That is, we first compute the score between every $\binom{r}{2} = \mathcal{O}(r^2)$ pair of components, and we then solve the assignment problem to determine the matching. The cost of computing the pairwise scores is $\mathcal{O}(r^2 \sum_{k=1}^{d} n_k)$, and the cost of solving the assignment problem is $\mathcal{O}(r^3)$ (Edmonds and Karp, 1972).

Definition 10.29 (Kruskal Tensor Similarity Score, 3-way) Suppose we are given two *column-normalized* Kruskal tensors of size $m \times n \times p$ and each having r components:

$$\mathcal{K} = [\![\boldsymbol{\lambda}; \mathbf{A}, \mathbf{B}, \mathbf{C}]\!] \quad \text{and} \quad \hat{\mathcal{K}} = [\![\bar{\boldsymbol{\lambda}}; \bar{\mathbf{A}}, \bar{\mathbf{B}}, \bar{\mathbf{C}}]\!].$$

The similarity **score** between $\mathcal{K}$ and $\bar{\mathcal{K}}$ is

$$\text{score}(\mathcal{K}, \bar{\mathcal{K}}) = \max_{\pi} \frac{1}{r} \sum_{j=1}^{r} \psi(\lambda_j, \bar{\lambda}_{\pi_j}) \, \langle \mathbf{a}_j, \bar{\mathbf{a}}_{\pi_j} \rangle \langle \mathbf{b}_j, \bar{\mathbf{b}}_{\pi_j} \rangle \langle \mathbf{c}_j, \bar{\mathbf{c}}_{\pi_j} \rangle,$$

where π ranges over the set of r-permutations and ψ is a function of the weights, such as Eq. (10.12). To ignore the weights, set $\psi(\lambda, \bar{\lambda}) = 1$.

10.8.2 Measuring Similarity of d-way Kruskal Tensors

We provide the general d-way score below.

Definition 10.30: Kruskal Tensor Similarity Score

Suppose we are given two *column-normalized* Kruskal tensors of size $n_1 \times n_2 \times \cdots \times n_d$, each having r components:

$$\mathcal{K} = [\![\boldsymbol{\lambda},\ \mathbf{A}_1, \mathbf{A}_2, \ldots, \mathbf{A}_d]\!] \quad \text{and} \quad \bar{\mathcal{K}} = [\![\bar{\boldsymbol{\lambda}},\ \bar{\mathbf{A}}_1, \bar{\mathbf{A}}_2, \ldots, \bar{\mathbf{A}}_d]\!].$$

The similarity **score** between $\mathcal{K}$ and $\bar{\mathcal{K}}$ is

$$\text{score}(\mathcal{K}, \bar{\mathcal{K}}) = \max_{\pi} \frac{1}{r} \sum_{j=1}^{r} \psi(\lambda_j, \bar{\lambda}_{\pi_j}) \prod_{k=1}^{d} \langle \mathbf{A}_k(:, j), \bar{\mathbf{A}}_k(:, \pi_j) \rangle,$$

where π ranges over the set of r-permutations and ψ is a function of the weights, such as Eq. (10.12). To ignore the weights, set $\psi(\lambda, \bar{\lambda}) = 1$.

All scores are in the range $[-1, 1]$. If the two Kruskal tensors are identical except for permutation, then their score is 1.

If $\mathcal{K}_B$ has $\hat{r} > r$ components, then the score can be used as is with the only difference that π is selected among all $\hat{r}$ permutations. We use the best r out of $\hat{r}$ components for the comparison, and the remainder are simply ignored.

***Remark* 10.31** (Absolute values on component scores) When we take the product of the factor inner products, negative signs can cancel out. Perhaps for this reason, Acar et al. (2011a) use the absolute value of the component scores, restricting the score to be in the range $[0, 1]$. This *could* give a high score to a component that is sign-flipped, but it would be unlikely that this would happen in practice. (This is how the `score` is implemented in Tensor Toolbox for MATLAB as of Version 3.4.)

Exercise 10.28 Consider the EEM tensor discussed in Sections 1.5.2 and 9.6. (a) Compute the rank-3 CP with 50 different starting points and determine the model that yields the minimal error. (b) Compute the similarity score of the other 49 solutions with the one that yielded the minimal error. (c) What are the range of similarity scores? (d) Visualize the best solution alongside a solution with a high similarity score. How do they compare? (e) Conversely, visualize the least similar solution alongside the best. How do they compare?

11 CP Alternating Least Squares Optimization

Computing a CP decomposition requires solving a nonlinear least squares optimization problem using an iterative algorithm. In this chapter, we cover what is arguably the most common approach for CP: solve for one factor matrix at a time, holding all the others fixed. Each subproblem is a linear least squares problem which can be solved exactly. We then cycle through the factor matrices, solving each in turn, so we have an *alternating* least squares method and thus refer to this as CP alternating least squares (CP-ALS). CP-ALS cycles repeatedly through all the factor matrices until convergence. The CP-ALS approach for 3-way tensors was proposed in the earliest papers on computing CP by Carroll and Chang (1970) and Harshman (1970).[1]

The ALS approach is not the only way to fit a CP model. Alternative optimization approaches such as gradient-based (CP-OPT) and *nonlinear* least squares (CP-NLS) are discussed in Chapters 12 and 13, respectively.

11.1 CP-ALS for 3-way Tensors

Suppose we want to compute the CP factorization $[\![\mathbf{A}, \mathbf{B}, \mathbf{C}]\!]$ with r components for the tensor $\mathcal{X} \in \mathbb{R}^{m \times n \times p}$. This requires solving

$$\min_{\mathbf{A},\mathbf{B},\mathbf{C}} \|\mathcal{X} - [\![\mathbf{A}, \mathbf{B}, \mathbf{C}]\!]\|^2 \quad \text{subject to} \quad \mathbf{A} \in \mathbb{R}^{m \times r}, \mathbf{B} \in \mathbb{R}^{n \times r}, \mathbf{C} \in \mathbb{R}^{p \times r}. \tag{11.1}$$

This is a nonlinear, nonconvex optimization problem. One approach is to *alternate* between the factor matrices, solving for each in turn while the others are fixed. We repeat this cycle until convergence. This is a form of block coordinate descent (see Section B.3.7), where the blocks are the factor matrices. The basic method is as follows:

CP-ALS Prototype, 3-way

> **while** not converged **do**
> $\quad \mathbf{A} \leftarrow \arg\min_{\mathbf{A}} \|\mathcal{X} - [\![\mathbf{A}, \mathbf{B}, \mathbf{C}]\!]\|^2$
> $\quad \mathbf{B} \leftarrow \arg\min_{\mathbf{B}} \|\mathcal{X} - [\![\mathbf{A}, \mathbf{B}, \mathbf{C}]\!]\|^2$
> $\quad \mathbf{C} \leftarrow \arg\min_{\mathbf{C}} \|\mathcal{X} - [\![\mathbf{A}, \mathbf{B}, \mathbf{C}]\!]\|^2$
> **end while**

[1] Harshman credits Robert Jennrich with the CP-ALS algorithm in his 1970 paper. This should not be confused with the simultaneous diagonalization algorithm that is often incorrectly attributed to Jennrich; see Kolda (2021b).

11.1.1 Least Squares Subproblem for 3-way Tensors

Each subproblem is a linear least squares problem. Consider the first subproblem:

$$\arg\min_{\mathbf{A}} \left\| \mathcal{X} - [\![\mathbf{A}, \mathbf{B}, \mathbf{C}]\!] \right\|^2,$$

with $\mathbf{B}$ and $\mathbf{C}$ fixed. The key to computing $\mathbf{A}$ is to unfold the tensor expression in the first mode. Using the unfolding of the Kruskal tensor yields

$$\left\| \mathcal{X} - [\![\mathbf{A}, \mathbf{B}, \mathbf{C}]\!] \right\|^2 = \left\| \mathbf{X}_{(1)} - \mathbf{A}(\mathbf{C} \odot \mathbf{B})^\intercal \right\|_F^2$$

(see Exercise 11.1). Now it may be apparent that solving for $\mathbf{A}$ is a linear least squares problem. To make it more obvious, we transpose the expression and reverse the terms to obtain, equivalently,

$$\left\| (\mathbf{C} \odot \mathbf{B})\mathbf{A}^\intercal - \mathbf{X}_{(1)}^\intercal \right\|_F^2, \tag{11.2}$$

so that the coefficient matrix is $\mathbf{C} \odot \mathbf{B}$ and the right-hand side is $\mathbf{X}_{(1)}^\intercal$, matching the format of a standard matrix least squares problem in Eq. (A.19). This problem is usually solved via the **normal equations**, which produces the linear system

$$(\mathbf{C} \odot \mathbf{B})^\intercal (\mathbf{C} \odot \mathbf{B})\mathbf{A}^\intercal = (\mathbf{C} \odot \mathbf{B})^\intercal \mathbf{X}_{(1)}^\intercal.$$

The coefficient matrix can be computed cheaply by using a property of the **Khatri–Rao product** (Proposition A.23), simplifying to

$$(\mathbf{C}^\intercal\mathbf{C} * \mathbf{B}^\intercal\mathbf{B})\mathbf{A}^\intercal = (\mathbf{C} \odot \mathbf{B})^\intercal \mathbf{X}_{(1)}^\intercal.$$

The $r \times r$ matrix $(\mathbf{C}^\intercal\mathbf{C} * \mathbf{B}^\intercal\mathbf{B})$ is symmetric positive definite if $(\mathbf{C} \odot \mathbf{B})$ is full rank (see Exercises 11.2 and 11.3), so we can solve for $\mathbf{A}$ using the Cholesky decomposition. Transposed, we have

$$\mathbf{A}(\mathbf{C}^\intercal\mathbf{C} * \mathbf{B}^\intercal\mathbf{B}) = \mathbf{X}_{(1)}(\mathbf{C} \odot \mathbf{B}). \tag{11.3}$$

The right-hand side of the normal equations is a matricized-tensor times Khatri–Rao product (MTTKRP) – see Section 3.5.

The computational complexity of the solution via the normal equations is as follows for a dense tensor:

- The MTTKRP costs $\mathcal{O}(mnpr)$.
- The Gramian matrices and their Hadamard product cost $\mathcal{O}(nr^2 + pr^2 + r^2)$.
- The Cholesky factorization costs $\mathcal{O}(r^3)$.
- The backsolves cost $\mathcal{O}(r^2 m)$.

The dominant cost is $\mathcal{O}(mnpr)$ for the MTTKRP.

Remark 11.1 (Structured tensors) If $\mathcal{X}$ has structure such as being a sparse tensor, a Kruskal tensor, or a Tucker tensor, the cost of computing the MTTKRP may be reduced, making CP-ALS significantly less computationally expensive than with dense inputs. See Section 11.2.4.

Exercise 11.1 Show $\left\| \mathcal{X} - [\![\mathbf{A}, \mathbf{B}, \mathbf{C}]\!] \right\|^2 = \left\| \mathbf{X}_{(1)} - \mathbf{A}(\mathbf{C} \odot \mathbf{B})^\intercal \right\|_F^2$. Hint: Use Proposition 10.10.

Exercise 11.2 Let $\mathbf{B} \in \mathbb{R}^{n \times r}$ and $\mathbf{C} \in \mathbb{R}^{p \times r}$. Prove that if $\operatorname{rank}(\mathbf{B}) = \operatorname{rank}(\mathbf{C}) = r$, then $\operatorname{rank}(\mathbf{C} \odot \mathbf{B}) = r$. Hint: Use Proposition A.24.

Exercise 11.3 If $\operatorname{rank}(\mathbf{C} \odot \mathbf{B}) = r$, prove $(\mathbf{C}^\intercal \mathbf{C} * \mathbf{B}^\intercal \mathbf{B})$ is symmetric positive definite. Hint: Use Proposition A.14.

Exercise 11.4 (Regularization) If we add regularization as described in Section 9.4.2, show that the normal equation for $\mathbf{A}$ given by Eq. (11.3) becomes

$$\mathbf{A}\big((\mathbf{C}^\intercal \mathbf{C} * \mathbf{B}^\intercal \mathbf{B}) + \rho \mathbf{I}_r\big) = \mathbf{X}_{(1)}(\mathbf{C} \odot \mathbf{B}).$$

Exercise 11.5 Derive solutions analogous to Eq. (11.3) for $\mathbf{B}$ and $\mathbf{C}$ via the second and third subproblems in CP-ALS.

***Remark* 11.2** (Linear solves) In many works, the solution of Eq. (11.3) is written in terms of $(\mathbf{C}^\intercal \mathbf{C} * \mathbf{B}^\intercal \mathbf{B})^{-1}$, the inverse of $(\mathbf{C}^\intercal \mathbf{C} * \mathbf{B}^\intercal \mathbf{B})$. We want to stress that we want to avoid explicitly creating the inverse (or pseudoinverse if singular). Instead, let $\mathbf{U} = \mathbf{X}_{(1)}(\mathbf{C} \odot \mathbf{B})$ and $\mathbf{V} = (\mathbf{C}^\intercal \mathbf{C} * \mathbf{B}^\intercal \mathbf{B})$, and then solve the linear system $\mathbf{A}\mathbf{V} = \mathbf{U}$ for $\mathbf{A}$ using Cholesky decomposition.

If the linear system is singular or ill-conditioned, then using QR decomposition or regularization may help. See also Remark 11.3.

***Remark* 11.3** (Solving least squares via QR rather than the normal equations) The least squares problem in Eq. (11.2) can be solved via QR rather than least squares (see Section A.7). This would be especially appropriate if $(\mathbf{C} \odot \mathbf{B})$ is ill-conditioned because the normal equations are more sensitive to roundoff error; however, this rarely occurs in practice. If $r < \min\{m, n, p\}$, the computational complexity using the QR solution is $\mathcal{O}(mnpr)$, which is the same as using the normal equations. Special care can be taken to avoid forming the Khatri–Rao product and its QR factorization explicitly; see Minster et al. (2023).

11.1.2 CP-ALS Algorithm for 3-way Tensors

A detailed CP-ALS algorithm for a 3-way tensor is provided in Algorithm 11.1. The inputs are the tensor, the desired rank, initial guesses for the factor matrices (an initial guess for $\mathbf{A}$ is not required since that is the first matrix that is computed), and algorithm parameters for the maximum number of iterations and stopping tolerance. The output is a CP decomposition that either has relative error below the threshold τ or is the result after MAXITERS iterations.

Algorithm 11.1 saves variables for reuse in several places, like computing the norm of $\mathcal{X}$ once in Line 2 and the column scalings in Line 19. The COLUMNNORMALIZE function used in Algorithm 11.1 rescales each column so that its norm is 1 and optionally returns a second argument with the original column norms. Strictly speaking, renormalization of the columns is unnecessary. However, it is a way to address the scaling ambiguity that could potentially manifest roundoff errors in extreme cases. Other normalizations are possible, such as scaling by the one norm (sum of absolute values of entries) or infinity norm (maximum entry).

Algorithm 11.1 CP-ALS for 3-way Tensor

Require: data tensor $\mathcal{X} \in \mathbb{R}^{m \times n \times p}$, CP rank $r \in \mathbb{N}$, convergence tolerance $\tau > 0$, maximum iterations $\text{MAXITERS} \in \mathbb{N}$

Ensure: CP model $[\![\boldsymbol{\lambda}; \mathbf{A}, \mathbf{B}, \mathbf{C}]\!]$ with r components such that $[\![\boldsymbol{\lambda}; \mathbf{A}, \mathbf{B}, \mathbf{C}]\!] \approx \mathcal{X}$

function CP-ALS($\mathcal{X}, r, \tau$, MAXITERS)
  $\chi \leftarrow \|\mathcal{X}\|$
  initialize $\mathbf{B} \in \mathbb{R}^{n \times r}$, $\mathbf{C} \in \mathbb{R}^{p \times r}$ ▷ Alternatively, pass as inputs
  $\mathbf{S}_2 \leftarrow \mathbf{B}^\intercal\mathbf{B}$, $\mathbf{S}_3 \leftarrow \mathbf{C}^\intercal\mathbf{C}$
  for $t = 1, 2, \ldots,$ MAXITERS **do**
    $\mathbf{U}_1 \leftarrow \mathbf{X}_{(1)}(\mathbf{C} \odot \mathbf{B})$ ▷ MTTKRP
    $\mathbf{V}_1 \leftarrow \mathbf{S}_3 * \mathbf{S}_2$
    $\mathbf{A} \leftarrow$ solution of $\mathbf{A}\mathbf{V}_1 = \mathbf{U}_1$
    $\mathbf{A} \leftarrow$ COLUMNNORMALIZE($\mathbf{A}$)
    $\mathbf{S}_1 \leftarrow \mathbf{A}^\intercal\mathbf{A}$

    $\mathbf{U}_2 \leftarrow \mathbf{X}_{(2)}(\mathbf{C} \odot \mathbf{A})$ ▷ MTTKRP
    $\mathbf{V}_2 \leftarrow \mathbf{S}_3 * \mathbf{S}_1$
    $\mathbf{B} \leftarrow$ solution of $\mathbf{B}\mathbf{V}_2 = \mathbf{U}_2$
    $\mathbf{B} \leftarrow$ COLUMNNORMALIZE($\mathbf{B}$)
    $\mathbf{S}_2 \leftarrow \mathbf{B}^\intercal\mathbf{B}$

    $\mathbf{U}_3 \leftarrow \mathbf{X}_{(3)}(\mathbf{B} \odot \mathbf{A})$ ▷ MTTKRP
    $\mathbf{V}_3 \leftarrow \mathbf{S}_2 * \mathbf{S}_1$
    $\mathbf{C} \leftarrow$ solution of $\mathbf{C}\mathbf{V}_3 = \mathbf{U}_3$
    $\{\mathbf{C}, \boldsymbol{\lambda}\} \leftarrow$ COLUMNNORMALIZE($\mathbf{C}$) ▷ $\boldsymbol{\lambda}$ holds column norms
    $\mathbf{S}_3 \leftarrow \mathbf{C}^\intercal\mathbf{C}$

    $\alpha \leftarrow \mathbf{1}^\intercal\mathbf{C}^\intercal\mathbf{U}_3\boldsymbol{\lambda}$ ▷ $\alpha = \langle \mathcal{X}, [\![\mathbf{A}, \mathbf{B}, \mathbf{C}]\!] \rangle$
    $\beta \leftarrow \boldsymbol{\lambda}^\intercal(\mathbf{S}_3 * \mathbf{V}_3)\boldsymbol{\lambda}$ ▷ $\beta = \|[\![\mathbf{A}, \mathbf{B}, \mathbf{C}]\!]\|^2$
    $e_t \leftarrow (\chi^2 - 2\alpha + \beta)^{1/2}$ ▷ $e_t = \|\mathcal{X} - [\![\mathbf{A}, \mathbf{B}, \mathbf{C}]\!]\|$
    if $(t > 1)$ and $(e_t - e_{t-1} < \tau\chi)$ **then** ▷ Stop if decrease in relative error less than τ
      break
    end if
  end for
  Optional postprocessing to reorder components by weight and adjust signs
  return $\{\boldsymbol{\lambda}, \mathbf{A}, \mathbf{B}, \mathbf{C}\}$ ▷ CP model is $[\![\boldsymbol{\lambda}; \mathbf{A}, \mathbf{B}, \mathbf{C}]\!]$
end function

function COLUMNNORMALIZE($\mathbf{A}$)
  for $j = 1, 2, \ldots, r$ **do** ▷ r = number of columns in $\mathbf{A}$
    $\lambda_j \leftarrow \|\mathbf{a}_j\|_2$ ▷ $\mathbf{a}_j = j$th column of $\mathbf{A}$
    $\mathbf{a}_j \leftarrow \mathbf{a}_j / \lambda_j$
  end for
  return $\{\mathbf{A}, \boldsymbol{\lambda}\}$
end function

Exercise 11.6 Consider Algorithm 11.1. (a) What is the cost of each step of Algorithm 11.1? (b) Assuming $r < \min\{mn, mp, np\}$, which step is the most expensive?

Lines 21–23 are steps in computing $e_t = \|\mathcal{X} - [\![\boldsymbol{\lambda}; \mathbf{A}, \mathbf{B}, \mathbf{C}]\!]\|$, as shown in Exercise 10.21 and discussed in more detail in Section 10.7.2. The method terminates when the change in relative error is less than τ, where the relative error is defined as

$$\text{relative error} = \frac{\|\mathcal{X} - [\![\boldsymbol{\lambda}; \mathbf{A}, \mathbf{B}, \mathbf{C}]\!]\|}{\|\mathcal{X}\|}.$$

The relative error at iteration t is $e_t/\mathcal{X}$ in the notation of Algorithm 11.1. The error is nonincreasing; see Exercise 11.7.

Exercise 11.7 Consider Algorithm 11.1. Prove $e_t \leq e_{t-1}$ for all $t > 1$.

> The error in CP-ALS is nonincreasing, i.e., the error at step $t+1$ is no greater than the error at step t.

11.2 CP-ALS for d-way Tensors

The d-way case follows the same reasoning as the 3-way case. Given a tensor $\mathcal{X} \in \mathbb{R}^{n_1 \times n_2 \times \cdots \times n_d}$, suppose we want to compute a CP factorization $[\![\boldsymbol{\lambda}; \mathbf{A}_1, \mathbf{A}_2, \ldots, \mathbf{A}_d]\!]$ with r components. If we use alternating optimization, solving for one factor matrix at a time while the others are fixed, the basic algorithm is

Prototype CP-ALS, d-way

while not converged **do**
  for $k = 1, 2, \ldots, d$ **do**
    $\mathbf{A}_k \leftarrow \arg\min_{\mathbf{A}_k} \|\mathcal{X} - [\![\mathbf{A}_1, \mathbf{A}_2, \ldots, \mathbf{A}_d]\!]\|^2$
  end for
end while

11.2.1 Least Squares Subproblem for d-way Tensors

The least squares problem for the kth factor matrix can be rewritten explicitly in matrix notation as

$$\min_{\mathbf{A}_k \in \mathbb{R}^{n_k \times r}} \|\mathbf{X}_{(k)} - \mathbf{A}_k(\mathbf{A}_d \odot \cdots \odot \mathbf{A}_{k+1} \odot \mathbf{A}_{k-1} \odot \cdots \odot \mathbf{A}_1)^{\intercal}\|_F. \tag{11.4}$$

Here we have used Proposition 10.10.

Exercise 11.8 Consider the least squares problem in Eq. (11.4).

(a) Write the problem in standard form, i.e., $\min_{\mathbf{X}} \|\mathbf{A}\mathbf{X} - \mathbf{B}\|_F^2$, where we say $\mathbf{A}$ is the coefficient matrix, $\mathbf{X}$ is the unknown, and $\mathbf{B}$ is the right-hand side.

(b) What is the size of the coefficient matrix? What is the cost of computing the Khatri–Rao product to form the coefficient matrix explicitly?

(c) What is the size of the right-hand side?

(d) What is the cost to solve the least squares problem via the normal equations, ignoring the structure of the coefficient matrix?

The normal equation for this least squares problem is

$$\mathbf{A}_k \mathbf{V}_k = \mathbf{X}_{(k)}(\mathbf{A}_d \odot \cdots \odot \mathbf{A}_{k+1} \odot \mathbf{A}_{k-1} \odot \cdots \odot \mathbf{A}_1), \tag{11.5}$$

where

$$\begin{aligned}\mathbf{V}_k &= (\mathbf{A}_d \odot \cdots \odot \mathbf{A}_{k+1} \odot \mathbf{A}_{k-1} \odot \cdots \odot \mathbf{A}_1)^{\intercal}(\mathbf{A}_d \odot \cdots \odot \mathbf{A}_{k+1} \odot \mathbf{A}_{k-1} \odot \cdots \odot \mathbf{A}_1)\\ &= \mathbf{A}_d^{\intercal}\mathbf{A}_d * \cdots * \mathbf{A}_{k+1}^{\intercal}\mathbf{A}_{k+1} * \mathbf{A}_{k-1}^{\intercal}\mathbf{A}_{k-1} * \cdots * \mathbf{A}_1^{\intercal}\mathbf{A}_1.\end{aligned}$$

Here we have used Proposition A.23 (applied repeatedly). We can solve the normal equations using a Cholesky decomposition. As in the 3-way case, the coefficient matrix $\mathbf{V}_k$ is $r \times r$, and the right-hand side is an MTTKRP. See also Remark 11.2.

Exercise 11.9 Consider the normal equations in Eq. (11.5).

(a) What is the cost to compute the MTTKRP, i.e., $\mathbf{X}_{(k)}(\mathbf{A}_d \odot \cdots \odot \mathbf{A}_{k+1} \odot \mathbf{A}_{k-1} \odot \cdots \odot \mathbf{A}_1)$? What is the size of the result?

(b) What is the cost to compute $\mathbf{V}_k$?

(c) Once the normal equations are formed, what is the remaining cost to solve for $\mathbf{A}_k$ via Cholesky factorization?

(d) Which step is most expensive?

11.2.2 CP-ALS Algorithm for d-way Tensors

We present a detailed version of CP-ALS for a d-way tensor in Algorithm 11.2. The inputs are the tensor, the desired rank, initial guesses for the factor matrices (an initial guess for $\mathbf{A}_1$ is not required since that is the first matrix that is computed), and algorithm parameters for the maximum number of iterations and stopping tolerance. Each outer iteration (indexed by t) cycles through all d factor matrices, optimizing each in turn. The output is a CP decomposition that either has relative error below the threshold τ or is the result after MAXITERS iterations. See Remark 11.2 regarding the linear solves in Line 11.

As in the 3-way case, the d-way CP-ALS procedure iterates until the change in the relative error goes below the specified convergence threshold (τ) or the maximum iterations (MAXITERS) is exceeded. This is similar to tracking the change of the objective function in optimization. Other stopping conditions are possible, such as tracking the change in the factor matrices and stopping when those changes become suitably small.

> The usual stopping criterion for CP-ALS is to stop when the change in relative error goes below a user-specified tolerance.

11.2.3 Complexity Analysis for CP-ALS

The costs of each line in an outer iteration of CP-ALS are given in Table 11.1. Before we derive the complexity of each line, we note that the computational complexity of the MTTKRPs involve the *product* of tensor dimensions. Every other cost is proportional to the *sum* of tensor dimensions (at most). This is because the MTTKRP is the only operation in the loop that involves the input tensor; therefore, it dominates the computational complexity.

> The most expensive step in CP-ALS is the MTTKRP.

The MTTKRP tensor operation is described in Section 3.5.2 and is computed directly for dense tensors by forming the Khatri–Rao product of the factor matrices followed by matrix multiplication with the unfolded tensor. Regardless of mode, the cost of an MTTKRP in an inner iteration is $\mathcal{O}(Nr)$, where $N = \prod_{k=1}^{d} n_k$.

Algorithm 11.2 CP-ALS for d-way Tensor

Require: data tensor $\mathfrak{X} \in \mathbb{R}^{n_1 \times n_2 \times \cdots \times n_d}$, rank $r \in \mathbb{N}$, convergence tolerance $\tau > 0$, maximum iterations MAXITERS $\in \mathbb{N}$
Ensure: CP model $[\![\boldsymbol{\lambda}; \mathbf{A}_1, \ldots, \mathbf{A}_d]\!]$ with r components such that $[\![\boldsymbol{\lambda}; \mathbf{A}_1, \ldots, \mathbf{A}_d]\!] \approx \mathfrak{X}$
1: **function** CP-ALS($\mathfrak{X}, r, \tau$, MAXITERS)
2: $\quad \mathcal{X} \leftarrow \|\mathfrak{X}\|$
3: $\quad$ **for** $k = 2, \ldots, d$ **do**
4: $\quad\quad$ initialize $\mathbf{A}_k \in \mathbb{R}^{n_k \times r}$ ▷ Alternatively, pass as inputs
5: $\quad\quad \mathbf{S}_k \leftarrow \mathbf{A}_k^{\mathsf{T}} \mathbf{A}_k$
6: $\quad$ **end for**
7: $\quad$ **for** $t = 1, \ldots,$ MAXITERS **do**
8: $\quad\quad$ **for** $k = 1, \ldots, d$ **do**
9: $\quad\quad\quad \mathbf{U}_k \leftarrow \mathbf{X}_{(k)}(\mathbf{A}_d \odot \cdots \odot \mathbf{A}_{k+1} \odot \mathbf{A}_{k-1} \odot \cdots \odot \mathbf{A}_1)$ ▷ MTTKRP
10: $\quad\quad\quad \mathbf{V}_k \leftarrow \mathbf{S}_d * \cdots * \mathbf{S}_{k+1} * \mathbf{S}_{k-1} * \cdots * \mathbf{S}_1$
11: $\quad\quad\quad \mathbf{A}_k \leftarrow$ solution of $\mathbf{A}_k \mathbf{V}_k = \mathbf{U}_k$
12: $\quad\quad\quad \{\, \mathbf{A}_k, \boldsymbol{\lambda} \,\} \leftarrow$ COLUMNNORMALIZE($\mathbf{A}_k$) ▷ See Algorithm 11.1
13: $\quad\quad\quad \mathbf{S}_k \leftarrow \mathbf{A}_k^{\mathsf{T}} \mathbf{A}_k$
14: $\quad\quad$ **end for**
15: $\quad\quad \alpha \leftarrow \mathbf{1}^{\mathsf{T}} \mathbf{A}_d^{\mathsf{T}} \mathbf{U}_d \boldsymbol{\lambda}$ ▷ $\alpha = \langle \mathfrak{X}, [\![\boldsymbol{\lambda}; \mathbf{A}_1, \mathbf{A}_2, \ldots, \mathbf{A}_d]\!] \rangle$
16: $\quad\quad \beta \leftarrow \boldsymbol{\lambda}^{\mathsf{T}} (\mathbf{S}_d * \mathbf{V}_d) \boldsymbol{\lambda}$ ▷ $\beta = \| [\![\boldsymbol{\lambda}; \mathbf{A}_1, \mathbf{A}_2, \ldots, \mathbf{A}_d]\!] \|^2$
17: $\quad\quad e_t \leftarrow (\mathcal{X}^2 - 2\alpha + \beta)^{1/2}$ ▷ $e_t = \| \mathfrak{X} - [\![\boldsymbol{\lambda}; \mathbf{A}_1, \mathbf{A}_2, \ldots, \mathbf{A}_d]\!] \|$
18: $\quad\quad$ **if** $(t > 1)$ and $(e_{t-1} - e_t < \tau \mathcal{X})$ **then**
19: $\quad\quad\quad$ **break** ▷ Stop if decrease in relative error less than τ
20: $\quad\quad$ **end if**
21: $\quad$ **end for**
22: $\quad$ *Optional postprocessing to reorder components by weight and adjust signs*
23: $\quad$ **return** $\{\, \boldsymbol{\lambda}, \mathbf{A}_1, \mathbf{A}_2, \ldots, \mathbf{A}_d \,\}$ ▷ CP model is $[\![\boldsymbol{\lambda}; \mathbf{A}_1, \mathbf{A}_2, \ldots, \mathbf{A}_d]\!]$
24: **end function**

Each outer loop requires d MTTKRP calculations, which can be performed independently for a cost of $\mathcal{O}(dNr)$. The cost can be reduced to $\mathcal{O}(Nr)$ by reusing intermediate quantities across MTTKRPs in different modes instead of recomputing those quantities; see the discussion of memoization in Section 3.6.2. Because this optimization reduces the computational complexity by a factor of approximately $d/2$, it can have a significant impact on the running time of CP-ALS without sacrificing accuracy or convergence.

The costs of the other lines are lower-order terms in the overall complexity. The linear solves and Gram computations in Lines 11 and 13 are the next most expensive operations after the MTTKRPs. In mode k, the costs are dominated by the triangular solves involving the Cholesky factor of $\mathbf{V}_k$ and computing the Gram matrix $\mathbf{S}_k$, which both cost $\mathcal{O}(n_k r^2)$. Summing over all modes yields the cost in Table 11.1. The Hadamard products computed in Line 10 each cost $\mathcal{O}(r^2)$ multiplications, and there are $d(d-2)$ of them to perform in direct evaluation. Like the MTTKRPs, the cost can be reduced by a factor of $\mathcal{O}(d)$ using memoization; see Exercise 11.10. Normalization in Line 12 involves only a couple of passes over each factor matrix, and the cost of efficient computation of the error in Lines 15–17 depends only on a single tensor dimension. These costs are typically negligible. If the error computation is performed directly to ensure high accuracy as discussed in Section 10.7.2, then its cost is comparable to a single MTTKRP.

Table 11.1 CP-ALS per-outer-iteration computational complexity for rank-r CP decomposition of (dense) tensor of size $n_1 \times n_2 \times \cdots \times n_d$ with $N = \prod_{k=1}^{d} n_k$

Calculation	Line(s)	Complexity	See also
MTTKRP	Line 9	$\mathcal{O}(Nr)$	Section 3.5.2
Hadamard product	Exercise 11.10	$\mathcal{O}(dr^2)$	Section 3.6.2
Linear solve	Line 11	$\mathcal{O}(dr^3 + r^2 \sum_{k=1}^{d} n_k)$	Section A.6.4
Normalization	Line 12	$\mathcal{O}(r \sum_{k=1}^{d} n_k)$	
Gram	Line 13	$\mathcal{O}(r^2 \sum_{k=1}^{d} n_k)$	Section A.4.1
Error	Lines 15–17	$\mathcal{O}(rn_d + r^2)$	Section 10.7.2

Exercise 11.10 Consider the computation of

$$\mathbf{V}_k = \mathbf{S}_d * \cdots * \mathbf{S}_{k+1} * \mathbf{S}_{k-1} * \cdots * \mathbf{S}_1$$

at iteration k in Line 10 of Algorithm 11.2. Define the matrices

$$\mathbf{L}_k = \mathbf{S}_d * \cdots * \mathbf{S}_{k+1} \quad \text{and} \quad \mathbf{R}_k = \mathbf{S}_{k-1} * \cdots * \mathbf{S}_1$$

so that $\mathbf{V}_k = \mathbf{L}_k \mathbf{R}_k$ for $1 < k < d$. (a) Show that pre-computing all $\mathbf{L}_k$ matrices can be performed using $\mathcal{O}(d)$ Hadamard products at the beginning of each outer iteration. (b) Show that $\mathbf{V}_k$ and $\mathbf{R}_{k+1}$ can be computed from $\mathbf{L}_k$ and $\mathbf{R}_k$ using two Hadamard products at iteration k, yielding a total of $\mathcal{O}(d)$ Hadamard products per outer iteration.

11.2.4 CP-ALS with Sparse and Structured Tensors

There are only two lines in CP-ALS (Algorithm 11.2) that use the tensor $\mathcal{X}$: the norm calculation in Line 2 and the MTTKRP in Line 9. The former is computed only once at a cost of $\mathcal{O}(N)$ for a dense tensor $\mathcal{X}$ of size $n_1 \times n_2 \times \cdots \times n_d$ with $N = \prod_{k=1}^{d} n_k$. The latter is the most expensive operation, requiring $\mathcal{O}(Nr)$ operations per CP-ALS iteration.

If the tensor has special structure, we can compute MTTKRPs and the norm more efficiently. For example, if $\mathcal{X}$ is a sparse tensor, then we can efficiently compute the MTTKRP and norm per Sections 3.7.2 and 3.7.4. In particular, the complexity of a single MTTKRP involving a sparse tensor can be reduced from $\mathcal{O}(Nr)$ down to $\mathcal{O}(dqr)$, where q is the number of nonzeros in the tensor.

There are other structures we can exploit as well. For instance, if $\mathcal{X}$ is a Tucker tensor, then we can compute the MTTKRP and norm as described in Sections 5.7.1 and 5.7.3. In the case of a Tucker tensor with orthonormal factor matrices, we can compute a CP decomposition of only the Tucker core (see Section 17.2). Likewise, if $\mathcal{X}$ is a Kruskal tensor (where the number of components is larger than the anticipated rank), then we can compute the MTTKRP and norm as described in Sections 10.7.1 and 10.7.3. For further discussion of sparse and structured tensors, see Bader and Kolda (2007).

Exercise 11.11 How does the computational cost of Eq. (11.3) change if $\mathcal{X}$ is a sparse tensor with $\text{nnz}(\mathcal{X}) \ll mnp$?

We can gain efficiencies in computing CP-ALS with an efficient method for MTTKRP for sparse or structured tensors.

Remark 11.4 (Norm in CP-ALS is dispensable) The norm is not critical to the algorithm. It is used solely in computing the error-based stopping criterion, which is not essential.

11.3 Further Notes on CP-ALS

As Kolda and Bader (2009) say, CP-ALS is the "workhorse" algorithm for computing the CP decomposition. It is easy to implement and relatively efficient. We discuss a few further ideas below.

Nonnegativity We may impose nonnegativity on each least squares solve to obtain nonnegative factor matrices. A classic method for solving a linear least squares problem with nonnegativity constraints is Lawson and Hanson (1974), and Bro and De Jong (1997) have a faster version that is amenable to use in an iterative method, such as CP-ALS. These methods are guaranteed to find an exact solution in a finite number of steps. See also Kim et al. (2014) for an overview of different methods.

Convergence and Rate of Convergence Let e_t denote the error of CP-ALS at iteration t, as in Algorithm 11.1 or Algorithm 11.2. It can be shown that $e_{t+1} \leq e_t$ for all t, so the error never increases in CP-ALS; see Exercise 11.7. Since the error is also bounded below by 0, the sequence $\{ e_t \}$ must converge. We cannot prove that the iterates themselves converge without additional assumptions (see, e.g., Uschmajew, 2012). However, the iterates seem to always converge to a stationary point in practice.

Sketched Least Squares The least squares problems in ALS are tall and thin, making them amenable to randomized methods for solving least squares problems. This has inspired both methods and related analyses; see Cheng et al. (2016), Battaglino et al. (2018), Jin et al. (2020), Malik and Becker (2020), and Larsen and Kolda (2022).

11.4 CP-ALS on Data Tensors

We have already studied CP-ALS on the EEM tensor in the introductory chapter on CP (Section 9.6), and recommend reviewing this material.

Additionally, we illustrate the results of this chapter on the 4-way Chicago crime tensor as described in Section 1.5.4. This is a tensor of size $365 \times 24 \times 77 \times 12$, where entry (i, j, k, ℓ) indicates the number of crimes on day i (out of 365) and hour j (of 24) in community k (of 77) and of type ℓ (of 12). Since this is a 4-way tensor, a rank-r CP model will be of the form

$$\mathcal{M} = [\![\mathbf{A}_1, \mathbf{A}_2, \mathbf{A}_3, \mathbf{A}_4]\!],$$

where $\mathbf{A}_1 \in \mathbb{R}^{365 \times r}$, $\mathbf{A}_2 \in \mathbb{R}^{24 \times r}$, $\mathbf{A}_3 \in \mathbb{R}^{77 \times r}$, and $\mathbf{A}_4 \in \mathbb{R}^{12 \times r}$.

In Fig. 11.1, we plot the rank versus the relative error. For each rank, we run CP-ALS three times with different initial guesses. First, observe that the relative error is over 90%. Although this error is quite high, we will still find interpretable patterns in the data. Second, there is no clear best rank. Some examination of the components may be in order to make a determination. We will use rank $r = 7$ in the subsequent example because it balances reducing the relative error with model parsimony.

Remark 11.5 (CP-ALS parameters) For running CP-ALS on the Chicago crime tensor, we used $\tau = 10^{-4}$ and MAXITERS $= 50$.

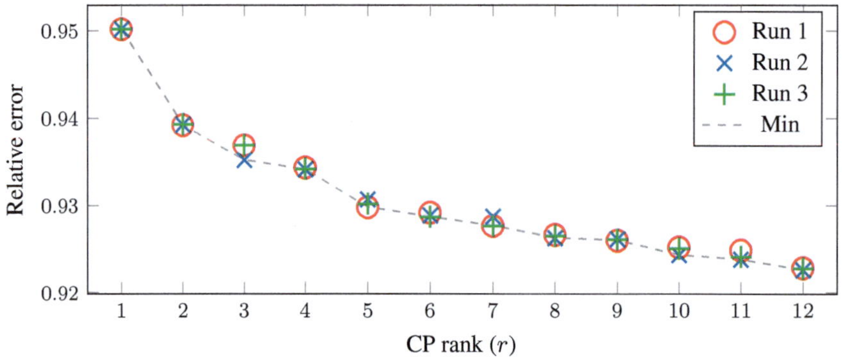

Figure 11.1 CP rank versus relative error for the Chicago crime tensor.

The results of the rank-7 CP decomposition are shown in Figs. 11.2 and 11.3. The first component corresponds to the day and is of length 365, the beginning of each month is indicated by a vertical gridline, and 0 is indicated by a horizontal gray line. The second component corresponds to the hour, with hour 0 corresponding to midnight to 12:59 a.m., and so on. The third component corresponds to community area, and map visualizations are provided in Fig. 11.3. The fourth component corresponds to crime type. The components are presented in order of overall magnitude and have been normalized to unit norm *except* the day component, which reflects the weight of the component overall.

We can make a few observations about the components:

- Component 1 is most active in the areas known as "Near North" and "Loop," which are heavily populated by tourists. We see a pattern of crime reports mainly during daytime and evening hours, peaking at 5–7 p.m. The main crime type is theft, followed by deceptive practice. These crimes are active throughout the year.
- Component 2 is arguably the main trend as it is fairly consistent across the days, hours, communities, and crimes (with the exception of deceptive practice).
- Component 3 is an outlier component focused on a few dates (early August), the evening hours, peaking around 10 p.m., a single community (Loop area), and a single crime type (theft). This corresponds with the Lollapalooza festival, which took place in Grant Park in the Loop area on August 1–4. Some of the elements of the first factor in this component are negative, making it harder to interpret.
- Component 4 is mainly narcotics, in the western part of the city, throughout the year, and mainly during the daytime, with peaks around 10 a.m. and 7 p.m.
- Component 5 has interesting time behavior, likely corresponding to the ways in which some crimes are reported. The main crimes are deceptive practice and theft. The unusual time pattern is peaks at the start of each month and at the hours of noon, midnight, and 9 a.m. These seem to indicate crimes that lacked the specificity of a date and time, so these were just recorded as the first of the month and an arbitrary time.

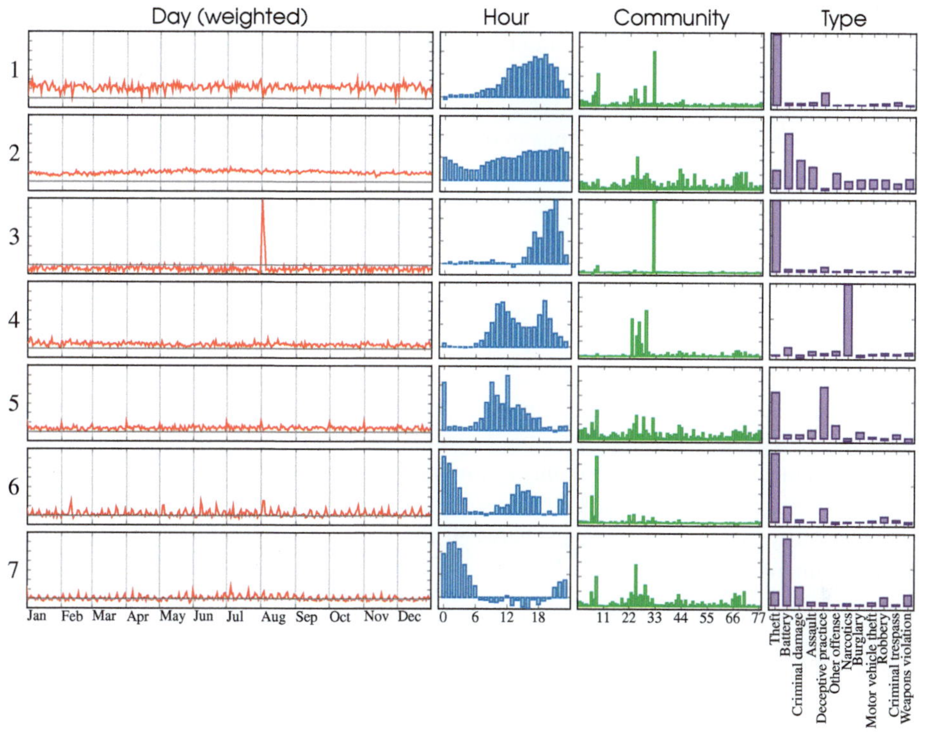

Figure 11.2 Chicago 2019 crime tensor rank-7 CP factors. Each row represents one component, sorted from largest to smallest magnitude. The factors for hour, community, and (crime) type are normalized to length 1. The factor for day holds the weight of the component. The horizontal line shown with each day factor is at 0.

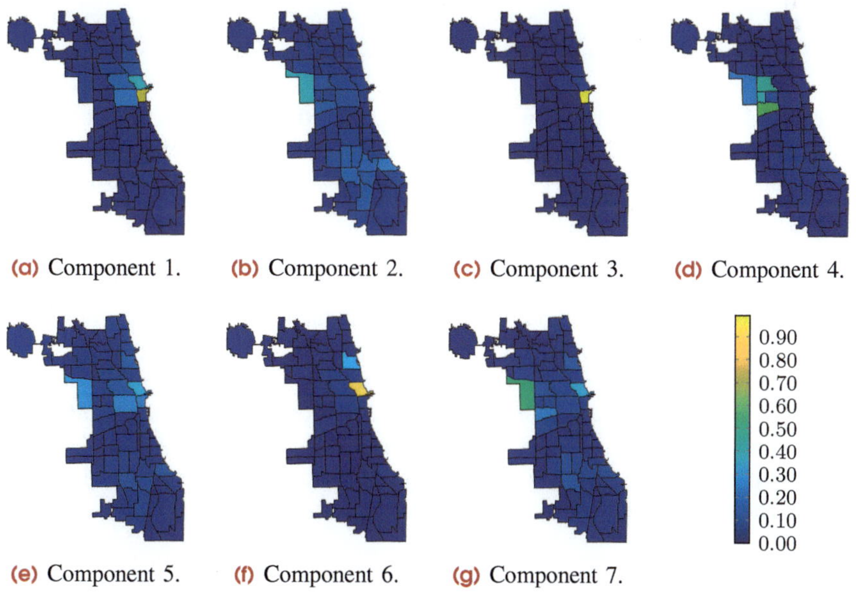

Figure 11.3 Map visualization for factor 3 of Fig. 11.2.

- Component 6 is somewhat similar to component 1, but with more of a focus on crimes in the middle of the night and more focused geographically on the tourist areas.
- Component 7 is broadly crimes in the middle of the night, with battery and criminal damage being the main crimes.

***Remark* 11.6** (CP versus GCP on Chicago crime tensor) In Section 9.8, we analyzed the Chicago 2019 crime data using GCP (to be covered in Chapter 15) and obtained somewhat different results. One cause for concern with CP is that the relative error is very high, over 90%. Further, the results from CP are arguably less interesting. For instance, component 3 of the CP decomposition in Figs. 11.2 and 11.3 focuses on just a few days in August (these dates and the locations identified correspond with the Lollapalooza festival that took place in Grant Park in the Loop area on August 1–4). The GCP results are more balanced and able to incorporate the high number of reports on those few days as a spike in time for a more general component. The CP factors have some negative entries, which also impacts interpretability. The main difference between CP and GCP is the objective functions. CP uses the sum of squared errors (SSE):

$$\sum_{i=1}^{365}\sum_{j=1}^{24}\sum_{k=1}^{77}\sum_{\ell=1}^{12}\left(m_{ijk\ell} - x_{ijk\ell}\right)^2,$$

whereas GCP uses a KL divergence loss function:

$$\sum_{i=1}^{365}\sum_{j=1}^{24}\sum_{k=1}^{77}\sum_{\ell=1}^{12} m_{ijk\ell} - x_{ijk\ell}\log(m_{ijk\ell}).$$

Exercise 11.12 Contrast these components to those found by GCP in Section 9.8. What is similar? What is different?

Exercise 11.13 (a) Implement 3-way CP-ALS (Algorithm 11.1). (b) Test it on the EEM dataset; see Sections 1.5.2 and 9.6. (c) Run the method with $r = 3$ several times using different starting point and save the best solution. (d) Does it compute the same decomposition as shown in Section 9.6? (e) Which step is the most expensive?

Exercise 11.14 (a) Implement CP-ALS as in Algorithm 11.2. (b) Create test problems with known rank, with and without noise, to test the method. We recommend trying both 3- and 4-way tensors, of sizes $100 \times 80 \times 60$ and $r = 10$ and $50 \times 40 \times 30 \times 20$ and $r = 8$. Try generating random factor matrices, e.g., using the Tensor Toolbox command `A=matrandnorm(n,r)` as well as matrices that have **congruent** factors via `A=matrandcong(n,r,gamma)`, which ensures that $(\mathbf{a}_i^\intercal \mathbf{a}_j)/(\|\mathbf{a}_i\|_2\|\mathbf{a}_j\|_2) = \gamma$ for all pairs of columns of $\mathbf{A}$. For $\gamma = 0$, all columns are orthogonal. For $\gamma = 1$, all columns are identical. The problems generally become more difficult for $\gamma \geq 0.5$.

Exercise 11.15 Generate a figure comparing rank and relative error for one of the test problems you created in Exercise 11.14. Be sure to compute the fit for multiple starting points for each choice of rank.

Exercise 11.16 Test your implementation of 3-way CP-ALS (Algorithm 11.1) on the Chicago dataset to reproduce the results in this section. (a) Compute the relative error for different ranks (using multiple starts). (b) Visualize the components for rank $r = 7$. (c) (Bonus) Try a different rank (e.g., $r = 6$). Explain how the results change.

Exercise 11.17 (a) Implement CP-ALS for sparse tensors; see Section 3.7. (b) Compare its performance to CP-ALS for dense tensors on the Chicago crime 2019 tensor for a reasonable rank (e.g., $r = 7$). (c) Do they obtain similar relative errors and solutions? (d) How do their times compare? (e) For each method, which step is most expensive? Discuss.

***Remark* 11.7 (Larger Chicago crime tensor)** The Chicago crime 2019 tensor is small enough that there is no major advantage to handling it as a sparse tensor. The advantage is pronounced, however, if running on a larger dataset. To test this, a larger sparse Chicago crime dataset is available at `https://gitlab.com/tensors/tensor_data_chicago_crime`. This dataset spans 2002–2022 for a total of 7484 days (April 22, 2002–October 17, 2022).

12 CP Gradient-Based Optimization

In this chapter, we consider general gradient-based optimization methods that minimize the loss with respect to all factor matrices simultaneously. By gradient-based optimization methods, we refer to those methods that require only function values and gradients and assume no special problem structure. In other words, the user need only provide functionality to evaluate the function and gradient, so we focus on how to compute these. This enables us to use a variety of general-purpose optimization methods, including gradient descent and quasi-Newton methods, as well as methods for constrained optimization. We refer to this class of methods as CP-OPT.

For context, other chapters consider the special structure of the problem. In Chapter 11, we discussed the ALS approach for computing CP, a form of alternating optimization wherein we solve for one block of variables at a time using the special structure that each subproblem is a *linear* least squares problem. In Chapter 13, we will consider the *nonlinear* least squares (NLS) structure and discuss how to solve it using a damped Gauss–Newton method with an iterative solver for the Gauss–Newton system.

12.1 CP Optimization Problem

A typical optimization problem (see Appendix B) is formulated in terms of a vector-valued function $f : \mathbb{R}^n \to \mathbb{R}$ as

$$\min_{\mathbf{v} \in \mathbb{R}^n} f(\mathbf{v}).$$

The prototypical gradient-based optimization method computes a search direction based on the gradient $\nabla f : \mathbb{R}^n \to \mathbb{R}^n$. For example, the method of steepest descent uses $\mathbf{d}_k = -\nabla f(\mathbf{v}_k)$ and a limited-memory quasi-Newton method uses a more complex calculation involving information from previous iterations. The step length can be fixed (usually called a learning rate) or computed using a line search. A line search will typically involve function and gradient evaluations to determine the suitability of the proposed step. Convergence is generally checked using the norm of the gradient. We discuss considerations in the choice of method in Section 12.3.

Prototypical Optimization Method

$\mathbf{v}_0 \leftarrow$ initial guess
repeat $k = 0, 1, \ldots$
  $\mathbf{d}_k \leftarrow$ compute search direction depending on $\nabla f(\mathbf{v}_k)$
  $\alpha_k \leftarrow$ step length in direction $\mathbf{d}_k$, potentially requiring $f(\mathbf{v}_k + \alpha \mathbf{d}_k)$ and $\nabla f(\mathbf{v}_k + \alpha \mathbf{d}_k)$ for different values of α
  $\mathbf{v}_{k+1} \leftarrow \mathbf{v}_k + \alpha_k \mathbf{d}_k$
until converged

The key to using an optimization method, therefore, is being able to provide a method for computing functions and gradients of iterates. This is the focus of this chapter. The first issue is that CP is solving for the CP factor *matrices*. So, how do we reconcile the fact that the variables in the CP fitting problem are the factor matrices? We have to reorganize these into a single vector for the purposes of the optimization.

> We must express the optimization problem as a function of a vector in order to use standard optimization approaches.

12.1.1 CP Optimization Formulation for 3-way CP

For a 3-way tensor $\mathcal{X} \in \mathbb{R}^{m \times n \times p}$, the rank-$r$ CP is the solution to the following minimization problem:

$$\min_{\mathbf{A},\mathbf{B},\mathbf{C}} \frac{1}{2} \| \mathcal{X} - [\![\mathbf{A},\mathbf{B},\mathbf{C}]\!] \|^2 \quad \text{subject to} \quad \mathbf{A} \in \mathbb{R}^{m \times r},\ \mathbf{B} \in \mathbb{R}^{n \times r},\ \mathbf{C} \in \mathbb{R}^{p \times r}. \tag{12.1}$$

To write this as a function with a vector input, we present operations that convert a Kruskal tensor to and from a vector.

Conversion of a Kruskal tensor to a vector stacks the vectorized factor matrices:

$$\mathbf{v} = \texttt{mats2vec}(\mathbf{A},\mathbf{B},\mathbf{C}) \equiv \begin{bmatrix} \text{vec}(\mathbf{A}) \\ \text{vec}(\mathbf{B}) \\ \text{vec}(\mathbf{C}) \end{bmatrix} \in \mathbb{R}^{mr+nr+pr}.$$

The converse is somewhat trickier to express mathematically, but it reduces to unpacking the array into three segments and reshaping them into matrices:

$$\begin{aligned} &\texttt{vec2mats}(\mathbf{v}, m, n, p, r) = \{ \mathbf{A}, \mathbf{B}, \mathbf{C} \}, \\ &\qquad \text{where} \quad \begin{aligned} \mathbf{A} &= \text{reshape}(\mathbf{v}(1 : mr), m \times r), \\ \mathbf{B} &= \text{reshape}(\mathbf{v}(mr+1 : mr+nr), n \times r), \\ \mathbf{C} &= \text{reshape}(\mathbf{v}(mr+nr+1 : mr+nr+pr), p \times r). \end{aligned} \end{aligned} \tag{12.2}$$

Note that the size of the tensor and the number of factors is needed to figure out how to reassemble the elements of $\mathbf{v}$ into the constituent factor matrices. We may write just $\texttt{vec2mats}\mathbf{v}$ when the sizes are clear by context.

With these transformations, we can rewrite the optimization problem in terms of the function $f : \mathbb{R}^{(m+n+p)r} \to \mathbb{R}$:

$$\begin{aligned} \min_{\mathbf{v}} \quad & f(\mathbf{v}) \equiv \frac{1}{2} \| \mathcal{X} - [\![\mathbf{A},\mathbf{B},\mathbf{C}]\!] \|^2, \\ \text{where} \quad & \{ \mathbf{A}, \mathbf{B}, \mathbf{C} \} = \texttt{vec2mats}(\mathbf{v}, m, n, p, r). \end{aligned} \tag{12.3}$$

We will usually write the optimization in terms of factor matrices as in Eq. (12.1), but there is an implicit transformation to Eq. (12.3) in order to use optimization solvers.

> ***Remark* 12.1** (Where are the weights?) We assume throughout this chapter that the Kruskal tensor component weights are equal to 1 and so can be ignored. This enables us to leave the factor matrices unconstrained, though there is still a scaling ambiguity.

12.1.2 CP Optimization Formulation for d-way CP

For a d-way tensor $\mathcal{X} \in \mathbb{R}^{n_1 \times n_2 \times \cdots \times n_d}$, we can compute a rank-$r$ CP as the solution to the following minimization problem:

$$\min_{\{\mathbf{A}_k\}} \frac{1}{2} \left\| \mathcal{X} - [\![\mathbf{A}_1, \mathbf{A}_2, \ldots, \mathbf{A}_d]\!] \right\|^2 \quad \text{subject to} \quad \mathbf{A}_k \in \mathbb{R}^{n_k \times r} \quad \text{for all} \quad k \in [d].$$

The conversion functions are analogous to the 3-way case. Converting a Kruskal tensor to a vector stacks the vectorized factor matrices. The converse reduces to unpacking the array into d segments and reshaping into factor matrices, and it requires the factor matrix sizes.

Definition 12.2: Kruskal Tensor Components to Vector (`mats2vec`)

Conversion of a Kruskal tensor's components, $\mathbf{A}_k \in \mathbb{R}^{n_k \times r}$ for $k \in [d]$, to a vector is accomplished by stacking the vectorized factor matrices as

$$\mathbf{v} = \texttt{mats2vec}(\mathbf{A}_1, \mathbf{A}_2, \ldots, \mathbf{A}_d) \equiv \begin{bmatrix} \text{vec}(\mathbf{A}_1) \\ \text{vec}(\mathbf{A}_2) \\ \vdots \\ \text{vec}(\mathbf{A}_d) \end{bmatrix} \in \mathbb{R}^{r(n_1+n_2+\cdots+n_d)}.$$

Definition 12.3: Vector to Kruskal Tensor Components (`vec2mats`)

Given the sizes of the intended Kruskal tensor $\big(\{n_1, n_2, \ldots, n_d\}$ and $r\big)$ and a vector $\mathbf{v}$ of length $r\sum_{k=1}^{d} n_k$, we can convert $\mathbf{v}$ into the components of a Kruskal tensor via

$$\texttt{vec2mats}(\mathbf{v}, n_1, n_2, \ldots, n_d, r) = \{\mathbf{A}_1, \mathbf{A}_2, \ldots, \mathbf{A}_d\},$$

$$\text{where} \quad i_k = 1 + r\sum_{\ell=1}^{k-1} n_\ell, \quad j_k = r\sum_{\ell=1}^{k} n_\ell, \quad \text{and}$$

$$\mathbf{A}_k = \text{reshape}(\mathbf{v}(i_k : j_k), n_k \times r) \quad \text{for all} \quad k \in [d]. \qquad (12.4)$$

***Remark* 12.4 (Conversion shorthand)** Converting a vector representation into a Kruskal tensor requires specifying the sizes of all the factor matrices. However, we will omit the sizes when the context is clear; in other words, $\texttt{vec2mats}(\mathbf{v})$ is shorthand for $\texttt{vec2mats}(\mathbf{v}, n_1, n_2, \ldots, n_d, r)$.

With these transformations, we can rewrite the optimization problem as a function $f : \mathbb{R}^{r(n_1+n_2+\cdots+n_d)} \to \mathbb{R}$:

$$\begin{aligned} &\min_{\mathbf{v}} \quad f(\mathbf{v}) \equiv \frac{1}{2} \left\| \mathcal{X} - [\![\mathbf{A}_1, \mathbf{A}_2, \ldots, \mathbf{A}_d]\!] \right\|^2, \\ &\text{where} \quad \{\mathbf{A}_1, \mathbf{A}_2, \ldots, \mathbf{A}_d\} = \texttt{vec2mats}(\mathbf{v}). \end{aligned} \qquad (12.5)$$

This transformation between the Kruskal tensor and the vector is usually done "under the hood" and not written out explicitly. In other words, if we write $f(\mathbf{A}_1, \mathbf{A}_2, \ldots, \mathbf{A}_d)$, then we treat f simply as a function of $r(n_1 + n_2 + \cdots + n_d)$ variables and compute its gradients in terms of $f(\mathbf{v})$, where $\mathbf{v} = \texttt{mats2vec}(\mathbf{A}_1, \mathbf{A}_2, \ldots, \mathbf{A}_d)$.

12.2 Gradients for CP

Recall that we stack the vectorized factor matrices to consider f as a function of a vector. The gradient is computed with respect to each (vectorized) factor matrix, and then these are stacked to form the gradient. In the 3-way case, for example, we need to compute

$$\nabla f = \begin{bmatrix} \frac{\partial f}{\partial \operatorname{vec}(\mathbf{A})} \\ \frac{\partial f}{\partial \operatorname{vec}(\mathbf{B})} \\ \frac{\partial f}{\partial \operatorname{vec}(\mathbf{C})} \end{bmatrix} \in \mathbb{R}^{r(m+n+p)}. \tag{12.6}$$

It is convenient to look at each partial gradient separately. We employ colloquial notation so that the gradient is the same shape as the original input, for example,

$$\frac{\partial f}{\partial \mathbf{A}} \equiv \operatorname{reshape}\left(\frac{\partial f}{\partial \operatorname{vec}(\mathbf{A})}, m \times r\right) \quad \text{and, conversely,} \quad \frac{\partial f}{\partial \operatorname{vec}(\mathbf{A})} = \operatorname{vec}\left(\frac{\partial f}{\partial \mathbf{A}}\right).$$

We stress that we are always computing $\frac{\partial f}{\partial \operatorname{vec}(\mathbf{A})}$, regardless of how it is written. We review some relevant matrix calculus before proceeding to compute the gradients for CP.

12.2.1 Preliminaries for Computing CP Gradients

We start by reviewing some multi-variable calculus topics addressed in Section B.1. The **gradient** (Definition B.1) of a function $f : \mathbb{R}^n \to \mathbb{R}$ is a vector of partial derivatives denoted by $\nabla f : \mathbb{R}^n \to \mathbb{R}^n$ and defined by

$$[\nabla f(\mathbf{x})]_i = \frac{\partial f}{\partial x_i} \quad \text{for all} \quad i \in [n].$$

We let $\frac{\partial f}{\partial \mathbf{u}}$ denote the partial gradient of f with respect to a subset of variables $\mathbf{u}$. We restate Proposition B.2 since it will be useful.

Proposition 12.5 (Vector 2-norm Gradient) *Let $f(\mathbf{x}) = \frac{1}{2}\|\mathbf{x}\|_2^2$. Then $\nabla f(\mathbf{x}) = \mathbf{x}$.*

For a vector-valued function $\mathbf{f} : \mathbb{R}^n \to \mathbb{R}^m$, its **Jacobian** (Definition B.5) is the matrix-valued function $D\mathbf{f} : \mathbb{R}^n \to \mathbb{R}^{m \times n}$ defined by

$$[D\mathbf{f}(\mathbf{x})]_{ij} = \frac{\partial f_i}{\partial x_j}(\mathbf{x}) \quad \text{for all} \quad (i,j) \in [m] \otimes [n].$$

We let $\frac{d\mathbf{f}}{d\mathbf{u}}$ denote the partial Jacobian of $\mathbf{f}$ with respect to a subset of variables $\mathbf{u}$.

For a real-valued function $f : \mathbb{R}^n \to \mathbb{R}$, because we follow the convention of column-oriented gradients, we have the property that the gradient is the *transpose* of the Jacobian, i.e., $\nabla f = [Df]^\intercal : \mathbb{R}^n \to \mathbb{R}^n$. Likewise, $\frac{\partial f}{\partial \mathbf{u}} = [\frac{df}{d\mathbf{u}}]^\intercal : \mathbb{R}^n \to \mathbb{R}^n$.

We present one key specialized proposition on the multivariate chain rule (Theorem B.11).

Proposition 12.6 (Specialized Chain Rule) *Let $\mathbf{h} : \mathbb{R}^n \to \mathbb{R}^p$, let $g : \mathbb{R}^p \to \mathbb{R}$, and define $f = g \circ \mathbf{h} : \mathbb{R}^n \to \mathbb{R}$. Then the gradient of $f(\mathbf{x})$ is given by*

$$\nabla f(\mathbf{x}) = \underbrace{[D\mathbf{h}(\mathbf{x})]^\intercal}_{n \times p} \underbrace{\nabla g(\mathbf{h}(\mathbf{x}))}_{p \times 1}.$$

Next, we recall an important property of the Kronecker product from Eq. (A.11e) in Section A.4.3. We present the special case that the first matrix is the identity. For any matrices $\mathbf{X} \in \mathbb{R}^{m \times p}$ and $\mathbf{Y} \in \mathbb{R}^{n \times p}$, we have

$$\text{vec}(\mathbf{X}\mathbf{Y}^\intercal) = \text{vec}(\mathbf{I}_m \mathbf{X}\mathbf{Y}^\intercal) = (\mathbf{Y} \otimes \mathbf{I}_m)\,\text{vec}(\mathbf{X}). \tag{12.7}$$

Lastly, with reference to Definition 2.24, recall that the tensor perfect shuffle permutation $\mathbf{P}_k$ is such that

$$\text{vec}(\mathbf{X}_{(k)}) = \mathbf{P}_k\,\text{vec}(\mathcal{X}). \tag{12.8}$$

Since the mode-1 unfolding is identical to that of the original tensor, we have $\mathbf{P}_1 = \mathbf{I}$.

12.2.2 CP Gradient for 3-way Tensors

To compute the gradient with respect to each factor matrix, we write f in a convenient form for application of the chain rule (Proposition 12.6):

$$f(\mathbf{A},\mathbf{B},\mathbf{C}) = \frac{1}{2}\left\|\mathcal{X} - [\![\mathbf{A},\mathbf{B},\mathbf{C}]\!]\right\|^2 = \frac{1}{2}\left\|\text{vec}(\mathcal{X}) - \text{vec}\big([\![\mathbf{A},\mathbf{B},\mathbf{C}]\!]\big)\right\|_2^2.$$

Before we apply the chain rule, it is useful to compute the Jacobians for the vectorized Kruskal tensors with respect to the factor matrices. These are given below.

Proposition 12.7 (3-way Kruskal Tensor Jacobians) *Let $\mathbf{A} \in \mathbb{R}^{m \times r}$, $\mathbf{B} \in \mathbb{R}^{n \times r}$, and $\mathbf{C} \in \mathbb{R}^{p \times r}$. Then the partial Jacobians of the vectorized Kruskal tensor operation $\mathbf{h}(\mathbf{A},\mathbf{B},\mathbf{C}) = \text{vec}([\![\mathbf{A},\mathbf{B},\mathbf{C}]\!])$ are*

$$\begin{aligned}
\frac{d\mathbf{h}}{d\,\text{vec}(\mathbf{A})} &= \quad (\mathbf{C} \odot \mathbf{B}) \otimes \mathbf{I}_m, \\
\frac{d\mathbf{h}}{d\,\text{vec}(\mathbf{B})} &= \mathbf{P}_2^\intercal\big[(\mathbf{C} \odot \mathbf{A}) \otimes \mathbf{I}_n\big], \quad \textit{and} \\
\frac{d\mathbf{h}}{d\,\text{vec}(\mathbf{C})} &= \mathbf{P}_3^\intercal\big[(\mathbf{B} \odot \mathbf{A}) \otimes \mathbf{I}_p\big],
\end{aligned}$$

where $\mathbf{P}_k$ is the tensor perfect shuffle permutation, such that $\text{vec}(\mathcal{X}) = \mathbf{P}_k^\intercal\,\text{vec}(\mathbf{X}_{(k)})$.

Proof. From the definition of a Jacobian, for a function $\mathbf{f}(\mathbf{v}) = \mathbf{A}\mathbf{v}$, we have $D\mathbf{f} = \mathbf{A}$. Applying Eqs. (12.7) and (12.8), the result follows from rewriting the function in terms of mode-k unfoldings:

$$\begin{aligned}
\text{vec}([\![\mathbf{A},\mathbf{B},\mathbf{C}]\!]) = \quad &\text{vec}\big(\mathbf{A}(\mathbf{C} \odot \mathbf{B})^\intercal\big) = \quad \big[(\mathbf{C} \odot \mathbf{B}) \otimes \mathbf{I}_m\big]\,\text{vec}(\mathbf{A}) \\
= \mathbf{P}_2^\intercal\,&\text{vec}\big(\mathbf{B}(\mathbf{C} \odot \mathbf{A})^\intercal\big) = \mathbf{P}_2^\intercal\big[(\mathbf{C} \odot \mathbf{A}) \otimes \mathbf{I}_n\big]\,\text{vec}(\mathbf{B}) \\
= \mathbf{P}_3^\intercal\,&\text{vec}\big(\mathbf{C}(\mathbf{B} \odot \mathbf{A})^\intercal\big) = \mathbf{P}_3^\intercal\big[(\mathbf{B} \odot \mathbf{A}) \otimes \mathbf{I}_p\big]\,\text{vec}(\mathbf{C}).
\end{aligned}$$ □

Using the result above, it is now possible to derive the gradient for the CP objective function in terms of the factor matrices.

Theorem 12.8 (CP Gradient) *Let* $f(\mathbf{A},\mathbf{B},\mathbf{C}) = \frac{1}{2}\|\mathcal{X} - [\![\mathbf{A},\mathbf{B},\mathbf{C}]\!]\|^2$. *Then its partial gradients are*

$$\frac{\partial f}{\partial \operatorname{vec}(\mathbf{A})} = \operatorname{vec}\big(\mathbf{A}(\mathbf{C}^\intercal\mathbf{C} * \mathbf{B}^\intercal\mathbf{B}) - \mathbf{X}_{(1)}(\mathbf{C} \odot \mathbf{B})\big), \tag{12.9a}$$

$$\frac{\partial f}{\partial \operatorname{vec}(\mathbf{B})} = \operatorname{vec}\big(\mathbf{B}(\mathbf{C}^\intercal\mathbf{C} * \mathbf{A}^\intercal\mathbf{A}) - \mathbf{X}_{(2)}(\mathbf{C} \odot \mathbf{A})\big), \tag{12.9b}$$

$$\frac{\partial f}{\partial \operatorname{vec}(\mathbf{C})} = \operatorname{vec}\big(\mathbf{C}(\mathbf{B}^\intercal\mathbf{B} * \mathbf{A}^\intercal\mathbf{A}) - \mathbf{X}_{(3)}(\mathbf{B} \odot \mathbf{A})\big). \tag{12.9c}$$

Before we provide the proof, we provide an alternative expression as a corollary.

Corollary 12.9 (CP Gradient, Matrix Form) *Let* $f(\mathbf{A},\mathbf{B},\mathbf{C}) = \frac{1}{2}\|\mathcal{X} - [\![\mathbf{A},\mathbf{B},\mathbf{C}]\!]\|^2$. *Its partial gradients can be equivalently expressed as*

$$\frac{\partial f}{\partial \mathbf{A}} = \mathbf{A}(\mathbf{C}^\intercal\mathbf{C} * \mathbf{B}^\intercal\mathbf{B}) - \mathbf{X}_{(1)}(\mathbf{C} \odot \mathbf{B}), \tag{12.10a}$$

$$\frac{\partial f}{\partial \mathbf{B}} = \mathbf{B}(\mathbf{C}^\intercal\mathbf{C} * \mathbf{A}^\intercal\mathbf{A}) - \mathbf{X}_{(2)}(\mathbf{C} \odot \mathbf{A}), \tag{12.10b}$$

$$\frac{\partial f}{\partial \mathbf{C}} = \mathbf{C}(\mathbf{B}^\intercal\mathbf{B} * \mathbf{A}^\intercal\mathbf{A}) - \mathbf{X}_{(3)}(\mathbf{B} \odot \mathbf{A}). \tag{12.10c}$$

Proof of Theorem 12.8. Let us consider computing the partial gradient of f with respect to $\operatorname{vec}(\mathbf{B})$. Define functions $g : \mathbb{R}^{mnp} \to \mathbb{R}$ and $\phi : \mathbb{R}^{r(m+n+p)} \to \mathbb{R}^{mnp}$ as

$$g(\mathbf{v}) = \frac{1}{2}\|\mathbf{v}\|_2^2 \quad \text{and} \quad \phi(\mathbf{A},\mathbf{B},\mathbf{C}) = \operatorname{vec}\big([\![\mathbf{A},\mathbf{B},\mathbf{C}]\!] - \mathcal{X}\big).$$

Then, observing that $f = g \circ \phi$, we compute the gradient via the chain rule. By Proposition 12.5, we have $\nabla g(\mathbf{v}) = \mathbf{v}$. Since $\phi(\mathbf{A},\mathbf{B},\mathbf{C}) = \operatorname{vec}\big([\![\mathbf{A},\mathbf{B},\mathbf{C}]\!]\big) - \operatorname{vec}(\mathcal{X})$ and $\operatorname{vec}(\mathcal{X})$ is a constant, we need only consider the $\operatorname{vec}\big([\![\mathbf{A},\mathbf{B},\mathbf{C}]\!]\big)$ term in computing the Jacobian of ϕ and can apply Proposition 12.7 directly.

Thus,

$$\begin{aligned}
\frac{\partial f}{\partial \operatorname{vec}(\mathbf{B})} &= \left[\frac{d\phi}{d\operatorname{vec}(\mathbf{B})}\right]^\intercal \nabla g(\phi) && \text{by Proposition 12.6} \\
&= \Big(\mathbf{P}_2^\intercal\big[(\mathbf{C}\odot\mathbf{A})\otimes\mathbf{I}_n\big]\Big)^\intercal \operatorname{vec}\big([\![\mathbf{A},\mathbf{B},\mathbf{C}]\!] - \mathcal{X}\big) && \text{by Propositions 12.5 and 12.7} \\
&= \big[(\mathbf{C}\odot\mathbf{A})^\intercal\otimes\mathbf{I}_n\big]\mathbf{P}_2\operatorname{vec}\big([\![\mathbf{A},\mathbf{B},\mathbf{C}]\!] - \mathcal{X}\big) && \text{by Eq. (A.11b)} \\
&= \big[(\mathbf{C}\odot\mathbf{A})^\intercal\otimes\mathbf{I}_n\big]\operatorname{vec}\big(\mathbf{B}(\mathbf{C}\odot\mathbf{A})^\intercal - \mathbf{X}_{(2)}\big) && \text{by Eq. (12.8)} \\
&= \operatorname{vec}\big[\big(\mathbf{B}(\mathbf{C}\odot\mathbf{A})^\intercal - \mathbf{X}_{(2)}\big)(\mathbf{C}\odot\mathbf{A})\big] && \text{by Eq. (12.7)} \\
&= \operatorname{vec}\big[\mathbf{B}(\mathbf{C}^\intercal\mathbf{C} * \mathbf{A}^\intercal\mathbf{A}) - \mathbf{X}_{(2)}(\mathbf{C}\odot\mathbf{A})\big] && \text{by Proposition A.23.}
\end{aligned}$$

Reshaping the result yields Eq. (12.10b). We leave the partial gradients with respect to $\mathbf{A}$ and $\mathbf{C}$ as Exercise 12.1. □

Exercise 12.1 Complete the proof of Theorem 12.8 for $\mathbf{A}$ and $\mathbf{C}$.

Remark 12.10 (Connection between CP-OPT and CP-ALS) The CP-ALS algorithm discussed in Chapter 11 solves for one block of variables at a time. We can alternatively derive CP-ALS from this optimization formulation. Per the first-order optimality conditions (Theorem B.19), any minimizer $f(\mathbf{A}, \mathbf{B}, \mathbf{C})$ with respect to $\mathbf{A}$ will have a zero gradient:

$$\frac{\partial f}{\partial \mathbf{A}} = \mathbf{A}(\mathbf{C}^{\mathsf{T}}\mathbf{C} * \mathbf{B}^{\mathsf{T}}\mathbf{B}) - \mathbf{X}_{(1)}(\mathbf{C} \odot \mathbf{B}) = \mathbf{0}.$$

Solving this is equivalent to solving the linear system

$$\mathbf{A}(\mathbf{C}^{\mathsf{T}}\mathbf{C} * \mathbf{B}^{\mathsf{T}}\mathbf{B}) = \mathbf{X}_{(1)}(\mathbf{C} \odot \mathbf{B}),$$

which is exactly the normal equations for the ALS subproblem to update $\mathbf{A}$; see Eq. (11.3).

The pseudocode for computing the CP function and gradient is shown in Algorithm 12.2. We precompute the norm squared of $\mathcal{X}$ (for a cost of $\mathcal{O}(mnp)$ for dense $\mathcal{X}$) and pass this in as χ. We assume the input is in vectorized form and has to be unpacked via `vec2mats` before computing the function and gradient; likewise, we return the gradient in vectorized form. Recall that the notation $\langle \mathbf{A}, \mathbf{B} \rangle$ for two same-sized matrices $\mathbf{A}$ and $\mathbf{B}$ is the inner product: $\langle \mathbf{A}, \mathbf{B} \rangle = \text{vec}(\mathbf{A})^{\mathsf{T}} \text{vec}(\mathbf{B})$. There are a few minor efficiencies, as follows. We save the $r \times r$ Gram matrices, each of which is used twice is subsequent computations. We save subparts of the gradient with respect to $\mathbf{C}$ for use in calculating f. It is possible to realize further efficiencies since the algorithm is computing a sequence of MTTKRPs; see Section 3.6.2.

Algorithm 12.1 Computing CP Function and Gradient for 3-way Tensor

Require: data tensor $\mathcal{X} \in \mathbb{R}^{m \times n \times p}$, $\chi = \|\mathcal{X}\|^2$, input vector $\mathbf{v} \in \mathbb{R}^{r(m+n+p)}$
Ensure: $f = \frac{1}{2}\left\|\mathcal{X} - [\![\mathbf{A}, \mathbf{B}, \mathbf{C}]\!]\right\|^2$ and $\mathbf{g} = \nabla f$, where $\{\mathbf{A}, \mathbf{B}, \mathbf{C}\} = \texttt{vec2mats}(\mathbf{v})$

function CP-FG($\mathcal{X}$, χ, $\mathbf{v}$)
  $\{\mathbf{A}, \mathbf{B}, \mathbf{C}\} \leftarrow \texttt{vec2mats}(\mathbf{v})$
  $\mathbf{S}_1 \leftarrow \mathbf{A}^{\mathsf{T}}\mathbf{A}$
  $\mathbf{S}_2 \leftarrow \mathbf{B}^{\mathsf{T}}\mathbf{B}$
  $\mathbf{S}_3 \leftarrow \mathbf{C}^{\mathsf{T}}\mathbf{C}$
  $\mathbf{G}_1 \leftarrow \mathbf{A}(\mathbf{S}_3 * \mathbf{S}_2) - \mathbf{X}_{(1)}(\mathbf{C} \odot \mathbf{B})$ ▷ $\mathbf{G}_1 = \frac{\partial f}{\partial \mathbf{A}}$
  $\mathbf{G}_2 \leftarrow \mathbf{B}(\mathbf{S}_3 * \mathbf{S}_1) - \mathbf{X}_{(2)}(\mathbf{C} \odot \mathbf{A})$ ▷ $\mathbf{G}_2 = \frac{\partial f}{\partial \mathbf{B}}$
  $\mathbf{V}_3 \leftarrow \mathbf{S}_2 * \mathbf{S}_1$ ▷ Saving for reuse
  $\mathbf{U}_3 \leftarrow \mathbf{X}_{(3)}(\mathbf{B} \odot \mathbf{A})$ ▷ Saving for reuse
  $\mathbf{G}_3 \leftarrow \mathbf{C}\mathbf{V}_3 - \mathbf{U}_3$ ▷ $\mathbf{G}_3 = \frac{\partial f}{\partial \mathbf{C}}$
  $f \leftarrow \frac{1}{2}\chi - \langle \mathbf{C}, \mathbf{U}_3 \rangle + \frac{1}{2}\langle \mathbf{V}_3, \mathbf{S}_3 \rangle$ ▷ $f = \frac{1}{2}\left\|\mathcal{X} - [\![\mathbf{A}, \mathbf{B}, \mathbf{C}]\!]\right\|^2$
  $\mathbf{g} \leftarrow \texttt{mats2vec}(\mathbf{G}_1, \mathbf{G}_2, \mathbf{G}_3)$
  return $\{f, \mathbf{g}\}$
end function

Exercise 12.2 Compare the computational complexity of one outer iteration of 3-way CP-ALS and computing the gradients as in Algorithm 12.1. Which is more costly?

12.2.3 CP Gradient for d-way Tensors

As in the 3-way case, we can rewrite the objective function in a convenient form for application of the chain rule:

$$f(\mathbf{A}_1, \mathbf{A}_2, \ldots, \mathbf{A}_d) = \frac{1}{2}\Big\|\mathrm{vec}(\mathcal{X}) - \mathrm{vec}(\llbracket \mathbf{A}_1, \mathbf{A}_2, \ldots, \mathbf{A}_d \rrbracket)\Big\|_2^2.$$

The gradient has the form

$$\nabla f = \begin{bmatrix} \frac{\partial f}{\partial\, \mathrm{vec}(\mathbf{A}_1)} \\ \vdots \\ \frac{\partial f}{\partial\, \mathrm{vec}(\mathbf{A}_d)} \end{bmatrix} \in \mathbb{R}^{n_1 r + \cdots + n_d r}.$$

We consider the derivative of f with respect to each factor matrix in the d-way case.

It is first useful to consider the generalization of Proposition 12.7 to the d-way case for computing the Jacobian of the vectorized Kruskal tensor.

Proposition 12.11 (Kruskal Tensor Jacobian, d-way) *Let* $\mathbf{A}_k \in \mathbb{R}^{n_k \times r}$ *for* $k \in [d]$. *The* k*th partial Jacobian of* $\mathbf{h}(\mathbf{A}_1, \mathbf{A}_2, \ldots, \mathbf{A}_d) \equiv \mathrm{vec}(\llbracket \mathbf{A}_1, \mathbf{A}_2, \ldots, \mathbf{A}_d \rrbracket)$ *is*

$$\frac{d\mathbf{h}}{d\,\mathrm{vec}(\mathbf{A}_k)} = \mathbf{P}_k^\intercal \left[(\mathbf{A}_d \odot \cdots \odot \mathbf{A}_{k+1} \odot \mathbf{A}_{k-1} \odot \cdots \odot \mathbf{A}_1) \otimes \mathbf{I}_{n_k} \right] \quad \textit{for all} \quad k \in [d],$$

where $\mathbf{P}_k$ *is the tensor perfect shuffle permutation, such that* $\mathrm{vec}(\mathcal{X}) = \mathbf{P}_k^\intercal \mathrm{vec}(\mathbf{X}_{(k)})$.

Exercise 12.3 Prove Proposition 12.11.

We can follow reasoning analogous to the 3-way case to derive the gradients.

Proposition 12.12: CP Gradient, d-way

Let $f(\mathbf{A}_1, \mathbf{A}_2, \ldots, \mathbf{A}_d) = \frac{1}{2}\|\mathcal{X} - \llbracket \mathbf{A}_1, \mathbf{A}_2, \ldots, \mathbf{A}_d \rrbracket\|^2$. *Then*

$$\frac{\partial f}{\partial\, \mathrm{vec}(\mathbf{A}_k)} = \mathrm{vec}\big(\mathbf{A}_k \mathbf{V}_k - \mathbf{X}_{(k)} \mathbf{Z}_k\big) \quad \textit{or, equivalently,} \quad \frac{\partial f}{\partial \mathbf{A}_k} = \mathbf{A}_k \mathbf{V}_k - \mathbf{X}_{(k)} \mathbf{Z}_k,$$

where

$$\mathbf{Z}_k \equiv \mathbf{A}_d \odot \cdots \odot \mathbf{A}_{k+1} \odot \mathbf{A}_{k-1} \odot \cdots \odot \mathbf{A}_1 \quad \textit{and}$$
$$\mathbf{V}_k \equiv \mathbf{A}_d^\intercal \mathbf{A}_d * \cdots * \mathbf{A}_{k+1}^\intercal \mathbf{A}_{k+1} * \mathbf{A}_{k-1}^\intercal \mathbf{A}_{k-1} * \cdots * \mathbf{A}_1^\intercal \mathbf{A}_1.$$

Exercise 12.4 Prove Proposition 12.12. For the chain rule, use $f = g \circ \phi$ with $g(\mathbf{v}) = \frac{1}{2}\|\mathbf{v}\|^2$ and

$$\phi(\mathbf{A}_1, \mathbf{A}_2, \ldots, \mathbf{A}_d) = \mathrm{vec}(\llbracket \mathbf{A}_1, \mathbf{A}_2, \ldots, \mathbf{A}_d \rrbracket) - \mathrm{vec}(\mathcal{X}).$$

Exercise 12.5 Consider f, $\mathbf{Z}_k$, and $\mathbf{V}_k$ as defined in Proposition 12.12. Suppose that $\|\mathcal{X}\|^2$, $\mathbf{X}_{(k)}$, $\mathbf{Z}_k$, and $\mathbf{V}_k$ have already been computed. How many additional operations does it cost to compute $f(\mathbf{A}_1, \mathbf{A}_2, \ldots, \mathbf{A}_d)$? Hint: $\|\mathcal{X} - \mathcal{Y}\|^2 = \|\mathcal{X}\|^2 + \|\mathcal{Y}\|^2 - 2\langle \mathcal{X}, \mathcal{Y} \rangle$.

Exercise 12.6 (Explicit Weights) Let $f(\boldsymbol{\lambda}, \mathbf{A}_1, \ldots, \mathbf{A}_d) = \frac{1}{2}\left\|\mathcal{X} - [\![\boldsymbol{\lambda}; \mathbf{A}_1, \ldots, \mathbf{A}_d]\!]\right\|^2$. What is $\frac{\partial f}{\partial \mathbf{A}_k}$ and $\frac{\partial f}{\partial \boldsymbol{\lambda}}$?

The pseudocode for computing the CP function and gradient is shown in Algorithm 12.2. We precompute the norm squared of $\mathcal{X}$, for a cost of $\mathcal{O}(\prod_{k=1}^{d} n_k)$ for dense $\mathcal{X}$, and pass this in as X. We assume the input is in vectorized form and has to be unpacked via `vec2mats` before computing the function and gradient; likewise, we return the gradient in vectorized form. Recall that the notation $\langle \mathbf{A}, \mathbf{B} \rangle$ for two same-sized matrices $\mathbf{A}$ and $\mathbf{B}$ is the inner product: $\langle \mathbf{A}, \mathbf{B} \rangle = \text{vec}(\mathbf{A})^\intercal \text{vec}(\mathbf{B})$.

Algorithm 12.2 Computing CP Function and Gradient for d-way Tensor

Require: data tensor $\mathcal{X} \in \mathbb{R}^{n_1 \times n_2 \times \cdots \times n_d}$, $X = \|\mathcal{X}\|$, input vector $\mathbf{v} \in \mathbb{R}^{r(n_1+n_2+\cdots+n_d)}$
Ensure: $f = \frac{1}{2}\|\mathcal{X} - [\![\mathbf{A}_1, \mathbf{A}_2, \ldots, \mathbf{A}_d]\!]\|^2$, where $\{\mathbf{A}_1, \mathbf{A}_2, \ldots, \mathbf{A}_d\} =$ `vec2mats`$(\mathbf{v})$ and $\mathbf{g} = \nabla f$

1: **function** CP-FG($\mathcal{X}$, X, $\mathbf{v}$)
2: $\quad \{\mathbf{A}_1, \mathbf{A}_2, \ldots, \mathbf{A}_d\} \leftarrow$ `vec2mats`$(\mathbf{v})$
3: $\quad$ **for** $k = 1, \ldots, d$ **do**
4: $\quad\quad \mathbf{S}_k \leftarrow \mathbf{A}_k^\intercal \mathbf{A}_k$
5: $\quad$ **end for**
6: $\quad$ **for** $k = 1, \ldots, d$ **do**
7: $\quad\quad \mathbf{U}_k \leftarrow \mathbf{X}_{(k)}(\mathbf{A}_d \odot \cdots \odot \mathbf{A}_{k+1} \odot \mathbf{A}_{k-1} \odot \cdots \odot \mathbf{A}_1)$ ▷ Seq. of MTTKRPs
8: $\quad\quad \mathbf{V}_k \leftarrow \mathbf{S}_d * \cdots * \mathbf{S}_{k+1} * \mathbf{S}_{k-1} * \cdots * \mathbf{S}_1$
9: $\quad\quad \mathbf{G}_k \leftarrow \mathbf{A}_k \mathbf{V}_k - \mathbf{U}_k$ ▷ $\mathbf{G}_k = \frac{\partial f}{\partial \mathbf{A}_k}$
10: $\quad$ **end for**
11: $\quad f \leftarrow \frac{1}{2}X^2 - \langle \mathbf{A}_d, \mathbf{U}_d \rangle + \frac{1}{2}\langle \mathbf{V}_d, \mathbf{S}_d \rangle$ ▷ $f = \frac{1}{2}\left\|\mathcal{X} - [\![\mathbf{A}_1, \ldots, \mathbf{A}_d]\!]\right\|^2$
12: $\quad \mathbf{g} \leftarrow$ `mats2vec`$(\mathbf{G}_1, \mathbf{G}_2, \ldots, \mathbf{G}_d)$
13: $\quad$ **return** $\{f, \mathbf{g}\}$
14: **end function**

Exercise 12.7 Show that Line 11 of Algorithm 12.2 computes the correct function value. (See also Exercise 12.5.)

Exercise 12.8 (Regularization) Let

$$f = \frac{1}{2}\|\mathcal{X} - [\![\mathbf{A}_1, \mathbf{A}_2, \ldots, \mathbf{A}_d]\!]\|^2 + \nu \left(\sum_{k=1}^{d} \|\mathbf{A}_k\|_F^2 \right).$$

What is $\frac{\partial f}{\partial\, \text{vec}(\mathbf{A}_k)}$?

Exercise 12.9 Implement Algorithm 12.2 using existing functions for MTTRKP (or a sequence of MTTKRPs).

12.2.4 Complexity Analysis for Computing CP Gradient

The costs of each line of Algorithm 12.2 for computing the CP function value and gradient are given in Table 12.1. Note the similarity with the costs of an iteration of the CP-ALS algorithm (see Table 11.1 in Section 11.2.3). Before we derive the complexity of each line, we note that the cost of only the MTTKRPs involve the quantity $N = \prod_{k=1}^{d} n_k$, the *product* of tensor dimensions. Other costs are proportional to the *sum* of tensor dimensions

$\sum_{k=1}^{d} n_k$. This is because the MTTKRP is the only operation in the loop that involves the input tensor; therefore, it dominates the computational complexity.

The computation of the Gram matrices in Line 4 costs $\mathcal{O}(r^2 \sum_{k=1}^{d} n_k)$. The MTTKRPs in Line 7 each cost $\mathcal{O}(Nr)$, but reusing intermediate quantities (memoization), as described in Section 3.6.2, reduces the cost by a factor of d. The computation of the Hadamard products in Line 8 costs $\mathcal{O}(d^2 r^2)$. This cost can also be reduced by a factor of $\mathcal{O}(d)$ using Exercise 11.10. Computing the partial gradients using matrix multiplication in Line 9 costs another $\mathcal{O}(r^2 \sum_{k=1}^{d} n_k)$ operation. Given the precomputed quantities for each mode, the CP function value can be computed very cheaply using two matrix inner products with matrices that have dimensions $n_d \times r$ and $r \times r$, respectively, as described in Section 10.7.2. Hence, as $N \gg \sum_{k=1}^{d} n_k$, the MTTKRP computation typically dominates the cost of Algorithm 12.2.

Table 12.1 CP-FG computational complexity for rank-r CP decomposition of dense tensor of size $n_1 \times n_2 \times \cdots \times n_d$ with $N = \prod_{k=1}^{d} n_k$

Calculation	Line(s)	Complexity	See also
Gram	Line 4	$\mathcal{O}(r^2 \sum_{k=1}^{d} n_k)$	Section A.4.1
MTTKRP	Line 7	$\mathcal{O}(Nr)$	Section 3.6.2
Hadamard product	Line 8	$\mathcal{O}(dr^2)$	Exercise 11.10
Gradient assembly	Line 9	$\mathcal{O}(r^2 \sum_{k=1}^{d} n_k)$	Section A.3.6
Function	Line 11	$\mathcal{O}(rn_d + r^2)$	Section 10.7.2

***Remark* 12.13 (Computations with sparse $\mathcal{X}$)** If $\mathcal{X}$ is sparse, then the MTTKRP cost is reduced to $\mathcal{O}(\text{nnz}(\mathcal{X}) r d^2)$; see Section 3.7.

12.3 CP-OPT Method

We have provided the tools for computing the function and gradient, enabling us to use any gradient-based optimization method. We do, however, have some recommendations of appropriate optimization algorithms to use.

A major consideration in choosing an optimization algorithm is its expense per iteration. For simplicity, consider computing the rank-r CP decomposition of a d-way tensor of size $n_1 \times n_2 \times \cdots \times n_d$. The computational complexity of an optimization method depends in part on the number of variables, and for CP we have

$$\text{number of optimization variables} = r \sum_{k=1}^{d} n_k.$$

Any gradient-based algorithm computes the gradient at a cost of $\mathcal{O}(Nr)$, where $N = \prod_{k=1}^{d} n_k$, as described in Section 12.2.4. Thus, methods with computation costs that are linear in the number of variables, such as gradient descent and (limited-memory) quasi-Newton methods, will have per-iteration complexity dominated by the computation of the CP gradient.

We can also consider a method whose storage and computation are quadratic in the number of variables, such as BFGS (see Section B.3.4). Its computation and storage would be proportional to $\mathcal{O}((r\sum_{k=1}^{d} n_k)^2)$. This computational cost is dominated by that of the CP gradient as long as $r(\sum_{k=1}^{d} n_k)^2 < N$, which is a reasonable assumption but certainly not guaranteed. In the case of sparse input tensors, the cost of the CP gradient computation becomes cheaper (proportional to the number of nonzeros), so the quadratic costs of BFGS are more likely to become a bottleneck. This is the reason the less expensive methods are generally recommended.

Gradient descent (see Section B.3.2) is a viable method since its cost per iteration is linear in the number of variables. A limited-memory quasi-Newton method, such as L-BFGS (see Section B.3.5), has cost proportion to m times the number of optimization variables, where m is the limited-memory parameter ($m = 5$ is a typical choice). So the per-iteration cost is still dominated by the gradient computation for this method. L-BFGS generally converges in fewer iterations than gradient descent and is our recommendation for most users. There is also a bound-constrained version, L-BFGS-B (Byrd et al., 1995). Other first-order optimization methods many be considered, such as momentum-based methods or various first-order methods for constrained optimization (see, e.g., Wright and Recht, 2022).

> Limited-memory BFGS (L-BFGS) is the default recommendation for optimization in CP-OPT.

Implementations of the aforementioned methods are readily available, requiring the user to provide a procedure for evaluating the function and gradient. As discussed in Section 12.1, from the point of view of the optimization algorithm, this procedure should take a vector-valued input $\mathbf{v}$ and return the function value $f(\mathbf{v})$ and gradient $\nabla f(\mathbf{v})$. In the 3-way case, we use Algorithm 12.1, and in the d-way case, we use Algorithm 12.2.

Once we are able to compute the function and gradient, we have the basic ingredients for working with an optimization method. There are a few other practical considerations.

Scaling and Stopping Most optimization methods use something like the following conditions to determine when to stop:

1. the relative change in function value is sufficiently small, or
2. the norm of the gradient is sufficiently small.

Both the 2-norm and infinity-norm are popular choices in measuring the gradient. It is important to investigate the settings for these. If they are too loose, the optimization routine may exit prematurely. If they are too tight, it may run much longer than necessary. The relative change in the function value should be insensitive to scaling, but the gradient is not.

Exercise 12.10 Implement Algorithm 12.2 and connect it with a suitable optimization method such as L-BFGS.

12.4 CP-OPT on Data Tensors

We revisit the EEM tensor from Section 9.6. Recall that the EEM tensor, denoted here by $\mathcal{X}$, is of size $18 \times 251 \times 21$. We consider an optimization problem of the form

$$\min_{\mathbf{v} \in \mathbb{R}^{290r}} \quad f(\mathbf{v}) \equiv \left\| \mathcal{X} - [\![\mathbf{A}, \mathbf{B}, \mathbf{C}]\!] \right\|^2 + \nu \|\mathbf{v}\|_2^2,$$
$$\text{where} \quad \{ \mathbf{A}, \mathbf{B}, \mathbf{C} \} = \texttt{vec2mats}(\mathbf{v}) \quad \text{and} \quad \mathbf{v} \geq \ell.$$

Here $\mathbf{v}$ represents the matrices $\mathbf{A}$, $\mathbf{B}$, and $\mathbf{C}$ vectorized and stacked. The constraint $\mathbf{v} \geq \ell$ is to be interpreted elementwise, i.e., every entry to every factor matrix is greater than ℓ. The value ν is the regularization parameter.

> ***Remark* 12.14 (Computational methodology)** For the CP-OPT optimization method, we use L-BFGS-B with the following settings, per Zhu et al. (1997). The memory parameter (`m`) is 5. The maximum number of iterations (`maxIts`) is 1000. The maximum number of total iterations including inner iterations for the line search (`maxTotalIts`) is 10,000. The convergence tolerance depends on two values: the projected gradient tolerance (`pgtol`) is `1e-5` and the function tolerance divided by machine epsilon (`factr`) is `1e-9/eps` or `4.5e6`.

On the EEM tensor, we compare the best of five runs each with $r = 3$, $\nu = 0$, and $\ell = 0$ for the CP-OPT (using L-BFGS-B) solution in Fig. 12.1. Since CP-ALS and CP-OPT are solving the same problem, we do not see a pronounced difference between them on most problems. We see only a tiny difference in the second factor, where the nonnegativity constraint plays a role. You will investigate further in Exercise 12.11.

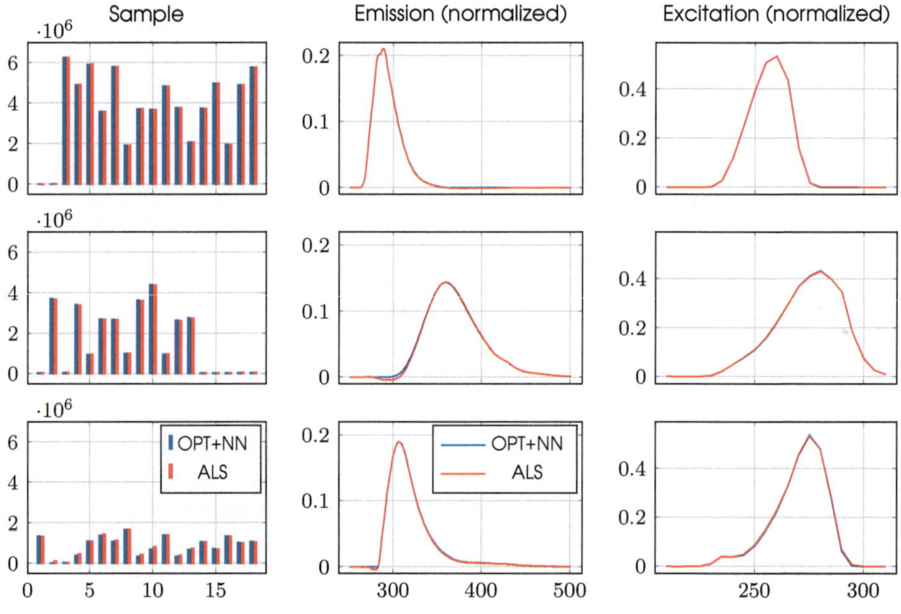

Figure 12.1 CP-OPT, using L-BFGS-B with nonnegativity constraint (NN) and no regularization, versus CP-ALS to compute rank $r = 3$ decomposition of the EEM tensor.

Exercise 12.11 Let us compare some different approaches for computing the rank-3 CP decomposition of the EEM tensor:

- CP-ALS,
- CP-OPT with $\ell = -\infty$ (no lower bound) and $\nu = 0$ (no regularization),
- CP-OPT with $\ell = -\infty$ and $\nu = 10^7$ (regularization),
- CP-OPT with $\ell = 0$ (nonnegativity constraint) and $\nu = 0$, and
- CP-OPT with $\ell = 0$ and $\nu = 10^7$.

Here we recommend CP-OPT with L-BFGS-B and the settings described in Remark 12.14. Run each method five times with different starting points and save the best solution (according to the relative error). (a) How would you *expect* the relative errors to compare? In other words, should adding a nonnegativity constraint lead to a solution with a lower relative error? What about regularization? (b) How do the relative errors actually compare? (c) Visualize the solutions from the different methods. How do they compare?

Regularization plays a more important role in situations where the model rank is larger than the true rank. Since we generally do not know the true rank in advance, this can be important. Figure 12.2 compares CP-OPT (using L-BFGS-B) without and with regularization ($\nu = 10^7$). Both methods use a lower bound of 0. The sample (first) mode is weighted, while the other two modes are normalized to norm 1. Observe that the regularized solution has negligible fourth and fifth components. The emission and excitation components of these factors are relatively strange-looking, but this is irrelevant since they are unimportant. The unregularized solution, on the other hand, has split some of the components. Component 1 has split into components 1 and 4, while component 2 has split into components 2 and 4. The main challenge is choosing the regularization parameter. This is explored further in Exercise 12.12.

Exercise 12.12 Let us compare some different approaches for computing the rank-4 and rank-5 CP decomposition of the EEM tensor:

- CP-ALS,
- CP-OPT with $\ell = -\infty$ (no lower bound) and $\nu = 0$ (no regularization),
- CP-OPT with $\ell = -\infty$ and $\nu = 10^7$ (regularization),
- CP-OPT with $\ell = 0$ (nonnegativity constraint) and $\nu = 0$, and
- CP-OPT with $\ell = 0$ and $\nu = 10^7$.

Here we recommend CP-OPT with L-BFGS-B and the settings described in Remark 12.14. Run each method five times with different starting points and save the best solution (according to the relative error). (a) How would you *expect* the relative errors to compare? In other words, should adding a nonnegativity constraint lead to a solution with a lower relative error? What about regularization? (b) How do the relative errors actually compare? (c) Visualize the solutions from the different methods. How do they compare? (d) What happens for different values of ν, such as 10^6 or 10^8?

Exercise 12.13 (a) Implement a version of d-way CP-OPT for sparse tensors that avoids forming any dense tensors. (b) Apply to the (sparse) Chicago crime dataset to compute a rank-7 decomposition, using lower bounds to constrain the factors to be positive. (Recommend using L-BFGS-B with the settings in Remark 12.14 with the exception that the function tolerance divided by machine epsilon (`factr`) is `1e-4/eps` or `4.5e+11`.) (c) Do the same with an implementation for dense data. (Use the same settings.) (d) How do the sparse and dense implementations compare in terms of runtime?

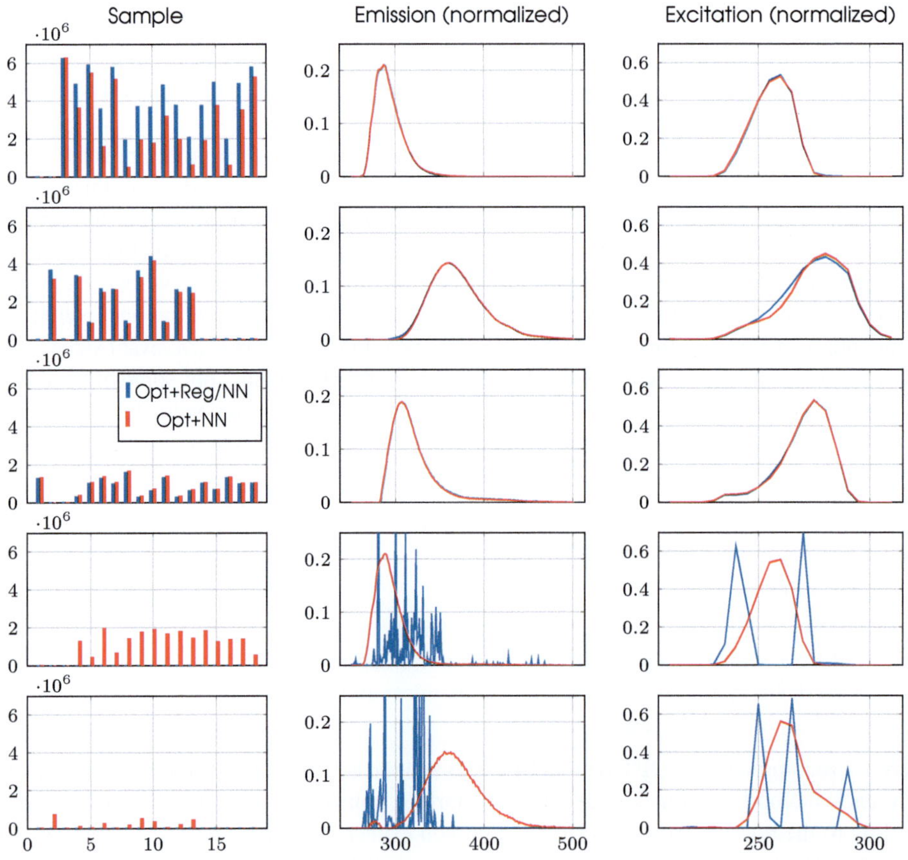

Figure 12.2 Comparison of CP-OPT, using L-BFGS-B with and without regularization, on a rank-5 decomposition of EEM tensor.

13 CP Nonlinear Least Squares Optimization

In this chapter, we consider the nonlinear least squares structure of the CP optimization problem to develop Gauss–Newton methods, which have been in use for CP decomposition since the work of Paatero (1997). We build on Chapter 12, in which we considered gradient-based optimization methods for computing CP. An advantage of a Gauss–Newton method is that it may achieve quadratic convergence, which is superior to the gradient-based methods that achieve only linear or superlinear convergence. However, Gauss–Newton methods require solving a large linear system at each iteration, which can be prohibitively expensive if the system is solved directly, even if the special structure of the CP problem is taken into account (Phan et al., 2013b). However, solving the linear system approximately via an iterative preconditioned conjugate gradient method reduces the cost per iteration to be on par with other gradient-based methods (Sorber et al., 2013; Vervliet and De Lathauwer, 2019), and this is our focus. This class of methods is referred to as CP-NLS.

13.1 CP Nonlinear Least Squares Problem

A nonlinear least squares problem is a structured optimization problem of the form

$$\min_{\mathbf{v}\in\mathbb{R}^n} f(\mathbf{v}) \equiv \frac{1}{2}\,\|\boldsymbol{\phi}(\mathbf{v})\|_2^2, \tag{13.1}$$

where $\boldsymbol{\phi} : \mathbb{R}^n \to \mathbb{R}^m$ is a nonlinear function. As discussed in Section B.3.6, the gradient of f is $\nabla f = \mathbf{J}^\intercal \boldsymbol{\phi}$, where $\mathbf{J} : \mathbb{R}^n \to \mathbb{R}^{n\times m}$ is the Jacobian of $\boldsymbol{\phi}$. A Gauss–Newton optimization method exploits the least squares problem structure by approximating the second-order Hessian $\nabla^2 f$ with a Gauss–Newton matrix $\mathbf{J}^\intercal\mathbf{J}$. It thereby achieves a faster rate of convergence than gradient descent, which uses only first-order information. The basic structure of the method is as follows.

Prototypical Nonlinear Least Squares Method

$\mathbf{v}_0 \leftarrow$ initial guess
repeat $k = 0, 1, \ldots$
  $\lambda_k \leftarrow$ damping parameter for iteration k
  $\mathbf{d}_k \leftarrow$ solution to $\big(\mathbf{J}(\mathbf{v}_k)^\intercal \mathbf{J}(\mathbf{v}_k) + \lambda_k \mathbf{I}\big)\mathbf{d}_k = -\nabla f(\mathbf{v}_k)$
  $\alpha_k \leftarrow$ step length in direction $\mathbf{d}_k$, potentially requiring $f(\mathbf{v}_k + \alpha \mathbf{d}_k)$ and $\nabla f(\mathbf{v}_k + \alpha \mathbf{d}_k)$ for different values of α
  $\mathbf{v}_{k+1} \leftarrow \mathbf{v}_k + \alpha_k \mathbf{d}_k$
until converged

Since the Gauss–Newton matrix $\mathbf{J}^\intercal\mathbf{J}$ can be singular, we add a damping parameter, $\lambda\mathbf{I}$, to enforce positive definiteness. Various strategies can be used for setting the damping parameter λ_k at each iteration, and for performing the line search to determine α_k, similar to the gradient-based optimization methods discussed in Chapter 12. These choices are largely independent of the structure of the CP objective function. We focus our attention on how to solve the Gauss–Newton linear system for the search direction $\mathbf{d}_k$ because we can exploit the CP-specific structure of the problem. Since a direct method such as Cholesky (see Section A.6.4) would be prohibitively expensive, we describe how to solve the linear system iteratively using the preconditioned conjugate gradient method (see Section A.6.4).

13.1.1 CP Jacobian for 3-way Tensors

For a rank-r CP decomposition of a 3-way tensor $\mathcal{X} \in \mathbb{R}^{m \times n \times p}$, the ϕ function in the nonlinear least squares problem in Eq. (13.1) is

$$\phi(\mathbf{v}) = \text{vec}([\![\mathbf{A}, \mathbf{B}, \mathbf{C}]\!] - \mathcal{X}), \quad \text{where} \quad \{\mathbf{A}, \mathbf{B}, \mathbf{C}\} = \texttt{vec2mats}(\mathbf{v}).$$

The transformation `vec2mats` between the vector and matrices is the same as for CP-OPT; see Section 12.1.1.

Consider the Jacobian $\mathbf{J} \equiv D\phi$. If we let $\mathbf{h}(\mathbf{v}) = \text{vec}([\![\mathbf{A}, \mathbf{B}, \mathbf{C}]\!])$, then $\phi(\mathbf{v}) = \mathbf{h}(\mathbf{v}) - \text{vec}(\mathcal{X})$. Since the Jacobian of $\text{vec}(\mathcal{X})$ is zero, the Jacobian of ϕ is simply the Jacobian of $\mathbf{h}$, as given by Proposition 12.7:

$$\mathbf{J} = \begin{bmatrix} \mathbf{J}_{\mathbf{A}} & \mathbf{J}_{\mathbf{B}} & \mathbf{J}_{\mathbf{C}} \end{bmatrix} \in \mathbb{R}^{mnp \times r(m+n+p)}, \tag{13.2a}$$

where

$$\mathbf{J}_{\mathbf{A}} \equiv \frac{d\phi}{d\,\text{vec}(\mathbf{A})} = (\mathbf{C} \odot \mathbf{B}) \otimes \mathbf{I}_m \in \mathbb{R}^{mnp \times rm}, \tag{13.2b}$$

$$\mathbf{J}_{\mathbf{B}} \equiv \frac{d\phi}{d\,\text{vec}(\mathbf{B})} = \mathbf{P}_2^{\mathsf{T}}[(\mathbf{C} \odot \mathbf{A}) \otimes \mathbf{I}_n] \in \mathbb{R}^{mnp \times rn}, \tag{13.2c}$$

$$\mathbf{J}_{\mathbf{C}} \equiv \frac{d\phi}{d\,\text{vec}(\mathbf{C})} = \mathbf{P}_3^{\mathsf{T}}[(\mathbf{B} \odot \mathbf{A}) \otimes \mathbf{I}_p] \in \mathbb{R}^{mnp \times rp}. \tag{13.2d}$$

Recall that $\mathbf{P}_k$ is the tensor perfect shuffle matrix, such that $\text{vec}(\mathcal{X}) = \mathbf{P}_k^{\mathsf{T}} \text{vec}(\mathbf{X}_{(k)})$, and $\mathbf{P}_1$ is not written explicitly because it is the identity matrix.

The Kronecker products with identity matrices and tensor perfect shuffle transformations make the Jacobian highly structured. Figure 13.1 shows the nonzero patterns for different sizes and ranks. Exploiting this structure is key to efficient calculations with the Jacobians.

13.1.2 CP Jacobian for d-way Tensors

Considering a rank-r CP decomposition of a d-way tensor $\mathcal{X} \in \mathbb{R}^{n_1 \times n_2 \times \cdots \times n_d}$, the ϕ function in the nonlinear least squares problem in Eq. (13.1) is

$$\phi(\mathbf{v}) = \text{vec}([\![\mathbf{A}_1, \ldots, \mathbf{A}_d]\!] - \mathcal{X}), \quad \text{where} \quad \{\mathbf{A}_1, \ldots, \mathbf{A}_d\} = \texttt{vec2mats}(\mathbf{v}).$$

The transformation `vec2mats` between the vector and matrices is the same as for CP-OPT; see Section 12.1.2.

To compute the Jacobian $\mathbf{J} \equiv D\phi$, we employ Proposition 12.11, using analogous reasoning to the 3-way case:

$$\mathbf{J} = \begin{bmatrix} \mathbf{J}_1 & \mathbf{J}_2 & \cdots & \mathbf{J}_d \end{bmatrix} \in \mathbb{R}^{(n_1 n_2 \cdots n_d) \times r(n_1+n_2+\cdots+n_d)}, \tag{13.3a}$$

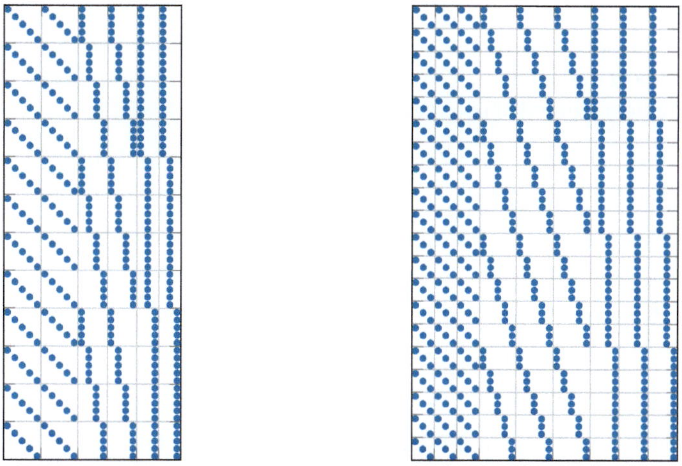

(a) Tensor size $5 \times 4 \times 3$ and CP rank $r = 2$. **(b)** Tensor size $3 \times 5 \times 4$ and CP rank $r = 3$.

Figure 13.1 Nonzero patterns of Jacobians for different sizes and ranks.

where for all $k \in [d]$, we let $\mathbf{J}_k \equiv \frac{d\phi}{d\,\mathrm{vec}(\mathbf{A}_k)}$, and so

$$\mathbf{J}_k = \mathbf{P}_k^\intercal[(\mathbf{A}_d \odot \cdots \odot \mathbf{A}_{k+1} \odot \mathbf{A}_{k-1} \odot \cdots \odot \mathbf{A}_1) \otimes \mathbf{I}_{n_k}] \in \mathbb{R}^{(n_1 n_2 \cdots n_d) \times r n_k}. \quad (13.3b)$$

As before, $\mathbf{P}_k$ is the tensor perfect shuffle matrix, such that $\mathrm{vec}(\mathcal{X}) = \mathbf{P}_k^\intercal \mathrm{vec}(\mathbf{X}_{(k)})$.

13.2 Solving the Gauss–Newton Linear System

At every iteration of a nonlinear least squares method, we have to solve the damped Gauss–Newton linear system of the form:

$$(\mathbf{J}^\intercal \mathbf{J} + \lambda \mathbf{I})\mathbf{d} = -\nabla f. \quad (13.4)$$

This is a linear system of equations in $r(m + n + p)$ variables in the 3-way case and $r(n_1 + n_2 + \cdots n_d)$ variables in the d-way case. The damping parameter $\lambda \geq 0$ is generally chosen to ensure the matrix $\mathbf{J}^\intercal \mathbf{J} + \lambda \mathbf{I}$ is positive definite.

As mentioned in the introduction, Gauss–Newton methods were employed by Paatero (1997). However, even though the number of iterations is typically fewer than for other approaches, a comparison of algorithms by Tomasi and Bro (2006) showed that Gauss–Newton methods can be slow due to the cost of solving Eq. (13.4) with a direct method at every iteration. Phan et al. (2013b) provided more efficient ways to form the inverse of the matrix by exploiting the structure of the CP problem, but this still did not make Gauss–Newton competitive enough with gradient-based methods. However, inexact Gauss–Newton methods, which approximately solve Eq. (13.4) using a preconditioned conjugate gradient method, are much cheaper per iteration and more competitive with other approaches (Sorber et al., 2013; Vervliet and De Lathauwer, 2019).

A preconditioned conjugate gradient method is an iterative method with a per-iteration cost proportional to the cost of multiplying the matrix times a vector. For a dense linear system, iterative methods have cost quadratic in the number of variables per iteration rather than cubic for direct methods, such as Cholesky decomposition. For sparse or structured linear systems, the cost of iterative methods can be even lower. See Section A.6.4 for further details. The linear system in Eq. (13.4) is highly structured, so this makes a preconditioned conjugate gradient method appealing.

In addition to computing the gradient, there are two operations that need to be efficient in order to make preconditioned conjugate gradient methods efficient for solving Eq. (13.4):

1. First, we need to *apply* the approximate Hessian, by which we mean computing the matrix–vector product $(\mathbf{J}^\intercal\mathbf{J} + \lambda\mathbf{I})\bar{\mathbf{v}}$.
2. Second, we need a *preconditioner* $\mathbf{M} \approx \mathbf{J}^\intercal\mathbf{J} + \lambda\mathbf{I}$, such that linear systems of the form $\mathbf{M}\mathbf{x} = \mathbf{y}$ are expeditious to solve.

In the remainder of this chapter, we focus on these operations.

In terms of computational complexity, the cost of computing the gradient is $\mathcal{O}(Nr)$, where $N = \prod_{k=1}^{d} n_k$ (see Section 12.2.4). Each iteration of a preconditioned conjugate gradient method requires an application of the approximate Hessian and an application of the preconditioner. As we will see in Sections 13.2.3 and 13.2.4, the cost of each of these two operations is $\mathcal{O}(r^2 \sum_{k=1}^{d} n_k)$. Thus, each iteration of CP-NLS using inexact Gauss–Newton is dominated by the gradient computation as long as $cr \sum_{k=1}^{d} n_k < N$, where c is the number of preconditioned conjugate gradient iterations.

13.2.1 Applying Approximate CP Hessian for 3-way Tensors

We consider fast computation of $(\mathbf{J}^\intercal\mathbf{J}+\lambda\mathbf{I})\bar{\mathbf{v}}$ for the 3-way case. Rather than forming $\mathbf{J}$ or $\mathbf{J}^\intercal\mathbf{J}$ explicitly, we use the structure of these matrices to compute the matrix–vector product without computing any explicit Kronecker or Khatri–Rao products. From Eq. (13.2a), the block structure of $\mathbf{J}^\intercal\mathbf{J}$ is

$$\mathbf{J}^\intercal\mathbf{J} = \begin{bmatrix} \mathbf{J}_\mathrm{A}^\intercal\mathbf{J}_\mathrm{A} & \mathbf{J}_\mathrm{A}^\intercal\mathbf{J}_\mathrm{B} & \mathbf{J}_\mathrm{A}^\intercal\mathbf{J}_\mathrm{C} \\ \mathbf{J}_\mathrm{B}^\intercal\mathbf{J}_\mathrm{A} & \mathbf{J}_\mathrm{B}^\intercal\mathbf{J}_\mathrm{B} & \mathbf{J}_\mathrm{B}^\intercal\mathbf{J}_\mathrm{C} \\ \mathbf{J}_\mathrm{C}^\intercal\mathbf{J}_\mathrm{A} & \mathbf{J}_\mathrm{C}^\intercal\mathbf{J}_\mathrm{B} & \mathbf{J}_\mathrm{C}^\intercal\mathbf{J}_\mathrm{C} \end{bmatrix}.$$

Consider a vector $\bar{\mathbf{v}} \in \mathbb{R}^{(m+n+p)r}$, and let $\{\, \bar{\mathbf{A}}, \bar{\mathbf{B}}, \bar{\mathbf{C}} \,\} = \texttt{vec2mats}(\bar{\mathbf{v}})$. Then

$$\mathbf{J}^\intercal\mathbf{J}\bar{\mathbf{v}} = \begin{bmatrix} \mathbf{J}_\mathrm{A}^\intercal\mathbf{J}_\mathrm{A}\,\mathrm{vec}(\bar{\mathbf{A}}) + \mathbf{J}_\mathrm{A}^\intercal\mathbf{J}_\mathrm{B}\,\mathrm{vec}(\bar{\mathbf{B}}) + \mathbf{J}_\mathrm{A}^\intercal\mathbf{J}_\mathrm{C}\,\mathrm{vec}(\bar{\mathbf{C}}) \\ \mathbf{J}_\mathrm{B}^\intercal\mathbf{J}_\mathrm{A}\,\mathrm{vec}(\bar{\mathbf{A}}) + \mathbf{J}_\mathrm{B}^\intercal\mathbf{J}_\mathrm{B}\,\mathrm{vec}(\bar{\mathbf{B}}) + \mathbf{J}_\mathrm{B}^\intercal\mathbf{J}_\mathrm{C}\,\mathrm{vec}(\bar{\mathbf{C}}) \\ \mathbf{J}_\mathrm{C}^\intercal\mathbf{J}_\mathrm{A}\,\mathrm{vec}(\bar{\mathbf{A}}) + \mathbf{J}_\mathrm{C}^\intercal\mathbf{J}_\mathrm{B}\,\mathrm{vec}(\bar{\mathbf{B}}) + \mathbf{J}_\mathrm{C}^\intercal\mathbf{J}_\mathrm{C}\,\mathrm{vec}(\bar{\mathbf{C}}) \end{bmatrix}.$$

Consider the structure of one of the terms corresponding to an off-diagonal block of $\mathbf{J}^\intercal\mathbf{J}$:

$$\begin{aligned}
\mathbf{J}_\mathrm{A}^\intercal\mathbf{J}_\mathrm{B}\,\mathrm{vec}(\bar{\mathbf{B}}) &= \mathbf{J}_\mathrm{A}^\intercal\mathbf{P}_2^\intercal\big[(\mathbf{C}\odot\mathbf{A})\otimes\mathbf{I}_n\big]\,\mathrm{vec}(\bar{\mathbf{B}}) && \text{from Eq. (13.2c)} \\
&= \mathbf{J}_\mathrm{A}^\intercal\mathbf{P}_2^\intercal\,\mathrm{vec}\big(\bar{\mathbf{B}}(\mathbf{C}\odot\mathbf{A})^\intercal\big) && \text{from Eq. (A.11e)} \\
&= \mathbf{J}_\mathrm{A}^\intercal\,\mathrm{vec}\big([\![\mathbf{A},\bar{\mathbf{B}},\mathbf{C}]\!]\big) && \text{from definition of } \mathbf{P}_2 \\
&= \mathbf{J}_\mathrm{A}^\intercal\,\mathrm{vec}\big(\mathbf{A}(\mathbf{C}\odot\bar{\mathbf{B}})^\intercal\big) && \text{from Proposition 10.8} \\
&= \big[(\mathbf{C}\odot\mathbf{B})\otimes\mathbf{I}_m\big]^\intercal\,\mathrm{vec}\big(\mathbf{A}(\mathbf{C}\odot\bar{\mathbf{B}})^\intercal\big) && \text{from Eq. (13.2b)} \\
&= \mathrm{vec}\big(\mathbf{A}(\mathbf{C}\odot\bar{\mathbf{B}})^\intercal(\mathbf{C}\odot\mathbf{B})\big) && \text{from Eq. (A.11e)} \\
&= \mathrm{vec}\big(\mathbf{A}(\mathbf{C}^\intercal\mathbf{C} * \bar{\mathbf{B}}^\intercal\mathbf{B})\big) && \text{from Proposition A.23.} \quad (13.5)
\end{aligned}$$

The other eight terms can be simplified similarly (see Exercise 13.1), which means we can compute $\mathbf{J}^\intercal\mathbf{J}$ times a vector efficiently as elucidated in Proposition 13.1.

Proposition 13.1: Applying Gauss–Newton Matrix for 3-way Tensor

For a tensor $\mathcal{X}$ *of size* $m \times n \times p$ *and a same-sized Kruskal tensor* $[\![\mathbf{A}, \mathbf{B}, \mathbf{C}]\!]$ *of rank* r*, let* $\mathbf{J}$ *be the Jacobian of the function* $\phi(\mathbf{v}) = \operatorname{vec}([\![\mathbf{A}, \mathbf{B}, \mathbf{C}]\!] - \mathcal{X})$*, where* $\{\mathbf{A}, \mathbf{B}, \mathbf{C}\} = \texttt{vec2mats}(\mathbf{v})$*. For a vector* $\bar{\mathbf{v}} \in \mathbb{R}^{r(m+n+p)}$*, let* $\{\bar{\mathbf{A}}, \bar{\mathbf{B}}, \bar{\mathbf{C}}\} = \texttt{vec2mats}(\bar{\mathbf{v}})$*. Then*

$$\mathbf{J}^\intercal\mathbf{J}\bar{\mathbf{v}} = \begin{bmatrix} \operatorname{vec}\big(\bar{\mathbf{A}}(\mathbf{B}^\intercal\mathbf{B} * \mathbf{C}^\intercal\mathbf{C}) + \mathbf{A}(\bar{\mathbf{B}}^\intercal\mathbf{B} * \mathbf{C}^\intercal\mathbf{C}) + \mathbf{A}(\mathbf{B}^\intercal\mathbf{B} * \bar{\mathbf{C}}^\intercal\mathbf{C})\big) \\ \operatorname{vec}\big(\mathbf{B}(\bar{\mathbf{A}}^\intercal\mathbf{A} * \mathbf{C}^\intercal\mathbf{C}) + \bar{\mathbf{B}}(\mathbf{A}^\intercal\mathbf{A} * \mathbf{C}^\intercal\mathbf{C}) + \mathbf{B}(\mathbf{A}^\intercal\mathbf{A} * \bar{\mathbf{C}}^\intercal\mathbf{C})\big) \\ \operatorname{vec}\big(\mathbf{C}(\bar{\mathbf{A}}^\intercal\mathbf{A} * \mathbf{B}^\intercal\mathbf{B}) + \mathbf{C}(\mathbf{A}^\intercal\mathbf{A} * \bar{\mathbf{B}}^\intercal\mathbf{B}) + \bar{\mathbf{C}}(\mathbf{A}^\intercal\mathbf{A} * \mathbf{B}^\intercal\mathbf{B})\big) \end{bmatrix}.$$

Exercise 13.1 Prove Proposition 13.1.

Using this structure, Algorithm 13.1 shows how to compute $(\mathbf{J}^\intercal\mathbf{J} + \lambda\mathbf{I})\bar{\mathbf{v}}$. The algorithm takes two vectors as input. The vector $\mathbf{v}$ is the current iterate in the Gauss–Newton method on which the Jacobian $\mathbf{J}$ is based, and the vector $\bar{\mathbf{v}}$ is the vector to be multiplied. The total cost is $\mathcal{O}(r^2(m+n+p))$.

Algorithm 13.1 Applying CP-NLS Approximate Hessian for 3-way Tensor

Require: $\mathbf{v}, \bar{\mathbf{v}} \in \mathbb{R}^{r(m+n+p)}$, where $\mathbf{v}$ determines $\mathbf{J}$ and $\bar{\mathbf{v}}$ is the input vector, $\lambda \geq 0$
Ensure: $\tilde{\mathbf{v}} = (\mathbf{J}^\intercal\mathbf{J} + \lambda\mathbf{I})\bar{\mathbf{v}}$, where $\mathbf{J}$ is the Jacobian of $\phi(\mathbf{v})$

function CP-APPLY-JTJ($\mathbf{v}, \bar{\mathbf{v}}, \lambda, m, n, p, r$)
  $\{\mathbf{A}, \mathbf{B}, \mathbf{C}\} \leftarrow \texttt{vec2mats}(\mathbf{v}, m, n, p, r)$ ▷ Determines Jacobian
  $\{\bar{\mathbf{A}}, \bar{\mathbf{B}}, \bar{\mathbf{C}}\} \leftarrow \texttt{vec2mats}(\bar{\mathbf{v}}, m, n, p, r)$ ▷ Unpack input vector
  $\mathbf{S_A} \leftarrow \mathbf{A}^\intercal\mathbf{A}$
  $\mathbf{S_B} \leftarrow \mathbf{B}^\intercal\mathbf{B}$ } Calculate Gram matrices
  $\mathbf{S_C} \leftarrow \mathbf{C}^\intercal\mathbf{C}$
  $\bar{\mathbf{S}}_\mathbf{A} \leftarrow \bar{\mathbf{A}}^\intercal\mathbf{A}$
  $\bar{\mathbf{S}}_\mathbf{B} \leftarrow \bar{\mathbf{B}}^\intercal\mathbf{B}$ } Calculate cross matrices
  $\bar{\mathbf{S}}_\mathbf{C} \leftarrow \bar{\mathbf{C}}^\intercal\mathbf{C}$
  $\tilde{\mathbf{A}} \leftarrow \bar{\mathbf{A}}(\mathbf{S_B} * \mathbf{S_C} + \lambda\mathbf{I}) + \mathbf{A}(\bar{\mathbf{S}}_\mathbf{B} * \mathbf{S_C} + \mathbf{S_B} * \bar{\mathbf{S}}_\mathbf{C})$
  $\tilde{\mathbf{B}} \leftarrow \bar{\mathbf{B}}(\mathbf{S_A} * \mathbf{S_C} + \lambda\mathbf{I}) + \mathbf{B}(\bar{\mathbf{S}}_\mathbf{A} * \mathbf{S_C} + \mathbf{S_A} * \bar{\mathbf{S}}_\mathbf{C})$ } Calculate result blockwise
  $\tilde{\mathbf{C}} \leftarrow \bar{\mathbf{C}}(\mathbf{S_A} * \mathbf{S_B} + \lambda\mathbf{I}) + \mathbf{C}(\bar{\mathbf{S}}_\mathbf{A} * \mathbf{S_B} + \mathbf{S_A} * \bar{\mathbf{S}}_\mathbf{B})$
  $\tilde{\mathbf{v}} = \texttt{mats2vec}(\tilde{\mathbf{A}}, \tilde{\mathbf{B}}, \tilde{\mathbf{C}})$ ▷ Pack output vector
  return $\tilde{\mathbf{v}}$
end function

13.2.2 Preconditioning in Approximate Gauss–Newton for 3-way Tensors

Preconditioning enables a conjugate gradient linear solver to converge in few iterations. The goal is to find a matrix $\mathbf{M}$ that captures some of the structure of the original matrix while being fast to invert. To choose an appropriate preconditioner, we consider the structure of the Gauss–Newton matrix, elucidated in Proposition 13.2. The proof follows reasoning similar to Sidiropoulos et al. (2017, section VIII).

Proposition 13.2: Explicit Gauss–Newton Matrix for 3-way Tensors

For a tensor $\mathcal{X}$ *of size* $m \times n \times p$ *and a same-sized Kruskal tensor* $[\![\mathbf{A}, \mathbf{B}, \mathbf{C}]\!]$ *of rank* r, *let* $\mathbf{J}$ *be the Jacobian of the function* $\phi(\mathbf{v}) = \text{vec}([\![\mathbf{A}, \mathbf{B}, \mathbf{C}]\!] - \mathcal{X})$, *where* $\{\, \mathbf{A}, \mathbf{B}, \mathbf{C} \,\} =$ `vec2mats`$(\mathbf{v})$. *Then we have*

$$\mathbf{J}^\intercal\mathbf{J} = \begin{bmatrix} (\mathbf{B}^\intercal\mathbf{B} * \mathbf{C}^\intercal\mathbf{C}) \otimes \mathbf{I}_m & (\mathbf{I}_r \otimes \mathbf{A})\mathbf{\Psi}_{\mathbf{C}}(\mathbf{I}_r \otimes \mathbf{B}^\intercal) & (\mathbf{I}_r \otimes \mathbf{A})\mathbf{\Psi}_{\mathbf{B}}(\mathbf{I}_r \otimes \mathbf{C}^\intercal) \\ (\mathbf{I}_r \otimes \mathbf{B})\mathbf{\Psi}_{\mathbf{C}}(\mathbf{I}_r \otimes \mathbf{A}^\intercal) & (\mathbf{A}^\intercal\mathbf{A} * \mathbf{C}^\intercal\mathbf{C}) \otimes \mathbf{I}_n & (\mathbf{I}_r \otimes \mathbf{B})\mathbf{\Psi}_{\mathbf{A}}(\mathbf{I}_r \otimes \mathbf{C}^\intercal) \\ (\mathbf{I}_r \otimes \mathbf{C})\mathbf{\Psi}_{\mathbf{B}}(\mathbf{I}_r \otimes \mathbf{A}^\intercal) & (\mathbf{I}_r \otimes \mathbf{C})\mathbf{\Psi}_{\mathbf{A}}(\mathbf{I}_r \otimes \mathbf{B}^\intercal) & (\mathbf{A}^\intercal\mathbf{A} * \mathbf{B}^\intercal\mathbf{B}) \otimes \mathbf{I}_p \end{bmatrix},$$

where for any matrix $\mathbf{X}$ *with* r *columns, we define* $\mathbf{\Psi}_{\mathbf{X}} = \mathbf{P}_{r,r}\,\text{diag}(\text{vec}(\mathbf{X}^\intercal\mathbf{X}))$ *and* $\mathbf{P}_{r,r}$ *is the* (r,r)*-perfect shuffle matrix of size* $r^2 \times r^2$.

Proof. The expressions for the blocks of $\mathbf{J}^\intercal\mathbf{J}$ can be verified by applying them to arbitrary vectors and comparing the results to successive application of partial Jacobians as described in Section 13.2.1. For example, to verify $\mathbf{J}_{\mathbf{A}}^\intercal\mathbf{J}_{\mathbf{B}} = (\mathbf{I}_r \otimes \mathbf{A})\mathbf{\Psi}_{\mathbf{C}}(\mathbf{I}_r \otimes \mathbf{B}^\intercal)$, we consider for an arbitrary $\bar{\mathbf{B}}$,

$$\begin{aligned} &(\mathbf{I}_r \otimes \mathbf{A})\mathbf{\Psi}_{\mathbf{C}}(\mathbf{I}_r \otimes \mathbf{B}^\intercal)\,\text{vec}(\bar{\mathbf{B}}) \\ &\quad = (\mathbf{I}_r \otimes \mathbf{A})\mathbf{\Psi}_{\mathbf{C}}\,\text{vec}(\mathbf{B}^\intercal\bar{\mathbf{B}}) && \text{from Eq. (A.11e)} \\ &\quad = (\mathbf{I}_r \otimes \mathbf{A})\mathbf{P}_{r,r}\,\text{diag}(\text{vec}(\mathbf{C}^\intercal\mathbf{C}))\,\text{vec}(\mathbf{B}^\intercal\bar{\mathbf{B}}) && \text{from definition of } \mathbf{\Psi}_{\mathbf{C}} \\ &\quad = (\mathbf{I}_r \otimes \mathbf{A})\mathbf{P}_{r,r}\,\text{vec}(\mathbf{C}^\intercal\mathbf{C} * \mathbf{B}^\intercal\bar{\mathbf{B}}) && \text{from Exercise A.25} \\ &\quad = (\mathbf{I}_r \otimes \mathbf{A})\,\text{vec}(\mathbf{C}^\intercal\mathbf{C} * \bar{\mathbf{B}}^\intercal\mathbf{B}) && \text{from Definition A.10} \\ &\quad = \text{vec}(\mathbf{A}(\mathbf{C}^\intercal\mathbf{C} * \bar{\mathbf{B}}^\intercal\mathbf{B})) && \text{from Eq. (A.11e),} \end{aligned}$$

which matches Eq. (13.5). The remainder of the proof follows the same reasoning and so is omitted. □

Our goal is to choose a preconditioner $\mathbf{M} \approx \mathbf{J}^\intercal\mathbf{J} + \lambda\mathbf{I}$ such that computing $\mathbf{M}^{-1}\bar{\mathbf{v}}$ is expeditious for an arbitrary vector $\bar{\mathbf{v}}$. Let $\{\, \mathbf{A}_{\bar{\mathbf{v}}}, \mathbf{B}_{\bar{\mathbf{v}}}, \mathbf{C}_{\bar{\mathbf{v}}} \,\} =$ `vec2mats`$(\bar{\mathbf{v}})$. The structure of $\mathbf{J}^\intercal\mathbf{J}$ hints at an effective block-diagonal preconditioner. For instance, the first diagonal block of $\mathbf{J}^\intercal\mathbf{J} + \lambda\mathbf{I}_{r(m+n+p)}$ is

$$\mathbf{J}_{\mathbf{A}}^\intercal\mathbf{J}_{\mathbf{A}} + \lambda\mathbf{I}_{mr} = (\mathbf{B}^\intercal\mathbf{B} * \mathbf{C}^\intercal\mathbf{C}) \otimes \mathbf{I}_m + \lambda\mathbf{I}_{mr} = (\mathbf{B}^\intercal\mathbf{B} * \mathbf{C}^\intercal\mathbf{C} + \lambda\mathbf{I}_r) \otimes \mathbf{I}_m.$$

It is efficient to apply the inverse of this to the first block component of $\bar{\mathbf{v}}$:

$$\begin{aligned} &((\mathbf{B}^\intercal\mathbf{B} * \mathbf{C}^\intercal\mathbf{C} + \lambda\mathbf{I}_r) \otimes \mathbf{I}_m)^{-1}\,\text{vec}(\mathbf{A}_{\bar{\mathbf{v}}}) \\ &\qquad = ((\mathbf{B}^\intercal\mathbf{B} * \mathbf{C}^\intercal\mathbf{C} + \lambda\mathbf{I}_r)^{-1} \otimes \mathbf{I}_m)\,\text{vec}(\mathbf{A}_{\bar{\mathbf{v}}}) && \text{by Eq. (A.11c)} \\ &\qquad = \text{vec}(\mathbf{A}_{\bar{\mathbf{v}}}(\mathbf{B}^\intercal\mathbf{B} * \mathbf{C}^\intercal\mathbf{C} + \lambda\mathbf{I}_r)^{-1}) && \text{by Eq. (A.11e).} \end{aligned}$$

Applying the inverse of the diagonal block amounts to a Cholesky decomposition of the $r \times r$ matrix $\mathbf{B}^\intercal\mathbf{B} * \mathbf{C}^\intercal\mathbf{C} + \lambda\mathbf{I}_r$ (which needs to happen only once and can be used repeatedly for different values of $\bar{\mathbf{v}}$ in the iterative linear solve) and $2m$ triangular solves with the Cholesky factor (per value of $\bar{\mathbf{v}}$). In fact, applying the inverse of $\mathbf{J}_{\mathbf{A}}^\intercal\mathbf{J}_{\mathbf{A}} + \lambda\mathbf{I}_{mr}$ is the same computational cost as solving the normal equations to update $\mathbf{A}$ in a CP-ALS subiteration (see Eq. (11.3)), though with a slightly modified coefficient matrix and different right-hand-side matrix. Applying the inverses of $\mathbf{J}_{\mathbf{B}}^\intercal\mathbf{J}_{\mathbf{B}} + \lambda\mathbf{I}_{nr}$ and $\mathbf{J}_{\mathbf{C}}^\intercal\mathbf{J}_{\mathbf{C}} + \lambda\mathbf{I}_{pr}$ can be done similarly.

Hence, the block diagonal of $\mathbf{J}^\intercal\mathbf{J} + \lambda\mathbf{I}_{r(m+n+p)}$, given by

$$\mathbf{M} = \begin{bmatrix} (\mathbf{B}^\intercal\mathbf{B} * \mathbf{C}^\intercal\mathbf{C} + \lambda\mathbf{I}_r) \otimes \mathbf{I}_m & 0 & 0 \\ 0 & (\mathbf{A}^\intercal\mathbf{A} * \mathbf{C}^\intercal\mathbf{C} + \lambda\mathbf{I}_r) \otimes \mathbf{I}_n & 0 \\ 0 & 0 & (\mathbf{A}^\intercal\mathbf{A} * \mathbf{B}^\intercal\mathbf{B} + \lambda\mathbf{I}_r) \otimes \mathbf{I}_p \end{bmatrix},$$

is a good preconditioner because

$$\mathbf{M}^{-1}\bar{\mathbf{v}} = \begin{bmatrix} \operatorname{vec}\big(\mathbf{A}_{\bar{\mathbf{v}}}(\mathbf{B}^\intercal\mathbf{B} * \mathbf{C}^\intercal\mathbf{C} + \lambda\mathbf{I}_r)^{-1}\big) \\ \operatorname{vec}\big(\mathbf{B}_{\bar{\mathbf{v}}}(\mathbf{A}^\intercal\mathbf{A} * \mathbf{C}^\intercal\mathbf{C} + \lambda\mathbf{I}_r)^{-1}\big) \\ \operatorname{vec}\big(\mathbf{C}_{\bar{\mathbf{v}}}(\mathbf{A}^\intercal\mathbf{A} * \mathbf{B}^\intercal\mathbf{B} + \lambda\mathbf{I}_r)^{-1}\big) \end{bmatrix}.$$

Thus, with very little extra cost per conjugate gradient iteration, we can accelerate its convergence and reduce the cost of each Gauss–Newton linear solve.

13.2.3 Applying Approximate CP Hessian for d-way Tensors

We consider fast computation of $(\mathbf{J}^\intercal\mathbf{J} + \lambda\mathbf{I})\bar{\mathbf{v}}$ for the d-way case, where $\mathbf{J}$ has the structure in Eq. (13.3). As in the 3-way case, we use the structure of these matrices to compute the matrix–vector product without computing any explicit Kronecker or Khatri–Rao products.

The Gauss–Newton matrix $\mathbf{J}^\intercal\mathbf{J}$ can be expressed blockwise as

$$\mathbf{J}^\intercal\mathbf{J} = \begin{bmatrix} \mathbf{J}_1^\intercal\mathbf{J}_1 & \mathbf{J}_1^\intercal\mathbf{J}_2 & \cdots & \mathbf{J}_1^\intercal\mathbf{J}_d \\ \mathbf{J}_2^\intercal\mathbf{J}_1 & \mathbf{J}_2^\intercal\mathbf{J}_2 & \cdots & \mathbf{J}_2^\intercal\mathbf{J}_d \\ \vdots & \vdots & \ddots & \vdots \\ \mathbf{J}_d^\intercal\mathbf{J}_1 & \mathbf{J}_d^\intercal\mathbf{J}_2 & \cdots & \mathbf{J}_d^\intercal\mathbf{J}_d \end{bmatrix}.$$

The (k,ℓ) block has size $rn_k \times rn_\ell$.

We can compute $\mathbf{J}^\intercal\mathbf{J}$ times a vector $\bar{\mathbf{v}}$ of length $r(n_1 + n_2 + \cdots + n_d)$ as follows. Let $\{\bar{\mathbf{A}}_1, \bar{\mathbf{A}}_2, \dots, \bar{\mathbf{A}}_d\} = \texttt{vec2mats}(\bar{\mathbf{v}})$ so that $\bar{\mathbf{A}}_k \in \mathbb{R}^{n_k \times r}$. Then we have

$$\mathbf{J}^\intercal\mathbf{J}\bar{\mathbf{v}} = \begin{bmatrix} \mathbf{J}_1^\intercal\mathbf{J}_1 \operatorname{vec}(\bar{\mathbf{A}}_1) + \mathbf{J}_1^\intercal\mathbf{J}_2 \operatorname{vec}(\bar{\mathbf{A}}_2) + \cdots + \mathbf{J}_1^\intercal\mathbf{J}_d \operatorname{vec}(\bar{\mathbf{A}}_d) \\ \mathbf{J}_2^\intercal\mathbf{J}_1 \operatorname{vec}(\bar{\mathbf{A}}_1) + \mathbf{J}_2^\intercal\mathbf{J}_2 \operatorname{vec}(\bar{\mathbf{A}}_2) + \cdots + \mathbf{J}_2^\intercal\mathbf{J}_d \operatorname{vec}(\bar{\mathbf{A}}_d) \\ \vdots \\ \mathbf{J}_d^\intercal\mathbf{J}_1 \operatorname{vec}(\bar{\mathbf{A}}_1) + \mathbf{J}_d^\intercal\mathbf{J}_2 \operatorname{vec}(\bar{\mathbf{A}}_2) + \cdots + \mathbf{J}_d^\intercal\mathbf{J}_d \operatorname{vec}(\bar{\mathbf{A}}_d) \end{bmatrix}. \tag{13.6}$$

We consider how to efficiently compute terms of the forms $\mathbf{J}_k^\intercal\mathbf{J}_k \operatorname{vec}(\bar{\mathbf{A}}_k)$ and $\mathbf{J}_k^\intercal\mathbf{J}_\ell \operatorname{vec}(\bar{\mathbf{A}}_\ell)$. To do this, we define some useful quantities. We first have Khatri–Rao products:

$$\mathbf{Z}_k = \bigodot_{\substack{h=d \\ h\neq k}}^{1} \mathbf{A}_h, \quad \mathbf{Z}_{k,\ell} = \bigodot_{\substack{h=d \\ h\neq k,\ell}}^{1} \mathbf{A}_h, \quad \text{and} \quad \bar{\mathbf{Z}}_{k,\ell} = \bigodot_{\substack{h=d \\ h\neq k}}^{\ell+1} \mathbf{A}_h \odot \bar{\mathbf{A}}_\ell \odot \bigodot_{\substack{h=\ell-1 \\ h\neq k}}^{1} \mathbf{A}_h. \tag{13.7}$$

The matrix $\mathbf{Z}_k$ is the Khatri–Rao product of all factor matrices except the kth, and we have used this notation before in discussing CP-ALS and CP-OPT. The matrix $\mathbf{Z}_{k,\ell}$ is the Khatri–Rao product of all factor matrices except the kth and the ℓth. Finally, the matrix

$\bar{\mathbf{Z}}_{k,\ell}$ is the same size as $\mathbf{Z}_k$ and is the Khatri–Rao of all factor matrices except the k and with $\bar{\mathbf{A}}_\ell$ swapped in for $\mathbf{A}_\ell$.

Further, we define some analogous Hadamard products:

$$\mathbf{V}_k = \mathop{\Large\ast}_{\substack{h=1\\h\neq k}}^{d} \mathbf{A}_h^\intercal \mathbf{A}_h, \quad \mathbf{V}_{k,\ell} = \mathop{\Large\ast}_{\substack{h=1\\h\neq k,\ell}}^{d} \mathbf{A}_h^\intercal \mathbf{A}_h, \quad \text{and} \quad \bar{\mathbf{V}}_{k,\ell} = \mathbf{V}_{k,\ell} \ast \bar{\mathbf{A}}_\ell^\intercal \mathbf{A}_\ell. \tag{13.8}$$

These matrices come from products of the $\mathbf{Z}$ matrices, as shown in Exercise 13.2.

Exercise 13.2 Show the following:

$$\mathbf{V}_k = \mathbf{Z}_k^\intercal \mathbf{Z}_k, \quad \mathbf{V}_{k,\ell} = \mathbf{Z}_{k,\ell}^\intercal \mathbf{Z}_{k,\ell}, \quad \text{and} \quad \bar{\mathbf{V}}_{k,\ell} = \bar{\mathbf{Z}}_{k,\ell}^\intercal \mathbf{Z}_k.$$

Hint: Use Proposition A.23.

Proposition 13.3: Applying Gauss–Newton Matrix for d-way Tensor

For a tensor $\mathcal{X}$ of size $n_1 \times n_2 \times \cdots \times n_d$ and a same-sized Kruskal tensor $[\![\mathbf{A}_1, \mathbf{A}_2, \ldots, \mathbf{A}_d]\!]$ of rank r, let $\mathbf{J}$ be the Jacobian of the function

$$\phi(\mathbf{v}) = \text{vec}([\![\mathbf{A}_1, \mathbf{A}_2, \ldots, \mathbf{A}_d]\!] - \mathcal{X}), \quad \textit{where} \quad \{\, \mathbf{A}_1, \mathbf{A}_2, \ldots, \mathbf{A}_d \,\} = \texttt{vec2mats}(\mathbf{v}).$$

For a vector $\bar{\mathbf{v}} \in \mathbb{R}^{r(n_1+n_2+\cdots+n_d)}$, let $\{\, \bar{\mathbf{A}}_1, \bar{\mathbf{A}}_2, \ldots, \bar{\mathbf{A}}_d \,\} = \texttt{vec2mats}(\bar{\mathbf{v}})$. Then

$$\mathbf{J}^\intercal \mathbf{J} \bar{\mathbf{v}} = \begin{bmatrix} \text{vec}\big(\bar{\mathbf{A}}_1 \mathbf{V}_1 + \mathbf{A}_1 \bar{\mathbf{V}}_{1,2} + \cdots + \mathbf{A}_1 \bar{\mathbf{V}}_{1,d}\big) \\ \text{vec}\big(\mathbf{A}_2 \bar{\mathbf{V}}_{2,1} + \bar{\mathbf{A}}_2 \mathbf{V}_2 + \cdots + \mathbf{A}_2 \bar{\mathbf{V}}_{2,d}\big) \\ \vdots \\ \text{vec}\big(\mathbf{A}_d \bar{\mathbf{V}}_{d,1} + \mathbf{A}_d \bar{\mathbf{V}}_{d,2} + \cdots + \bar{\mathbf{A}}_d \mathbf{V}_d\big) \end{bmatrix},$$

where $\mathbf{V}_k$ and $\bar{\mathbf{V}}_{k,\ell}$ are the $r \times r$ matrices defined in Eq. (13.8).

Proof. Using Eq. (13.6), we show that each summand in the vectorized blocks has the right form, i.e., considering each $\mathbf{J}_k^\intercal \mathbf{J}_\ell \,\text{vec}(\bar{\mathbf{A}}_\ell)$. For $k = \ell$, we have

$$\begin{aligned} \mathbf{J}_k^\intercal \mathbf{J}_k \,\text{vec}(\bar{\mathbf{A}}_k) &= (\mathbf{Z}_k^\intercal \otimes \mathbf{I}_{n_k}) \mathbf{P}_k \mathbf{P}_k^\intercal (\mathbf{Z}_k \otimes \mathbf{I}_{n_k}) \,\text{vec}(\bar{\mathbf{A}}_k) && \text{from Eqs. (A.11b) and (13.3)} \\ &= (\mathbf{Z}_k^\intercal \otimes \mathbf{I}_{n_k}) \,\text{vec}(\bar{\mathbf{A}}_k \mathbf{Z}_k^\intercal) && \text{from Eq. (A.11e) and } \mathbf{P}_k \mathbf{P}_k^\intercal = \mathbf{I} \\ &= \text{vec}(\bar{\mathbf{A}}_k \mathbf{Z}_k^\intercal \mathbf{Z}_k) && \text{from Eq. (A.11e)} \\ &= \text{vec}(\bar{\mathbf{A}}_k \mathbf{V}_k) && \text{from Exercise 13.2.} \end{aligned}$$

For $k \neq \ell$, we have

$$\begin{aligned} \mathbf{J}_k^\intercal \mathbf{J}_\ell \,\text{vec}(\bar{\mathbf{A}}_\ell) &= (\mathbf{Z}_k^\intercal \otimes \mathbf{I}_{n_k}) \mathbf{P}_k \mathbf{P}_\ell^\intercal (\mathbf{Z}_\ell \otimes \mathbf{I}_{n_\ell}) \,\text{vec}(\bar{\mathbf{A}}_\ell) && \text{from Eqs. (A.11b) and (13.3)} \\ &= (\mathbf{Z}_k^\intercal \otimes \mathbf{I}_{n_k}) \mathbf{P}_k \mathbf{P}_\ell^\intercal \,\text{vec}(\bar{\mathbf{A}}_\ell \mathbf{Z}_\ell^\intercal) && \text{from Eq. (A.11e)} \\ &= (\mathbf{Z}_k^\intercal \otimes \mathbf{I}_{n_k}) \,\text{vec}(\mathbf{A}_k \bar{\mathbf{Z}}_{k,\ell}^\intercal) && \text{from Exercise 13.3 and Eq. (13.3)} \\ &= \text{vec}(\mathbf{A}_k \bar{\mathbf{Z}}_{k,\ell}^\intercal \mathbf{Z}_k) && \text{from Eq. (A.11e)} \\ &= \text{vec}(\mathbf{A}_k \bar{\mathbf{V}}_{k,\ell}) && \text{from Exercise 13.2.} \end{aligned}$$

Hence, the claim. □

Exercise 13.3 Let $\mathcal{T} = [\![\mathbf{A}_1, \mathbf{A}_2, \ldots, \mathbf{A}_d]\!]$. For $k \in [d]$, let $\mathbf{P}_k$ be the tensor perfect shuffle matrix, such that $\text{vec}(\mathcal{T}) = \mathbf{P}_k^{\mathsf{T}} \text{vec}(\mathbf{T}_{(k)})$. Show

$$\begin{aligned}\text{vec}\big(\mathbf{A}_k(\mathbf{A}_d \odot \cdots \odot \mathbf{A}_{k+1} \odot \mathbf{A}_{k-1} \odot \cdots \odot \mathbf{A}_1)^{\mathsf{T}}\big) \\ = \mathbf{P}_k \mathbf{P}_\ell^{\mathsf{T}} \text{vec}\big(\mathbf{A}_\ell(\mathbf{A}_d \odot \cdots \odot \mathbf{A}_{\ell+1} \odot \mathbf{A}_{\ell-1} \odot \cdots \odot \mathbf{A}_1)^{\mathsf{T}}\big).\end{aligned}$$

Using the structure of $\mathbf{J}^{\mathsf{T}}\mathbf{J}\bar{\mathbf{v}}$ in Proposition 13.3, Algorithm 13.2 shows how to compute $(\mathbf{J}^{\mathsf{T}}\mathbf{J} + \lambda\mathbf{I})\bar{\mathbf{v}}$. The algorithm takes two vectors as input. The vector $\mathbf{v}$ is the current iterate in the Gauss–Newton method at which the Jacobian is evaluated, and the vector $\bar{\mathbf{v}}$ is the vector to be multiplied.

Algorithm 13.2 Applying CP-NLS Approximate Hessian for d-way Tensor

Require: $\mathbf{v}, \bar{\mathbf{v}} \in \mathbb{R}^{r(n_1+n_2+\cdots+n_d)}$, where $\mathbf{v}$ determines Jacobian, $\bar{\mathbf{v}}$ is input vector, $\lambda \geq 0$
Ensure: $\tilde{\mathbf{v}} = (\mathbf{J}^{\mathsf{T}}\mathbf{J} + \lambda\mathbf{I})\bar{\mathbf{v}}$, where $\mathbf{J}$ is the Jacobian of $\phi(\mathbf{v})$

1: **function** CP-APPLY-JTJ($\mathbf{v}, \bar{\mathbf{v}}, \lambda, n_1, n_2, \ldots, n_d, r$)
2: $\quad \{\mathbf{A}_1, \mathbf{A}_2, \ldots, \mathbf{A}_d\} =$ `vec2mats`$(\mathbf{v}, n_1, n_2, \ldots, n_d, r)$ ▷ Determines Jacobian
3: $\quad \{\bar{\mathbf{A}}_1, \bar{\mathbf{A}}_2, \ldots, \bar{\mathbf{A}}_d\} =$ `vec2mats`$(\bar{\mathbf{v}}, n_1, n_2, \ldots, n_d, r)$ ▷ Unpack input vector
4: $\quad$ **for** $k = 1, \ldots, d$ **do**
5: $\quad\quad \mathbf{S}_k \leftarrow \mathbf{A}_k^{\mathsf{T}}\mathbf{A}_k$ ▷ Calculate Gram matrices
6: $\quad\quad \bar{\mathbf{S}}_k \leftarrow \bar{\mathbf{A}}_k^{\mathsf{T}}\mathbf{A}_k$ ▷ Calculate cross matrices
7: $\quad$ **end for**
8: $\quad$ **for** $k = 1, \ldots, d$ **do**
9: $\quad\quad \mathbf{V}_k \leftarrow \ast_{h \neq k} \mathbf{S}_h$ ▷ "Diagonal" factor
10: $\quad\quad \bar{\mathbf{V}}_k \leftarrow \mathbf{0}_{r \times r}$
11: $\quad\quad$ **for** $\ell = 1, \ldots, k-1, k+1, \ldots, d$ **do**
12: $\quad\quad\quad \bar{\mathbf{V}}_{k,\ell} \leftarrow \ast_{h \neq k,\ell} \mathbf{S}_h \ast \bar{\mathbf{S}}_\ell$
13: $\quad\quad\quad \bar{\mathbf{V}}_k \leftarrow \bar{\mathbf{V}}_k + \bar{\mathbf{V}}_{k,\ell}$ ▷ Accumulate "off-diagonal" factors
14: $\quad\quad$ **end for**
15: $\quad\quad \tilde{\mathbf{A}}_k \leftarrow \bar{\mathbf{A}}_k(\mathbf{V}_k + \lambda\mathbf{I}_r) + \mathbf{A}_k\bar{\mathbf{V}}_k$
16: $\quad$ **end for**
17: $\quad \tilde{\mathbf{v}} =$ `mats2vec`$(\tilde{\mathbf{A}}_1, \tilde{\mathbf{A}}_2, \ldots, \tilde{\mathbf{A}}_d)$ ▷ Pack output vector
18: $\quad$ **return** $\tilde{\mathbf{v}}$
19: **end function**

Exercise 13.4 Implement Algorithm 13.2.

Complexity Analysis

Lines 5, 6, and 15 involve multiplying matrices of size $n_k \times r$ and $r \times r$ in mode k. Thus, the cost of each line is $\mathcal{O}(r^2 \sum_{k=1}^{d} n_k)$ for one application of the approximate Hessian.

In computing the Hadamard products, Line 9 costs $\mathcal{O}(d^2 r^2)$ and Line 12 has a cost of $\mathcal{O}(d^3 r^2)$. Memoization can reduce both of these costs by a factor of $\mathcal{O}(d)$ (see Exercise 11.10 for Line 9).

The total cost is thus dominated by $\mathcal{O}(r^2 \sum_{k=1}^{d} n_k)$. The computations involving only the current iterate in the Gauss–Newton method (vector $\mathbf{v}$) do not vary over conjugate gradient iterations. So Lines 5 and 9 can be avoided by precomputing those quantities and passing them into the function, which reduces the computational cost of Algorithm 13.2 by a constant factor.

13.2.4 Preconditioning in Approximate Gauss–Newton for d-way Tensors

We consider preconditioning in the d-way case, first identifying the explicit Gauss–Newton matrix in Proposition 13.4.

Proposition 13.4: Explicit Gauss–Newton Matrix for d-way Tensors

For a tensor $\mathcal{X}$ of size $n_1 \times n_2 \times \cdots \times n_d$ and a same-sized Kruskal tensor $[\![\mathbf{A}_1, \mathbf{A}_2, \ldots, \mathbf{A}_d]\!]$ of rank r, let $\mathbf{J}$ be the Jacobian of the function $\phi(\mathbf{v}) = \text{vec}([\![\mathbf{A}_1, \mathbf{A}_2, \ldots, \mathbf{A}_d]\!] - \mathcal{X})$, where $\{\mathbf{A}_1, \mathbf{A}_2, \ldots, \mathbf{A}_d\} = \texttt{vec2mats}(\mathbf{v})$. Then we have that the blocks of $\mathbf{J}^\intercal \mathbf{J}$ are given by

$$\mathbf{J}_k^\intercal \mathbf{J}_\ell = \begin{cases} \mathbf{V}_k \otimes \mathbf{I}_r & \text{if } \ell = k \\ (\mathbf{I}_r \otimes \mathbf{A}_k)\mathbf{P}_{r,r} \operatorname{diag}\big(\text{vec}(\mathbf{V}_{k,\ell})\big)(\mathbf{I}_r \otimes \mathbf{A}_\ell) & \text{if } \ell \neq k \end{cases}, \tag{13.9}$$

where $\mathbf{P}_{r,r}$ is the (r,r)-perfect shuffle matrix of size $r^2 \times r^2$.

Just as in the 3-way case, we can employ a cheap and effective preconditioner for conjugate gradients. The diagonal blocks of $\mathbf{J}^\intercal\mathbf{J} + \lambda\mathbf{I}$ have Kronecker structure that makes it easy to apply their inverses. That is, for each $k \in [d]$, $\mathbf{J}_k^\intercal \mathbf{J}_k + \lambda \mathbf{I}_{n_k r} = (\mathbf{V}_k + \lambda \mathbf{I}_r) \otimes \mathbf{I}_{n_k}$, so applying the inverse of the kth diagonal block amounts to a single Cholesky decomposition of the $r \times r$ matrix $\mathbf{V}_k + \lambda \mathbf{I}_r$ and $2n_k$ triangular solves with the Cholesky factor. The overall cost of applying the preconditioner is then $\mathcal{O}(dr^3 + r^2 \sum_{k=1}^d n_k)$. Note that this coefficient matrix is nearly the same as the one from the normal equations to update $\mathbf{A}_k$ in a CP-ALS subiteration (see Eq. (11.5)), though with a different right-hand-side matrix. Thus, with very little extra cost per conjugate gradient iteration, we can accelerate the convergence of conjugate gradients and reduce the cost of each Gauss–Newton iteration.

Exercise 13.5 Prove Eq. (13.9).

13.3 CP-NLS on Data Tensors

We consider a synthetic tensor to illustrate the convergence advantages of methods that exploit the least squares structure. We create a $250 \times 250 \times 250$ tensor with exact rank 10 (no noise) from factor matrices that are constructed to have specified pairwise *congruence* values. A factor congruence value $\gamma \in [0,1]$ means that for each pair of distinct columns $\mathbf{u}$ and $\mathbf{v}$ in a factor matrix, the cosine of the angle between $\mathbf{u}$ and $\mathbf{v}$ is γ, i.e., $\mathbf{u}^\intercal\mathbf{v}/(\|\mathbf{u}\|_2\|\mathbf{v}\|_2) = \gamma$. Congruence values near 0 yield easier problems because the factors are nearly orthogonal and easy to separate; congruence values near 1 yield harder problems because the factors are close together and hard to separate. If the factor matrices are generated as standard normal random matrices, the congruence values are close to 0.

Figure 13.2 shows a comparison of CP-NLS and CP-ALS on synthetic tensors with congruence values of $\gamma = 0.1$ and $\gamma = 0.8$. Here we plot the relative error versus iteration for the best of 10 trials (i.e., the trial with the lowest final function value). Bear in mind that the cost per iteration is roughly 2–3 times higher for CP-NLS than CP-ALS.

Remark 13.5 (Computational methodology) For CP-NLS, we use the Gauss–Newton method with an iterative preconditioned conjugate gradient (PCG) linear solver and backtracking line search using the following settings. The damping parameter λ for the Gauss–Newton matrix is set to 0. The maximum number of PCG iterations is set to 20, and the tolerance (for the relative magnitude of the residual within PCG) is set to `1e-4`. The tolerance for both CP-NLS and CP-ALS, with respect to change in relative error, is set to `1e-10`, and the maximum number of iterations is 500.

For congruence value $\gamma = 0.1$, NLS converges in about half as many iterations. However, since ALS is cheaper per iteration, the total runtime is similar.

In the case of congruence $\gamma = 0.8$, we see a stark difference in the number of iterations to converge. ALS converges linearly and achieves a relative error of only `1e-6` after 500 iterations. The convergence rate of NLS is quadratic, and it converges to a relative error near machine precision after 35 iterations. In this case, even with a higher cost per iteration, the NLS method solves the problem in much less time than ALS.

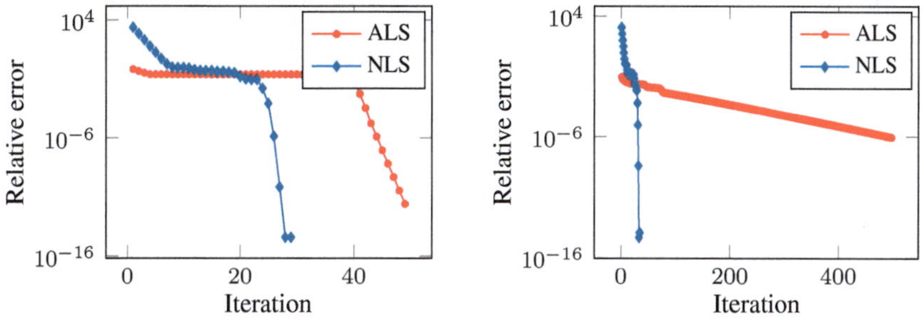

(a) Congruence $\gamma = 0.1$. (b) Congruence $\gamma = 0.8$.

Figure 13.2 Convergence of best of 10 trials of CP-NLS and CP-ALS on $250 \times 250 \times 250$ synthetic tensors of rank 10 (no noise). Congruence γ measures the similarity of the vectors in the factor matrices, and higher values mean the problem is more challenging.

Note that with no noise added to this problem, the minimum function value is 0. As described in Section B.3.6, the Gauss–Newton matrix is a particularly good approximation of the Hessian in this case as the iterates approach the solution. You will explore in Exercise 13.6 how the convergence behavior changes with noise added to the problem.

Exercise 13.6 Create test problems with known rank, with and without noise, to test the convergence of CP-NLS. Generate three random 250×10 factor matrices with specified congruence $\gamma = \{0.1, 0.8\}$, e.g., using the Tensor Toolbox command `A=matrandcong(n,r,gamma)`. If $\mathcal{X}$ is the tensor with exact rank 10, compute $\mathcal{Z} = \mathcal{X} + \eta \frac{\|\mathcal{X}\|}{\|\mathcal{N}\|} \cdot \mathcal{N}$, where η is the fraction of noise to add and $\mathcal{N}$ is a randomly generated tensor. How does convergence behavior vary across $\eta = \{0, 0.0001, 0.1\}$? Be sure to try from multiple random starts.

Exercise 13.7 Implement CP-NLS using existing implementations for computing the CP gradient (see Exercise 12.9), the preconditioned conjugate gradient method, and applying the approximate Hessian (see Exercise 13.4).

Exercise 13.8 Using an existing implementation of CP-NLS, compare the results for computing a rank-3 CP decomposition of the EEM tensor using CP-NLS with the results using CP-ALS and CP-OPT, as in Exercise 12.11.

14 CP Algorithms for Incomplete or Scarce Data

In many real-world data analysis tasks, we have to work with tensors that are incomplete, meaning that some entries are missing. This chapter considers the problem of computing CP for incomplete tensors, even when most of the data is missing. We refer to the later case with only a sparse set of known entries as scarce (Kolda and Duersch, 2017).

Example 14.1 (Incomplete Tensor) An incomplete tensor $\mathcal{X} \in \mathbb{R}^{2\times 2\times 2}$ is

$$\mathcal{X}(:,:,1) = \begin{bmatrix} 8 & 7 \\ ? & ? \end{bmatrix} \quad \text{and} \quad \mathcal{X}(:,:,2) = \begin{bmatrix} ? & ? \\ 0 & 5 \end{bmatrix},$$

where ? denotes a missing value.

Incomplete tensors are prevalent in real-world scenarios. For instance, Fig. 14.1 shows the EEM tensor from Fig. 1.8 *before preprocessing filled in the missing data*; the white areas indicate regions devoid of accurate data. This data was collected using fluorescence spectroscopy, and a phenomenon known as Rayleigh scattering makes it impossible to collect accurate data in certain regions.

We consider the problem of computing CP for tensors with incomplete data. We are not necessarily focused on the problem of filling in missing data, though the techniques we discuss can be used for that purpose, as we will do with the EEM tensor. Primarily, we focus on computing the CP factorization when some or even the majority of data is missing. There are many different techniques to handle missing data, depending on how much data is missing and under what circumstances (Tomasi and Bro, 2005). We described expectation maximization (EM) in Section 9.5.2, but this is primarily useful when only a handful of entries are missing and may require extensive computation. In this chapter, we focus on optimization approaches whereby missing data are not used in the model fitting (Acar et al., 2010, 2011b). This enables us to compute low-rank CP factorizations in extreme cases where the vast majority of the data is missing.

> We say a tensor is **incomplete** if one or more entries is unknown. We say an incomplete tensor is **scarce** if most of the data is missing.

Throughout the chapter, we assume that the missing data is missing at random rather than due to some inherent property that might lead to bias in computing the CP model.

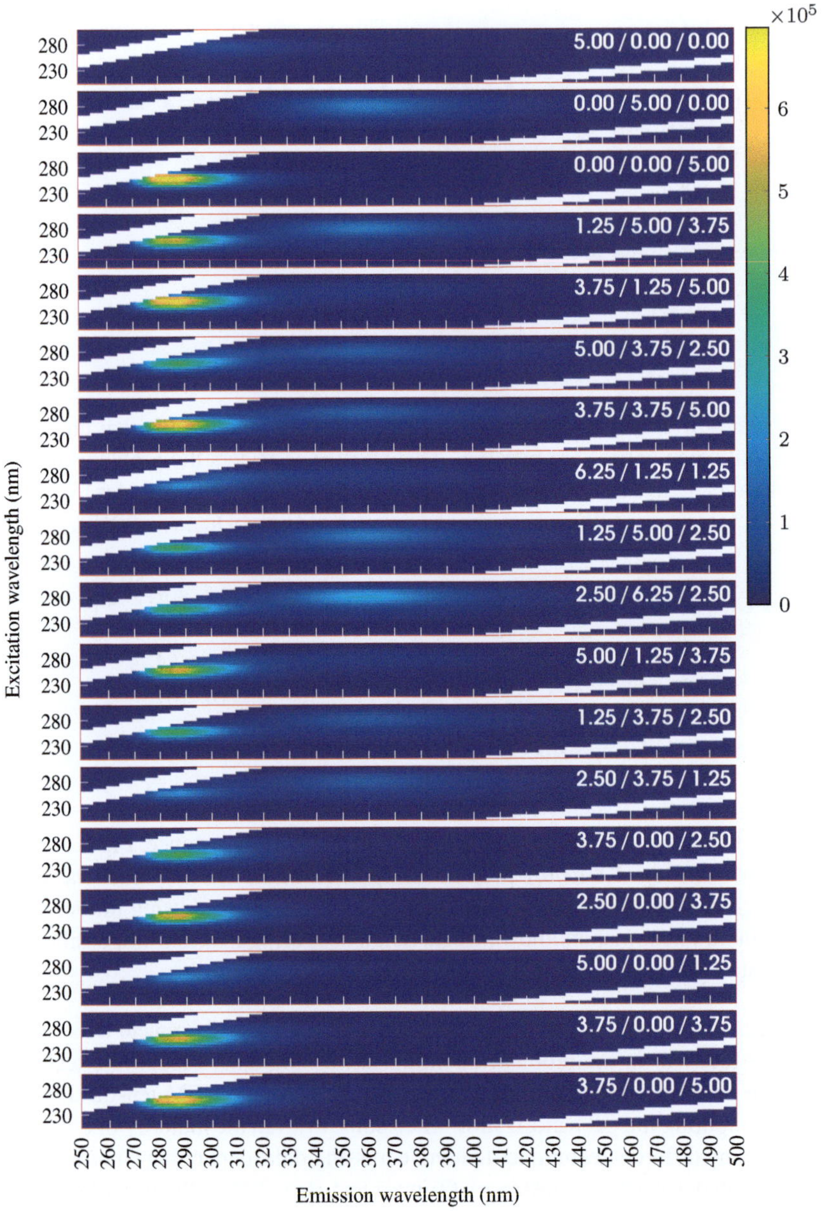

Figure 14.1 EEM matrices from fluorescence spectroscopy experiments on 18 samples. Each sample is labeled with the concentrations of the three chemical compounds (Val-Tyr-Val/Try-Gly/Phe). The white regions show where the data was not acquired.

14.1 Representing Incomplete or Scarce Data

Before we can formulate the mathematical problem, we need notation and mechanisms for working with incomplete tensors. Without loss of generality, we assume that the indices of the known values are known explicitly and that the missing values are occupied by some numerical value such that multiplication by 0 will result in a 0.

Remark 14.1 (Representing missing values) There is no standard for representing missing values in terms of data representations. NaN is the IEEE arithmetic representation for not-a-number, but this is not necessarily consistent across languages and computer architectures. Oftentimes, missing values are represented by a value that would not otherwise appear in the data, such as 99 or -1 or 0. Some care is needed in preprocessing data with missing values to ensure the right conventions are used. It may also be worth noting that multiplication of a NaN by any other value is still a NaN, so replacing NaNs with 0s requires explicitly setting those values.

14.1.1 Known Value Indicator Set

We define the **known value indicator set**, denoted here by Ω, to be the indices of the known entries for an incomplete tensor. The complement of the indicator set is the **missing value indicator set**, denoted by Ω^c.

Example 14.2 (Known Value Indicator Set) For the tensor

$$\mathcal{X}(:,:,1) = \begin{bmatrix} 8 & 7 \\ ? & ? \end{bmatrix} \quad \text{and} \quad \mathcal{X}(:,:,2) = \begin{bmatrix} ? & ? \\ 0 & 5 \end{bmatrix},$$

the known value indicator set is

$$\Omega = \{\,(1,1,1),(1,2,1),(2,1,2),(2,2,2)\,\}.$$

Exercise 14.1 For Example 14.2, what is Ω^c?

If only a few entries are missing, it may be more efficient to store Ω^c than Ω, since Ω can then be determined implicitly. The set of indices in Ω or Ω^c can be stored as tuples, linearized indices, or as a weight tensor, discussed in the next subsection.

14.1.2 Known Value Selection Matrix

For an indicator set Ω for tensors of a given size, we can define a **known value selection matrix**, $\mathbf{S}_\Omega$, such that multiplying $\mathbf{S}_\Omega^\intercal$ times a vectorized tensor extracts the elements in Ω.

Supposing Ω has q entries and is for tensors of size $m \times n \times p$, then $\mathbf{S}_\Omega \in \mathbb{R}^{mnp \times q}$. It is a subset of the columns of the $mnp \times mnp$ identity matrix. Specifically, it extracts the columns in the set $\{\,\mathbb{L}(i,j,k) : (i,j,k) \in \Omega\,\}$. Recall that $\mathbb{L}(i,j,k) = i + m(j-1) + mn(k-1)$ is the linear index; see Section 2.1.1.

Since $\mathbf{S}_\Omega$ is a subset of columns from the $mnp \times mnp$ identity matrix, it is an orthonormal matrix. From this, we can form an orthogonal projector $\mathbf{S}_\Omega \mathbf{S}_\Omega^\intercal$ that has the property of zeroing out the entries of a vectorized tensor that are not in Ω. In general, $\mathbf{S}_\Omega$ is a very large matrix that we would not form explicitly, but it is useful in our mathematical discussions, and its action can be easily implemented.

Example 14.3 (Known Value Selection Matrix) The known value selection matrix for $\Omega = \{ (1,1,1), (1,2,1), (2,1,2), (2,2,2) \}$, is

$$\mathbf{S}_\Omega = \begin{bmatrix} 1 & 0 & 0 & 0 \\ 0 & 0 & 0 & 0 \\ 0 & 1 & 0 & 0 \\ 0 & 0 & 0 & 0 \\ 0 & 0 & 0 & 0 \\ 0 & 0 & 1 & 0 \\ 0 & 0 & 0 & 0 \\ 0 & 0 & 0 & 1 \end{bmatrix}. \tag{14.1}$$

For the tensor

$$\mathcal{X}(:,:,1) = \begin{bmatrix} 8 & 7 \\ -100 & 150 \end{bmatrix} \quad \text{and} \quad \mathcal{X}(:,:,2) = \begin{bmatrix} 100 & -250 \\ 0 & 5 \end{bmatrix},$$

we have

$$\mathbf{S}_\Omega^\mathsf{T} \operatorname{vec}(\mathcal{X}) = \begin{bmatrix} 8 \\ 7 \\ 0 \\ 5 \end{bmatrix}.$$

Setting $\operatorname{vec}(\mathcal{Y}) = \mathbf{S}_\Omega \mathbf{S}_\Omega^\mathsf{T} \operatorname{vec}(\mathcal{X})$ yields

$$\mathcal{Y}(:,:,1) = \begin{bmatrix} 8 & 7 \\ 0 & 0 \end{bmatrix} \quad \text{and} \quad \mathcal{Y}(:,:,2) = \begin{bmatrix} 0 & 0 \\ 0 & 5 \end{bmatrix}.$$

We have $y_{ijk} = 0$ for every $(i,j,k) \in \Omega$, but observe carefully that not every 0 in $\mathcal{Y}$ corresponds to an index in Ω.

14.1.3 Known Value Weight Tensor

For a known value indicator set Ω, we can define a **known value weight tensor** $\mathcal{W}_\Omega$ that has 1s for known entries and 0s elsewhere. For instance, in the 3-way case, $\mathcal{W}_\Omega$ would be defined as

$$\mathcal{W}_\Omega(i,j,k) = \begin{cases} 1 & \text{if } (i,j,k) \in \Omega \\ 0 & \text{otherwise} \end{cases}. \tag{14.2}$$

Computing the Hadamard (elementwise) product of any tensor and $\mathcal{W}_\Omega$ has the effect of zeroing out any entry $(i,j,k) \notin \Omega$.

Exercise 14.2 In Example 14.2, what is the weight tensor and corresponding indicator set Ω?

The known value weight tensor is an alternative way to achieve the effect of the orthogonal projection with the known value selection matrix. Specifically,

$$\operatorname{vec}(\mathcal{W}_\Omega * \mathcal{X}) = \mathbf{S}_\Omega \mathbf{S}_\Omega^\mathsf{T} \operatorname{vec}(\mathcal{X}). \tag{14.3}$$

14.2 Missing Data CP Function and Gradient

We express the function for the missing data problem and compute its gradient.

14.2.1 Missing Data CP Function and Gradient: 3-way

Let $\mathcal{X}$ be a tensor of size $m \times n \times p$ that has $q < mnp$ observed entries. Let Ω denote its indicator set:

$$\Omega = \{\, (i,j,k) \mid x_{ijk} \text{ is observed} \,\} \subseteq [m] \otimes [n] \otimes [p].$$

The CP minimization problem that ignores the unknown entries is

$$\min_{\mathbf{A},\mathbf{B},\mathbf{C}} \tilde{f}(\mathbf{A},\mathbf{B},\mathbf{C}) \equiv \frac{1}{2} \sum_{(i,j,k)\in\Omega} \left(x_{ijk} - \sum_{\ell=1}^{r} a_{i\ell} b_{j\ell} c_{k\ell} \right)^2 = \frac{1}{2} \left\| \mathcal{W}_\Omega * (\mathcal{X} - [\![\mathbf{A},\mathbf{B},\mathbf{C}]\!]) \right\|^2,$$

where $\mathcal{W}_\Omega$ is the weight tensor defined as in Eq. (14.2), so we can refer to this as a **weighted** optimization problem. This objective function picks out the squared errors for only the observed entries.

Let us consider the gradient with respect to $\operatorname{vec}(\mathbf{B})$. For computing the gradient, it is useful to write the objective in terms of a vectorized version using Eq. (14.3):

$$\tilde{f}(\mathbf{A},\mathbf{B},\mathbf{C}) = \frac{1}{2} \left\| \mathbf{S}_\Omega \mathbf{S}_\Omega^\intercal \operatorname{vec}\big(\mathcal{X} - [\![\mathbf{A},\mathbf{B},\mathbf{C}]\!]\big) \right\|_2^2. \tag{14.4}$$

As we did in the all-at-once optimization approach in Section 12.2.2, we can compute the gradient using the chain rule (Proposition 12.6). We write $\tilde{f} = g \circ \mathbf{h}$ as a composition of functions where $g : \mathbb{R}^{mnp} \to \mathbb{R}$ and $h : \mathbb{R}^{(m+n+p)r} \to \mathbb{R}^{mnp}$ are defined as follows:

$$g(\bar{\mathbf{x}}) = \frac{1}{2} \left\| \mathbf{S}_\Omega \mathbf{S}_\Omega^\intercal \big(\operatorname{vec}(\mathcal{X}) - \bar{\mathbf{x}}\big) \right\|_2^2 \quad \text{and} \quad \mathbf{h}(\mathbf{A},\mathbf{B},\mathbf{C}) = \operatorname{vec}\big([\![\mathbf{A},\mathbf{B},\mathbf{C}]\!]\big).$$

Exercise 14.3 Let $\mathbf{A}$ be an $m \times n$ matrix and $\mathbf{x}, \bar{\mathbf{x}} \in \mathbb{R}^n$ and show the gradient of $g(\bar{\mathbf{x}}) = \|\mathbf{A}(\mathbf{x} - \bar{\mathbf{x}})\|_2^2$ is $\nabla g(\bar{\mathbf{x}}) = \mathbf{A}^\intercal \mathbf{A}(\bar{\mathbf{x}} - \mathbf{x})$. Hint: This is similar to Proposition 12.5.

By Exercise 14.3, the gradient of g is

$$\nabla g(\bar{\mathbf{x}}) = \big(\mathbf{S}_\Omega \mathbf{S}_\Omega^\intercal\big)^\intercal \mathbf{S}_\Omega \mathbf{S}_\Omega^\intercal \big(\bar{\mathbf{x}} - \operatorname{vec}(\mathcal{X})\big) = \mathbf{S}_\Omega \mathbf{S}_\Omega^\intercal \big(\bar{\mathbf{x}} - \operatorname{vec}(\mathcal{X})\big).$$

Thus, plugging in $\mathbf{h}(\mathbf{A},\mathbf{B},\mathbf{C})$ for $\bar{\mathbf{x}}$ yields

$$\nabla g\big(\mathbf{h}(\mathbf{A},\mathbf{B},\mathbf{C})\big) = \mathbf{S}_\Omega \mathbf{S}_\Omega^\intercal \operatorname{vec}([\![\mathbf{A},\mathbf{B},\mathbf{C}]\!] - \mathcal{X}) = \operatorname{vec}\big(\mathcal{W}_\Omega * ([\![\mathbf{A},\mathbf{B},\mathbf{C}]\!] - \mathcal{X})\big).$$

Finally, the partial Jacobian of $\mathbf{h}$ with respect to $\operatorname{vec}(\mathbf{B})$ is given by Proposition 12.7. Denoting the weighted residual as

$$\mathcal{Y} = \mathcal{W}_\Omega * (\mathcal{X} - [\![\mathbf{A},\mathbf{B},\mathbf{C}]\!]) \tag{14.5}$$

and plugging these components into the chain rule (Proposition 12.6) yields

$$\begin{aligned}
\frac{\partial \tilde{f}}{\partial \operatorname{vec}(\mathbf{B})} &= \left[\frac{d\mathbf{h}}{d \operatorname{vec}(\mathbf{B})} \right]^\intercal \nabla g(\mathbf{h}) &\quad (14.6)\\
&= \big[(\mathbf{C} \odot \mathbf{A})^\intercal \otimes \mathbf{I}_n\big] \mathbf{P}_2 \operatorname{vec}(-\mathcal{Y}) &\quad (14.7)\\
&= \big[(\mathbf{C} \odot \mathbf{A})^\intercal \otimes \mathbf{I}_n\big] \operatorname{vec}(-\mathbf{Y}_{(2)})\\
&= \operatorname{vec}\big[-\mathbf{Y}_{(2)}(\mathbf{C} \odot \mathbf{A})\big].
\end{aligned}$$

Recall that $\mathbf{P}_2$ is the permutation such that $\mathbf{P}_2 \operatorname{vec}(\mathcal{X}) = \operatorname{vec}(\mathbf{X}_{(2)})$ for any $m \times n \times p$ tensor $\mathcal{X}$.

Following similar logic for $\mathbf{A}$ and $\mathbf{C}$ (left as an exercise), we have the following result.

Proposition 14.2 *Let $\mathcal{X}$ be an incomplete 3-way tensor whose known entries are indexed in Ω, and let $\mathcal{W}_\Omega$ be the corresponding weight tensor with 1s for entries in Ω and 0s elsewhere. Consider the weighted objective function $\tilde{f}(\mathbf{A}, \mathbf{B}, \mathbf{C}) = \frac{1}{2}\|\mathcal{W}_\Omega * (\mathcal{X} - [\![\mathbf{A}, \mathbf{B}, \mathbf{C}]\!])\|^2$. Define $\mathcal{Y} \equiv \mathcal{W}_\Omega * (\mathcal{X} - [\![\mathbf{A}, \mathbf{B}, \mathbf{C}]\!])$. Then*

$$\frac{\partial \tilde{f}}{\partial \operatorname{vec}(\mathbf{A})} = \operatorname{vec}\big[-\mathbf{Y}_{(1)}(\mathbf{C} \odot \mathbf{B})\big],$$
$$\frac{\partial \tilde{f}}{\partial \operatorname{vec}(\mathbf{B})} = \operatorname{vec}\big[-\mathbf{Y}_{(2)}(\mathbf{C} \odot \mathbf{A})\big],$$
$$\frac{\partial \tilde{f}}{\partial \operatorname{vec}(\mathbf{C})} = \operatorname{vec}\big[-\mathbf{Y}_{(3)}(\mathbf{B} \odot \mathbf{A})\big].$$

Equivalently, in matrix notation

$$\frac{\partial \tilde{f}}{\partial \mathbf{A}} = -\mathbf{Y}_{(1)}(\mathbf{C} \odot \mathbf{B}), \quad \frac{\partial \tilde{f}}{\partial \mathbf{B}} = -\mathbf{Y}_{(2)}(\mathbf{C} \odot \mathbf{A}), \quad \frac{\partial \tilde{f}}{\partial \mathbf{C}} = -\mathbf{Y}_{(3)}(\mathbf{B} \odot \mathbf{A}).$$

Exercise 14.4 Prove Proposition 14.2 for the gradients with respect to $\mathbf{A}$ and $\mathbf{C}$.

The weighted residual tensor $\mathcal{Y}$ is the residual between $\mathcal{X}$ and the model $[\![\mathbf{A}, \mathbf{B}, \mathbf{C}]\!]$ with values corresponding to missing entries in $\mathcal{X}$ zeroed out. This means that those (unknown) differences between the data tensor and the model do not contribute toward the gradient. Though it may not be obvious, this formula is nearly identical to the gradient for the problem with no missing data.

14.2.2 Missing Data CP Function and Gradient: d-way

The situation in the d-way case is analogous. We assume we have a tensor $\mathcal{X}$ of size $n_1 \times n_2 \times \cdots \times n_d$ that has $q < \prod_{k=1}^{d} n_k$ observed entries, and we let Ω be the indicator set:

$$\Omega = \{\, (i_1, i_2, \ldots, i_d) \mid x_{i_1 i_2 \cdots i_d} \text{ is observed} \,\} \subset [n_1] \otimes [n_2] \otimes \cdots \otimes [n_d].$$

The weight tensor $\mathcal{W}_\Omega$ in the d-way case is a tensor of size $n_1 \times n_2 \times \cdots \times n_d$ with

$$\mathcal{W}_\Omega(i_1, i_2, \ldots, i_d) = \begin{cases} 1 & \text{if } (i_1, i_2, \ldots, i_d) \in \Omega \\ 0 & \text{otherwise} \end{cases}.$$

We can express the problem as a weighted optimization problem:

$$\min_{\mathbf{A}_1, \mathbf{A}_2, \ldots, \mathbf{A}_d} \tilde{f}(\mathbf{A}_1, \mathbf{A}_2, \ldots, \mathbf{A}_d) \equiv \frac{1}{2}\Big\|\mathcal{W}_\Omega * (\mathcal{X} - [\![\mathbf{A}_1, \mathbf{A}_2, \ldots, \mathbf{A}_d]\!])\Big\|^2.$$

The following proposition derives the gradient.

Proposition 14.3 *Let $\mathcal{X}$ be an incomplete d-way tensor whose known entries are indexed in Ω, and let $\mathcal{W}_\Omega$ be the corresponding weight tensor with 1s for entries in Ω and 0s elsewhere. Consider the weighted objective function*

$$\tilde{f}(\mathbf{A}_1, \mathbf{A}_2, \ldots, \mathbf{A}_d) = \frac{1}{2}\left\| \mathcal{W}_\Omega * (\mathcal{X} - [\![\mathbf{A}_1, \mathbf{A}_2, \ldots, \mathbf{A}_d]\!]) \right\|_2^2.$$

Define the weighted residual tensor

$$\mathcal{Y} = \mathcal{W}_\Omega * (\mathcal{X} - [\![\mathbf{A}_1, \mathbf{A}_2, \ldots, \mathbf{A}_d]\!]).$$

Then, for all $k \in [d]$, we have

$$\frac{\partial \tilde{f}}{\partial \operatorname{vec}(\mathbf{A}_k)} = -\operatorname{vec}\big[\mathbf{Y}_{(k)}(\mathbf{A}_d \odot \cdots \odot \mathbf{A}_{k+1} \odot \mathbf{A}_{k-1} \odot \cdots \odot \mathbf{A}_1)\big].$$

Equivalently, in matrix notation we have

$$\frac{\partial \tilde{f}}{\partial \mathbf{A}_k} = -\mathbf{Y}_{(k)}(\mathbf{A}_d \odot \cdots \odot \mathbf{A}_{k+1} \odot \mathbf{A}_{k-1} \odot \cdots \odot \mathbf{A}_1).$$

The proof follows the same logic as the 3-way case and is left as an exercise.

Exercise 14.5 Prove Proposition 14.3. You will need to use the permutation matrix $\mathbf{P}_k$, such that $\mathbf{P}_k \operatorname{vec}(\mathcal{X}) = \operatorname{vec}(\mathbf{X}_{(k)})$ for any tensor $\mathcal{X}$ of size $n_1 \times n_2 \times \cdots \times n_d$.

14.3 Weighted All-at-Once Optimization

With formulations for the gradients, we can apply a first-order optimization method and follow the same advice as in the case of no missing data for handling regularization, constraints, and so on. As with CP-OPT, we provide the tools for computing the function and gradient, enabling us to use any first-order optimization method, such as L-BFGS. We refer to this methodology as CP-WOPT (weighted optimization). The same considerations apply here as for CP-OPT; see Section 12.3 for further discussion.

14.3.1 CP-WOPT Method

We show the algorithm for computing the function and gradients in the case of missing data in Algorithm 14.1. In the case of no missing data, Algorithm 12.2 does not form an explicit weighted residual tensor and computes the function value implicitly. Unfortunately, Algorithm 14.1 needs the weighted residual tensor explicitly.

Line 3 of Algorithm 14.1 computes the weighted residual tensor, $\mathcal{Y}$. Assuming that the weight tensor $\mathcal{W}_\Omega$ is dense, we can explicitly construct the full Kruskal tensor (see Section 10.6), take its difference with $\mathcal{X}$, and then zero out any entries corresponding to missing entries. The norm of the tensor $\mathcal{Y}$ computed in Line 4 is the function value, and the sequence of MTTKRPs (see Section 3.6.2) with $\mathcal{Y}$ in Lines 5–7 computes the gradient.

Exercise 14.6 Assuming $\mathbf{W}_\Omega$ is dense, analyze the computational complexity of Algorithm 14.1.

Unfortunately, even if $\mathcal{X}$ is sparse, the weighted residual tensor is dense. However, if $\mathcal{X}$

Algorithm 14.1 Computing CP-WOPT Function and Gradient for d-way Tensor

Require: data and weight tensors $\mathcal{X}, \mathcal{W}_\Omega \in \mathbb{R}^{n_1 \times \cdots \times n_d}$, input vector $\mathbf{v} \in \mathbb{R}^{r(n_1+\cdots+n_d)}$
Ensure: $\tilde{f} = \frac{1}{2}\left\| \mathcal{W}_\Omega * (\mathcal{X} - [\![\mathbf{A}_1, \mathbf{A}_2, \dots, \mathbf{A}_d]\!]) \right\|^2$ and $\tilde{\mathbf{g}} = \nabla \tilde{f}$,
where $\{\mathbf{A}_1, \mathbf{A}_2, \dots, \mathbf{A}_d\} = \texttt{vec2mats}(\mathbf{v})$

1: **function** CP-FG($\mathcal{X}$, $\mathcal{W}_\Omega$, $\mathbf{v}$)
2: $\quad \{\mathbf{A}_1, \mathbf{A}_2, \dots, \mathbf{A}_d\} \leftarrow \texttt{vec2mats}(\mathbf{v})$
3: $\quad \mathcal{Y} \leftarrow \mathcal{W}_\Omega * (\mathcal{X} - [\![\mathbf{A}_1, \mathbf{A}_2, \dots, \mathbf{A}_d]\!])$ ▷ Weighted residual tensor
4: $\quad \tilde{f} \leftarrow \|\mathcal{Y}\|^2$ ▷ $\tilde{f} = \frac{1}{2}\left\| \mathcal{W}_\Omega * (\mathcal{X} - [\![\mathbf{A}_1, \mathbf{A}_2, \dots, \mathbf{A}_d]\!]) \right\|^2$
5: $\quad$ **for** $k = 1, \dots, d$ **do** ▷ Sequence of MTTKRPs
6: $\qquad \tilde{\mathbf{G}}_k \leftarrow -\mathbf{Y}_{(k)}(\mathbf{A}_d \odot \cdots \odot \mathbf{A}_{k+1} \odot \mathbf{A}_{k-1} \odot \cdots \odot \mathbf{A}_1)$ ▷ $\tilde{\mathbf{G}}_k = \frac{\partial \tilde{f}}{\partial \mathbf{A}_k}$
7: $\quad$ **end for**
8: $\quad \tilde{\mathbf{g}} \leftarrow \texttt{mats2vec}(\tilde{\mathbf{G}}_1, \tilde{\mathbf{G}}_2, \dots, \tilde{\mathbf{G}}_d)$
9: $\quad$ **return** $\{\tilde{f}, \tilde{\mathbf{g}}\}$
10: **end function**

is scarce (and so $\mathcal{W}_\Omega$ is sparse), then the tensor $\mathcal{Y}$ will be sparse and can be computed efficiently, as we discuss in the next section.

14.3.2 Special Handling of Scarce Tensors

If the tensor $\mathcal{X}$ is scarce, then Algorithm 14.1 can be more efficient. Since $\mathcal{X}$ is scarce, then $\mathcal{W}_\Omega$ must be a sparse tensor with 0s for unknown (masked) entries and 1s for known (unmasked entries). We can store this as a sparse tensor: $\mathcal{W}_\Omega = [\![\boldsymbol{\Omega}, \mathbf{1}]\!]$, where $\boldsymbol{\Omega}$ is the matrix representation of the set Ω.

If $\mathcal{W}_\Omega$ is sparse, then the weighted residual tensor $\mathcal{Y} = \mathcal{W}_\Omega * (\mathcal{X} - [\![\mathbf{A}_1, \mathbf{A}_2, \dots, \mathbf{A}_d]\!])$, computed in Line 3 of Algorithm 14.1, must be sparse with the same sparsity pattern as $\mathcal{W}_\Omega$. We write this as two terms:

$$\mathcal{Y} = \mathcal{W}_\Omega * \mathcal{X} - \mathcal{W}_\Omega * [\![\mathbf{A}_1, \mathbf{A}_2, \dots, \mathbf{A}_d]\!].$$

For the first term, if we let the vector $\mathbf{v}$ denote the known values of $\mathcal{X}$ in the order specified by $\boldsymbol{\Omega}$, then the masked version is a sparse tensor: $\mathcal{W}_\Omega * \mathcal{X} = [\![\boldsymbol{\Omega}, \mathbf{v}]\!]$.

The second term is a masked full operation; see Section 10.6.3. It will also have the same sparsity pattern as $\mathcal{W}_\Omega$, so we can compute $\hat{\mathbf{v}}$ such that $[\![\boldsymbol{\Omega}, \hat{\mathbf{v}}]\!] = \mathcal{W}_\Omega * [\![\mathbf{A}_1, \mathbf{A}_2, \dots, \mathbf{A}_d]\!]$.

Finally, the sparse tensor $\mathcal{Y}$ is given by $\mathcal{Y} = [\![\boldsymbol{\Omega}, \bar{\mathbf{v}}]\!]$, where $\bar{\mathbf{v}} = \mathbf{v} - \hat{\mathbf{v}}$.

There are some implementation nuances in that some values in $\mathbf{v}$, $\hat{\mathbf{v}}$, and $\bar{\mathbf{v}}$ may be 0. In the sparse tensors using these vectors, the 0 entries can be filtered or ignored.

The remaining parts of the algorithm are efficient because $\mathcal{Y}$ is sparse. The norm in Line 4 is with respect to the sparse tensor (see Section 3.7.2) and the sequence of MTTKRPs computed in Line 6 is with a sparse tensor (see Sections 3.7.3 and 3.7.4).

> If $\mathcal{X}$ is scarce, the gradient can be computed in time proportional to the number of known entries in $\mathcal{X}$.

Exercise 14.7 Assuming $\mathcal{W}_\Omega$ is sparse ($\mathcal{X}$ is scarce), analyze the computational complexity of Algorithm 14.1 and compare to the case that $\mathcal{W}_\Omega$ is dense.

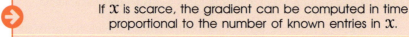

14.4 Weighted Alternating Optimization

For the alternating optimization approach, a form of block coordinate descent, we sequentially set each gradient to zero and solve for the corresponding factor matrix. We refer to this approach as CP-WALS (weighted alternating least squares). In the 3-way case, this would look like the following.

CP-WALS Prototype

while not converged **do**
  $\mathbf{A} \leftarrow$ solution to $\frac{\partial \tilde{f}}{\partial \mathbf{A}}(\mathbf{A}, \mathbf{B}, \mathbf{C}) = \mathbf{0}$
  $\mathbf{B} \leftarrow$ solution to $\frac{\partial \tilde{f}}{\partial \mathbf{B}}(\mathbf{A}, \mathbf{B}, \mathbf{C}) = \mathbf{0}$
  $\mathbf{C} \leftarrow$ solution to $\frac{\partial \tilde{f}}{\partial \mathbf{C}}(\mathbf{A}, \mathbf{B}, \mathbf{C}) = \mathbf{0}$
end while

Though it may not be obvious, this is also a least squares problem, albeit not the same one as in the standard case. We consider the case of solving for $\mathbf{B}$ given a 3-way tensor $\mathcal{X}$ with known elements Ω, and fixed values for $\mathbf{A}$ and $\mathbf{C}$. Recall from Eq. (14.6) that we can write the gradient as

$$\frac{\partial \tilde{f}}{\partial \operatorname{vec}(\mathbf{B})} = \left[(\mathbf{C} \odot \mathbf{A})^{\intercal} \otimes \mathbf{I}_n\right] \mathbf{P}_2 \operatorname{vec}(-\mathcal{Y}).$$

Here $\mathbf{P}_2$ is the tensor perfect shuffle matrix, such that $\mathbf{P}_2 \operatorname{vec}(\mathcal{X}) = \operatorname{vec}(\mathbf{X}_2)$.

Recalling also that $\operatorname{vec}(\mathcal{Y}) = \mathbf{S}_\Omega \mathbf{S}_\Omega^{\intercal} \operatorname{vec}(\mathcal{X} - [\![\mathbf{A}, \mathbf{B}, \mathbf{C}]\!])$ and setting the gradient equal to zero yields

$$\left[(\mathbf{C} \odot \mathbf{A})^{\intercal} \otimes \mathbf{I}_n\right] \mathbf{P}_2 \mathbf{S}_\Omega \mathbf{S}_\Omega^{\intercal} \operatorname{vec}([\![\mathbf{A}, \mathbf{B}, \mathbf{C}]\!] - \mathcal{X}) = 0.$$

If we let $q = |\Omega|$ and define

$$\mathbf{U}_2 = \mathbf{S}_\Omega^{\intercal} \mathbf{P}_2^{\intercal} \left[(\mathbf{C} \odot \mathbf{A}) \otimes \mathbf{I}_n\right] \in \mathbb{R}^{q \times nr},$$

then we have

$$\begin{aligned}
\mathbf{U}_2^{\intercal} \mathbf{S}_\Omega^{\intercal} \operatorname{vec}([\![\mathbf{A}, \mathbf{B}, \mathbf{C}]\!]) &= \mathbf{U}_2^{\intercal} \mathbf{S}_\Omega^{\intercal} \operatorname{vec}(\mathcal{X}) \\
\mathbf{U}_2^{\intercal} \mathbf{S}_\Omega^{\intercal} \mathbf{P}_2^{\intercal} \operatorname{vec}\left(\mathbf{B}(\mathbf{C} \odot \mathbf{A})^{\intercal}\right) &= \mathbf{U}_2^{\intercal} \mathbf{S}_\Omega^{\intercal} \operatorname{vec}(\mathcal{X}) \\
\mathbf{U}_2^{\intercal} \mathbf{S}_\Omega^{\intercal} \mathbf{P}_2^{\intercal} \left[(\mathbf{C} \odot \mathbf{A}) \otimes \mathbf{I}_n\right] \operatorname{vec}(\mathbf{B}) &= \mathbf{U}_2^{\intercal} \mathbf{S}_\Omega^{\intercal} \operatorname{vec}(\mathcal{X}) \\
\mathbf{U}_2^{\intercal} \mathbf{U}_2 \operatorname{vec}(\mathbf{B}) &= \mathbf{U}_2^{\intercal} \mathbf{S}_\Omega^{\intercal} \operatorname{vec}(\mathcal{X}).
\end{aligned}$$

Setting $\mathbf{x} = \mathbf{S}_\Omega^{\intercal} \operatorname{vec}(\mathcal{X})$, this can be viewed as the normal equations for the least squares problem:

$$\min \frac{1}{2} \|\mathbf{U}_2 \operatorname{vec}(\mathbf{B}) - \mathbf{x}\|_2^2.$$

Exercise 14.8 Given $\mathcal{X} \in \mathbb{R}^{m \times n \times p}$, known value indicator set Ω, and setting $\mathbf{U}_2 = \mathbf{S}_\Omega^{\intercal} \mathbf{P}_2^{\intercal} \left[(\mathbf{C} \odot \mathbf{A}) \otimes \mathbf{I}_n\right]$, where $\mathbf{P}_2$ is such that $\mathbf{P}_2 \operatorname{vec}(\mathcal{X}) = \operatorname{vec}(\mathbf{X}_2)$, show that

$$\left\|\mathcal{W}_\Omega * (\mathcal{X} - [\![\mathbf{A}, \mathbf{B}, \mathbf{C}]\!])\right\|^2 = \left\|\mathbf{U}_2 \operatorname{vec}(\mathbf{B}) - \mathbf{S}_\Omega^{\intercal} \operatorname{vec}(\mathcal{X})\right\|_2^2.$$

The matrix $\mathbf{S}_\Omega^\mathsf{T}$ can be viewed as picking out particular rows of the matrix $\big[(\mathbf{C} \odot \mathbf{A}) \otimes \mathbf{I}_n\big]$ (with $\mathbf{P}_2$ ensuring the ordering is consistent). Specifically, the resulting matrix and right-hand side are

$$\mathbf{U}_2 = \Big[\big(\mathbf{C}(k,:) * \mathbf{A}(i,:)\big) \otimes \mathbf{I}_n(j,:)\Big]_{(i,j,k)\in\Omega} \quad \text{and} \quad \mathbf{x} = \Big[x_{ijk}\Big]_{(i,j,k)\in\Omega}.$$

The intermediate matrix $\big[(\mathbf{C} \odot \mathbf{A}) \otimes \mathbf{I}_n\big]$ is potentially expensive to form. However, we can use the special structure of $\mathbf{U}_2$ to form it directly and more cheaply in the case that $q \ll mnp$ (i.e., $\mathcal{X}$ is scarce).

A final observation is that the least squares problem can be decoupled into n independent least squares problems, one per row of $\mathbf{B}$. Define $\Omega_j \equiv \{\,(i,k) \mid (i,j,k) \in \Omega\,\}$ for all $j \in [n]$, and consider the subset of equations corresponding to Ω_j:

$$\Big[\big(\mathbf{C}(k,:) * \mathbf{A}(i,:)\big) \otimes \mathbf{I}_n(j,:)\Big]_{(i,k)\in\Omega_j} \operatorname{vec}(\mathbf{B}) = \Big[x_{ijk}\Big]_{(i,k)\in\Omega_j}.$$

Using the rule for Kronecker products in Eq. (A.11e), we can rewrite this as

$$\operatorname{vec}\Bigg(\underbrace{\mathbf{I}_n(j,:)}_{1\times n}\underbrace{\mathbf{B}}_{n\times r}\underbrace{\Big[\mathbf{C}(k,:) * \mathbf{A}(i,:)\Big]^\mathsf{T}_{(i,k)\in\Omega_j}}_{r\times|\Omega_j|}\Bigg) = \Big[x_{ijk}\Big]_{(i,k)\in\Omega_j},$$

which (realizing vec on a row vector has the effect of a transpose) simplifies to

$$\Big[\mathbf{C}(k,:) * \mathbf{A}(i,:)\Big]_{(i,k)\in\Omega_j} \mathbf{B}(j,:)^\mathsf{T} = \Big[x_{ijk}\Big]_{(i,k)\in\Omega_j}.$$

So, the least squares problems for the individual rows are decoupled and can be solved independently (and in parallel).

14.5 Example: CP-WOPT on EEM Tensor

We revisit the EEM tensor from fluorescence spectroscopy as described in Section 1.5.2 and used in Section 9.6, but now look at the *raw* data. The raw data for EEM omits emission data in an interval of 10 nm from the excitation wavelength in order to avoid first-order Rayleigh scatter (Acar et al., 2014), and these entries are indicated by NaN. Additionally, some entries are negative due to measurement errors.

14.5.1 Computing CP on EEM with Missing Data

The EEM tensor is of size $18 \times 251 \times 21$, and the raw data has 7398 (7.8%) missing entries. We let Ω denote the known value indicator set, so $|\Omega| = 7398$. The remaining entries are in the range $[-1.0405\text{e+}04, 6.9768\text{e+}05]$. There are 4935 (5.2%) negative entries, though the data is ideally nonnegative. The missing data is indicated by white regions in Fig. 14.1.

Before we discuss applying weighted optimization (WOPT) to this data, we mention one technique that is often used in practice: filling in missing data with the average of the known values. In other words, construct a tensor $\bar{\mathcal{X}}$ such that

$$\bar{x}_{ijk} = \begin{cases} x_{ijk} & \text{if } (i,j,k) \in \Omega \\ \frac{1}{|\Omega|}\sum_{i\in\Omega} x_{ijk} & \text{otherwise} \end{cases}.$$

We can then apply standard methods for computing the CP decomposition to the tensor $\bar{\mathcal{X}}$. We will compare WOPT to this heuristic approach, which we call FILL+OPT.

To compute CP with weighted optimization, we construct a known value weight tensor $\mathcal{W}_\Omega$ as in Eq. (14.2). Then, we solve the WOPT problem

$$\min_{\mathbf{v}\in\mathbb{R}^{290r}} \quad \tilde{f}(\mathbf{v}) \equiv \left\| \mathcal{W}_\Omega * (\mathcal{X} - [\![\mathbf{A},\mathbf{B},\mathbf{C}]\!]) \right\|^2$$
$$\text{subject to} \quad \{\mathbf{A},\mathbf{B},\mathbf{C}\} = \texttt{vec2mats}(\mathbf{v}) \quad \text{and} \quad \mathbf{v} \geq \mathbf{0}.$$

Here $\mathbf{v}$ represents the matrices $\mathbf{A}$, $\mathbf{B}$, and $\mathbf{C}$ vectorized and stacked. The constraint $\mathbf{v} \geq \mathbf{0}$ is to be interpreted elementwise, i.e., every entry to every factor matrix is greater than 0.

We compare FILL+OPT and WOPT on the raw EEM tensor. We run each method five times and take the best solution according to each objective function. The results are shown in Fig. 14.2, and the WOPT solution is somewhat better than FILL+OPT.

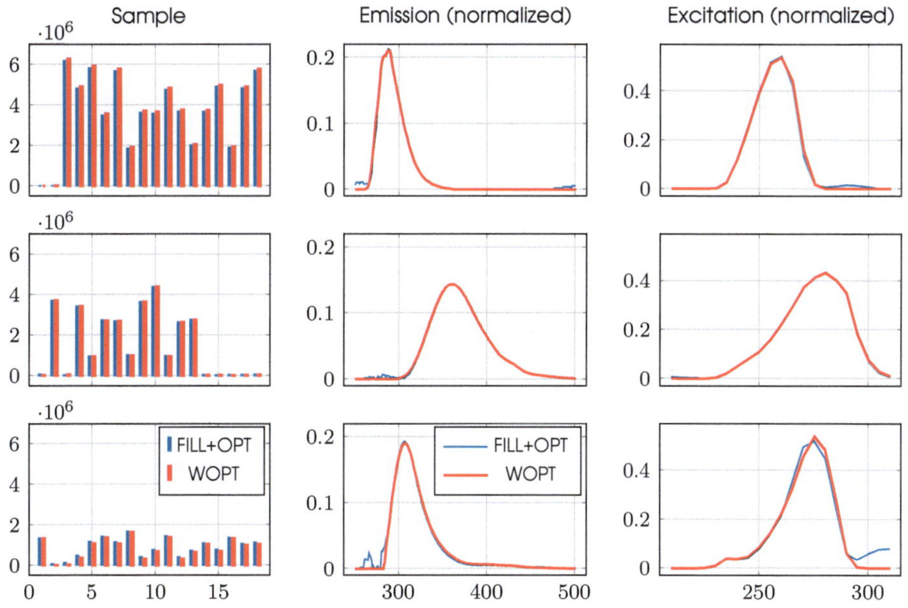

Figure 14.2 Comparison of weighted optimization (WOPT) and filling in missing data with average known entry (FILL+OPT) on the raw EEM tensor of size $18 \times 251 \times 21$ with 7.8% missing entries. Both formulations have nonnegativity constraints and compute a rank $r = 3$ decomposition.

Exercise 14.9 Implement Algorithm 14.1 and reproduce the experiment used to generate Fig. 14.2.

Exercise 14.10 Implement the EM algorithm from Section 9.5.2. Compare its performance to CP-WOPT in terms of time and solution quality.

Exercise 14.11 Implement CP-WALS, outlined in Section 14.4. Compare its performance to CP-WOPT in terms of time and solution quality.

14.5.2 EEM Tensor with Even More Missing Data

We make the problem more difficult by removing additional data. We remove an additional 50% of the known entries at random. The result is a tensor with 51,138 (53.9%) missing entries. We run the same experiment as before and show the results in Fig. 14.3. With a larger degree of missing data, the difference between naively filling in the missing entries with an average value and using weighted optimization is dramatic. The FILL+OPT approach cannot recover the third component, but the weighted optimization yields the same result as before.

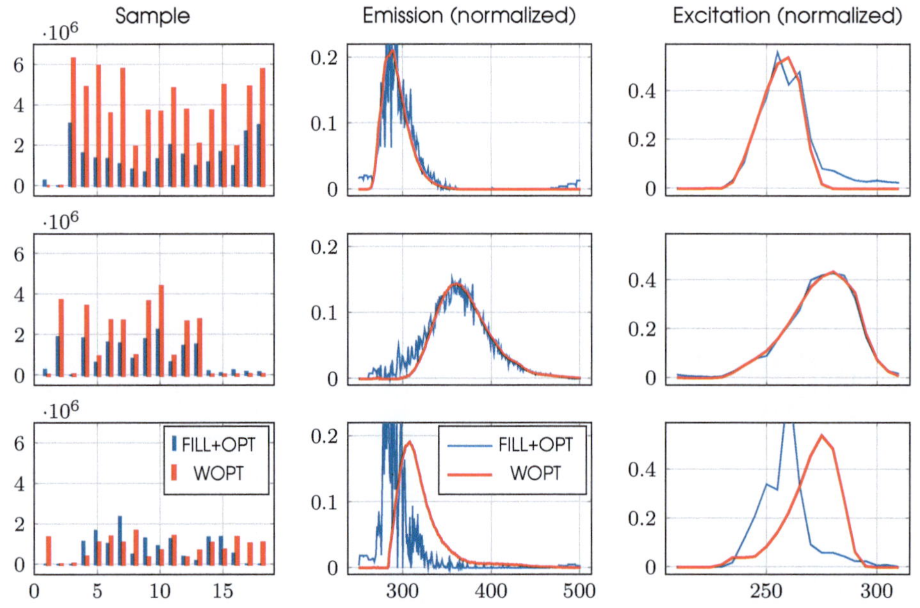

Figure 14.3 Comparing weighted optimization (WOPT) and filling in missing data with average entry (FILL+OPT) on the EEM tensor of size $18 \times 251 \times 21$ with 53.9% missing entries. Both formulations have nonnegativity constraints and compute a rank $r = 3$ decomposition.

Exercise 14.12 Start with the raw EEM tensor and remove a portion (ρ) of the entries. Compare FILL+OPT and WOPT on this tensor, as we did in the experiment that produced Fig. 14.3. (a) Use $\rho = 0.25$. (b) Use $\rho = 0.5$ (reproducing Fig. 14.3). (c) Use $\rho = 0.75$.

15 Generalized CP Decomposition

In this chapter, we consider generalizing the *loss* function used in computing a low-rank CP model. We refer to this as *generalized* CP (GCP) decomposition. The specific GCP formulation that we discuss here was introduced by Hong et al. (2020); however, different loss functions have been promoted in various contexts before that work. For instance, several authors have promoted Kullback–Leibler (KL) divergence for count tensors, starting with Welling and Weber (2001) and also including Chi and Kolda (2012), Hansen et al. (2015), and Shashua and Hazan (2005). Alpha and beta divergences have been proposed for nonnegative data by Cichocki et al. (2007). These formulations fit within the GCP framework. GCP is also sometimes referred to as non-least-squares cost (Vandecappelle et al., 2020).

In this chapter, we discuss the concept of generalized loss functions in Section 15.1 and some choices for loss functions in Section 15.2. We cast this as an optimization formulation in Section 15.3, compute the gradient in Section 15.4, and discuss its optimization in Section 15.5. Finally, we consider application to the monkey BMI tensor in Section 15.6 and the Chicago crime tensor in Section 15.7.

15.1 Generalized Loss Functions

The GCP minimization problem for $\mathcal{X} \in \mathbb{R}^{m \times n \times p}$ computes a rank-r Kruskal tensor $\mathcal{Y} = \llbracket \mathbf{A}, \mathbf{B}, \mathbf{C} \rrbracket$ that minimizes a GCP loss function that sums the differences between $\mathcal{X}$ and $\mathcal{Y}$ at each element. The general problem for a 3-way tensor is

$$\min_{\mathbf{A},\mathbf{B},\mathbf{C}} f(\mathbf{A}, \mathbf{B}, \mathbf{C}) \equiv \sum_{i=1}^{m} \sum_{j=1}^{n} \sum_{k=1}^{p} f_{ijk}(y_{ijk}) \quad \text{subject to} \quad \mathcal{Y} = \llbracket \mathbf{A}, \mathbf{B}, \mathbf{C} \rrbracket,$$

where $f : \mathbb{R}^{(m+n+p)r} \to \mathbb{R}$ is called the *loss function* and $f_{ijk} : \mathbb{R} \to \mathbb{R}$ is called the *elementwise loss function*. Each function f_{ijk} depends on entry (i, j, k) of $\mathcal{X}$, the data tensor, for its definition and evaluates entry (i, j, k) of $\mathcal{Y}$, which depends on the inputs $\{ \mathbf{A}, \mathbf{B}, \mathbf{C} \}$, to compute some metric of similarity or distance.

GCP encapsulates standard CP if f is the sum of squared errors (SSE):

$$f_{ijk}(y_{ijk}) = (x_{ijk} - y_{ijk})^2.$$

In terms of other functions, KL divergence is useful for count data (Chi and Kolda, 2012; Hong et al., 2020; Welling and Weber, 2001), in which case the choice for the elementwise loss function is

$$f_{ijk}(y_{ijk}) = y_{ijk} - x_{ijk} \log y_{ijk}.$$

These and other options are discussed in Section 15.2.

The GCP loss function for a d-way tensor $\mathcal{X} \in \mathbb{R}^{n_1 \times n_2 \times \cdots \times n_d}$ and $\mathcal{Y} = [\![\mathbf{A}_1, \mathbf{A}_2, \ldots, \mathbf{A}_d]\!]$ is the same except that the summation is over all d modes rather than only three:

$$\begin{aligned} \min_{\mathbf{A}_1, \mathbf{A}_2, \ldots, \mathbf{A}_d} \quad & f(\mathbf{A}_1, \mathbf{A}_2, \ldots, \mathbf{A}_d) \equiv \sum_{i_1=1}^{n_1} \sum_{i_2=1}^{n_2} \cdots \sum_{i_d=1}^{n_d} f_{i_1 i_2 \cdots i_d}(y_{i_1 i_2 \cdots i_d}) \\ \text{subject to} \quad & \mathcal{Y} = [\![\mathbf{A}_1, \mathbf{A}_2, \ldots, \mathbf{A}_d]\!]. \end{aligned}$$

As in the above, the elementwise loss function $f_{i_1 i_2 \cdots i_d}$ depends on $x_{i_1 i_2 \cdots i_d}$.

To simplify the notation, we can write the GCP loss function using **multi-index notation**, where $\boldsymbol{i} \equiv (i_1, i_2, \ldots, i_d)$.

Definition 15.1 (GCP Loss Function) For a tensor $\mathcal{X} \in \mathbb{R}^{n_1 \times n_2 \times \cdots \times n_d}$, the GCP loss function is

$$f(\mathbf{A}_1, \mathbf{A}_2, \ldots, \mathbf{A}_d) \equiv \sum_{\boldsymbol{i} \in \mathcal{I}} f_{\boldsymbol{i}}(y_{\boldsymbol{i}}) \quad \text{subject to} \quad \mathcal{Y} = [\![\mathbf{A}_1, \mathbf{A}_2, \ldots, \mathbf{A}_d]\!],$$

where $\boldsymbol{i} \equiv (i_1, i_2, \ldots, i_d)$, $\mathcal{I} = [n_1] \otimes [n_2] \otimes \cdots \otimes [n_d]$ is the set of all multi-indices, and each elementwise loss function $f_{\boldsymbol{i}} : \mathbb{R} \to \mathbb{R}$ depends on $x_{\boldsymbol{i}}$.

15.2 Choices for Loss Functions

There are many ways to select the loss function, f. It can be heuristic or derived from some specific principles, and we discuss some options in this section. The general requirement we impose (for ease of fitting the model using optimization) is that each $f_{\boldsymbol{i}} : \mathbb{R} \to \mathbb{R}$ be continuously differentiable.

One methodology is based on statistical maximum likelihood estimation; see Section C.2. In this case, we think of each $x_{\boldsymbol{i}}$ as a random variable drawn from a random distribution defined by $p : \mathbb{R} \to \mathbb{R}$, a parameterized probability distribution function (pdf) or probability mass function (pmf). The parametrization depends (perhaps indirectly) on $y_{\boldsymbol{i}}$. In other words, we presume that

$$x_{\boldsymbol{i}} \sim p(x_{\boldsymbol{i}} | \theta_{\boldsymbol{i}}), \quad \text{where} \quad \theta_{\boldsymbol{i}} = L(y_{\boldsymbol{i}}).$$

Here $L : \mathbb{R} \to \mathbb{R}$ is an invertible real-valued **link function** that maps $y_{\boldsymbol{i}}$ to some *natural parameter* $\theta_{\boldsymbol{i}}$ of the distribution. The idea of a natural parameter will make more sense as we delve into examples in the sections that follow. Under this assumption, our objective is to maximize the likelihood of the low-rank CP model $\mathcal{Y}$ given $\mathcal{X}$, i.e., to solve

$$\max_{\mathbf{A}_1, \mathbf{A}_2, \ldots, \mathbf{A}_d} \prod_{\boldsymbol{i} \in \mathcal{I}} p(x_{\boldsymbol{i}} | L(y_{\boldsymbol{i}})), \quad \text{subject to} \quad \mathcal{Y} = [\![\mathbf{A}_1, \mathbf{A}_2, \ldots, \mathbf{A}_d]\!].$$

Working with the product is inconvenient and potentially problematic (e.g., underflow errors can occur in finite precision arithmetic). For this reason, we apply the (natural) log, which does not change the maximizer because it is monotonic. Further, it is convenient to cast this as a minimization problem by taking its negative. So, rather than computing the maximum likelihood, we instead compute the minimum negative log-likelihood. This results in the following minimization problem:

$$\min_{\mathbf{A}_1,\mathbf{A}_2,\ldots,\mathbf{A}_d} f \equiv \sum_{i\in\mathcal{I}} -\log p\big(x_i|L(y_i)\big) \quad \text{subject to} \quad \mathcal{Y} = [\![\mathbf{A}_1, \mathbf{A}_2, \ldots, \mathbf{A}_d]\!]. \tag{15.1}$$

Hence, the elementwise loss function is $f_i(y_i) = -\log p\big(x_i|L(y_i)\big)$. We give examples of using this methodology for real-valued, count, binary, and nonnegative data in the subsequent discussion.

15.2.1 Sum of Squared Errors (Normal-Distributed Data)

In this subsection, we show that the standard CP elementwise loss function, $f_i(y_i) = (x_i - y_i)^2$ can be derived under the assumption that the data is low-rank plus white noise. Specifically, assume

$$\mathcal{X} = \mathcal{Y} + \mathcal{E},$$

where $\mathcal{Y}$ is a low-rank tensor and $\mathcal{E}$ is a noise tensor, such that $\varepsilon_i \sim \mathcal{N}(0,\sigma)$ for all $i \in \mathcal{I}$ and σ is some fixed constant across all entries. We can rewrite this as

$$x_i \sim y_i + \varepsilon_i \quad \text{with} \quad \varepsilon_i \sim \mathcal{N}(0,\sigma) \quad \text{for all} \quad i \in \mathcal{I}.$$

Alternatively, we can think of x_i being normally distributed with mean y_i and standard deviation σ, so that we have

$$x_i \sim \mathcal{N}(y_i, \sigma) \quad \text{for all} \quad i \in \mathcal{I}.$$

Plugging the negative log likelihood for the normal distribution from Eq. (C.4) into Eq. (15.1) with $\mu_i = L(y_i) \equiv y_i$ yields the negative log likelihood of $\mathcal{Y}$:

$$f \equiv \frac{1}{2\sigma^2}\sum_{i\in\mathcal{I}}(x_i - y_i)^2 - \underbrace{|\mathcal{I}|\log(\sqrt{\pi\sigma^2})}_{\text{constant}}.$$

We can drop the constant term and constant multiplicative factor to simplify to the standard CP loss function:

$$f \equiv \sum_{i\in\mathcal{I}}(x_i - y_i)^2.$$

The elementwise loss function for several sample values of x_i is shown in Fig. 15.1. The elementwise loss function is minimized when $y_i = x_i$, though we cannot achieve this for all entries because $\mathcal{Y}$ is low rank.

Exercise 15.1 (a) What is the derivative of the Gaussian elementwise loss function: $f(y) = (x - y)^2$, where x is a constant? (b) Prove that $y = x$ is a stationary point.

15.2.2 Logistic Regression (Binary Data)

Suppose the data in $\mathcal{X}$ is binary with values in $\{0, 1\}$. In this case, it may be reasonable to assume the data is Bernoulli distributed; see Section C.3.2. This means we assume

$$x_i \sim \text{Bernoulli}(\rho_i), \quad \text{where} \quad \rho_i \in [0,1] \quad \text{for all} \quad i \in \mathcal{I}.$$

The parameter ρ_i is the probability of observing a 1. We have to link the natural parameter to the model: $\rho_i = L(y_i)$. We have three ways we could make this link.

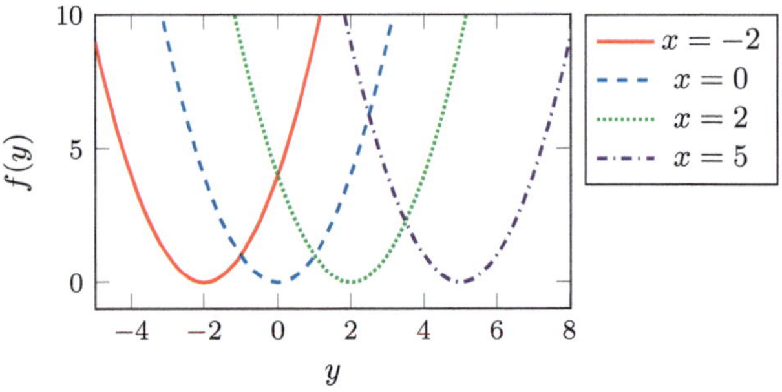

Figure 15.1 Gaussian elementwise loss function $f(y) = (x - y)^2$ for several fixed values of $x \in \mathbb{R}$.

One option is to simply define $L(y_i) = y_i$. However, this approach has the major disadvantage that y_i must be constrained to $[0, 1]$. This is a nonlinear constraint with respect to the entries for the model factor matrices. For this reason, we do not consider this approach further.

A second option is to define the link as $L(y_i) = y_i/(1+y_i)$. This means that y_i represents the **odds** of observing a 1, and we need only constrain y_i to be nonnegative. This link is especially nice for data where 0 represents something very common (i.e., the default) and 1s are somewhat rare.

Exercise 15.2 Let $\rho \in [0, 1]$ be the probability of an event. Prove that $\rho = y/(1 + y)$ if and only if $y = \rho/(1 - \rho)$ is the odds of the event.

Plugging the negative log likelihood for the Bernoulli distribution from Eq. (C.6) into Eq. (15.1) with $\rho_i = L(y_i) = y_i/(1 + y_i)$ yields the negative log likelihood of $\boldsymbol{\mathcal{Y}}$ to be

$$f \equiv \sum_{\boldsymbol{i} \in \mathcal{I}} \log(1 + y_{\boldsymbol{i}}) - x_{\boldsymbol{i}} \log y_{\boldsymbol{i}} \quad \text{with} \quad y_{\boldsymbol{i}} \geq 0 \text{ for all } \boldsymbol{i} \in \mathcal{I}.$$

The elementwise loss function for both sample values of x_i is shown in Fig. 15.2a. If $x_i = 0$, the elementwise loss function is minimized at $y_i = 0$. If $x_i = 1$, the elementwise loss function is minimized at $y_i = +\infty$.

Exercise 15.3 (a) What is the derivative for the Bernoulli elementwise loss function with log link, $f(y) = \log(1 + y) - x \log y$? (b) Prove that the minimizer is $y = 0$ if $x = 0$. Hint: Use Proposition B.25.

A third option is to define the link as $L(y_i) = e^{y_i}/(1 + e^{y_i})$. This means that $e^{y_i} = \rho_i/(1 - \rho_i)$ represents the **log-odds** of observing a 1, and y_i is unconstrained.

Exercise 15.4 Let $\rho \in [0, 1]$ be the probability of an event. Prove that $\rho = e^y/(1 + e^y)$ if and only if $y = \log(\rho/(1 - \rho))$ is the log-odds of the event.

Plugging the negative log likelihood for the Bernoulli distribution from Eq. (C.6) into Eq. (15.1) with $\rho_i = L(y_i) = e^{y_i}/(1 + e^{y_i})$ yields the negative log likelihood of $\boldsymbol{\mathcal{Y}}$ to be

$$f \equiv \sum_{\boldsymbol{i} \in \mathcal{I}} \log(1 + e^{y_{\boldsymbol{i}}}) - x_{\boldsymbol{i}} y_{\boldsymbol{i}}.$$

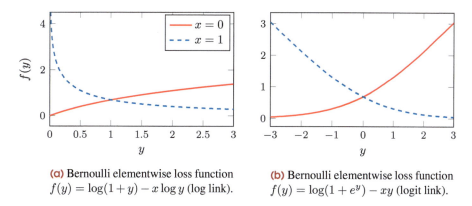

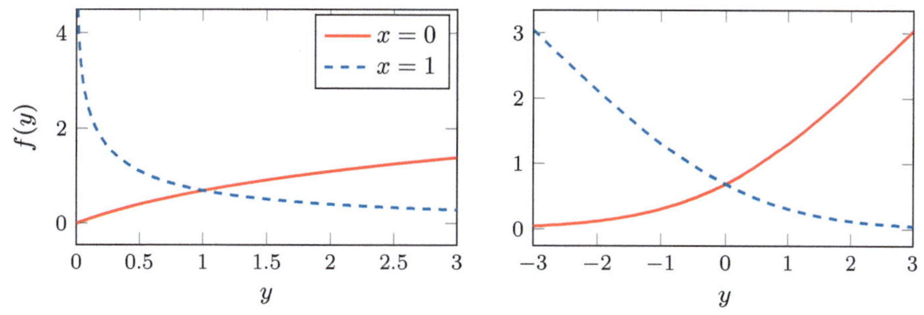

(a) Bernoulli elementwise loss function $f(y) = \log(1 + y) - x \log y$ (log link).

(b) Bernoulli elementwise loss function $f(y) = \log(1 + e^y) - xy$ (logit link).

Figure 15.2 Bernoulli elementwise loss functions with different links.

The elementwise loss function for $x_i \in \{0, 1\}$ is shown in Fig. 15.2b. If $x_i = 0$, the elementwise loss function is minimized at $y_i = -\infty$. If $x_i = 1$, the elementwise loss function is minimized at $y_i = +\infty$.

Exercise 15.5 What is the derivative for the Bernoulli elementwise loss function with logit link, $f_i(y_i) = \log(1 + e^{y_i}) - x_i y_i$?

15.2.3 KL Divergence (Count Data)

Suppose the data in $\mathfrak{X}$ is count data, i.e., values in $\mathbb{N} \equiv \{0, 1, 2, \ldots\}$. In this case, it may be reasonable to assume the data is Poisson distributed; see Section C.3.3. This means we assume

$$x_i \sim \text{Poisson}(\lambda_i), \quad \text{where} \quad \lambda_i \geq 0 \quad \text{for all} \quad \boldsymbol{i} \in \mathcal{I}.$$

The parameter λ_i is the mean and need not be an integer. We have to link the natural parameter to the model: $\rho_i = L(y_i)$. We have two ways we could make this link.

One option is to simply define $L(y_i) = y_i$. This means that y_i represents the expected value of x_i, and we need only constrain y_i to be positive.

Plugging the negative log likelihood for the Poisson distribution from Eq. (C.8) into Eq. (15.1) with $\lambda_i = L(y_i) = y_i$ yields the negative log likelihood of $\mathfrak{Y}$ to be

$$f \equiv \sum_{\boldsymbol{i} \in \mathcal{I}} y_i - x_i \log y_i + \underbrace{\log x_i!}_{\text{constant w.r.t. } \mathfrak{Y}} \qquad \text{with} \quad y_i > 0 \text{ for all } \boldsymbol{i} \in \mathcal{I}.$$

This is the KL divergence. The last term does not involve y_i and so can be ignored for the purposes of optimization, leading to an elementwise loss function of the form $f_i(y_i) = y_i - x_i \log y_i$. Hence, the objective function becomes

$$f = \sum_{\boldsymbol{i} \in \mathcal{I}} y_i - x_i \log y_i \quad \text{with} \quad y_i > 0 \text{ for all } \boldsymbol{i} \in \mathcal{I}.$$

The constraint that y_i be strictly positive can be difficult to enforce. In practice, we use $f_i(y_i) = y_i - x_i \log(y_i + \varepsilon)$, where ε is a very small constant, and then constrain $y_i \geq 0$.

The elementwise loss function for sample values of x_i is shown in Fig. 15.3a. The loss function is minimized at $y_i = x_i$.

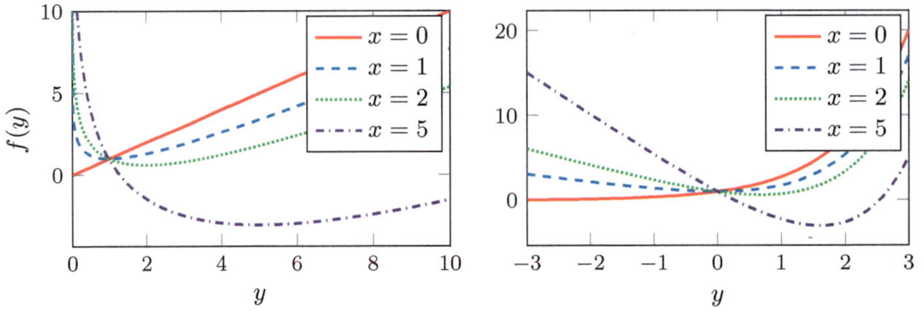

(a) Poisson elementwise loss function $f(y) = y - x \log y$ (identity link)

(b) Poisson elementwise loss function $f(y) = e^y - xy$ (log link).

Figure 15.3 Poisson elementwise loss functions for several fixed values of $x \in \mathbb{N}$.

Another option is to define $L(y_i) = e^{y_i}$. This means that e^{y_i} represents the expected value of x_i, and y_i is unconstrained.

Plugging the negative log likelihood for the Poisson distribution from Eq. (C.8) into Eq. (15.1) with $\lambda_i = L(y_i) = e^{y_i}$ yields the negative log likelihood of $\mathcal{Y}$ to be

$$f \equiv \sum_{i \in \mathcal{I}} e^{y_i} - x_i y_i + \underbrace{\log x_i!}_{\text{constant w.r.t. } \mathcal{Y}} \qquad \text{with} \quad y_i > 0 \text{ for all } i \in \mathcal{I}.$$

The last term does not involve y_i and so can be ignored for the purposes of optimization, leading to an elementwise loss function of the form $f_i(y_i) = e^m - xm$. Hence, the objective function becomes

$$f \equiv \sum_{i \in \mathcal{I}} e^{y_i} - x_i y_i \quad \text{with} \quad y_i > 0 \text{ for all } i \in \mathcal{I}.$$

The elementwise loss function for sample values of x_i is shown in Fig. 15.3b. The loss function is minimized at $e^{y_i} = x_i$. For $x_i = 0$, this means the optimal value of y_i is $-\infty$.

Exercise 15.6 (a) What is the derivative for the Poisson elementwise loss function with identity link, $f(y) = y - x \log y$ for fixed x? (b) Prove that $y = x$ satisfies the optimality conditions for nonnegativity constraints (see Proposition B.25) for all $x \geq 0$ (assume $0 \log 0 = 0$ for the case of $x = 0$).

Exercise 15.7 (a) What is the derivative for the Poisson elementwise loss function with log link, $f(y) = e^y - xy$ with fixed x? (b) Prove that $y = \log x$ satisfies the optimality conditions for nonnegativity constraints (see Proposition B.25) for all $x > 0$.

15.2.4 Loss Functions for Nonnegative Data

There are many distributions for nonnegative data.

Gamma distribution

One general option is the gamma distribution, which includes some well-known distributions as special cases; see Section C.3.4. The gamma function is only defined for strictly positive data, and it has two parameters:

$$x_i \sim \text{Gamma}(K, \theta_i), \quad \text{where} \quad \theta_i > 0 \text{ for all } i \in \mathcal{I}.$$

We assume K is constant and use the link function $\theta_i = L(i) = y_i/K$, which means $y_i = K\theta_i = \mathbb{E}[x_i]$.

Plugging the negative log likelihood for the gamma distribution from Eq. (C.10) into Eq. (15.1) with $\theta_i = L(i) = y_i/K$ yields the negative log likelihood of $\mathcal{Y}$ to be

$$\sum_{i \in \mathcal{I}} \underbrace{\log \Gamma(K)}_{\text{constant}} + K \log \frac{y_i}{K} \underbrace{+K \log x_i +}_{\text{constant w.r.t } \mathcal{Y}} \frac{Kx_i}{y_i}, \quad \text{where} \quad y_i > 0 \text{ for all } \boldsymbol{i} \in \mathcal{I}.$$

Removing terms that do not involved y_i and factoring out K, which can both be ignored for the purposes of optimization, the elementwise loss function is $f_i(y_i) = \log y_i + \frac{x_i}{y_i}$ with the constraint $y_i > 0$, so the overall loss function is

$$f \equiv \sum_{i \in \mathcal{I}} \log y_i + \frac{x_i}{y_i}, \quad \text{where} \quad y_i > 0 \text{ for all } \boldsymbol{i} \in \mathcal{I}.$$

In practice, we use $f_i(y_i) = \log(y_i + \varepsilon) + \frac{x_i}{y_i + \varepsilon}$, where ε is a very small constant, and then we can relax the constraint to $y_i \geq 0$.

The elementwise loss function is shown in Fig. 15.4. The loss function is minimized when $y_i = x_i$.

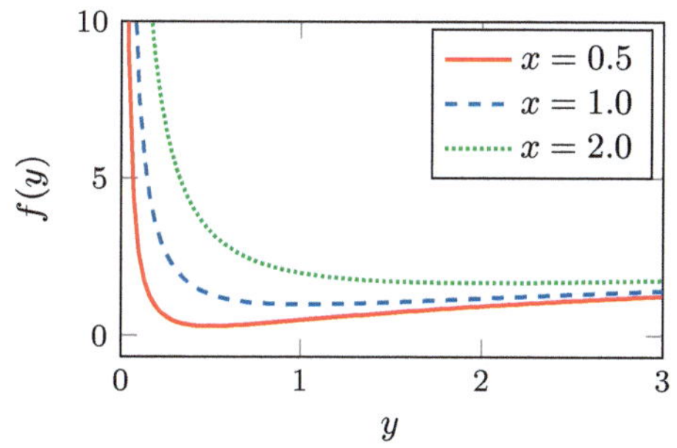

Figure 15.4 Gamma elementwise loss function $f(y) = \log y + x/y$ for several fixed $x \in \mathbb{R}$ with $x > 0$.

Exercise 15.8 (a) What is the derivative for the gamma elementwise loss function: $f_i(y_i) = \log y_i - \frac{x_i}{y_i}$? (b) Prove that $y_i = x_i$ satisfies the optimality conditions for nonnegativity constraints (see Proposition B.25) for all $x_i > 0$.

Beta Divergence

Another popular loss function for nonnegative data is the β-divergence (Cichocki and Amari, 2010; Cichocki et al., 2007; Févotte and Idier, 2011), though this does not derive from a distribution. The origin of β-divergence is attributed to Basu et al. (1998) and Mihoko and Eguchi (2002). For fixed x and β, the β-divergence is defined as

$$\beta\text{-divergence}(y) = \begin{cases} \frac{1}{\beta(\beta-1)} \left(x^\beta + (\beta - 1) y^\beta - \beta x y^{\beta-1} \right) & \text{if } \beta \in \mathbb{R} \setminus \{0, 1\} \\ x \log \frac{x}{y} - x + y & \text{if } \beta = 1 \\ \frac{x}{y} - \log \frac{x}{y} - 1 & \text{if } \beta = 0 \end{cases}.$$

For $\beta \in \mathbb{R} \setminus \{0, 1\}$, ignoring the terms that are constant with respect to the optimization, the loss function becomes

$$f \equiv \sum_{\boldsymbol{i} \in \mathcal{I}} \frac{1}{\beta} y_{\boldsymbol{i}}^{\beta} - \frac{1}{\beta - 1} x_{\boldsymbol{i}} y_{\boldsymbol{i}}^{\beta-1}, \quad \text{where} \quad y_{\boldsymbol{i}} \geq 0 \text{ for all } \boldsymbol{i} \in \mathcal{I}.$$

Loss functions for different values of β are shown in Fig. 15.5.

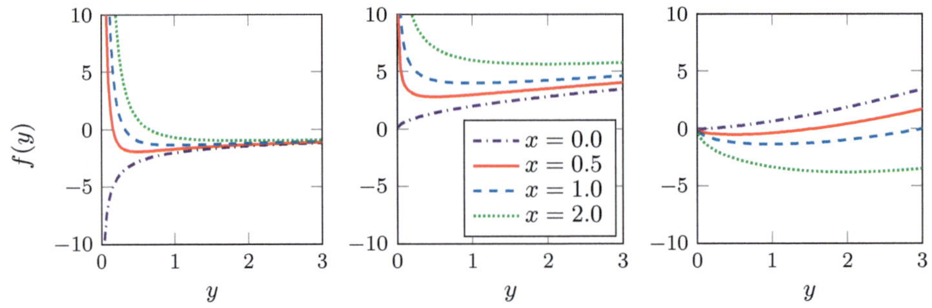

(a) $\beta = -0.5$. (b) $\beta = 0.5$. (c) $\beta = 1.5$.

Figure 15.5 Beta divergence elementwise loss function $f(y) = \frac{y^{\beta}}{\beta} - \frac{xy^{\beta-1}}{\beta-1}$ for different values of parameter β and several fixed $x \in \mathbb{R}$ with $x \geq 0$.

Exercise 15.9 (a) What is the derivative for the beta divergence elementwise loss function with $\beta \notin \{0, 1\}$: $f(y) = y^{\beta}/\beta - xy^{\beta-1}/(\beta - 1)$? (b) Prove that $y = x$ satisfies the optimality conditions for nonnegativity constraints (see Proposition B.25) for all $x > 0$.

The case of $\beta = 0$ reduces to the same loss function as for the gamma distribution.

Exercise 15.10 Prove that the elementwise loss function for $\beta = 0$ can be simplified to the same as that for the gamma distribution with identity link, $f(y) = \log y + x/y$.

The case of $\beta = 1$ reduces to the same loss function as for the Poisson distribution.

Exercise 15.11 Prove that the elementwise loss function for $\beta = 1$ can be simplified to the same as that for Poisson with identity link, $f(y) = y - x \log y$.

15.2.5 Robust Loss Functions

One heuristic choice is the so-called *Huber loss* (Huber, 1964) which is a robust loss function (Hastie et al., 2009). For threshold Δ, the Huber elementwise loss function is

$$f_{\boldsymbol{i}}(y_{\boldsymbol{i}}) \equiv \begin{cases} (x_{\boldsymbol{i}} - y_{\boldsymbol{i}})^2 & \text{if } |x_{\boldsymbol{i}} - y_{\boldsymbol{i}}| \leq \Delta \\ 2\Delta|x_{\boldsymbol{i}} - y_{\boldsymbol{i}}| - \Delta^2 & \text{otherwise} \end{cases}. \tag{15.2}$$

We compare the Huber loss to the usual CP loss in Fig. 15.6. The Huber loss increases more slowly away from the minimizer, making it more robust against outliers.

Exercise 15.12 (a) What is the derivative for the Huber elementwise loss function? (b) Prove that $y = x$ satisfies the optimality conditions for nonnegativity constraints (see Proposition B.25) for all $x > 0$.

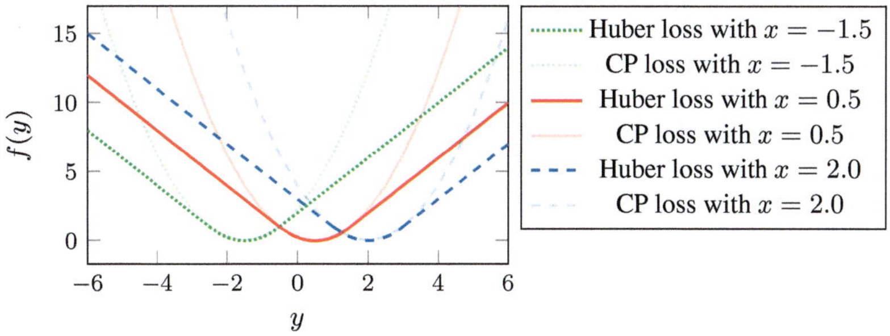

Figure 15.6 Comparison of Huber loss (with $\Delta = 1.0$) and CP loss for several fixed $x \in \mathbb{R}$.

15.2.6 Summary of Loss Functions

We summarize the options for the elementwise loss function in Table 15.1. In some cases, strict positivity is required on y. However, we can add a small ε to relax this constraint. Essentially, this indicates that we can never have $y_{\boldsymbol{i}} = 0$ if $x_{\boldsymbol{i}} \neq 0$. In the table, we provide a fix in the loss function, but it is also possible to design $\mathcal{Y}$ itself to have an extra "noise" component, per Remark 15.2.

***Remark* 15.2 (Handling strict positivity)** Consider a case where strict positivity is required, such as the Bernoulli odds link. To compute a 3-way rank-r GCP decomposition $\mathcal{Y} = [\![\mathbf{A}, \mathbf{B}, \mathbf{C}]\!]$ that satisfies *strict* positivity, we can optimize over a rank-$(r+1)$ decomposition of the form

$$\tilde{\mathcal{Y}} = [\![\mathbf{A}, \mathbf{B}, \mathbf{C}]\!] + \tau \mathbf{1} \circ \mathbf{1} \circ \mathbf{1},$$

where $\tau > 0$ is a regularization parameter, $\mathbf{1}$ represents a vector of all 1s, and $\mathbf{A}, \mathbf{B}, \mathbf{C}$ are only required to be nonnegative rather than strictly positive.

Table 15.1 Options for elementwise loss functions in GCP. Here subscripts $\boldsymbol{i}$ are omitted, the data tensor element is x, and the CP model element is y. Notation "≥ 0" indicates strict inequality is technically required; however, functions are adjusted by adding a small positive constant "$+\,\varepsilon$" to justify only nonnegativity.

Name	$f(y)$	**Constraints**
Gaussian (standard CP loss)	$(x-y)^2$	$x, y \in \mathbb{R}$
Bernoulli (odds link)	$\log(1+y) - x\log(y+\varepsilon)$	$x \in \{0,1\}, y \geq 0$
Bernoulli (logit link)	$\log(1+e^y) - xy$	$x \in \{0,1\}, y \in \mathbb{R}$
Poisson (identity link)	$y - x\log(y+\varepsilon)$	$x \in \mathbb{N}, y \geq 0$
Poisson (log link)	$e^y - xy$	$x \in \mathbb{N}, y \in \mathbb{R}$
Gamma (affine link)	$x/(y+\varepsilon) + \log(y+\varepsilon)$	$x \geq 0, y \geq 0$
Beta divergence ($\beta \notin \{0,1\}$)	$y^\beta/\beta + xy^{\beta-1}/(\beta-1)$	$x, y \geq 0$
Huber (robust loss)	$\begin{cases} (x-y)^2 & \text{if } \lvert x-y \rvert \leq \Delta \\ 2\Delta\lvert x-y\rvert - \Delta^2 & \text{otherwise} \end{cases}$	$x, y \in \mathbb{R}$

Exercise 15.13 How does handling strict positivity as described in Remark 15.2 compare to adding ε in certain places as prescribed in Table 15.1.

15.3 Optimization Formulation

We now consider the optimization formulation, which generalizes the discussion of optimization for CP in Chapter 12. We cast the optimization problem in terms of minimizing a function $f(\mathbf{v})$, where $\mathbf{v}$ is a vector. We can convert between a vector representation and Kruskal tensor representation using the `mats2vec` and `vec2mats` operations as discussed in Section 12.1.

15.3.1 GCP for 3-way Tensors

For a 3-way tensor $\mathcal{X} \in \mathbb{R}^{m \times n \times p}$, elementwise loss function $f_{ijk}(y_{ijk})$, and rank r, we can formulate the GCP optimization problem as

$$\begin{aligned} \min_{\mathbf{v} \in \mathbb{R}^{r(m+n+p)}} \quad & f(\mathbf{v}) \equiv \sum_{i=1}^{m} \sum_{j=1}^{n} \sum_{k=1}^{p} f_{ijk}(y_{ijk}), \\ \text{where} \quad & \{\, \mathbf{A}, \mathbf{B}, \mathbf{C} \,\} = \texttt{vec2mats}(\mathbf{v}) \quad \text{and} \quad \mathcal{Y} = [\![\mathbf{A}, \mathbf{B}, \mathbf{C}]\!]. \end{aligned} \tag{15.3}$$

15.3.2 GCP for d-way Tensors

For a d-way tensor $\mathcal{X} \in \mathbb{R}^{n_1 \times n_2 \times \cdots \times n_d}$, elementwise loss function $f_{i_1,i_2,\ldots,i_d}(y_{i_1,i_2,\ldots,i_d})$, and rank r, we can formulate the GCP optimization problem as

$$\begin{aligned} \min_{\mathbf{v} \in \mathbb{R}^{r(n_1+n_2+\cdots+n_d)}} \quad & f(\mathbf{v}) \equiv \sum_{i_1=1}^{n_1} \sum_{i_2=1}^{n_2} \cdots \sum_{i_d=1}^{n_d} f_{i_1,i_2,\ldots,i_d}(y_{i_1,i_2,\ldots,i_d}), \\ \text{where} \quad & \{\, \mathbf{A}_1, \mathbf{A}_2, \ldots, \mathbf{A}_d \,\} = \texttt{vec2mats}(\mathbf{v}), \\ & \mathcal{Y} = [\![\mathbf{A}_1, \mathbf{A}_2, \ldots, \mathbf{A}_d]\!]. \end{aligned} \tag{15.4}$$

15.3.3 Properties and Extensions of GCP Decompositions

Because $\mathcal{Y}$ is a Kruskal tensor, it is subject to scaling and permutation ambiguities. The scaling ambiguity, in particular, may confound the optimization method. In such a situation, regularization can be added in the same way as for standard CP; see Section 9.4.2.

We may also consider adding constraints, such as nonnegativity of the factor matrices to ensure that $\mathcal{Y}$ is nonnegative; see Section 9.5.1.

15.4 GCP Gradient and First-Order Optimization

For computing the GCP gradient, we assume that f is continuously differentiable, which depends on the choice for the elementwise loss functions.

15.4.1 GCP Gradient for 3-way Tensors

Consider the optimization problem Eq. (15.3), where the function $f : \mathbb{R}^{r(m+n+p)} \to \mathbb{R}$. To compute the partial gradient of f with respect to $\text{vec}(\mathbf{B})$, we write $f = g \circ \mathbf{h}$, where

$$\mathcal{Y} = [\![\mathbf{A}, \mathbf{B}, \mathbf{C}]\!], \quad \mathbf{h}(\mathbf{A}, \mathbf{B}, \mathbf{C}) = \text{vec}(\mathcal{Y}), \quad \text{and} \quad g(\text{vec}(\mathcal{Y})) = \sum_{i=1}^{m} \sum_{j=1}^{n} \sum_{k=1}^{p} f_{ijk}(y_{ijk}).$$

We define the **elementwise derivative tensor** $\mathcal{D} \in \mathbb{R}^{m \times n \times p}$, such that

$$\mathcal{D}(i,j,k) \equiv f'_{ijk}(y_{ijk}) \quad \text{for all} \quad (i,j,k) \in [m] \otimes [n] \otimes [p].$$

Then $\nabla g(\text{vec}(\mathcal{Y})) = \text{vec}(\mathcal{D})$. Via the chain rule (Theorem B.11), using the partial Jacobian of $\mathbf{h}$ with respect to $\text{vec}(\mathbf{B})$ given in Proposition 12.7, we have

$$\begin{aligned}\frac{\partial f}{\partial \mathbf{B}}(\text{vec}(\mathbf{B})) &= \left[\frac{d\mathbf{h}}{d\,\text{vec}(\mathbf{B})}\right]^{\mathsf{T}} \nabla g(\mathbf{h}(\mathbf{A},\mathbf{B},\mathbf{C}))\\ &= \left(\mathbf{P}_2^{\mathsf{T}}\left[(\mathbf{C}\odot\mathbf{A})\otimes\mathbf{I}_n\right]\right)^{\mathsf{T}} \text{vec}(\mathcal{D})\\ &= \left[(\mathbf{C}\odot\mathbf{A})^{\mathsf{T}}\otimes\mathbf{I}_n\right]\mathbf{P}_2\,\text{vec}(\mathcal{D})\\ &= \left[(\mathbf{C}\odot\mathbf{A})^{\mathsf{T}}\otimes\mathbf{I}_n\right]\text{vec}(\mathbf{D}_{(2)})\\ &= \text{vec}\Big(\mathbf{D}_{(2)}(\mathbf{C}\odot\mathbf{A})\Big).\end{aligned}$$

The result is summarized in Proposition 15.3. We assume there is a tensor $\mathcal{X} \in \mathbb{R}^{m\times n\times p}$ and that f_{ijk} depends on x_{ijk}.

Proposition 15.3 (GCP Gradient, 3-way) *Let the GCP objective function be given by*

$$f(\mathbf{A},\mathbf{B},\mathbf{C}) = \sum_{i=1}^{m}\sum_{j=1}^{n}\sum_{k=1}^{p} f_{ijk}(y_{ijk}), \quad \textit{where} \quad \mathcal{Y} = [\![\mathbf{A},\mathbf{B},\mathbf{C}]\!].$$

Define the elementwise derivative tensor $\mathcal{D} \in \mathbb{R}^{m\times n\times p}$, *such that* $\mathcal{D}(i,j,k) = f'_{ijk}(i,j,k)$ *for all* $(i,j,k) \in [m]\otimes[n]\otimes[p]$. *Then*

$$\nabla f = \begin{bmatrix} \text{vec}\Big(\mathbf{D}_{(1)}(\mathbf{C}\odot\mathbf{B})\Big)\\ \text{vec}\Big(\mathbf{D}_{(2)}(\mathbf{C}\odot\mathbf{A})\Big)\\ \text{vec}\Big(\mathbf{D}_{(3)}(\mathbf{B}\odot\mathbf{A})\Big)\end{bmatrix}.$$

Equivalently, in matrix notation,

$$\frac{\partial f}{\partial \mathbf{A}} = \mathbf{D}_{(1)}(\mathbf{C}\odot\mathbf{B}), \quad \frac{\partial f}{\partial \mathbf{B}} = \mathbf{D}_{(2)}(\mathbf{C}\odot\mathbf{A}), \quad \textit{and} \quad \frac{\partial f}{\partial \mathbf{C}} = \mathbf{D}_{(3)}(\mathbf{B}\odot\mathbf{A}).$$

Exercise 15.14 Show that the elementwise derivative tensor is $\mathcal{D} = \mathcal{X} - \mathcal{Y}$ if $f_{ijk}(y_{ijk}) = \frac{1}{2}(x_{ijk} - y_{ijk})^2$.

Exercise 15.15 Finish the proof for Proposition 15.3 by proving the gradients with respect to $\mathbf{A}$ and $\mathbf{C}$.

Exercise 15.16 Write an algorithm for computing the 3-way GCP function and gradient.

15.4.2 GCP Gradient for d-way Tensors

The d-way gradient is analogous to the 3-way case. Consider the optimization problem from Section 15.3.2, where the function $f : \mathbb{R}^{r(n_1+n_2+\cdots+n_d)} \to \mathbb{R}$. The GCP objective function is the sum of subfunctions. Specifically, we assume there is a tensor $\mathcal{X} \in \mathbb{R}^{n_1\times n_2\times\cdots\times n_d}$ and that f_i depends on x_i.

Proposition 15.4 (d-way GCP gradient) *Let the GCP objective function be given by*

$$f(\mathbf{A}_1, \mathbf{A}_2, \ldots, \mathbf{A}_d) = \sum_{\boldsymbol{i} \in \mathcal{I}} f_{\boldsymbol{i}}, (y_{\boldsymbol{i}}) \quad \textit{where} \quad \boldsymbol{\mathcal{Y}} = [\![\mathbf{A}_1, \mathbf{A}_2, \ldots, \mathbf{A}_d]\!].$$

Here $\boldsymbol{i} \equiv (i_1, i_2, \ldots, i_d)$ *and* $\mathcal{I} = [n_1] \otimes [n_2] \otimes \cdots \otimes [n_d]$. *Then, for each* $k \in [d]$,

$$\frac{\partial f}{\partial \operatorname{vec}(\mathbf{A}_k)} = \operatorname{vec}\Big(\mathbf{D}_{(k)}\big(\mathbf{A}_d \odot \cdots \odot \mathbf{A}_{k+1} \odot \mathbf{A}_{k-1} \odot \cdots \odot \mathbf{A}_1\big)\Big).$$

Here, for all $k \in [d]$, $\boldsymbol{\mathcal{D}} \in \mathbb{R}^{n_1 \times n_2 \times \cdots \times n_d}$ *is the elementwise derivative tensor, such that* $\boldsymbol{\mathcal{D}}(\boldsymbol{i}) \equiv f'_{\boldsymbol{i}}(y_{\boldsymbol{i}})$ *for all* $\boldsymbol{i} \in \mathcal{I}$. *Equivalently, in matrix notation, we have*

$$\frac{\partial f}{\partial \mathbf{A}_k} = \mathbf{D}_{(k)}\big(\mathbf{A}_d \odot \cdots \odot \mathbf{A}_{k+1} \odot \mathbf{A}_{k-1} \odot \cdots \odot \mathbf{A}_1\big).$$

Proof. To compute the partial gradient of f with respect to $\operatorname{vec}(\mathbf{A}_k)$, we write $f = g \circ \mathbf{h}$ as a composition of functions. The function $h(\mathbf{A}_1, \mathbf{A}_2, \ldots, \mathbf{A}_d) = \operatorname{vec}([\![\mathbf{A}_1, \mathbf{A}_2, \ldots, \mathbf{A}_d]\!]) = \operatorname{vec}(\boldsymbol{\mathcal{Y}})$, and its partial Jacobian with respect to $\operatorname{vec}(\mathbf{A}_k)$ is given in Proposition 12.11. The function g is

$$g(\operatorname{vec}(\boldsymbol{\mathcal{Y}})) = \sum_{i_1=1}^{n_1} \sum_{i_2=1}^{n_2} \cdots \sum_{i_d=1}^{n_d} f_{i_1 i_2 \cdots i_d}(y_{i_1 i_2 \cdots i_d}).$$

Then $\nabla g(\operatorname{vec}(\boldsymbol{\mathcal{Y}})) = \operatorname{vec}(\boldsymbol{\mathcal{D}})$. Via the chain rule (Theorem B.11), we have

$$\begin{aligned}
\frac{\partial f}{\partial \operatorname{vec}(\mathbf{A}_k)} &= \left[\frac{d\mathbf{h}}{d \operatorname{vec}(\mathbf{A}_k)}\right]^{\mathsf{T}} \nabla g(h(\mathbf{A}_1, \mathbf{A}_2, \ldots, \mathbf{A}_d)) \\
&= \Big(\mathbf{P}_k^{\mathsf{T}}\big[(\mathbf{A}_d \odot \cdots \odot \mathbf{A}_{k+1} \odot \mathbf{A}_{k-1} \odot \cdots \odot \mathbf{A}_1) \otimes \mathbf{I}_{n_k}\big]\Big)^{\mathsf{T}} \operatorname{vec}(\boldsymbol{\mathcal{D}}) \\
&= \big[(\mathbf{A}_d \odot \cdots \odot \mathbf{A}_{k+1} \odot \mathbf{A}_{k-1} \odot \cdots \odot \mathbf{A}_1)^{\mathsf{T}} \otimes \mathbf{I}_{n_k}\big] \mathbf{P}_k \operatorname{vec}(\boldsymbol{\mathcal{D}}) \\
&= \big[(\mathbf{A}_d \odot \cdots \odot \mathbf{A}_{k+1} \odot \mathbf{A}_{k-1} \odot \cdots \odot \mathbf{A}_1)^{\mathsf{T}} \otimes \mathbf{I}_{n_k}\big] \operatorname{vec}\big(\mathbf{D}_{(k)}\big) \\
&= \operatorname{vec}\big(\mathbf{D}_{(k)}(\mathbf{A}_d \odot \cdots \odot \mathbf{A}_{k+1} \odot \mathbf{A}_{k-1} \odot \cdots \odot \mathbf{A}_1)\big).
\end{aligned}$$ □

As in the case with CP-OPT, there is no *specific* GCP-OPT algorithm. Instead, we give an algorithm to compute the GCP function and gradient in Algorithm 15.1, which can be combined with any first-order optimization method. See Section 12.3 for considerations in choosing an appropriate optimization method; we recommend limited-memory BFGS (L-BFGS) or its bound-constrained version (L-BFGS-B).

15.5 GCP-OPT Method

Just as for CP-OPT, we have algorithms for computing the function and gradient, so we can use any gradient-based optimization method. We refer the reader to Section 12.3 for a discussion of the options. Since many of the methods have bound constraints, we recommend using L-BFGS-B as the default optimization method.

Bound-constrained limited-memory BFGS (L-BFGS) is the recommendation for optimization in GCP-OPT.

Algorithm 15.1 Computing GCP Function and Gradient for d-way Tensor

Require: data tensor $\mathcal{X} \in \mathbb{R}^{n_1 \times \cdots \times n_d}$, input vector $\mathbf{v} \in \mathbb{R}^{r(n_1+n_2+\cdots+n_d)}$
Ensure: $f = \sum_{i_1=1}^{n_1} \sum_{i_2=1}^{n_2} \cdots \sum_{i_d=1}^{n_d} f_{i_1,i_2,\ldots,i_d}(y_{i_1,i_2,\ldots,i_d})$ and $\mathbf{g} = \nabla f$
for $\{\mathbf{A}_1, \mathbf{A}_2, \ldots, \mathbf{A}_d\} = \texttt{vec2mats}(\mathbf{v})$ and $\mathcal{Y} = [\![\mathbf{A}_1, \mathbf{A}_2, \ldots, \mathbf{A}_d]\!]$

function GCP-FG($\mathcal{X}$, $\mathbf{v}$)
  $\{\mathbf{A}_1, \mathbf{A}_2, \ldots, \mathbf{A}_d\} \leftarrow \texttt{vec2mats}(\mathbf{v})$
  $\mathcal{Y} \leftarrow [\![\mathbf{A}_1, \mathbf{A}_2, \ldots, \mathbf{A}_d]\!]$ ▷ Explicit full Kruskal tensor
  $f \leftarrow 0$
  for $(i_1, i_2, \ldots, i_d) \in [n_1] \otimes [n_2] \otimes \cdots \otimes [n_d]$ **do**
    $f \leftarrow f + f_{i_1,i_2,\ldots,i_d}(y_{i_1,i_2,\ldots,i_d})$
    $\mathcal{D}(i_1, i_2, \ldots, i_d) \leftarrow f'_{i_1,i_2,\ldots,i_d}(y_{i_1,i_2,\ldots,i_d})$ ▷ Elementwise derivative tensor
  end for
  for $k = 1, \ldots, d$ **do** ▷ Sequence of MTTKRPs
    $\mathbf{G}_k \leftarrow -\mathbf{D}_{(k)}(\mathbf{A}_d \odot \cdots \odot \mathbf{A}_{k+1} \odot \mathbf{A}_{k-1} \odot \cdots \odot \mathbf{A}_1)$ ▷ $\mathbf{G}_k = \frac{\partial \tilde{f}}{\partial \mathbf{A}_k}$
  end for
  $\mathbf{g} \leftarrow \texttt{mats2vec}(\mathbf{G}_1, \mathbf{G}_2, \ldots, \mathbf{G}_d)$
  return $\{f, \mathbf{g}\}$
end function

Several of the GCP elementwise loss functions $f(y)$ have a requirement that y is strictly positive: $y > 0$. This will not work with a method such as L-BFGS-B because it only handles inequalities of the form $y \geq 0$ (nonnegativity). In this case, it is generally sufficient to replace y everywhere in the elementwise function with $y + \varepsilon$, where ε is a small value, such as 10^{-10}.

15.6 Example: GCP-OPT on Monkey BMI Tensor

We revisit the monkey BMI tensor from Section 9.7. In this experiment, a monkey uses a brain–machine interface to move a cursor to a target location at an angle of 0, 90, 180, or 270 degrees relative to the starting point. After achieving the target, the monkey must hold the cursor at the target location for 500 ms. The data is normalized so that the first half of each trial is target acquisition and the second half is holding the cursor at the target. Data is recorded from 88 neurons over 88 trials. The number of trials for each target is documented in Table 1.2. The resulting tensor is of size

$$43 \text{ neurons } \times 200 \text{ timesteps } \times 88 \text{ trials.}$$

To use GCP, we want to specify an appropriate loss function, which generally requires some experimentation, trial, and error.

We considered different loss functions and ultimately settled on the **Huber loss** in Eq. (15.2) with $\Delta = 0.001$. We use a small value of Δ because the values of $\mathcal{X}$ are very small, ranging between 0 and 0.187 with a median value of 0.010. Hence, using $\Delta = 0.001$ means that the Huber loss acts like standard least squares if the model is within 10% of the median value and otherwise acts like (scaled) absolute value loss.

An illustration of an eight-component GCP factorization with Huber loss is shown in Fig. 15.7. We plot each component as a row in the image. Along each row, the first plot is a bar chart plotting the neuron activity levels, normalized to the norm of the component. Additionally, the neurons were sorted according to total activity across all trials, from most to least active. The middle is a plot of the time mode, scaled to norm 1. The right is a scatter plot of the different trials, scaled to norm 1. Each dot in the scatter chart is colored by the target angle. The tensor decomposition did not have access to which trial corresponded to which target; thus, any correlations between the components and the targets are learned from only the neural activity data.

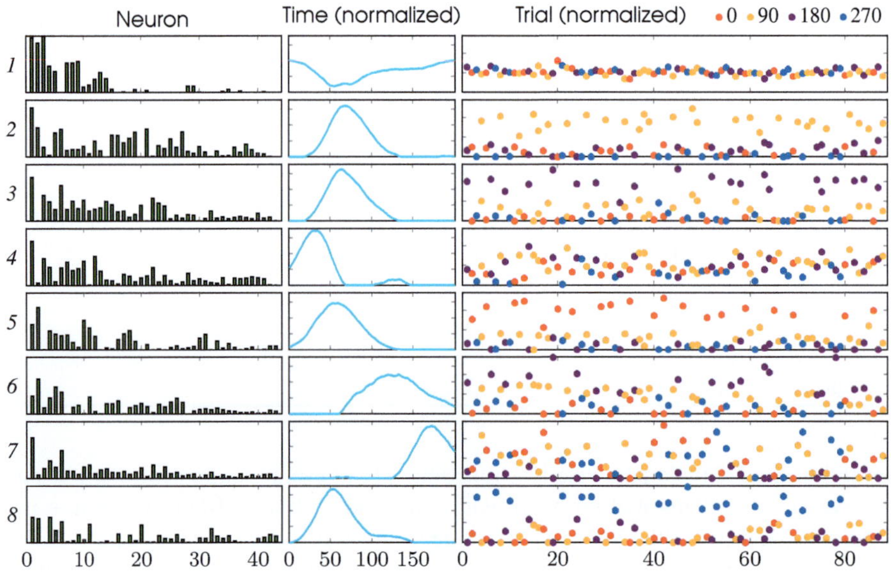

Figure 15.7 Rank-8 GCP decomposition of monkey BMI tensor with Huber loss ($\Delta = 0.001$).

We make a few observations about these experimental results:

- Component 1 is active consistently across all trials, based on examining the third factor in that component. We hypothesize that this is background brain activity.
- Component 2 separates the 90-degree (yellow) targets. This target corresponds to the highest number of trials (see Table 1.2) and so it is not surprising that this component has the largest magnitude of the target-specific components.
- Component 3 separates the 180-degree (purple) targets.
- Component 4 has no clear patterns of activity in terms of trials, but appears to correspond to activity at the beginning of each trial based on the time profile in the second factor of the component.
- Component 5 separates the 0-degree (red) targets, with the exception of the lowest red marker.
- Components 6 and 7 have no clear patterns of activity in terms of trials, but appear to correspond to activity in the second half of the trials, which is when the cursor is being held at the target location.
- Component 8 separates the 270-degree (blue) targets. This target corresponds to the lowest number of trials (see Table 1.2) and so it is not surprising that this component has the smallest magnitude of the target-specific components.

In general, these GCP results are appealing because they separate the four trials and also show other activities that have reasonable interpretations. For instance, components 6 and 7 seem to correspond to the holding activity in the second half of the trial.

Remark 15.5 (Optimization methodology) For GCP, we use L-BFGS-B as the optimization method with the following settings per Zhu et al. (1997). The memory parameter (`m`) is 5. The maximum number of iterations (`maxIts`) is 250. The convergence tolerance depends on two values: the projected gradient tolerance (`pgtol`) is `1e-7` and the function tolerance divided by machine epsilon (`factr`) is `1e-7/eps` or `4.5e8`.

Exercise 15.17 (a) Implement GCP-OPT. (b) Reproduce the results in Fig. 15.7. (c) Further, cluster the trials using k-means to produce a confusion matrix as in Table 9.1.

Exercise 15.18 Try other objective functions. How does the interpretability compare with Huber loss?

15.7 Example: GCP-OPT on Chicago Crime Tensor

We have given an example of using GCP on the Chicago crime tensor in Section 9.8.

Exercise 15.19 (a) Implement GCP-OPT. (b) Using Poisson with identity link (also known as KL divergence), run GCP-OPT at various ranks for the Chicago crime tensor, reproducing Fig. 9.12.

Exercise 15.20 (a) Compare the results of Poisson with identity link and Poisson with log link for rank $r = 7$. (b) Provide an interpretation of each. (c) Which do you think is more useful?

16 CP Tensor Rank and Special Topics

In this chapter, we consider algebraic properties of tensor rank and implications for computing CP. We cover the fact that computing the rank is NP-hard, ill-posedness, and the notion of border rank. We explore the connection between rank, border rank, and fast matrix multiplication. We show how to algebraically compute the rank and rank decomposition of any $2 \times 2 \times 2$ tensor and some more general low-rank tenors.

16.1 Tensor Rank

Recall from Section 10.1 that a rank-1 tensor is an outer product of vectors. The rank of a tensor is the number of rank-1 tensors needed to *exactly* reconstruct it.

Definition 16.1: Tensor Rank, 3-way

The **rank** of a tensor $\mathcal{X} \in \mathbb{R}^{m \times n \times p}$ is

$$\operatorname{rank}(\mathcal{X}) = \min \left\{ r \in \mathbb{N} \mid \mathcal{X} = [\![\mathbf{A}, \mathbf{B}, \mathbf{C}]\!] \text{ with } \mathbf{A} \in \mathbb{R}^{m \times r}, \mathbf{B} \in \mathbb{R}^{n \times r}, \mathbf{C} \in \mathbb{R}^{n \times r} \right\}.$$

Definition 16.2: Tensor Rank, d-way

The **rank** of a tensor $\mathcal{X} \in \mathbb{R}^{n_1 \times n_2 \times \cdots \times n_d}$ is

$$\operatorname{rank}(\mathcal{X}) = \min \left\{ r \in \mathbb{N} \mid \mathcal{X} = [\![\mathbf{A}_1, \mathbf{A}_2, \ldots, \mathbf{A}_d]\!] \text{ with } \mathbf{A}_k \in \mathbb{R}^{n_k \times r} \text{ for all } k \in [d] \right\}.$$

The definition is analogous to matrix rank (the number of rank-1 matrices that sum to the original matrix), but many of its properties differ. Notably, the rank of a real-valued tensor can be different over $\mathbb{R}$ and $\mathbb{C}$. In this book, we focus exclusively on the rank over $\mathbb{R}$, excepting Example 16.1 that illustrates a tensor with different ranks over $\mathbb{R}$ and $\mathbb{C}$.

Example 16.1 (Different Ranks over $\mathbb{R}$ and $\mathbb{C}$) Consider the $2 \times 2 \times 2$ tensor $\mathcal{X}$ given by

$$\mathcal{X}(:,:,1) = \begin{bmatrix} 1 & 0 \\ 0 & -1 \end{bmatrix} \quad \text{and} \quad \mathcal{X}(:,:,2) = \begin{bmatrix} 0 & 1 \\ 1 & 0 \end{bmatrix}.$$

We want its rank decomposition $\mathcal{X} = [\![\mathbf{A}, \mathbf{B}, \mathbf{C}]\!]$. Over $\mathbb{R}$, $\operatorname{rank}(\mathcal{X}) = 3$ with

$$\mathbf{A} = \begin{bmatrix} 1 & 0 & 1 \\ 0 & 1 & 1 \end{bmatrix}, \quad \mathbf{B} = \begin{bmatrix} 1 & 0 & 1 \\ 0 & 1 & 1 \end{bmatrix}, \quad \text{and} \quad \mathbf{C} = \begin{bmatrix} 1 & -1 & 0 \\ -1 & -1 & 1 \end{bmatrix}.$$

We will discuss how to compute the rank of $\mathcal{X}$ over $\mathbb{R}$ later in Exercise 16.27. In contrast, over $\mathbb{C}$, $\text{rank}(\mathcal{X}) = 2$, with

$$\mathbf{A} = \frac{1}{\sqrt{2}}\begin{bmatrix} 1 & 1 \\ -i & i \end{bmatrix}, \quad \mathbf{B} = \frac{1}{\sqrt{2}}\begin{bmatrix} 1 & 1 \\ -i & i \end{bmatrix}, \quad \text{and} \quad \mathbf{C} = \begin{bmatrix} 1 & 1 \\ i & -i \end{bmatrix},$$

where $i = \sqrt{-1}$.

Exercise 16.1 For both the real and complex factorizations in Example 9.1, verify that these produce the tensor $\mathcal{X}$.

Rank of a tensor is unchanged by permutation or TTM with nonsingular matrix.

Exercise 16.2 (Rank Unaffected by TTM with Nonsingular Matrix) Define $\mathcal{Y} = \mathcal{X} \times_k \mathbf{U}$, where $\mathbf{U}$ is a nonsingular matrix of appropriate size. Prove $\text{rank}(\mathcal{Y}) = \text{rank}(\mathcal{X})$. Hint: First prove $\text{rank}(\mathcal{Y}) \leq \text{rank}(\mathcal{X})$, and then reverse the roles of $\mathcal{Y}$ and $\mathcal{X}$ to get equality.

Exercise 16.3 (Rank Unaffected by Permutation) Define $\mathcal{Y} = \mathbb{P}(\mathcal{X}, \pi)$, where π is a permutation of the modes of $\mathcal{X}$. Prove $\text{rank}(\mathcal{Y}) = \text{rank}(\mathcal{X})$. Hint: First prove $\text{rank}(\mathcal{Y}) \leq \text{rank}(\mathcal{X})$, and then reverse the roles of $\mathcal{Y}$ and $\mathcal{X}$ to get equality.

16.2 Tensor Rank is NP-Hard

There are well-known methods for determining the rank of an arbitrary matrix. In contrast, there are no methods for determining the rank for an arbitrary tensor. Hillar and Lim (2013) have shown that computing the rank of a tensor (and most tensor problems) is NP-hard, based on the work of Håstad (1990).

Theorem 16.3 (Tensor Rank in NP-Hard, Hillar and Lim, 2013) *For any real-valued tensor $\mathcal{X} \in \mathbb{R}^{m \times n \times p}$ and $r \in \mathbb{N}$, it is NP-hard to determine if* $\text{rank}(\mathcal{X}) \leq r$.

In Section 16.6.3, we discuss an infamous $9 \times 9 \times 9$ tensor whose rank is unknown, and so far only bounded between 19 and 23.

For data science applications, we generally do not know or need to know the exact rank, so we use various heuristics to choose an approximate rank. This may be thought of as finding the best low-rank approximation. Unfortunately, de Silva and Lim (2008) have shown that some low-rank approximation problems are ill-posed. In Section 16.5, we show an example of a tensor of rank 3 that has no best rank-2 approximation. Although de Silva and Lim (2008) have also shown that the set of tensors that do not have a best rank-k approximation has positive probability over any continuous distribution on tensors, this issue is rarely encountered in data analysis applications.

16.3 Maximum Rank

Although we cannot compute the rank of a tensor in general, we could perhaps settle for knowing the maximum (attainable) rank of tensors of a given size. For example, in the case of an $m \times n$ matrix, we know its maximum rank is $\min\{m, n\}$. We formally define the notion of maximum rank for a given tensor size.

Definition 16.4 (Maximum Rank) The **maximum rank** for tensors of size $n_1 \times n_2 \times \cdots \times n_d$ is the largest *attainable* rank for that size:

$$\text{max-rank}(n_1 \times n_2 \times \cdots \times n_d) \equiv \max \{ \operatorname{rank}(\mathcal{X}) \mid \mathcal{X} \in \mathbb{R}^{n_1 \times n_2 \times \cdots \times n_d} \}.$$

Unfortunately, with the exception of a few special cases, maximum ranks for most higher-order tensors are unknown. The special cases where the maximum rank is known are listed in Table 16.1. The first result for $2 \times m \times n$ tensors implies that $2 \times 2 \times 2$ has maximum rank of 3. Thus, the tensor in Example 16.1 achieved the maximum rank (over $\mathbb{R}$) for its size.

Table 16.1 Known maximum tensor ranks. Order of dimensions does not change rank, so sizes are sorted from smallest to largest.

Tensor size	Maximum rank	Source
$2 \times m \times n \ (m \leq n)$	$m + \min \{ m, \lfloor n/2 \rfloor \}$	JáJá (1979); Kruskal (1989)
$3 \times 3 \times 3$	5	Kruskal (1989)
$3 \times 7 \times 7$	8	Atkinson and Stephens (1979)
$2 \times 4 \times 4$	6	ten Berge (2000b)

We can derive (see Exercise 16.4) a weak upper bound on the maximal rank:

$$\text{max-rank}(n_1 \times n_2 \times \cdots \times n_d) \leq \min_k \prod_{\substack{\ell=1 \\ \ell \neq k}}^{d} n_\ell = \frac{\prod_{k=1}^{d} n_k}{\max_k n_k}. \tag{16.1}$$

In other words, the maximum rank is the product of all dimensions except the largest one.

Exercise 16.4 Prove Eq. (16.1). Hint: This connects to matrix factorization.

Slightly better bounds are known for $m \times n \times p$ tensors where $p \leq mn - 1$ (Atkinson and Lloyd, 1983; Atkinson and Stephens, 1979). If $p = mn - 1$, we can bound the maximum rank as $mn - 1$ versus mn in Eq. (16.1). If $p \leq mn - 2$, there is only one tensor with rank $mn - 1$ and the remainder have maximum rank $mn - 2$.

16.4 Typical Rank

Suppose we create a random $m \times n$ matrix by filling it with standard normal random values. With probability 1, its rank is equal to $\min \{ m, n \}$. We consider the same question about a random $m \times n \times p$ tensor.

Definition 16.5 (Typical Rank) The **typical rank(s)** for tensors of size $n_1 \times n_2 \times \cdots \times n_d$ is the *set* of all ranks that occur with probability greater than 0, for any continuous distribution $\mathcal{D}(n_1, \ldots, n_d)$ over the set of all such tensors. In other words,

$$\text{typical-rank}(n_1 \times \cdots \times n_d) \equiv \{ r \mid \operatorname{Prob} \{ \operatorname{rank}(\mathcal{X}) = r \mid \mathcal{X} \sim \mathcal{D}(n_1, \ldots, n_d) \} > 0 \}.$$

In most cases, the typical rank is unknown. The exception is for 3-way tensors, where some progress has been made. A summary of the known typical ranks is provided in Table 16.2. It is possible that the typical is different than the maximal rank. For example, we know from Table 16.1 that $2 \times 4 \times 4$ tensors have a maximum rank of 6, whereas Table 16.2 shows that the typical ranks are $\{ 4, 5 \}$.

Table 16.2 Known typical ranks over $\mathbb{R}$ for tensors of size $m \times n \times p$. Without loss of generality (since the order of the modes does not impact rank), $2 \leq m \leq n \leq p$.

Size	Typical rank	Source
$2 \times n \times n$	$\{n, n+1\}$	ten Berge and Kiers (1999)
$3 \times 3 \times 3$	5	ten Berge and Stegeman (2006)
$3 \times 3 \times 5$	$\{5, 6\}$	ten Berge (2004)
$3 \times 4 \times 8$	$\{8, 9\}$	Sumi et al. (2013)
$3 \times 5 \times 9$	$\{9, 10\}$	Choulakian (2010); ten Berge (2011)
$4 \times 4 \times 12$	$\{12, 13\}$	Friedland (2012)
$m \times n \times n(m-1)$ $m > 2$, n odd	$n(m-1)$	ten Berge (2000b)
$m \times n \times p$ $n(m-1) < p < mn$	p	ten Berge and Kiers (1999); ten Berge (2000b)
$m \times n \times p$ $p \geq mn$	mn	ten Berge and Kiers (1999); ten Berge (2000b)

The typical ranks of $2 \times m \times n$ tensors have been completely characterized by ten Berge and Kiers (1999). If the size of the first mode is greater than 2, then we rely primarily on the results of ten Berge (2000b). For $p = n(m-1)$, in contrast to the results for $m = 2$, the typical rank depends on whether n is even or odd. If n is odd, the typical rank is p; however, if n is even, we do not know what the typical rank is. It is conjectured to be $\{p, p+1\}$. We only know for sure for the smallest cases listed in the table. See ten Berge (2011) for further details and other results such as lower bounds, computational estimates, rank of symmetric tensors, etc.

> The maximum and typical ranks of tensors (over $\mathbb{R}$) are unknown except in a few special cases.

Exercise 16.5 Using Table 16.2, give the typical ranks for tensors of size (a) $2 \times 2 \times 3$ and (b) $2 \times 3 \times 3$.

16.5 Border Rank

The best rank-k approximation *may not exist* (de Silva and Lim, 2008). Example 16.2 provides a famous illustration of this problem, and other examples can be found in Bini et al. (1979) and Paatero (2000). To this end, Bini et al. (1979) defined the important concept of border rank, which considers whether or not a tensor is a limit point of a sequence of lower-rank tensors.

Definition 16.6 (Border Rank) The **border rank** of a tensor $\mathcal{X}$ is given by

$$\text{border-rank}(\mathcal{X}) = \min\{\, r \mid \text{ for any } \varepsilon > 0, \text{ there exists } \mathcal{Y} \text{ such that } \operatorname{rank}(\mathcal{Y}) = r \text{ and } \|\mathcal{X} - \mathcal{Y}\| < \varepsilon \,\}.$$

Example 16.2 (Border Rank $\neq$ Rank, from Paatero, 2000 and de Silva and Lim, 2008) Let $\mathbf{a}_1, \mathbf{a}_2 \in \mathbb{R}^m$, $\mathbf{b}_1, \mathbf{b}_2 \in \mathbb{R}^n$, and $\mathbf{c}_1, \mathbf{c}_2 \in \mathbb{R}^p$. Define the tensor $\mathcal{X} \in \mathbb{R}^{m \times n \times p}$ by

$$\mathcal{X} = \mathbf{a}_1 \circ \mathbf{b}_1 \circ \mathbf{c}_2 + \mathbf{a}_1 \circ \mathbf{b}_2 \circ \mathbf{c}_1 + \mathbf{a}_2 \circ \mathbf{b}_1 \circ \mathbf{c}_1.$$

It can be shown that $\text{rank}(\mathcal{X}) = 3$. However, $\mathcal{X}$ can be approximated arbitrarily well by a rank-2 tensor $\mathcal{Y}$ defined by

$$\mathcal{Y} = \alpha \left(\mathbf{a}_1 + \frac{1}{\alpha}\mathbf{a}_2 \right) \circ \left(\mathbf{b}_1 + \frac{1}{\alpha}\mathbf{b}_2 \right) \circ \left(\mathbf{c}_1 + \frac{1}{\alpha}\mathbf{c}_2 \right) - \alpha \mathbf{a}_1 \circ \mathbf{b}_1 \circ \mathbf{c}_1.$$

If we expand out the terms of the first component of $\mathcal{Y}$, we see

$$\begin{aligned} \mathcal{Y} &= \alpha \mathbf{a}_1 \circ \mathbf{b}_1 \circ \mathbf{c}_1 + \mathbf{a}_1 \circ \mathbf{b}_1 \circ \mathbf{c}_2 + \mathbf{a}_1 \circ \mathbf{b}_2 \circ \mathbf{c}_1 + \mathbf{a}_2 \circ \mathbf{b}_1 \circ \mathbf{c}_1 \\ &\quad + \frac{1}{\alpha}\mathbf{a}_1 \circ \mathbf{b}_2 \circ \mathbf{c}_2 + \frac{1}{\alpha}\mathbf{a}_2 \circ \mathbf{b}_1 \circ \mathbf{c}_2 + \frac{1}{\alpha}\mathbf{a}_2 \circ \mathbf{b}_1 \circ \mathbf{c}_2 + \frac{1}{\alpha^2}\mathbf{a}_2 \circ \mathbf{b}_2 \circ \mathbf{c}_2 \\ &\quad - \alpha \mathbf{a}_1 \circ \mathbf{b}_1 \circ \mathbf{c}_1 \\ &= \mathcal{X} + \frac{1}{\alpha}\left(\mathbf{a}_1 \circ \mathbf{b}_2 \circ \mathbf{c}_2 + \mathbf{a}_2 \circ \mathbf{b}_1 \circ \mathbf{c}_2 + \mathbf{a}_2 \circ \mathbf{b}_2 \circ \mathbf{c}_1 + \frac{1}{\alpha}\mathbf{a}_2 \circ \mathbf{b}_2 \circ \mathbf{c}_2 \right). \end{aligned}$$

Hence,

$$\lim_{\alpha \to +\infty} \|\mathcal{X} - \mathcal{Y}\| =$$

$$\lim_{\alpha \to +\infty} \frac{1}{\sqrt{\alpha}} \left\| \mathbf{a}_1 \circ \mathbf{b}_2 \circ \mathbf{c}_2 + \mathbf{a}_2 \circ \mathbf{b}_1 \circ \mathbf{c}_2 + \mathbf{a}_2 \circ \mathbf{b}_2 \circ \mathbf{c}_1 + \frac{1}{\alpha}\mathbf{a}_2 \circ \mathbf{b}_2 \circ \mathbf{c}_2 \right\| = 0$$

This means that $\mathcal{X}$ can be approximated arbitrarily closely by a rank-2 tensor, but $\mathcal{Y}$ converges to a rank-3 tensor,

$$\lim_{\alpha \to +\infty} \mathcal{Y} = \mathcal{X}.$$

This is only possible because the norms of the components of $\mathcal{Y}$ diverge. The space of all rank-2 tensors is not closed, so a sequence can converge to something outside of the space of rank-2 tensors.

In Example 16.2, $\text{border-rank}(\mathcal{X}) = 2$ even though $\text{rank}(\mathcal{X}) = 3$. We revisit the border rank in Section 16.6.

Exercise 16.6 (Border Rank $\leq$ Rank) Prove $\text{border-rank}(\mathcal{X}) \leq \text{rank}(\mathcal{X})$.

16.6 Connections to Arithmetic Complexity

Tensor rank is fundamental to several deep questions in arithmetic complexity, including the complexity of matrix–matrix multiplication. Dense matrix–matrix multiplication is a fundamental computation in a wide variety of applications such as deep learning, computational simulation, and image processing. To approach the problem of reducing its arithmetic complexity, we frame the problem in terms of evaluating bilinear forms.

Definition 16.7 (Bilinear Form) A **bilinear form** is a function that maps a pair of vectors to a scalar and is linear in each of its input vectors: $f : \mathbb{R}^m \times \mathbb{R}^n \to \mathbb{R}$.

Proposition 16.8 (Matrix Representation of Bilinear Form) *If $f : \mathbb{R}^m \times \mathbb{R}^n \to \mathbb{R}$ is a bilinear form, then there exists $\mathbf{M} \in \mathbb{R}^{m \times n}$ such that $f(\mathbf{u}, \mathbf{v}) = \mathbf{u}^\intercal \mathbf{M} \mathbf{v}$ for all $\mathbf{u} \in \mathbb{R}^m$ and $\mathbf{v} \in \mathbb{R}^m$.*

If we have a set of p bilinear forms to be evaluated on the same pair of inputs, then we have a vector-valued function $\mathbf{f} : \mathbb{R}^m \times \mathbb{R}^n \to \mathbb{R}^p$ that corresponds to a 3-way tensor $\mathcal{X}$ such that the kth bilinear form is

$$f_k(\mathbf{u}, \mathbf{v}) = \mathbf{u}^\intercal \mathbf{X}_k \mathbf{v} = \sum_{i=1}^{m} \sum_{j=1}^{n} x_{ijk} u_i v_j, \tag{16.2}$$

where $\mathbf{X}_k = \mathcal{X}(:,:,k)$ is the kth frontal slice. In TTM notation, we have

$$\mathbf{f}(\mathbf{u}, \mathbf{v}) = \mathcal{X} \times_1 \mathbf{u}^\intercal \times_2 \mathbf{v}^\intercal.$$

In the case that the elements of the input vectors $\mathbf{u}$ and $\mathbf{v}$ are objects for which multiplication is more expensive than addition or scalar multiplication (e.g., matrices), we can reduce the complexity of the evaluation of $\mathbf{f}(\mathbf{u}, \mathbf{v})$ by minimizing the number of **active multiplications** between elements of $\mathbf{u}$ and elements of $\mathbf{v}$. Evaluating Eq. (16.2) directly requires an active multiplication for every nonzero entry in $\mathcal{X}$. We assume this cost is dominated by the active multiplications rather than the scaling and accumulation operations. The reason for this assumption will become clear later.

Suppose we have an exact CP decomposition of the tensor $\mathcal{X} = [\![\mathbf{A}, \mathbf{B}, \mathbf{C}]\!]$ of rank r: $\mathcal{X} = \sum_{\ell=1}^{r} \mathbf{a}_\ell \circ \mathbf{b}_\ell \circ \mathbf{c}_\ell$. Then we can express the set of bilinear forms as

$$\mathbf{f}(\mathbf{u}, \mathbf{v}) = \left(\sum_{\ell=1}^{r} \mathbf{a}_\ell \circ \mathbf{b}_\ell \circ \mathbf{c}_\ell \right) \times_1 \mathbf{u}^\intercal \times_2 \mathbf{v}^\intercal = \sum_{\ell=1}^{r} (\mathbf{a}_\ell^\intercal \mathbf{u})\,(\mathbf{b}_\ell^\intercal \mathbf{v})\,\mathbf{c}_\ell.$$

Evaluating this expression requires computing $\mathbf{a}_\ell^\intercal \mathbf{u}$ and $\mathbf{b}_\ell^\intercal \mathbf{v}$ for each $\ell \in [r]$, but because the elements of $\mathbf{A}$ and $\mathbf{B}$ are scalars, this amounts to taking linear combinations of elements of $\mathbf{u}$ and $\mathbf{v}$. The number of costly operations, the active multiplications, is exactly the rank of the decomposition r. Scaling and summing over the vectors $\mathbf{c}_\ell$ also corresponds to taking linear combinations of the outputs of the active multiplications. Thus, minimizing the complexity of the evaluation of $\mathbf{f}$ corresponds to finding an exact CP decomposition of the tensor $\mathcal{X}$ with minimal rank.

Casting the arithmetic complexity question as a CP decomposition problem does not make it easier to solve, since tensor rank is still NP-hard. However, we can use numerical methods to compute approximate solutions and employ heuristics like regularization to try to find exact decompositions. This has been successful for matrix–matrix multiplication when the matrix dimensions are small (Ballard et al., 2018; Benson and Ballard, 2015; Brent, 1970; Johnson and McLoughlin, 1986; Smirnov, 2013).

16.6.1 Multiplying Complex Numbers

A simple example of a set of bilinear forms is the multiplication of two complex numbers:

$$(u_1 + u_2 i)(v_1 + v_2 i) = (u_1 v_1 - u_2 v_2) + (u_1 v_2 + u_2 v_1) i \equiv w_1 + w_2 i,$$

where $i \equiv \sqrt{-1}$. We can represent a complex number as a vector containing the real part and imaginary part, yielding the expression as a pair of bilinear forms:

$$\begin{bmatrix} w_1 \\ w_2 \end{bmatrix} = \begin{bmatrix} u_1v_1 - u_2v_2 \\ u_1v_2 + u_2v_1 \end{bmatrix}.$$

Letting $\mathbf{X}_k \equiv \mathcal{X}(:,:,k)$ denote the frontal slices, the corresponding tensor representation is

$$\mathbf{X}_1 = \begin{bmatrix} 1 & 0 \\ 0 & -1 \end{bmatrix} \quad \text{and} \quad \mathbf{X}_2 = \begin{bmatrix} 0 & 1 \\ 1 & 0 \end{bmatrix}. \tag{16.3}$$

We can write this in terms of four active multiplications (denoted m_1 through m_4), one per nonzero:

$$\begin{bmatrix} w_1 \\ w_2 \end{bmatrix} = \begin{bmatrix} m_1 - m_2 \\ m_3 + m_4 \end{bmatrix}, \quad \text{where} \quad \begin{aligned} m_1 &= u_1v_1, \\ m_2 &= u_2v_2, \\ m_3 &= u_1v_2, \\ m_4 &= u_2v_1. \end{aligned} \tag{16.4}$$

Correspondingly, we can write $\mathcal{X}$ as the sum of four rank-1 components (one per active multiplication). In other words, we can decompose $\mathcal{X} = [\![\mathbf{A}, \mathbf{B}, \mathbf{C}]\!]$ with

$$\mathbf{A} = \begin{bmatrix} 1 & 0 & 1 & 0 \\ 0 & 1 & 0 & 1 \end{bmatrix}, \quad \mathbf{B} = \begin{bmatrix} 1 & 0 & 0 & 1 \\ 0 & 1 & 1 & 0 \end{bmatrix}, \quad \text{and} \quad \mathbf{C} = \begin{bmatrix} 1 & -1 & 0 & 0 \\ 0 & 0 & 1 & 1 \end{bmatrix}.$$

The way to read this is that the columns of $\mathbf{A}$ say which parts of the vector $\mathbf{u} = \left[\begin{smallmatrix} u_1 \\ u_2 \end{smallmatrix}\right]$ go into each active multiplication and likewise for the columns of $\mathbf{B}$ and the vector $\mathbf{v} = \left[\begin{smallmatrix} v_1 \\ v_2 \end{smallmatrix}\right]$. Finally, each *row* of the matrix $\mathbf{C}$ dictates the combination of the active multiplications.

However, we know from Table 16.1 that the maximum rank of a $2 \times 2 \times 2$ tensor is 3. In fact, this is the tensor we considered in Example 16.1, which has rank 3. The rank-3 decomposition is $\mathcal{X} = [\![\mathbf{A}, \mathbf{B}, \mathbf{C}]\!]$ with

$$\mathbf{A} = \begin{bmatrix} 1 & 0 & 1 \\ 0 & 1 & 1 \end{bmatrix}, \quad \mathbf{B} = \begin{bmatrix} 1 & 0 & 1 \\ 0 & 1 & 1 \end{bmatrix}, \quad \text{and} \quad \mathbf{C} = \begin{bmatrix} 1 & -1 & 0 \\ -1 & -1 & 1 \end{bmatrix}. \tag{16.5}$$

Since this decomposition is rank 3, there are three active multiplications as follows (reading off the combinations from the columns of $\mathbf{A}$ and $\mathbf{B}$), and the rows of $\mathbf{C}$ yield the linear combinations of the active multiplications:

$$\begin{bmatrix} w_1 \\ w_2 \end{bmatrix} = \begin{bmatrix} m_1 - m_2 \\ -m_1 - m_2 + m_3 \end{bmatrix}, \quad \text{where} \quad \begin{aligned} m_1 &= u_1v_1, \\ m_2 &= u_2v_2, \\ m_3 &= (u_1 + u_2)(v_1 + v_2). \end{aligned} \tag{16.6}$$

Here m_1, m_2, m_3 represent the three active multiplications. This method is known as the 3M method for complex multiplication (Higham, 1992).

The standard evaluation of Eq. (16.4) requires four active multiplications and two additions/subtractions, whereas the 3M method given by Eq. (16.6) requires three active multiplications and five additions/subtractions.

Exercise 16.7 Explain how $\mathcal{X}$ in Eq. (16.3) corresponds to multiplying complex numbers.

Exercise 16.8 Verify that Eq. (16.5) is a rank-3 decomposition of $\mathcal{X}$ in Eq. (16.3).

Exercise 16.9 Compute a CP decomposition of $\mathcal{X}$ in Eq. (16.3) using a computational method. Why is the computed solution not the same as Eq. (16.5)?

16.6.2 Strassen's 2 × 2 Matrix Multiplication

Consider the multiplication of two 2×2 matrices: $\mathbf{W} = \mathbf{U}\mathbf{V}$ written out is

$$\begin{bmatrix} w_{11} & w_{12} \\ w_{21} & w_{22} \end{bmatrix} = \begin{bmatrix} u_{11}v_{11} + u_{12}v_{21} & u_{11}v_{12} + u_{12}v_{22} \\ u_{21}v_{11} + u_{22}v_{21} & u_{21}v_{12} + u_{22}v_{22} \end{bmatrix}.$$

Each of the four elements of the output matrix is a bilinear form involving the two input matrices (each considered as a vector of length 4). The set of bilinear forms corresponds to a $4 \times 4 \times 4$ tensor with eight nonzeros, analogous to the construction of the complex multiplication tensor.

In order to expose a special kind of symmetry in the tensor, called cyclic symmetry, we use columnwise (natural) linearization for the input matrices and rowwise (reverse) linearization of the output; in other words, we use $\text{vec}(\mathbf{U})$, $\text{vec}(\mathbf{V})$, and $\text{vec}(\mathbf{W}^{\mathsf{T}})$. The frontal slices of the corresponding $4 \times 4 \times 4$ tensor are

$$\mathbf{X}_1 = \begin{bmatrix} 1&0&0&0 \\ 0&0&0&0 \\ 0&1&0&0 \\ 0&0&0&0 \end{bmatrix}, \mathbf{X}_2 = \begin{bmatrix} 0&0&1&0 \\ 0&0&0&0 \\ 0&0&0&1 \\ 0&0&0&0 \end{bmatrix}, \mathbf{X}_3 = \begin{bmatrix} 0&0&0&0 \\ 1&0&0&0 \\ 0&0&0&0 \\ 0&1&0&0 \end{bmatrix}, \mathbf{X}_4 = \begin{bmatrix} 0&0&0&0 \\ 0&0&1&0 \\ 0&0&0&0 \\ 0&0&0&1 \end{bmatrix}, \tag{16.7}$$

yielding $\text{vec}(\mathbf{W}^{\mathsf{T}}) = \mathcal{X} \times_1 \text{vec}(\mathbf{U})^{\mathsf{T}} \times_2 \text{vec}(\mathbf{V})^{\mathsf{T}}$. An interesting feature of this representation is that $\mathcal{X}$ is invariant under cyclic permutations of the indices: $x_{ijk} = x_{kij} = x_{jki}$ for all $i, j, k \in [4]$.

We can see that direct evaluation performs eight active multiplications, one for each nonzero, and four additions. This equates to the computations

$$\begin{bmatrix} w_{11} \\ w_{12} \\ w_{21} \\ w_{22} \end{bmatrix} = \begin{bmatrix} m_1 + m_2 \\ m_3 + m_4 \\ m_5 + m_6 \\ m_7 + m_8 \end{bmatrix}, \quad \text{where} \quad \begin{aligned} m_1 &= u_{11}v_{11}, & m_2 &= u_{12}v_{21}, \\ m_3 &= u_{11}v_{12}, & m_4 &= u_{12}v_{22}, \\ m_5 &= u_{21}v_{11}, & m_6 &= u_{22}v_{21}, \\ m_7 &= u_{21}v_{12}, & m_8 &= u_{22}v_{22}. \end{aligned}$$

Strassen (1969) showed there is a rank-7 decomposition, $\mathcal{X} = [\![\mathbf{A}, \mathbf{B}, \mathbf{C}]\!]$ with

$$\mathbf{A} = \begin{bmatrix} 1&0&1&0&1&-1&0 \\ 0&1&0&0&0&1&0 \\ 0&0&0&0&1&0&1 \\ 1&1&0&1&0&0&-1 \end{bmatrix}, \mathbf{B} = \begin{bmatrix} 1&1&0&-1&0&1&0 \\ 0&0&0&1&0&0&1 \\ 0&0&1&0&0&1&0 \\ 1&0&-1&0&1&0&1 \end{bmatrix}, \mathbf{C} = \begin{bmatrix} 1&0&0&1&-1&0&1 \\ 0&0&1&0&1&0&0 \\ 0&1&0&1&0&0&0 \\ 1&-1&1&0&0&1&0 \end{bmatrix}. \tag{16.8}$$

Remark 16.9 (Cyclic permutation invariance) This decomposition is invariant under cyclic permutation, meaning $\mathcal{X} = [\![\mathbf{A}, \mathbf{B}, \mathbf{C}]\!] = [\![\mathbf{B}, \mathbf{C}, \mathbf{A}]\!] = [\![\mathbf{C}, \mathbf{A}, \mathbf{B}]\!]$. This is a consequence of the cyclic symmetry of $\mathcal{X}$. All cyclic permutations of the factor matrices yield valid decompositions. These three decompositions differ only by permutation (see Definition 10.12).

Similar to the 3M method for multiplying complex numbers, this decomposition specifies an algorithm. The columns of $\mathbf{A}$ give the linear combinations of the entries of $\text{vec}(\mathbf{U})$, and the columns of $\mathbf{B}$ give the linear combinations of the entries of $\text{vec}(\mathbf{V})$ that feed into the active multiplications, denoted by m_ℓ. The rows of $\mathbf{C}$ provide the linear combinations of active multiplications corresponding to $\text{vec}(\mathbf{W}^\mathsf{T})$. In this way, matrix–matrix multiplication can be performed using 7 active multiplications and 18 additions/subtractions:

$$\begin{bmatrix} w_{11} \\ w_{12} \\ w_{21} \\ w_{22} \end{bmatrix} = \begin{bmatrix} m_1 + m_4 - m_5 + m_7 \\ m_3 + m_5 \\ m_2 + m_4 \\ m_1 - m_2 + m_3 + m_6 \end{bmatrix}, \quad \text{where} \quad \begin{aligned} m_1 &= (u_{11} + u_{22})(v_{11} + v_{22}), \\ m_2 &= (u_{21} + u_{22})v_{11}, \\ m_3 &= u_{11}(v_{12} - v_{22}), \\ m_4 &= u_{22}(v_{21} - v_{11}), \\ m_5 &= (u_{11} + u_{12})v_{22}, \\ m_6 &= (u_{21} - u_{11})(v_{11} + v_{12}), \\ m_7 &= (u_{12} - u_{22})(v_{21} + v_{22}). \end{aligned} \tag{16.9}$$

The correspondence between the factor matrices and the computations can be seen, for example, by considering the last columns of each of the matrices, which together as a component correspond to m_7. The seventh column of $\mathbf{A}$ has a 1 in the third row and a -1 in the fourth row, which corresponds to the linear combination $u_{12} - u_{22}$, as the elements of $\mathbf{A}$ have been linearized in natural order. Likewise, the seventh column of $\mathbf{B}$ has 1s in the second and fourth rows, which corresponds to the linear combination $v_{21} + v_{22}$. These two linear combinations are the inputs to the m_7 multiply. The seventh column of $\mathbf{C}$ encodes how m_7 contributes to the output elements: because there is a 1 only in the first row, m_7 is added only to the output element w_{11}.

The real power of this low-rank decomposition for a tiny matrix multiplication is that it applies to *block* matrices and, moreover, can be applied recursively. First, consider the block case. If the entries of $\mathbf{U}$, $\mathbf{V}$, and $\mathbf{W}$ are $n \times n$ matrices, then each active multiplication costs $\mathcal{O}(n^3)$ (assuming direct matrix–matrix multiplication) and each addition costs $\mathcal{O}(n^2)$. This implies that for large N, Strassen's method reduces computation by a factor of approximately $8/7$. Second, we gain even more savings when we consider recursive application of the method. Matrices of dimension $n \times n$ can be partitioned into 2×2 block matrices with dimensions $n/2 \times n/2$ (or close to it if n is not even), and we can perform each of the seven active multiplications recursively. This means that $n \times n$ multiplication can be performed with arithmetic complexity $\mathcal{O}(n^{\log_2 7}) = \mathcal{O}(n^{2.8074})$ rather than $\mathcal{O}(n^3)$. The seemingly small improvement in the exponent is significant for large n, and it leads to improved running times in practice (Benson and Ballard, 2015; Huang et al., 2016; Lipshitz et al., 2012).

The rank of this $4 \times 4 \times 4$ tensor for 2×2 matrix multiplication is 7 (Landsberg, 2006; Winograd, 1971), so it is not possible to improve the exponent any further when considering a 2×2 partitioning. It is possible to reduce the hidden constant by optimizing the base case dimension within the recursion, reducing the number of additions/subtractions per Winograd's variant (Higham, 2002) and using an alternative basis to represent the matrices as proposed by Karstadt and Schwartz (2020).

Exercise 16.10 Verify that $\mathcal{X} = [\![\mathbf{A}, \mathbf{B}, \mathbf{C}]\!]$ for $\mathcal{X}$ in Eq. (16.7) and the factors in Eq. (16.8).

Exercise 16.11 (a) Compute a rank-7 factorization of $\mathcal{X}$ in Eq. (16.7) using a computational method. (b) How does the solution compare with Eq. (16.8)? (c) How might you find a solution with only entries in $\{-1, 0, 1\}$?

16.6.3 3 × 3 Matrix Multiplication

In order to find matrix multiplication algorithms with reduced arithmetic complexity, we can consider larger base cases (changing both the rank and the base of the logarithm in the recursion). The multiplication of two 3×3 matrices corresponds to a $9 \times 9 \times 9$ tensor $\mathcal{X}$ such that every entry is 0 except for 27 entries equal to 1. If we linearize the input matrices columnwise and the output matrix rowwise, this tensor is

$$x_{ijk} = \begin{cases} 1 & (i,j,k) \in \Omega \\ 0 & \text{otherwise} \end{cases}, \text{ where } \Omega = \left\{ \begin{array}{l} (1,1,1),(5,5,5),(9,9,9), \\ (1,2,4),(2,4,1),(4,1,2), \\ (1,3,7),(3,7,1),(7,1,3), \\ (2,4,5),(4,5,2),(5,2,4), \\ (2,6,7),(6,7,2),(7,2,6), \\ (3,4,8),(4,8,3),(8,3,4), \\ (3,7,9),(7,9,3),(9,3,7), \\ (5,6,8),(6,8,5),(8,5,6), \\ (6,8,9),(8,9,6),(9,6,8) \end{array} \right\}. \tag{16.10}$$

This tensor also has cyclic symmetry: $x_{ijk} = x_{kij} = x_{jki}$ for all (i,j,k). There exist exact CP decompositions with $r = 23$ (Laderman, 1976), including some that are invariant under cyclic permutation (Ballard et al., 2018); but there is no rank decomposition. Instead, we know only that the rank is between $r = 19$ (Bläser, 2003) and $r = 23$.

The recursive algorithm based on the $r = 23$ decomposition has complexity $\mathcal{O}(n^{\log_3 23}) = \mathcal{O}(n^{2.8541})$. If a rank $r = 21$ decomposition is discovered, then it will yield a matrix multiplication algorithm with complexity $\mathcal{O}(n^{\log_3 21}) = \mathcal{O}(n^{2.7713})$, which is better than Strassen's algorithm for the 2×2 case.

Exercise 16.12 Show how the tensor in Eq. (16.10) corresponds to 3×3 times 3×3 matrix–matrix multiplication.

Exercise 16.13 Compute a rank-23 decomposition of the $\mathcal{X}$ corresponding to 3×3 matrix multiplication.

16.6.4 General Matrix Multiplication

We are not restricted to considering only the case of square matrix multiplication. We can consider a base case of multiplying $m \times n$ and $n \times p$ matrices for any triplet of integers $\langle m,n,p \rangle$. The $mn \times np \times mp$ tensor representing matrix multiplication with these dimensions is defined entrywise by

$$\mathcal{X}^{\langle m,n,p \rangle}(a + (b-1)m, c + (d-1)n, e + (f-1)p) = \delta_{fa}\delta_{bc}\delta_{de}$$

for $f, a \in [m]$, $b, c \in [n]$, and $d, e \in [p]$, where δ_{ij} is the Kronecker delta function that is 1 if $i = j$ and 0 otherwise (Brent, 1970). The Kronecker deltas ensure that nonzero entries in the tensor correspond to subscripts that match between pairs of matrices, as each scalar multiplication within matrix multiplication has the form $u_{ij}v_{jk}$, which contributes to w_{ik}. The tensor can be generated using the following pseudocode:

Tensor for $m \times n$ and $n \times p$ Matrix–Matrix Multiplication

$\mathcal{X} = 0$ $\quad \triangleright \mathcal{X} \in \mathbb{R}^{mn \times np \times mp}$
for $i = 1$ to m **do**
  for $j = 1$ to n **do**
    for $k = 1$ to p **do**
      $\mathcal{X}(i + (j-1)m, j + (k-1)n, k + (i-1)p) = 1$
    end for
  end for
end for

As before, this uses natural linearization of the input matrices and reverse linearization of the output matrix, which exposes the tensor's cyclic symmetry when $m = n = p$.

If we have a rank-r decomposition of $\mathcal{X}^{\langle m,n,p\rangle}$ as a base case, then we can combine it with the corresponding cyclically permuted decompositions for $\langle p, m, n\rangle$ and $\langle n, p, m\rangle$, to obtain a rank-r^3 decomposition for $\langle mnp, mnp, mnp\rangle$. We can think of this combination of algorithms as alternating recursive steps among the three recursive rules. This implies a matrix multiplication algorithm for $N \times N$ matrices with complexity $\mathcal{O}(N^{3\log_{mnp} r})$.

Another transformation of a CP decomposition for $\langle m, n, p\rangle$ yields a CP decomposition of $\langle n, m, p\rangle$. This means that, along with the cyclic permutation transformation, an algorithm for $\langle m, n, p\rangle$ yields algorithms for all five of the other permutations of the dimensions (Hopcroft and Musinski, 1973). Table 16.3 lists several small base case dimension triplets and the best-known rank upper bounds, along with the exponent for the corresponding matrix multiplication algorithm.

Table 16.3 Rank upper bounds on tensors corresponding to $m \times n$ times $n \times p$ matrix multiplication. Without loss of generality (since the order of the modes does not impact rank of the matrix–matrix multiplication), we assume $m \leq n \leq p$. The exponent α means that the corresponding matrix–matrix multiply for two $N \times N$ matrices has arithmetic complexity $\mathcal{O}(N^{\alpha})$ based on recursive application of matrix–matrix multiplication.

$\langle m, n, p\rangle$	Rank bound	Exponent (α)	Citation
$\langle 2, 2, 2\rangle$	7	2.81	Strassen (1969)
$\langle 2, 3, 3\rangle$	15	2.81	Hopcroft and Kerr (1971)
$\langle 3, 3, 3\rangle$	23	2.85	Laderman (1976)
$\langle 3, 3, 4\rangle$	29	2.82	Smirnov (2013)
$\langle 2, 5, 5\rangle$	40	2.83	Hopcroft and Kerr (1971)
$\langle 3, 3, 6\rangle$	40	2.77	Smirnov (2013)
$\langle 3, 4, 5\rangle$	47	2.82	Fawzi et al. (2022)
$\langle 4, 4, 4\rangle$	49	2.81	Strassen (1969)
$\langle 3, 5, 5\rangle$	58	2.82	Sedoglavic and Smirnov (2021)
$\langle 4, 4, 5\rangle$	62	2.83	Kauers and Moosbauer (2023)
$\langle 4, 5, 5\rangle$	76	2.82	Fawzi et al. (2022)
$\langle 5, 5, 5\rangle$	97	2.84	Kauers and Moosbauer (2023)

The list is certainly not exhaustive, as progress continues to be made. Most of the examples are just upper bounds on rank given by a particular CP decomposition of that rank, leaving gaps between the best-known lower and upper bounds. Most of the algorithms have been discovered using computer-aided search. Ballard et al. (2018), Benson and Ballard (2015), Brent (1970), Johnson and McLoughlin (1986), Sedoglavic and Smirnov (2021), and Smirnov (2013) use variants of common algorithms for computing CP decompositions, such as CP-ALS (Chapter 11) and CP-NLS (Chapter 13), and more recent approaches have used deep learning (Fawzi et al., 2022) and combinatorial techniques (Kauers and Moosbauer, 2023).

Exercise 16.14 (a) Form the tensor $\mathfrak{X}^{\langle 2,3,3\rangle}$ corresponding to matrix–matrix multiplication for matrices of size 2×3 and 3×3. (b) Compute its rank-15 factorization.

16.6.5 Arbitrary Precision Approximating Algorithms

Recall that the border rank of a tensor is the smallest r such that for any approximation error there exists a rank-r CP approximation within that error (Definition 16.6). If the border rank of a particular matrix multiplication tensor is smaller than its rank, it means that we can (in infinite precision) compute an arbitrarily precise approximation of a matrix product more cheaply than computing it exactly. These are known as arbitrary precision approximating (APA) algorithms.

The first APA algorithm was demonstrated for multiplying 2×2 matrices where one input matrix has a 0 entry (Bini et al., 1979). This is used to construct an APA algorithm for $\langle 3, 2, 2\rangle$ based on a rank-10 CP decomposition, as shown in Example 16.3.

Example 16.3 (Rank-10 APA Decomposition for $\langle \mathbf{3}, \mathbf{2}, \mathbf{2}\rangle$ Matrix Multiplication from Bini et al., 1979) Given the parametrized factor matrices

$$\mathbf{A}(\varepsilon) = \begin{bmatrix} 1 & 0 & 1 & 0 & 1 & 0 & 0 & 0 & 0 & 0 \\ 0 & 0 & 0 & 0 & 0 & 1 & 0 & 1 & 0 & 1 \\ 0 & 0 & 0 & 0 & 0 & 0 & 0 & 0 & \varepsilon & \varepsilon \\ 0 & 0 & 0 & \varepsilon & \varepsilon & 0 & 0 & 0 & 0 & 0 \\ 1 & 1 & 0 & 1 & 0 & 0 & 0 & 0 & 0 & 0 \\ 0 & 0 & 0 & 0 & 0 & 1 & 1 & 0 & 1 & 0 \end{bmatrix},$$

$$\mathbf{B}(\varepsilon) = \begin{bmatrix} \varepsilon & 0 & 0 & -\varepsilon & 0 & 1 & 1 & -1 & 1 & 0 \\ 0 & -1 & 0 & 1 & 0 & 0 & 0 & 0 & \varepsilon & 0 \\ 0 & 0 & 0 & 0 & \varepsilon & 0 & 0 & -1 & 0 & 1 \\ 1 & -1 & 1 & 0 & 1 & \varepsilon & 0 & 0 & 0 & -\varepsilon \end{bmatrix},$$

$$\mathbf{C}(\varepsilon) = \begin{bmatrix} 1/\varepsilon & 1/\varepsilon & -1/\varepsilon & 1/\varepsilon & 0 & 0 & 0 & 0 & 0 & 0 \\ 0 & 0 & -1/\varepsilon & 0 & 1/\varepsilon & 0 & 0 & 0 & 0 & 0 \\ 0 & 0 & 0 & 1 & 0 & 1 & 0 & 0 & -1 & 0 \\ 1 & 0 & 0 & 0 & -1 & 0 & 0 & 0 & 0 & 1 \\ 0 & 0 & 0 & 0 & 0 & 0 & -1/\varepsilon & 0 & 1/\varepsilon & 0 \\ 0 & 0 & 0 & 0 & 0 & 1/\varepsilon & -1/\varepsilon & 1/\varepsilon & 0 & 1/\varepsilon \end{bmatrix},$$

we have

$$\lim_{\varepsilon \to 0} [\![\mathbf{A}(\varepsilon), \mathbf{B}(\varepsilon), \mathbf{C}(\varepsilon)]\!] = \mathfrak{X}^{\langle 3,2,2\rangle}.$$

The rank of $\mathfrak{X}^{\langle 3,2,2\rangle}$ is 11 (Bläser, 2003), so the border rank and rank differ. The exponent for the complexity of square matrix multiplication based on this algorithm is $3 \log_{12} 10 \approx 2.78$, which is better than Strassen's $\langle 2, 2, 2\rangle$ algorithm, but it computes only an approximate matrix multiplication result.

In exact arithmetic, APA algorithms can be transformed into exact algorithms with an overhead of a polylogarithmic factor (Bini, 1980). In finite precision, APA algorithms must navigate a trade-off between the approximation error of the algorithm and the roundoff error, but the optimal value of the parameter ε can be computed from properties of the algorithm (Bini et al., 1980).

APA algorithms enable much faster decrease in the exponent of the complexity of matrix multiplication. Strassen's $\langle 2,2,2\rangle$ algorithm is beaten by an exact algorithm only after the base case is enlarged to $\langle 6,3,3\rangle$. APA algorithms have thus far been key to obtaining exponents that are competitive with the current world record of 2.371552 for a theoretical algorithm (Williams et al., 2024). Alas, the algorithms with the best exponents are not practical: they involve base cases of infeasible size, have large constant factors, and incur numerical difficulties since they are inexact.

Exercise 16.15 Verify Example 16.3.

16.7 CP Uniqueness

An important property of a tensor rank decomposition is *uniqueness*. When we say a tensor decomposition is unique, we mean it is "essentially" unique up to inherent permutation and scaling ambiguities; see Definitions 10.15 and 10.18. Uniqueness means there is only one rank decomposition for a given tensor. It is worth remembering that low-rank matrix decompositions are not unique, as discussed in Section 10.5. Likewise, the Tucker decomposition is not unique; see Section 5.3. If a decomposition is unique, it improves interpretation.

In the results below, the properties of the factor matrices can be used to determine if the factorization is essentially unique. Before we explain those conditions, we need Definition 16.10.

Definition 16.10: k-rank (Kruskal, 1989)

The **k-rank** of a matrix $\mathbf{A}$, denoted $\text{k-rank}(\mathbf{A})$, is the maximum value of k such that *any* k columns of $\mathbf{A}$ are linearly independent.

Exercise 16.16 Let

$$\mathbf{A} = \begin{bmatrix} 1 & 2 & 4 \\ 1 & 2 & 2 \end{bmatrix} \quad \text{and} \quad \mathbf{B} = \begin{bmatrix} 2 & 2 & 4 \\ 0 & 2 & 2 \end{bmatrix}.$$

(a) What is $\text{rank}(\mathbf{A})$? What is $\text{k-rank}(\mathbf{A})$? (b) What is $\text{rank}(\mathbf{B})$? What is $\text{k-rank}(\mathbf{B})$?

Proposition 16.11 (Upper Bounding k-rank, Kruskal, 1989) *For any matrix* $\mathbf{A} \in \mathbb{R}^{n\times r}$, $\text{k-rank}(\mathbf{A}) \leq \text{rank}(\mathbf{A})$.

Exercise 16.17 Prove Proposition 16.11.

Proposition 16.12 (Full Rank Matrix k-rank) *Let* $\mathbf{A} \in \mathbb{R}^{n\times r}$ *with* $r \leq n$. *If* $\text{rank}(\mathbf{A}) = r$, *then* $\text{k-rank}(\mathbf{A}) = r$.

Exercise 16.18 Prove Proposition 16.12.

If $\mathbf{A}$ is orthonormal, then its rank and k-rank are both equal to r. Otherwise, the k-rank is not necessarily easy to compute, but we can lower bound it by using a result from compressed sensing. In compressed sensing, the **spark** of a matrix is defined to be the minimum number of linearly dependent columns. Thus, $\text{spark}(\mathbf{A}) = \text{k-rank}(\mathbf{A}) + 1$, and so results on the spark can be used for the k-rank.

Proposition 16.13 (Lower Bounding k-rank, Elad, 2010, lemma 2.1) *For any matrix* $\mathbf{A} = [\,\mathbf{a}_1\,\mathbf{a}_2 \cdots \mathbf{a}_r\,] \in \mathbb{R}^{n \times r}$ *that is not orthonormal,*

$$\text{k-rank}(\mathbf{A}) \geq \min\left\{ r, \frac{1}{\mu(\mathbf{A})} \right\}, \quad \textit{where} \quad \mu(\mathbf{A}) = \max_{i \neq j} \frac{\mathbf{a}_i^{\mathsf{T}} \mathbf{a}_j}{\|\mathbf{a}_i\|_2 \|\mathbf{a}_j\|_2}.$$

The value $\mu(\mathbf{A})$ *is called the coherence of* $\mathbf{A}$.

The first uniqueness result is due to Kruskal (1977) and says that an r-component Kruskal tensor $\mathcal{K} = [\![\mathbf{A}, \mathbf{B}, \mathbf{C}]\!]$ is essentially unique if the k-ranks of the factor matrices sum to $2r + 2$. This would be satisfied, for instance, if $r < \min\{\,m, n, p\,\}$ and every factor matrix is full rank.

Theorem 16.14: Kruskal Uniqueness (Kruskal, 1977)

A Kruskal tensor $\mathcal{K} = [\![\mathbf{A}, \mathbf{B}, \mathbf{C}]\!]$ *with r components is essentially unique if*

$$\text{k-rank}(\mathbf{A}) + \text{k-rank}(\mathbf{B}) + \text{k-rank}(\mathbf{C}) \geq 2r + 2. \tag{16.11}$$

Equation (16.11) is a sufficient but not a necessary condition. For instance, Eq. (16.11) cannot hold for $r = 1$, but the uniqueness in this case has been proved by Harshman (1972). For $r \in \{\,2, 3\,\}$, ten Berge and Sidiriopolous (2002) showed that Eq. (16.11) is necessary. See also Stegeman and Sidiropoulos (2007) for further discussion and details of the proof. This result has been generalized to the d-way case as follows.

Theorem 16.15: Kruskal Uniqueness (Sidiropoulos and Bro, 2000)

A Kruskal tensor $\mathcal{K} = [\![\mathbf{A}_1, \mathbf{A}_2, \ldots, \mathbf{A}_d]\!]$ *with r components is essentially unique if*

$$\sum_{k=1}^{d} \text{k-rank}(\mathbf{A}_k) \geq 2r + d - 1. \tag{16.12}$$

Exercise 16.19 Using Theorem 16.15, prove that the r-component Kruskal tensor $\mathcal{K} = [\![\mathbf{A}_1, \mathbf{A}_2, \ldots, \mathbf{A}_d]\!]$ is (essentially) unique if $r \geq 2$ and $\text{k-rank}(\mathbf{A}_k) = r$ for all k.

Eq. (16.12) is sufficient but not necessary for uniqueness. Conversely, there are some necessary conditions.

Theorem 16.16 (Nonuniqueness of CP, Liu and Sidiropoulos, 2001) *If*

$$\min\{\,\text{rank}(\mathbf{A}_d \odot \cdots \odot \mathbf{A}_{k+1} \odot \mathbf{A}_{k-1} \odot \cdots \odot \mathbf{A}_1) \mid k \in [d]\,\} < r,$$

then the r-component Kruskal tensor $\mathcal{K} = [\![\mathbf{A}_1, \mathbf{A}_2, \ldots, \mathbf{A}_d]\!]$ *is* not *essentially unique.*

Exercise 16.20 Prove Theorem 16.16 using Proposition 10.10 and facts from Section A.7 to show that if

$$k^* = \arg\min \{ \operatorname{rank}(\mathbf{A}_d \odot \cdots \odot \mathbf{A}_{k+1} \odot \mathbf{A}_{k-1} \odot \cdots \odot \mathbf{A}_1) \mid k \in [d] \},$$

then there are infinitely many $\tilde{\mathbf{A}}_{k^*}$ that satisfy

$$[\![\mathbf{A}_1, \mathbf{A}_2, \ldots, \mathbf{A}_d]\!] = [\![\mathbf{A}_1, \ldots, \mathbf{A}_{k^*-1}, \tilde{\mathbf{A}}_{k^*}, \mathbf{A}_{k^*+1}, \ldots, \mathbf{A}_d]\!].$$

Exercise 16.21 Using Theorem 16.16 and the properties of the KRP, prove that the rank decomposition in Example 9.1 is not unique.

16.8 Direct Computation of Rank for Certain Tensors

In general, computing the rank and the rank decomposition is NP-hard. However, there are a few particular instances where we can compute the tensor rank or decomposition algebraically (by which we mean using matrix eigendecompositions). In general, these results are not especially practical, but they have some utility in exposing what is theoretically possible. They assume that the tensor is exact (no experimental noise or uncertainty) and that various quantities such as matrix eigenvalues can be computed. Perhaps the most important takeaway from this section is how little is known about tensor rank, with only a small number of situations well characterized.

As a preliminary, we consider a special identity for all 3-way tensors. If $\mathcal{X} = [\![\mathbf{A}, \mathbf{B}, \mathbf{C}]\!] \in \mathbb{R}^{m \times n \times p}$, we can write the kth frontal slice $\mathbf{X}_k \equiv \mathcal{X}(:,:,k)$ as

$$\mathbf{X}_k = \sum_{\ell=1}^{r} c_{k\ell}\, \mathbf{a}_\ell \mathbf{b}_\ell^\intercal = \mathbf{A} \operatorname{diag}\big(\mathbf{C}(k,:)\big)\mathbf{B}^\intercal \quad \text{for all} \quad k \in [p]. \tag{16.13}$$

We will work extensively with the frontal slices and this expression in this section.

16.8.1 Rank-1 Tensors

It is always possible to determine if a tensor is exactly rank 1 by considering the ranks of its mode-k unfoldings.

3-way Tensors

We can test whether or not a tensor is rank 1 by computing the ranks of its unfoldings. A 3-way tensor is rank 1 if at least two unfoldings are rank 1.

Theorem 16.17 (Conditions for Rank-1 Tensor, 3-way) *Let* $\mathcal{X} \in \mathbb{R}^{m \times n \times p}$. *If any two of its three mode-k unfoldings are rank 1, then* $\operatorname{rank}(\mathcal{X}) = 1$.

Proof. By definition, the rank of $\mathcal{X}$ is unchanged by any permutation of the modes. Thus, without loss of generality, we assume that $\operatorname{rank}(\mathbf{X}_{(1)}) = \operatorname{rank}(\mathbf{X}_{(3)}) = 1$.

Let the frontal slices of $\mathcal{X}$ be denoted as $\mathbf{X}_k \equiv \mathcal{X}(:,:,k)$ for all $k \in [p]$. Recall (see Section 2.3.1) that the unfoldings are such that

$$\mathbf{X}_{(1)} = \begin{bmatrix} \mathbf{X}_1 & \mathbf{X}_2 & \cdots & \mathbf{X}_p \end{bmatrix} \in \mathbb{R}^{m \times np}, \tag{16.14}$$

$$\mathbf{X}_{(3)}^\intercal = \begin{bmatrix} \operatorname{vec}(\mathbf{X}_1) & \operatorname{vec}(\mathbf{X}_2) & \cdots & \operatorname{vec}(\mathbf{X}_p) \end{bmatrix} \in \mathbb{R}^{mn \times p}. \tag{16.15}$$

Since $\mathbf{X}_{(3)}$ is rank 1, we have

$$\mathbf{X}_{(3)} = \mathbf{c}\mathbf{z}^{\mathsf{T}} \quad \text{for some} \quad \mathbf{c} \in \mathbb{R}^p \text{ and } \mathbf{z} \in \mathbb{R}^{mn}.$$

From Eq. (16.15), this means $\mathrm{vec}(\mathbf{X}_k) = c_k\mathbf{z}$ for all $k \in [p]$. Or, equivalently, $\mathbf{X}_k = c_k\mathbf{Z}$, where $\mathbf{Z} = \mathrm{reshape}(\mathbf{z}, m \times n)$.

Now, since $\mathbf{X}_{(1)}$ is rank 1, Eq. (16.14) implies each $\mathbf{X}_k$ is also rank 1. Thus, $\mathbf{Z}$ must be rank 1 and so can be expressed as

$$\mathbf{Z} = \mathbf{a}\mathbf{b}^{\mathsf{T}} \quad \text{for some} \quad \mathbf{a} \in \mathbb{R}^m \text{ and } \mathbf{b} \in \mathbb{R}^n.$$

Finally, we have

$$\mathbf{X}_{(3)} = \mathbf{c}\,\mathrm{vec}(\mathbf{Z})^{\mathsf{T}} = \mathbf{c}\,\mathrm{vec}(\mathbf{a}\mathbf{b}^{\mathsf{T}})^{\mathsf{T}} = \mathbf{c}(\mathbf{b} \otimes \mathbf{a})^{\mathsf{T}} \quad \Rightarrow \quad \mathcal{X} = \mathbf{a} \bigcirc \mathbf{b} \bigcirc \mathbf{c}.$$

The last step comes from Proposition 3.7. □

Exercise 16.22 Let $\mathcal{X} \in \mathbb{R}^{m\times n\times p}$. Prove the following: If $\mathrm{rank}(\mathcal{X}) = 1$, then $\mathrm{rank}(\mathbf{X}_{(1)}) = \mathrm{rank}(\mathbf{X}_{(2)}) = \mathrm{rank}(\mathbf{X}_{(3)}) = 1$.

d-way Tensors

We can extend this idea for d-way tensors. A sufficient condition for a d-way tensor to be rank 1 is that $d-1$ of its unfoldings are rank 1.

Theorem 16.18 (Conditions for Rank-1 Tensor) *Let $\mathcal{X} \in \mathbb{R}^{n_1\times n_2\times\cdots\times n_d}$. If $d-1$ of its d mode-k unfolding are rank 1, then* $\mathrm{rank}(\mathcal{X}) = 1$.

Proof. We do a proof by induction. We know the result holds for $d = 3$ from Theorem 16.17. So, we assume that the result holds for every $d' < d$ and prove it for d.

By definition, the rank of $\mathcal{X}$ is unchanged by any permutation of the modes. Thus, without loss of generality, we assume $\mathrm{rank}\big(\mathbf{X}_{(k)}\big) = 1$ for all $k > 1$.

Let the frontal hyperslices of $\mathcal{X}$ be denoted as $\mathcal{Y}_j = \mathcal{X}(:, \ldots, :, j)$ for all $j \in [n_d]$. From Exercise 2.32, we have

$$\mathbf{X}_{(d)}^{\mathsf{T}} = \begin{bmatrix}\mathrm{vec}(\mathcal{Y}_1) & \mathrm{vec}(\mathcal{Y}_2) & \cdots & \mathrm{vec}(\mathcal{Y}_{n_d})\end{bmatrix} \in \mathbb{R}^{N_d\times n_d}, \tag{16.16}$$

where $N_d = \prod_{k=1}^{d-1} n_k$.

Since $\mathrm{rank}\big(\mathbf{X}_{(d)}\big) = 1$, we have

$$\mathbf{X}_{(d)} = \mathbf{b}\mathbf{z}^{\mathsf{T}} \quad \text{for some} \quad \mathbf{b} \in \mathbb{R}^{n_d} \text{ and } \mathbf{z} \in \mathbb{R}^{N_d}.$$

From Eq. (16.16), this means $\mathrm{vec}\big(\mathcal{Y}^{(j)}\big) = b_j\mathbf{z}$ for all $j \in [n_d]$. Or, equivalently, $\mathcal{Y}_j = b_j\mathcal{Z}$, where $\mathcal{Z} = \mathrm{reshape}(\mathbf{z}, n_1 \times n_2 \times \cdots \times n_{d-1})$ is a tensor of order $d-1$.

From Exercise 2.33, we can relate the ranks of the unfoldings: $\mathbf{Y}_{(k)}^{(j)}$ is rank 1 if $\mathbf{X}_{(k)}$ is rank 1. We have $\mathrm{rank}\big(\mathbf{X}_{(k)}\big) = 1$ for $k \in 2, \ldots, d-1$. Since $\mathcal{Z}$ is a multiple of $\mathcal{Y}^{(j)}$ for any $j \in [d-1]$, we have that $d-2$ of its unfoldings have rank 1. By the induction assumption, $\mathcal{Z}$ has rank 1.

Thus, setting $\mathbf{a}_d = \mathbf{b}$ and $\mathcal{Z} = \mathbf{a}_1 \bigcirc \mathbf{a}_2 \bigcirc \cdots \bigcirc \mathbf{a}_{d-1}$ (since it is rank 1), we have

$$\mathbf{X}_{(d)} = \mathbf{a}_d \operatorname{vec}(\mathbf{Z})^\intercal = \mathbf{a}_d \operatorname{vec}(\mathbf{a}_{d-1} \otimes \cdots \otimes \mathbf{a}_1)^\intercal \quad \Rightarrow \quad \mathcal{X} = \mathbf{a}_1 \bigcirc \mathbf{a}_2 \bigcirc \cdots \bigcirc \mathbf{a}_d.$$

The last step comes from Proposition 3.10. □

Exercise 16.23 Provide an algorithm for computing the rank-1 factorization of a d-way tensor where $\mathbf{X}_{(k)}$ is rank 1 for $k \in \{2, 3, \ldots, d\}$.

16.8.2 Rank of 2 × 2 × 2 Tensors

We can compute the rank of a $2 \times 2 \times 2$ tensor directly. From the discussion in the previous subsection, we can easily check whether a $2 \times 2 \times 2$ tensor is rank 1. We consider some special cases before our main result.

For the special case of a superdiagonal tensor, the rank is 2.

Proposition 16.19 (Superdiagonal $2 \times 2 \times 2$ is Rank 2, ten Berge, 1991) *Let $\mathcal{X} \in \mathbb{R}^{2\times 2\times 2}$. If $\mathcal{X}$ is superdiagonal, meaning*

$$\mathcal{X}(:,:,1) = \begin{bmatrix} \alpha & 0 \\ 0 & 0 \end{bmatrix} \quad \textit{and} \quad \mathcal{X}(:,:,2) = \begin{bmatrix} 0 & 0 \\ 0 & \beta \end{bmatrix},$$

then $\operatorname{rank}(\mathcal{X}) = 2$.

Exercise 16.24 Prove Proposition 16.19.

The following result says that if every slice is rank 1, then either the tensor is rank 1 or the tensor is superdiagonal (and thus rank 2 by the prior result).

Proposition 16.20 (ten Berge, 1991) *A nonzero tensor $\mathcal{X} \in \mathbb{R}^{2\times 2\times 2}$ is rank 1 if and only if every frontal, lateral, and horizontal slice is at most rank 1* and *$\mathcal{X}$ is not superdiagonal.*

Proof. One direction is left as Exercise 16.25.

For the other direction, we assume every nonzero frontal, lateral, and horizontal slice is rank 1. We will prove that either $\operatorname{rank}(\mathcal{X}) = 1$ or $\mathcal{X}$ is superdiagonal.

Without loss of generality, we assume the tensor has been permuted so that $\mathcal{X}(1,1,1)$ is nonzero. We denote the frontal slices as $\mathbf{X}_k \equiv \mathcal{X}(:,:,k)$ for $k \in \{1, 2\}$.

Case I: Zero slice (rank 1). First, consider the case that some slice is zero. Without loss of generality, assume the tensor is permuted so that the frontal slice $\mathbf{X}_2$ is the zero slice. Then $\mathbf{X}_{(1)} = [\mathbf{X}_1 \; \mathbf{0}]$ and $\mathbf{X}_{(3)}^\intercal = [\operatorname{vec}(\mathbf{X}_1) \; \mathbf{0}]$ are both rank 1, so by Theorem 16.17, $\operatorname{rank}(\mathcal{X}) = 1$.

Case II: No zero slice (rank 1). Because every slice is rank 1, the frontal slices have the form

$$\mathbf{X}_1 = \begin{bmatrix} \mathbf{a} & \alpha \mathbf{a} \end{bmatrix} = \begin{bmatrix} a_1 & \alpha a_1 \\ a_2 & \alpha a_2 \end{bmatrix} \quad \text{and} \quad \mathbf{X}_2 = \begin{bmatrix} \beta \mathbf{b} & \gamma \mathbf{b} \end{bmatrix} = \begin{bmatrix} \beta b_1 & \gamma b_1 \\ \beta b_2 & \gamma b_2 \end{bmatrix}.$$

Here $a_1 \neq 0$ because of the assumption that element $\mathcal{X}(1,1,1) \neq 0$. Likewise, $\mathbf{b} \neq 0$ and either β or γ must be nonzero, but not both, because no slice is entirely zero.

Case IIa: b $\propto$ a (rank 1). First, consider the possibility that $\mathbf{b} = \mathbf{a}$ (since β and γ are arbitrary, this is just a simplification of $\mathbf{b}$ proportional to $\mathbf{a}$). Since the horizontal slices are nonzero, we know

$$\mathcal{X}(1,:,:) = \begin{bmatrix} a_1 & \alpha a_1 \\ \beta b_1 & \gamma b_1 \end{bmatrix} = \begin{bmatrix} a_1 & \alpha a_1 \\ \beta a_1 & \gamma a_1 \end{bmatrix}$$

has rank 1 and so $\gamma = \alpha\beta$. Thus, both

$$\mathbf{X}_{(1)} = \begin{bmatrix} \mathbf{a} & \alpha\mathbf{a} & \beta\mathbf{a} & \gamma\mathbf{a} \end{bmatrix} \quad \text{and} \quad \mathbf{X}_{(2)} = \begin{bmatrix} \mathbf{a}^\intercal & \beta\mathbf{a}^\intercal \\ \alpha\mathbf{a}^\intercal & \alpha\beta\mathbf{a}^\intercal \end{bmatrix}$$

are rank 1, so $\operatorname{rank}(\mathcal{X}) = 1$ by Theorem 16.17.

Case IIb: b $\not\propto$ a (superdiagonal). Second, assume $\mathbf{b}$ is not proportional to $\mathbf{a}$. The rank-1 lateral slices are

$$\mathcal{X}(:,1,:) = \begin{bmatrix} \mathbf{a} & \beta\mathbf{b} \end{bmatrix} \quad \text{and} \quad \mathcal{X}(:,2,:) = \begin{bmatrix} \alpha\mathbf{a} & \gamma\mathbf{b} \end{bmatrix}.$$

Since these are rank 1, we must have $\beta = 0$. Since $\beta = 0$, $\gamma \neq 0$ since they cannot both be 0. Hence, $\alpha = 0$. Without loss of generality (since $\mathbf{b}$ is arbitrary), we assume $\gamma = 1$. So, the rank-1 nonzero horizontal slices are

$$\mathcal{X}(1,:,:) = \begin{bmatrix} a_1 & 0 \\ 0 & b_1 \end{bmatrix} \quad \text{and} \quad \mathcal{X}(2,:,:) = \begin{bmatrix} a_2 & 0 \\ 0 & b_2 \end{bmatrix}.$$

Since we assume $a_1 \neq 0$, it must be the case that $b_1 = 0$. Since $\mathbf{b} \neq 0$, it must be the case that $b_2 = 0$. Hence, $a_2 = 0$. Thus, $\mathcal{X}$ is superdiagonal. □

Exercise 16.25 Prove the following: if a tensor $\mathcal{X} \in \mathbb{R}^{2\times2\times2}$ is rank 1, then every frontal, lateral, and horizontal slice is at most rank 1.

By the following proposition, except for special cases we can check, we can always assume that the first frontal slice is nonsingular.

Proposition 16.21 *Let $\mathcal{X} \in \mathbb{R}^{2\times2\times2}$. If $\operatorname{rank}(\mathcal{X}) > 1$ and $\mathcal{X}$ is not superdiagonal, then there exists a mode permutation π and a 2×2 matrix permutation $\mathbf{P}$ such that $\mathcal{Y} = \mathbb{P}(\mathcal{X}, \pi) \times_3 \mathbf{P}$ and its first frontal slice, $\mathcal{Y}(:,:,1)$, is nonsingular.*

Proof. By Proposition 16.20, there must be at least one frontal, horizontal, or lateral slice that is full rank. Choose π so that this slice is a frontal slice (i.e., after permuting the modes, either $\mathbf{X}_1$ or $\mathbf{X}_2$ is nonsingular). If $\mathbf{X}_1$ is singular, then we multiply $\mathcal{X}$ by the permutation matrix $\mathbf{P} = \left[\begin{smallmatrix} 0 & 1 \\ 1 & 0 \end{smallmatrix}\right]$ in mode 3 to swap the slices. Hence, the claim. □

The cases we have dealt with thus far (rank 1, superdiagonal) are unusual in the sense that a real-valued tensor with entries chosen at random from a continuous distribution (e.g., normal or uniform) has probability 0. The main case of interest, which occurs with probability 1, is that the first frontal slice is nonsingular.

First, we formally prove that the maximum rank of a $2 \times 2 \times 2$ tensor is 3, following the constructive proof from ten Berge (1991).

Theorem 16.22 (Maximum Rank of $2 \times 2 \times 2$ is 3, JáJá, 1979; Kruskal, 1983; ten Berge, 1991) *The maximum rank of a $2 \times 2 \times 2$ tensor is 3.*

Proof. Let $\mathbf{X}_1$ and $\mathbf{X}_2$ denote the frontal slices of $\mathcal{X} \in \mathbb{R}^{2\times 2\times 2}$. Without loss of generality, assume $\operatorname{rank}(\mathcal{X}) > 1$ and that $\mathbf{X}_1$ is nonsingular. (By Proposition 16.21, there must be a nonsingular slice, and the rank is invariant to permutation.)

Define $\mathbf{Y} = \mathbf{X}_2\mathbf{X}_1^{-1}$,

$$\mathbf{A} = \begin{bmatrix} 1 & 0 & y_{12} \\ 0 & 1 & y_{21} \end{bmatrix}, \quad \mathbf{B} = \mathbf{X}_1^{\intercal} \begin{bmatrix} 1 & 0 & 1 \\ 0 & 1 & 1 \end{bmatrix}, \quad \text{and} \quad \mathbf{C} = \begin{bmatrix} 1 & 1 & 0 \\ y_{11} - y_{12} & y_{22} - y_{21} & 1 \end{bmatrix}.$$

Then the first frontal slice of $[\![\mathbf{A}, \mathbf{B}, \mathbf{C}]\!]$ is $\mathbf{A} \operatorname{diag}(\mathbf{C}(1,:))\mathbf{B}^{\intercal}$ per Eq. (16.13), which yields

$$\begin{bmatrix} 1 & 0 & y_{12} \\ 0 & 1 & y_{21} \end{bmatrix} \begin{bmatrix} 1 & 0 & 0 \\ 0 & 1 & 0 \\ 0 & 0 & 0 \end{bmatrix} \begin{bmatrix} 1 & 0 & 1 \\ 0 & 1 & 1 \end{bmatrix} \mathbf{X}_1 = \mathbf{X}_1,$$

and the second frontal slice is $\mathbf{A} \operatorname{diag}(\mathbf{C}(2,:))\mathbf{B}^{\intercal}$, which yields

$$\begin{bmatrix} 1 & 0 & y_{12} \\ 0 & 1 & y_{21} \end{bmatrix} \begin{bmatrix} y_{11} - y_{12} & 0 & 0 \\ 0 & y_{22} - y_{21} & 0 \\ 0 & 0 & 1 \end{bmatrix} \begin{bmatrix} 1 & 0 & 1 \\ 0 & 1 & 1 \end{bmatrix} \mathbf{X}_1 = \mathbf{Y}\mathbf{X}_1 = \mathbf{X}_2.$$

Hence, the maximum rank is 3 because we can write any $\mathcal{X}$ using three components: $\mathcal{X} = [\![\mathbf{A}, \mathbf{B}, \mathbf{C}]\!]$ with $\mathbf{A}, \mathbf{B}, \mathbf{C} \in \mathbb{R}^{2\times 3}$. □

So, the remaining question is how to differentiate between ranks 2 and 3 for tensors of rank greater than 1 and not superdiagonal. In this case, we consider the eigendecomposition of the matrix $\mathbf{X}_2\mathbf{X}_1^{-1}$. If it is *diagonalizable*, which means we can write $\mathbf{X}_2\mathbf{X}_1^{-1} = \mathbf{U}\boldsymbol{\Lambda}\mathbf{U}^{-1}$ for some nonsingular matrix $\mathbf{U}$ and diagonal matrix $\boldsymbol{\Lambda}$, then $\operatorname{rank}(\mathcal{X}) = 2$; otherwise, $\operatorname{rank}(\mathcal{X}) = 3$.

Theorem 16.23 (ten Berge, 1991) *Let* $\mathcal{X} \in \mathbb{R}^{2\times 2\times 2}$ *with* $\operatorname{rank}(\mathcal{X}) > 1$ *and* $\mathbf{X}_1$ *nonsingular. Then* $\operatorname{rank}(\mathcal{X}) = 2$ *if and only if* $\mathbf{X}_2\mathbf{X}_1^{-1}$ *is diagonalizable. Otherwise,* $\operatorname{rank}(\mathcal{X}) = 3$.

Proof. Let $\mathbf{X}_1$ and $\mathbf{X}_2$ denote the frontal slices of $\mathcal{X}$. By the assumption that $\operatorname{rank}(\mathcal{X}) > 1$ and Theorem 16.22, we know that $\operatorname{rank}(\mathcal{X}) \in \{2, 3\}$.

If $\operatorname{rank}(\mathcal{X}) = 2$, then $\mathcal{X} = [\![\mathbf{A}, \mathbf{B}, \mathbf{C}]\!]$ with $\mathbf{A}, \mathbf{B}, \mathbf{C} \in \mathbb{R}^{2\times 2}$. Hence, by Eq. (16.13),

$$\mathbf{X}_1 = \mathbf{A}\begin{bmatrix} c_{11} & 0 \\ 0 & c_{12} \end{bmatrix}\mathbf{B}^{\intercal} \quad \text{and} \quad \mathbf{X}_2 = \mathbf{A}\begin{bmatrix} c_{21} & 0 \\ 0 & c_{22} \end{bmatrix}\mathbf{B}^{\intercal}.$$

Since $\mathbf{X}_1$ is nonsingular, we know $\mathbf{A}$ and $\mathbf{B}$ are nonsingular and c_{11} and c_{12} are nonzero. Thus, we can write

$$\mathbf{X}_2\mathbf{X}_1^{-1} = \mathbf{A}\begin{bmatrix} c_{21}/c_{11} & 0 \\ 0 & c_{22}/c_{12} \end{bmatrix}\mathbf{A}^{-1},$$

so $\mathbf{X}_2\mathbf{X}_1^{-1}$ is diagonalizable.

Conversely, if $\mathbf{X}_2\mathbf{X}_1^{-1}$ is diagonalizable, then can write its eigenvalue decompositions as $\mathbf{U}\boldsymbol{\Lambda}\mathbf{U}^{\intercal}$, where $\boldsymbol{\Lambda} = \operatorname{diag}(\lambda_1, \lambda_2)$. Set $\mathbf{A} = \mathbf{U}$, $\mathbf{B}^{\intercal} = \mathbf{U}^{-1}\mathbf{X}_1$, and $\mathbf{C} = \begin{bmatrix} 1 & 1 \\ \lambda_1 & \lambda_2 \end{bmatrix}$. Since

$$\mathbf{X}_1 = \mathbf{U}\mathbf{U}^{-1}\mathbf{X}_1 = \mathbf{A} \operatorname{diag}(\mathbf{C}(1,:))\mathbf{B}^{\intercal} \quad \text{and} \quad \mathbf{X}_2 = \mathbf{U}\boldsymbol{\Lambda}\mathbf{U}^{-1}\mathbf{X}_1 = \mathbf{A} \operatorname{diag}(\mathbf{C}(2,:))\mathbf{B}^{\intercal},$$

we prove by construction that $\mathcal{X} = [\![\mathbf{A}, \mathbf{B}, \mathbf{C}]\!]$ has rank 2. If $\operatorname{rank}(\mathcal{X}) \neq 2$, we must have $\operatorname{rank}(\mathcal{X}) = 3$ by process of elimination. □

Remark 16.24 (Do not use explicit inverses) To compute $\mathbf{Y} = \mathbf{X}_2\mathbf{X}_1^{-1}$, do not compute the inverse of $\mathbf{X}_1$ explicitly; instead, solve the system $\mathbf{Y}\mathbf{X}_1 = \mathbf{X}_2$ for $\mathbf{Y}$.

Ten Berge (1991, relying in part on Kruskal, 1989) shows that we can use a special calculation to determine the rank. Define

$$\Delta \equiv (x_{122}x_{211} + x_{111}x_{222} - x_{112}x_{221} - x_{121}x_{212})^2 - 4(x_{121}x_{112} - x_{111}x_{122})(x_{221}x_{212} - x_{211}x_{222}).$$

This is the **discriminant** of $\det(\mathbf{X}_2\mathbf{X}_1^{-1} - \lambda\mathbf{I}) = 0$, where det denotes the **determinant**. The roots of this polynomial are the eigenvalues of $\mathbf{X}_2\mathbf{X}_1^{-1}$. The value of Δ determines the rank as follows:

$$\begin{cases} \Delta > 0 & \Rightarrow \operatorname{rank}(\mathcal{X}) = 2 \\ \Delta < 0 & \Rightarrow \operatorname{rank}(\mathcal{X}) = 3 \\ \Delta = 0 & \Rightarrow \operatorname{rank}(\mathcal{X}) \in \{0,1,2,3\} \end{cases}.$$

The quantity Δ is also known as **Cayley's hyperdeterminant** of a $2 \times 2 \times 2$ tensor (de Silva and Lim, 2008). As discussed in Section 16.4 and derived earlier in this section, the typical ranks of $2 \times 2 \times 2$ tensors are $\{2,3\}$. In other words, if you choose a tensor at random, it has rank 2 or rank 3 with probability 1.

The cases where $\Delta = 0$ occur with probability 0 for tensors drawn at random, but we can still determine the rank (de Silva and Lim, 2008). If $\Delta = 0$, the rank can be inferred by additionally considering the ranks of the unfoldings:

$$\Delta = 0 \quad \text{and} \quad \begin{array}{rl} \operatorname{rank}(\mathbf{X}_{(1)}) = \operatorname{rank}(\mathbf{X}_{(2)}) = \operatorname{rank}(\mathbf{X}_{(3)}) = 0 & \Rightarrow \operatorname{rank}(\mathcal{X}) = 0, \\ \operatorname{rank}(\mathbf{X}_{(1)}) = \operatorname{rank}(\mathbf{X}_{(2)}) = \operatorname{rank}(\mathbf{X}_{(3)}) = 1 & \Rightarrow \operatorname{rank}(\mathcal{X}) = 1, \\ \operatorname{rank}(\mathbf{X}_{(1)}) = \operatorname{rank}(\mathbf{X}_{(2)}) = \operatorname{rank}(\mathbf{X}_{(3)}) = 2 & \Rightarrow \operatorname{rank}(\mathcal{X}) = 3, \\ \text{otherwise} & \Rightarrow \operatorname{rank}(\mathcal{X}) = 2. \end{array}$$

Exercise 16.26 (a) What is the rank of the tensor $\mathcal{X}$ whose frontal slices are

$$\mathbf{X}_1 = \begin{bmatrix} 1 & 0 \\ 0 & 0 \end{bmatrix} \quad \text{and} \quad \mathbf{X}_2 = \begin{bmatrix} 0 & 0 \\ 1 & 0 \end{bmatrix}?$$

(b) What is the rank of the tensor $\mathcal{X}$ whose frontal slices are

$$\mathbf{X}_1 = \begin{bmatrix} 1 & 0 \\ 0 & 0 \end{bmatrix} \quad \text{and} \quad \mathbf{X}_2 = \begin{bmatrix} 0 & 1 \\ 1 & 0 \end{bmatrix}?$$

Exercise 16.27 Prove that the rank (over $\mathbb{R}$) of the tensor in Example 16.1 is 3.

Exercise 16.28 Generate 100,000 tensors of size $2\times2\times2$ with independent random entries. Give the breakdown by rank if the random entries are (a) normal distributed with mean 0 and standard deviation 1, (b) uniformly distributed on $[-1,1]$, (c) 1 with probability $1/2$ and 0 otherwise, and (d) 1 with probability $1/2$ and -1 otherwise. Discuss the differences in these results.

Exercise 16.29 Construct a tensor $\mathcal{X} = [\![\mathbf{A}, \mathbf{B}, \mathbf{C}]\!]$, where $\mathbf{A}, \mathbf{B}, \mathbf{C} \in \mathbb{R}^{2\times 3}$ and the entries of each factor matrix are drawn from a standard normal distribution. Compute the $2 \times 2 \times 2$ tensor $\mathcal{X}$ explicitly, and then compute its rank. Repeat this 100,000 times. What is the breakdown of the ranks?

16.8.3 Rank of $n \times n \times 2$ Tensors

We can extend some of the analysis of the previous subsection to tensors of size $n \times n \times 2$. As discussed in Section 16.4, the typical ranks of $n \times n \times 2$ tensors are $\{n, n+1\}$. If a tensor's first frontal slice is nonsingular, we can check if its rank is n. Further, if the tensor has rank n, we can construct its decomposition. The proof of the next result is adapted from ten Berge (1991).

Theorem 16.25 (Decomposing $n \times n \times 2$ Tensors of Rank n) *Let $\mathcal{X} \in \mathbb{R}^{n\times n\times 2}$ with frontal slices denoted $\mathbf{X}_1$ and $\mathbf{X}_2$, and let $\mathbf{X}_1$ be nonsingular. Then $\operatorname{rank}(\mathcal{X}) = n$ if and only if $\mathbf{X}_2\mathbf{X}_1^{-1}$ is diagonalizable, i.e., there exists a nonsingular $\mathbf{U} \in \mathbb{R}^{n\times n}$ and vector $\boldsymbol{\lambda} \in \mathbb{R}^n$ such that*

$$\mathbf{X}_2\mathbf{X}_1^{-1} = \mathbf{U}\operatorname{diag}(\boldsymbol{\lambda})\mathbf{U}^{-1}.$$

In this case, $\mathcal{X}$ has a rank-n CP decomposition of the form

$$\mathcal{X} = \left[\!\!\left[\mathbf{U}, (\mathbf{U}^{-1}\mathbf{X}_1)^{\intercal}, ([\mathbf{1}_n\ \boldsymbol{\lambda}])^{\intercal}\right]\!\!\right]. \tag{16.17}$$

Proof. If $\operatorname{rank}(\mathcal{X}) = n$, then $\mathcal{X} = [\![\mathbf{A}, \mathbf{B}, \mathbf{C}]\!]$, where $\mathbf{A}, \mathbf{B} \in \mathbb{R}^{n\times n}$ and $\mathbf{C} \in \mathbb{R}^{2\times n}$. Thus, we can write

$$\mathbf{X}_1 = \mathbf{A}\begin{bmatrix} c_{11} & \cdots & 0 \\ \vdots & \ddots & \vdots \\ 0 & \cdots & c_{1n} \end{bmatrix}\mathbf{B}^{\intercal} \quad \text{and} \quad \mathbf{X}_2 = \mathbf{A}\begin{bmatrix} c_{21} & \cdots & 0 \\ \vdots & \ddots & \vdots \\ 0 & \cdots & c_{2n} \end{bmatrix}\mathbf{B}^{\intercal}.$$

Since we have assumed that $\mathbf{X}_1$ is invertible, its multiplicands are all nonsingular and the diagonal entries c_{1j} are all nonzero. Consequently, $\mathbf{X}_2\mathbf{X}_1^{-1}$ is diagonalizable as

$$\mathbf{X}_2\mathbf{X}_1^{-1} = \mathbf{A}\begin{bmatrix} c_{21}/c_{11} & \cdots & 0 \\ \vdots & \ddots & \vdots \\ 0 & \cdots & c_{2n}/c_{1n} \end{bmatrix}\mathbf{A}^{-1}.$$

Conversely, assume $\mathbf{X}_2\mathbf{X}_1^{-1}$ can be written as

$$\mathbf{X}_2\mathbf{X}_1^{-1} = \mathbf{U}\boldsymbol{\Lambda}\mathbf{U}^{-1}, \quad \text{where} \quad \boldsymbol{\Lambda} = \operatorname{diag}(\lambda_1, \lambda_2, \ldots, \lambda_n).$$

Defining $\mathbf{A} = \mathbf{U}$ and $\mathbf{B}^{\intercal} = \mathbf{U}^{-1}\mathbf{X}_1$, we have

$$\mathbf{X}_1 = \mathbf{U}\mathbf{B}^{\intercal} = \mathbf{A}\mathbf{B}^{\intercal} \quad \text{and} \quad \mathbf{X}_2 = \mathbf{U}\boldsymbol{\Lambda}\mathbf{U}^{-1}\mathbf{X}_1 = \mathbf{A}\boldsymbol{\Lambda}\mathbf{B}^{\intercal}.$$

Defining

$$\mathbf{C} = \begin{bmatrix} 1 & 1 & \cdots & 1 \\ \lambda_1 & \lambda_2 & \cdots & \lambda_n \end{bmatrix},$$

we can see that $\mathcal{X}$ has rank n since $\mathcal{X} = [\![\mathbf{A}, \mathbf{B}, \mathbf{C}]\!]$. Moreover, this is the decomposition given in Eq. (16.17). □

The requirement in the above result that $\mathbf{X}_1$ be invertible is a **generic** requirement. In other words, if you choose a tensor at random with entries from a continuous distribution, its frontal slice will be nonsingular. In practice, if we have a situation where $\mathbf{X}_1$ is not invertible, we can modify $\mathcal{X}$ by, for instance, permuting the frontal slices.

As a consequence of the above result, we obtain the following corollary that generically characterizes the space of all $n \times n \times 2$ tensors. See the discussion in ten Berge (1991) for further details.

Corollary 16.26 (Generic Characterization of $n \times n \times 2$ Tensors) *Let $\mathcal{X} \in \mathbb{R}^{n \times n \times 2}$, and let $\mathbf{X}_1$ and $\mathbf{X}_2$ denote its frontal slices. With probability 1, either (a) $\mathbf{X}_2\mathbf{X}_1^{-1}$ exists and is diagonalizable so that* $\text{rank}(\mathcal{X}) = n$*, or (b)* $\text{rank}(\mathcal{X}) = n + 1$.

From Corollary 16.26, we can estimate the proportion of $n \times n \times 2$ tensors with ranks n and $n + 1$ via numerical experiments, and the results for $n \in \{2, 3, \ldots, 9\}$ are shown in Table 16.4. Using results from random matrix theory, Bergqvist (2013) and Bergqvist and Forrester (2011) have shown that the probability of a $2 \times 2 \times 2$ tensor having rank 2 is exactly $\pi/4 \approx 0.7854$ and that the probability of a $3 \times 3 \times 2$ tensor having rank 3 is exactly $1/2$. The theory aligns perfectly with Table 16.4. Unfortunately, these results have not been extended to larger n. Nevertheless, the proportion of $n \times n \times 2$ tensors of rank n is decreasing as n grows.

Table 16.4 Numerical estimation of proportion of $n \times n \times 2$ tensors having ranks n and $n + 1$. Data generated from 100,000 tensors with standard normal random values, using Corollary 16.26 to determine if the rank is n.

n	Tensor size	Rank $= n$	Rank $= n+1$
2	$2 \times 2 \times 2$	78.505 %	21.495 %
3	$3 \times 3 \times 2$	50.043 %	49.957 %
4	$4 \times 4 \times 2$	26.159 %	73.841 %
5	$5 \times 5 \times 2$	11.067 %	88.933 %
6	$6 \times 6 \times 2$	3.863 %	96.137 %
7	$7 \times 7 \times 2$	1.163 %	98.837 %
8	$8 \times 8 \times 2$	0.233 %	99.767 %
9	$9 \times 9 \times 2$	0.057 %	99.943 %

Exercise 16.30 Recreate the computational experiments used to produce Table 16.4 and validate the results.

16.8.4 Direct Computation of CP for Certain $m \times n \times p$ Tensors

Dating back to Harshman (1972), there has been a series of papers (Domanov and De Lathauwer, 2014; Evert et al., 2022; Leurgans et al., 1993; Sanchez and Kowalski, 1990) on direct computation of the CP decomposition for 3-way tensors $\mathcal{X} \in \mathbb{R}^{m \times n \times p}$ when the rank is $\text{rank}(\mathcal{X}) \leq \min\{m, n\}$ and the factors satisfy certain conditions. In general, most tensors will not satisfy these criteria, and so this direct method has limited utility; additionally, Beltrán et al. (2019) have shown that direct computation is numerically unstable. Nevertheless, we discuss these techniques for the sake of completeness and refer the interested reader to Domanov and De Lathauwer (2014) for further discussion.

The basic idea relates to our discussion in the prior subsection on decomposing a tensor of size $n \times n \times 2$. Extending those ideas, it is possible to algebraically (using matrix eigendecompositions) compute a CP decomposition of certain $m \times n \times p$ tensors. Specifically, for a tensor $\mathcal{X} \in \mathbb{R}^{m \times n \times p}$ we require that the rank is bounded as

$$\operatorname{rank}(\mathcal{X}) = r \leq \min\{m, n\}. \tag{16.18}$$

Further, we assume that the rank decomposition $\mathcal{X} = [\![\mathbf{A}, \mathbf{B}, \mathbf{C}]\!]$ satisfies

$$\operatorname{rank}(\mathbf{A}) = \operatorname{rank}(\mathbf{B}) = r \quad \text{and} \quad \text{k-rank}(\mathbf{C}) = 2. \tag{16.19}$$

Under these conditions, the rank decomposition is unique (Theorem 16.14), and we can compute it as we describe below.

Reducing First Two Modes We can compute orthonormal matrices $\mathbf{U} \in \mathbb{R}^{m \times r}$ and $\mathbf{V} \in \mathbb{R}^{n \times r}$, such that they span the mode-1 and mode-2 fibers of $\mathcal{X}$, respectively. It is typically recommended to compute $\mathbf{U}$ and $\mathbf{V}$ via the HOSVD (Evert et al., 2022). Let

$$\bar{\mathcal{X}} = \mathcal{X} \times_1 \mathbf{U}^\intercal \times_2 \mathbf{V}^\intercal \in \mathbb{R}^{r \times r \times p}.$$

Then $\operatorname{rank}(\bar{\mathcal{X}}) = \operatorname{rank}(\mathcal{X})$ by Exercise 16.31.

Exercise 16.31 Let $\mathcal{X} \in \mathbb{R}^{n_1 \times n_2 \times \cdots \times n_d}$. Prove the following. If $\mathbf{U}_k$ spans the column space of $\mathbf{X}_{(k)}$, then $\operatorname{rank}(\mathcal{X}) = \operatorname{rank}(\mathcal{X} \times_k \mathbf{U}_k^\intercal)$.

We can derive the rank decomposition of $\bar{\mathcal{X}}$ from that of $\mathcal{X}$:

$$\bar{\mathcal{X}} = [\![\underbrace{\mathbf{U}^\intercal \mathbf{A}}_{\bar{\mathbf{A}}}, \underbrace{\mathbf{V}^\intercal \mathbf{B}}_{\bar{\mathbf{B}}}, \mathbf{C}]\!]. \tag{16.20}$$

Moreover, this rank decomposition is unique.

Exercise 16.32 Prove that the rank decomposition of $\bar{\mathcal{X}}$ in Eq. (16.20) is unique. Hint: Use Eq. (16.19).

Decomposing Reduced Tensor From Eq. (16.20), we have that

$$\bar{\mathcal{X}} = \sum_{\ell=1}^{r} \bar{\mathbf{a}}_\ell \circ \bar{\mathbf{b}}_\ell \circ \mathbf{c}_\ell.$$

This implies that the frontal slices of $\bar{\mathcal{X}}$ can be written as:

$$\bar{\mathbf{X}}_k = \sum_{\ell=1}^{r} c_{k\ell} \bar{\mathbf{a}}_\ell \bar{\mathbf{b}}_\ell^\intercal = \bar{\mathbf{A}} \operatorname{diag}(\mathbf{C}(k,:)) \bar{\mathbf{B}}^\intercal \quad \text{for all} \quad k \in [p].$$

The idea of reducing the third mode is that we need only two frontal slices to uniquely determine the factorization of $\mathcal{X}$ using the connection to the generalized eigenvalue decomposition (GEVD) of a matrix pencil. The expressions

$$\bar{\mathbf{X}}_1 = \bar{\mathbf{A}} \begin{bmatrix} c_{11} & \cdots & 0 \\ \vdots & \ddots & \vdots \\ 0 & \cdots & c_{1r} \end{bmatrix} \bar{\mathbf{B}}^\intercal \quad \text{and} \quad \bar{\mathbf{X}}_2 = \bar{\mathbf{A}} \begin{bmatrix} c_{21} & \cdots & 0 \\ \vdots & \ddots & \vdots \\ 0 & \cdots & c_{2r} \end{bmatrix} \bar{\mathbf{B}}^\intercal$$

give the Kronecker canonical form of the matrix pencil $(\bar{\mathbf{X}}_1, \bar{\mathbf{X}}_2)$. Here $\bar{\mathbf{A}}$ and $\bar{\mathbf{B}}$ are matrices of generalized eigenvectors and the ratios $c_{1\ell}/c_{2\ell}$ for $\ell \in [r]$ are the generalized eigenvalues (which can be infinite). Thus, by solving the generalized eigenproblem on the first two slices of $\bar{\mathcal{X}}$, we can recover the first two CP factor matrices for the entire tensor $\bar{\mathcal{X}}$.

In fact, we can choose any two slices or, more generally, choose any orthonormal $\mathbf{W} \in \mathbb{R}^{p \times 2}$ and compute

$$\hat{\mathcal{X}} = \bar{\mathcal{X}} \times_3 \mathbf{W}^\intercal.$$

Given $\hat{\mathcal{X}} \in \mathbb{R}^{r \times r \times 2}$, we compute the GEVD of the matrix pencil $(\hat{\mathbf{X}}_1, \hat{\mathbf{X}}_2)$. As described above, the generalized eigenvectors correspond to the CP factors $\hat{\mathbf{A}}$ and $\hat{\mathbf{B}}$ of $\hat{\mathcal{X}}$ (and $\bar{\mathcal{X}}$).

Translating to Original Tensor Finally, we have

$$\mathbf{A} = \mathbf{U}\bar{\mathbf{A}} = \mathbf{U}\hat{\mathbf{A}} \quad \text{and} \quad \mathbf{B} = \mathbf{V}\bar{\mathbf{B}} = \mathbf{U}\hat{\mathbf{B}}.$$

We can compute the $\mathbf{C}$ matrix by solving the linear least squares problem directly since we know $\mathbf{A}$ and $\mathbf{B}$; that is, $\mathbf{C}$ is the solution to

$$\mathbf{C}(\mathbf{A}^\intercal\mathbf{A} * \mathbf{B}^\intercal\mathbf{B}) = \mathbf{X}_{(3)}(\mathbf{B} \odot \mathbf{A}),$$

as in the CP-ALS algorithm (Chapter 11).

Discussion Several important cautionary notes on computing CP directly are in order:

- The tensor must be *exactly* low rank.
- Arbitrary tensors $\mathcal{X} \in \mathbb{R}^{m \times n \times p}$ are not guaranteed to satisfy $\operatorname{rank}(\mathcal{X}) \leq \min\{m, n\}$.
- The rank and properties of the factor matrices must be known in advance.
- Even when the above conditions are satisfied, numerical instability can be an issue despite the use of numerically stable methods for the matrix computations like the GEVD (Beltrán et al., 2019).

16.9 Greedy Computation

One method that might seem natural for computing a low-rank CP approximation is a *greedy* approach whereby we compute one component at a time, getting the best rank-1 approximation to the current residual. In general, this approach does not produce a best rank-k approximation (Kolda, 2001, 2003). Exercise 16.33 walks through an example where the best rank-1 approximation is not a component of the best rank-2 approximation, illustrating why a greedy method to compute a CP factorization is ill-advised.

Exercise 16.33 (Adapted from Example 4.3 of Smilde et al., 2004) Define $\mathcal{X} \in \mathbb{R}^{2 \times 2 \times 2}$ via its frontal slices to be

$$\mathcal{X}(:,:,1) = \begin{bmatrix} 14 & 10 \\ 11 & 9 \end{bmatrix}, \quad \mathcal{X}(:,:,2) = \begin{bmatrix} 14 & 6 \\ 8 & 4 \end{bmatrix}.$$

(a) Compute the best rank-1 approximation (this can be done via the methods learned for Tucker decomposition), which we denote as $\mathcal{Y}_1$. What is the norm of the residual, $\|\mathcal{X} - \mathcal{Y}_1\|$?

(b) Compute the best rank-1 approximation of $\mathcal{R}_1 = \mathcal{X} - \mathcal{Y}_1$, denoted as $\mathcal{Y}_2$. Let $\mathcal{Y} = \mathcal{Y}_1 + \mathcal{Y}_2$. What is the rank of $\mathcal{Y}$? What is $\|\mathcal{X} - \mathcal{Y}\|$?

(c) Show that $\mathcal{Z} = [\![\mathbf{A}, \mathbf{B}, \mathbf{C}]\!]$ is a rank factorization of $\mathcal{X}$ with

$$\mathbf{A} = \begin{bmatrix} 1 & 2 \\ 1 & 1 \end{bmatrix}, \quad \mathbf{B} = \begin{bmatrix} 2 & 3 \\ 2 & 1 \end{bmatrix}, \quad \text{and} \quad \mathbf{C} = \begin{bmatrix} 4 & 1 \\ 1 & 2 \end{bmatrix}.$$

(d) Choose the largest of the two components $\mathcal{Z}$, denoted as $\mathcal{Z}_1$. Compute the norm of the residual for this rank-1 approximation $\|\mathcal{X} - \mathcal{Z}_1\|$.

(e) Which rank-1 approximation is better, $\mathcal{Y}_1$ or $\mathcal{Z}_1$? Which rank-2 approximation is better, $\mathcal{Y}$ or $\mathcal{Z}$?

(f) (Bonus) If you continue to build the best rank-1 factorization, $\mathcal{Y}_{k+1}$, to the residual $\mathcal{R}_k = \mathcal{R}_{k-1} - \mathcal{Y}_k$, how long does it take before $\|\mathcal{R}_k\| = 0$?

The greedy method for computing CP (i.e., sequentially computing the best rank-1 approximation of the current residual) does not yield a rank decomposition nor a best rank-k decomposition.

Part IV

Closing Observations

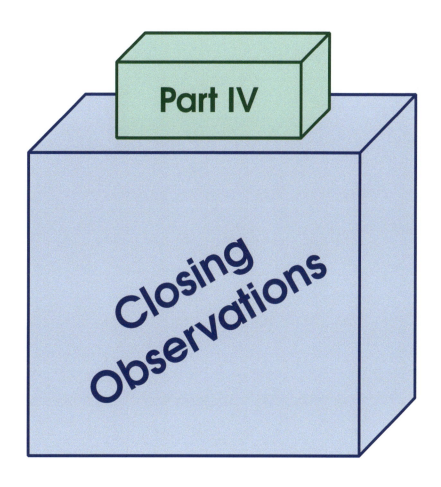

17 Closing Observations

We close with some observations. In Section 17.1, we discuss the choice of decomposition, both matrix versus tensor and Tucker/TT versus CP. We consider the connections between CP and Tucker, including their equivalence for orthogonally decomposable (ODECO) tensors. In Section 17.2, we discuss Tucker compression to accelerate CP decomposition. In Section 17.3, we consider symmetric tensors, including their connection to homogeneous polynomials, symmetric versions of Tucker and CP, and tensor eigenvalues. Finally, in Section 17.4, we briefly review a variety of other tensor decompositions: t-SVD, hierarchical tensor decomposition, tensor ring decomposition, block decompositions, and infinite dimensional decompositions.

17.1 Comparing Matrix and Tensor Decompositions

Now that we have learned about several tensor decompositions, we can compare their utility in various settings. At a high level, Tucker and TT decompositions are recommended for **data compression** because we can control the level of accuracy and compute quasi-optimal approximations. In contrast, CP decomposition is most useful for **interpretation** since it is often identifiable (i.e., essentially unique) and its factors can be interpreted. We also include matrix decomposition in our comparison discussion – specifically, SVD and nonnegative matrix factorization (NMF).

We provide an overview of the properties of the decompositions in Table A.1 for d-way tensors of size $n_1 \times n_2 \times \cdots \times n_d$. The sizes of the decompositions are in big-O notation using $n = \max_k n_k$ and $r = \max_k r_k$ for Tucker and TT ranks. The ranks are fundamentally different for each decomposition, which is emphasized by subscripts on the ranks. We consider the SVD and NMF of a "square" unfolding of the tensor so that the maximum dimension of the matrix is roughly proportional to $\mathcal{O}(n^{\lceil d/2 \rceil})$.

17.1.1 Decomposition Overview

We briefly remind the reader about the decompositions being compared. Consider a d-way tensor $\mathcal{X} \in \mathbb{R}^{n_1 \times n_2 \times \cdots \times n_d}$. Let $\mathcal{R}$ and $\mathcal{C}$ partition the d modes, define $p = \prod_{k \in \mathcal{R}} n_k$ and $q = \prod_{k \in \mathcal{C}} n_k$, and let $\mathbf{X} \equiv \mathbf{X}_{(\mathcal{R} \times \mathcal{C})} \in \mathbb{R}^{p \times q}$ be an unfolding of $\mathcal{X}$.

Tucker Decomposition The **Tucker decomposition** of rank $(r_1, r_2, \ldots, r_d)$ can be expressed as

$$\mathcal{X} \approx [\![\mathcal{G}; \mathbf{U}_1, \mathbf{U}_2, \ldots, \mathbf{U}_d]\!].$$

The **core tensor** $\mathcal{G}$ is of size $r_1 \times r_2 \times \cdots \times r_d$. For the purposes of the comparison discussion, we assume $r_k \leq n_k$ for all $k \in [d]$. The **factor matrices** are such that $\mathbf{U}_k \in$

Table 17.1 Comparison of tensor and matrix decompositions on d-way tensor of maximum dimension n. Let $r = \max_k r_k$ for Tucker and TT decomposition ranks and assume maximum dimension of unfolding for SVD and NMF is $\mathcal{O}(n^{\lceil d/2 \rceil})$. Ranks are not the same for different decompositions.

Trait	Tucker	TT	CP	SVD	NMF
Size (order of magnitude)	r_{Tucker}^d	$r_{\text{TT}}^2 nd$	$r_{\text{CP}}\, nd$	$r_{\text{SVD}}\, n^{\lceil d/2 \rceil}$	$r_{\text{NMF}}\, n^{\lceil d/2 \rceil}$
Computable rank	✓	✓	✗	✓	✗
Quasi-optimal	✓	✓	✗	✓	✗
Orthonormal factors	✓	✓	✗	✓	✗
Unique (generically)	✗	✗	✓	✓	✗

$\mathbb{R}^{n_k \times r_k}$ for all $k \in [d]$. Each factor matrix may have a different number of columns, in contrast to the factor matrices for CP. Without loss of generality (see Section 5.4), we assume the factor matrices are orthonormal. Using HOSVD (Algorithm 6.3) or ST-HOSVD (Algorithm 6.5), we can always determine ranks and compute a Tucker decomposition to achieve a specified error (including 0). The total size of the decomposition is $\prod_{k=1}^d r_k + \sum_{k=1}^d n_k r_k$.

TT Decomposition The **TT decomposition** of rank $(r_1, r_2, \ldots, r_{d-1})$ can be expressed as

$$\mathcal{X} \approx [\![\mathcal{G}_1, \mathcal{G}_2, \ldots, \mathcal{G}_d]\!],$$

representing a series of tensor contractions. The components of the TT decomposition are 3-way tensors $\mathcal{G}_k \in \mathbb{R}^{r_{k-1} \times n_k \times r_k}$ for all $k \in [d]$, with $r_0 = r_d = 1$ so that the first and last components are matrices. Using Algorithm 8.2, we can always determine ranks and compute a TT decomposition to achieve a specified error (including 0). Similarly to Tucker factor matrices, TT components (except the last) can be orthogonalized (that is, so that one of their unfoldings is an orthonormal matrix). For TT, we may have $r_k > n_k$. We stress that the ranks for TT are not directly comparable with the ranks for Tucker. The total size of the decomposition is $\sum_{k=1}^d r_{k-1} r_k n_k$.

CP Decomposition The **CP decomposition** of rank r can be expressed as

$$\mathcal{X} \approx [\![\mathbf{A}_1, \mathbf{A}_2, \ldots, \mathbf{A}_d]\!].$$

The **factor matrices** are $\mathbf{A}_k \in \mathbb{R}^{n_k \times r}$ and have no special structure, such as orthogonality. Every factor matrix has the same number of columns, in contrast to Tucker. It is NP-hard to determine the exact rank or the rank to achieve a specified error. Further, it is possible that $r > \max_k n_k$. The rank of CP is not directly comparable to the ranks for Tucker or TT. The total size is $r \sum_{k=1}^d n_k$.

Truncated SVD The truncated rank-r **SVD** can be written as

$$\mathbf{X} \approx \mathbf{U} \boldsymbol{\Sigma} \mathbf{V}^\intercal.$$

It is always the case that $r \leq \min\{p, q\}$. Here $\mathbf{U} \in \mathbb{R}^{p \times r}$ is an orthonormal matrix of the left singular vectors, $\mathbf{V} \in \mathbb{R}^{q \times r}$ is an orthonormal matrix of the right singular vectors, and $\boldsymbol{\Sigma}$ is a diagonal matrix with the singular values on the diagonal, in decreasing order. Using the SVD, we can also compute a truncated SVD that achieves a specified error. This is also known as **principal component analysis (PCA)**. The total size is $r(p+q)$.

Nonnegative Matrix Factorization (NMF) The rank-r **nonnegative matrix factorization (NMF)** problem can be written as

$$\mathbf{X} \approx \mathbf{A}\mathbf{B}^{\mathsf{T}},$$

where $\mathbf{A} \in \mathbb{R}^{p \times r}$ and $\mathbf{B} \in \mathbb{R}^{q \times r}$ are nonnegative matrices. The total size is $r(p+q)$. NMF is a low-rank matrix factorization that shares some properties with CP, such as being NP-hard to compute (Vavasis, 2009).

17.1.2 Decomposition Size

For simplicity, consider a tensor with $n = n_1 = \cdots = n_d$.

For Tucker, we can always assume $r_k \leq n_k$. Assuming $r = r_1 = \cdots = r_d$ for the Tucker decomposition, its size is $\mathcal{O}(r^d + dnr)$. Hence, Tucker is exponential in d and so we lament that Tucker suffers from the **curse of dimensionality**. This is primarily an issue for very high-order tensors.

For TT, the ranks satisfy only $r_k \leq \min\{\, r_{k-1}n, n^{d-k}\,\}$. If we assume the TT decomposition also has all its ranks equal (which is not generally the case), its size is $\mathcal{O}(dnr^2)$. As this is not exponential in d, this is often used as an argument for the superiority of TT. The ranks for TT are fundamentally different than those of Tucker. There are examples where, for the same relative error, TT is larger because the TT ranks are significantly larger than the Tucker ranks. Experimentation may be needed to determine which decomposition is best for any particular tensor.

The size of the CP decomposition is $\mathcal{O}(dnr)$, making it very compact. However, the r for CP may be large and we do not know tight upper bounds, only that $r \leq \prod_{k=1}^{d} n_k / \max_k n_k$.

Matrix decompositions suffer from the curse of dimensionality because at least one dimension must be $n^{\lceil d/2 \rceil}$, so the size of at least one factor matrix is exponential. If there is low-rank tensor structure in the data, then tensor decompositions will be smaller.

17.1.3 Computability and Quasi-Optimality

We consider whether or not optimal decompositions are computable. To start, we consider the case for matrices. For a matrix, we can compute the SVD directly with a predictable number of operations, yielding the matrix rank and optimal rank-k decompositions. But matrices are not always easily factorized. If we consider the case of NMF, the problem of determining the nonnegative rank is NP-hard (Vavasis, 2009) and computing the decomposition or a best rank-k approximation is a nonconvex optimization problem.

Now consider the case for a d-way tensor. It is always possible to find the multilinear ranks and compute an exact Tucker decomposition. Moreover, some of the methods for computing the Tucker decomposition are guaranteed to produce a decomposition that is within $\sqrt{d}$ of the best possible decomposition for the specified size (see Section 7.4). Similar results hold for TT (see Theorem 8.7).

In the case of CP, however, computing the rank is NP-hard. Further, even if we know the rank, we have a nonconvex nonlinear program to solve (except for some special 3-way tensors; see Section 16.8.4). Finally, the problem of computing a low-rank decomposition may be ill-posed (see Section 16.5).

We can determine the ranks for an exact or ε-approximate Tucker decomposition. In contrast, there is no straightforward algorithm for determining the rank for an exact or ε-accurate CP decomposition.

17.1.4 Factor Orthogonality

Tucker factor matrices can always be transformed to be **orthonormal (matrix)** (see Section 5.4), as can TT cores. In contrast, CP factor matrices are generally not orthonormal. In the matrix case, the truncated SVD produces orthonormal factor matrices, while NMF does not.

CP factor matrices are not orthonormal; in contrast, Tucker factor matrices can always be made orthonormal.

17.1.5 Uniqueness

As discussed in Section 16.7, the CP decomposition is **essentially unique** under mild conditions on the factor matrices. In contrast, the Tucker decomposition is never unique; see Section 5.3. This means that the factors of a Tucker model are not directly interpretable. Instead, only the subspace spanned by columns of a factor matrix is unchanged by transformations.

CP is (essentially) unique under mild conditions, but Tucker is never unique.

17.1.6 Interpreting CP as Tucker

It is possible to express CP in Tucker tensor format. For instance, we can express the rank-r Kruskal tensor $[\![\boldsymbol{\lambda}; \mathbf{A}, \mathbf{B}, \mathbf{C}]\!]$ as a rank-(r, r, r) Tucker tensor $[\![\mathcal{G}; \mathbf{A}, \mathbf{B}, \mathbf{C}]\!]$, where $\mathcal{G} \in \mathbb{R}^{r \times r \times r}$ with

$$g_{ijk} = \begin{cases} \lambda_i & \text{if } i = j = k \\ 0 & \text{otherwise} \end{cases}.$$

Even though CP can be written as a Tucker tensor, the representation may not have minimal multirank. For example, if the factor matrices are not full column rank, there is a lower-multirank Tucker decomposition.

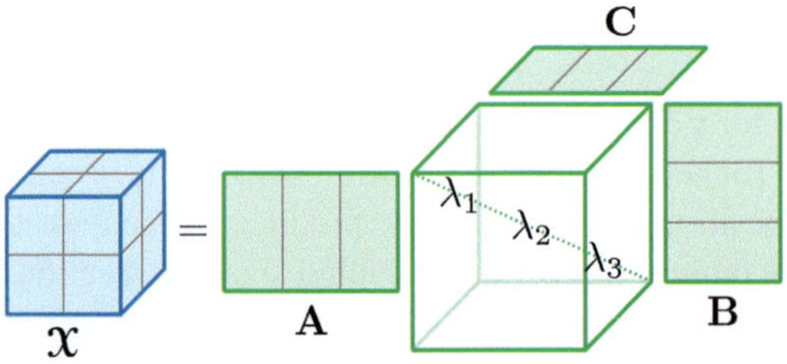

Figure 17.1 CP expressed as Tucker: rank-3 CP decomposition $\mathcal{X} = [\![\boldsymbol{\lambda}; \mathbf{A}, \mathbf{B}, \mathbf{C}]\!]$ of $2 \times 2 \times 2$ tensor expressed as Tucker tensor with factor matrices of size 2×3 that are not full column rank.

17.1.7 Interpreting Tucker as CP

Conversely, we can express a rank-(q,r,s) Tucker tensor as a rank-(qrs) Kruskal tensor (see Exercise 17.1). Consider a rank-(q,r,s) Tucker tensor $[\![\mathcal{G};\mathbf{U},\mathbf{V},\mathbf{W}]\!] \in \mathbb{R}^{m\times n\times p}$. We can write this as a weighted Kruskal tensor by observing

$$\mathcal{X} = \sum_{\alpha=1}^{q}\sum_{\beta=1}^{r}\sum_{\gamma=1}^{s} g_{\alpha\beta\gamma}\, \mathbf{u}_\alpha \circ \mathbf{v}_\beta \circ \mathbf{w}_\gamma.$$

We illustrate this in Fig. 17.2. Even though this is a Kruskal tensor, there is a lower-rank CP decomposition since its maximum rank is $\max\{\,qr, qs, rs\,\}$.

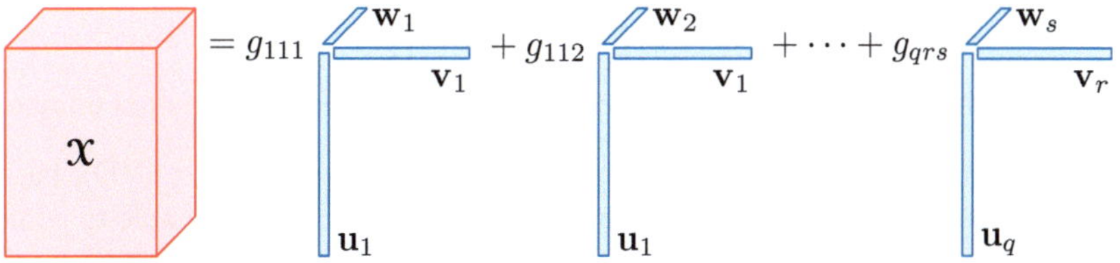

Figure 17.2 Tucker expressed as a Kruskal tensor: $\mathcal{X} = [\![\mathcal{G};\mathbf{U},\mathbf{V},\mathbf{W}]\!]$ with core $\mathcal{G}$ of size $q \times r \times s$ as the sum of qrs rank-1 tensors.

Exercise 17.1 (Writing a Tucker Tensor as a Kruskal Tensor) Consider a rank-(q,r,s) Tucker tensor $[\![\mathcal{G};\mathbf{U},\mathbf{V},\mathbf{W}]\!] \in \mathbb{R}^{m\times n\times p}$. Prove that we can express this as a rank-(qrs) Kruskal tensor $[\![\boldsymbol{\lambda};\mathbf{A},\mathbf{B},\mathbf{C}]\!]$, such that

$$\boldsymbol{\lambda} = \operatorname{vec}(\mathcal{G}), \qquad \mathbf{A} = \left(\mathbf{U}^{\mathsf{T}} \odot \mathbf{1}_{rs\times m}\right)^{\mathsf{T}},$$
$$\mathbf{B} = \left(\mathbf{1}_{q\times n} \odot \mathbf{V}^{\mathsf{T}} \odot \mathbf{1}_{s\times n}\right)^{\mathsf{T}}, \quad \text{and} \qquad \mathbf{C} = \left(\mathbf{1}_{qr\times p} \odot \mathbf{W}^{\mathsf{T}}\right)^{\mathsf{T}}.$$

Here $\mathbf{1}$ represents the all-1s matrix of the specified size.

17.1.8 CP and Tucker Equivalence for Orthogonally Decomposable Tensors

The set of tensors that admit orthogonal CP decompositions are a special subclass referred to as **ODECO**, short for orthogonally decomposable (see, e.g., Anandkumar et al., 2014; Robeva, 2014). ODECO tensors are interesting for study because they have nice theoretical properties. In particular, they can be decomposed in a greedy fashion, one rank-1 factor at a time, subtracting that from the residual, and continuing. As a result, it is also straightforward to determine the tensor rank. Each rank-1 factor can be computed by HOOI with multirank $(1,1,\cdots,1)$, for example. Unfortunately, ODECO tensors occur with probability 0, limiting the applications (Kolda, 2001, 2003, 2015b).

17.1.9 Comparing Matrix and Tensor Decomposition

Both the Tucker and CP decompositions can be viewed as extensions of the matrix SVD, as summarized in Table 17.2.

For Tucker, the factor matrices can be orthogonalized (similar to the SVD), but the core tensor is allowed to be dense (dissimilar to the SVD). We can use the SVD to compute the optimal rank-r matrix approximation of a matrix, and we can use HOSVD (Algorithm 6.3) or ST-HOSVD (Algorithm 6.5) to compute a quasi-optimal rank-$(r_1, r_2, \ldots, r_d)$ Tucker

Table 17.2 Matrix SVD properties for Tucker and CP

SVD property	Orthogonal factors	Diagonal "core"	Optimal low-rank	Unique
Tucker	✓	✗	Quasi-optimal low-rank	✗
CP	✗	✓	✗	✓

decomposition, meaning that the approximation is within $\sqrt{d}$ of optimal (see Section 7.4). The SVD is unique as long as the singular values are distinct, but this is not the case for Tucker (see Section 5.3). The matrix SVD can be written using Tucker-like notation as follows:

$$\mathbf{X} = \mathbf{U}\boldsymbol{\Sigma}\mathbf{V}^{\intercal} = \boldsymbol{\Sigma} \times_1 \mathbf{U} \times_2 \mathbf{V}.$$

If we do not restrict $\boldsymbol{\Sigma}$ to be diagonal, then this matrix decomposition is not unique.

For CP, the factor matrices are generally not orthogonal (dissimilar to SVD), but we can think of it as having a diagonal core (similar to SVD). We may not be able to compute an optimal low-rank CP decomposition since it is a nonconvex nonlinear optimization problem and potentially ill-posed (see Section 16.2). On the other hand, CP is unique under mild conditions (Section 9.2.3), similar to SVD. The similarity is that we can write SVD as the sum of rank-1 outer products:

$$\mathbf{X} = \mathbf{U}\boldsymbol{\Sigma}\mathbf{V}^{\intercal} = \sum_{j=1}^{r} \sigma_j \, \mathbf{u}_j \circ \mathbf{v}_j,$$

similar to the outer product expression for CP.

17.2 CANDELINC: Tucker Preprocessing for CP

Tucker compression (exact or inexact) can be a helpful preprocessing step before computing CP because it may reduce the CP iteration cost.

When computing the CP decomposition for a large tensor, we can extract a reduced Tucker core representation, compute CP for that, and then transform the result to a CP decomposition of the original tensor, using the properties of Kruskal and Tucker tensors. In the literature, this has been referred to as CANDECOMP with linear constraints and abbreviated as CANDELINC (Bro and Andersson, 1998; Carroll et al., 1980). See Fig. 17.3 for an illustration in the 3-way case.

Exact CANDELINC Suppose we have a tensor $\mathcal{X} \in \mathbb{R}^{n_1 \times n_2 \times \cdots \times n_d}$ with an exact Tucker decomposition

$$\mathcal{X} = [\![\mathcal{G}; \mathbf{U}_1, \mathbf{U}_2, \ldots, \mathbf{U}_d]\!], \tag{17.1}$$

where $\mathcal{G} \in \mathbb{R}^{m_1 \times m_2 \times \cdots \times m_d}$ and $\mathbf{U}_k \in \mathbb{R}^{n_k \times m_k}$ are orthonormal for all $k \in [d]$. Then we can compute a rank-r CP factorization of $\mathcal{G}$:

$$\mathcal{G} \approx [\![\mathbf{A}_1, \mathbf{A}_2, \ldots, \mathbf{A}_d]\!], \tag{17.2}$$

where $\mathbf{A}_k \in \mathbb{R}^{m_k \times r}$ for all $k \in [d]$. Then this is easily translated to a CP decomposition of $\mathcal{X}$:

$$\mathcal{X} \approx [\![\mathbf{U}_1\mathbf{A}_1, \mathbf{U}_2\mathbf{A}_2, \ldots, \mathbf{U}_d\mathbf{A}_d]\!]. \tag{17.3}$$

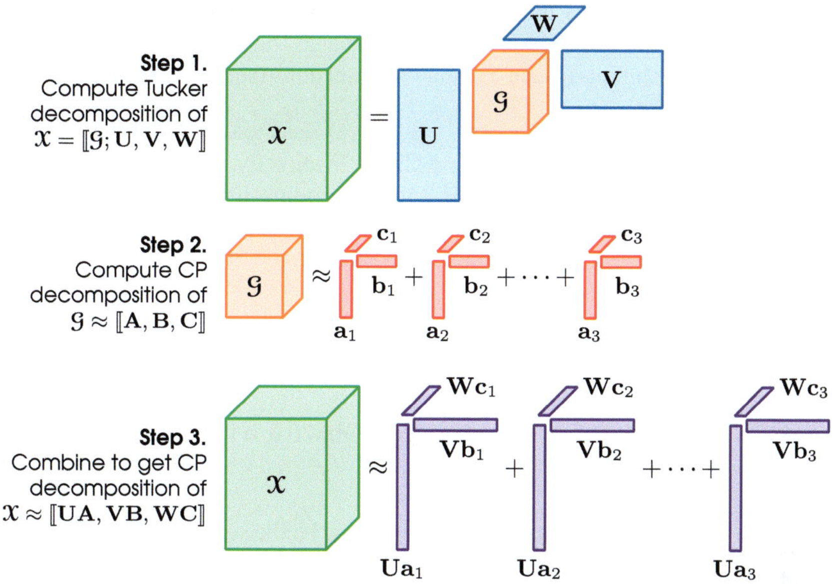

Figure 17.3 CANDELINC: Tucker preprocessing for computing CP.

Additionally, the error is retained:

$$\big\|\mathcal{X} - [\![\mathbf{U}_1\mathbf{A}_1, \ldots, \mathbf{U}_d\mathbf{A}_d]\!]\big\| = \big\|\mathcal{G} - [\![\mathbf{A}_1, \ldots, \mathbf{A}_d]\!]\big\|. \tag{17.4}$$

Exercise 17.2 Prove Eqs. (17.3) and (17.4).

> Computing CP of the core of an exact Tucker decomposition with orthonormal factor matrices is equivalent to computing CP on the original tensor.

Inexact CANDELINC This approach also works when the decomposition is inexact. Let $\mathbf{U}_k \in \mathbb{R}^{n_k \times m_k}$ be orthonormal for all $k \in [d]$ and

$$\mathcal{G} = \mathcal{X} \times_1 \mathbf{U}_1^\intercal \cdots \times_d \mathbf{U}_d^\intercal,$$

such that $\mathcal{X} \approx [\![\mathcal{G}; \mathbf{U}_1, \mathbf{U}_2, \ldots, \mathbf{U}_d]\!]$. Next, compute an approximate CP decomposition of $\mathcal{G}$:

$$\mathcal{G} \approx [\![\mathbf{A}_1, \mathbf{A}_2, \ldots, \mathbf{A}_d]\!].$$

Then we have

$$\mathcal{X} \approx [\![\mathbf{U}_1\mathbf{A}_1, \mathbf{U}_2\mathbf{A}_2, \ldots, \mathbf{U}_d\mathbf{A}_d]\!].$$

The error nicely decomposes into the sum of the Tucker approximation error plus the CP on the core:

$$\begin{aligned}
&\big\|\mathcal{X} - [\![\mathbf{U}_1\mathbf{A}_1, \ldots, \mathbf{U}_d\mathbf{A}_d]\!]\big\|^2 \\
&\quad \leq \big\|\mathcal{X} - [\![\mathcal{G}; \mathbf{U}_1, \ldots, \mathbf{U}_d]\!]\big\|^2 + \big\|[\![\mathcal{G}; \mathbf{U}_1, \ldots, \mathbf{U}_d]\!] - [\![\mathbf{U}_1\mathbf{A}_1, \ldots, \mathbf{U}_d\mathbf{A}_d]\!]\big\|^2 \\
&\quad = \underbrace{\|\mathcal{X}\|^2 - \|\mathcal{G}\|^2}_{\text{Tucker error}} + \underbrace{\big\|\mathcal{G} - [\![\mathbf{A}_1, \mathbf{A}_2, \ldots, \mathbf{A}_d]\!]\big\|^2}_{\text{CP on core error}}.
\end{aligned}$$

It can be advantageous to pay the one-time cost of computing the ST-HOSVD to reduce the per-iteration cost of CP; see Exercise 17.3. This analysis also opens the door to dimensionality reduction techniques, such as random projections (see, e.g., Zhou et al., 2014).

Exercise 17.3 (CANDELINC Complexity) (a) For a dense tensor $\mathcal{X}$, what is the per iteration computation complexity of computing CP for $\mathcal{X}$ directly versus CP for $\mathcal{G}$? (b) What is the computational cost of computing the Tucker decomposition of $\mathcal{X}$ using ST-HOSVD? (c) What is the computational cost of converting the CP decomposition of $\mathcal{G}$ into a CP decomposition of $\mathcal{X}$? (d) How do the complexities of each step of CANDELINC change if $\mathcal{X}$ is a sparse tensor?

17.3 Symmetric Tensors

Definition 17.1 (Symmetric Tensor) A tensor is **symmetric** if its entries are invariant under all permutations of the indices.

By definition, every mode of a symmetric tensor must be the same size. For a 3-way tensor $\mathcal{A} \in \mathbb{R}^{n \times n \times n}$, symmetry means that

$$a_{ijk} = a_{ikj} = a_{jik} = a_{jki} = a_{kij} = a_{kji} \quad \text{for all} \quad (i, j, k) \in [n] \otimes [n] \otimes [n].$$

Example 17.1 (Symmetric Tensor) The tensor $\mathcal{A} \in \mathbb{R}^{3 \times 3 \times 3}$ whose frontal slices are given by

$$\mathbf{A}_1 = \begin{bmatrix} 6 & 7 & 0 \\ 7 & 8 & 1 \\ 0 & 1 & 5 \end{bmatrix}, \quad \mathbf{A}_2 = \begin{bmatrix} 7 & 8 & 1 \\ 8 & 2 & 9 \\ 1 & 9 & 3 \end{bmatrix}, \quad \text{and} \quad \mathbf{A}_3 = \begin{bmatrix} 0 & 1 & 5 \\ 1 & 9 & 3 \\ 5 & 3 & 4 \end{bmatrix}$$

is a symmetric tensor. It has 10 unique entries.

Exercise 17.4 Write down the unique entries and where they appear (e.g., $a_{311} = a_{131} = a_{311} = 0$) for $\mathcal{A}$ in Example 17.1.

Exercise 17.5 For symmetric $\mathcal{A} \in \mathbb{R}^{n \times n \times n \times n}$, list all the entries that are equal to $a_{ijk\ell}$.

Proposition 17.2 (Symmetric Tensor Unique Entries, Ballard et al., 2011) *The number of unique entries in a d-way symmetric tensor $\mathcal{A} \in \mathbb{R}^{n \times n \times \cdots \times n}$ is given by the binomial coefficient*

$$\binom{n+d-1}{d} = \frac{n^d}{d!} + \mathcal{O}(n^{d-1}).$$

Exercise 17.6 How many unique entries does a symmetric 3-way tensor of dimension $n = 4$ have?

A common operation for a symmetric tensor is to compute its inner product with a symmetric vector outer product, defined as follows.

Definition 17.3 (Symmetric Tensor Times Vector Outer Product) Let $\mathcal{A}$ be a symmetric d-way tensor of size $n \times n \times \cdots \times n$ and let $\mathbf{x} \in \mathbb{R}^n$. Then we let $\mathcal{A}\mathbf{x}^{\otimes d}$ denote

$$\mathcal{A}\mathbf{x}^{\otimes d} \equiv \langle \mathcal{A}, \underbrace{\mathbf{x} \circ \mathbf{x} \circ \cdots \circ \mathbf{x}}_{d \text{ times}} \rangle = \sum_{i_1=1}^{n} \sum_{i_2=1}^{n} \cdots \sum_{i_d=1}^{n} a_{i_1 i_2 \cdots i_d} x_{i_1} x_{i_2} \cdots x_{i_d}. \quad (17.5)$$

We can consider this product as a series of contractions with the vector in each mode, as illustrated in Fig. 17.4. We can perform this computation more efficiently by exploiting symmetry and performing computations only with unique entries (Proposition 17.2).

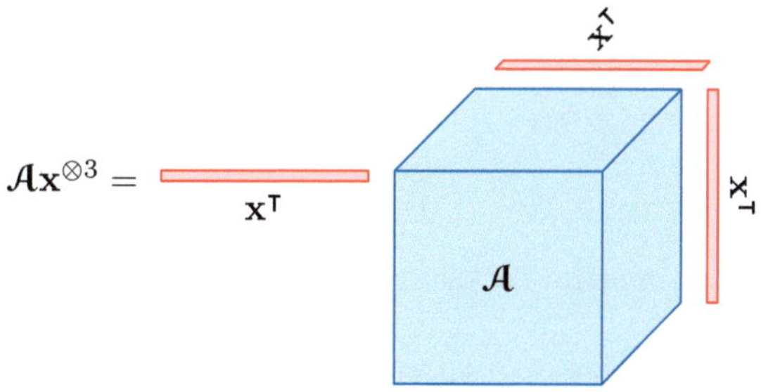

Figure 17.4 Symmetric tensor times vector $\mathcal{A}\mathbf{x}^{\otimes 3}$ (i.e., $\mathcal{A} \times_1 \mathbf{x}^\mathsf{T} \times_2 \mathbf{x}^\mathsf{T} \times_3 \mathbf{x}^\mathsf{T}$).

Symmetric tensors can be used to express homogeneous polynomials. For example, let $\mathcal{A}$ be a symmetric 3-way tensor of size $3 \times 3 \times 3$ and let $\mathbf{v} = \begin{bmatrix} x \\ y \\ z \end{bmatrix} \in \mathbb{R}^3$. Then

$$\begin{aligned} \mathcal{A}\mathbf{v}^{\otimes 3} &= a_{111}x^3 + a_{222}y^3 + a_{333}z^3 \\ &\quad + (a_{112} + a_{121} + a_{211})x^2y + (a_{113} + a_{131} + a_{311})x^2z \\ &\quad + (a_{122} + a_{212} + a_{221})xy^2 + (a_{223} + a_{232} + a_{322})y^2z \\ &\quad + (a_{133} + a_{313} + a_{331})xz^2 + (a_{233} + a_{323} + a_{332})yz^2 \\ &\quad + (a_{123} + a_{132} + a_{213} + a_{213} + a_{312} + a_{321})xyz. \end{aligned}$$

Remark 17.4 (Connection to homogeneous polynomials) The product $\mathcal{A}\mathbf{x}^{\otimes d}$ is a homogeneous polynomial of degree d in $\mathbf{x}$. This relationship means that tools from algebraic geometry for factoring polynomials can potentially be useful in decomposing symmetric tensors (Brachat et al., 2010).

This product is similar to $\mathbf{x}^\mathsf{T}\mathbf{A}\mathbf{x}$ for a symmetric $n \times n$ matrix $\mathbf{A}$. This motivates a notion of positive definiteness for tensors.

Definition 17.5 (Symmetric Positive Definite Tensor) Let $\mathcal{A}$ be a symmetric tensor of order d and dimension n. We say $\mathcal{A}$ is **positive definite** if $\mathcal{A}\mathbf{x}^{\otimes d} > 0$ for all $\mathbf{x} \in \mathbb{R}^n$ with $\mathbf{x} \neq 0$.

Exercise 17.7 Prove that only even-order tensors can be positive definite.

17.3.1 Symmetric Tucker Decomposition

For a symmetric tensor, we can impose symmetry on its decomposition. If $\mathcal{A} \in \mathbb{R}^{n\times n\times n}$ is symmetric, then we can find a symmetric Tucker decomposition of the form

$$\mathcal{A} = \mathcal{G} \times_1 \mathbf{U} \times_2 \mathbf{U} \times_3 \mathbf{U},$$

where $\mathcal{G} \in \mathbb{R}^{r\times r\times r}$ is symmetric and $\mathbf{U} \in \mathbb{R}^{n\times r}$ is orthogonal; see Fig. 17.5. The methodology can be extended to order d in a straightforward way. The next exercise describes a computational method and proves that it is quasi-optimal.

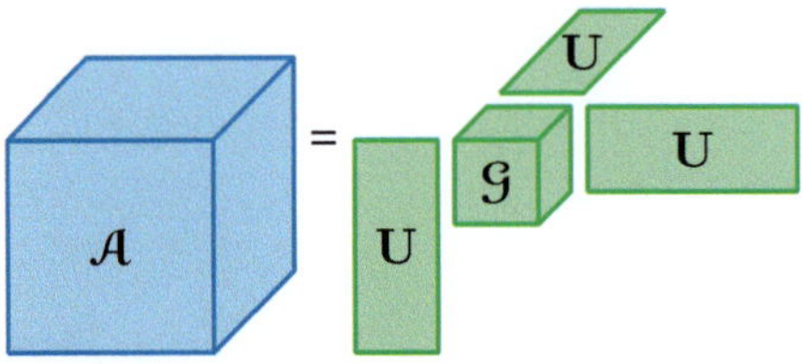

Figure 17.5 Symmetric Tucker decomposition: $\mathcal{X} = [\![\mathcal{G}; \mathbf{U}, \mathbf{U}, \mathbf{U}]\!]$.

Exercise 17.8 Suppose $\mathcal{A} \in \mathbb{R}^{n\times n\times n}$ is symmetric. Let $\mathbf{U}$ denote the r leading left singular vectors of $\mathbf{A}_{(1)}$, and define $\mathcal{G} = \mathcal{A} \times_1 \mathbf{U}^\intercal \times_2 \mathbf{U}^\intercal \times_3 \mathbf{U}^\intercal$. (a) Prove $\mathcal{G}$ is symmetric. (b) Prove $[\![\mathcal{G}; \mathbf{U}, \mathbf{U}, \mathbf{U}]\!]$ is within $\sqrt{3}$ of the optimal rank-(r, r, r) symmetric decomposition.

17.3.2 Symmetric CP Decomposition

Similar to the Tucker decomposition, if $\mathcal{A}$ is a d-way tensor of size $n \times n \times \cdots \times n$, then we can find a symmetric CP decomposition of the form

$$\mathcal{A} = \sum_{\ell=1}^{r} \lambda_\ell \mathbf{x}_\ell^{\otimes d}.$$

If d is even, multiplying $\mathbf{x}_\ell$ by -1 has no impact on the summation; therefore, explicit weights are needed to allow for subtraction of rank-1 components. The symmetric decomposition for a 3-way tensor is illustrated in Fig. 17.6.

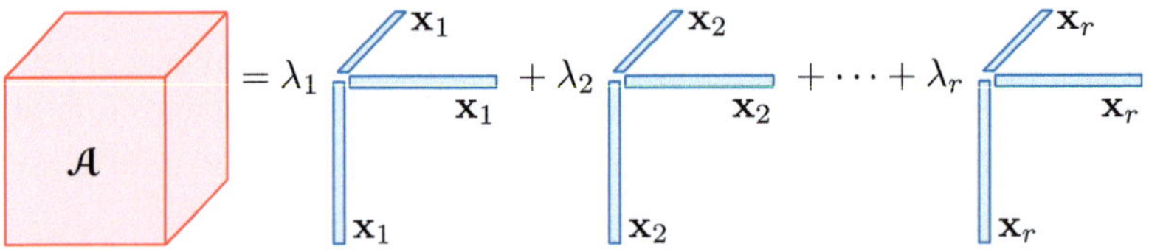

Figure 17.6 Symmetric CP decomposition: $\mathcal{A} = \sum_{\ell=1}^{r} \lambda_\ell \mathbf{x}_\ell^{\otimes d}$.

See Kolda (2015a) for discussion of numerical methods for symmetric CP decomposition and how methods for nonsymmetric CP may also be successful (due to uniqueness properties of CP). See also Section 9.5.4.

Exercise 17.9 Define $f(\boldsymbol{\lambda}, \mathbf{x}_1, \ldots, \mathbf{x}_r) = \|\mathcal{A} - \sum_{\ell=1}^{r} \lambda_\ell \mathbf{x}_\ell^{\otimes d}\|^2$. (a) What is $\frac{\partial f}{\partial \boldsymbol{\lambda}}$? (b) What is $\frac{\partial f}{\partial \mathbf{x}_j}$ for $j \in [r]$?

17.3.3 Tensor Eigenproblems

The generalized symmetric matrix eigenproblem is defined as follows. For an $n \times n$ symmetric matrix $\mathbf{A}$ and a symmetric positive definite $n \times n$ matrix $\mathbf{B}$, find a $\lambda \in \mathbb{R}$ and $\mathbf{x} \in \mathbb{R}^n$ such that $\mathbf{A}\mathbf{x} = \lambda \mathbf{B}\mathbf{x}$. If $\mathbf{B} = \mathbf{I}$, the $n \times n$ identity matrix, then we have the standard matrix eigenproblem: solve $\mathbf{A}\mathbf{x} = \lambda \mathbf{x}$. In this subsection, we consider the extension of the (generalized) matrix eigenproblem to symmetric tensors.

Preliminaries We define the analog for matrix–vector multiplication. Let $\mathcal{A}$ be a symmetric d-way tensor of dimension n. For $\mathbf{x} \in \mathbb{R}^n$, the tensor $\mathbf{x}^{\otimes(d-1)}$ is a $(d-1)$-way tensor of dimension n. The contraction of these tensor is denoted as $\mathcal{A}\mathbf{x}^{\otimes(d-1)}$, results in a vector of length n, and is defined by

$$[\mathcal{A}\mathbf{x}^{\otimes(d-1)}]_{i_1} \equiv \sum_{i_2=1}^{n} \cdots \sum_{i_d=1}^{n} a_{i_1 i_2 \cdots i_d} x_{i_2} \cdots x_{i_d} \quad \text{for all} \quad i_i \in [n].$$

This is illustrated for a 3-way tensor in Fig. 17.7.

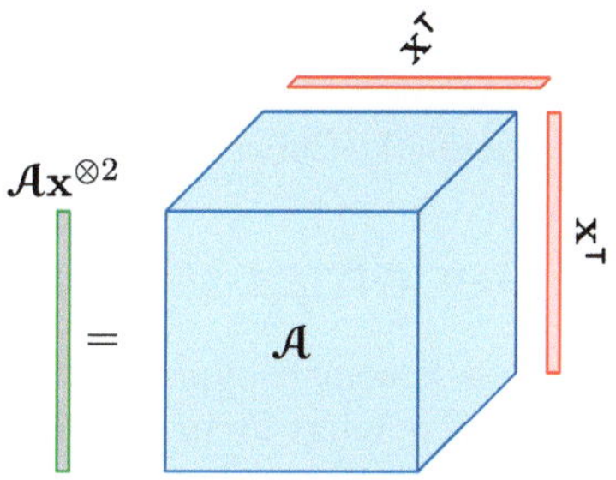

Figure 17.7 Symmetric tensor operation $\mathcal{A}\mathbf{x}^{\otimes 2}$ envisioned as $\mathcal{A} \times_2 \mathbf{x}^\intercal \times_3 \mathbf{x}^\intercal$.

Exercise 17.10 Prove $\mathcal{A}\mathbf{x}^{\otimes d} = \mathbf{x}^\intercal(\mathcal{A}\mathbf{x}^{\otimes(d-1)})$, where $\mathcal{A}\mathbf{x}^{\otimes d}$ is as defined in Eq. (17.5).

Generalized Tensor Eigenvalues and Special Cases We start with the most general definition for tensor eigenpairs, and then present several special cases. The following definition (with $\hat{d} = d$) was proposed by Chang et al. (2009) and later generalized by Cui et al. (2014) (under the name $\mathcal{B}$-eigenpair).

Definition 17.6: Generalized Tensor Eigenpair

Let $\mathcal{A}$ and $\mathcal{B}$ be symmetric tensors of dimension n and order d and $\hat{d}$, respectively. Further, assume $\mathcal{B}$ is positive definite. We say $(\lambda, \mathbf{x})$ with $\lambda \in \mathbb{R}$ and $\mathbf{x} \in \mathbb{R}^n \setminus \{\mathbf{0}\}$ is a **generalized eigenpair** if

$$\mathcal{A}\mathbf{x}^{\otimes(d-1)} = \lambda \mathcal{B}\mathbf{x}^{\otimes(\hat{d}-1)}.$$

Exercise 17.11 Prove that any generalized tensor eigenvalue satisfies

$$\lambda = \frac{\mathcal{A}\mathbf{x}^{\otimes d}}{\mathcal{B}\mathbf{x}^{\otimes \hat{d}}}.$$

Now we consider some special cases.

Definition 17.7 (Z-eigenpair, Qi, 2005 and Lim, 2005) Let $\mathcal{A}$ be a symmetric tensor of order d and dimension n. We say $(\lambda, \mathbf{x})$ with $\lambda \in \mathbb{R}$ and $\mathbf{x} \in \mathbb{R}^n$ is a **Z-eigenpair** if

$$\mathcal{A}\mathbf{x}^{\otimes(d-1)} = \lambda\mathbf{x} \quad \text{and} \quad \|\mathbf{x}\|_2 = 1.$$

Exercise 17.12 For what choice of $\hat{d}$ and $\mathcal{B}$ is the Z-eigenpair a special case of the generalized eigenpair?

Definition 17.8 (H-eigenpair, Qi, 2005 and Lim, 2005) Let $\mathcal{A}$ be a symmetric tensor of order d and dimension n. We say $(\lambda, \mathbf{x})$ with $\lambda \in \mathbb{R}$ and $\mathbf{x} \in \mathbb{R}^n \setminus \{\,\mathbf{0}\,\}$ is an **H-eigenpair** if

$$\mathcal{A}\mathbf{x}^{\otimes(d-1)} = \lambda\mathbf{x}^{[d-1]},$$

where $\mathbf{x}^{[d-1]}$ denotes elementwise power.

Exercise 17.13 For $\hat{d} = d$, for what choice of $\mathcal{B}$ is an H-eigenpair a special case of a generalized eigenpair?

Cartwright and Sturmfels (2013) bound the number of Z-eigenpairs of a symmetric tensor. Iterative power methods can be used to efficiently compute stable eigenpairs; see Kofidis and Regalia (2002), Kolda and Mayo (2011, 2014), and Regalia and Kofidis (2003). To compute *all* real eigenvalues sequentially, Cui et al. (2014) use semidefinite programming.

17.4 Other Tensor Decompositions

There are a multitude of other tensor decompositions that we do not cover in detail; instead, we provide very brief overviews and pointers for more information.

17.4.1 Tensor SVD (t-SVD)

The **tensor SVD (t-SVD)** is a special decomposition of a 3-way tensor introduced by Kilmer and Martin (2011) and extended in subsequent works; see Kilmer et al. (2021) and references therein. A key advantage of the t-SVD is that it can be used to find an optimal low-rank approximation akin to matrix SVD. The premise of the t-SVD is that it operates on the frontal slices of a transformed 3-way tensor. Given a tensor $\mathcal{X} \in \mathbb{R}^{m \times n \times p}$, the t-SVD decomposes the frontal slices of the tensor $\hat{\mathcal{X}} = \mathcal{X} \times_3 \mathbf{M}$, where $\mathbf{M}$ is an invertible $p \times p$ matrix. In the original paper (Kilmer and Martin, 2011), $\mathbf{M}$ is a discrete Fourier transform. The resulting decomposition has elegant mathematical properties and is effective for compressing image data (Kilmer et al., 2021) and tensor completion (Zhang and Aeron, 2017).

17.4.2 Hierarchical Tensor Decomposition

The **hierarchical tensor decomposition**, also known as hierarchical Tucker decomposition (Grasedyck, 2010; Hackbusch and Kühn, 2009), successively divides a tensor into products of smaller tensors. This decomposition is premised on the fact that any d-way tensor can be divided into the product of two tensors of order α and β where $\alpha + \beta = d + 2$. We can successively repeat this process until every tensor is at most order 3.

Consider, for example, a 5-way tensor $\mathcal{X} \in \mathbb{R}^{n_1 \times \cdots \times n_5}$. Let $\mathbf{X}_{(\{1,2,3\} \times \{4,5\})}$ denote the tensor unfolding of $\mathcal{X}$ of size $(n_1 n_2 n_3) \times (n_4 n_5)$. Compute a matrix factorization such that $\mathbf{X}_{(\{1,2,3\} \times \{4,5\})} \approx \mathbf{AB}$, where $\mathbf{A} \in \mathbb{R}^{n_1 n_2 n_3 \times r}$ and $\mathbf{B} \in \mathbb{R}^{r \times n_4 n_4}$. Finally, reshape

$\mathbf{A}$ into a 4-way tensor $\mathcal{A}$ of size $n_1 \times n_2 \times n_3 \times r$, and reshape $\mathbf{B}$ into a 3-way tensor $\mathcal{B}$ of size $r \times n_4 \times n_5$. Then $\mathcal{X}$ is approximated by the tensor contraction of $\mathbf{A}$ and $\mathbf{B}$ along the mode of size r. This is shown as the first step of Fig. 17.8. We can repeat this process, splitting the 4-way tensor $\mathcal{A}$ into the product of two 3-way tensors, as shown in the second step of Fig. 17.8.

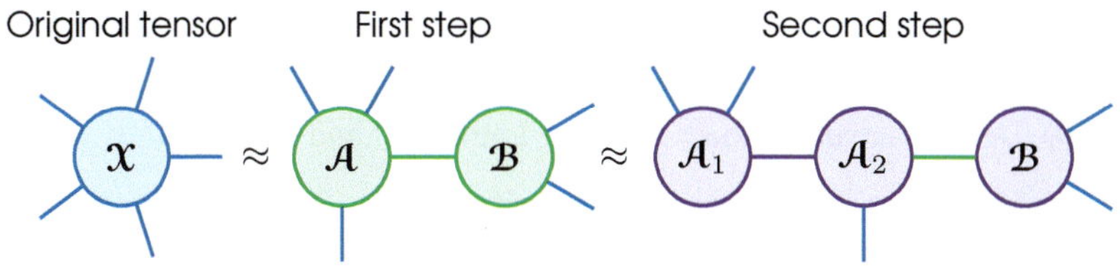

Figure 17.8 Hierarchical tensor decomposition network process: 5-way tensor $\mathcal{X}$ approximated by contraction of 4-way tensor $\mathcal{A}$ and 3-way tensor $\mathcal{B}$; then $\mathcal{A}$ split into contraction of 3-way tensors $\mathcal{A}_1$ and $\mathcal{A}_2$.

The division of the modes in a split operation is arbitrary. In fact, hierarchical tensor decomposition contains TT decomposition as a special case. The main challenge in hierarchical tensor decomposition is choosing the sequence of divisions. See Grasedyck et al. (2013) for an overview including a detailed treatment of hierarchical tensor decomposition.

17.4.3 Tensor Ring Decomposition

Like TT, the **tensor ring decomposition** (Zhao et al., 2016) also decomposes a d-way tensor into a series of tensor contractions of 3-way tensors. The difference is that the first and last 3-way tensors are also contracted.

Let $\mathcal{X} \in \mathbb{R}^{n_1 \times n_2 \times \cdots \times n_d}$ be a given tensor and let ranks $(r_1, r_2, \ldots, r_d)$ be given. The tensor ring decomposition finds 3-way tensors $\mathcal{G}_k \in \mathbb{R}^{r_k \times n_k \times r_{k+1}}$ for $k \in [d-1]$ and $\mathcal{G}_d \in \mathbb{R}^{r_d \times n_d \times r_1}$, such that

$$\mathcal{X}(i_1, i_2, \ldots, i_d) = \sum_{\alpha_1=1}^{r_1} \sum_{\alpha_2=1}^{r_2} \cdots \sum_{\alpha_d=1}^{r_d} \mathcal{G}_1(\alpha_1, i_1, \alpha_2)\mathcal{G}_2(\alpha_2, i_2, \alpha_3) \cdots \mathcal{G}_d(\alpha_d, i_d, \alpha_1)$$
$$\text{for all} \quad (i_1, i_2, \ldots, i_d) \in [n_1] \otimes [n_2] \otimes \cdots \otimes [n_d].$$

This is illustrated for a 5-way tensor using tensor networks in Fig. 17.9.

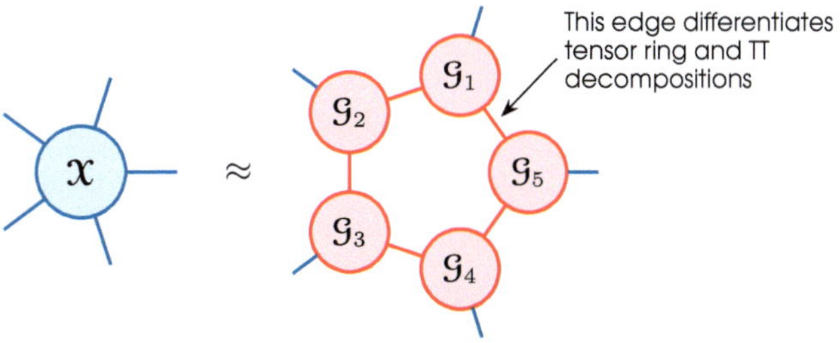

Figure 17.9 Tensor ring decomposition: a 5-way tensor decomposed into contraction of five 3-way tensors.

Tensor ring contrasts with TT and hierarchical tensor decomposition in that there is no direct algorithm for computing the tensor ring decomposition; instead, it must be computed iteratively.

17.4.4 CP–Tucker Hybrid Block Decomposition

A CP decomposition writes a tensor as the sum of rank-1 factors; equivalently, we could envision the decomposition as a sum of rank-(1,1,1) factors. We can then generalize this to consider other multiranks for the factors, writing the decomposition as a sum of Tucker decompositions. Several researchers have proposed **block CP decompositions**; see Bro et al. (2009), De Lathauwer (2008a,b), and De Lathauwer and Nion (2008).

Consider the 3-way case, computing a decomposition of $\mathcal{X} \in \mathbb{R}^{m \times n \times p}$. For a block decomposition, we have to specify the number of blocks, b, and the size of each block, (q_ℓ, r_ℓ, s_ℓ) for each $\ell \in [b]$. Then we find

$$\mathcal{G}_\ell \in \mathbb{R}^{q_\ell \times r_\ell \times s_\ell}, \; \mathbf{U}_\ell \in \mathbb{R}^{m \times q_\ell}, \; \mathbf{V}_\ell \in \mathbb{R}^{n \times r_\ell}, \text{ and } \mathbf{W}_\ell \in \mathbb{R}^{p \times s_\ell} \quad \text{for each} \quad \ell \in [b],$$

such that

$$\mathcal{X} \approx \sum_{\ell=1}^{b} [\![\mathcal{G}_\ell; \mathbf{U}_\ell, \mathbf{V}_\ell, \mathbf{W}_\ell]\!].$$

Elementwise, this means

$$x_{ijk} \approx \sum_{\ell=1}^{b} \sum_{\alpha=1}^{q_\ell} \sum_{\beta=1}^{r_\ell} \sum_{\gamma=1}^{s_\ell} \mathcal{G}_\ell(\alpha, \beta, \gamma) \mathbf{U}_\ell(i, \alpha) \mathbf{V}_\ell(j, \beta) \mathbf{W}_\ell(k, \gamma).$$

An example 3-way block decomposition is illustrated in Fig. 17.10.

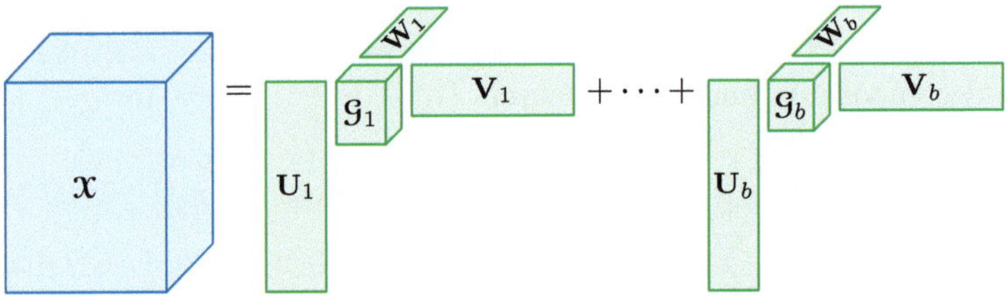

Figure 17.10 Hybrid CP–Tucker decomposition.

If the number of blocks is 1 ($b = 1$), then this reduces to Tucker decomposition. At the other extreme, if $q_\ell = r_\ell = s_\ell = 1$ for all $\ell \in [b]$, this reduces to CP. One challenge of the block tensor decomposition is choosing appropriate block sizes.

17.4.5 Infinite Dimensional Decompositions

A 3-way tensor $\mathcal{X}$ of size $m \times n \times p$ can be viewed as an **operator** from the domain $[m] \otimes [n] \otimes [p]$ to $\mathbb{R}$. The domain of $\mathcal{X}$ is finite, and $\mathcal{X}(i, j, k)$ is evaluating the operator $\mathcal{X}$ at (i, j, k) and returning a real value.

Consider a real-valued operator $f : \mathbb{R}^3 \to \mathbb{R}$. The domain of f is $\mathbb{R} \otimes \mathbb{R} \otimes \mathbb{R}$, and $f(x, y, z)$ returns a real value. This is analogous to $\mathcal{X}$ except that the domain of f is infinite whereas the domain of $\mathcal{X}$ is finite.

Continuing from that viewpoint, we can consider an infinite dimensional analog to CP. Let $f : \mathbb{R}^3 \to \mathbb{R}$. The goal is to write the real-valued trivariate (three-variable) function f as the sum of products of real-valued univariate (one-variable) functions. In other words, the goal is to find r and functions

$$\phi_\ell : \mathbb{R} \to \mathbb{R}, \quad \psi_\ell : \mathbb{R} \to \mathbb{R}, \quad \text{and} \quad \rho_\ell : \mathbb{R} \to \mathbb{R} \quad \text{for all} \quad \ell \in [r],$$

such that

$$f(x, y, z) \approx \sum_{\ell=1}^{r} \phi_\ell(x)\psi_\ell(y)\rho_\ell(z).$$

In the d-variate case, consider a function $f : \mathbb{R}^d \to \mathbb{R}$. We what to find r and functions

$$\phi_\ell^{(k)} : \mathbb{R} \to \mathbb{R} \quad \text{for all} \quad \ell \in [r] \text{ and } k \in [d],$$

such that

$$f(x_1, x_2, \ldots, x_d) = \sum_{\ell=1}^{r} \phi_\ell^{(1)}(x_1)\phi_\ell^{(2)}(x_2) \cdots \phi_\ell^{(d)}(x_d).$$

Many functions have such **separated representations**, meaning that a multivariate function can be written in terms of univariate functions, as illustrated in Example 17.2.

Example 17.2 (Infinite-Dimensional CP, Beylkin and Mohlenkamp, 2002) Let

$$f(x_1, x_2, \ldots, x_d) = \sin\left(\sum_{k=1}^{d} x_k\right). \tag{17.6}$$

Then f has a separated representation,

$$f(x_1, x_2, \ldots, x_d) = \sum_{\ell=1}^{d} \prod_{k=1}^{d} \phi_\ell^{(k)}(x_k), \tag{17.7a}$$

where

$$\phi_\ell^{(k)}(x) = \begin{cases} \sin(x) & \text{if } k = \ell \\ \frac{\sin(x+\alpha_k-\alpha_j)}{\sin(\alpha_k-\alpha_j)} & \text{if } k \neq j \end{cases}, \tag{17.7b}$$

and the constants $\{\alpha_1, \alpha_2, \ldots, \alpha_d\}$ are any values such that $\sin(\alpha_k - \alpha_\ell) \neq 0$ for all $j \neq k \in [d]$.

Exercise 17.14 Verify Example 17.2 computationally by evaluating f using both Eq. (17.6) and Eq. (17.7) and comparing the results for different inputs.

For bivariate functions, $f : \mathbb{R}^2 \to \mathbb{R}$, the continuous version of the matrix SVD is called the Karhunen–Loéve transformation.

In the realm of tensors, the earliest work is that of Beylkin and Mohlenkamp (2002, 2005).

Appendices

A Numerical Linear Algebra Principles and Methods

This appendix covers topics from numerical linear algebra that are useful throughout the book, but it is far from a complete treatment. For more coverage of these subjects, we recommend the textbooks of Demmel (1997), Golub and Van Loan (2013), Strang (2016), and Trefethen and Bau (1997).

A.1 Complexity and Big-O Notation

Since this is a book on computational methods for tensors, we will often be concerned with the expense of the algorithms we propose, especially when comparing different algorithms. To compare algorithms, we compute various measures as functions of input size.

One key measure of algorithmic performance is the number of computational operations, which we refer to as **computational complexity**. This is computed by counting scalar arithmetic operations. Because the scalars are nearly always represented as floating point numbers, we refer to these as flops, short for floating point operations.

Example A.1 (Computational Complexity) Let $\mathbf{x}$ be a vector of length n whose ith entry is denoted by x_i. Consider the computation:

$$f(\mathbf{x}) = \sqrt{\sum_{i=1}^{n} x_i^2}.$$

The input is length n, and we can compute $f(\mathbf{x})$ via n multiplications, $n-1$ additions, and 1 square root, for a total of $2n$ scalar operations.

> The **computational complexity** of an algorithm is the number of scalar operations it performs as a function of the input size.

Complexity as a function of the inputs is key to predicting the **scalability** of a method. For this reason, we often use **big-O notation** to bound the limiting behavior of the complexity as its input tends toward infinity. Loosely speaking, big-O notation strips constants and lower-order terms. For instance, $2n^2 + 10n = \mathcal{O}(n^2)$. Rigorously, big-O notation is defined as:

$$f(n) = \mathcal{O}\big(g(n)\big) \quad \text{if and only if} \quad f(n) \leq Cg(n) \text{ for all } n \geq N,$$

for some constants C and N.

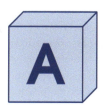

> Big-O notation strips constants and lower-order terms: $2n^2+10n = \mathcal{O}(n^2)$.

The appeal of big-O notation is that it excises architecture- and implementation-specific details. This way, we need not distinguish between the costs of different scalar operations (e.g., addition versus multiplication versus square root), hardware-specific combinations of operations such as multiply–add, and many nuances of implementation. Hence, the computational complexity for Example A.1 is $\mathcal{O}(n)$, independent of architecture, the precise method for computing the sum of n values, and so on.

Though we prefer lower-complexity algorithms, big-O complexity does not solely determine the best algorithm. If one method costs $100n$ and another costs $2n$, we likely prefer the latter even though both methods are $\mathcal{O}(n)$.

Another key measure of algorithmic performance is the amount of storage required, which we refer to as **memory complexity**. This is computed by evaluating the maximum storage needed at any point in an algorithm. To be more specific, we have to consider the programming language and architecture. For instance, in C, an integer uses 32 bits, a long integer uses 64 bits, a float uses 32 bits, and a double uses 64 bits. For instance, assuming we store all values as double precision, Example A.1 requires $64n$ bits to store the input, and 64 bits to store the running sum and final square root, for a total storage complexity of $64(n + 1)$ bits. As with computational complexity, we are generally only interested in asymptotic complexity, in which case we can say more simply that the memory complexity is $\mathcal{O}(n)$. This removes consideration of the differences in representation for single precision, double precision, etc.

> The **memory complexity** of an algorithm is the maximum number of scalar values that need to be stored as a function of the input size.

A related metric is the amount of data movement required by an algorithm, which we refer to as the **I/O complexity**. This is a measure of how much data needs to move between different memory locations in the course of an algorithm. The different places could be physically distinct machines or simply different levels of memory hierarchy. In addition to computational complexity, this can impact the overall runtime of an algorithm.

A.2 Finite Precision and Numerical Stability

Most of the computations we consider involve real numbers that are stored in a finite precision format known as **floating point**. As mentioned in Section A.1, float is a format that uses 32 bits for each number, and double uses 64 bits. You can think of these formats in terms of scientific notation (with base 2): a number is represented as $\pm\ (1 + f) \cdot 2^e$. In these formats, 1 bit specifies the sign of the number, and the remaining bits are partitioned into fractional bits that specify f and exponent bits that specify e.

Because of finite precision, we cannot store all real numbers exactly (π is an irrational number that would require an infinite number of bits, for example), and we cannot perform all arithmetic operations exactly. The error incurred during finite precision arithmetic is known as **roundoff error**. Floating point formats such as float and double ensure that roundoff error is small *relative* to the sizes of the numbers involved in the arithmetic. The size of this relative error is known as **machine precision**, and it is determined by the number of fractional bits in the format. Machine precision is approximately 10^{-8} for float and 10^{-16} for double. For example, $|\pi - \hat{\pi}|/|\pi| \approx 10^{-16}$, if $\hat{\pi}$ is the finite representation of π

using double precision.

The **numerical stability** of solving a problem refers to how sensitive the solution is to small changes to the input. In a stable scenario, small changes to the input lead to small changes in the output, but small changes to the input of an unstable system can lead to unacceptably large changes in the solution. This idea is important in the context of finite precision because roundoff error introduces small changes that can be amplified by numerical instability. When solving problems in linear algebra, numerical instability can come from the particular input data for the problem or from the algorithm we use to solve the problem. If the problem's input data causes instability, we call the input **ill conditioned**; otherwise it is **well conditioned**.

An algorithm is **numerically stable** if it produces a solution whose error depends only on the conditioning of the problem. That is, a numerically stable algorithm does not add any extra exacerbation of roundoff error. For a numerically stable algorithm and a well-conditioned problem, the error of the final output is on the order of machine precision, so that even if there are many arithmetic operations performed by the algorithm, each with their own roundoff errors, that error does not accumulate in a detrimental way.

> A **numerically stable algorithm** produces a solution that is as accurate as possible, subject to the precision used and the conditioning of the input.

For many problems, there are several possible methods to use, each with its own computational complexity and numerical stability. Often the fastest method is not the most numerically stable. For well-conditioned inputs, the fastest method may produce solutions to well-conditions inputs that are just as accurate as more stable but slower methods. On the other hand, numerically stable algorithms do not always guarantee an accurate answer, as ill-conditioned inputs can still produce solutions that are highly sensitive to roundoff error. For a detailed treatment of numerical stability with a particular focus on matrix computations, see Higham (2002).

A.3 Vectors and Matrices

Calculations with vectors and matrices are the foundation for computations with tensors, so we review associated definitions and basic operations.

A.3.1 Definitions

A **scalar** is a single number. We represent these with lowercase letters, e.g., $x = 1$. To specify that x is a real-valued scalar, we write $x \in \mathbb{R}$, where $\mathbb{R}$ denotes the set of all real numbers.

A **vector** is a one-dimensional array of scalars. We represent vectors throughout by lowercase boldface roman letters. If $\mathbf{x}$ is a real-valued vector of size n, then we write $\mathbf{x} \in \mathbb{R}^n$. We use the shorthand $[n] \equiv \{1, \dots, n\}$. Entry $i \in [n]$ of $\mathbf{x}$ is denoted as $\mathbf{x}(i)$ or compactly as x_i.

A **matrix** is a two-dimensional array of numbers. We represent matrices throughout by uppercase boldface Roman letters. If $\mathbf{A}$ is a real-valued matrix of size $m \times n$, then we write $\mathbf{A} \in \mathbb{R}^{m \times n}$. More generally, entry $(i, j) \in [m] \otimes [n]$ of $\mathbf{A}$ is denoted $\mathbf{A}(i, j)$ or a_{ij}. The notation $[m] \otimes [n]$ is compact notation for the set $\{ (i, j) : i \in [m], j \in [n] \}$. We write the jth column of $\mathbf{A}$ as $\mathbf{a}_j$.

The **vectorization** of a matrix $\mathbf{A} \in \mathbb{R}^{m \times n}$ stacks its columns into a vector:

$$\text{vec}(\mathbf{A}) = \begin{bmatrix} \mathbf{a}_1 \\ \mathbf{a}_2 \\ \vdots \\ \mathbf{a}_n \end{bmatrix} \in \mathbb{R}^{mn}.$$

Given a matrix $\mathbf{A} \in \mathbb{R}^{m \times n}$, we let $\text{nnz}(\mathbf{A})$ denote the number of nonzeros of the matrix. A matrix is **sparse** if the vast majority of its entries are 0, i.e., $\text{nnz}(\mathbf{A}) \ll mn$. Otherwise, the matrix is **dense**. A dense matrix is usually stored in vectorized format as a list of mn values, so its storage complexity is $\mathcal{O}(mn)$. A sparse matrix can be stored as a list of coordinates and nonzeros:

$$\{ (i, j, a_{ij}) \mid a_{ij} \neq 0 \}.$$

Thus, if $\mathbf{A}$ is sparse, its storage complexity is $\mathcal{O}(\text{nnz}(\mathbf{A}))$.

The **transpose** of a matrix reverses its row and column indicies as follows. If $\mathbf{A} \in \mathbb{R}^{m \times n}$ and $\mathbf{B} = \mathbf{A}^\mathsf{T}$, then $\mathbf{B} \in \mathbb{R}^{n \times m}$ and $b_{ji} = a_{ij}$ for all $(i, j) \in [m] \otimes [n]$.

A matrix $\mathbf{A} \in \mathbb{R}^{m \times n}$ is **square** if $m = n$.

A square matrix $\mathbf{A} \in \mathbb{R}^{n \times n}$ is **symmetric** if $a_{ij} = a_{ji}$ for all $(i, j) \in [n] \otimes [n]$.

If $\mathbf{A} \in \mathbb{R}^{n \times n}$, then $\text{diag}(\mathbf{A}) = \begin{bmatrix} a_{11} & a_{22} & \cdots & a_{nn} \end{bmatrix}^\mathsf{T} \in \mathbb{R}^n$ is the vector of its diagonal entries. The **trace** of $\mathbf{A}$ is the sum of its diagonal entries: $\text{trace}(\mathbf{A}) = \sum_{i=1}^n a_{ii}$.

A matrix $\mathbf{A} \in \mathbb{R}^{n \times n}$ is called **diagonal** if $a_{ij} = 0$ for all $i \neq j$. If $\mathbf{x} \in \mathbb{R}^n$ is a vector, then $\mathbf{A} = \text{diag}(\mathbf{x})$ is an $n \times n$ diagonal matrix such that $a_{ii} = x_i$ for all $i \in [n]$, i.e., $\mathbf{x}$ is on $\mathbf{A}$'s diagonal.

The $n \times n$ **identity matrix** is a square diagonal matrix with 1s along it diagonal, denoted $\mathbf{I}$ (or $\mathbf{I}_n$ if the size is ambiguous).

A rectangular matrix $\mathbf{A} \in \mathbb{R}^{m \times n}$ is called **upper triangular** if $a_{ij} = 0$ for all $i > j$, and it is called **lower triangular** if $a_{ij} = 0$ for all $i < j$.

A.3.2 Vector Inner Product and Norms

The **inner product** of two same-sized vectors $\mathbf{a}, \mathbf{b} \in \mathbb{R}^n$ produces a scalar, is denoted as $\langle \mathbf{a}, \mathbf{b} \rangle$, and defined as

$$\langle \mathbf{a}, \mathbf{b} \rangle \equiv \sum_{i=1}^n a_i b_i.$$

The computational complexity of the inner product is $\mathcal{O}(n)$.

Exercise A.1 For $\mathbf{a}, \mathbf{b} \in \mathbb{R}^n$, show $\langle \mathbf{a}, \mathbf{b} \rangle = \langle \mathbf{b}, \mathbf{a} \rangle$.

The **norm** of a vector $\mathbf{a} \in \mathbb{R}^n$ is the square root of its inner product with itself:

$$\|\mathbf{a}\|_2 \equiv \sqrt{\langle \mathbf{a}, \mathbf{a} \rangle} = \sqrt{\sum_{i=1}^n a_i^2}.$$

The ℓ_2-norm is denoted by $\| \cdot \|_2$.

Exercise A.2 For $\mathbf{a} \in \mathbb{R}^n$, show $\|\mathbf{a}\|_2 \geq 0$. Further, show $\|\mathbf{a}\|_2 = 0$ if and only if $\mathbf{a} = \mathbf{0}$, the all-0s vector.

Proposition A.1 (Vector Difference Norm) *For* $\mathbf{a}, \mathbf{b} \in \mathbb{R}^n$,

$$\|\mathbf{a} - \mathbf{b}\|_2^2 = \|\mathbf{a}\|_2^2 + \|\mathbf{b}\|_2^2 - 2\langle \mathbf{a}, \mathbf{b} \rangle.$$

Exercise A.3 Prove Proposition A.1.

The inner product between two vectors can be used to determine how aligned they are per Proposition A.2.

Proposition A.2 (Cosine and Inner Product) *Let* θ *denote the angle between vectors* $\mathbf{a}, \mathbf{b} \in \mathbb{R}^n$. *Then*

$$\cos\theta = \frac{\langle \mathbf{a}, \mathbf{b} \rangle}{\|\mathbf{a}\|_2 \|\mathbf{b}\|_2}.$$

We say two same-sized vectors are **orthogonal** if $\langle \mathbf{a}, \mathbf{b} \rangle = 0$.

Exercise A.4 Prove that vectors $\mathbf{a}, \mathbf{b} \in \mathbb{R}^n$ are orthogonal if and only if the angle between them is $\pi/2$ (90 degrees) or $-\pi/2$ (-90 degrees).

Exercise A.5 (Cauchy–Schwartz Inequality) For $\mathbf{a}, \mathbf{b} \in \mathbb{R}^n$, show $\langle \mathbf{a}, \mathbf{b} \rangle \leq \|\mathbf{a}\|_2 \|\mathbf{b}\|_2$.

A.3.3 Matrix Inner Product and Norms

We can extend the inner product to matrices.

The **inner product** of two same-sized matrices $\mathbf{A}, \mathbf{B} \in \mathbb{R}^{m \times n}$ is expressed as $\langle \mathbf{A}, \mathbf{B} \rangle$ and defined as

$$\langle \mathbf{A}, \mathbf{B} \rangle \equiv \sum_{i=1}^{m} \sum_{j=1}^{n} a_{ij} b_{ij}.$$

Exercise A.6 Let $\mathbf{A}, \mathbf{B} \in \mathbb{R}^{m \times n}$, and show

$$\langle \mathbf{A}, \mathbf{B} \rangle = \sum_{j=1}^{n} \langle \mathbf{a}_j, \mathbf{b}_j \rangle = \big\langle \text{vec}(\mathbf{A}), \text{vec}(\mathbf{B}) \big\rangle.$$

For a matrix $\mathbf{A} \in \mathbb{R}^{m \times n}$, its (Frobenius) **norm** is

$$\|\mathbf{A}\|_F \equiv \sqrt{\langle \mathbf{A}, \mathbf{A} \rangle} = \sqrt{\sum_{i=1}^{m} \sum_{j=1}^{n} a_{ij}^2}.$$

The Frobenius norm is denoted by $\|\cdot\|_F$.

Exercise A.7 Let $\mathbf{A} \in \mathbb{R}^{m \times n}$, and show $\|\mathbf{A}\|_F^2 = \sum_{j=1}^{n} \|\mathbf{a}_j\|_2^2 = \|\text{vec}(\mathbf{A})\|_2^2$.

Exercise A.8 Let $\mathbf{A} \in \mathbb{R}^{m \times n}$, and show the complexity of computing $\|\mathbf{A}\|_F$ is $\mathcal{O}(nm)$ if $\mathbf{A}$ is dense and $\mathcal{O}\big(\text{nnz}(\mathbf{A})\big)$ if $\mathbf{A}$ is sparse.

A.3.4 Vector Outer Product

The inner product of two vectors creates a scalar (reductive). In contrast, the outer product of two vectors creates a matrix (expansive).

Given two vectors $\mathbf{a} \in \mathbb{R}^m, \mathbf{b} \in \mathbb{R}^n$, their **vector outer product** is

$$\mathbf{C} = \mathbf{a} \bigcirc \mathbf{b} \in \mathbb{R}^{m \times n}, \quad \text{where} \quad c_{ij} = a_i b_j \quad \text{for all} \quad (i,j) \in [m] \otimes [n].$$

The computational complexity of the outer product is $\mathcal{O}(mn)$.

Remark A.3 (Outer product notation) The vector outer product is usually written as $\mathbf{a}\mathbf{b}^\mathsf{T}$, but we use the notation $\mathbf{a} \bigcirc \mathbf{b}$ because it is easier to generalize for our tensor discussion.

Exercise A.9 Prove that $\|\mathbf{a} \bigcirc \mathbf{b}\|_F = \|\mathbf{a}\|_2 \|\mathbf{b}\|_2$.

A.3.5 Matrix–Vector Product

Given a matrix $\mathbf{A} \in \mathbb{R}^{m \times n}$ and vector $\mathbf{x} \in \mathbb{R}^n$, the **matrix–vector product** is

$$\mathbf{y} = \mathbf{A}\mathbf{x} \in \mathbb{R}^m, \quad \text{where} \quad y_i = \sum_{j=1}^{n} a_{ij} x_j \quad \text{for all} \quad i \in [m].$$

The computational complexity of the matrix–vector product is $\mathcal{O}(mn)$, and it can be reduced to $\mathcal{O}(\text{nnz}(\mathbf{A}))$ if $\mathbf{A}$ is sparse.

Proposition A.4 (Matrix–Vector and Inner Products) *For $\mathbf{A} \in \mathbb{R}^{m \times n}$, $\mathbf{x} \in \mathbb{R}^n$, and $\mathbf{y} \in \mathbb{R}^m$,*

$$\langle \mathbf{A}\mathbf{x}, \mathbf{y} \rangle = \langle \mathbf{x}, \mathbf{A}^\mathsf{T}\mathbf{y} \rangle.$$

Proof. Using definitions of inner product and matrix–vector product, we have

$$\langle \mathbf{A}\mathbf{x}, \mathbf{y} \rangle = \sum_{i=1}^{m} \left(\sum_{j=1}^{n} a_{ij} x_j \right) y_i = \sum_{j=1}^{n} x_j \left(\sum_{i=1}^{m} a_{ij} y_i \right) = \langle \mathbf{x}, \mathbf{A}^\mathsf{T}\mathbf{y} \rangle. \qquad \square$$

Exercise A.10 Let $\mathbf{I}$ be the $n \times n$ identity matrix. Prove $\mathbf{I}\mathbf{x} = \mathbf{x}$ for any vector $\mathbf{x} \in \mathbb{R}^n$.

Exercise A.11 Let $\mathbf{a} \in \mathbb{R}^m, \mathbf{b} \in \mathbb{R}^n$, and show $\mathbf{a} \bigcirc \mathbf{b} = \mathbf{a}\mathbf{b}^\mathsf{T}$.

A.3.6 Matrix–Matrix Product

Given two matrices $\mathbf{A} \in \mathbb{R}^{m \times p}, \mathbf{B} \in \mathbb{R}^{p \times n}$, their **matrix product** is

$$\mathbf{C} = \mathbf{A}\mathbf{B} \in \mathbb{R}^{m \times n}, \quad \text{where} \quad c_{ij} = \sum_{k=1}^{p} a_{ik} b_{kj} \quad \text{for all} \quad (i,j) \in [m] \otimes [n],$$

and the cost to compute $\mathbf{C}$ is $\mathcal{O}(mnp)$.

The matrix product has several useful properties:

$$\begin{aligned} \text{right distributive:} \quad & (\mathbf{A}+\mathbf{B})\mathbf{C} = \mathbf{AC}+\mathbf{BC}, && \text{(A.1a)} \\ \text{left distributive:} \quad & \mathbf{C}(\mathbf{A}+\mathbf{B}) = \mathbf{CA}+\mathbf{CB}, && \text{(A.1b)} \\ \text{associative:} \quad & \mathbf{A}(\mathbf{BC}) = (\mathbf{AB})\mathbf{C}, && \text{(A.1c)} \\ \text{transposition:} \quad & (\mathbf{AB})^\mathsf{T} = \mathbf{B}^\mathsf{T}\mathbf{A}^\mathsf{T}. && \text{(A.1d)} \end{aligned}$$

In general, matrix multiplication is not commutative, i.e., $\mathbf{AB} \neq \mathbf{BA}$, even for square matrices.

Exercise A.12 For $\mathbf{a}, \mathbf{b} \in \mathbb{R}^n$, prove $\mathbf{a}^\mathsf{T}\mathbf{b} = \langle \mathbf{a}, \mathbf{b} \rangle$.

Exercise A.13 Given two matrices $\mathbf{A} = \begin{bmatrix} \mathbf{a}_1 & \mathbf{a}_2 & \cdots & \mathbf{a}_r \end{bmatrix} \in \mathbb{R}^{m \times r}$ and $\mathbf{B} = \begin{bmatrix} \mathbf{b}_1 & \mathbf{b}_2 & \cdots & \mathbf{b}_r \end{bmatrix} \in \mathbb{R}^{n \times r}$, prove

$$\mathbf{AB}^\mathsf{T} = \sum_{j=1}^{r} \mathbf{a}_j \bigcirc \mathbf{b}_j.$$

Exercise A.14 Prove Eq. (A.1d).

Exercise A.15 Prove $\operatorname{trace}(\mathbf{A}^\mathsf{T}\mathbf{B}) = \langle \mathbf{A}, \mathbf{B} \rangle$.

A.3.7 Matrix Inverse

Given a matrix $\mathbf{A} \in \mathbb{R}^{n \times n}$, if there exists a matrix $\mathbf{B} \in \mathbb{R}^{n \times n}$ that satisfies

$$\mathbf{AB} = \mathbf{BA} = \mathbf{I},$$

then the matrix $\mathbf{B}$ is denoted $\mathbf{A}^{-1}$ and called the **inverse** of $\mathbf{A}$.

If $\mathbf{A}^{-1}$ exists, $\mathbf{A}$ is called **invertible** or **nonsingular**; otherwise, $\mathbf{A}$ is called **singular**. Only a square matrix can be invertible.

If $\mathbf{A} \in \mathbb{R}^{n \times n}$ is invertible, then

$$(\mathbf{A}^\mathsf{T})^{-1} = (\mathbf{A}^{-1})^\mathsf{T}.$$

If two matrices $\mathbf{A}, \mathbf{B} \in \mathbb{R}^{n \times n}$ are both invertible, then $\mathbf{AB}$ is invertible and

$$(\mathbf{AB})^{-1} = \mathbf{B}^{-1}\mathbf{A}^{-1}.$$

If two matrices $\mathbf{A}, \mathbf{B} \in \mathbb{R}^{n \times n}$ and $\mathbf{C} = \mathbf{AB}$ is invertible, then both $\mathbf{A}$ and $\mathbf{B}$ are also invertible.

***Remark* A.5 (Avoiding matrix inverse)** In most cases, we want to avoid explicitly computing matrix inverses. This is discussed further in the context of linear systems (Section A.6).

A.3.8 Positive Definiteness

A square matrix $\mathbf{A} \in \mathbb{R}^{n \times n}$ is **positive definite** if

$$\mathbf{x}^\mathsf{T}\mathbf{A}\mathbf{x} > 0 \quad \text{for all} \quad \mathbf{x} \in \mathbb{R}^n \quad \text{such that} \quad \mathbf{x} \neq \mathbf{0}.$$

Any symmetric positive definite matrix is invertible. We say the matrix is **positive semidefinite** if

$$\mathbf{x}^\mathsf{T}\mathbf{A}\mathbf{x} \geq 0 \quad \text{for all} \quad \mathbf{x} \in \mathbb{R}^n.$$

Analogous definitions apply for negative (semi-)definiteness. In the case of symmetric matrices, positive (semi-)definiteness can also be characterized by the eigenvalues of the matrix, as described in Section A.5.4.

Exercise A.16 Let $\mathbf{A} \in \mathbb{R}^{m \times n}$ with $m \geq n$. Prove $\mathbf{A}^\mathsf{T}\mathbf{A}$ is positive semidefinite.

A.3.9 Vector Span and Subspace Dimension

We say a set of vectors $\{\mathbf{x}_1, \mathbf{x}_2, \ldots, \mathbf{x}_p\} \subset \mathbb{R}^n$ is **linearly dependent** if there exists nontrivial weights $\{\alpha_i\}_{i=1}^p$ such that

$$\sum_{i=1}^p \alpha_i \mathbf{x}_i = \mathbf{0}.$$

Otherwise, the set is said to be **linearly independent**.

A set of vectors $\{\mathbf{x}_1, \mathbf{x}_2, \ldots, \mathbf{x}_p\} \subset \mathbb{R}^n$ is called **(pairwise) orthogonal** if $\mathbf{x}_i^\mathsf{T}\mathbf{x}_j = 0$ for all $i \neq j$. The set is called **orthonormal** if, additionally, $\|\mathbf{x}_i\|_2 = 1$ for all $i \in [p]$.

Exercise A.17 Prove that every orthonormal set is linearly independent.

The **span** of a set of vectors $\{\mathbf{x}_1, \mathbf{x}_2, \ldots, \mathbf{x}_p\} \subset \mathbb{R}^n$ is the subspace defined by all linear combinations of its vectors:

$$\operatorname{span}\{\mathbf{x}_1, \mathbf{x}_2, \ldots, \mathbf{x}_p\} = \left\{ \sum_{i=1}^p \alpha_i \mathbf{x}_i \in \mathbb{R}^n \;\middle|\; \alpha_i \in \mathbb{R} \text{ for } i \in [p] \right\} \subseteq \mathbb{R}^n.$$

Let $\mathcal{X} = \operatorname{span}\{\mathbf{x}_1, \mathbf{x}_2, \ldots, \mathbf{x}_p\}$. The **dimension** of $\mathcal{X}$, denoted $\dim(\mathcal{X})$ is equal to the minimum number of (linearly independent) vectors whose span is equal to $\mathcal{X}$. That set of vectors is called a **basis** for the subset. Every linear subspace has an **orthonormal basis**. By definition, $\dim(\mathcal{X}) \leq \min\{n, p\}$.

The **orthogonal complement** to $\mathcal{X}$ is

$$\mathcal{X}^\perp = \{\mathbf{y} \in \mathbb{R}^n \mid \mathbf{y}^\mathsf{T}\mathbf{x} = 0 \text{ for all } \mathbf{x} \in \mathcal{X}\}.$$

If $\dim(\mathcal{X}) = n$, then $\mathcal{X}^\perp = \emptyset$. Further, $\dim(\mathcal{X}) + \dim(\mathcal{X}^\perp) = n$.

Example A.2 (Subspace Orthonormal Basis and Orthogonal Complement) The subspace

$$\mathcal{X} = \operatorname{span}\left\{ \begin{bmatrix} 1 \\ 0 \\ 1 \end{bmatrix}, \begin{bmatrix} 1 \\ 1 \\ 1 \end{bmatrix}, \begin{bmatrix} 2 \\ -1 \\ 2 \end{bmatrix} \right\}$$

has dimension less than three because the vectors are not linearly independent. Any of the three vectors can be written as a linear combination of the other two. Moreover, $\dim(\mathcal{X}) = 2$ because it has an orthogonal basis given by

$$\left\{ \begin{bmatrix} 1 \\ 0 \\ 1 \end{bmatrix}, \begin{bmatrix} 0 \\ 1 \\ 0 \end{bmatrix} \right\}.$$

Finally, $\dim(\mathcal{X}^\perp) = 1$, and it can be verified that

$$\mathcal{X}^\perp = \operatorname{span}\left\{ \begin{bmatrix} 1 \\ 0 \\ -1 \end{bmatrix} \right\}.$$

Exercise A.18 Given two vectors $\mathbf{a} \in \mathbb{R}^m, \mathbf{b} \in \mathbb{R}^n$, and $\mathbf{C} = \mathbf{a} \bigcirc \mathbf{b}$, prove that for any $\mathbf{x} \in \mathbb{R}^n$, $\mathbf{Cx} \in \operatorname{span}\{\mathbf{a}\}$.

A.3.10 Matrix Range and Rank

The **range** of a matrix $\mathbf{A} = \begin{bmatrix} \mathbf{a}_1 & \cdots & \mathbf{a}_n \end{bmatrix} \in \mathbb{R}^{m \times n}$ is the span of its columns: $\operatorname{range}(\mathbf{A}) = \operatorname{span}\{\mathbf{a}_1, \mathbf{a}_2, \ldots, \mathbf{a}_n\}$. The **rank** of a matrix $\mathbf{A}$ is the dimension of its range. If $m \geq n = \operatorname{rank}(\mathbf{A})$, then we say that $\mathbf{A}$ is **full rank**, i.e., the columns of $\mathbf{A}$ are linearly independent. The range and rank of a matrix are specified by the SVD of the matrix, as described in Section A.5.3.

Proposition A.6 (Matrix Rank Properties, Horn and Johnson, 1985) *Let* $\mathbf{A} \in \mathbb{R}^{m \times n}$ *and* $\mathbf{B} \in \mathbb{R}^{n \times p}$. *Then we have the following useful properties of the matrix rank:*

(a) $\operatorname{rank}(\mathbf{A}) = \operatorname{rank}(\mathbf{A}^\mathsf{T})$.
(b) $\operatorname{rank}(\mathbf{A}) \leq \min\{m, n\}$.
(c) $\operatorname{rank}(\mathbf{A}) + \operatorname{rank}(\mathbf{B}) - p \leq \operatorname{rank}(\mathbf{AB}) \leq \min\{\operatorname{rank}(\mathbf{A}), \operatorname{rank}(\mathbf{B})\}$.
(d) *If* $n = 1$, *then* $\operatorname{rank}(\mathbf{AB}) = 1$.
(e) *If* $m = n$ *and* $\operatorname{rank}(\mathbf{A}) = n$, *the* $\mathbf{A}$ *is invertible.*
(f) *If* $m \geq n$ *and* $\operatorname{rank}(\mathbf{A}) = n$, *then* $\mathbf{A}^\mathsf{T}\mathbf{A}$ *is full rank and therefore invertible.*
(g) *If* $\mathbf{U} \in \mathbb{R}^{m \times m}$ *and* $\mathbf{V} \in \mathbb{R}^{n \times n}$ *are nonsingular, then* $\operatorname{rank}(\mathbf{A}) = \operatorname{rank}(\mathbf{UA}) = \operatorname{rank}(\mathbf{AV}) = \operatorname{rank}(\mathbf{UAV})$.

Exercise A.19 Prove Proposition A.6g using Proposition A.6c.

A.3.11 Orthonormal and Orthogonal Matrices

We say a matrix $\mathbf{U} \in \mathbb{R}^{m \times n}$ with $m \geq n$ is **column orthonormal**, or simply **orthonormal**, if its columns form an orthonormal set, i.e.,

$$\mathbf{u}_i^\mathsf{T} \mathbf{u}_j = \begin{cases} 1 & \text{if } i = j \\ 0 & \text{if } i \neq j \end{cases} \quad \text{for all} \quad i, j \in [n].$$

In other words, $\mathbf{U}^\mathsf{T}\mathbf{U} = \mathbf{I}_n$, the $n \times n$ identity matrix. Conversely, a matrix whose transpose is column orthonormal is called **row orthonormal**, i.e., its rows form an orthonormal set of vectors.

If $\mathbf{U} \in \mathbb{R}^{m \times n}$ with $m > n$ is orthonormal, then there exists an **orthogonal complement** matrix $\mathbf{U}^\perp \in \mathbb{R}^{m \times (m-n)}$ such that $\mathbf{V} = \begin{bmatrix} \mathbf{U} & \mathbf{U}^\perp \end{bmatrix}$ is orthogonal.

Proposition A.7 (Orthonormal Matrix Properties) *If* $\mathbf{U} \in \mathbb{R}^{m \times n}$ *with* $m > n$ *is (column) orthonormal, then*

$$\mathbf{U}^\mathsf{T}\mathbf{U} = \mathbf{I}_n, \tag{A.2a}$$

$$\|\mathbf{U}\mathbf{x}\|_2 = \|\mathbf{x}\|_2 \quad \textit{for all} \quad \mathbf{x} \in \mathbb{R}^n, \tag{A.2b}$$

$$\|\mathbf{U}^\mathsf{T}\mathbf{y}\|_2 \leq \|\mathbf{y}\|_2 \quad \textit{for all} \quad \mathbf{y} \in \mathbb{R}^m, \tag{A.2c}$$

$$\|\mathbf{U}\mathbf{A}\|_F = \|\mathbf{A}\|_F \quad \textit{for all} \quad \mathbf{A} \in \mathbb{R}^{n \times p}, \tag{A.2d}$$

$$\|\mathbf{U}^\mathsf{T}\mathbf{B}\|_F \leq \|\mathbf{B}\|_F \quad \textit{for all} \quad \mathbf{B} \in \mathbb{R}^{m \times p}. \tag{A.2e}$$

Exercise A.20 Give an analogous proposition to Proposition A.7 for a row orthonormal matrix.

A square (column and row) orthonormal matrix $\mathbf{U} \in \mathbb{R}^{n \times n}$ is called **orthogonal**. This nomenclature is a bit confusing because an orthogonal matrix means that its columns are not just pairwise orthogonal but also have unit norm.

An **orthonormal matrix** has columns that are unit length and pairwise orthogonal. An **orthogonal matrix** is a *square* orthonormal matrix.

Proposition A.8 (Orthogonal Matrix Properties) *If* $\mathbf{U} \in \mathbb{R}^{n \times n}$ *is orthogonal, then the following properties hold:*

$$\mathbf{U}^{-1} = \mathbf{U}^\mathsf{T}, \tag{A.3a}$$

$$\mathbf{U}^\mathsf{T}\mathbf{U} = \mathbf{U}\mathbf{U}^\mathsf{T} = \mathbf{I}, \tag{A.3b}$$

$$\langle \mathbf{U}\mathbf{x}, \mathbf{U}\mathbf{y} \rangle = \langle \mathbf{x}, \mathbf{y} \rangle \quad \textit{for all} \quad \mathbf{x}, \mathbf{y} \in \mathbb{R}^n, \tag{A.3c}$$

$$\|\mathbf{U}\mathbf{x}\|_2 = \|\mathbf{U}^\mathsf{T}\mathbf{x}\|_2 = \|\mathbf{x}\|_2 \quad \textit{for all} \quad \mathbf{x} \in \mathbb{R}^n, \tag{A.3d}$$

$$\|\mathbf{U}\mathbf{A}\|_F = \|\mathbf{U}^\mathsf{T}\mathbf{A}\|_F = \|\mathbf{A}\|_F \quad \textit{for all} \quad \mathbf{A} \in \mathbb{R}^{n \times p}. \tag{A.3e}$$

Exercise A.21 Prove Eq. (A.3e).

Orthogonal Projectors For an orthonormal matrix $\mathbf{U} \in \mathbb{R}^{m \times n}$ with $m > n$, it is *not* the case that $\mathbf{U}\mathbf{U}^\mathsf{T} = \mathbf{I}_n$. Instead, the matrix $\mathbf{U}\mathbf{U}^\mathsf{T}$ is called an **orthogonal projector**. An orthogonal projector should not be confused with an orthogonal matrix. The matrix $\mathbf{I}_m - \mathbf{U}\mathbf{U}^\mathsf{T}$ is called the **complementary orthogonal projector**. We can also prove useful properties involving orthogonal projectors, as follows.

Proposition A.9 (Orthogonal Projector Properties) *If* $\mathbf{U} \in \mathbb{R}^{m\times n}$ *is orthonormal and* $\mathbf{A}, \mathbf{B} \in \mathbb{R}^{m\times p}$, *then*

$$\langle \mathbf{U}\mathbf{U}^\top \mathbf{A}, (\mathbf{I} - \mathbf{U}\mathbf{U}^\top)\mathbf{B}\rangle = 0, \quad \textit{and} \tag{A.4a}$$

$$\|\mathbf{A}\|_F^2 = \|\mathbf{U}\mathbf{U}^\top \mathbf{A}\|_F^2 + \|(\mathbf{I} - \mathbf{U}\mathbf{U}^\top)\mathbf{A}\|_F^2. \tag{A.4b}$$

Proof. From Proposition A.4 and the fact that $\mathbf{U}$ is orthonormal, we have

$$\langle \mathbf{U}\mathbf{U}^\top \mathbf{A}, (\mathbf{I} - \mathbf{U}\mathbf{U}^\top)\mathbf{B}\rangle = \langle \mathbf{A}, \mathbf{U}\mathbf{U}^\top(\mathbf{I} - \mathbf{U}\mathbf{U}^\top)\mathbf{B}\rangle = \langle \mathbf{A}, (\mathbf{U}\mathbf{U}^\top - \mathbf{U}\mathbf{U}^\top\mathbf{U}\mathbf{U}^\top)\mathbf{B}\rangle = 0.$$

Then we can use this fact to see that

$$\begin{aligned}
\|\mathbf{A}\|_F^2 &= \|\mathbf{U}\mathbf{U}^\top \mathbf{A} + (\mathbf{I} - \mathbf{U}\mathbf{U}^\top)\mathbf{A}\|_F^2 \\
&= \langle \mathbf{U}\mathbf{U}^\top \mathbf{A} + (\mathbf{I} - \mathbf{U}\mathbf{U}^\top)\mathbf{A}, \mathbf{U}\mathbf{U}^\top \mathbf{A} + (\mathbf{I} - \mathbf{U}\mathbf{U}^\top)\mathbf{A}\rangle \\
&= \langle \mathbf{U}\mathbf{U}^\top \mathbf{A}, \mathbf{U}\mathbf{U}^\top \mathbf{A}\rangle + 2\langle \mathbf{U}\mathbf{U}^\top \mathbf{A}, (\mathbf{I} - \mathbf{U}\mathbf{U}^\top)\mathbf{A}\rangle + \langle (\mathbf{I} - \mathbf{U}\mathbf{U}^\top)\mathbf{A}, (\mathbf{I} - \mathbf{U}\mathbf{U}^\top)\mathbf{A}\rangle \\
&= \|\mathbf{U}\mathbf{U}^\top \mathbf{A}\|_F^2 + \|(\mathbf{I} - \mathbf{U}\mathbf{U}^\top)\mathbf{A}\|_F^2.
\end{aligned}$$

□

A.3.12 Permutation Matrices

A **permutation matrix** $\mathbf{P} \in \mathbb{R}^{n\times n}$ is a special orthogonal matrix, such that $\mathbf{y} = \mathbf{P}\mathbf{x}$ is a rearrangement of the entries of $\mathbf{x}$. A permutation matrix $\mathbf{P}$ is all 0s except for a single 1 in each row and in each column. For example,

$$\mathbf{P} = \begin{bmatrix} 0 & 1 & 0 \\ 1 & 0 & 0 \\ 0 & 0 & 1 \end{bmatrix} \tag{A.5}$$

is a permutation matrix, representing the permutation $\boldsymbol{\pi} = (2, 1, 3)$. Conversely, given a permutation $\boldsymbol{\pi}$ of $[n]$, the corresponding permutation matrix $\mathbf{P} \in \mathbb{R}^{n\times n}$ is defined by

$$p_{ij} = \begin{cases} 1 & \text{if } j = \pi_i \\ 0 & \text{otherwise} \end{cases}.$$

Exercise A.22 Let $\mathbf{A} \in \mathbb{R}^{3\times 3}$ and let $\mathbf{P}$ be the permutation matrix in Eq. (A.5). (a) How does $\mathbf{B} = \mathbf{P}\mathbf{A}$ differ from $\mathbf{A}$? (b) How does $\mathbf{C} = \mathbf{A}\mathbf{P}$ differ from $\mathbf{A}$?

Permutation matrices need not be formed explicitly. If we want to compute $\mathbf{y} = \mathbf{P}\mathbf{x}$ and we know π, we can instead just execute the following loop:

Permutation with Explicit Matrix

```
for i = 1, ..., n do
    y(i) ← x(π_i)
end for
```

This has *no* computation, only memory movement.

Perfect Shuffle One important permutation matrix rearranges the elements of a vectorized matrix to correspond to its transpose.

Definition A.10 (Matrix Perfect Shuffle) A **perfect shuffle** matrix is a permutation matrix $\mathbf{P}$ such that

$$\mathbf{P}\,\text{vec}(\mathbf{A}) = \text{vec}(\mathbf{A}^\intercal)$$

for a matrix $\mathbf{A}$ of size $m \times n$. This is also known as the **commutation matrix**.

Proposition A.11 (Matrix Perfect Shuffle) *The permutation* π *defined by*

$$\pi_k = \big((k-1) \bmod n\big)\, m + \lceil k/n \rceil \quad \textit{for all} \quad k \in [mn] \tag{A.6}$$

produces the (m,n)*-perfect shuffle matrix.*

See Magnus and Neudecker (1979) for more on commutation matrices.

A.4 Other Matrix Products

A few other matrix products come up in the context of tensor decompositions.

A.4.1 Gram Matrix

The **Gram matrix** of a set of vectors $\{\, \mathbf{x}_1, \mathbf{x}_2, \ldots, \mathbf{x}_n \,\}$ is given by $\mathbf{X}^\intercal\mathbf{X}$, where $\mathbf{X}$ is the matrix whose columns are the vectors $\mathbf{x}_j$: $\mathbf{X} = \begin{bmatrix} \mathbf{x}_1 & \mathbf{x}_2 & \cdots & \mathbf{x}_n \end{bmatrix}$.

Proposition A.12 (Symmetric Positive Semidefinite Gram) *Any Gram matrix* $\mathbf{X}^\intercal\mathbf{X}$ *is symmetric positive semidefinite.*

Proof. Suppose $\mathbf{X} \in \mathbb{R}^{m\times n}$. We can see that $\mathbf{X}^\intercal\mathbf{X}$ is symmetric because

$$(\mathbf{X}^\intercal\mathbf{X})^\intercal = \mathbf{X}^\intercal(\mathbf{X}^\intercal)^\intercal = \mathbf{X}^\intercal\mathbf{X}.$$

The first step used Eq. (A.1d). We can see that it is positive semidefinite as follows. For any $\mathbf{y} \in \mathbb{R}^n$, define $\mathbf{z} = \mathbf{X}\mathbf{y}$. Then

$$\mathbf{y}(\mathbf{X}^\intercal\mathbf{X})\mathbf{y} = (\mathbf{X}\mathbf{y})^\intercal(\mathbf{X}\mathbf{y}) = \mathbf{z}^\intercal\mathbf{z} = \|\mathbf{z}\|_2^2 \geq 0. \qquad \square$$

Proposition A.13 (Gram Matrix Rank, Horn and Johnson, 1985) *The rank of* $\mathbf{X}^\intercal\mathbf{X}$ *equals the dimension of the span of the columns of* $\mathbf{X}$*, i.e.,* $\text{rank}(\mathbf{X}^\intercal\mathbf{X}) = \text{rank}(\mathbf{X})$. *Further, the columns of* $\mathbf{X}$ *are linearly independent if and only if* $\mathbf{X}^\intercal\mathbf{X}$ *is positive definite.*

A.4.2 Matrix Hadamard Product

Given two same-sized matrices $\mathbf{A}, \mathbf{B} \in \mathbb{R}^{m\times n}$, their **Hadamard product** or **elementwise product** is

$$\mathbf{C} = \mathbf{A} * \mathbf{B} \in \mathbb{R}^{m\times n}, \quad \text{where} \quad c_{ij} = a_{ij}b_{ij} \quad \text{for all} \quad (i,j) \in [m] \otimes [n].$$

This is also known sometimes as the **Schur product** (Horn and Johnson, 1985).

Elementwise, the Hadamard product of matrices $\mathbf{A}, \mathbf{B} \in \mathbb{R}^{m \times n}$ is

$$\underbrace{\begin{bmatrix} a_{11} & \cdots & a_{1n} \\ \vdots & \ddots & \vdots \\ a_{m1} & \cdots & a_{mn} \end{bmatrix}}_{\mathbf{A}} * \underbrace{\begin{bmatrix} b_{11} & \cdots & b_{1n} \\ \vdots & \ddots & \vdots \\ b_{m1} & \cdots & b_{mn} \end{bmatrix}}_{\mathbf{B}} = \underbrace{\begin{bmatrix} a_{11}b_{11} & \cdots & a_{1n}b_{1n} \\ \vdots & \ddots & \vdots \\ a_{m1}b_{m1} & \cdots & a_{mn}b_{mn} \end{bmatrix}}_{\mathbf{A} * \mathbf{B}}.$$

The Hadamard product is

$$\text{commutative:} \quad \mathbf{A} * \mathbf{B} = \mathbf{B} * \mathbf{A}, \tag{A.7}$$

$$\text{distributive:} \quad \mathbf{A} * (\mathbf{B} + \mathbf{C}) = (\mathbf{A} * \mathbf{B}) + (\mathbf{A} * \mathbf{C}), \tag{A.8}$$

$$\text{associative:} \quad (\mathbf{A} * \mathbf{B}) * \mathbf{C} = \mathbf{A} * (\mathbf{B} * \mathbf{C}). \tag{A.9}$$

Example A.3 (Hadamard Product) The Hadamard product has many uses in the context of tensors and elsewhere, including masking regions of a matrix. For instance, we can mask the lower right corner of a matrix as follows:

$$\begin{bmatrix} 0.81 & 0.63 & 0.96 & 0.96 \\ 0.91 & 0.10 & 0.96 & 0.49 \\ 0.13 & 0.28 & 0.16 & 0.80 \\ 0.91 & 0.55 & 0.97 & 0.14 \end{bmatrix} * \begin{bmatrix} 1 & 1 & 1 & 1 \\ 1 & 1 & 1 & 1 \\ 1 & 1 & 0 & 0 \\ 1 & 1 & 0 & 0 \end{bmatrix} = \begin{bmatrix} 0.81 & 0.63 & 0.96 & 0.96 \\ 0.91 & 0.10 & 0.96 & 0.49 \\ 0.13 & 0.28 & 0 & 0 \\ 0.91 & 0.55 & 0 & 0 \end{bmatrix}.$$

Exercise A.23 Prove that if $\mathbf{C} = \mathbf{A} * \mathbf{B}$, then $\text{vec}(\mathbf{C}) = \text{vec}(\mathbf{A}) * \text{vec}(\mathbf{B})$.

Exercise A.24 For $\mathbf{a}, \mathbf{c} \in \mathbb{R}^m$, and $\mathbf{b}, \mathbf{d} \in \mathbb{R}^n$, prove that $\mathbf{a}\mathbf{b}^\intercal * \mathbf{c}\mathbf{d}^\intercal = (\mathbf{a} * \mathbf{c})(\mathbf{b} * \mathbf{d})^\intercal$.

Exercise A.25 For $\mathbf{a}, \mathbf{b} \in \mathbb{R}^n$, prove that $\mathbf{a} * \mathbf{b} = \text{diag}(\mathbf{a})\mathbf{b}$.

Proposition A.14 (Schur Product Theorem, Horn and Johnson, 1985) *Let $\mathbf{A}, \mathbf{B} \in \mathbb{R}^{n \times n}$. If $\mathbf{A}$ and $\mathbf{B}$ are symmetric positive definite, then $\mathbf{A} * \mathbf{B}$ is positive definite. If $\mathbf{A}$ and $\mathbf{B}$ are symmetric positive semidefinite, then $\mathbf{A} * \mathbf{B}$ is positive semidefinite.*

Proposition A.15 (Hadamard Product Rank Upper Bound, Horn and Johnson, 1991) *Let $\mathbf{A}, \mathbf{B} \in \mathbb{R}^{m \times n}$. Then*

$$\text{rank}(\mathbf{A} * \mathbf{B}) \leq \text{rank}(\mathbf{A}) \, \text{rank}(\mathbf{B}).$$

Proposition A.16 (Hadamard Product Rank Lower Bound, Horn and Yang, 2020, corollary 5) *If $\mathbf{A}, \mathbf{B} \in \mathbb{R}^{n \times n}$ are symmetric positive semidefinite and have no 0 diagonal entries, then*

$$\text{rank}(\mathbf{A} * \mathbf{B}) \geq \max \{ \text{rank}(\mathbf{A}), \text{rank}(\mathbf{B}) \}.$$

A.4.3 Matrix Kronecker Product

The Kronecker product is, in a sense, the matrix analog of the vector outer product. The analogy is not quite complete because the outer product of two vectors results in a matrix, whereas the Kronecker product of two matrices is still a matrix. We see in Chapter 3 that a rearrangement of output of the Kronecker product of two matrices yields a 4-way tensor that is equivalent to their (tensor) outer product; conversely, every tensor product has an *unfolding* that can be expressed as the Kronecker product of two matrices.

Definition A.17: Matrix Kronecker Product

Given two matrices $\mathbf{A} \in \mathbb{R}^{m_1 \times n_1}$ and $\mathbf{B} \in \mathbb{R}^{m_2 \times n_2}$, their **Kronecker product** is

$$\mathbf{C} = \mathbf{A} \otimes \mathbf{B} \in \mathbb{R}^{m_1 m_2 \times n_1 n_2}, \quad \text{where} \quad c_{k\ell} = a_{i_1 j_1} b_{i_2 j_2}, \tag{A.10a}$$

and the relationship between (k, ℓ), (i_1, j_1), and (i_2, j_2) is as follows.
Given input indices $(i_1, j_1, i_2, j_2) \in [m_1] \otimes [n_1] \otimes [m_2] \otimes [n_2]$,

$$k = (i_1 - 1)m_2 + i_2 \quad \text{and} \quad \ell = (j_1 - 1)n_2 + j_2. \tag{A.10b}$$

Conversely, given output index $(k, \ell) \in [m_1 m_2] \otimes [n_1 n_2]$,

$$\begin{aligned} i_1 &= \lceil k/m_2 \rceil, & j_1 &= \lceil \ell/n_2 \rceil, \\ i_2 &= ((k-1) \bmod m_2) + 1, & j_2 &= ((\ell-1) \bmod n_2) + 1. \end{aligned} \tag{A.10c}$$

Elementwise, the Kronecker product of $\mathbf{A} \in \mathbb{R}^{m \times n}$ and $\mathbf{B} \in \mathbb{R}^{p \times q}$ is

$$\underbrace{\overset{n}{\begin{bmatrix} a_{11} & \cdots & a_{1n} \\ \vdots & \ddots & \vdots \\ a_{m1} & \cdots & a_{mn} \end{bmatrix}}}_{\mathbf{A}}_{m} \otimes \underbrace{\overset{q}{\begin{bmatrix} b_{11} & \cdots & b_{1q} \\ \vdots & \ddots & \vdots \\ b_{p1} & \cdots & b_{pq} \end{bmatrix}}}_{\mathbf{B}}_{p} = \underbrace{\overset{nq}{\begin{bmatrix} a_{11}b_{11} & \cdots & a_{11}b_{1q} & \cdots\cdots & a_{1n}b_{11} & \cdots & a_{1n}b_{1q} \\ \vdots & \ddots & \vdots & \ddots & \vdots & \ddots & \vdots \\ a_{11}b_{p1} & \cdots & a_{11}b_{pq} & \cdots\cdots & a_{1n}b_{p1} & \cdots & a_{1n}b_{pq} \\ \vdots & & & \ddots & & & \vdots \\ a_{m1}b_{11} & \cdots & a_{m1}b_{1q} & \cdots\cdots & a_{mn}b_{11} & \cdots & a_{mn}b_{1q} \\ \vdots & \ddots & \vdots & \ddots & \vdots & \ddots & \vdots \\ a_{m1}b_{p1} & \cdots & a_{m1}b_{pq} & \cdots\cdots & a_{mn}b_{p1} & \cdots & a_{mn}b_{pq} \end{bmatrix}}}_{\mathbf{A} \otimes \mathbf{B}}_{mp}.$$

The Kronecker product is much bigger than its inputs: its total size is the product of the total size of the inputs.

One way to express the Kronecker product is in block format as

$$\mathbf{A} \otimes \mathbf{B} = \begin{bmatrix} a_{11}\mathbf{B} & a_{12}\mathbf{B} & \cdots & a_{1n}\mathbf{B} \\ a_{21}\mathbf{B} & a_{22}\mathbf{B} & \cdots & a_{2n}\mathbf{B} \\ \vdots & \vdots & \ddots & \vdots \\ a_{m1}\mathbf{B} & a_{m2}\mathbf{B} & \cdots & a_{mn}\mathbf{B} \end{bmatrix}.$$

The Kronecker product has several other useful properties, including associativity, as follows.

Proposition A.18: Kronecker Product Properties

The following are properties of the Kronecker product:

$$\mathbf{A} \otimes \mathbf{B} \otimes \mathbf{C} = (\mathbf{A} \otimes \mathbf{B}) \otimes \mathbf{C} = \mathbf{A} \otimes (\mathbf{B} \otimes \mathbf{C}), \tag{A.11a}$$
$$(\mathbf{A} \otimes \mathbf{B})^\mathsf{T} = \mathbf{A}^\mathsf{T} \otimes \mathbf{B}^\mathsf{T}, \tag{A.11b}$$
$$(\mathbf{A} \otimes \mathbf{B})^{-1} = \mathbf{A}^{-1} \otimes \mathbf{B}^{-1}, \tag{A.11c}$$
$$(\mathbf{A} \otimes \mathbf{B})(\mathbf{C} \otimes \mathbf{D}) = (\mathbf{AC}) \otimes (\mathbf{BD}), \tag{A.11d}$$
$$\operatorname{vec}(\mathbf{ACB}^\mathsf{T}) = (\mathbf{B} \otimes \mathbf{A}) \operatorname{vec}(\mathbf{C}), \tag{A.11e}$$
$$\operatorname{rank}(\mathbf{A} \otimes \mathbf{B}) = \operatorname{rank}(\mathbf{A}) \operatorname{rank}(\mathbf{B}). \tag{A.11f}$$

For Eq. (A.11d), *it is required that the sizes are conforming: the number of rows in* $\mathbf{C}$ *is equal to the number of columns in* $\mathbf{A}$ *and likewise for* $\mathbf{D}$ *and* $\mathbf{B}$. *Likewise for Eq.* (A.11e), *the number of columns in* $\mathbf{A}$ *is equal to the number of rows in* $\mathbf{C}$, *and the number of columns in* $\mathbf{B}$ *is equal to the number of columns in* $\mathbf{C}$.

Exercise A.26 Prove Eq. (A.11e).

Exercise A.27 Let $\mathbf{U} \in \mathbb{R}^{m \times n}$ with $m > n$ and $\mathbf{V} \in \mathbb{R}^{p \times q}$ with $p > q$ be orthonormal matrices. Show $\mathbf{U} \otimes \mathbf{V}$ is orthonormal.

Exercise A.28 Prove $\|\mathbf{A} \otimes \mathbf{B}\|_F^2 = \|\mathbf{A}\|_F^2 \|\mathbf{B}\|_F^2$.

Example A.4 (Kronecker Product) An example Kronecker product is

$$\begin{bmatrix} 5 & 3 & 5 \\ 4 & 5 & 5 \end{bmatrix} \otimes \begin{bmatrix} 1 & 4 \\ 6 & 6 \end{bmatrix} = \begin{bmatrix} 5 & 20 & 3 & 12 & 5 & 20 \\ 30 & 30 & 18 & 18 & 30 & 30 \\ 4 & 16 & 5 & 20 & 5 & 20 \\ 24 & 24 & 30 & 30 & 30 & 30 \end{bmatrix}.$$

The Kronecker operator does not commute; in other words, it is not the case that $\mathbf{A} \otimes \mathbf{B} = \mathbf{B} \otimes \mathbf{A}$ for arbitrary $\mathbf{A}, \mathbf{B}$. However, the only difference is a permutation of the rows and columns, as elucidated in the next result.

Proposition A.19 (Kronecker-Perfect Shuffle Connection, Magnus and Neudecker, 1979) *Let* $\mathbf{A} \in \mathbb{R}^{m \times p}$ *and* $\mathbf{B} \in \mathbb{R}^{n \times q}$. *Then*

$$\mathbf{A} \otimes \mathbf{B} = \mathbf{P}(\mathbf{B} \otimes \mathbf{A})\mathbf{Q}^\mathsf{T},$$

where $\mathbf{P}$ *and* $\mathbf{Q}$ *are* (m, n)*- and* (p, q)*-perfect shuffle permutation matrices, respectively.*

The **vector Kronecker product** is a special case of the matrix Kronecker product. We use its properties often enough that we deem it worthwhile to consider them specially. As in the matrix case, the Kronecker product of two vectors combines all possible products of the entries. If the inputs are vectors of length m and n, then the output is of length mn.

Definition A.20: Vector Kronecker Product

For two vectors $\mathbf{a} \in \mathbb{R}^m, \mathbf{b} \in \mathbb{R}^n$, their **Kronecker product** is

$$\mathbf{v} = \mathbf{a} \otimes \mathbf{b} \in \mathbb{R}^{mn} \quad \Leftrightarrow \quad v_k = a_i b_j, \text{ where } k = n(i-1)+j. \tag{A.12}$$

Exercise A.29 Let $\mathbf{v} = \mathbf{a} \otimes \mathbf{b}$, where $\mathbf{a} \in \mathbb{R}^m$ and $\mathbf{b} \in \mathbb{R}^n$. Given index $k \in [mn]$, what are the i and j such that $v_k = a_i b_j$?

Elementwise, the Kronecker product can be written as

$$m\downarrow \underbrace{\begin{bmatrix} a_1 \\ a_2 \\ \vdots \\ a_m \end{bmatrix}}_{\mathbf{a}} \otimes \; n\downarrow \underbrace{\begin{bmatrix} b_1 \\ b_2 \\ \vdots \\ b_n \end{bmatrix}}_{\mathbf{b}} = mn\downarrow \underbrace{\begin{bmatrix} a_1 b_1 \\ \vdots \\ a_1 b_n \\ \vdots \\ \vdots \\ a_m b_1 \\ \vdots \\ a_m b_n \end{bmatrix}}_{\mathbf{a} \otimes \mathbf{b}}.$$

More compactly, we have

$$\mathbf{a} \otimes \mathbf{b} = \begin{bmatrix} a_1 \mathbf{b} \\ a_2 \mathbf{b} \\ \vdots \\ a_m \mathbf{b} \end{bmatrix}.$$

Exercise A.30 (Connection of Vector Outer Product and Kronecker Product) Let $\mathbf{a} \in \mathbb{R}^m, \mathbf{b} \in \mathbb{R}^n$. Prove $\text{vec}(\mathbf{a} \bigcirc \mathbf{b}) = \mathbf{b} \otimes \mathbf{a}$.

A.4.4 Matrix Khatri–Rao Product

The Khatri–Rao product computes the columnwise Kronecker product of its inputs. Its utility is in working with sums of vector outer products, and we show below how a low-rank matrix factorization can be expressed using the Khatri–Rao product. The Khatri–Rao product has an intimate relationships with *sums* of rank-1 tensors, which we explore in Chapter 10.

Definition A.21: Matrix Khatri–Rao Product (KRP)

Given two matrices with the same number of columns $\mathbf{A} \in \mathbb{R}^{m \times r}$ and $\mathbf{B} \in \mathbb{R}^{n \times r}$, their **Khatri–Rao product** is

$$\mathbf{C} = \mathbf{A} \odot \mathbf{B} \in \mathbb{R}^{mn \times r}, \quad \text{where} \quad c_{k\ell} = a_{i\ell} b_{j\ell}, \tag{A.13a}$$

and the relationship between $(k) \in [mn]$ and $(i,j) \in [m] \otimes [n]$ is

$$k = (i-1)n + j. \tag{A.13b}$$

In terms of the columns of $\mathbf{A}$ and $\mathbf{B}$, we have $\mathbf{c}_\ell = \mathbf{a}_\ell \otimes \mathbf{b}_\ell$ for all $\ell \in [r]$:

$$\mathbf{C} = \begin{bmatrix} | & | & & | \\ \mathbf{a}_1 \otimes \mathbf{b}_1 & \mathbf{a}_2 \otimes \mathbf{b}_2 & \cdots & \mathbf{a}_r \otimes \mathbf{b}_r \\ | & | & & | \end{bmatrix}.$$

This also means that the kth row of $\mathbf{A} \odot \mathbf{B}$ is the Hadamard product of the ith row of $\mathbf{A}$ and the jth row of $\mathbf{B}$, where $k = (i-1)n + j$. Writing the Khatri–Rao product out completely, we get

$$\underbrace{\overset{\xrightarrow{\;r\;}}{m\downarrow\begin{bmatrix} a_{11} & \cdots & a_{1r} \\ \vdots & \ddots & \vdots \\ a_{m1} & \cdots & a_{mr} \end{bmatrix}}}_{\mathbf{A}} \odot \underbrace{\overset{\xrightarrow{\;r\;}}{n\downarrow\begin{bmatrix} b_{11} & \cdots & b_{1r} \\ \vdots & \ddots & \vdots \\ b_{n1} & \cdots & b_{nr} \end{bmatrix}}}_{\mathbf{B}} = \underbrace{\overset{\xrightarrow{\;r\;}}{mn\downarrow\begin{bmatrix} a_{11}b_{11} & a_{12}b_{12} & \cdots & a_{1r}b_{1r} \\ \vdots & \vdots & \ddots & \vdots \\ a_{11}b_{n1} & a_{12}b_{n2} & \cdots & a_{1r}b_{nr} \\ \vdots & \vdots & \ddots & \vdots \\ a_{m1}b_{11} & a_{m2}b_{12} & \cdots & a_{mr}b_{1r} \\ \vdots & \vdots & \ddots & \vdots \\ a_{m1}b_{n1} & a_{m2}b_{n2} & \cdots & a_{mr}b_{nr} \end{bmatrix}}}_{\mathbf{A} \odot \mathbf{B}}.$$

Example A.5 (Khatri–Rao product) An example Khatri–Rao product is

$$\begin{bmatrix} 5 & 2 & 3 & 1 \\ 2 & 2 & 4 & 5 \end{bmatrix} \odot \begin{bmatrix} 3 & 3 & 4 & 1 \\ 5 & 1 & 2 & 5 \\ 2 & 1 & 5 & 3 \end{bmatrix} = \begin{bmatrix} 15 & 6 & 12 & 1 \\ 25 & 2 & 6 & 5 \\ 10 & 2 & 15 & 3 \\ 6 & 6 & 16 & 5 \\ 10 & 2 & 8 & 25 \\ 4 & 2 & 20 & 15 \end{bmatrix}.$$

Exercise A.31 Suppose $\mathbf{X} \in \mathbb{R}^{m \times n}$ has a factorization of the form

$$\mathbf{X} = \mathbf{U}\boldsymbol{\Sigma}\mathbf{V}^\intercal = \sum_{j=1}^{r} \sigma_i \mathbf{u}_i \mathbf{v}_j^\intercal,$$

where $\mathbf{U} \in \mathbb{R}^{m \times r}$, $\mathbf{V} \in \mathbb{R}^{n \times r}$, and $\boldsymbol{\Sigma} = \operatorname{diag}(\boldsymbol{\sigma})$ with $\boldsymbol{\sigma} \in \mathbb{R}^r$. Prove

$$\operatorname{vec}(\mathbf{X}) = (\mathbf{V} \odot \mathbf{U})\boldsymbol{\sigma}.$$

Exercise A.32 Prove $\|\mathbf{A} \odot \mathbf{B}\|_F^2 \leq \|\mathbf{A} \otimes \mathbf{B}\|_F^2 = \|\mathbf{A}\|_F^2 \|\mathbf{B}\|_F^2$.

Proposition A.22 (Multiplying Kronecker and Khatri–Rao Products) *Given matrices* $\mathbf{A} \in \mathbb{R}^{m \times n}, \mathbf{B} \in \mathbb{R}^{p \times q}, \mathbf{C} \in \mathbb{R}^{n \times r}, \mathbf{D} \in \mathbb{R}^{q \times r}$,

$$(\mathbf{A} \otimes \mathbf{B})(\mathbf{C} \odot \mathbf{D}) = (\mathbf{AC}) \odot (\mathbf{BD}).$$

Table A.1 Leading term of computational cost of numerically stable algorithms for matrix factorizations of $m \times n$ matrix with $m \geq n$

Decomposition	**Square** $(m = n)$	**Rectangular** $(m > n)$	**Comments**
LU	$\frac{2}{3}n^3$		Must be square
Cholesky	$\frac{1}{3}n^3$		Must be symmetric positive definite
QR	$\frac{4}{3}n^3$	$2mn^2$	Cost doubles for explicit $\mathbf{Q}$
SVD	$\frac{20}{3}n^3$	$6mn^2$	For computing all singular vectors
Sym. EVD	$\frac{10}{3}n^3$		Must be symmetric

Proof. We can rewrite the product as

$$\begin{aligned}(\mathbf{A} \otimes \mathbf{B})(\mathbf{C} \odot \mathbf{D}) &= (\mathbf{A} \otimes \mathbf{B}) \begin{bmatrix}\mathbf{c}_1 \otimes \mathbf{d}_1 & \cdots & \mathbf{c}_r \otimes \mathbf{d}_r\end{bmatrix} \\ &= \begin{bmatrix}(\mathbf{A} \otimes \mathbf{B})(\mathbf{c}_1 \otimes \mathbf{d}_1) & \cdots & (\mathbf{A} \otimes \mathbf{B})(\mathbf{c}_r \otimes \mathbf{d}_r)\end{bmatrix} \\ &= \begin{bmatrix}\mathbf{A}\mathbf{c}_1 \otimes \mathbf{B}\mathbf{d}_1 & \cdots & \mathbf{A}\mathbf{c}_r \otimes \mathbf{B}\mathbf{d}_r\end{bmatrix} \\ &= \begin{bmatrix}[\mathbf{AC}]_1 \otimes [\mathbf{BD}]_1 & \cdots & [\mathbf{AC}]_r \otimes [\mathbf{BD}]_r\end{bmatrix} \\ &= (\mathbf{AC}) \odot (\mathbf{BD}).\end{aligned}$$

The product of Kronecker products is simplified in the third line using Eq. (A.11d). □

Proposition A.23 (Khatri–Rao Product Gram) *Given matrices* $\mathbf{A} \in \mathbb{R}^{m \times r}, \mathbf{B} \in \mathbb{R}^{n \times r}, \mathbf{C} \in \mathbb{R}^{m \times s}, \mathbf{D} \in \mathbb{R}^{n \times s}$,

$$(\mathbf{A} \odot \mathbf{B})^\intercal (\mathbf{C} \odot \mathbf{D}) = (\mathbf{A}^\intercal \mathbf{C}) * (\mathbf{B}^\intercal \mathbf{D}).$$

Exercise A.33 Prove Proposition A.23.

Proposition A.24 (Khatri–Rao Product Rank Bound, ten Berge, 2000a) *Let matrices* $\mathbf{A} \in \mathbb{R}^{m \times r}, \mathbf{B} \in \mathbb{R}^{n \times r}$. *If* $\mathbf{A}$ *and* $\mathbf{B}$ *have no all-0 columns, then*

$$\operatorname{rank}(\mathbf{A} \odot \mathbf{B}) \geq \max \{ \operatorname{rank}(\mathbf{A}), \operatorname{rank}(\mathbf{B}) \}.$$

Exercise A.34 Prove Proposition A.24. Hint: Use Propositions A.13, A.16, and A.23.

A.5 Matrix Decompositions

We consider several different matrix decompositions: LU, Cholesky, QR, SVD, and eigenvalue decomposition (EVD). All have roughly the same cost for a square $n \times n$ matrix: $\mathcal{O}(n^3)$. However, the leading term varies from $\frac{1}{3}$ up to $\frac{20}{3}$. The SVD is often the most convenient and intuitive matrix factorization in a mathematical sense, but any other factorization will be more efficient computationally and preferred in practice if it can serve an equivalent role. We summarize the leading term of the computational cost for each method in Table A.1.

A.5.1 LU and Cholesky Decompositions

Let $\mathbf{A} \in \mathbb{R}^{n \times n}$ be a nonsingular matrix. Its **LU decomposition** is expressed as

$$\mathbf{PA} = \mathbf{LU},$$

where $\mathbf{P}$ is a permutation matrix, $\mathbf{L}$ is lower triangular, and $\mathbf{U}$ is upper triangular, each with the same dimensions as $\mathbf{A}$. Ignoring the permutation of $\mathbf{A}$, we can visualize this as in Fig. A.1. The most common algorithm for computing this decomposition is called Gaussian elimination, requires $\frac{2}{3}n^3$ flops, and performs row permutations (known as partial pivoting) that are encoded in the matrix $\mathbf{P}$.

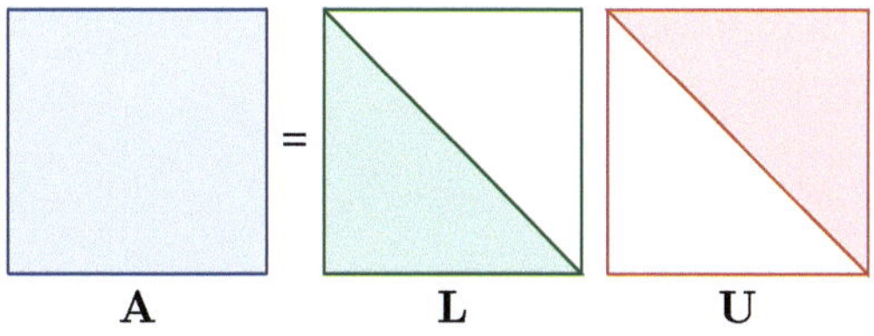

Figure A.1 LU decomposition.

Suppose further that $\mathbf{A} \in \mathbb{R}^{n \times n}$ is symmetric and positive definite (see Section A.3.8). Then its **Cholesky decomposition** is

$$\mathbf{A} = \mathbf{L}\mathbf{L}^\intercal,$$

where $\mathbf{L} \in \mathbb{R}^{n \times n}$ is lower triangular. The algorithm for computing the Cholesky decomposition requires $\frac{1}{3}n^3$ flops, which is half the cost of LU because the algorithm exploits symmetry. Because of the positive definiteness, no row or column permutations are required to maintain numerical stability. The Cholesky factorization can be visualized as in Fig. A.2.

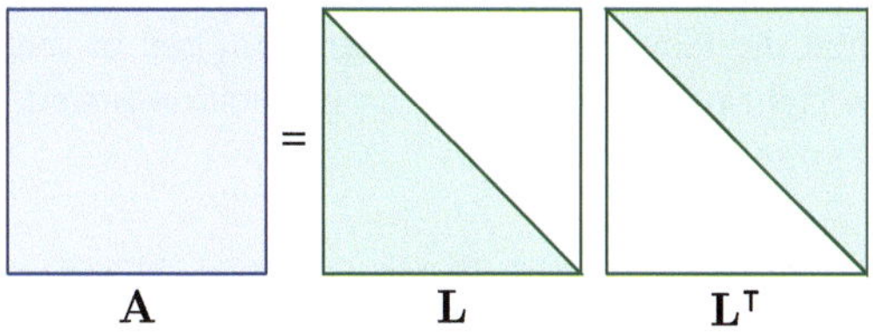

Figure A.2 Cholesky factorization.

These two decompositions are most commonly used to solve linear systems, as described in Section A.6. For more details, see Demmel (1997, chapter 2) or Trefethen and Bau (1997, part IV).

> The **LU and Cholesky decompositions** are most useful for the solution of linear systems and factors the (permuted) input matrix into the product of a lower triangular matrix and an upper triangular matrix.

A.5.2 QR Decomposition

Let $\mathbf{A} \in \mathbb{R}^{m \times n}$ with $m \geq n$. Then its **QR decomposition** is

$$\mathbf{A} = \bar{\mathbf{Q}}\bar{\mathbf{R}} = \begin{bmatrix}\mathbf{Q} & \mathbf{Q}^{\perp}\end{bmatrix} \begin{bmatrix}\mathbf{R} \\ \mathbf{0}\end{bmatrix} = \mathbf{Q}\mathbf{R}. \tag{A.14}$$

Here $\bar{\mathbf{Q}} \in \mathbb{R}^{m \times m}$ is orthogonal, $\mathbf{Q} \in \mathbb{R}^{m \times n}$ is a matrix whose orthonormal columns span the column space of $\mathbf{A}$, and $\mathbf{Q}^{\perp} \in \mathbb{R}^{m \times (m-n)}$ is the orthogonal complement of $\mathbf{Q}$. The matrix $\bar{\mathbf{R}}$ is an upper triangular matrix of size $m \times n$, with $\mathbf{R}$ of size $n \times n$ and the zero block of size $(m-n) \times n$. The QR decomposition exists for matrices with $m < n$ as well, but we ignore that case here. In computations, we generally use the **economy** or **compact** QR decomposition given by the last term $\mathbf{A} = \mathbf{QR}$. We can visualize this as in Fig. A.3.

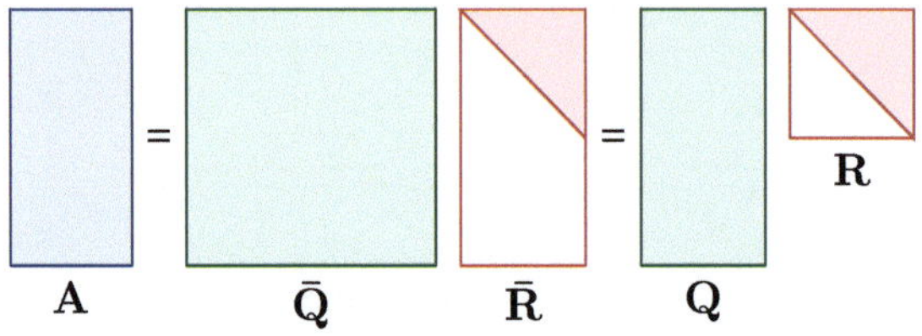

Figure A.3 QR factorization.

The most common algorithm for computing the QR decomposition is called Householder QR, which is numerically stable, costs $2mn^2 - \frac{2}{3}n^3$ flops, and represents $\mathbf{Q}$ in an implicit form. Using the implicit form, the matrix–vector products $\mathbf{Qb}$ and $\mathbf{Q}^{\mathsf{T}}\mathbf{b}$ for $\mathbf{b} \in \mathbb{R}^m$ are each computed with $2mn + 2n^2$ flops. An explicit (compact) $\mathbf{Q}$ can be constructed at an additional cost of $2mn^2 - \frac{2}{3}n^3$ flops. The QR decomposition is often used to solve linear least squares problems (as described in Section A.7) and to find an orthonormal basis for the column space of a full-rank matrix, i.e., $\text{range}(\mathbf{Q}) = \text{range}(\mathbf{A})$.

A QR decomposition always exists and can be computed stably, even if $\mathbf{A}$ is not full rank. When $\mathbf{A}$ is full rank, the QR decomposition is unique up to the signs of columns of $\mathbf{Q}$. If $\mathbf{A}$ has rank $r < n$, then the Householder QR algorithm can be augmented with column pivoting (equivalent to right multiplication by a permutation matrix) in order to compute $\mathbf{Q} \in \mathbb{R}^{m \times r}$ such that $\text{range}(\mathbf{Q}) = \text{range}(\mathbf{A})$.

> The **QR decomposition** decomposes a matrix into an orthonormal matrix ($\mathbf{Q}$) times an upper triangular matrix ($\mathbf{R}$). It is used in the solution of least squares problems, and the $\mathbf{Q}$ matrix is also an orthonormal basis for the column space of the input matrix.

For more details, see Demmel (1997, section 3.4) or Trefethen and Bau (1997, lecture 7).

A.5.3 Singular Value Decomposition

Let $\mathbf{A} \in \mathbb{R}^{m \times n}$. Its **SVD** is

$$\mathbf{A} = \bar{\mathbf{U}}\bar{\boldsymbol{\Sigma}}\bar{\mathbf{V}} = \begin{bmatrix}\mathbf{U} & \mathbf{U}^{\perp}\end{bmatrix} \underbrace{\begin{bmatrix}\boldsymbol{\Sigma} & \mathbf{0} \\ \mathbf{0} & \mathbf{0}\end{bmatrix}}_{\bar{\boldsymbol{\Sigma}}} \begin{bmatrix}\mathbf{V} & \mathbf{V}^{\perp}\end{bmatrix}^{\mathsf{T}} = \mathbf{U}\boldsymbol{\Sigma}\mathbf{V}^{\mathsf{T}}.$$

Here $\bar{\mathbf{U}} \in \mathbb{R}^{m\times m}$ and $\bar{\mathbf{V}} \in \mathbb{R}^{n\times n}$ are orthogonal matrices. The matrix $\bar{\mathbf{\Sigma}} \in \mathbb{R}^{m\times n}$ is a diagonal matrix with diagonal entries

$$\sigma_1 \geq \sigma_2 \geq \cdots \geq \sigma_{\min\{m,n\}} \geq 0.$$

The number of nonzero diagonal values is the matrix rank (i.e., $\operatorname{rank}(\mathbf{A}) = r$), and we let $\mathbf{\Sigma}$ be the $r \times r$ submatrix with positive diagonal entries.

The columns of $\mathbf{U} \in \mathbb{R}^{m\times r}$ are an orthonormal basis for the range of $\mathbf{A}$, and likewise for $\mathbf{V} \in \mathbb{R}^{n\times r}$ and the range of $\mathbf{A}^\mathsf{T}$.

Exercise A.35 Let $\mathbf{A} = \mathbf{U\Sigma V}^\mathsf{T}$ be the SVD of a matrix $\mathbf{A}$. Prove $\|\mathbf{A}\|_F^2 = \sum_{i=1}^r \sigma_i^2$.

The SVD can be visualized as in Fig. A.4. Here we show the nonzero diagonal entries as colored blocks and the 0 diagonal entries as open blocks.

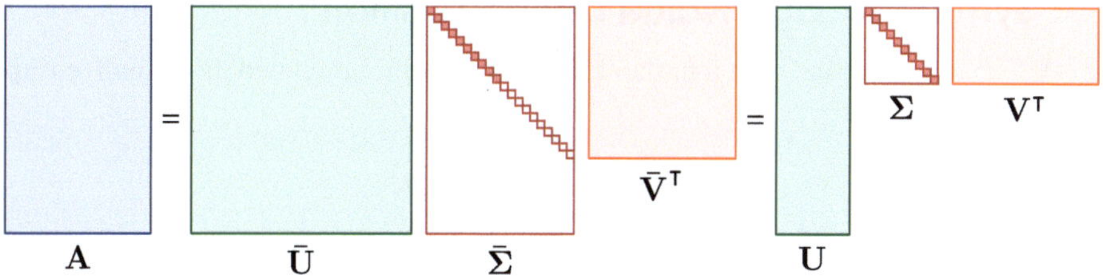

Figure A.4 Singular value decomposition.

We often use the **economy** or **compact** SVD given by

$$\mathbf{A} = \mathbf{U\Sigma V}^\mathsf{T} = \sum_{k=1}^{r} \sigma_k \mathbf{u}_k \mathbf{v}_k^\mathsf{T}.$$

Here $\mathbf{\Sigma} = \operatorname{diag}(\sigma_1, \ldots, \sigma_r)$, and $\mathbf{U} = [\mathbf{u}_1, \ldots, \mathbf{u}_r] \in \mathbb{R}^{m\times r}$, $\mathbf{V} = [\mathbf{v}_1, \ldots, \mathbf{v}_r] \in \mathbb{R}^{n\times r}$ are orthonormal matrices. Each term in the SVD summation expression is a rank-1 matrix, so it shows that $\mathbf{A}$ can be decomposed as the sum of r rank-1 matrices.

We refer to σ_k as the kth **singular value**, $\mathbf{u}_k$ as the kth **left singular vector**, and $\mathbf{v}_k$ as the kth **right singular vector**. The singular values and vectors can be alternatively defined as satisfying the following conditions:

$$\mathbf{A}^\mathsf{T}\mathbf{u}_k = \sigma_k \mathbf{v}_k \quad \text{and} \quad \mathbf{A}\mathbf{v}_k = \sigma_k \mathbf{u}_k.$$

If σ_k is distinct, then its left and right singular vectors are unique (up to sign). More generally, if all the singular values are distinct, then the SVD is **unique**, up to sign ambiguity.

The **condition number** of a matrix generally refers to the ratio of the largest singular value to the smallest: $\sigma_1/\sigma_{\min\{m,n\}}$. When this ratio is small (close to 1), we say the matrix is **well conditioned**, and when it is large (close to the reciprocal of machine precision), we say it is **ill conditioned**. If a matrix is not full rank, then its condition number is infinite.

The **SVD** decomposes a matrix into the sum of r rank-1 matrices, where r is the rank of the input matrix. The singular values can be used to determine the matrix rank and norm. The left and right singular vectors (corresponding to nonzero singular values) provide orthonormal bases for the column and row spaces, respectively.

There is no closed-form solution for computing the SVD. However, the methods are such that the dominant cost depends only on the size of matrix, i.e., there is no dependency on the singular values, and the iterative parts have lower-order costs. The cost of computing the SVD is $\mathcal{O}(\min\{mn^2, m^2n\})$. The hidden constant can vary from 1 up to almost 7, depending on the relative sizes of m and n and the algorithm used (see Section A.5.5). See also Demmel (1997, section 5.4) or Trefethen and Bau (1997, lecture 31).

If the full SVD is not required (e.g., only the largest several singular values are desired), then iterative methods can be more efficient than computing the full SVD, particularly when the matrix is large and sparse. We discuss these issues in further detail in Section A.8.

Exercise A.36 (a) Prove that if $\mathbf{A} \in \mathbb{R}^{m \times n}$ is full rank with $m \geq n$, then $\mathbf{A}^\intercal\mathbf{A}$ is full rank. (b) How does the condition number of $\mathbf{A}$ compare with that of $\mathbf{A}^\intercal\mathbf{A}$?

A.5.4 Symmetric Eigenvalue Decomposition

If $\mathbf{A} \in \mathbb{R}^{n \times n}$ is symmetric, then it has an **EVD**, also sometimes called the **eigendecomposition**, given by

$$\mathbf{A} = \mathbf{U}\mathbf{\Lambda}\mathbf{U}^\intercal = \sum_{i=1}^{n} \lambda_i \mathbf{u}_i \mathbf{u}_i^\intercal,$$

where $\mathbf{U}$ is an $n \times n$ orthogonal matrix and $\mathbf{\Lambda} = \operatorname{diag}(\lambda_1, \lambda_2, \ldots, \lambda_n)$ is a (real) diagonal matrix. We refer to the λ_i values as the **eigenvalues** and the $\mathbf{u}_i$ vectors as the **eigenvectors**. These **eigenpairs** $(\lambda_i, \mathbf{u}_i)$ satisfy

$$\mathbf{A}\mathbf{u}_i = \lambda_i \mathbf{u}_i \quad \text{for all} \quad i \in [n].$$

If λ_i is distinct, then $\mathbf{u}_i$ is unique up to sign.

We can visualize the matrix eigendecomposition as in Fig. A.5. Here, again, the solid blocks in the diagonal matrix $\mathbf{\Lambda}$ denote nonzeros and the open blocks denote zeros.

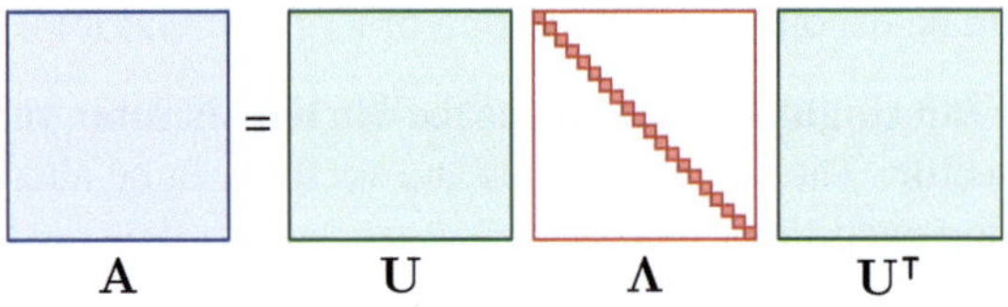

Figure A.5 Symmetric eigenvalue decomposition.

> The **EVD** of a symmetric matrix decomposes a symmetric matrix into its eigenvectors and eigenvalues.

A symmetric matrix $\mathbf{A}$ is **positive definite** if and only if all its eigenvalues are positive: $\lambda_i > 0$ for all $i \in [n]$. The matrix $\mathbf{A}$ is **positive semidefinite** if and only if all its eigenvalues are nonnegative: $\lambda_i \geq 0$ for all $i \in [n]$. Likewise, a **negative definite** matrix has all negative eigenvalues, a **negative semidefinite** matrix has all nonpositive eigenvalues. Symmetric matrices with both positive and negative eigenvalues are called **indefinite**.

Algorithms for computing the symmetric eigendecomposition must be iterative. However, the dominant costs depend only on the matrix dimensions, and the iterative parts have lower-order costs. The cost of computing a symmetric eigendecomposition is approximately $\frac{10}{3}n^3$. For more details, see Demmel (1997, section 5.3) or Trefethen and Bau (1997, part V).

Exercise A.37 (a) Prove that if a symmetric matrix $\mathbf{A}$ is positive definite then all its eigenvalues are positive. (b) Prove that if a symmetric matrix $\mathbf{A}$ is positive semidefinite then all its eigenvalues are nonnegative.

A.5.5 Detailed Costs of Computing the SVD

In this section we will derive the leading constants of the cost of direct methods for computing the SVD, which depends on several factors. We will assume that all singular values are computed. Let $\mathbf{A}$ be $m \times n$, and assume $m \leq n$ (otherwise we can apply the following analysis to $\mathbf{A}^\mathsf{T}$).

Square Case

In the case that $\mathbf{A}$ is square or nearly square (i.e., $n/m \leq 5/3$), we compute the SVD in a three-step process. This first step transforms $\mathbf{A}$ into a bidiagonal matrix (a matrix that is 0 except for the main diagonal and 1-diagonal either just above or just below the main diagonal) using a process known as Golub–Kahan bidiagonalization. The second step applies an iterative method to compute the SVD of the bidiagonal matrix. Finally, the third step back-transforms to obtain the singular vectors of the original matrix. That is, for input matrix $\mathbf{A}$, the first step computes $\mathbf{A} = \mathbf{U}_0\mathbf{B}\mathbf{V}_0^\mathsf{T}$ for bidiagonal $\mathbf{B}$, the second step computes $\mathbf{B} = \mathbf{U}_\mathbf{B}\mathbf{\Sigma}\mathbf{V}_\mathbf{B}^\mathsf{T}$, and the third step computes $\mathbf{U} = \mathbf{U}_0\mathbf{U}_\mathbf{B}$ and $\mathbf{V} = \mathbf{V}_\mathbf{B}\mathbf{V}_0$, so that

$$\mathbf{A} = \mathbf{U}_0\mathbf{B}\mathbf{V}_0^\mathsf{T} = \mathbf{U}_0\mathbf{U}_\mathbf{B}\mathbf{\Sigma}\mathbf{V}_\mathbf{B}^\mathsf{T}\mathbf{V}_0^\mathsf{T} = \mathbf{U}\mathbf{\Sigma}\mathbf{V}^\mathsf{T}.$$

If $m = n$, the first step costs $\frac{8}{3}n^3$, the second step is $\mathcal{O}(n^2)$, and the third step costs $2n^3$ for each set of singular vectors. Thus, the cost is $\frac{20}{3}n^3$ for the full SVD. When not all singular vectors are desired, the cost can be reduced. In particular, if only the first k left singular vectors are desired, then this cost can be reduced to $\frac{8}{3}n^3 + 2n^2k$.

Rectangular Case

In the case that $\mathbf{A}$ is rectangular (i.e., $n/m > 5/3$), we consider two different methods. The first is known as Lawson–Hanson–Chan bidiagonalization (Trefethen and Bau, 1997) and is a cheaper variation on the method described for square matrices: (1) compute a compact QR decomposition of $\mathbf{A}^\mathsf{T}$, (2) compute the SVD of the square triangular factor $\mathbf{R}$ using the method described above, and (3) transform the right singular vectors using the orthonormal factor $\mathbf{Q}$ if desired. If we have the compact QR decomposition $\mathbf{A}^\mathsf{T} = \mathbf{Q}\mathbf{R}$ and the SVD $\mathbf{R}^\mathsf{T} = \mathbf{U}\mathbf{\Sigma}\mathbf{V}_\mathbf{R}^\mathsf{T}$, then

$$\mathbf{A} = (\mathbf{U}\mathbf{\Sigma}\mathbf{V}_\mathbf{R}^\mathsf{T})\,\mathbf{Q}^\mathsf{T} = \mathbf{U}\mathbf{\Sigma}\,(\mathbf{Q}\mathbf{V}_\mathbf{R})^\mathsf{T} = \mathbf{U}\mathbf{\Sigma}\mathbf{V}^\mathsf{T}$$

is the SVD of $\mathbf{A}$. If $m \ll n$, then for the full SVD, the cost of the QR decomposition is $2m^2n + \mathcal{O}(m^3)$, the cost of SVD of $\mathbf{R}$ is $\mathcal{O}(m^3)$, and the cost of computing $\mathbf{V} = \mathbf{Q}\mathbf{V}_R$ is $4m^2n$. Again, when not all singular vectors are desired, the cost can be reduced. If only the first k left singular vectors are desired, then the cost is dominated by that of the QR: $2m^2n$.

The second method for the rectangular case relies on a connection between the SVD of a matrix and the eigendecomposition of its Gram matrices. If $\mathbf{A} = \mathbf{U}\mathbf{\Sigma}\mathbf{V}^\mathsf{T}$ is the compact

SVD of $\mathbf{A}$ (with square $\boldsymbol{\Sigma}$), then

$$\mathbf{A}\mathbf{A}^\top = \mathbf{U}\boldsymbol{\Sigma}\mathbf{V}^\top\mathbf{V}\boldsymbol{\Sigma}^\top\mathbf{U}^\top = \mathbf{U}\boldsymbol{\Sigma}^2\mathbf{U}^\top. \tag{A.15}$$

As $\mathbf{A}\mathbf{A}^\top$ is an $m \times m$ symmetric matrix, $\mathbf{U}$ is orthogonal, and $\boldsymbol{\Sigma}^2$ is diagonal, Eq. (A.15) is the symmetric eigendecomposition as described in Section A.5.4. That is, the eigenvectors of $\mathbf{A}\mathbf{A}^\top$ are the left singular vectors of $\mathbf{A}$, and the eigenvalues of $\mathbf{A}\mathbf{A}^\top$ are the squares of the singular values of $\mathbf{A}$. Thus, we can compute the singular values and left singular vectors $\mathbf{U}$ of $\mathbf{A}$ by forming $\mathbf{A}\mathbf{A}^\top$, computing its eigendecomposition, and then taking square roots of the computed eigenvalues and sorting them by their magnitudes. We can also recover the right singular vectors $\mathbf{V}$ by computing $\mathbf{V} = \boldsymbol{\Sigma}^{-1}\mathbf{U}^\top\mathbf{A}$, assuming $\mathbf{A}$ has full rank. The cost of this approach to computing the full SVD includes m^2n for computing $\mathbf{A}\mathbf{A}^\top$, $\mathcal{O}(m^3)$ for the symmetric eigendecomposition, and $2m^2n$ for computing $\mathbf{V}$. If only the first k left singular vectors are required, then the cost is dominated by m^2n from forming $\mathbf{A}\mathbf{A}^\top$.

As in the case of solving linear least squares, the choice of algorithm is problem-dependent. The method based on computing the Gram matrix is computationally cheaper when the matrix is rectangular (about half the cost when only left singular vectors are desired), but it is also less accurate. In particular, the Gram matrix method does not compute small singular values as accurately as the direct method when the matrix is ill conditioned. Thus, the Gram matrix method is preferred when the accuracy of small singular values is not required.

A.6 Solving Linear Equations

A **linear system** of equations in n variables, $x_1, \ldots, x_n$ can be expressed in matrix notation as

$$\mathbf{A}\mathbf{x} = \mathbf{b},$$

where $\mathbf{A}$ is an $n \times n$ square matrix and $\mathbf{b}$ is an n-vector. We can visualize this as in Fig. A.6

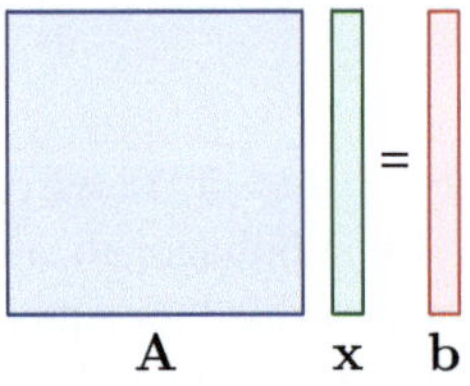

Figure A.6 Linear equation $\mathbf{A}\mathbf{x} = \mathbf{b}$.

If $\mathbf{A}$ is nonsingular, then there exists a unique solution $\mathbf{x} = \mathbf{A}^{-1}\mathbf{b}$. Otherwise, there may be no solution or infinitely many solutions.

We rarely compute the explicit inverse $\mathbf{A}^{-1}$ and instead focus on cheaper and more numerically stable approaches to computing the solution $\mathbf{x}$. A linear system can be solved in straightforward ways when $\mathbf{A}$ has special structure (such as being diagonal, orthogonal, or triangular). If $\mathbf{A}$ does not have special structure, then direct methods are based on first factoring $\mathbf{A}$ into a product of matrices that do have special structure and then solving a sequence of linear systems with each factor.

See Demmel (1997, chapter 2) and Trefethen and Bau (1997, part IV) for full treatments of methods for solving linear systems.

A.6.1 Solving Diagonal Linear Equations

If $\mathbf{A}$ is an $n \times n$ diagonal matrix, then all the equations in $\mathbf{Ax} = \mathbf{b}$ are independent and the ith equation is simply $a_{ii}x_i = b_i$. Therefore, the solution is given by $x_i = b_i/a_{ii}$ for each $1 \leq i \leq n$, which takes n operations to compute.

A.6.2 Solving Orthogonal Linear Equations

If $\mathbf{A}$ is an $n \times n$ orthogonal matrix, then we can multiply both sides of $\mathbf{Ax} = \mathbf{b}$ by $\mathbf{A}^\mathsf{T}$ and use the fact that $\mathbf{A}^\mathsf{T}\mathbf{A} = \mathbf{I}$ to see that $\mathbf{x} = \mathbf{A}^\mathsf{T}\mathbf{b}$. This has the cost of a matrix vector product, or $2n^2 + \mathcal{O}(n)$ computational operations.

A.6.3 Solving Triangular Linear Equations

Suppose $\mathbf{A}$ is an $n \times n$ lower triangular matrix, and we are solving $\mathbf{Ax} = \mathbf{b}$. The first equation is $a_{11}x_1 = b_1$, so we can compute $x_1 = b_1/a_{11}$ directly. The second equation is $a_{21}x_1 + a_{22}x_2 = b_2$, and we can substitute the value we just computed for x_1 to compute $x_2 = (b_2 - a_{21}x_1)/a_{22}$. Following in that way, for each x_i we can substitute previously computed values:

$$x_i = \frac{b_i - \sum_{j=1}^{i-1} a_{ij}x_j}{a_{ii}}.$$

This process is called **forward substitution**. For upper triangular matrices, we can compute the entries of $\mathbf{x}$ in the opposite order using a similar technique known as **back substitution**. Either way, it requires $n^2 + \mathcal{O}(n)$ computational operations.

A.6.4 Solving Symmetric Positive Definite Linear Equations

If $\mathbf{A}$ is an $n \times n$ symmetric positive definite matrix, we can use its **Cholesky decomposition** to solve $\mathbf{Ax} = \mathbf{b}$, using

$$\mathbf{Ax} = \mathbf{LL}^\mathsf{T}\mathbf{x} = \mathbf{Ly} = \mathbf{b},$$

where we define $\mathbf{y} = \mathbf{L}^\mathsf{T}\mathbf{x}$. Thus, we can solve $\mathbf{Ly} = \mathbf{b}$ for $\mathbf{y}$ using forward substitution (because $\mathbf{L}$ is lower triangular), and then we can solve $\mathbf{L}^\mathsf{T}\mathbf{x} = \mathbf{y}$ for $\mathbf{x}$ using backward substitution (because $\mathbf{L}^\mathsf{T}$ is upper triangular). The substitution process requires only $\mathcal{O}(n^2)$ flops, much less than the $\frac{1}{3}n^3$ cost of computing the Cholesky decomposition.

Multiple Right-Hand Sides As most of the work in solving a linear system is spent computing the decomposition of the coefficient matrix, we can solve multiple linear systems with the same coefficient matrix cheaply by reusing the decomposition. In other words, if we are solving

$$\mathbf{AX} = \mathbf{B}, \tag{A.16}$$

where $\mathbf{A}$ is an $n \times n$ symmetric positive definite matrix and $\mathbf{B}$ is an $n \times k$ matrix, then the solution matrix $\mathbf{X}$ of size $n \times k$ can be computed in $\frac{1}{3}n^3 + 2n^2k + \mathcal{O}(n^2 + nk)$ computational operations.

Iterative Methods for Sparse or Structured Systems When $\mathbf{A}$ is large and sparse or structured, then iterative methods may be more efficient than direct Cholesky decomposition, particularly when full accuracy is not required. For symmetric positive definite matrices, the **(preconditioned) conjugate gradient method** is commonly used. The algorithm requires only a means of applying the matrix to a vector, so the matrix need not be explicitly stored. The computation for each iteration is typically dominated by the matrix–vector product involving $\mathbf{A}$, which costs $\mathcal{O}(\mathrm{nnz}(\mathbf{A}))$ for sparse matrices, and the rate of convergence depends on the condition number of the matrix.

Remark A.25 (Implicit matrices in conjugate gradients) Iterative linear solvers such as the conjugate gradient method require only a means to apply the coefficient matrix to a vector. For sparse matrices this means that the cost per iteration is often dominated by the $\mathcal{O}(\mathrm{nnz}(\mathbf{A}))$ cost of a sparse matrix–vector product. It also means that the user does not need to provide an explicit representation of the matrix, as conjugate gradients requires only a method of applying it to a vector.

For well-conditioned problems, the conjugate gradient method can converge quickly; preconditioning can help to improve convergence for ill-conditioned problems. Preconditioning a linear system $\mathbf{A}\mathbf{x} = \mathbf{b}$ refers to employing a matrix $\mathbf{M}$ and solving the related system $\mathbf{M}^{-1}\mathbf{A}\mathbf{x} = \mathbf{M}^{-1}\mathbf{b}$ using the iterative method. Effective preconditioners are ones that balance the approximation $\mathbf{M} \approx \mathbf{A}$ with a cheap means of applying $\mathbf{M}^{-1}$. We want the matrix $\mathbf{M}^{-1}\mathbf{A}$ to have favorable convergence properties, but in each iteration we must apply $\mathbf{A}$ and then apply $\mathbf{M}^{-1}$, as shown in the following pseudocode for a preconditioned conjugate method.

Preconditioned Conjugate Gradient Method

$\mathbf{x}_0 = 0, \mathbf{r}_0 = \mathbf{b}, \mathbf{y}_0 = \mathbf{M}^{-1}\mathbf{b}, \mathbf{p}_1 = \mathbf{y}_0, \beta_0 = \mathbf{y}_0^\top \mathbf{r}_0$
repeat $k = 1, 2, \ldots$
  $\mathbf{z} = \mathbf{A}\mathbf{p}_k$ ▷ Application of coefficient matrix
  $\nu_k = \frac{\beta_{k-1}}{\mathbf{p}_k^\top \mathbf{z}}$
  $\mathbf{x}_k = \mathbf{x}_{k-1} + \nu_k \mathbf{p}_k$
  $\mathbf{r}_k = \mathbf{r}_{k-1} - \nu_k \mathbf{z}$
  $\mathbf{y}_k = \mathbf{M}^{-1}\mathbf{r}_k$ ▷ Application of preconditioner
  $\beta_k = \mathbf{y}_k^\top \mathbf{r}_k$
  $\mathbf{p}_{k+1} = \mathbf{y}_k + \frac{\beta_k}{\beta_{k-1}}\mathbf{p}_k$
until converged

Here, in each iteration, $\mathbf{x}$ is the approximate solution to the linear system, $\mathbf{r}$ is the residual vector, and $\mathbf{p}$ is the search direction. Each iteration requires one application of the coefficient matrix and one application of the preconditioner, which typically dominate the computational cost. To employ preconditioned conjugate gradients, the user must specify the right-hand side $\mathbf{b}$ and the explicit matrices $\mathbf{A}$ and $\mathbf{M}^{-1}$, or the user can specify methods for implicitly applying one or both of $\mathbf{A}$ and $\mathbf{M}^{-1}$. See Demmel (1997, chapter 6) or Trefethen and Bau (1997, lecture 35) for more details.

A.6.5 Solving Nonsymmetric Linear Equations

We will not generally need to solve general linear systems, but we touch upon this topic briefly for completeness.

Consider the solution of $\mathbf{A}\mathbf{x} = \mathbf{b}$ for a general $n \times n$ square matrix $\mathbf{A}$. In this case, we use the **LU decomposition**, $\mathbf{P}\mathbf{A} = \mathbf{L}\mathbf{U}$, where $\mathbf{P}$ is a permutation matrix, $\mathbf{L}$ is lower triangular, and $\mathbf{U}$ is upper triangular. Then we can solve for $\mathbf{x}$ in a way similar to the symmetric positive definite case, with forward and back substitution involving the triangular factors, but also permuting the final solution according to $\mathbf{P}^\top$. Forward and backward substitution requires $\mathcal{O}(n^2)$ flops, which is dominated by the $\frac{2}{3}n^3$ cost of computing the LU decomposition.

Iterative methods such as generalized minimum residual (GMRES) are also commonly used for solving general linear systems when $\mathbf{A}$ is large and sparse or structured. As with the conjugate gradient method, the cost of these method is dominated by matrix–vector products, and their rate of convergence depends on properties of the matrix and can be improved via preconditioning. See Demmel (1997, chapter 6) or Trefethen and Bau (1997, lecture 35) for more details.

Exercise A.38 Compare the costs of solving an $n \times n$ nonsymmetric linear system via the following three decompositions: LU, QR, and SVD. Be sure to include the cost of both computing the decomposition and using it to solve the system.

A.7 Linear Least Squares Problems

A linear least squares problem in n variables $x_1, \ldots, x_n$ has the form

$$\min_{\mathbf{x} \in \mathbb{R}^n} \|\mathbf{A}\mathbf{x} - \mathbf{b}\|_2 , \tag{A.17}$$

where $\mathbf{A}$ is an $m \times n$ matrix and $\mathbf{b} \in \mathbb{R}^m$. We refer to the quantity $\mathbf{A}\mathbf{x} - \mathbf{b}$ as the **residual** of the least squares problem. If $m > n$, we have more equations than variables and cannot achieve a 0 residual unless $\mathbf{b} \in \text{range}(\mathbf{A})$. Problems where $m > n$ are referred to as **overdetermined**. Such problems occur frequently in tensor decomposition and so are the main focus of our discussion. The overdetermined least squares problem can be visualized as in Fig. A.7.

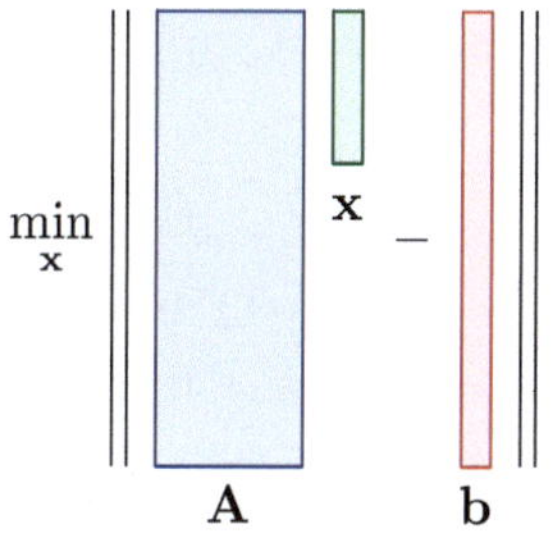

Figure A.7 Least squares problem: $\min_{\mathbf{x}} \|\mathbf{A}\mathbf{x} - \mathbf{b}\|_2$.

We discuss several different solution methods in the subsections that follow. In general, the solution to this problem is unique if $\mathbf{A}$ has full rank; otherwise, there are infinitely many minimizers.

See Demmel (1997, chapter 3) and Trefethen and Bau (1997, part II) for full treatments of methods for solving linear least squares problems.

Exercise A.39 Prove that if $\mathbf{A}$ is not full rank, then there are infinitely many solutions of Eq. (A.17).

A.7.1 Solving Least Squares via Normal Equations

The simplest method for minimizing a linear least squares problem is solving the associated **normal equations**, which form a linear system of equations. For Eq. (A.17), the normal equations are

$$\mathbf{A}^{\mathsf{T}}\mathbf{A}\mathbf{x} = \mathbf{A}^{\mathsf{T}}\mathbf{b}. \tag{A.18}$$

This expression can be derived by computing the gradient of the objective function and setting it equal to zero (see Example B.2). That is, an $\mathbf{x}$ that solves Eq. (A.18) is a stationary point of Eq. (A.17), and because the optimization problem is convex, it is a global minimizer (see Theorem B.24).

Exercise A.40 Prove that if $\mathbf{A}$ is full rank, $\mathbf{A}^\mathsf{T}\mathbf{A}$ is symmetric and positive definite.

The cost of the normal equations method includes the cost of forming the $n \times n$ coefficient matrix $\mathbf{A}^\mathsf{T}\mathbf{A}$ and the right-hand side $\mathbf{A}^\mathsf{T}\mathbf{b} \in \mathbb{R}^n$ and that of solving the linear system. When $\mathbf{A}$ is $m \times n$ with $m > n$, nearly all of the computation occurs in computing $\mathbf{A}^\mathsf{T}\mathbf{A}$, which costs $mn^2 + \mathcal{O}(n^2)$ flops. Forming $\mathbf{A}^\mathsf{T}\mathbf{b}$ requires $2mn + \mathcal{O}(n)$ flops. As explained in Section A.6.4, solving the $n \times n$ symmetric positive definite linear system costs $\frac{1}{3}n^3 + \mathcal{O}(n^2)$ flops.

A.7.2 Solving Least Squares via QR

The QR decomposition can be used to solve the linear least squares problem in Eq. (A.17) as follows. Let $\mathbf{A} = \bar{\mathbf{Q}}\bar{\mathbf{R}}$ be the (full) QR decomposition with the partitioning specified by Eq. (A.14) so that $\bar{\mathbf{Q}} = \begin{bmatrix}\mathbf{Q} & \mathbf{Q}^\perp\end{bmatrix}$ is an $m \times m$ orthogonal matrix and $\bar{\mathbf{R}} = \begin{bmatrix}\mathbf{R} \\ \mathbf{0}\end{bmatrix}$ is an $m \times n$ upper triangular matrix. Then

$$
\begin{aligned}
\|\mathbf{A}\mathbf{x} - \mathbf{b}\|_2^2 &= \left\|\bar{\mathbf{Q}}\bar{\mathbf{R}}\mathbf{x} - \mathbf{b}\right\|_2^2 \\
&= \left\|\bar{\mathbf{Q}}^\mathsf{T}(\bar{\mathbf{Q}}\bar{\mathbf{R}}\mathbf{x} - \mathbf{b})\right\|_2^2 \\
&= \left\|\bar{\mathbf{R}}\mathbf{x} - \bar{\mathbf{Q}}^\mathsf{T}\mathbf{b}\right\|_2^2 \\
&= \left\|\begin{bmatrix}\mathbf{R} \\ \mathbf{0}\end{bmatrix}\mathbf{x} - \begin{bmatrix}\mathbf{Q}^\mathsf{T} \\ (\mathbf{Q}^\perp)^\mathsf{T}\end{bmatrix}\mathbf{b}\right\|_2^2 \\
&= \left\|\begin{bmatrix}\mathbf{R}\mathbf{x} - \mathbf{Q}^\mathsf{T}\mathbf{b} \\ -(\mathbf{Q}^\perp)^\mathsf{T}\mathbf{b}\end{bmatrix}\right\|_2^2 \\
&= \left\|\mathbf{R}\mathbf{x} - \mathbf{Q}^\mathsf{T}\mathbf{b}\right\|_2^2 + \left\|(\mathbf{Q}^\perp)^\mathsf{T}\mathbf{b}\right\|_2^2.
\end{aligned}
$$

This formulation divides $\mathbf{b}$ into the component that is in the range of $\mathbf{A}$ and the component that is not. Because the second term is independent of $\mathbf{x}$, a minimizer of $\|\mathbf{R}\mathbf{x} - \mathbf{Q}^\mathsf{T}\mathbf{b}\|_2$ is a minimizer of $\|\mathbf{A}\mathbf{x} - \mathbf{b}\|_2$. Here $\mathbf{R}$ is an $n \times n$ upper triangular matrix. If $\mathbf{A}$ is full rank, then $\mathbf{R}$ is nonsingular, so we can solve the linear system $\mathbf{R}\mathbf{x} = \mathbf{Q}^\mathsf{T}\mathbf{b}$ for the minimizing $\mathbf{x}$ using back-substitution. In other words, the solution to Eq. (A.17) is

$$
\mathbf{x}^* = \mathbf{R}^{-1}\mathbf{Q}^\mathsf{T}\mathbf{b} \quad \text{with (minimal) residual} \quad \left\|\mathbf{A}\mathbf{x}^* - \mathbf{b}\right\|_2 = \left\|(\mathbf{Q}^\perp)^\mathsf{T}\mathbf{b}\right\|_2.
$$

We only need the economy QR decomposition to compute this solution. We discuss the case where $\mathbf{A}$ is not full rank in the next subsection.

The computational cost of the QR solution for least squares are the costs of

- computing the economy QR decomposition $\mathbf{A} = \mathbf{Q}\mathbf{R}$, $2mn^2 + \mathcal{O}(n^3)$;
- computing the right-hand side $\mathbf{Q}^\mathsf{T}\mathbf{b}$, $2mn + \mathcal{O}(n^2)$; and
- solving the triangular linear system, $n^2 + \mathcal{O}(n)$.

> The QR decomposition is a numerically stable method for solving least squares problems, and the cost for solving a problem with an $m \times n$ matrix $\mathbf{A}$ of full rank is $\mathcal{O}(mn^2)$ computational operations.

A.7.3 Solving Least Squares via SVD

We can pursue an analogous solution using the SVD. Assume we have the (full) SVD of $\mathbf{A}$, such that

$$\mathbf{A} = \bar{\mathbf{U}}\bar{\boldsymbol{\Sigma}}\bar{\mathbf{V}}^{\mathsf{T}} = \begin{bmatrix}\mathbf{U} & \mathbf{U}^{\perp}\end{bmatrix} \underbrace{\begin{bmatrix}\boldsymbol{\Sigma} & \mathbf{0} \\ \mathbf{0} & \mathbf{0}\end{bmatrix}}_{\bar{\boldsymbol{\Sigma}}} \begin{bmatrix}\mathbf{V} & \mathbf{V}^{\perp}\end{bmatrix}^{\mathsf{T}} = \mathbf{U}\boldsymbol{\Sigma}\mathbf{V}^{\mathsf{T}}.$$

If $r = \operatorname{rank}(\mathbf{A})$, then $\mathbf{U} \in \mathbb{R}^{m\times r}$, $\mathbf{V} \in \mathbb{R}^{n\times r}$ are orthonormal matrices, $\bar{\mathbf{U}}$ and $\bar{\mathbf{V}}$ are square orthogonal matrices, and $\boldsymbol{\Sigma} \in \mathbb{R}^{r\times r}$ is a nonsingular diagonal matrix.

Using reasoning analogous to the solution with QR, we can rewrite the least squares problem using the SVD, but here we need not assume that $\mathbf{A}$ is full rank. We have

$$\begin{aligned}\|\mathbf{A}\mathbf{x} - \mathbf{b}\|_2^2 &= \left\|\bar{\boldsymbol{\Sigma}}\bar{\mathbf{V}}^{\mathsf{T}}\mathbf{x} - \bar{\mathbf{U}}^{\mathsf{T}}\mathbf{b}\right\|_2^2 \\ &= \left\|\boldsymbol{\Sigma}\mathbf{V}^{\mathsf{T}}\mathbf{x} - \mathbf{U}^{\mathsf{T}}\mathbf{b}\right\|_2^2 + \left\|(\bar{\mathbf{U}}^{\perp})^{\mathsf{T}}\mathbf{b}\right\|_2^2.\end{aligned}$$

We can find $\mathbf{x}^*$ such that $\boldsymbol{\Sigma}\mathbf{V}^{\mathsf{T}}\mathbf{x} = \mathbf{U}^{\mathsf{T}}\mathbf{b}$, so the solution is thus

$$\mathbf{x}^* = \mathbf{V}\boldsymbol{\Sigma}^{-1}\mathbf{U}^{\mathsf{T}}\mathbf{b} \quad \text{with (minimal) residual} \quad \left\|\mathbf{A}\mathbf{x} - \mathbf{b}\right\|_2^2 = \left\|(\bar{\mathbf{U}}^{\perp})^{\mathsf{T}}\mathbf{b}\right\|_2^2,$$

which is the unique solution if $\mathbf{A}$ is full rank and the **minimum norm** solution if $\mathbf{A}$ is not full rank. The matrix $\mathbf{A}^{\dagger} \equiv \mathbf{V}\boldsymbol{\Sigma}^{-1}\mathbf{U}^{\mathsf{T}}$ is called the **Moore–Penrose pseudoinverse**. Like the matrix inverse for linear systems, the pseudoinverse lets us express the solution of linear least squares problems mathematically as $\mathbf{x} = \mathbf{A}^{\dagger}\mathbf{b}$, but is rarely computed explicitly.

Exercise A.41 Consider the least squares problem in Eq. (A.17) where $\mathbf{A}$ is not full rank, i.e., $r < n$. Prove that $\mathbf{x}^* = \mathbf{V}\boldsymbol{\Sigma}^{-1}\mathbf{U}^{\mathsf{T}}\mathbf{b}$ is the minimum norm solution. In other words, consider the set of all possible solutions,

$$\mathcal{S} = \left\{ \mathbf{y} \;\middle|\; \|\mathbf{A}\mathbf{y} - \mathbf{b}\|_2 = \|(\bar{\mathbf{U}}^{\perp})^{\mathsf{T}}\mathbf{b}\|_2^2 \right\},$$

and show $\|\mathbf{x}\|_2 \leq \|\mathbf{y}\|_2$ for all $\mathbf{y} \in \mathcal{S}$.

Exercise A.42 Using the SVD, show that the solution of the normal equations Eq. (A.18) is that same as the solution of Eq. (A.17) using the SVD:

$$\mathbf{x}^* = \mathbf{V}\boldsymbol{\Sigma}^{-1}\mathbf{U}^{\mathsf{T}}\mathbf{b}.$$

A.7.4 Choice of Least Squares Solver

The choice of method for solving linear least squares problems is problem-dependent. When $m > n$, the normal equations method is about half the cost of the QR decomposition method: the dominating costs are forming $\mathbf{A}^{\mathsf{T}}\mathbf{A}$ and computing the QR decomposition, which cost mn^2 and $2mn^2$ flops, respectively, assuming a single right-hand side. However, the normal equations method is less numerically stable than using QR. That is, when $\mathbf{A}$ is nearly low rank or ill conditioned, then the computed solution from the normal equations is more sensitive to the floating point errors that occur during the computation. For well-conditioned problems, both methods produce accurate solutions and the normal equations method is typically preferred because of its efficiency.

If the coefficient matrix $\mathbf{A}$ is low rank (or very ill conditioned), then other slightly more expensive methods should be used. In this case, the solution is not unique, and the computed solution can be very sensitive to floating point error. The SVD of $\mathbf{A}$ can be used to compute the minimum-norm solution among all minimizers, or the QR decomposition algorithm can be extended to use column pivoting to find the solution with the fewest nonzeros among all minimizers.

If $\mathbf{A}$ is large and sparse or structured, then iterative methods may be more efficient for solving the least squares problem. One approach is to solve the normal equations iteratively, using the preconditioned conjugate gradient method, for example. Because the preconditioned conjugate gradient method relies only on the matrix–vector product ($\mathbf{A}^\mathsf{T}\mathbf{A}\mathbf{y}$ in this case), the method can avoid forming $\mathbf{A}^\mathsf{T}\mathbf{A}$ explicitly and compute the result by first multiplying by $\mathbf{A}^\mathsf{T}$ and then multiplying by $\mathbf{A}$. Another approach is to apply an iterative method, such as LSQR (Paige and Saunders, 1982), which also involves matrix–vector products with $\mathbf{A}$ and $\mathbf{A}^\mathsf{T}$. LSQR is more robust than the conjugate gradient method applied to the normal equations for ill-conditioned problems.

A.7.5 Multiple Right-Hand-Sides Version of Least Squares

As in the case of linear systems, we can efficiently solve the matrix version of this problem, written as

$$\min_{\mathbf{X}\in\mathbb{R}^{n\times k}} \|\mathbf{A}\mathbf{X} - \mathbf{B}\|_F\,, \tag{A.19}$$

where $\mathbf{A} \in \mathbb{R}^{m\times n}$ and $\mathbf{B} \in \mathbb{R}^{n\times k}$. The normal equations for this problem are

$$\mathbf{A}^\mathsf{T}\mathbf{A}\mathbf{X} = \mathbf{A}^\mathsf{T}\mathbf{B},$$

which is a linear system with multiple right-hand sides that can be solved using a single Cholesky decomposition with total cost $mn^2 + 2mnk + \mathcal{O}(n^3)$ computational operations. Likewise, given the compact QR decomposition $\mathbf{A} = \mathbf{Q}\mathbf{R}$, we can solve

$$\mathbf{R}\mathbf{X} = \mathbf{Q}^\mathsf{T}\mathbf{B}$$

with a cost of $2mn^2 + 4mnk + \mathcal{O}(n^3)$ operations (by applying the implicit form of $\mathbf{Q}^\mathsf{T}$ to $\mathbf{B}$) or $4mn^2 + 2mnnk + \mathcal{O}(n^3)$ operations (by forming and multiplying $\mathbf{B}$ by an explicit $\mathbf{Q}^\mathsf{T}$). These costs imply that when k is small relative to n, the normal equations approach is about half the cost of using QR. When k is large relative to n, then the two methods have roughly the same arithmetic cost.

A.8 Low-Rank Matrix Approximation

Let $\mathbf{X} \in \mathbb{R}^{m\times n}$. The goal of **low-rank matrix approximation** is to find a matrix $\hat{\mathbf{X}} \approx \mathbf{X}$ with $\operatorname{rank}(\hat{\mathbf{X}}) = k \ll \min\{m, n\}$. We measure the approximation error using the norm of the residual matrix: $\|\mathbf{X} - \hat{\mathbf{X}}\|_F$. In some cases we seek the best possible approximation subject to a fixed rank k (Section A.8.1), and in other cases we seek the lowest-rank approximation that satisfies a given error threshold (Section A.8.2). We can visualize a rank-k factorization as Fig. A.8, where $\mathbf{A} \in \mathbb{R}^{m\times k}$ and $\mathbf{B} \in \mathbb{R}^{n\times k}$.

The matrix low-rank approximation problem is an optimization problem, but it is special in that it has a closed-form solution. In particular, we can solve this problem using the SVD as elucidated in one of the key theorems of linear algebra.

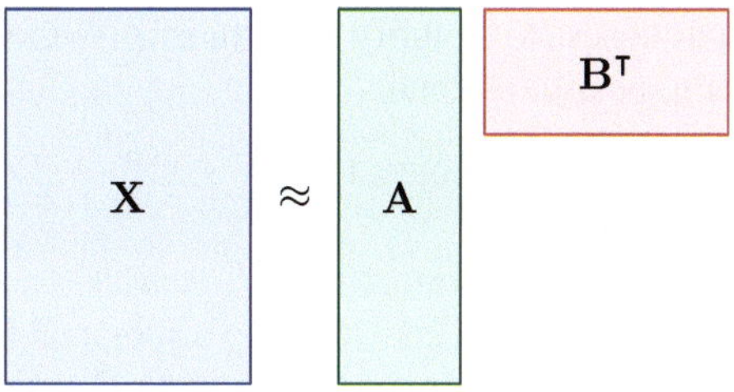

Figure A.8 Low-rank approximate matrix factorization.

Theorem A.26 (SVD and Matrix Approximation, Eckhart and Young, 1936) *Let* $\mathbf{X} \in \mathbb{R}^{m\times n}$ *with* $r = \operatorname{rank}(\mathbf{X})$. *Denote its compact SVD by* $\mathbf{X} = \mathbf{U}\boldsymbol{\Sigma}\mathbf{V}^\mathsf{T} = \sum_{i=1}^{r} \sigma_i \mathbf{u}_i \mathbf{v}_i^\mathsf{T}$. *For* $k < r$, *the best rank-*k *approximation to* $\mathbf{X}$ *is the rank-*k *truncated SVD,*

$$\mathbf{X}_k = \mathbf{U}_k\boldsymbol{\Sigma}_k\mathbf{V}_k^\mathsf{T} = \mathbf{U}_k\mathbf{U}_k^\mathsf{T}\mathbf{X} = \mathbf{X}\mathbf{V}_k\mathbf{V}_k^\mathsf{T} = \sum_{i=1}^{k} \sigma_i \mathbf{u}_i \mathbf{v}_i^\mathsf{T},$$

where $\mathbf{U}_k$ *and* $\mathbf{V}_k$ *are the first* k *columns of* $\mathbf{U}$ *and* $\mathbf{V}$, $\boldsymbol{\Sigma}_k = \operatorname{diag}(\sigma_1, \ldots, \sigma_k)$, *and*

$$\|\mathbf{X} - \mathbf{X}_k\|_F^2 = \sum_{i=k+1}^{r} \sigma_i^2.$$

The best rank-k approximation is achieved using the rank-k truncated SVD.

Computing the rank-k truncated SVD can be done using a direct method for the full SVD. Some computation can be saved when only the leading k singular values and vectors are desired, but direct methods still require $\mathcal{O}(\min\{mn^2, m^2n\})$ as described in Section A.5.3 (recall that "direct" methods for the SVD include a cheap iterative component). If $\mathbf{X}$ is large and sparse and $k \ll \min\{m, n\}$, then iterative methods, such as Golub–Kahan–Lanczos bidiagonalization, can be much more efficient than computing the full SVD (Golub and Kahan, 1965; Gu, 2015). The algorithms require applying $\mathbf{X}$ and $\mathbf{X}^\mathsf{T}$ to vectors or blocks of vectors at each iteration, and convergence depends on the singular values of $\mathbf{X}$.

Exercise A.43 Let $\mathbf{X} = \mathbf{U}\boldsymbol{\Sigma}\mathbf{V}^\mathsf{T}$ and $\mathbf{X}_k = \mathbf{U}_k\boldsymbol{\Sigma}_k\mathbf{V}_k^\mathsf{T}$. Prove

$$\|\mathbf{X} - \mathbf{X}_k\|_F^2 = \sum_{i=k+1}^{r} \sigma_i^2.$$

A.8.1 Specified Rank

Because a matrix of rank no more than k can be written as a product of two rectangular matrices, we can express this problem as

$$\min_{\mathbf{A},\mathbf{B}} \|\mathbf{X} - \mathbf{A}\mathbf{B}^\mathsf{T}\|_F \quad \text{subject to} \quad \mathbf{A} \in \mathbb{R}^{m\times k}, \mathbf{B} \in \mathbb{R}^{n\times k}. \tag{A.20}$$

The low-rank approximation problem Eq. (A.20) does not have a unique solution for the following reason. If we let $\mathbf{M}$ be any $k \times k$ nonsingular matrix besides the identity and define $\hat{\mathbf{A}} = \mathbf{A}\mathbf{M} \neq \mathbf{A}$ and $\hat{\mathbf{B}} = \mathbf{B}\mathbf{M}^{-\mathsf{T}} \neq \mathbf{B}$, then $\hat{\mathbf{A}}\hat{\mathbf{B}}^\mathsf{T} = \mathbf{A}\mathbf{B}^\mathsf{T}$. Hence, there are infinitely many equivalent solutions.

We can exploit this nonuniqueness to simplify the problem. Without loss of generality, we can restrict the first factor to be orthonormal:

$$\min_{\mathbf{W},\mathbf{B}} \|\mathbf{X} - \mathbf{W}\mathbf{B}^\mathsf{T}\|_F \quad \text{subject to} \quad \mathbf{W} \in \mathbb{O}^{m\times k}, \mathbf{B} \in \mathbb{R}^{n\times k}, \tag{A.21}$$

where $\mathbb{O}^{m\times k}$ denotes the set of orthonormal $m \times k$ matrices, also known as the Stiefel manifold. Equation (A.21) is sometimes known as the orthogonal Procrustes problem. The advantage of this restriction is that we can easily eliminate $\mathbf{B}$ from the problem. Given an orthonormal matrix $\mathbf{W}$, the optimal $\mathbf{B}$ is given by $\mathbf{B} = \mathbf{X}^\mathsf{T}\mathbf{W}$, as can be derived from the associated linear least squares problem. Thus, we can rewrite Eq. (A.20) as a minimization problem over a single variable matrix:

$$\min_{\mathbf{W}} \|(\mathbf{I} - \mathbf{W}\mathbf{W}^\mathsf{T})\mathbf{X}\|_F \quad \text{subject to} \quad \mathbf{W} \in \mathbb{O}^{m\times k}. \tag{A.22}$$

The restriction to orthonormal matrices is not enough to obtain uniqueness. If we let $\mathbf{Q}$ be any $k \times k$ orthogonal matrix besides the identity and define $\hat{\mathbf{W}} = \mathbf{W}\mathbf{Q} \neq \mathbf{W}$, then $\hat{\mathbf{W}}\hat{\mathbf{W}}^\mathsf{T}\mathbf{X} = \mathbf{W}\mathbf{W}^\mathsf{T}\mathbf{X}$. The intuition for this nonuniqueness is that for this problem, the optimal solution corresponds to a subspace rather than a particular matrix. The matrix we wish to compute is an orthonormal basis of the subspace, but it is not unique.

Given the formulation of Eq. (A.22), we can apply Theorem A.26 to solve the problem. With the kth truncated SVD $\mathbf{X}_k = \mathbf{U}_k\mathbf{\Sigma}_k\mathbf{V}_k^\mathsf{T}$, we let $\mathbf{W} = \mathbf{U}_k$, and we see that $\mathbf{U}_k^\mathsf{T}\mathbf{X} = \mathbf{\Sigma}_k\mathbf{V}_k^\mathsf{T}$ so that $\mathbf{W}\mathbf{W}^\mathsf{T}\mathbf{X} = \mathbf{X}_k$. Thus, the first k left singular vectors of $\mathbf{X}$ form a basis of the optimal subspace.

We can simplify the notation further by observing that $\mathbf{I}-\mathbf{W}\mathbf{W}^\mathsf{T}$ is an orthogonal projector and applying Propositions A.7 and A.8. We have that

$$\|(\mathbf{I} - \mathbf{W}\mathbf{W}^\mathsf{T})\mathbf{X}\|_F^2 = \|\mathbf{X}\|_F^2 - \|\mathbf{W}\mathbf{W}^\mathsf{T}\mathbf{X}\|_F^2 = \|\mathbf{X}\|_F^2 - \|\mathbf{W}^\mathsf{T}\mathbf{X}\|_F^2 .$$

Thus, a solution to Eq. (A.22) is also a solution of

$$\max_{\mathbf{W}} \|\mathbf{W}^\mathsf{T}\mathbf{X}\|_F \quad \text{subject to} \quad \mathbf{W} \in \mathbb{O}^{m\times k}. \tag{A.23}$$

The leading k left singular vectors of $\mathbf{X}$, or any k vectors that span that subspace, form the solution to Eq. (A.23).

A.8.2 Specified Error

Another formulation of the low-rank matrix approximation problem is to minimize the rank of the approximation subject to a relative error threshold. That is, given $\varepsilon > 0$, we can reformulate Eq. (A.22) to

$$\min k \quad \text{subject to} \quad \mathbf{W} \in \mathbb{O}^{m\times k} \text{ and } \|(\mathbf{I} - \mathbf{W}\mathbf{W}^\mathsf{T})\,\mathbf{X}\|_F \leq \varepsilon\,\|\mathbf{X}\|_F . \tag{A.24}$$

As Theorem A.26 applies to every value of k, we can solve this formulation by considering only the truncated SVDs. Thus, we choose the smallest k such that

$$\|\mathbf{X} - \mathbf{X}_k\|_F = \|(\mathbf{I} - \mathbf{U}_k\mathbf{U}_k^\mathsf{T})\,\mathbf{X}\|_F \leq \varepsilon\,\|\mathbf{X}\|_F ,$$

where $\mathbf{X}_k$ is the rank-k truncated SVD, or equivalently,

$$k = \min\left\{ \tilde{k} \in [n] \;\middle|\; \sum_{i=\tilde{k}+1}^{n} \sigma_i^2 \leq \varepsilon^2 \sum_{i=1}^{n} \sigma_i^2 \right\}, \tag{A.25}$$

where σ_i is the ith singular value of $\mathbf{X}$.

Evaluating Eq. (A.25) directly requires first computing all singular values, which costs $\mathcal{O}(\min\{mn^2, m^2n\})$. Iterative methods can be employed for this formulation, in which case the left-hand side of the inequality is approximated as

$$\sum_{i=\tilde{k}+1}^{n} \sigma_i^2 \approx \|\mathbf{X}\|_F^2 - \sum_{i=1}^{\tilde{k}} \hat{\sigma}_i^2,$$

where $\hat{\sigma}_i$ is the approximately computed ith singular value.

The rank-constrained maximization problem in Eq. (A.23) has the following error-constrained formulation:

$$\min k \quad \text{subject to} \quad \mathbf{W} \in \mathbb{O}^{m\times k} \text{ and } \|\mathbf{W}^\mathsf{T}\mathbf{X}\|_F \geq \sqrt{1-\varepsilon^2}\,\|\mathbf{X}\|_F\,. \tag{A.26}$$

Exercise A.44 Prove that Eq. (A.24) and Eq. (A.26) have equivalent solutions.

A.8.3 Extensions of Low-Rank Matrix Approximation

Other than by their dimensions, the variable matrices in Eq. (A.20) are not constrained. In many cases, imposing additional constraints on $\mathbf{A}$ and $\mathbf{B}$ can uncover more relevant structure in the data matrix. For example, nonnegative matrix factorization (Lee and Seung, 1999; Paatero and Tapper, 1994) imposes nonnegativity on $\mathbf{A}$ and $\mathbf{B}$, which can improve interpretability when $\mathbf{X}$ is nonnegative. Another complication occurs when some entries of $\mathbf{X}$ are unknown (i.e., there is missing data). In these cases, the SVD no longer provides a guaranteed solution, and more general optimization techniques must be employed.

A.9 Software Libraries for Linear Algebra

In general, we should rely on matrix software libraries rather than coding our own implementations because the software libraries have been tuned to achieve high performance.

The standard libraries are **BLAS** and **LAPACK**. BLAS stands for Basic Linear Algebra Subroutines and includes functions for performing operations on matrices and vectors. LAPACK stands for Linear Algebra PACKage and includes functions for computing matrix decompositions and solving the fundamental problems of numerical linear algebra, including linear systems, least squares problems, and eigenvalue and singular value problems. These two libraries have high-performance implementations on most architectures, including multicore CPUs, GPUs, and clusters of processors. Examples include OpenBLAS, BLIS, Intel's Math Kernel Library, NVIDIA's cuBLAS, and the AMD Core Math Library.

User-friendly interfaces have been provided so that code written in high-level languages, such as MATLAB and Python, can benefit from the high performance of BLAS and LAPACK implementations.

A.9.1 Representing Matrices in Memory

Matrices are stored in contiguous arrays in memory. The BLAS and LAPACK interfaces require that matrices are internally ordered either in **column-** or **row-major** order. Column-major order is the natural ordering as defined in Section 2.1, where each column is contiguous within the array. Row-major order is the reverse ordering, where each row is contiguous. See Fig. A.9 for an illustration. If a matrix is stored in column-major, its transpose is stored by the same array but in row-major. The interfaces are flexible enough to handle matrix transposes without any reordering, so it is rarely necessary to store a separate explicit matrix transpose in memory.

(a) Column-major. (b) Row-major.

Figure A.9 Comparing column- and row-major orderings.

In order to utilize the subroutines provided by BLAS and LAPACK, the input matrices must be in either column- or row-major. If they are not, the matrices need to be reordered in memory, which can be a slow process. This cost of reordering is often worth paying in order to benefit from the high performance of the libraries. A better alternative is to follow the convention of column- and row-major as much as possible, which is what MATLAB and Python do.

A.9.2 BLAS Hierarchy

BLAS functions are partitioned into three "levels" according to their computational complexity. Level-1 BLAS functions perform vector–vector operations, such as dot products and vector norms. For vectors of dimension n, the computational complexity is $\mathcal{O}(n)$. Level-2 BLAS functions perform matrix–vector operations, such as matrix–vector multiplication and vector outer product (whose output is a matrix). The complexity of BLAS-2 functions is $\mathcal{O}(n^2)$. Level-3 BLAS covers matrix–matrix operations, including matrix–matrix multiplication and triangular solve with multiple right-hand sides; these operations have complexity $\mathcal{O}(n^3)$. For more details on BLAS, see Blackford et al. (2002).

Not all levels of the BLAS achieve high performance. The ratio of computation to data of a particular operation is known as its arithmetic intensity. Level-1 BLAS performs $\mathcal{O}(n)$ computation on $\mathcal{O}(n)$ data, and Level-2 BLAS performs $\mathcal{O}(n^2)$ computation on $\mathcal{O}(n^2)$ data, so they both have an arithmetic intensity of $\mathcal{O}(1)$ (a constant). Level-3 BLAS performs $\mathcal{O}(n^3)$ computations on $\mathcal{O}(n^2)$ data, so those routines have an arithmetic intensity of $\mathcal{O}(n)$.

Higher arithmetic intensity allows for more reuse of data in cache, particularly as n gets large, which translates to higher performance. That is, while Level-3 BLAS involves more computation than Level-1 and Level-2 routines, they run faster. Matrix–matrix multiplication is one of the most efficient computations that can be performed on most computers, often running at over 90% of the peak speed of the processing units. Level-1 and Level-2 BLAS are bottlenecked by the speed of memory access, which is much slower than processor speeds.

Thus, when casting computation into calls to BLAS, using Level-3 routines is crucial in order to achieve high performance. LAPACK routines, which implement higher-level matrix computations, generally cast the bulk of their computations using the Level-3 BLAS. This is the key to the high performance of those routines. For more on LAPACK, see Anderson et al. (1999).

In some cases, multiple related calls to BLAS routines can be "batched" to improve performance. Often the operations involve the same computation with the same (often small) dimensions but on different data. Because of the regularity of the computation and independence across data access, low-level optimizations and multiple levels of parallelization can yield large performance improvements. The interface for this type of operation has been standardized into the Batched BLAS (Abdelfattah et al., 2021).

B Optimization Principles and Methods

The goal of this appendix is to give the reader a few basic tools to use and choose optimization methods for fitting tensor decompositions. We briefly survey matrix calculus so that we have tools for differentiation that we need for tensor decompositions. We also aim to familiarize the reader with basic optimization concepts (e.g., definition of a minimizer), the computations needed for calling an optimization (e.g., computing the gradient), and a quick guide to useful optimization methods available in various optimization software packages. We direct the reader to, e.g., Brookes (2020) for more on matrix calculus and to Nocedal and Wright (2006) and Wright and Recht (2022) for more on numerical optimization.

B.1 Multivariable Calculus

B.1.1 First Derivatives

We begin derivatives of real-valued multivariate functions, $f : \mathbb{R}^n \to \mathbb{R}$. The objective functions of optimization problems are scalar valued; that is, they take as input a vector of n variables and output a scalar value.

Definition B.1 (Gradient) For a continuously differentiable multivariate function,

$$f : \mathbb{R}^n \to \mathbb{R},$$

its first derivative is called the **gradient**, denoted $\nabla f : \mathbb{R}^n \to \mathbb{R}^n$ and defined as

$$\nabla f = \begin{bmatrix} \frac{\partial f}{\partial x_1} \\ \frac{\partial f}{\partial x_2} \\ \vdots \\ \frac{\partial f}{\partial x_n} \end{bmatrix},$$

where $\frac{\partial f}{\partial x_i}$ denotes the partial derivative of f with respect to x_i.

We use the convention that the gradient is oriented as a column vector, matching the size of the input vector. The next propositions can be verified by applying the definition directly.

Proposition B.2 (Gradient of Norm Squared) *If* $f(\mathbf{x}) = \frac{1}{2}\|\mathbf{x}\|_2^2$, *then* $\nabla f(\mathbf{x}) = \mathbf{x}$.

Proof. To verify, we compute the partial derivative to see that

$$[\nabla f(\mathbf{x})]_i = \frac{\partial f}{\partial x_i}(\mathbf{x}) = \frac{\partial}{\partial x_i}\left[\frac{1}{2}\sum_{j=1}^{n} x_j^2\right] = \frac{1}{2}\sum_{j=1}^{n}\frac{\partial}{\partial x_i}\left[x_j^2\right] = x_i$$

for all $i \in [n]$. □

Proposition B.3 (Gradient of Dot Product) *If* $f(\mathbf{x}) = \mathbf{y}^\mathsf{T}\mathbf{x}$ *for* $\mathbf{y} \in \mathbb{R}^n$, *then* $\nabla f(\mathbf{x}) = \mathbf{y}$.

Multivariate functions can be expressed as functions of multiple sets of variables, taking as input two or more vectors. For example, a function $f : \mathbb{R}^{m+n} \to \mathbb{R}$ may be expressed as $f(\mathbf{x}, \mathbf{y})$ with $\mathbf{x} \in \mathbb{R}^m$ and $\mathbf{y} \in \mathbb{R}^n$, which is equivalent to $f(\mathbf{v})$ with $\mathbf{v} \in \mathbb{R}^{m+n}$ a concatenation of $\mathbf{x}$ and $\mathbf{y}$. We can express the gradient of such a function by partitioning the entries conformally and using partial derivative notation.

Definition B.4 (Partial Gradient) The **partial gradient** of $f : \mathbb{R}^n \to \mathbb{R}$ is the gradient of f with respect to a subset $\mathbf{x} \in \mathbb{R}^p$ of the inputs and denoted as $\frac{\partial f}{\partial \mathbf{x}} \in \mathbb{R}^p$.

For a function $f : \mathbb{R}^{p+q} \to \mathbb{R}$ expressed as $f(\mathbf{x}, \mathbf{y})$ with $\mathbf{x} \in \mathbb{R}^p$ and $\mathbf{y} \in \mathbb{R}^q$, the (full) gradient is the assembly of the partial gradients:

$$\nabla f(\mathbf{v}) = \begin{bmatrix} \frac{\partial f}{\partial \mathbf{x}}(\mathbf{v}) \\ \frac{\partial f}{\partial \mathbf{y}}(\mathbf{v}) \end{bmatrix} \quad \text{with} \quad \mathbf{v} = \begin{bmatrix} \mathbf{x} \\ \mathbf{y} \end{bmatrix}.$$

We may also write the gradient using partial gradient notation so that the differentiation variable is clear. For instance, in the example we just gave, we could write $\frac{\partial f}{\partial \mathbf{v}}(\mathbf{v})$ instead of $\nabla f(\mathbf{v})$.

Next, we consider derivatives of vector-valued multivariate functions, $\mathbf{f} : \mathbb{R}^n \to \mathbb{R}^m$. We think of this as m real-valued functions organized into a column vector.

Definition B.5 (Jacobian) For a continuously differentiable vector-valued multivariate function,

$$\mathbf{f}(\mathbf{x}) = \begin{bmatrix} f_1(\mathbf{x}) \\ \vdots \\ f_m(\mathbf{x}) \end{bmatrix} \in \mathbb{R}^m,$$

its first derivative is called the **Jacobian**, denoted $D\mathbf{f} : \mathbb{R}^n \to \mathbb{R}^{m \times n}$ and defined as

$$D\mathbf{f} = \begin{bmatrix} (\nabla f_1)^\mathsf{T} \\ (\nabla f_2)^\mathsf{T} \\ \vdots \\ (\nabla f_m)^\mathsf{T} \end{bmatrix} = \begin{bmatrix} \frac{\partial f_1}{\partial x_1} & \frac{\partial f_1}{\partial x_2} & \cdots & \frac{\partial f_1}{\partial x_n} \\ \frac{\partial f_2}{\partial x_1} & \frac{\partial f_2}{\partial x_2} & \cdots & \frac{\partial f_2}{\partial x_n} \\ \vdots & \vdots & \ddots & \vdots \\ \frac{\partial f_m}{\partial x_1} & \frac{\partial f_m}{\partial x_2} & \cdots & \frac{\partial f_m}{\partial x_n} \end{bmatrix},$$

where $\frac{\partial f_i}{\partial x_j}$ denotes the partial derivative of f_i with respect to x_j.

For a scalar-valued function ($m = 1$), the gradient is the *transpose* of the Jacobian.

Remark B.6 (Jacobian of a scalar-valued function) For a function $f : \mathbb{R}^n \to \mathbb{R}$, we have $Df \in \mathbb{R}^{1\times n}$ (a row vector) and $\nabla f \in \mathbb{R}^n$ (a column vector). The gradient is the *transpose* of the Jacobian; in other words, $\nabla f = [Df]^\intercal$.

The following examples can be verified by direct application of the definition.

Example B.1 (Jacobian) The Jacobian of

$$\mathbf{f}(x,y) = \begin{bmatrix} x+y \\ x^2 y \\ y^3 \end{bmatrix} \quad \text{is} \quad D\mathbf{f}(x,y) = \begin{bmatrix} 1 & 1 \\ 2xy & x^2 \\ 0 & 3y^2 \end{bmatrix}.$$

Proposition B.7 (Jacobian of a Linear Function) *If* $\mathbf{f}(\mathbf{x}) = \mathbf{A}\mathbf{x} - \mathbf{b}$ *for* $\mathbf{A} \in \mathbb{R}^{m\times n}$ *and* $\mathbf{b} \in \mathbb{R}^m$, *then* $D\mathbf{f}(\mathbf{x}) = \mathbf{A}$.

Proof. To verify, we compute the partial derivative of an arbitrary component function with respect to an arbitrary element:

$$[D\mathbf{f}(\mathbf{x})]_{ij} = \frac{\partial f_i}{\partial x_j}(\mathbf{x}) = \frac{\partial}{\partial x_j}\left[\sum_{k=1}^{n} a_{ik}x_k - b_i\right] = \sum_{k=1}^{n} \frac{\partial}{\partial x_j}[a_{ik}x_k] = a_{ij}. \qquad \square$$

Just as we have partial gradients, we can also have partial Jacobians.

Definition B.8 (Partial Jacobian) The **partial Jacobian** of $\mathbf{f} : \mathbb{R}^n \to \mathbb{R}^m$ is the Jacobian of $\mathbf{f}$ with respect to a subset $\mathbf{x} \in \mathbb{R}^p$ of the inputs and denoted as $\frac{d\mathbf{f}}{d\mathbf{x}} \in \mathbb{R}^{m\times p}$.

For a function $\mathbf{f} : \mathbb{R}^{p+q} \to \mathbb{R}^m$ expressed as $\mathbf{f}(\mathbf{x}, \mathbf{y})$ with $\mathbf{x} \in \mathbb{R}^p$ and $\mathbf{y} \in \mathbb{R}^q$, we have

$$D\mathbf{f} = \begin{bmatrix} \frac{d\mathbf{f}}{d\mathbf{x}} & \frac{d\mathbf{f}}{d\mathbf{y}} \end{bmatrix},$$

where $\frac{d\mathbf{f}}{d\mathbf{x}}$ is $m \times p$ and $\frac{d\mathbf{f}}{d\mathbf{y}}$ is $m \times q$ and the partial Jacobians.

Properties of derivatives generalize nicely from single-variable functions to multivariate functions. For example, it is straightforward to verify that gradients and Jacobians are linear.

Proposition B.9 (Linearity of the Jacobian) *Let* $\mathbf{h}(\mathbf{x}) = \alpha\mathbf{f}(\mathbf{x}) + \beta\mathbf{g}(\mathbf{x})$, *where* $\alpha, \beta \in \mathbb{R}$ *and* $\mathbf{f}, \mathbf{g} : \mathbb{R}^n \to \mathbb{R}^m$. *Then*

$$D\mathbf{h}(\mathbf{x}) = \alpha D\mathbf{f}(\mathbf{x}) + \beta D\mathbf{g}(\mathbf{x}).$$

The product rule for single-variable functions generalizes to the dot product rule.

Proposition B.10 (Dot Product Rule) *Let* $\mathbf{f}, \mathbf{g} : \mathbb{R}^n \to \mathbb{R}^m$. *Then*

$$\nabla\big(\mathbf{f}(\mathbf{x})^\mathsf{T}\mathbf{g}(\mathbf{x})\big) = D\mathbf{f}(\mathbf{x})^\mathsf{T}\mathbf{g}(\mathbf{x}) + D\mathbf{g}(\mathbf{x})^\mathsf{T}\mathbf{f}(\mathbf{x}).$$

Proof. Define $h(\mathbf{x}) = \mathbf{f}(\mathbf{x})^\mathsf{T}\mathbf{g}(\mathbf{x}) = \sum_{i=1}^m f_i(\mathbf{x})g_i(\mathbf{x})$. Then

$$\begin{aligned}\frac{\partial h}{\partial x_j}(\mathbf{x}) &= \sum_{i=1}^m \frac{\partial}{\partial x_j}[f_i(\mathbf{x})g_i(\mathbf{x})] \\ &= \sum_{i=1}^m \frac{\partial f_i}{\partial x_j}(\mathbf{x})g_i(\mathbf{x}) + \frac{\partial g_i}{\partial x_j}(\mathbf{x})f_i(\mathbf{x}) \\ &= \sum_{i=1}^m [D\mathbf{f}(\mathbf{x})]_{ij}\, g_i(\mathbf{x}) + [D\mathbf{g}(\mathbf{x})]_{ij}\, f_i(\mathbf{x}).\end{aligned}$$

□

Exercise B.1 Let $f(\mathbf{x}) = \mathbf{x}^\mathsf{T}\mathbf{A}\mathbf{x}$. Use Proposition B.10 to show $\nabla f(\mathbf{x}) = (\mathbf{A} + \mathbf{A}^\mathsf{T})\mathbf{x}$.

The chain rule also generalizes; see, e.g., Colley (2006, theorem 5.3) for details of the proof.

Theorem B.11 (Multivariate Chain Rule) *Let* $\mathbf{f} = \mathbf{g} \circ \mathbf{h}$, *where* $\mathbf{f} : \mathbb{R}^m \to \mathbb{R}^p$, $\mathbf{g} : \mathbb{R}^n \to \mathbb{R}^p$, *and* $\mathbf{h} : \mathbb{R}^m \to \mathbb{R}^n$. *Then*

$$D\mathbf{f}(\mathbf{x}) = \underbrace{D\mathbf{g}\big(\mathbf{h}(\mathbf{x})\big)}_{p\times n}\,\underbrace{D\mathbf{h}(\mathbf{x})}_{n\times m} \in \mathbb{R}^{p\times m}.$$

If $p = 1$, *this specializes to*

$$\nabla f(\mathbf{x}) = \underbrace{[D\mathbf{h}(\mathbf{x})]^\mathsf{T}}_{m\times n}\,\underbrace{\nabla g\big(\mathbf{h}(\mathbf{x})\big)}_{n\times 1} \in \mathbb{R}^{m\times 1}.$$

Example B.2 (Linear Least Squares Gradient) If $f(\mathbf{x}) = \frac{1}{2}\|\mathbf{A}\mathbf{x} - \mathbf{b}\|_2^2$ for $\mathbf{A} \in \mathbb{R}^{m\times n}$, $\mathbf{b} \in \mathbb{R}^m$, then

$$\nabla f(\mathbf{x}) = \mathbf{A}^\mathsf{T}\mathbf{A}\mathbf{x} - \mathbf{A}^\mathsf{T}\mathbf{b}.$$

To verify, observe that $f = g \circ \mathbf{h}$ with $g(\mathbf{y}) = \frac{1}{2}\|\mathbf{y}\|_2^2$ and $\mathbf{h}(\mathbf{x}) = \mathbf{A}\mathbf{x} - \mathbf{b}$, and apply the multivariate chain rule and results of Propositions B.2 and B.7. Setting the gradient equal to zero yields the normal equations associated with minimizing the linear least squares function f (see Section A.7.1).

B.1.2 Second Derivatives

The second derivative of a multivariate function is the first derivative of the gradient. For a scalar-valued multivariate function $f : \mathbb{R}^n \to \mathbb{R}$, its gradient $\nabla f : \mathbb{R}^n \to \mathbb{R}^n$ is vector-valued, so the derivative of the gradient is a square Jacobian matrix called the Hessian.

Definition B.12 (Hessian) The **Hessian** of a twice continuously differentiable $f : \mathbb{R}^n \to \mathbb{R}$ is denoted as $\nabla^2 f : \mathbb{R}^n \to \mathbb{R}^{n\times n}$ and defined as the symmetric matrix

$$\nabla^2 f = \begin{bmatrix} \frac{\partial^2 f}{\partial x_1 \partial x_1} & \frac{\partial^2 f}{\partial x_1 \partial x_2} & \cdots & \frac{\partial^2 f}{\partial x_1 \partial x_n} \\ \frac{\partial^2 f}{\partial x_2 \partial x_1} & \frac{\partial^2 f}{\partial x_2 \partial x_2} & \cdots & \frac{\partial^2 f}{\partial x_2 \partial x_n} \\ \vdots & \vdots & \ddots & \vdots \\ \frac{\partial^2 f}{\partial x_1 \partial x_n} & \frac{\partial^2 f}{\partial x_n \partial x_2} & \cdots & \frac{\partial^2 f}{\partial x_n \partial x_n} \end{bmatrix},$$

where $\frac{\partial^2 f}{\partial x_i \partial x_j}$ denotes the partial derivative of $\frac{\partial f}{\partial x_j}$ with respect to x_i and has the property of symmetry: $\frac{\partial^2 f}{\partial x_i \partial x_j} = \frac{\partial^2 f}{\partial x_j \partial x_i}$.

Example B.3 (Linear Least Squares Hessian) If $f(\mathbf{x}) = \frac{1}{2}\|\mathbf{A}\mathbf{x} - \mathbf{b}\|_2^2$ for $\mathbf{A} \in \mathbb{R}^{m\times n}$, $\mathbf{b}\in\mathbb{R}^m$, then $\nabla^2 f(\mathbf{x}) = \mathbf{A}^\mathsf{T}\mathbf{A}$.

Second derivatives of vector-valued multivariate functions and other higher derivatives can also be defined (they are tensors!) but we will not need them in this book.

Exercise B.2 Compute the gradient and Hessian of the function

$$f(x, y) = c(y - x^2)^2 + (1 - x)^2.$$

B.1.3 Matrix Calculus

An important class of functions for our purposes are scalar-valued functions of a matrix, such as $f(\mathbf{A}) = \frac{1}{2}\|\mathbf{A}\|_F^2$. For the rules of differentiation discussed above to apply, functions need to be described in terms of vector inputs and outputs. Thus, a function $f : \mathbb{R}^{m\times n} \to \mathbb{R}$ is better approached as a function $f : \mathbb{R}^{mn} \to \mathbb{R}$. In other words, a function $f(\mathbf{A})$ must be differentiated as a function of $f(\operatorname{vec}(\mathbf{A}))$, in which case $\nabla f : \mathbb{R}^{mn} \to \mathbb{R}^{mn}$. However, we can express its gradient colloquially in matrix notation (i.e., $\nabla f : \mathbb{R}^{m\times n} \to \mathbb{R}^{m\times n}$) by reshaping the vector $\frac{\partial f}{\partial \operatorname{vec}(\mathbf{A})}$ into a matrix $\frac{\partial f}{\partial \mathbf{A}}$ with the same dimensions as $\mathbf{A}$. In other words,

$$\frac{\partial f}{\partial \operatorname{vec}(\mathbf{A})} = \operatorname{vec}\left(\frac{\partial f}{\partial \mathbf{A}}\right) \quad \Leftrightarrow \quad \frac{\partial f}{\partial \mathbf{A}} = \operatorname{reshape}\left(\frac{\partial f}{\partial \operatorname{vec}(\mathbf{A})}, m \times n\right).$$

Either expression is acceptable as ∇f and equivalent so long as the context is understood.

Example B.4 (Gradient of Frobenius Norm Squared) Let $f(\mathbf{A}) = \frac{1}{2}\|\mathbf{A}\|_F^2$ for $\mathbf{A} \in \mathbb{R}^{m\times n}$. To compute the gradient of f with respect to $\mathbf{A}$, we can consider f as a function from $\mathbb{R}^{mn}$ to $\mathbb{R}$: $f(\operatorname{vec}(\mathbf{A})) = \frac{1}{2}\|\mathbf{A}\|_F^2 = \frac{1}{2}\|\operatorname{vec}(\mathbf{A})\|_2^2$. From Proposition B.2, we know $\frac{\partial f}{\partial \operatorname{vec}(\mathbf{A})}(\operatorname{vec}(\mathbf{A})) = \operatorname{vec}(\mathbf{A})$. Equivalently, we can write

$$\nabla f(\mathbf{A}) = \mathbf{A}.$$

To express a function of a matrix $\mathbf{A}$ in terms of $\operatorname{vec}(\mathbf{A})$, the following property of the Kronecker product from Eq. (A.11e) is often key:

$$\operatorname{vec}(\mathbf{B}\mathbf{A}\mathbf{C}^\mathsf{T}) = (\mathbf{C} \otimes \mathbf{B}) \operatorname{vec}(\mathbf{A}).$$

Example B.5 (Using Kronecker Product Identity to Compute Gradient) Let $f(\mathbf{A}) = \mathbf{x}^\mathsf{T}\mathbf{A}\mathbf{y}$, where $\mathbf{A} \in \mathbb{R}^{m\times n}$, $\mathbf{x} \in \mathbb{R}^m$, and $\mathbf{y} \in \mathbb{R}^n$. To compute the gradient of f in terms of $\mathbf{A}$, applying Eq. (A.11e) yields

$$f\big(\text{vec}(\mathbf{A})\big) = \text{vec}(\mathbf{x}^\mathsf{T}\mathbf{A}\mathbf{y}) = (\mathbf{y}^\mathsf{T} \otimes \mathbf{x}^\mathsf{T})\,\text{vec}(\mathbf{A}).$$

If we consider f as a function on $\text{vec}(\mathbf{A}) \in \mathbb{R}^{mn}$, then by Proposition B.3,

$$\nabla f(\text{vec}(\mathbf{A})) = \mathbf{y} \otimes \mathbf{x}.$$

Finally, to convert to matrix notation, we use the fact that $\text{vec}(\mathbf{x}\mathbf{y}^\mathsf{T}) = \mathbf{y} \otimes \mathbf{x}$ to write

$$\nabla f(\mathbf{A}) = \mathbf{x}\mathbf{y}^\mathsf{T} \in \mathbb{R}^{m\times n}.$$

In the case of matrix-valued functions of matrices, such as $\mathbf{F}(\mathbf{B}) = \mathbf{X} - \mathbf{A}\mathbf{B}^\mathsf{T}$, both the input and the output are matrices. In this case, we still vectorize both input and output in order to express the first derivative (the Jacobian). Unlike the gradient, the Jacobian does not have the same size as the input.

Recall from Definition A.10 that the $m\times n$ perfect shuffle permutation matrix $\mathbf{P} \in \mathbb{R}^{mn\times mn}$ is such that for any $m \times n$ matrix $\mathbf{A}$,

$$\mathbf{P}\,\text{vec}(\mathbf{A}) = \text{vec}(\mathbf{A}^\mathsf{T}) \quad \text{and} \quad \text{vec}(\mathbf{A}) = \mathbf{P}^\mathsf{T}\,\text{vec}(\mathbf{A}^\mathsf{T}).$$

Example B.6 (Perfect Shuffle in Gradient Computation) Let $\mathbf{F} : \mathbb{R}^{n\times r} \to \mathbb{R}^{m\times n}$ be defined as $\mathbf{F}(\mathbf{B}) = \mathbf{X} - \mathbf{A}\mathbf{B}^\mathsf{T}$ with $\mathbf{X} \in \mathbb{R}^{m\times n}$, $\mathbf{A} \in \mathbb{R}^{m\times r}$, and $\mathbf{B} \in \mathbb{R}^{n\times r}$. Let $\mathbf{f} \equiv \text{vec}(\mathbf{F}) : \mathbb{R}^{nr} \to \mathbb{R}^{mn}$ be the vectorized function with respect to a vectorized input so that by Definition A.10 and Eq. (A.11e),

$$\begin{aligned}\mathbf{f}(\text{vec}(\mathbf{B})) &= \text{vec}(\mathbf{X} - \mathbf{A}\mathbf{B}^\mathsf{T})\\ &= \text{vec}(\mathbf{X}) - \mathbf{P}^\mathsf{T}\,\text{vec}(\mathbf{B}\mathbf{A}^\mathsf{T})\\ &= \text{vec}(\mathbf{X}) - \mathbf{P}^\mathsf{T}(\mathbf{A} \otimes \mathbf{I}_n)\,\text{vec}(\mathbf{B}),\end{aligned}$$

where $\mathbf{P}$ is the $m \times n$ perfect shuffle permutation matrix. Applying Proposition B.7 yields

$$D\mathbf{f}(\text{vec}(\mathbf{B})) = -\mathbf{P}^\mathsf{T}(\mathbf{A} \otimes \mathbf{I}_n) \in \mathbb{R}^{mn\times nr}.$$

We now combine matrix calculus and the chain rule to derive the gradient for the matrix low-rank approximation problem (see Section A.8). While the unconstrained version of the problem is solved via the SVD, we derive the gradient here because it is useful when the variable matrices are constrained and because it is a simpler version of the tensor CP problem addressed in Part III. First, consider the low-rank matrix approximation objective function as an optimization problem in only one factor matrix.

Example B.7 (Gradient for Low-Rank Matrix Approximation) Let $f(\mathbf{B}) = \frac{1}{2}\|\mathbf{X} - \mathbf{A}\mathbf{B}^\mathsf{T}\|_F^2$, where $\mathbf{X} \in \mathbb{R}^{m\times n}$, $\mathbf{A} \in \mathbb{R}^{m\times r}$, and $\mathbf{B} \in \mathbb{R}^{n\times r}$. So that we can apply the chain rule, we rewrite $f = g \circ \mathbf{h}$ with

$$g(\mathbf{v}) = \frac{1}{2}\|\mathbf{v}\|_2^2 \quad \text{and} \quad \mathbf{h}(\text{vec}(\mathbf{B})) = \text{vec}(\mathbf{X} - \mathbf{A}\mathbf{B}^\mathsf{T}).$$

Applying the chain rule (Theorem B.11) and the result of Example B.6, where $\mathbf{P}$ is the $m \times n$ perfect shuffle permutation matrix, we have

$$\begin{aligned}\nabla f(\text{vec}(\mathbf{B})) &= \left[-\mathbf{P}^\mathsf{T}(\mathbf{A} \otimes \mathbf{I}_n)\right]^\mathsf{T} \text{vec}(\mathbf{X} - \mathbf{A}\mathbf{B}^\mathsf{T}) \\ &= (\mathbf{A}^\mathsf{T} \otimes \mathbf{I}_n)\mathbf{P}\,\text{vec}(\mathbf{A}\mathbf{B}^\mathsf{T} - \mathbf{X}) \\ &= (\mathbf{A}^\mathsf{T} \otimes \mathbf{I}_n)\,\text{vec}(\mathbf{B}\mathbf{A}^\mathsf{T} - \mathbf{X}^\mathsf{T}) \\ &= \text{vec}((\mathbf{B}\mathbf{A}^\mathsf{T} - \mathbf{X}^\mathsf{T})\mathbf{A}).\end{aligned}$$

Finally, reshaping to matrix form, we have

$$\nabla f(\mathbf{B}) = (\mathbf{A}\mathbf{B}^\mathsf{T} - \mathbf{X})^\mathsf{T}\mathbf{A}.$$

Exercise B.3 Let $f(\mathbf{A}) = \frac{1}{2}\|\mathbf{X} - \mathbf{A}\mathbf{B}^\mathsf{T}\|_F^2$ and prove that $\nabla f(\mathbf{A}) = (\mathbf{A}\mathbf{B}^\mathsf{T} - \mathbf{X})\mathbf{B}$.

More generally, we can consider the low-rank matrix approximation problem's objective function as a function of both factor matrices:

$$f(\mathbf{A}, \mathbf{B}) = \frac{1}{2}\|\mathbf{X} - \mathbf{A}\mathbf{B}^\mathsf{T}\|_F^2.$$

In this case, we can denote the gradient of f to have the same shape as the inputs (a pair of matrices) using partial derivative notation (see Definition B.4). From Example B.7 and Exercise B.3, we have

$$\nabla f\left(\begin{bmatrix}\text{vec}(\mathbf{A}) \\ \text{vec}(\mathbf{B})\end{bmatrix}\right) = \begin{bmatrix}\frac{\partial f}{\partial\,\text{vec}(\mathbf{A})} \\ \frac{\partial f}{\partial\,\text{vec}(\mathbf{B})}\end{bmatrix} = \begin{bmatrix}\text{vec}\left((\mathbf{A}\mathbf{B}^\mathsf{T} - \mathbf{X})\mathbf{B}\right) \\ \text{vec}\left((\mathbf{A}\mathbf{B}^\mathsf{T} - \mathbf{X})^\mathsf{T}\mathbf{A}\right)\end{bmatrix}.$$

We summarize the key results in Table B.1. For more information on matrix calculus, see, e.g., Brookes (2020).

B.2 Principles of Unconstrained Optimization

A **minimization** problem has the form

$$\min_{\mathbf{x}\in\mathbb{R}^n} f(\mathbf{x}), \quad \text{where} \quad f : \mathbb{R}^n \to \mathbb{R}. \tag{B.1}$$

The function f measures, for example, how well a model that depends on the input $\mathbf{x}$ fits some observed data, with $f(\mathbf{x}) = 0$ indicating a perfect match. We usually want to find the vector $\mathbf{x}$ that best fits the data and yields the smallest value for $f(\mathbf{x})$. If f is twice continuously differentiable, then we have a variety of methods to solve this problem, including gradient descent (Section B.3.2), Newton's method (Section B.3.3), quasi-Newton methods (Sections B.3.4 and B.3.5), and block coordinate descent (also known as alternating optimization, see Section B.3.7).

Table B.1 First derivatives for vector- and matrix-valued functions

Function	Derivative
$f(\mathbf{x}) = \frac{1}{2}\|\mathbf{x}\|_2^2$	$\nabla f(\mathbf{x}) = \mathbf{x}$
$f(\mathbf{x}) = \mathbf{y}^\mathsf{T}\mathbf{x}$	$\nabla f(\mathbf{x}) = \mathbf{y}$
$f(\mathbf{x}) = \mathbf{x}^\mathsf{T}\mathbf{A}\mathbf{x}$	$\nabla f(\mathbf{x}) = (\mathbf{A} + \mathbf{A}^\mathsf{T})\mathbf{x}$
$\mathbf{f}(\mathbf{x}) = \mathbf{A}\mathbf{x}$	$D\mathbf{f}(\mathbf{x}) = \mathbf{A}$
$f(\mathbf{x}) = \frac{1}{2}\|\mathbf{A}\mathbf{x} - \mathbf{b}\|_2^2$	$\nabla f(\mathbf{x}) = \mathbf{A}^\mathsf{T}\mathbf{A}\mathbf{x} - \mathbf{A}^\mathsf{T}\mathbf{b}$
$f(\mathbf{A}) = \mathbf{x}^\mathsf{T}\mathbf{A}\mathbf{y}$	$\nabla f(\mathbf{A}) = \mathbf{x}\mathbf{y}^\mathsf{T}$
$f(\mathbf{A}) = \frac{1}{2}\|\mathbf{A}\|_F^2$	$\nabla f(\mathbf{A}) = \mathbf{A}$
$f(\mathbf{A},\mathbf{B}) = \frac{1}{2}\|\mathbf{X} - \mathbf{A}\mathbf{B}^\mathsf{T}\|_F^2$	$\frac{\partial f}{\partial \mathbf{A}}(\mathbf{A},\mathbf{B}) = (\mathbf{A}\mathbf{B}^\mathsf{T} - \mathbf{X})\mathbf{B}$
$f(\mathbf{A},\mathbf{B}) = \frac{1}{2}\|\mathbf{X} - \mathbf{A}\mathbf{B}^\mathsf{T}\|_F^2$	$\frac{\partial f}{\partial \mathbf{B}}(\mathbf{A},\mathbf{B}) = (\mathbf{A}\mathbf{B}^\mathsf{T} - \mathbf{X})^\mathsf{T}\mathbf{A}$

Most of our problems are a special case of minimization known as **nonlinear least squares** and are of the form

$$\min_{\mathbf{x}\in\mathbb{R}^n} f(\mathbf{x}) \equiv \frac{1}{2}\sum_{i=1}^{m}\Big(\phi_i(\mathbf{x})\Big)^2, \quad \text{where} \quad \phi_i : \mathbb{R}^n \to \mathbb{R} \text{ for all } i \in [m]. \tag{B.2}$$

These problems have structure that allows for additional optimization approaches. For example, we have already discussed the case where each ϕ_i is linear in Section A.7. The Gauss–Newton method for nonlinear least squares is presented in Section B.3.6.

We say that these formulations are **unconstrained** because $\mathbf{x}$ can be any vector in $\mathbb{R}^n$. We discussed constrained optimization in Section B.5.

We focus here on minimization, but the definitions can be "flipped" for maximization problems, i.e., maximizing $f(\mathbf{x})$ is the same as minimizing $-f(\mathbf{x})$.

Before getting into the details of solution methods, we want to cover the basics. Our goal is to find the point $\mathbf{x}^*$ that yields the smallest value of f.

Definition B.13 (Global Minimizer) We say a point $\mathbf{x}_* \in \mathbb{R}^n$ is a **global minimizer** of $f : \mathbb{R}^n \to \mathbb{R}$ if $f(\mathbf{x}_*) \leq f(\mathbf{x})$ for all $\mathbf{x} \in \mathbb{R}^n$.

Generally, we can only guarantee that the point is a minimizer in a local region, rather than globally.

Definition B.14 (Local Minimizer) We say a point $\mathbf{x}_* \in \mathbb{R}^n$ is a **local minimizer** of $f : \mathbb{R}^n \to \mathbb{R}$ if there exists $\varepsilon > 0$ such that $f(\mathbf{x}_*) \leq f(\mathbf{x})$ for all $\mathbf{x} \in \mathbb{R}^n$ such that $\|\mathbf{x}-\mathbf{x}_*\|_2 < \varepsilon$.

Every global minimizer is also a local minimizer.

Example B.8 (Local and Global Minimizers and Maximizers) In Fig. B.1, we graph the function

$$f(\mathbf{x}) = 10(x_1^3 + x_2^5)e^{-(x_1^2+x_2^2)}. \tag{B.3}$$

We can see visually that it has a global minimizer, a local minimizer, a global maximizer, and a local maximizer. We give more rigorous ways to verify this below.

In the discussion that follows, we describe how to find these minimizers mathematically.

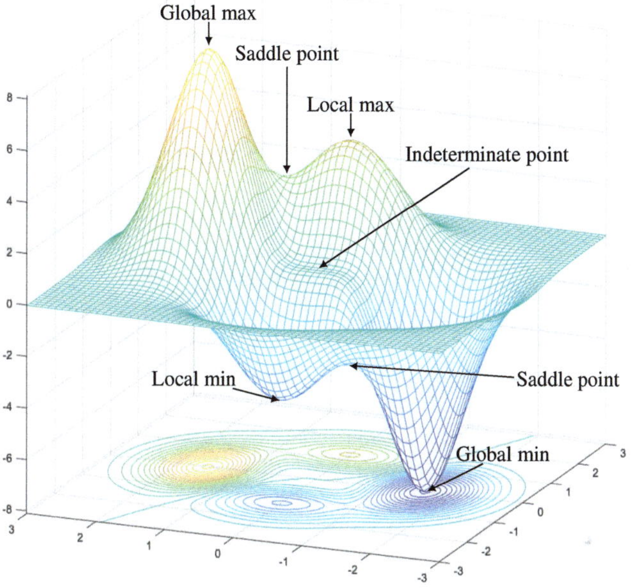

Figure B.1 The function $10(x_1^3 + x_2^5)e^{-(x_1^2+x_2^2)}$ has exactly seven stationary points.

B.2.1 Gradients and Stationary Points

For minimizing continuously differentiable functions, we make extensive use of the first derivative, or gradient (Definition B.1), as it indicates how the function is changing locally.

Example B.9 (Gradient of a Two-Dimensional Function) The gradient for $f(\mathbf{x}) = 10(x_1^3 + x_2^5)e^{-(x_1^2+x_2^2)}$, as shown in Fig. B.1, is given by

$$\nabla f(\mathbf{x}) = 10e^{-(x_1^2+x_2^2)} \begin{bmatrix} 3x_1^2 - 2x_1(x_1^3 + x_2^5) \\ 5x_2^4 - 2x_2(x_1^3 + x_2^5) \end{bmatrix}.$$

The negative gradient is important because it indicates which way is "downhill." Any direction that is within 90° of the negative gradient also points downhill.

Definition B.15 (Descent Direction) For a continuously differentiable function $f : \mathbb{R}^n \to \mathbb{R}$, we say $\mathbf{d}$ is a **descent direction** at the point $\mathbf{x}$ if $\langle \mathbf{d}, \nabla f(\mathbf{x}) \rangle < 0$.

For any continuously differentiable function, moving along a descent direction yields decrease, at least for a sufficiently short step. In other words, if $\nabla f(\mathbf{x}) \neq 0$ and $\mathbf{d}$ is such that $\langle \mathbf{d}, \nabla f(\mathbf{x}) \rangle < 0$, then there exists $\alpha > 0$ such that $f(\mathbf{x} + \alpha\mathbf{d}) < f(\mathbf{x})$. More formally, we have Proposition B.16.

Proposition B.16 (Descent Step Existence) *Let $f : \mathbb{R}^n \to \mathbb{R}$ be a continuously differentiable function. Let $\mathbf{x} \in \mathbb{R}^n$ be given and $\mathbf{d}$ be a descent direction at $\mathbf{x}$. Then there exists $\bar{\alpha} > 0$ such that*

$$f(\mathbf{x} + \alpha\mathbf{d}) < f(\mathbf{x}) \quad \textit{for all} \quad \alpha \in (0, \bar{\alpha}).$$

The rate of initial decrease is fastest in the direction of the negative gradient, and for this reason it is often called the direction of *steepest descent*.

Definition B.17 (Direction of Steepest Descent) For a continuously differentiable function $f : \mathbb{R}^n \to \mathbb{R}$, $\mathbf{d} = -\nabla f(\mathbf{x})$ is the direction of **steepest descent** at the point $\mathbf{x}$.

Example B.10 (Decrease in Steepest Descent Direction) Let $f(\mathbf{x})$ be as defined in Example B.9. Let $\mathbf{x}_0 = [-1\ 1]^\mathsf{T}$. Then its gradient is $\nabla f(\mathbf{x}_0) = [4.0601\ 6.7668]^\mathsf{T}$. We plot $f(\mathbf{x}_0 + \alpha\mathbf{d})$, where $\mathbf{d} = -\nabla f(\mathbf{x}_0)$ is the direction of steepest descent. The point at $\alpha = 0$ corresponds to $f(\mathbf{x}_0)$. As α increases, the function value initially decreases at the rate predicted by the linear model. As α increases further, the linear model becomes increasingly inaccurate, and the function value eventually increases again. So long as f is continuously differentiable, we are guaranteed that the function decreases for small enough values of α.

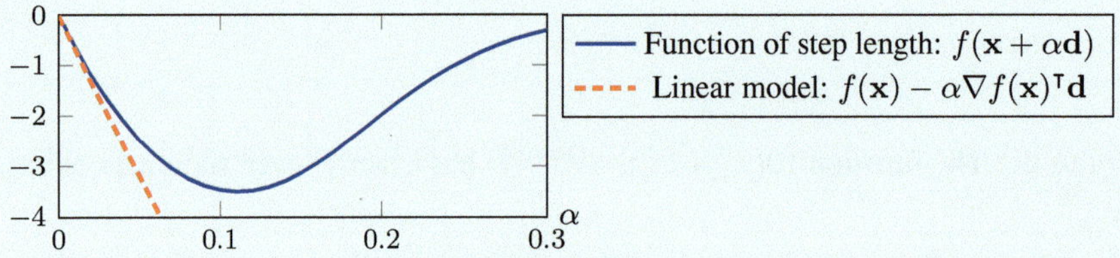

Exercise B.4 Let $f(\mathbf{x})$ be defined as in Example B.9. Let $\mathbf{x}_0 = [-1\ 1]^\mathsf{T}$. (a) Prove that $\mathbf{d} = [-1\ -1]$ is a descent direction. (b) Plot $f(\mathbf{x}_0 + \alpha\mathbf{d})$ for values of α ranging from 0 to 1. (c) What is its behavior?

Whenever the gradient is nonzero, we can *always* move along a descent direction to find a point with a lower function value. Therefore, any minimizer must have a zero gradient.

Definition B.18 (Stationary Point) A point $\mathbf{x}$ is a **stationary point** of f if $\nabla f(\mathbf{x}) = \mathbf{0}$.

Theorem B.19 (First-Order Necessary Conditions for Unconstrained Local Minimizer) *If f is continuously differentiable and $\mathbf{x}_*$ is a local minimizer of f, then $\nabla f(\mathbf{x}_*) = \mathbf{0}$.*

The converse is not true. A point can have a zero gradient and not be a minimizer. Finding a point with a zero gradient is a necessary but not sufficient condition for finding a minimizer.

Example B.11 (Necessary Condition is Not Sufficient for Local Minimizer) There are seven points that have zero gradient in Example B.9. They can be calculated by finding all the roots of $\nabla f(\mathbf{x}) = 0$, which we can reduce to finding all roots of this polynomial system:

$$3x_1^2 - 2x_1(x_1^3 + x_2^5) = 0$$
$$5x_2^4 - 2x_2(x_1^3 + x_2^5) = 0.$$

This function is simple enough that we can use techniques of abstract algebra to find all the roots (e.g., using the Symbolic Toolbox of MATLAB). There are seven real-valued roots, as follows:

$$(0,0), \quad (0, \pm\sqrt{5/2}), \quad (\pm\sqrt{3/2}, 0), \quad (1.0316, 0.8522), \quad (-1.0316, -0.8522).$$

The last two roots are of the form $(\frac{5}{3}\alpha^3, \alpha)$, where α is one of the two real roots of $z^6 + \frac{27}{125}z^2 - \frac{27}{50} = 0$. We see that only some of the stationary points correspond to minima.

B.2.2 Hessians and Optimality Conditions

For a function that is twice continuously differentiable, its Hessian is the matrix of second derivatives and describes the local curvature of the function. This can *sometimes* be useful in determining whether or not a stationary point is a local minimum. It cannot differentiate between a local or global minimum.

Example B.12 (Hessian of a Two-Dimensional Function) The Hessian of the function f from Example B.9 is

$$\nabla^2 f(\mathbf{x}) = 20e^{-x_1^2-x_2^2} \begin{bmatrix} (2x_1^2-1)(x_1^3-3x_1+x_2^5) & 2x_1^3-3x_1+2x_2^5-5x_2^3 \\ 2x_1^3-3x_1+2x_2^5-5x_2^3 & 2x_1^3x_2^2-x_1^3+2x_2^7-11x_2^5+10x_2^3 \end{bmatrix}.$$

Though this can be computed by hand, we recommend using the Symbolic Toolbox of MATLAB for this example.

Any minimizer must have a Hessian that is at least positive semidefinite. This means that if we move in any direction from the current point, the function locally stays flat or goes uphill.

Theorem B.20 (Second-Order Necessary Conditions for Unconstrained Local Minimizer) *If f is twice continuously differentiable and $\mathbf{x}_*$ is a local minimizer of f, then $\nabla^2 f(\mathbf{x}_*)$ is positive semidefinite.*

Unfortunately, having a positive semidefinite Hessian does not ensure that the point is a local minimizer. It might be, but it might not be as we see in the next example.

Example B.13 (Necessary Condition is Not Sufficient for Local Minimizer) Let $f(\mathbf{x})$ as in Example B.12 and consider the point $\mathbf{x} = [0 \ 0]^\intercal$. Its Hessian is the all-0 matrix: $\nabla^2 f(\mathbf{x}) = \left[\begin{smallmatrix} 0 & 0 \\ 0 & 0 \end{smallmatrix}\right]$. Although $\nabla^2 f(\mathbf{x})$ is positive semidefinite, the point $\mathbf{x}$ is not a local minimizer, as we can see in Fig. B.1. Some directions lead uphill and others downhill.

The only way we can *guarantee* that a stationary point $\mathbf{x}$ is a local minimizer is if all its Hessian's eigenvalues are positive. This means that every direction away from $\mathbf{x}$ points uphill.

Theorem B.21 (Second-Order Sufficient Conditions for Unconstrained Local Minimizer) *If f is twice continuously differentiable and $\nabla^2 f(\mathbf{x}_*)$ is positive definite, then $\mathbf{x}_*$ is a strict local minimizer.*

Conversely, if $\nabla^2 f(\mathbf{x})$ is negative definite, then $\mathbf{x}$ is a local maximum. If $\nabla^2 f(\mathbf{x})$ has both positive and negative eigenvalues, then locally there are some directions that go uphill and some that go downhill, which means that $\mathbf{x}$ is a **saddle point**. If the Hessian has 0 eigenvalues, the stationary point cannot be conclusively classified as a minimizer or maximizer.

Exercise B.5 Consider the stationary points of $f(\mathbf{x})$ as in Example B.11. (a) Compute the eigenvalues of the Hessian for each stationary point. (b) Which stationary points can be definitively characterized using their Hessian information? (c) Which cannot?

B.2.3 Convex Functions

Convex functions are a class of function that have only a single minimizer, which is thus the global minimizer.

Definition B.22 (Convex Function) We say a function $f : \mathbb{R}^n \to \mathbb{R}$ is **convex** if

$$f(\lambda\mathbf{x} + (1-\lambda)\mathbf{y}) \leq \lambda f(\mathbf{x}) + (1-\lambda)f(\mathbf{y})$$

for all $\lambda \in (0, 1)$ and any points $\mathbf{x}, \mathbf{y}$ in the domain of f. If f is continuously differentiable, an equivalent condition is that

$$f(\mathbf{x}) \geq f(\mathbf{y}) + \nabla f(\mathbf{y})^{\mathsf{T}}(\mathbf{x} - \mathbf{y})$$

for all $\mathbf{x}, \mathbf{y}$ in the domain of f.

Proposition B.23 (Convex Function Characterization) *If f is twice continuously differentiable and $\nabla^2 f$ is positive semidefinite on the domain of f, then f is convex.*

Example B.14 (Linear Least Squares is Convex) The function $f(\mathbf{x}) = \frac{1}{2}\|\mathbf{A}\mathbf{x} - \mathbf{b}\|_2^2$ is convex. From Example B.3, $\nabla^2 f(\mathbf{x}) = \mathbf{A}^{\mathsf{T}}\mathbf{A}$, which is positive semidefinite from Exercise A.16.

Exercise B.6 Let $f : \mathbb{R}^2 \to \mathbb{R}$ be defined as

$$f(\mathbf{x}) = 9x_1^2 + x_1x_2 + 6x_2^2.$$

(a) Derive the gradient and Hessian of f. (b) Prove that f is convex.

Theorem B.24 (Sufficient Conditions for Unconstrained Global Minimizer) *Any local minimizer of a convex function $f : \mathbb{R}^n \to \mathbb{R}$ is a global minimizer. If f is differentiable, then any stationary point is a global minimizer.*

Most of the functions we encounter in tensor decompositions are nonconvex. This means we may have no guarantee that a stationary point is a local or global minimizer. Convex functions are still important in tensor decomposition, however, because certain tensor methods have convex optimization *subproblems* (see Chapter 11).

B.3 Unconstrained Optimization Methods

It is unusual that we can find stationary points directly. Hence, most optimization methods are iterative, meaning they generate a sequence of iterates, $\{\mathbf{x}_k\}$, that should ideally converge to a local minimizer. We usually require downhill progress at each step:

$$f(\mathbf{x}_{k+1}) < f(\mathbf{x}_k).$$

For the optimization methods we consider, the iterates are of the form

$$\mathbf{x}_{k+1} = \mathbf{x}_k + \alpha_k \mathbf{d}_k,$$

where $\alpha_k > 0$ is called the **step length** and $\mathbf{d}_k$ is called the **search direction**. Different methods make different choices for $\mathbf{d}_k$.

B.3.1 Using Optimization Methods

Before we get into specific methods, we talk about some general notions. For the methods we discuss, there is never any guarantee of finding a global minimizer unless the function is convex. At best, we can hope to find a local minimizer. In general, if we require downhill progress at each step, we have a good chance of finding a minimizer. But any of the methods we discuss can get "stuck" at a stationary point that is not a local minimizer. When this happens, the iterates have usually converged to a saddle point, which looks like a local minimizer in some directions. The main technique to combat these potential pitfalls is to rerun the optimization method with different starting points.

Choosing the Step Length

Whatever method we use, we have to choose a step length, $\alpha_k > 0$, at each iteration. Ideally, α_k is such that the function value at the new iterate is less than that of the prior iterate:

$$f(\mathbf{x}_{k+1}) < f(\mathbf{x}_k), \quad \text{where} \quad \mathbf{x}_{k+1} = \mathbf{x}_k + \alpha_k \mathbf{d}_k. \tag{B.4}$$

If the step length α_k is fixed across iterates, it may be referred to as the **learning rate**. The difficulty with using a fixed learning rate is longer steps may not yield decrease in the objective value but small steps mean it takes a long time to converge.

Assuming $\mathbf{d}_k$ is a descent direction, there always exists $\alpha_k > 0$ that yields decrease per Proposition B.16. We could find this point by solving a one-dimensional optimization problem:

$$\alpha_k = \arg\min_{\alpha > 0} f(\mathbf{x}_k + \alpha \mathbf{d}_k).$$

However, solving this problem exactly can be expensive. Instead, we determine α_k via a **line search** such as the following:

Backtracking Line Search

Choose initial $\alpha_k > 0, \tau > 0$
while $f(\mathbf{x}_k + \alpha_k \mathbf{d}_k) \geq f(\mathbf{x}_k) + \tau\alpha\nabla f(\mathbf{x}_k)^{\mathsf{T}}\mathbf{d}_k$ **do**
  $\alpha_k \leftarrow \alpha_k/2$
end while

The backtracking linear search starts with an initial guess and decreases the step until it satisfies a **sufficient decrease** condition, i.e., obtains a decrease in the objective value that is as good as a fraction (τ) of the decrease predicted by a linear model. See, e.g., Nocedal and Wright (2006) for further details.

Convergence

We focus on line-search based methods that yield a sequence of optimization iterates that satisfy

$$f(\mathbf{x}_{k+1}) \leq f(\mathbf{x}_k) \quad \text{for all} \quad k = 1, 2, \ldots.$$

If f is unbounded below, then it is possible that $f(\mathbf{x}_k) \to -\infty$. Otherwise, if f is bounded below, $\{f(\mathbf{x}_k)\}$ is a decreasing sequence that is bounded below and therefore must converge to some f_*. By itself, this is not enough to ensure convergence to a stationary point. However, an appropriate line search ensures that an optimization method is **globally convergent**, meaning that it converges to a stationary point from any initial iterate $\mathbf{x}_0$. Global convergence should not be confused with convergence to a global minimum, which is not guaranteed by any of the methods we discuss here.

Rate of Convergence

When comparing methods, a natural question is how fast the method converges. Suppose that an optimization method produces a sequence of iterates $\{\,\mathbf{x}_k\,\}$ that converges to $\mathbf{x}_*$. We say that the method is **linearly convergent** if

$$\|\mathbf{x}_{k+1} - \mathbf{x}_*\|_2 \leq \beta\|\mathbf{x}_k - \mathbf{x}_*\|_2 \tag{B.5}$$

for some constant $0 < \beta < 1$ and all k sufficiently large. We say that the method is **superlinearly convergent** if

$$\lim_{k\to\infty} \frac{\|\mathbf{x}_{k+1} - \mathbf{x}_*\|_2}{\|\mathbf{x}_k - \mathbf{x}_*\|_2} = 0.$$

We say that the method is **quadratically convergent** if

$$\|\mathbf{x}_{k+1} - \mathbf{x}_*\|_2 \leq \beta\|\mathbf{x}_k - \mathbf{x}_*\|_2^2 \tag{B.6}$$

for some constant $\beta > 0$ and all k sufficiently large. These rates of convergence are asymptotic, so they only "kick in" when the iterates get sufficiently close to the minimizer.

Methods with a higher rate of convergence are not always faster because the cost per iteration is higher. There is some balance to be achieved between the cost per iteration and the progress per iteration, and this may be problem-specific.

B.3.2 Gradient Descent

Gradient descent, also known as steepest descent, chooses its search direction as

$$\mathbf{d}_k = -\nabla f(\mathbf{x}_k). \tag{B.7}$$

Using this direction, the local linear approximation of the function given by the first-order Taylor polynomial is

$$f(\mathbf{x}_k + \mathbf{d}_k) \approx f(\mathbf{x}_k) + \nabla f(\mathbf{x}_k)^\mathsf{T}(\mathbf{d}_k).$$

Minimizing the linear approximation suggests setting $\mathbf{d}_k$ to be the negative of the gradient (Eq. (B.7)) and α_k to be as large as possible. However, since the linear approximation is only accurate near $\mathbf{x}_k$, we should take a small step. A common approach is to use a line search to ensure decrease in the function value. With exact line search, gradient descent is linearly convergent.

The main advantage of steepest descent is its simplicity, requiring the computation of only the gradient. However, the linear convergence can be prohibitively slow. The preferred alternative to gradient descent is L-BFGS, discussed in Section B.3.5, which has the same asymptotic computational complexity, memory complexity, and rate of convergence while generally performing better in practice.

There are many versions of gradient descent that use a fixed learning rate, which may be appropriate with sufficient information about the properties of function; see, e.g., Wu et al. (2018). Related methods include Nesterov's method (Nesterov, 2012), stochastic gradient descent (SGD) (Robbins and Monro, 1951), and variants of SGD such as ADAM (Kingma and Ba, 2015).

B.3.3 Newton's Method

Newton's method incorporates curvature information into the search direction by using the Hessian. It sets the search direction to be the solution to **Newton's equation**:

$$\nabla^2 f(\mathbf{x}_k)\mathbf{d}_k = -\nabla f(\mathbf{x}_k). \tag{B.8}$$

The premise is that we can estimate the function using a second-order Taylor polynomial of the form

$$f(\mathbf{x}_k + \mathbf{d}_k) \approx f(\mathbf{x}_k) + \nabla f(\mathbf{x}_k)^\mathsf{T}\mathbf{d}_k + \frac{1}{2}\mathbf{d}_k^\mathsf{T}\nabla^2 f(\mathbf{x}_k)\mathbf{d}_k.$$

This quadratic approximation is minimized by the $\mathbf{d}_k$ that solves Eq. (B.8). As with the linear approximation used by gradient descent, the approximation is accurate only locally, so we require a line search or other method to determine an appropriate step.

Additionally, if the Hessian is not positive definite, the solution to Newton's equation is not guaranteed to be a descent direction. One method to obtain a descent direction is to add a multiple of the identity to the Hessian, solving

$$\left(\nabla^2 f(\mathbf{x}_k) + \lambda_k \mathbf{I}\right)\mathbf{d}_k = -\nabla f(\mathbf{x}_k)$$

for λ_k chosen large enough to make the coefficient matrix positive definite, but determining an appropriate λ_k can be expensive.

The fast convergence of Newton's method is only observed once the iterates are near enough to the solution. If the iterates are sufficiently close to a local minimizer with a positive definite Hessian, then taking a pure Newton step ensures a quadratic rate of convergence to the minimizer. In other words, no line search is needed (just set $\alpha = 1$) and the convergence rate is very fast. Further away, a line search is required.

The main disadvantage of Newton's method is the expense of computing the Hessian and solving the linear system to compute the search direction, requiring $\mathcal{O}(n^3)$ operations per iteration in general. One option is to use truncated Newton (Dembo and Steihaug, 1983), whereby the Newton equation is solved approximately using an iterative method such as preconditioned conjugate gradients, which can greatly reduce the cost by taking advantage of problem-specific structure in the Hessian, such as sparsity.

B.3.4 BFGS Optimization Method

Since the Hessian in Newton's method is expensive to compute and may not even be positive definite, an alternative is to use an approximation. The class of methods known as **quasi-Newton methods** use a quasi-Newton matrix that satisfies the secant condition:

$$\mathbf{B}_{k+1}\mathbf{s}_k = \mathbf{y}_k, \quad \text{where} \quad \begin{aligned} \mathbf{s}_k &= \mathbf{x}_{k+1} - \mathbf{x}_k, \\ \mathbf{y}_k &= \nabla f(\mathbf{x}_{k+1}) - \nabla f(\mathbf{x}_k). \end{aligned} \tag{B.9}$$

Using this Hessian approximation, the search direction at step k is the solution to

$$\mathbf{B}_k\mathbf{d}_k = -\nabla f(\mathbf{x}_k).$$

There is a family of different methods for picking $\mathbf{B}_k$, but the most notable one is the **BFGS** method that uses

$$\mathbf{B}_{k+1} = \mathbf{B}_k - \frac{\mathbf{B}_k\mathbf{s}_k\mathbf{s}_k^\mathsf{T}\mathbf{B}_k}{\mathbf{s}_k^\mathsf{T}\mathbf{B}_k\mathbf{s}_k} + \frac{\mathbf{y}_k\mathbf{y}_k^\mathsf{T}}{\mathbf{y}_k^\mathsf{T}\mathbf{s}_k}.$$

The initial choice of $\mathbf{B}_0$ is up to the user and can be simply the $n \times n$ identity matrix. The BFGS matrices are guaranteed to be positive definite if an appropriate line search is used. Moreover, the inverses can be updated *directly* according to

$$\mathbf{B}_{k+1}^{-1} = (\mathbf{I} - \rho_k\mathbf{s}_k\mathbf{y}_k^\mathsf{T})\mathbf{B}_k^{-1}(\mathbf{I} - \rho_k\mathbf{y}_k\mathbf{s}_k^\mathsf{T}) + \rho_k\mathbf{s}_k\mathbf{s}_k^\mathsf{T}, \quad \text{where} \quad \rho_k = \frac{1}{\mathbf{y}_k^\mathsf{T}\mathbf{s}_k},$$

which can be implemented using the symmetric rank-2 update,

$$\mathbf{B}_{k+1}^{-1} = \mathbf{B}_k^{-1} - \mathbf{s}_k\mathbf{w}_k^\mathsf{T} - \mathbf{w}_k\mathbf{s}_k^\mathsf{T}, \qquad \text{where} \quad \begin{aligned} \mathbf{w}_k &= \rho_k\left(\mathbf{z}_k - \tfrac{1}{2}(1 + \rho_k\mathbf{y}_k^\mathsf{T}\mathbf{z}_k)\mathbf{s}_k\right), \\ \mathbf{z}_k &= \mathbf{B}_k^{-1}\mathbf{y}_k. \end{aligned}$$

In this way, the update requires only $\mathcal{O}(n^2)$ operations per iteration, and applying the explicit inverse to compute the search direction,

$$\mathbf{d}_k = -\mathbf{B}_k^{-1}\nabla f(\mathbf{x}_k), \tag{B.10}$$

via a matrix–vector product also costs $\mathcal{O}(n^2)$ operations.

The name BFGS refers to the last names of its inventors (Broyden, Fletcher, Goldfarb, and Shanno). The main advantage of BFGS is that it is superlinearly convergent with a step length of 1 near the minimizer, assuming it converges to a strict local minimizer. As with Newton's method, it also requires a line search to get into the neighborhood of the local minimizer. It still has the disadvantage of requiring $\mathcal{O}(n^2)$ storage to store the approximate Hessian and $\mathcal{O}(n^2)$ work per iteration.

B.3.5 L-BFGS Optimization Method

The **limited-memory BFGS (L-BFGS)**, introduced by Nocedal (1980), overcomes the memory and computational disadvantages of BFGS by computing an update that incorporates only the m most-recent $\mathbf{s}_k$ and $\mathbf{y}_k$ vectors in such a way that it never actually forms or stores the quasi-Newton matrix explicitly. Instead, applying the implicitly stored approximation to $\mathbf{B}_k^{-1}$ to the gradient can be done by unrolling the recursive definition. Assuming the m updates are applied to the identity matrix, the L-BFGS two-loop recursion for computing

$$\mathbf{d}_k = -\tilde{\mathbf{B}}_k^{-1} \nabla f(\mathbf{x}_k), \tag{B.11}$$

where $\tilde{\mathbf{B}}_k$ is the L-BFGS matrix, is as follows.

L-BFGS Two-Loop Recursion

$\mathbf{d}_k = -\nabla f(\mathbf{x}_k)$
for $i = k-1$ **down to** $k-m$ **do**
  $\alpha_i \leftarrow \rho_i \mathbf{s}_i^\mathsf{T} \mathbf{d}_k$
  $\mathbf{d}_k \leftarrow \mathbf{d}_k - \alpha_i \mathbf{y}_i$
end for
for $i = k-m$ **to** $k-1$ **do**
  $\beta \leftarrow \rho_i \mathbf{y}_i^\mathsf{T} \mathbf{d}_k$
  $\mathbf{d}_k \leftarrow \mathbf{d}_k + (\alpha_i - \beta)\mathbf{s}_i$
end for

This reduces the memory requirements to $\mathcal{O}(mn)$ and the computational complexity to $\mathcal{O}(mn)$ per iteration, where m is typically chosen to be a small constant such as 5 or 20. Although it drops back to a linear rate of convergence, it is highly competitive with BFGS because each iteration is very fast. Because of the use of approximate second-order information, the linear convergence rate (β) is typically much faster than gradient descent as well.

L-BFGS is a popular optimization method because the cost per iteration is so low that it is often competitive with methods that have a faster rate of convergence (BFGS and Newton's method).

B.3.6 Damped Gauss–Newton for Least Squares Problems

An alternative approximation of the Hessian can be used in the special case of nonlinear least squares problems, i.e., a sum of squares form. These problems have the form in Eq. (B.2): $f(\mathbf{x}) = \frac{1}{2}\|\boldsymbol{\phi}(\mathbf{x})\|_2^2$, where $\boldsymbol{\phi} : \mathbb{R}^n \to \mathbb{R}^m$. If each function ϕ_i is affine, of the form $\phi_i(\mathbf{x}) = \mathbf{a}_i^\mathsf{T}\mathbf{x} + b_i$, then the problem is a *linear* least squares problem, so it can be solved using linear algebra as described in Section A.7. For nonlinear functions $\boldsymbol{\phi}$, the Gauss–Newton method computes a search direction using the linear approximation of $\boldsymbol{\phi}$ given by the first-order Taylor series:

$$\boldsymbol{\phi}(\mathbf{x}_k + \mathbf{d}_k) \approx \boldsymbol{\phi}(\mathbf{x}_k) + \mathbf{J}(\mathbf{x}_k)\mathbf{d}_k,$$

where $\mathbf{J} = D\boldsymbol{\phi}$ is the Jacobian operator as defined in Definition B.5.

Finding the $\mathbf{x}_{k+1}$ that minimizes this approximation of $f(\mathbf{x}_{k+1}) = \frac{1}{2}\|\boldsymbol{\phi}(\mathbf{x}_{k+1})\|_2^2$ is equivalent to finding the search direction $\mathbf{d}_k$ (with $\alpha_k = 1$) that solves

$$\min_{\mathbf{d}_k} \tfrac{1}{2}\|\boldsymbol{\phi}(\mathbf{x}_k) + \mathbf{J}(\mathbf{x}_k)\mathbf{d}_k\|_2^2,$$

which is a linear least squares problem. Using the normal equations to solve this problem (see Section A.7.1) yields

$$\mathbf{J}(\mathbf{x}_k)^\mathsf{T}\mathbf{J}(\mathbf{x}_k)\mathbf{d}_k = -\mathbf{J}(\mathbf{x}_k)^\mathsf{T}\boldsymbol{\phi}(\mathbf{x}_k). \tag{B.12}$$

The right-hand side of Eq. (B.12) is the negative gradient, i.e., $\nabla f(\mathbf{x}) = \mathbf{J}(\mathbf{x})^\mathsf{T}\boldsymbol{\phi}(\mathbf{x})$. We can see this by observing that $f = g \circ \boldsymbol{\phi}$ with $g(\mathbf{y}) = \frac{1}{2}\|\mathbf{y}\|_2^2$ and applying the multivariate chain rule (Theorem B.11).

Because the Jacobian can be rank deficient or ill conditioned, we often add a small value times the identity to the Gramian of the Jacobian. This ensures that the linear system is positive definite, and it plays the role of damping the size of the search direction. This **damped Gauss–Newton** search direction is the solution to the following system:

$$\left[\mathbf{J}(\mathbf{x}_k)^\mathsf{T}\mathbf{J}(\mathbf{x}_k) + \lambda_k\mathbf{I}\right]\mathbf{d}_k = -\nabla f(\mathbf{x}_k). \tag{B.13}$$

If λ_k is very large, the coefficient matrix tends toward a scaled identity matrix, and so the computed direction $\mathbf{d}_k$ tends toward the gradient descent search direction. Thus, the damping parameter represents a compromise between pure Gauss–Newton and gradient descent.

The matrix in Eq. (B.13) is an approximation to the Hessian, with an addition of $\lambda_k\mathbf{I}$ to ensure the system is positive definite. The Hessian of f is given by

$$\nabla^2 f(\mathbf{x}) = \mathbf{J}(\mathbf{x})^\mathsf{T}\mathbf{J}(\mathbf{x}) + \sum_{i=1}^{m} \phi_i(\mathbf{x})\,\nabla^2\phi_i(\mathbf{x}).$$

The Gauss–Newton method drops the second term, so it is accurate when that term is small. This can happen near the solution $\mathbf{x}_*$ if $f(\mathbf{x}_*) = 0$, which implies $\boldsymbol{\phi}(\mathbf{x}) \approx 0$ when $\mathbf{x} \approx \mathbf{x}_*$, or if the functions $\{\phi_i\}$ are nearly linear with small second derivatives. For this reason, Gauss–Newton is a popular method for numerically solving systems of nonlinear equations.

The main advantage of Gauss–Newton is that the approximate Hessian, $\mathbf{J}(\mathbf{x}_k)^\mathsf{T}\mathbf{J}(\mathbf{x}_k)$, can be computed from the Jacobian, which involves no second derivatives. Additionally, Eq. (B.12) can often be solved efficiently via an iterative method such as the conjugate gradient method (see Section A.6.4), similar to truncated Newton. The last advantage is that when the second term of the true Hessian is small, the convergence of Gauss–Newton can still be quadratic.

As with Newton's method, we may need to choose λ_k to ensure the resulting approximate Hessian is positive definite, but an advantage of Gauss–Newton is that the approximate Hessian is guaranteed to be semidefinite. Many strategies exist for tuning λ_k at each iteration, including the Levenberg–Marquardt method.

Exercise B.7 Derive the Jacobian $\mathbf{J} = D\boldsymbol{\phi}$, and compute $\mathbf{J}^\mathsf{T}\mathbf{J}$ for

$$\boldsymbol{\phi}(x, y, z) = \begin{bmatrix} xyz - a \\ x - b \\ y - c \\ z - d \end{bmatrix}.$$

B.3.7 Block Coordinate Descent

The optimization methods described in Sections B.3.2–B.3.6 update the entire vector $\mathbf{x}$ in each iteration. An alternative approach, known as **block coordinate descent** or **block nonlinear Gauss–Seidel**, is to update a block of elements of $\mathbf{x}$ at a time, holding all other blocks fixed. In this case, each iteration is performed via subiterations, each of which is a smaller optimization problem.

The advantage of this approach is that the subproblems are often much simpler to solve; for example, the function may be convex even if it is nonconvex over the entire vector. The disadvantage is that convergence can be slow, as the optimization considers blocks of elements in isolation rather than all together.

Consider the example

$$\min_{\mathbf{x}\in\mathbb{R}^n,\ \mathbf{y}\in\mathbb{R}^p} f(\mathbf{x},\mathbf{y}), \quad \text{where} \quad f:\mathbb{R}^{n+p}\to\mathbb{R}.$$

An optimization method like Newton's would concatenate vectors $\mathbf{x}$ and $\mathbf{y}$ and compute the search direction to update all $n+p$ elements at once. In a block coordinate descent method that partitions the elements into separate blocks $\mathbf{x}$ and $\mathbf{y}$, the kth iteration performs the following subiterations:

$$\begin{aligned}\mathbf{x}_{k+1} &= \arg\min_{\mathbf{x}\in\mathbb{R}^n} f(\mathbf{x},\mathbf{y}_k)\\ \mathbf{y}_{k+1} &= \arg\min_{\mathbf{y}\in\mathbb{R}^p} f(\mathbf{x}_{k+1},\mathbf{y}).\end{aligned}$$

The update for $\mathbf{y}$ in the second subiteration uses the most up-to-date values for $\mathbf{x}$ that are computed in the first subiteration. More generally, if a vector $\mathbf{x}$ is partitioned into d blocks $\{\mathbf{x}^{(i)}\}$ with $\mathbf{x}^{(i)}\in\mathbb{R}^{n_i}$ and $\sum_i n_i = n$, then the subiteration to update the ith block takes the form

$$\mathbf{x}_{k+1}^{(i)} = \arg\min_{\mathbf{x}^{(i)}\in\mathbb{R}^{n_i}} f\left(\mathbf{x}_{k+1}^{(1)},\ldots,\mathbf{x}_{k+1}^{(i-1)},\mathbf{x}^{(i)},\mathbf{x}_k^{(i+1)},\ldots,\mathbf{x}_k^{(d)}\right). \tag{B.14}$$

Block coordinate descent methods need not solve each subproblem exactly, but their main advantage is when the subproblems are convex and have a closed-form solution. If there is a unique solution to each subproblem, and the method computes it exactly, then block coordinate descent is guaranteed to converge to a stationary point. For more detail on the convergence guarantees, see Bertsekas (2016, section 3.7) and Gillis (2021, section 8.1.4).

Exercise B.8 Consider the optimization problem

$$\min_{\mathbf{x}\in\mathbb{R}^m,\ \mathbf{y}\in\mathbb{R}^m} \frac{1}{2}\left\|\mathbf{A}-\mathbf{x}\mathbf{y}^\mathsf{T}\right\|_F^2.$$

Devise a BCD method for solving it by specifying a partition of the variables and the update rule for solving each subproblem.

B.4 Example: Two-Dimensional Optimization

To illustrate the application of the optimization methods described in Sections B.3.2–B.3.4, B.3.6, and B.3.7 and compare their convergence properties, we consider the following optimization problem.

Example B.15 (Two-Dimensional Optimization Problem for Comparison of Methods) Consider the two-dimensional optimization problem $\min_{x,y} f(x,y)$, where

$$f(x,y) \equiv \frac{1}{2}\left[(x-1)^2 + (y-1)^2 + (xy)^2\right]. \qquad \text{(B.15)}$$

In order to apply gradient descent or a quasi-Newton method such as BFGS, we compute the gradient of Eq. (B.15):

$$\nabla f(x,y) = \begin{bmatrix} x - 1 + xy^2 \\ y - 1 + x^2 y \end{bmatrix}. \qquad \text{(B.16)}$$

To apply Newton's method, we need the gradient from Eq. (B.16) as well as the Hessian:

$$\nabla^2 f(x,y) = \begin{bmatrix} 1+y^2 & 2xy \\ 2xy & 1+x^2 \end{bmatrix}.$$

Noting that Example B.15 takes the form of a nonlinear least squares problem, where

$$\phi(x,y) = \begin{bmatrix} x-1 \\ y-1 \\ xy \end{bmatrix},$$

we can also apply the Gauss–Newton method. To this end, we compute the Jacobian of ϕ and its Gram matrix:

$$\mathbf{J}(x,y) = \begin{bmatrix} 1 & 0 \\ 0 & 1 \\ y & x \end{bmatrix} \quad \text{and} \quad \mathbf{J}^\mathsf{T}\mathbf{J}(x,y) = \begin{bmatrix} 1+y^2 & xy \\ xy & 1+x^2 \end{bmatrix}.$$

The Gauss–Newton matrix $\mathbf{J}^\mathsf{T}\mathbf{J}$ differs from the Hessian $\nabla^2 f$ in the off-diagonal entries.

We can also apply a (block) coordinate descent method, where the only possible partitioning of the variables is into the two individual variables x and y. When y is fixed, Eq. (B.15) is a quadratic function of x. Its unique minimum is attained at $x = \frac{1}{1+y^2}$. Likewise, f is a quadratic function of y when x is fixed, and its unique minimum is attained at $y = \frac{1}{1+x^2}$.

Although memory and computational cost are not an issue with this problem, we also apply L-BFGS with $m = 2$ using only the gradient to illustrate the difference in convergence behavior with BFGS.

The convergence behavior of all six methods is illustrated in Fig. B.2 and Table B.2, and we use abbreviations GD for gradient descent, GN for Gauss–Newton, and CD for coordinate descent. In this experiment, all methods start from the point $(x_0, y_0) = (\frac{1}{2}, \frac{1}{4})$. We use backtracking line search as described in Section B.3.1, though for this problem we observe function value increase and require backtracking only for the gradient descent method (and the first step of BFGS/L-BFGS). The convergence criterion we use is to test if the absolute change in objective function value is sufficiently small: $|f(\mathbf{x}_{k-1}) - f(\mathbf{x}_k)| < 10^{-14}$.

We make several observations from this simple example that are representative of the convergence behavior for these methods:

- Gradient descent requires the most iterations, and we observe linear convergence with a ratio of $\beta \approx 0.5$ (see Eq. (B.5)).
- Gauss–Newton converges more slowly than BFGS, as the error in the approximate Hessian is not small for this problem (e.g., the minimum function value is not close to 0).
- Coordinate descent requires fewer iterations than gradient descent, as we observe linear convergence with a ratio of $\beta \approx 0.4$ (see Eq. (B.5)), but it requires more iterations than the methods with superlinear convergence.
- L-BFGS (with $m = 2$) behaves similarly to BFGS in early iterations but requires more iterations overall because it loses superlinear convergence near the solution.
- BFGS exhibits superlinear convergence, requiring many fewer iterations than gradient descent but more than Newton's method.
- Newton's method requires the fewest iterations, and we observe quadratic convergence (see Eq. (B.6)).

We emphasize that the number of iterations is not the only factor that contributes to the time to convergence for realistic problems, as the cost per iteration of these methods varies widely for large n. Recall that the iterations of Newton's method are the most expensive, as they require evaluating the Hessian of size $\mathcal{O}(n^2)$ and solving a linear system with cost $\mathcal{O}(n^3)$, assuming a direct method like the Cholesky decomposition is used. The quasi-Newton method BFGS requires evaluating the gradient and storing an approximate Hessian of size $\mathcal{O}(n^2)$ but allows for a linear system solve with only $\mathcal{O}(n^2)$ cost. Gradient descent and L-BFGS are generally the cheapest gradient-based methods, as they involve only $\mathcal{O}(n)$ computation. We demonstrate only the basic versions of these methods in this example, variants such as truncated Newton, Gauss–Newton using the conjugate gradient method for the linear solve, and block coordinate descent all trade-off the cost per iteration with speed of convergence, and the most efficient method overall is typically problem-dependent.

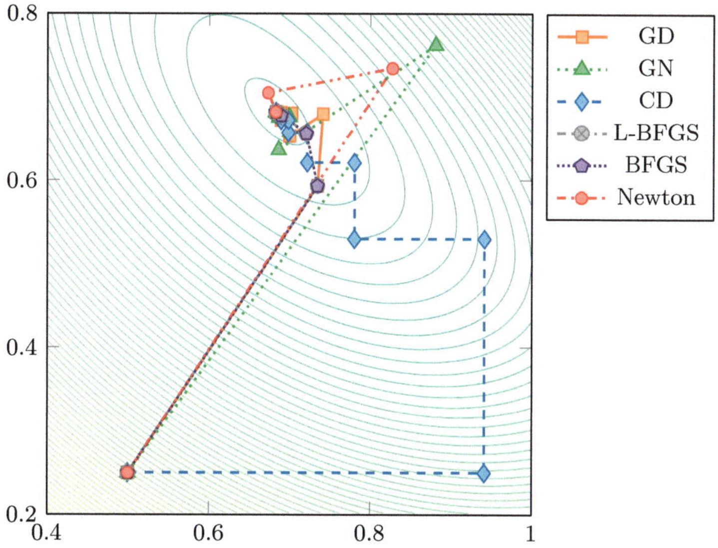

Figure B.2 Convergence of optimization methods for Example B.15.

Table B.2 Convergence behavior as measured by $\|\mathbf{x}_k - \mathbf{x}_*\|_2$ on Example B.15

k	GD	GN	CD	L-BFGS	BFGS	Newton
0	$4.7 \cdot 10^{-1}$	$4.7 \cdot 10^{-1}$	$4.7 \cdot 10^{-1}$	$4.7 \cdot 10^{-1}$	$4.7 \cdot 10^{-1}$	$4.7 \cdot 10^{-1}$
1	$1.0 \cdot 10^{-1}$	$2.1 \cdot 10^{-1}$	$3.0 \cdot 10^{-1}$	$1.0 \cdot 10^{-1}$	$1.0 \cdot 10^{-1}$	$1.5 \cdot 10^{-1}$
2	$5.9 \cdot 10^{-2}$	$4.6 \cdot 10^{-2}$	$1.2 \cdot 10^{-1}$	$4.6 \cdot 10^{-2}$	$4.6 \cdot 10^{-2}$	$2.5 \cdot 10^{-2}$
3	$3.4 \cdot 10^{-2}$	$1.8 \cdot 10^{-2}$	$4.6 \cdot 10^{-2}$	$7.9 \cdot 10^{-3}$	$7.9 \cdot 10^{-3}$	$3.8 \cdot 10^{-4}$
4	$1.9 \cdot 10^{-2}$	$7.8 \cdot 10^{-3}$	$1.9 \cdot 10^{-2}$	$1.3 \cdot 10^{-4}$	$1.3 \cdot 10^{-4}$	$4.8 \cdot 10^{-8}$
5	$1.1 \cdot 10^{-2}$	$3.6 \cdot 10^{-3}$	$7.5 \cdot 10^{-3}$	$5.2 \cdot 10^{-5}$	$2.0 \cdot 10^{-6}$	$1.9 \cdot 10^{-15}$
6	$6.2 \cdot 10^{-3}$	$1.7 \cdot 10^{-3}$	$3.0 \cdot 10^{-3}$	$3.0 \cdot 10^{-5}$	$9.6 \cdot 10^{-8}$	
7	$3.8 \cdot 10^{-3}$	$7.7 \cdot 10^{-4}$	$1.2 \cdot 10^{-3}$	$1.2 \cdot 10^{-6}$	$6.8 \cdot 10^{-12}$	
8	$2.0 \cdot 10^{-3}$	$3.6 \cdot 10^{-4}$	$4.9 \cdot 10^{-4}$	$9.2 \cdot 10^{-8}$		
9	$1.3 \cdot 10^{-3}$	$1.7 \cdot 10^{-4}$	$2.0 \cdot 10^{-4}$	$1.5 \cdot 10^{-8}$		
10	$6.5 \cdot 10^{-4}$	$7.7 \cdot 10^{-5}$	$8.0 \cdot 10^{-5}$			
11	$4.4 \cdot 10^{-4}$	$3.6 \cdot 10^{-5}$	$3.2 \cdot 10^{-5}$			
12	$2.2 \cdot 10^{-4}$	$1.7 \cdot 10^{-5}$	$1.3 \cdot 10^{-5}$			
13	$1.4 \cdot 10^{-4}$	$7.8 \cdot 10^{-6}$	$5.3 \cdot 10^{-6}$			
14	$7.2 \cdot 10^{-5}$	$3.6 \cdot 10^{-6}$	$2.1 \cdot 10^{-6}$			
15	$4.4 \cdot 10^{-5}$	$1.7 \cdot 10^{-6}$	$8.6 \cdot 10^{-7}$			
16	$2.4 \cdot 10^{-5}$	$7.9 \cdot 10^{-7}$	$3.5 \cdot 10^{-7}$			
17	$1.4 \cdot 10^{-5}$	$3.7 \cdot 10^{-7}$	$1.4 \cdot 10^{-7}$			
18	$8.2 \cdot 10^{-6}$	$1.7 \cdot 10^{-7}$				
19	$4.4 \cdot 10^{-6}$	$8.0 \cdot 10^{-8}$				
20	$2.8 \cdot 10^{-6}$					
21	$1.4 \cdot 10^{-6}$					
22	$9.4 \cdot 10^{-7}$					
23	$4.7 \cdot 10^{-7}$					
24	$3.2 \cdot 10^{-7}$					

Exercise B.9 Consider the function given in Exercise B.2:

$$f(x, y) = c(y - x^2)^2 + (1 - x)^2.$$

(a) Implement gradient descent, Newton's method, and Gauss–Newton to test them minimizing f for $c = 100$. Use backtracking line search for all methods.

(b) Report the convergence behavior as measured by $\|\mathbf{x}_k - \mathbf{x}_*\|_2$ for $\mathbf{x}_* = \mathbf{1}$ in a table.

(c) Find instances of linear and quadratic convergence in your results. Are they where you expected to find them?

(d) Adjust the parameter c to 1000 and to 1 and analyze the effects of that change on the behavior of the methods.

B.5 Constrained Optimization

We omit here a general discussion of constrained optimization and instead refer readers to Nocedal and Wright (2006, chapter 12). We just discuss a few of the simpler ideas that may be useful in our discussions.

The **constrained** multivariate optimization problem has the form

$$\begin{aligned} \min_{\mathbf{x} \in \mathbb{R}^n} \quad & f(\mathbf{x}), \qquad f : \mathbb{R}^n \to \mathbb{R}, \\ \text{subject to} \quad & \mathbf{c}(\mathbf{x}) \geq \mathbf{0}, \quad \mathbf{c} : \mathbb{R}^n \to \mathbb{R}^m. \end{aligned} \tag{B.17}$$

The constraints $\mathbf{c}(\mathbf{x}) \geq \mathbf{0}$ are inequality constraints. In general, bound constraints (e.g., $\boldsymbol{\ell} \leq \mathbf{x} \leq \mathbf{u}$) are the simplest to handle, then linear constraints (e.g., $\boldsymbol{\ell} \leq \mathbf{A}\mathbf{x} \leq \mathbf{u}$), and finally nonlinear constraints. A popular method for handling bound constraints is bound constrained L-BFGS (L-BFGS-B, Byrd et al., 1995). Nonlinear constraints are often handled by a penalty term, an interior point method, or something like the alternating direction method of multipliers (ADMM). For more information, see, e.g., Wright and Recht (2022, chapter 7).

Optimality Conditions for Nonnegativity Constraints

In the unconstrained case, any minimizer must satisfy the necessary condition that $\nabla f(\mathbf{x}^*) = \mathbf{0}$. However, in the case of nonnegativity constraints (i.e., $\mathbf{x} \geq \mathbf{0}$) the necessary conditions are

$$[\nabla f(\mathbf{x}^*)]_i \geq 0 \text{ if } x_i^* = 0,$$
$$[\nabla f(\mathbf{x}^*)]_i = 0 \text{ if } x_i^* > 0,$$

per Proposition B.25.

Proposition B.25 (First-Order Necessary Conditions for Nonnegative Local Minimizer, Chen and Plemmons, 2009) *Any solution* $\mathbf{x}^* \in \mathbb{R}^n$ *of*

$$\min_{\mathbf{x}\in\mathbb{R}^n} f(\mathbf{x}) \quad \textit{subject to} \quad \mathbf{x} \geq \mathbf{0}, \quad \textit{where} \quad f : \mathbb{R}^n \to \mathbb{R}, \tag{B.18}$$

must satisfy

$$\nabla f(\mathbf{x}^*) \geq \mathbf{0} \quad \textit{and} \quad \nabla f(\mathbf{x}^*)^\mathsf{T}\mathbf{x}^* = 0.$$

In the unconstrained case, optimization methods seek a solution $\mathbf{x}$ that satisfies the first-order necessary condition $\nabla f(\mathbf{x}) = \mathbf{0}$ (Theorem B.19). Thus, the norm of the gradient serves as a metric for how far from satisfying this necessary condition an iterate is, and it can be used as a stopping criterion. For problems with nonnegativity constraints, the **projected gradient**, also known as the **reduced gradient**, can be used to measure how far from satisfying the necessary conditions of Proposition B.25 an iterate is (Kim et al., 2014). In this case, the projected gradient $\nabla^{\text{proj}} f \in \mathbb{R}^n$ has entries given by

$$[\nabla^{\text{proj}} f(\mathbf{x})]_i = \begin{cases} 0 & \text{if } x_i = 0 \quad \text{and} \quad [\nabla f(\mathbf{x})]_i \geq 0 \\ [\nabla f(\mathbf{x})]_i & \text{otherwise} \end{cases}.$$

Checking that the norm of the projected gradient $\|\nabla^{\text{proj}} f(\mathbf{x})\|$ is sufficiently small can be used as a stopping criterion. The projected gradient for general bound-constrained optimization problems is used by L-BFGS-B (Byrd et al., 1995).

C Statistics and Probability

This appendix covers some essentials of statistics and probability. We cover basics of random variables in Section C.1, maximum likelihood estimators in Section C.2, and useful random variable distributions, such as Gaussian and Poisson in Section C.3. These topics are needed for our discussion of GCP tensor decomposition in Chapter 15. We also review principal component analysis (PCA) in Section C.4, which is a data analysis tool based on matrix decomposition and is useful for understanding tensor decompositions.

C.1 Random Variables

Random variables are unknowns that do not have a fixed value but instead represents a distribution of possible values. Before we discuss distributions, we start with some basics.

A scalar random variable is generally denoted with a capital letter such as X. Its realizations are then typically denoted with lower case letters, $x_1, x_2, \ldots$, etc. As we are dealing with vectors, matrices, and tensors, we usually do not use different notation for random variables and observations, leaving the distinctions to context. We do use the capital letter notation in our introduction, however.

C.1.1 Discrete Random Variables

A **discrete random variable** X has only a finite number of possible values. Let $\{ v_1, v_2, \ldots, v_n \}$ be the possible values of X.

The **probability mass function** (pmf) is a mapping from the set of possible values to the associated probabilities:

$$p : \{ v_1, v_2, \ldots, v_n \} \to [0, 1], \quad \text{such that} \quad p(x) \geq 0 \quad \text{and} \quad \sum_{i=1}^{n} p(v_i) = 1.$$

Thus, $p(v_i) = \text{Prob}\{X = v_i\}$. Then the **mean** or **expected value** of a discrete random value X with pmf p is

$$\mathbb{E}[X] = \sum_{i=1}^{n} v_i \, p(v_i).$$

The **variance** is

$$\text{Var}[X] = \sum_{i=1}^{n} \big(v_i - \mathbb{E}[X]\big)^2 \, p(v_i).$$

C.1.2 Continuous Random Variables

A **continuous random variable** X can take on any value within a range. The **probability density function** (pdf) is a mapping such that its integral yields the probability of X being in a range:

$$p : \mathbb{R} \to \mathbb{R}_+, \quad \text{such that} \quad \int_{-\infty}^{+\infty} p(x)dx = 1.$$

Thus, the probability that $X \in [a, b]$ is given as the following integral:

$$\text{Prob}\{a \leq X \leq b\} = \int_a^b p(x)dx.$$

The **mean** of the continuous random variable X is

$$\mathbb{E}[X] = \int_{-\infty}^{+\infty} x\, p(x)\, dx.$$

Its **variance** is

$$\text{Var}[X] = \int_{-\infty}^{+\infty} (x - \mathbb{E}[X])^2\, p(x)\, dx.$$

C.2 Maximum Likelihood Estimator

The idea of **maximum likelihood estimation (MLE)** in statistics is to choose the parameters of a statistical model such that the probability of the observed data is maximized.

Consider the situation where we have some model whose pdf (or pmf) is given by $p(x|\theta)$, where θ is one or more parameters to be optimized. If we have n observed instances of the random variable X, denoted $x_1, x_2, \ldots, x_n$, then maximizing the likelihood equates to solving

$$\max_\theta \prod_{i=1}^n p(x_i \,|\, \theta).$$

We typically work instead with a transformed version of the problem based on taking the logarithm (which is a monotonic function):

$$\max_\theta \sum_{i=1}^n \log p(x_i \,|\, \theta). \tag{C.1}$$

The optimum value of θ is called the **maximum likelihood estimate**. Many optimization methods prefer to do minimization, and the optimizer of Eq. (C.1) is equivalent to the optimizer of

$$\min_\theta \sum_{i=1}^n -\log p(x_i \,|\, \theta). \tag{C.2}$$

C.3 Useful Distributions

C.3.1 Gaussian Distribution and Sum of Squared Errors

The **Gaussian distribution**, also known as the **normal distribution**, of a random variable $X \in \mathbb{R}$ is defined by the pdf

$$p(x|\mu,\sigma) = \frac{e^{-(x-\mu)^2/(2\sigma^2)}}{\sqrt{2\pi\sigma^2}}. \tag{C.3}$$

The negative log-likelihood function is

$$-\log p(x|\mu,\sigma) = \frac{(x-\mu)^2}{2\sigma^2} - \log(\sqrt{\pi\sigma^2}). \tag{C.4}$$

We denote that X is normally distributed as $X \sim \mathcal{N}(\mu,\sigma)$. In this case,

$$\mathbb{E}[X] = \mu \quad \text{and} \quad \text{Var}[X] = \sigma^2.$$

Thus, the parameter μ is in fact the mean of the distribution and σ is the standard deviation (the square root of the variance). The pdfs for different means and standard deviations are shown in Fig. C.1.

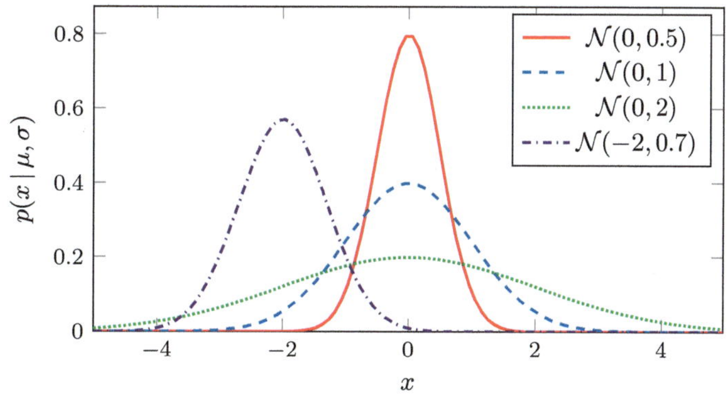

Figure C.1 Normal distributions $\mathcal{N}(\mu,\sigma)$ with mean μ and standard deviation σ.

C.3.2 Bernoulli Distribution and Logistic Regression for Binary Data

The **Bernoulli distribution** of a binary random variable $X \in \{0,1\}$ is defined by a parameter $\rho \in [0,1]$ that defines the probability of a 1. Hence, the pmf is

$$p(x \mid \rho) = \begin{cases} \rho & \text{if } x = 1 \\ (1-\rho) & \text{if } x = 0 \end{cases}.$$

This is usually written in the more compact form:

$$p(x \mid \rho) = \rho^x (1-\rho)^{1-x} \quad \text{for} \quad x \in \{0,1\}. \tag{C.5}$$

The negative log-likelihood is

$$-\log p(x \mid \rho) = \log\left(1 + \frac{\rho}{1-\rho}\right) - x\log\left(\frac{\rho}{1-\rho}\right). \tag{C.6}$$

The notation is $X \sim \text{Bernoulli}(\rho)$. In this case,

$$\mathbb{E}[X] = \rho \quad \text{and} \quad \text{Var}[X] = \rho(1-\rho).$$

Exercise C.1 Prove Eq. (C.6).

C.3.3 Poisson Distribution and KL Divergence for Count Data

The **Poisson distribution** of an integer random variable $X \in \{0, 1, 2, \ldots\}$ is defined by a parameter $\lambda > 0$ that is the mean. The pmf is

$$p(x \mid \lambda) = \frac{\lambda^x e^{-\lambda}}{x!} \quad \text{for} \quad x \in \{0, 1, 2, \ldots\}. \tag{C.7}$$

The negative log-likelihood is

$$-\log p(x \mid \lambda) = \lambda - x \log \lambda + \log x! \,. \tag{C.8}$$

The notation is $X \sim \text{Poisson}(\lambda)$, and

$$\mathbb{E}[X] = \text{Var}[X] = \lambda.$$

Examples of the discrete Poisson distribution are shown in Fig. C.2 with different values of λ. We use the gamma function, $\Gamma(x+1)$, to extend $x!$ and the Poisson pmfs to non-integral values, as given by the dotted lines. For low values of λ, the Poisson distribution is very different than a normal distribution with the same mean. However, for higher values of λ, the Poisson distribution is something like a discrete version of a normal distribution. For instance, see Fig. C.3 and notice how the Poisson and the normal distributions with identical means of 0.5 are very different, whereas the versions with means of 5 are starting to look very similar. To set the standard deviation of the normal distributions in these examples, the Gaussian pdf is constrained to be equal to the Poisson pmf at the mean ($\lambda = \mu$), which implies $\sigma^2 = \Gamma(\mu+1)/(\sqrt{2\pi}\,\mu^\mu\, e^{-\mu})$.

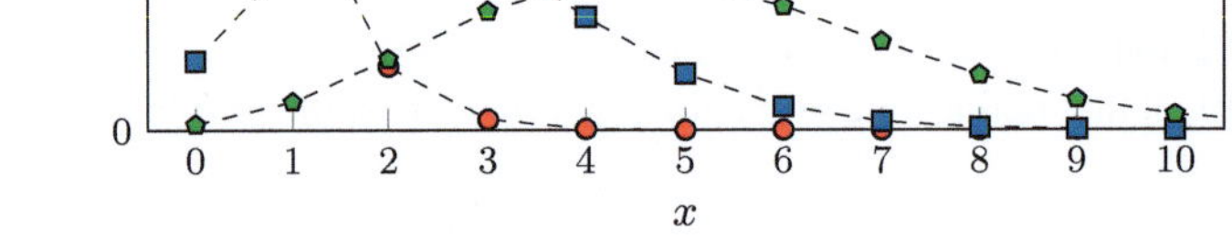

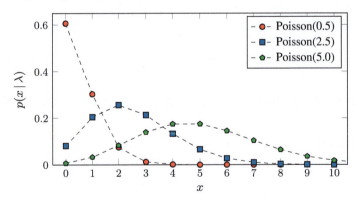

Figure C.2 Poisson distributions, Poisson(λ), with different means, λ.

C.3.4 Gamma Distribution for Continuous Nonnegative Data

The **gamma distribution** is for strictly positive continuous data with a pdf given by

$$p(x \mid k, \theta) = \frac{x^{k-1}}{\Gamma(k)\theta^k}\, e^{-x/\theta} \quad \text{for} \quad x > 0. \tag{C.9}$$

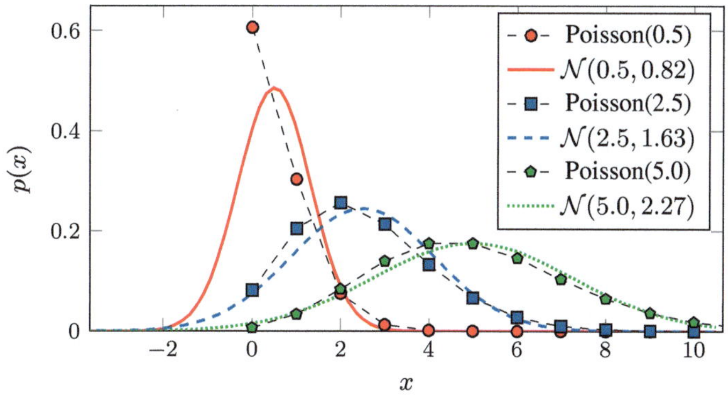

Figure C.3 Poisson versus normal distributions with identical means.

The parameters are the shape $k > 0$ and scale $\theta > 0$. For $k = 1$, this is the exponential distribution, and for $k = 2$, it is the chi-squared distribution. The negative log-likelihood is

$$-\log p(x \mid k, \theta) = \log \Gamma(k) + k \log \theta + k \log x + \frac{x}{\theta}. \tag{C.10}$$

The mean and variance are

$$\mathbb{E}[X] = k\theta \quad \text{and} \quad \text{Var}[X] = k\theta^2.$$

Some example gamma distributions are shown in Fig. C.4.

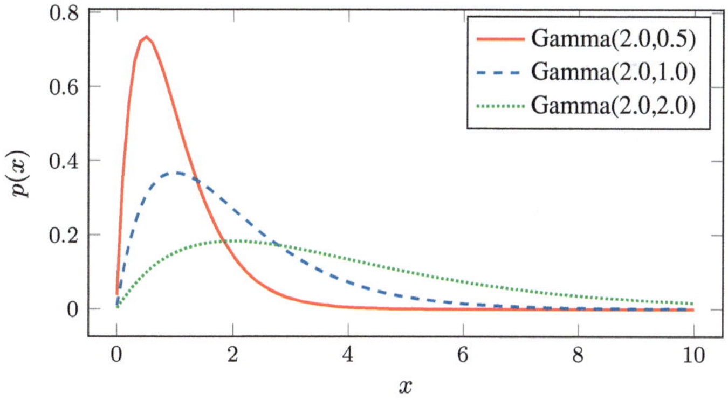

Figure C.4 Gamma distributions, $\text{Gamma}(k, \theta)$, with different values of θ.

The gamma distribution is sometimes parameterized instead by $\alpha = k$ and $\beta = 1/\theta$.

C.4 Principal Component Analysis

Principal component analysis (PCA) is a popular multivariate statistical technique. The goals of PCA include separating important information from noise, reducing the size of the data, identifying latent patterns, and analyzing the structure of the observations and the variables. This section provides a brief introduction to PCA. For more information, see Abdi and Williams (2010) and Jolliffe (2002).

The input to PCA is a data matrix $\mathbf{X} \in \mathbb{R}^{m \times n}$ corresponding to m objects and n features. The PCA decomposition is

$$\mathbf{X} = \mathbf{S}\mathbf{V}^{\mathsf{T}} = \sum_k \mathbf{s}_k \mathbf{v}_k^{\mathsf{T}},$$

as shown in Fig. C.5. We let k denote the number of principal components. The orthonormal matrix $\mathbf{V} \in \mathbb{R}^{n \times k}$ is referred to as the **loadings**. It is also known as the **principal axes** because its columns define the directions in feature space along which the variance of the data is maximized. The matrix $\mathbf{S} \in \mathbb{R}^{m \times k}$ is referred to as the **scores** or, more explicitly, the **principal component scores**. It represents the objects in the lower dimensional space defined by the principal axes.

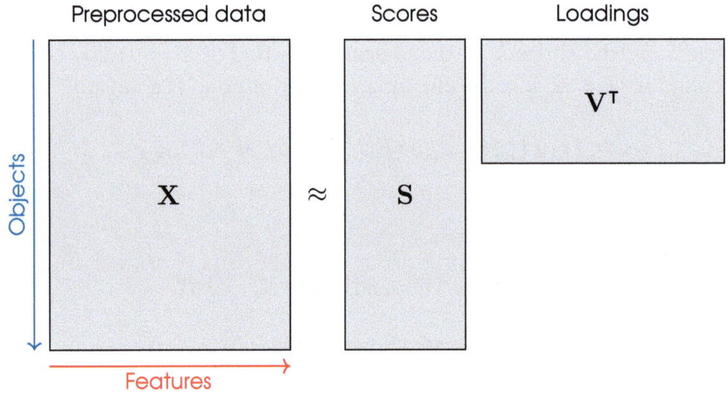

Figure C.5 PCA.

The orthogonal columns of $\mathbf{V}$ form a basis for a reduced k-dimensional space. The rows of $\mathbf{S}$ are representations of the objects in this new space. In other words, $\mathbf{X}(i,:)$ represents object i in the original n-dimensional feature space and $\mathbf{S}(i,:)$ represents object i in the reduced k-dimensional feature space. PCA scores are used for visualizing data, spectral clustering, etc.

Remark C.1 (Preprocessing the data matrix for PCA) In PCA, it is customary to assume that the data matrix is **centered**. Centering means that we subtract the average value in each column. After centering, each column has mean 0.

C.4.1 Computing PCA

In statistics, the way to compute PCA is as follows. The loading matrix $\mathbf{V}$ is the k principal eigenvectors of the **covariance matrix** $\mathbf{C} \equiv \mathbf{X}^{\mathsf{T}}\mathbf{X} \in \mathbb{R}^{n \times n}$. Recall from Section A.5.4 that the eigenvectors are orthonormal. The scores are then computed as $\mathbf{S} = \mathbf{X}\mathbf{V}$. Alternatively, we get the same scores and loadings from the SVD; see Section A.5.3. If the truncated rank-k SVD of $\mathbf{X}$ is $\mathbf{X} \approx \mathbf{U}\mathbf{\Sigma}\mathbf{V}^{\mathsf{T}}$, then the loadings are $\mathbf{V}$ and the scores are $\mathbf{S} = \mathbf{U}\mathbf{\Sigma}$. This viewpoint reveals that PCA is an optimal rank-k approximation; see Theorem A.26. By considering only the first k principal components, we reduce the dimensionality and mitigate noise in the data.

C.4.2 Example of PCA

We illustrate PCA on decathlon data from the 1988 Summer Olympics (Ballard, 2024). A decathlon comprises 10 track and field events: 100-meter dash, 110-meter hurdles, 400-meter run, 1500-meter run, long jump, high jump, pole vault, shot put, discus throw, and javelin throw. The raw times (for running events) and distances (for jumping and throwing events) are converted to point values using event-specific formulas, and the total scores determine the rankings. This dataset consists of scores for 33 athletes who competed and finished in the 1988 Olympics. The centered data is shown in Table C.1 and ranges from a low of -223 to a maximum 297.

Table C.1 Centered decathlon data

Id	100m	110h	400m	1500	Long	High	Pole	Shot	Disc	Jave
1	−12	−14	17	49	71	271	−16	94	142	28
2	72	68	74	22	75	−14	106	63	41	34
3	3	25	46	87	73	−14	137	16	26	71
4	129	36	9	−55	58	41	45	66	50	69
5	81	103	44	15	118	125	45	−22	14	−109
6	38	76	87	132	71	−14	137	−63	−24	−30
7	3	77	−4	−92	−21	69	297	11	−14	32
8	32	81	50	69	−45	13	14	86	−22	53
9	9	43	5	44	−5	41	45	35	0	105
10	−8	31	31	−98	34	−14	137	80	116	0
11	56	94	−32	−119	103	−14	14	86	−11	108
12	3	−12	11	131	49	−41	−16	33	2	96
13	38	6	49	123	36	69	75	−63	−58	−40
14	45	38	68	48	56	−14	−133	−21	31	107
15	36	−51	20	58	75	−14	−16	16	−14	68
16	23	28	−29	51	−14	41	45	35	17	−34
17	−57	−122	−92	−157	−92	13	14	131	171	202
18	−80	−3	−27	−60	−33	−41	45	102	88	11
19	27	64	62	92	−24	−41	14	−33	−41	−119
20	67	9	−20	−181	−17	−171	45	116	60	15
21	−70	−74	−34	65	53	−41	−45	−1	−72	114
22	−63	−25	−62	95	−29	41	−16	−9	−67	22
23	−40	5	−45	24	−14	13	−104	22	81	−57
24	−23	−44	−33	−9	−40	154	−45	−44	−74	−77
25	43	6	−22	−57	22	41	−75	−49	−88	−100
26	−29	−45	42	41	−73	69	−45	−141	−99	−61
27	20	−14	30	96	−38	−120	−16	−77	−88	−149
28	−68	−20	−87	−161	−31	−41	−45	14	71	−48
29	−14	−71	49	28	−57	−94	−104	−94	−89	−102
30	−65	−65	0	−107	−12	−146	−75	−61	−1	−89
31	−51	−102	−91	−114	−212	−67	−45	2	78	−25
32	−59	2	−48	−107	−165	−41	−218	−99	−74	−33
33	−80	−138	−67	42	12	−67	−190	−223	−162	−68

After centering, we apply PCA to the matrix $\mathbf{X} \in \mathbb{R}^{33\times 10}$ representing the athlete $\times$ event score data. We consider the first two principal components, so the decomposition is $\mathbf{X} \approx \mathbf{S}\mathbf{V}^\intercal$, where the scores are $\mathbf{S} \in \mathbb{R}^{33\times 2}$ and the loadings are $\mathbf{V} \in \mathbb{R}^{10\times 2}$. The first component explains 34% of the variance, and the first two components together explain 59% of the variance, meaning that $\|\mathbf{S}\|_F^2/\|\mathbf{X}\|_F^2 = 0.59$.

The scores for each athlete and loadings for each event are plotted in Fig. C.6. Figure C.6b plots the scores for each of the 33 athletes, with the x value corresponding to the first principle direction and the y value corresponding to the second principle direction. The points are color coded by the final ranking (1 to 33) and the top three finishers are explicitly labeled. Figure C.6a shows the loadings of each event with respect to the principal directions. The events are color-coded by type (run, jump, and throw).

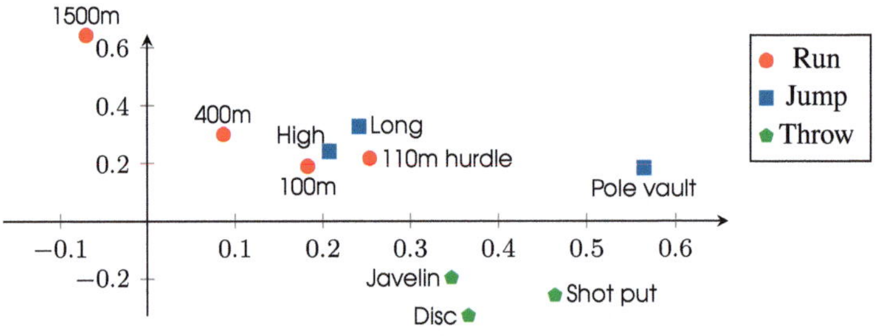

(a) Scatter plot of the first two PCA coefficients for each decathlon event. The x and y axes represents the event's weights in the first and second principal directions, respectively.

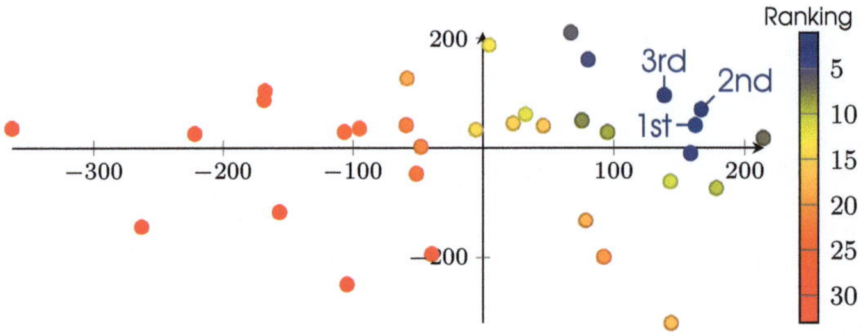

(b) Scatter plot of principal component scores for the athletes, color-coded by ranking. The x axis represents the first principal direction, and the y axis represents the second principal direction.

Figure C.6 PCA scores and loadings for decathlon data.

The first principal component describes 33% of the variance. In Fig. C.6a, we can examine which events contribute to this component. At one extreme are the pole vault and shot put, and the only negatively weighted event is the 1500-meter run. The pole vault incorporates abilities related to all events: running, jumping, and throwing, so perhaps it is not surprising that it is at an extreme. Indeed, the top three pole vaulters finished seventh, third, and sixth overall, respectively. The second principal component is orthogonal to the first and captures an additional 26% of the variance. It has throwing events (shot put, disc, javelin) at one extreme and again the 1500-meter run at the other extreme, which are at opposite ends of the endurance versus power spectrum. We can interpret this component as differentiating among the types of athlete, and it seems to differentiate faster runners from powerful throwers. Overall, we can see that throwing events are clustered in the lower right quadrant. The short-distance running events, along with the jumping events that are related to sprinting ability, are also clustered together in the upper right quadrant. The long-distance running (1500-meter run) and the pole vault are more unique events and are separated from the others.

In Fig. C.6b, we see the plots of the athletes with respect to their PCA scores. The first component divides the top-ranked athletes (positive values) and lowest ranked (negative values). The very top-ranked athletes have positive values in both the first and second components, and so they are clustered together.

Exercise C.2 Perform PCA on the *raw* data from the 1988 Summer Olympics decathlon using existing software for PCA or SVD. Your solution should provide (a) a discussion and justification of the preprocessing performed, (b) scatter plots of the first two PCA scores for each athlete and first two PCA coefficients for each event, (c) an interpretation of the first two principal components based on the values in the coefficient matrix, and (d) a comparison of the PCA results using points data with PCA results using raw data. Hint: The raw data has units of seconds and meters, which means the winner of each track event has the smallest value (shortest time) while the winner of each field event has the largest value (greatest distance). Be sure to take these differences into account in your interpretation.

References

Abdelfattah, A., Costa, T., Dongarra, J., et al. (2021). A set of batched basic linear algebra subprograms and LAPACK routines. *ACM Transactions on Mathematical Software* **47**(3), Article No. 21. DOI: 10.1145/3431921.

Abdi, H. and Williams, L. J. (2010). Principal component analysis. *WIREs Computational Statistics* **2**(4), 433–459. DOI: 10.1002/wics.101.

Acar, E., Dunlavy, D. M., Kolda, T. G., and Mørup, M. (2010). Scalable tensor factorizations with missing data. In *Proceedings of the 2010 SIAM International Conference on Data Mining (SDM'10)*, pp. 701–712. DOI: 10.1137/1.9781611972801.61.

Acar, E., Dunlavy, D. M., and Kolda, T. G. (2011a). A scalable optimization approach for fitting canonical tensor decompositions. *Journal of Chemometrics* **25**(2), 67–86. DOI: 10.1002/cem.1335.

Acar, E., Dunlavy, D. M., Kolda, T. G., and Mørup, M. (2011b). Scalable tensor factorizations for incomplete data. *Chemometrics and Intelligent Laboratory Systems* **106**(1), 41–56. DOI: 10.1016/j.chemolab.2010.08.004.

Acar, E., Papalexakis, E. E., Gürdeniz, G., et al. (2014). Structure-revealing data fusion. *BMC Bioinformatics* **15**(1). DOI: 10.1186/1471-2105-15-239.

Ahmadi-Asl, S., Abukhovich, S., Asante-Mensah, M. G., et al. (2021). Randomized algorithms for computation of Tucker decomposition and higher order SVD (HOSVD). *IEEE Access* **9**, 28684–28706. DOI: 10.1109/access.2021.3058103.

Anandkumar, A., Ge, R., Hsu, D., Kakade, S. M., and Telgarsky, M. (2014). Tensor decompositions for learning latent variable models. *Journal of Machine Learning Research* **15**(1), 2773–2832. URL: http://jmlr.org/papers/v15/anandkumar14b.html.

Anderson, E., Bai, Z., Bischof, C., et al. (1999). *LAPACK Users' Guide*. 3rd ed. Philadelphia: SIAM. DOI: 10.1137/1.9780898719604.

Atkinson, M. D. and Lloyd, S. (1983). The ranks of $m \times n \times (mn-2)$ tensors. *SIAM Journal on Computing* **12**(4), 611–615. DOI: 10.1137/0212041.

Atkinson, M. D. and Stephens, N. M. (1979). On the maximal multiplicative complexity of a family of bilinear forms. *Linear Algebra and Applications* **27**, 1–8. DOI: 10.1016/0024-3795(79)90026-0.

Austin, W., Ballard, G., and Kolda, T. G. (2016). Parallel tensor compression for large-scale scientific data. In *Proceedings of the 30th IEEE International Parallel and Distributed Processing Symposium (IPDPS'16)*, pp. 912–922. DOI: 10.1109/IPDPS.2016.67.

Bader, B. W. and Kolda, T. G. (2007). Efficient MATLAB computations with sparse and factored tensors. *SIAM Journal on Scientific Computing* **30**(1), 205–231. DOI: 10.1137/060676489.

Bader, B. W., Kolda, T. G., et al. (2023). *MATLAB Tensor Toolbox, Version 3.6*. URL: www.tensortoolbox.org (accessed July 29, 2024).

Ballard, G. (2024). *Decathlon Matrix Data*. URL: https://gitlab.com/tensors/matrix_data_decathlon (accessed July 29, 2024).

Ballard, G., Kolda, T. G., and Plantenga, T. (2011). Efficiently computing tensor eigenvalues on a GPU. In *Proceedings of the 2011 IEEE International Symposium on Parallel and Distributed Processing Workshops and PhD Forum (IPDPSW'11)*, pp. 1340–1348. DOI: 10.1109/IPDPS.2011.287.

Ballard, G., Ikenmeyer, C., Landsberg, J. M., and Ryder, N. (2018). The geometry of rank decompositions of matrix multiplication II: 3×3 matrices. *Journal of Pure and Applied Algebra* **223**(8), 3205–3224. DOI: 10.1016/j.jpaa.2018.10.014.

Ballard, G., Klinvex, A., and Kolda, T. G. (2020). TuckerMPI: a parallel C++/MPI software package for large-scale data compression via the Tucker tensor decomposition. *ACM Transactions on Mathematical Software* **46**(2), Article No. 13. DOI: 10.1145/3378445.

Ballard, G., Kolda, T. G., and Lindstrom, P. (2022). *Miranda Turbulent Flow Dataset.* URL: https://gitlab.com/tensors/tensor_data_miranda_sim (accessed July 29, 2024).

Basu, A., Harris, I. R., Hjort, N. L., and Jones, M. C. (1998). Robust and efficient estimation by minimising a density power divergence. *Biometrika* **85**(3), 549–559. DOI: 10.1093/biomet/85.3.549.

Battaglino, C., Ballard, G., and Kolda, T. G. (2018). A practical randomized CP tensor decomposition. *SIAM Journal on Matrix Analysis and Applications* **39**(2), 876–901. DOI: 10.1137/17M1112303.

Beltrán, C., Breiding, P., and Vannieuwenhoven, N. (2019). Pencil-based algorithms for tensor rank decomposition are not stable. *SIAM Journal on Matrix Analysis and Applications* **40**(2), 739–773. DOI: 10.1137/18m1200531.

Benson, A. R. and Ballard, G. (2015). A framework for practical parallel fast matrix multiplication. In *Proceedings of the 20th ACM SIGPLAN Symposium on Principles and Practice of Parallel Programming (PPoPP'15)*, pp. 42–53. DOI: 10.1145/2688500.2688513.

Bergqvist, G. (2013). Exact probabilities for typical ranks of $2 \times 2 \times 2$ and $3 \times 3 \times 2$ tensors. *Linear Algebra and its Applications* **438**(2), 663–667. DOI: 10.1016/j.laa.2011.02.041.

Bergqvist, G. and Forrester, P. (2011). Rank probabilities for real random $N \times N \times 2$ tensors. *Electronic Communications in Probability* **16**. DOI: 10.1214/ecp.v16-1655.

Bertsekas, D. P. (2016). *Nonlinear Programming*. 3rd ed. Belmont, MA: Athena Scientific.

Beylkin, G. and Mohlenkamp, M. J. (2002). Numerical operator calculus in higher dimensions. *Proceedings of the National Academy of Sciences* **99**(16), 10246–10251. DOI: 10.1073/pnas.112329799.

Beylkin, G. and Mohlenkamp, M. J. (2005). Algorithms for numerical analysis in high dimensions. *SIAM Journal on Scientific Computing* **26**(6), 2133–2159. DOI: 10.1137/040604959.

Bini, D. (1980). Relations between exact and approximate bilinear algorithms: applications. *CALCOLO* **17**(1), 87–97. DOI: 10.1007/BF02575865.

Bini, D., Capovani, M., Lotti, G., and Romani, F. (1979). $O(n^{2.7799})$ complexity for $n \times n$ approximate matrix multiplication. *Information Processing Letters* **8**(5), 234–235. DOI: 10.1016/0020-0190(79)90113-3.

Bini, D., Lotti, G., and Romani, F. (1980). Approximate solutions for the bilinear form computational problem. *SIAM Journal on Computing* **9**(4), 692–697. DOI: 10.1137/0209053.

Blackford, L. S., Demmel, J., Dongarra, J., et al. (2002). An updated set of Basic Linear Algebra Subroutines (BLAS). *ACM Transactions on Mathematical Software* **28**(2). DOI: 10.1145/567806.567807.

Bläser, M. (2003). On the complexity of the multiplication of matrices in small formats. *Journal of Complexity* **19**(1), 43–60. DOI: 10.1016/S0885-064X(02)00007-9.

Brachat, J., Comon, P., Mourrain, B., and Tsigaridas, E. (2010). Symmetric tensor decomposition. *Linear Algebra and its Applications* **433**(11–12), 1851–1872. DOI: 10.1016/j.laa.2010.06.046.

Brent, R. P. (1970). *Algorithms for Matrix Multiplication.* Tech. rep. STAN-CS-70-157. Stanford University, Department of Computer Science. URL: http://i.stanford.edu/pub/cstr/reports/cs/tr/70/157/CS-TR-70-157.pdf (accessed July 29, 2024).

Bro, R. and Andersson, C. A. (1998). Improving the speed of multi-way algorithms: Part II. Compression. *Chemometrics and Intelligent Laboratory Systems* **42**(1–2), 105–113. DOI: 10.1016/S0169-7439(98)00011-2.

Bro, R. and De Jong, S. (1997). A fast non-negativity-constrained least squares algorithm. *Journal of Chemometrics* **11**(5), 393–401. DOI: 10.1002/(SICI)1099-128X(199709/10)11:5<393::AID-CEM483>3.0.CO;2-L.

Bro, R. and Kiers, H. A. L. (2003). A new efficient method for determining the number of components in PARAFAC models. *Journal of Chemometrics* **17**(5), 274–286. DOI: 10.1002/cem.801.

Bro, R., Acar, E., and Kolda, T. G. (2008). Resolving the sign ambiguity in the singular value decomposition. *Journal of Chemometrics* **22**(2), 135–140. DOI: 10.1002/cem.1122.

Bro, R., Harshman, R. A., Sidiropoulos, N. D., and Lundy, M. E. (2009). Modeling multi-way data with linearly dependent loadings. *Journal of Chemometrics* **23**(7–8), 324–340. DOI: 10.1002/cem.1206.

Bro, R., Leardi, R., and Johnsen, L. G. (2013). Solving the sign indeterminacy for multiway models. *Journal of Chemometrics* **27**(3–4), 70–75. DOI: 10.1002/cem.2493.

Brookes, M. (2020). *The Matrix Reference Manual, Calculus Section.* URL: www.ee.ic.ac.uk/hp/staff/dmb/matrix/calculus.html (accessed July 29, 2024).

Buluç, A. and Gilbert, J. R. (2008). On the representation and multiplication of hypersparse matrices. In *IEEE International Symposium on Parallel and Distributed Processing (IPDPS'08).* DOI: 10.1109/ipdps.2008.4536313.

Byrd, R. H., Lu, P., Nocedal, J., and Zhu, C. (1995). A limited memory algorithm for bound constrained optimization. *SIAM Journal on Scientific Computing* **16**(5), 1190–1208. DOI: 10.1137/0916069.

Cabot, W. H. and Cook, A. W. (2006). Reynolds number effects on Rayleigh–Taylor instability with possible implications for type Ia supernovae. *Nature Physics* **2**(8), 562–568. DOI: 10.1038/nphys361.

Carroll, J. D. and Chang, J. J. (1970). Analysis of individual differences in multidimensional scaling via an N-way generalization of "Eckart–Young" decomposition. *Psychometrika* **35**, 283–319. DOI: 10.1007/BF02310791.

Carroll, J. D., Pruzansky, S., and Kruskal, J. B. (1980). CANDELINC: a general approach to multidimensional analysis of many-way arrays with linear constraints on parameters. *Psychometrika* **45**(1), 3–24. DOI: 10.1007/BF02293596.

Cartwright, D. and Sturmfels, B. (2013). The number of eigenvalues of a tensor. *Linear Algebra and its Applications* **438**(2), 942–952. DOI: 10.1016/j.laa.2011.05.040.

Cattell, R. B. (1944). Parallel proportional profiles and other principles for determining the choice of factors by rotation. *Psychometrika* **9**(4), 267–283. DOI: 10.1007/BF02288739.

Cattell, R. B. (1952). The three basic factor-analytic research designs: their interrelations and derivatives. *Psychological Bulletin* **49**, 499–452.

Chang, K. C., Pearson, K., and Zhang, T. (2009). On eigenvalue problems of real symmetric tensors. *Journal of Mathematical Analysis and Applications* **350**(1), 416–422. DOI: 10.1016/j.jmaa.2008.09.067.

Chen, D. and Plemmons, R. J. (2009). Nonnegativity constraints in numerical analysis. In *The Birth of Numerical Analysis*. Singapore: World Scientific, pp. 109–139. DOI: 10.1142/9789812836267_0008.

Cheng, D., Peng, R., Perros, I., and Liu, Y. (2016). SPALS: fast alternating least squares via implicit leverage scores sampling. In *Advances in Neural Information Processing Systems (NeurIPS'16).* URL: https://proceedings.neurips.cc/paper_files/paper/2016/file/f4f6dce2f3a0f9dada0c2b5b66452017-Paper.pdf.

Chi, E. C. and Kolda, T. G. (2012). On tensors, sparsity, and nonnegative factorizations. *SIAM Journal on Matrix Analysis and Applications* **33**(4), 1272–1299. DOI: 10.1137/110859063.

Choulakian, V. (2010). Some numerical results on the rank of generic three-way arrays over $\mathbb{R}$. *SIAM Journal on Matrix Analysis and Applications* **31**(4), 1541–1551. DOI: 10.1137/08073531X.

Cichocki, A. and Amari, S.-i. (2010). Families of alpha- beta- and gamma- divergences: flexible and robust measures of similarities. *Entropy* **12**(6), 1532–1568. DOI: 10.3390/e12061532.

Cichocki, A., Zdunek, R., Choi, S., Plemmons, R., and Amari, S.-I. (2007). Non-negative tensor factorization using alpha and beta divergences. In *Proceedings of the International Conference on Acoustics, Speech, and Signal Processing (ICASSP'07).* DOI: 10.1109/ICASSP.2007.367106.

Colley, S. J. (2006). *Vector Calculus.* 3rd ed. Hoboken: Prentice Hall.

Cui, C.-F., Dai, Y.-H., and Nie, J. (2014). All real eigenvalues of symmetric tensors. *SIAM Journal on Matrix Analysis and Applications* **35**(4), 1582–1601. DOI: 10.1137/140962292.

De Lathauwer, L. (2008a). Decompositions of a higher-order tensor in block terms – part I: lemmas for partitioned matrices. *SIAM Journal on Matrix Analysis and Applications* **30**(3), 1022–1032. DOI: 10.1137/060661685.

De Lathauwer, L. (2008b). Decompositions of a higher-order tensor in block terms – part II: definitions and uniqueness. *SIAM Journal on Matrix Analysis and Applications* **30**(3), 1033–1066. DOI: 10.1137/070690729.

De Lathauwer, L. and Nion, D. (2008). Decompositions of a higher-order tensor in block terms – part III: alternating least squares algorithms. *SIAM Journal on Matrix Analysis and Applications* **30**(3), 1067–1083. DOI: 10.1137/070690730.

De Lathauwer, L., De Moor, B., and Vandewalle, J. (2000a). A multilinear singular value decomposition. *SIAM Journal on Matrix Analysis and Applications* **21**(4), 1253–1278. DOI: 10.1137/S0895479896305696.

De Lathauwer, L., De Moor, B., and Vandewalle, J. (2000b). On the best rank-1 and rank-$(R_1, R_2, \ldots, R_N)$ approximation of higher-order tensors. *SIAM Journal on Matrix Analysis and Applications* **21**(4), 1324–1342. DOI: 10.1137/S0895479898346995.

de Silva, V. and Lim, L.-H. (2008). Tensor rank and the ill-posedness of the best low-rank approximation problem. *SIAM Journal on Matrix Analysis and Applications* **30**(3), 1084–1127. DOI: 10.1137/06066518X.

Dembo, R. S. and Steihaug, T. (1983). Truncated-Newton algorithms for large-scale unconstrained optimization. *Mathematical Programming* **26**(2), 190–212. DOI: 10.1007/BF02592055.

Demmel, J. (1997). *Applied Numerical Linear Algebra*. Philadelphia: SIAM.

Domanov, I. and De Lathauwer, L. (2014). Canonical polyadic decomposition of third-order tensors: reduction to generalized eigenvalue decomposition. *SIAM Journal on Matrix Analysis and Applications* **35**(2), 636–660. DOI: 10.1137/130916084.

Dunlavy, D. M., Johnson, N., et al. (2022). pyttb*: Python Tensor Toolbox*. URL: https://github.com/sandialabs/pyttb (accessed June 22, 2023).

Eckhart, C. and Young, G. (1936). The approximation of one matrix by another of lower rank. *Psychometrika* **1**(3), 211–218. DOI: 10.1007/BF02288367.

Edmonds, J. and Karp, R. M. (1972). Theoretical improvements in algorithmic efficiency for network flow problems. *Journal of the ACM* **19**(2), 248–264. DOI: 10.1145/321694.321699.

Elad, M. (2010). *Sparse and Redundant Representations*. New York: Springer.

Eldén, L. and Savas, B. (2009). A Newton–Grassmann method for computing the best multilinear rank-(r_1, r_2, r_3) approximation of a tensor. *SIAM Journal on Matrix Analysis and Applications* **31**(2), 248–271. DOI: 10.1137/070688316.

Eswar, S., Hayashi, K., Ballard, G., et al. (2021). PLANC: parallel low-rank approximation with nonnegativity constraints. *ACM Transactions on Mathematical Software* **47**(3). DOI: 10.1145/3432185.

Evert, E., Vandecappelle, M., and De Lathauwer, L. (2022). Canonical polyadic decomposition via the generalized Schur decomposition. *IEEE Signal Processing Letters* **29**, 937–941. DOI: 10.1109/lsp.2022.3156870.

Fackler, P. L. (2019). Algorithm 993: efficient computation with Kronecker products. *ACM Transactions on Mathematical Software* **45**(2), Article No. 22. DOI: 10.1145/3291041.

Fawzi, A., Balog, M., Huang, A., et al. (2022). Discovering faster matrix multiplication algorithms with reinforcement learning. *Nature* **610**, 47–53. DOI: 10.1038/s41586-022-05172-4.

Févotte, C. and Idier, J. (2011). Algorithms for nonnegative matrix factorization with the β-divergence. *Neural Computation* **23**(9), 2421–2456. DOI: 10.1162/NECO_a_00168.

Friedland, S. (2012). On the generic and typical ranks of 3-tensors. *Linear Algebra and Applications* **436**(3), 478–497. DOI: 10.1016/j.laa.2011.05.008.

Friedlander, M. P. and Hatz, K. (2008). Computing nonnegative tensor factorizations. *Computational Optimization and Applications* **23**(4), 631–647. DOI: 10.1080/10556780801996244.

Gillis, N. (2021). *Nonnegative Matrix Factorization*. Philadelphia: SIAM. DOI: 10.1137/1.9781611976410.

Golub, G. and Kahan, W. (1965). Calculating the singular values and pseudo-inverse of a matrix. *Journal of the Society for Industrial and Applied Mathematics Series B Numerical Analysis* **2**(2), 205–224. DOI: 10.1137/0702016.

Golub, G. H. and Van Loan, C. F. (2013). *Matrix Computations*. 4th ed. Baltimore: Johns Hopkins University Press.

Grasedyck, L. (2010). Hierarchical singular value decomposition of tensors. *SIAM Journal on Matrix Analysis and Applications* **31**(4), 2029–2054. DOI: 10.1137/090764189.

Grasedyck, L., Kressner, D., and Tobler, C. (2013). A literature survey of low-rank tensor approximation techniques. *GAMM-Mitteilungen* **36**(1), 53–78. DOI: 10.1002/gamm.201310004.

Gu, M. (2015). Subspace iteration randomization and singular value problems. *SIAM Journal on Scientific Computing* **37**(3), A1139–A1173. DOI: 10.1137/130938700.

Hackbusch, W. (2014). Numerical tensor calculus. *Acta Numerica* **23**, 651–742. DOI: 10.1017/S0962492914000087.

Hackbusch, W. (2019). *Tensor Spaces and Numerical Tensor Calculus*. 2nd ed. Cham: Springer. DOI: 10.1007/978-3-030-35554-8.

Hackbusch, W. and Kühn, S. (2009). A new scheme for the tensor representation. *Journal of Fourier Analysis and Applications* **15**(5), 706–722. DOI: 10.1007/s00041-009-9094-9.

Halko, N., Martinsson, P. G., and Tropp, J. A. (2011). Finding structure with randomness: probabilistic algorithms for constructing approximate matrix decompositions. *SIAM Review* **53**(2), 217–288. DOI: 10.1137/090771806.

Hansen, S., Plantenga, T., and Kolda, T. G. (2015). Newton-based optimization for Kullback–Leibler nonnegative tensor factorizations. *Optimization Methods and Software* **30**(5), 1002–1029. DOI: 10.1080/10556788.2015.1009977.

Harshman, R. A. (1970). Foundations of the PARAFAC procedure: models and conditions for an "explanatory" multi-modal factor analysis. *UCLA Working Papers in Phonetics* **16**, 1–84. URL: www.psychology.uwo.ca/faculty/harshman/wpppfac0.pdf (accessed July 29, 2024).

Harshman, R. A. (1972). Determination and proof of minimum uniqueness conditions for PARAFAC1. *UCLA working papers in phonetics* **22**, 111–117. URL: www.psychology.uwo.ca/faculty/harshman/wpppfac1.pdf (accessed July 29, 2024).

Håstad, J. (1990). Tensor rank is NP-complete. *Journal of Algorithms* **11**(4), 644–654. DOI: 10.1016/0196-6774(90)90014-6.

Hastie, T., Tibshrirani, R., and Friedman, J. (2009). *The Elements of Statistical Learning*. 2nd ed. New York: Springer. DOI: 10.1007/978-0-387-84858-7.

Helal, A. E., Laukemann, J., Checconi, F., et al. (2021). ALTO: adaptive linearized storage of sparse tensors. In *Proceedings of the 35th ACM International Conference on Supercomputing (ICS'21)*, pp. 404–416. DOI: 10.1145/3447818.3461703.

Higham, N. J. (1992). Stability of a method for multiplying complex matrices with three real matrix multiplications. *SIAM Journal on Matrix Analysis and Applications* **13**(3), 681–687. DOI: 10.1137/0613043.

Higham, N. J. (2002). *Accuracy and Stability of Numerical Algorithms*. 2nd ed. Philadelphia: SIAM.

Hillar, C. J. and Lim, L.-H. (2013). Most tensor problems are NP-hard. *Journal of the ACM* **60**(6), 1–39. DOI: 10.1145/2512329.

Hitchcock, F. L. (1927). The expression of a tensor or a polyadic as a sum of products. *Journal of Mathematics and Physics* **6**(1), 164–189. DOI: 10.1002/sapm192761164.

Hong, D., Kolda, T. G., and Duersch, J. A. (2020). Generalized canonical polyadic tensor decomposition. *SIAM Review* **62**(1), 133–163. DOI: 10.1137/18M1203626.

Hopcroft, J. E. and Kerr, L. R. (1971). On minimizing the number of multiplications necessary for matrix multiplication. *SIAM Journal on Applied Mathematics* **20**(1), 30–36. DOI: 10.1137/0120004.

Hopcroft, J. and Musinski, J. (1973). Duality applied to the complexity of matrix multiplication and other bilinear forms. *SIAM Journal on Computing* **2**(3), 159–173. DOI: 10.1137/0202013.

Horn, R. A. and Johnson, C. R. (1985). *Matrix Analysis*. Cambridge: Cambridge University Press.

Horn, R. A. and Johnson, C. R. (1991). *Topics in Matrix Analysis*. Cambridge: Cambridge University Press.

Horn, R. A. and Yang, Z. (2020). Rank of a Hadamard product. *Linear Algebra and its Applications* **591**, 87–98. DOI: 10.1016/j.laa.2020.01.005.

Huang, J., Smith, T. M., Henry, G. M., and van de Geijn, R. A. (2016). Strassen's algorithm reloaded. In *Proceedings of the International Conference for High Performance Computing, Networking, Storage and Analysis (SC'16)*. DOI: 10.5555/3014904.3014983.

Huber, P. J. (1964). Robust estimation of a location parameter. *Annals of Statistics* **53**(1), 73–101. DOI: 10.1214/aoms/1177703732.

JáJá, J. (1979). Optimal evaluation of pairs of bilinear forms. *SIAM Journal on Computing* **8**(3), 443–462. DOI: 10.1137/0208037.

Jin, R., Kolda, T. G., and Ward, R. (2020). Faster Johnson–Lindenstrauss transforms via Kronecker products. *Information and Inference: A Journal of the IMA*. DOI: 10.1093/imaiai/iaaa028.

Johnson, R. W. and McLoughlin, A. M. (1986). Noncommutative bilinear algorithms for 3×3 matrix multiplication. *SIAM Journal on Computing* **15**(2), 595–603. DOI: 10.1137/0215043.

Jolliffe, I. T. (2002). *Principal Component Analysis*. 2nd ed. Berlin: Springer-Verlag. DOI: 10.1007/b98835.

Kapteyn, A., Neudecker, H., and Wansbeek, T. (1986). An approach to n-mode components analysis. *Psychometrika* **51**(2), 269–275. DOI: 10.1007/BF02293984.

Karstadt, E. and Schwartz, O. (2020). Matrix multiplication, a little faster. *Journal of the ACM* **67**(1). DOI: 10.1145/3364504.

Kauers, M. and Moosbauer, J. (2023). Flip graphs for matrix multiplication. In *Proceedings of the 2023 International Symposium on Symbolic and Algebraic Computation*. DOI: 10.1145/3597066.3597120.

Kaya, O. and Robert, Y. (2019). Computing dense tensor decompositions with optimal dimension trees. *Algorithmica* **81**, 2092–2121. DOI: 10.1007/s00453-018-0525-3.

Kaya, O. and Uçar, B. (2015). Scalable sparse tensor decompositions in distributed memory systems. In *Proceedings of the International Conference for High Performance Computing, Networking, Storage and Analysis (SC'15)*. DOI: 10.1145/2807591.2807624.

Kaya, O. and Uçar, B. (2016). High-performance parallel algorithms for the Tucker decomposition of higher order sparse tensors. In *45th International Conference on Parallel Processing (ICPP'16)*. DOI: 10.1109/ICPP.2016.19.

Kiers, H. A. L. (1997). Weighted least squares fitting using ordinary least squares algorithms. *Psychometrika* **62**(2), 215–266. DOI: 10.1007/BF02295279.

Kiers, H. A. L. (2000). Towards a standardized notation and terminology in multiway analysis. *Journal of Chemometrics* **14**(3), 105–122. DOI: 10.1002/1099-128X(200005/06)14:3<105::AID-CEM582>3.0.CO;2-I.

Kilmer, M. E. and Martin, C. D. (2011). Factorization strategies for third-order tensors. *Linear Algebra and its Applications* **435**(3), 641–658. DOI: 10.1016/j.laa.2010.09.020.

Kilmer, M. E., Horesh, L., Avron, H., and Newman, E. (2021). Tensor–tensor algebra for optimal representation and compression of multiway data. *Proceedings of the National Academy of Sciences* **118**(28), e2015851118. DOI: 10.1073/pnas.2015851118.

Kim, J., He, Y., and Park, H. (2014). Algorithms for nonnegative matrix and tensor factorizations: a unified view based on block coordinate descent framework. *Journal of Global Optimization* **58**(2), 285–319. DOI: 10.1007/s10898-013-0035-4.

Kingma, D. P. and Ba, J. (2015). *Adam: A Method for Stochastic Optimization*. Published as a conference paper at the 3rd International Conference for Learning Representations, San Diego, 2015. arXiv: 1412.6980v9.

Kofidis, E. and Regalia, P. A. (2002). On the best rank-1 approximation of higher-order supersymmetric tensors. *SIAM Journal on Matrix Analysis and Applications* **23**(3), 863–884. DOI: 10.1137/S0895479801387413.

Kolda, T. G. (2001). Orthogonal tensor decompositions. *SIAM Journal on Matrix Analysis and Applications* **23**(1), 243–255. DOI: 10.1137/S0895479800368354.

Kolda, T. G. (2003). A counterexample to the possibility of an extension of the Eckart–Young low-rank approximation theorem for the orthogonal rank tensor decomposition. *SIAM Journal on Matrix Analysis and Applications* **24**(3), 762–767. DOI: 10.1137/S0895479801394465.

Kolda, T. G. (2015a). Numerical optimization for symmetric tensor decomposition. *Mathematical Programming B* **151**(1), 225–248. DOI: 10.1007/s10107-015-0895-0.

Kolda, T. G. (2015b). *Symmetric Orthogonal Tensor Decomposition Is Trivial.* arXiv: 1503.01375.

Kolda, T. G. (2021a). *EEM Tensor Data.* URL: https://gitlab.com/tensors/tensor_data_eem (accessed July 29, 2024).

Kolda, T. G. (2021b). *Will the Real Jennrich's Algorithm Please Stand Up?* URL: www.mathsci.ai/post/jennrich/ (accessed July 29, 2024).

Kolda, T. G. (2022a). *Monkey BMI Tensor Dataset.* URL: https://gitlab.com/tensors/tensor_data_monkey_bmi (accessed July 29, 2024).

Kolda, T. G. (2022b). *New Chicago Crime Tensor Dataset.* URL: https://gitlab.com/tensors/tensor_data_miranda_sim (accessed July 29, 2024).

Kolda, T. G. and Bader, B. W. (2009). Tensor decompositions and applications. *SIAM Review* **51**(3), 455–500. DOI: 10.1137/07070111X.

Kolda, T. and Duersch, J. (2017). *Sparse Versus Scarce.* URL: www.mathsci.ai/post/sparse-versus-scarce/ (accessed July 29, 2024).

Kolda, T. G. and Mayo, J. R. (2011). Shifted power method for computing tensor eigenpairs. *SIAM Journal on Matrix Analysis and Applications* **32**(4), 1095–1124. DOI: 10.1137/100801482.

Kolda, T. G. and Mayo, J. R. (2014). An adaptive shifted power method for computing generalized tensor eigenpairs. *SIAM Journal on Matrix Analysis and Applications* **35**(4), 1563–1581. DOI: 10.1137/140951758.

Kolda, T. G. and Sun, J. (2008). Scalable tensor decompositions for multi-aspect data mining. In *Proceedings of the 8th IEEE International Conference on Data Mining (ICDM'08)*, pp. 363–372. DOI: 10.1109/ICDM.2008.89.

Kolda, T. G., Bader, B. W., and Kenny, J. P. (2005). Higher-order web link analysis using multilinear algebra. In *Proceedings of the 5th IEEE International Conference on Data Mining (ICDM'05)*, pp. 242–249. DOI: 10.1109/ICDM.2005.77.

Kroonenberg, P. M. and De Leeuw, J. (1980). Principal component analysis of three-mode data by means of alternating least squares algorithms. *Psychometrika* **45**(1), 69–97. DOI: 10.1007/BF02293599.

Kruskal, J. B. (1977). Three-way arrays: rank and uniqueness of trilinear decompositions, with application to arithmetic complexity and statistics. *Linear Algebra and its Applications* **18**(2), 95–138. DOI: 10.1016/0024-3795(77)90069-6.

Kruskal, J. B. (1983). "Statement of some current results about three-way arrays." Unpublished manuscript, AT&T Bell Laboratories, Murray Hill, NJ. URL: http://three-mode.leidenuniv.nl/pdf/k/kruskal1983.pdf.

Kruskal, J. B. (1989). Rank, decomposition, and uniqueness for 3-way and N-way arrays. In *Multiway Data Analysis.* Ed. by R. Coppi and S. Bolasco. Amsterdam: North-Holland, pp. 7–18. URL: www.psychology.uwo.ca/faculty/harshman/jbkrank.pdf (accessed July 29, 2024).

Laderman, J. D. (1976). A noncommutative algorithm for multiplying 3×3 matrices using 23 multiplications. *Bulletin of the American Mathematical Society* **82**(1), 126–128. URL: www.ams.org/bull/1976-82-01/S0002-9904-1976-13988-2/S0002-9904-1976-13988-2.pdf (accessed July 29, 2024).

Landsberg, J. M. (2006). The border rank of the multiplication of 2×2 matrices is seven. *Journal of the American Mathematical Society* **19**, 447–459. DOI: 10.1090/S0894-0347-05-00506-0.

Larsen, B. W. and Kolda, T. G. (2022). Practical leverage-based sampling for low-rank tensor decomposition. *SIAM Journal on Matrix Analysis and Applications* **43**(3), 1488–1517. DOI: 10.1137/21m1441754.

Lawson, C. L. and Hanson, R. J. (1974). *Solving Least Squares Problems.* Hoboken: Prentice-Hall.

Lee, D. D. and Seung, H. S. (1999). Learning the parts of objects by non-negative matrix factorization. *Nature* **401**, 788–791. DOI: 10.1038/44565.

Lee, D. D. and Seung, H. S. (2001). Algorithms for non-negative matrix factorization. In *Advances in Neural Information Processing Systems (NIPS'00)*. Vol. 13, pp. 556–562. URL: https://proceedings.neurips.cc/paper_files/paper/2000/file/f9d1152547c0bde01830b7e8bd60024c-Paper.pdf (accessed July 29, 2024).

Leurgans, S. E., Ross, R. T., and Abel, R. B. (1993). A decomposition for three-way arrays. *SIAM Journal on Matrix Analysis and Applications* **14**(4), 1064–1083. DOI: 10.1137/0614071.

Li, J., Battaglino, C., Perros, I., Sun, J., and Vuduc, R. (2015). An input-adaptive and in-place approach to dense tensor-times-matrix multiply. In *Proceedings of the International Conference for High Performance Computing, Networking, Storage and Analysis (SC'15)*. DOI: 10.1145/2807591.2807671.

Li, J., Choi, J., Perros, I., Sun, J., and Vuduc, R. (2017). Model-driven sparse CP decomposition for higher-order tensors. In *IEEE International Parallel and Distributed Processing Symposium (IPDPS'17)*, pp. 1048–1057. DOI: 10.1109/ipdps.2017.80.

Li, J., Sun, J., and Vuduc, R. (2018). HiCOO: hierarchical storage of sparse tensors. In *International Conference for High Performance Computing, Networking, Storage and Analysis (SC'18)*, pp. 238–252. DOI: 10.1109/SC.2018.00022.

Lim, L.-H. (2005). Singular values and eigenvalues of tensors: a variational approach. In *Proceedings of the IEEE International Workshop on Computational Advances in Multi-Sensor Adaptive Processing (CAMSAP'05)*, pp. 129–132. DOI: 10.1109/CAMAP.2005.1574201.

Lipshitz, B., Ballard, G., Demmel, J., and Schwartz, O. (2012). Communication-avoiding parallel Strassen: implementation and performance. In *International Conference for High Performance Computing, Networking, Storage and Analysis (SC'12)*. DOI: 10.1109/sc.2012.33.

Liu, X. and Sidiropoulos, N. D. (2001). Cramér–Rao lower bounds for low-rank decomposition of multidimensional arrays. *IEEE Transactions on Signal Processing* **49**(9), 2074–2086. DOI: 10.1109/78.942635.

Magnus, J. R. and Neudecker, H. (1979). The commutation matrix: some properties and applications. *The Annals of Statistics* **7**(2), 381–394. DOI: 10.1214/aos/1176344621.

Malik, O. A. and Becker, S. (2018). Low-rank Tucker decomposition of large tensors using TensorSketch. In *Advances in Neural Information Processing Systems (NeurIPS'18)*, pp. 10116–10126. URL: https://proceedings.neurips.cc/paper_files/paper/2018/file/45a766fa266ea2ebeb6680fa139d2a3d-Paper.pdf (accessed July 29, 2024).

Malik, O. A. and Becker, S. (2020). Guarantees for the Kronecker fast Johnson–Lindenstrauss transform using a coherence and sampling argument. *Linear Algebra and its Applications* **602**, 120–137. DOI: 10.1016/j.laa.2020.05.004.

Mihoko, M. and Eguchi, S. (2002). Robust blind source separation by beta divergence. *Neural Computation* **14**(8), 1859–1886. DOI: 10.1162/089976602760128045.

Minster, R., Viviano, I., Liu, X., and Ballard, G. (2023). CP decomposition for tensors via alternating least squares with QR decomposition. *Numerical Linear Algebra with Applications*, e2511. DOI: 10.1002/nla.2511.

Minster, R., Li, Z., and Ballard, G. (2024). Parallel randomized Tucker decomposition algorithms. *SIAM Journal on Scientific Computing* **46**(2), A1186–A1213. DOI: 10.1137/22m1540363.

Möcks, J. (1988). Topographic components model for event-related potentials and some biophysical considerations. *IEEE Transactions on Biomedical Engineering* **35**(6), 482–484. DOI: 10.1109/10.2119.

Mørup, M., Hansen, L. K., and Arnfred, S. M. (2008). Algorithms for sparse nonnegative Tucker decompositions. *Neural Computation* **20**(8), 2112–2131. DOI: 10.1162/neco.2008.11-06-407.

Nesterov, Y. (2012). Gradient methods for minimizing composite functions. *Mathematical Programming* **140**(1), 125–161. DOI: 10.1007/s10107-012-0629-5.

Nocedal, J. (1980). Updating quasi-Newton matrices with limited storage. *Mathematics of Computation* **35**(151), 773–782. DOI: 10.2307/2006193.

Nocedal, J. and Wright, S. J. (2006). *Numerical Optimization*. 2nd ed. New York: Springer. DOI: 10.1007/978-0-387-40065-5.

Oseledets, I. V. (2011). Tensor-train decomposition. *SIAM Journal on Scientific Computing* **33**(5), 2295–2317. DOI: 10.1137/090752286.

Oseledets, I. V. and Tyrtyshnikov, E. E. (2009). Breaking the curse of dimensionality, or how to use SVD in many dimensions. *SIAM Journal on Scientific Computing* **31**(5), 3744–3759. DOI: 10.1137/090748330.

Oseledets, I. and Tyrtyshnikov, E. (2010). TT-cross approximation for multidimensional arrays. *Linear Algebra and its Applications* **432**(1), 70–88. DOI: 10.1016/j.laa.2009.07.024.

Paatero, P. (1997). A weighted non-negative least squares algorithm for three-way "PARAFAC" factor analysis. *Chemometrics and Intelligent Laboratory Systems* **38**(2), 223–242. DOI: 10.1016/S0169-7439(97)00031-2.

Paatero, P. (1999). The multilinear engine: a table-driven, least squares program for solving multilinear problems, including the n-way parallel factor analysis model. *Journal of Computational and Graphical Statistics* **8**(4), 854–888. DOI: 10.1080/10618600.1999.10474853.

Paatero, P. (2000). Construction and analysis of degenerate PARAFAC models. *Journal of Chemometrics* **14**(3), 285–299. DOI: 10.1002/1099-128X(200005/06)14:3<285::AID-CEM584>3.0.CO;2-1.

Paatero, P. and Tapper, U. (1994). Positive matrix factorization: a non-negative factor model with optimal utilization of error estimates of data values. *Environmetrics* **5**(2), 111–126. DOI: 10.1002/env.3170050203.

Paige, C. C. and Saunders, M. A. (1982). LSQR: an algorithm for sparse linear equations and sparse least squares. *ACM Transactions on Mathematical Software* **8**(1), 43–71. DOI: 10.1145/355984.355989.

Phan, A. H. and Cichocki, A. (2008). Fast and efficient algorithms for nonnegative Tucker decomposition. In *Advances in Neural Networks (ISNN'08)*. New York: Springer, pp. 772–782. DOI: 10.1007/978-3-540-87734-9_88.

Phan, A. H. and Cichocki, A. (2011). Extended HALS algorithm for nonnegative Tucker decomposition and its applications for multiway analysis and classification. *Neurocomputing* **74**(11), 1956–1969. DOI: 10.1016/j.neucom.2010.06.031.

Phan, A. H., Tichavský, P., and Cichocki, A. (2011). Fast damped Gauss–Newton algorithm for sparse and nonnegative tensor factorization. In *Proceedings of the IEEE International Conference on Acoustics, Speech, and Signal Processing (ICASSP'11)*, pp. 1988–1991. DOI: 10.1109/ICASSP.2011.5946900.

Phan, A.-H., Tichavský, P., and Cichocki, A. (2013a). Fast alternating LS algorithms for high order CANDECOMP/PARAFAC tensor factorizations. *IEEE Transactions on Signal Processing* **61**(19), 4834–4846. DOI: 10.1109/TSP.2013.2269903.

Phan, A.-H., Tichavský, P., and Cichocki, A. (2013b). Low complexity damped Gauss–Newton algorithms for CANDECOMP/PARAFAC. *SIAM Journal on Matrix Analysis and Applications* **34**(1), 126–147. DOI: 10.1137/100808034.

Phipps, E. and Kolda, T. G. (2019). Software for sparse tensor decomposition on emerging computing architectures. *SIAM Journal on Scientific Computing* **41**(3), C269–C290. DOI: 10.1137/18M1210691.

Qi, L. (2005). Eigenvalues of a real supersymmetric tensor. *Journal of Symbolic Computation* **40**, 1302–1324. DOI: 10.1016/j.jsc.2005.05.007.

Regalia, P. A. and Kofidis, E. (2003). Monotonic convergence of fixed-point algorithms for ICA. *IEEE Transactions on Neural Networks* **14**(4), 943–949. DOI: 10.1109/TNN.2003.813843.

Robbins, H. and Monro, S. (1951). A stochastic approximation method. *The Annals of Mathematical Statistics* **22**(3), 400–407. URL: www.jstor.org/stable/2236626 (accessed July 29, 2024).

Robeva, E. (2014). *Orthogonal Decomposition of Symmetric Tensors*. eprint: 1409.6685.

Royer, J.-P., Thirion-Moreau, N., and Comon, P. (2011). Computing the polyadic decomposition of nonnegative third order tensors. *Signal Processing* **91**(9), 2159–2171. DOI: 10.1016/j.sigpro.2011.03.006.

Sanchez, E. and Kowalski, B. R. (1990). Tensorial resolution: a direct trilinear decomposition. *Journal of Chemometrics* **4**(1), 29–45. DOI: 10.1002/cem.1180040105.

Sedoglavic, A. and Smirnov, A. V. (2021). The tensor rank of 5×5 matrices multiplication is bounded by 98 and its border rank by 89. DOI: 10.1145/3452143.3465537.

Shashua, A. and Hazan, T. (2005). Non-negative tensor factorization with applications to statistics and computer vision. In *Proceedings of the 22nd International Conference on Machine Learning (ICML'05)*, pp. 792–799. DOI: 10.1145/1102351.1102451.

Sherman, S. and Kolda, T. G. (2020). Estimating higher-order moments using symmetric tensor decomposition. *SIAM Journal on Matrix Analysis and Applications* **41**(3), 1369–1387. DOI: 10.1137/19m1299633.

Sidiropoulos, N. D. and Bro, R. (2000). On the uniqueness of multilinear decomposition of N-way arrays. *Journal of Chemometrics* **14**(3), 229–239. DOI: 10.1002/1099-128X(200005/06)14:3<229::AID-CEM587>3.0.CO;2-N.

Sidiropoulos, N. D., De Lathauwer, L., Fu, X., et al. (2017). Tensor decomposition for signal processing and machine learning. *IEEE Transactions on Signal Processing* **65**(13), 3551–3582. DOI: 10.1109/tsp.2017.2690524.

Smilde, A., Bro, R., and Geladi, P. (2004). *Multi-Way Analysis: Applications in the Chemical Sciences*. Chichester: Wiley.

Smirnov, A. V. (2013). The bilinear complexity and practical algorithms for matrix multiplication. *Computational Mathematics and Mathematical Physics* **53**(12), 1781–1795. DOI: 10.1134/S0965542513120129.

Smith, S. and Karypis, G. (2015). Tensor-matrix products with a compressed sparse tensor. In *Proceedings of the 5th Workshop on Irregular Applications: Architectures and Algorithms (IA^3'15)*. DOI: 10.1145/2833179.2833183.

Sorber, L., Van Barel, M., and De Lathauwer, L. (2013). Optimization-based algorithms for tensor decompositions: canonical polyadic decomposition, decomposition in rank-(Lr,Lr,1) terms, and a new generalization. *SIAM Journal on Optimization* **23**(2), 695–720. DOI: 10.1137/120868323.

Sorensen, M. and De Lathauwer, L. (2010). New simultaneous generalized Schur decomposition methods for the computation of the canonical polyadic decomposition. In *2010 Conference Record of the Forty Fourth Asilomar Conference on Signals, Systems and Computers*. DOI: 10.1109/ACSSC.2010.5757456.

Springer, P., Hammond, J. R., and Bientinesi, P. (2017). TTC: a high-performance compiler for tensor transpositions. *ACM Transactions on Mathematical Software* **44**(2), 1–21. DOI: 10.1145/3104988.

Stegeman, A. and Sidiropoulos, N. D. (2007). On Kruskal's uniqueness condition for the CANDECOMP/PARAFAC decomposition. *Linear Algebra and its Applications* **420**(2–3), 540–552. DOI: 10.1016/j.laa.2006.08.010.

Strang, G. (2016). *Introduction to Linear Algebra*. 5th ed. Wellesley: Wellesley-Cambridge Press.

Strassen, V. (1969). Gaussian elimination is not optimal. *Numerische Mathematik* **13**(4), 354–356. DOI: 10.1007/BF02165411.

Sumi, T., Sakata, T., and Miyazaki, M. (2013). Typical ranks for $m \times n \times (m-1)n$ tensors with $m \leq n$. *Linear Algebra and its Applications* **438**(2), 953–958. DOI: 10.1016/j.laa.2011.08.009.

Sun, Y., Guo, Y., Luo, C., Tropp, J., and Udell, M. (2020). Low-rank Tucker approximation of a tensor from streaming data. *SIAM Journal on Mathematics of Data Science* **2**(4), 1123–1150. DOI: 10.1137/19m1257718.

ten Berge, J. M. F. (1991). Kruskal's polynomial for $2 \times 2 \times 2$ arrays and a generalization to $2 \times n \times n$ arrays. *Psychometrika* **56**(4), 631–636. DOI: 10.1007/BF02294495.

ten Berge, J. (2000a). "The k-rank of a Khatri–Rao product." Unpublished Note, Heijmans Institute of Psychological Research, University of Groningen, the Netherlands.

ten Berge, J. M. F. (2000b). The typical rank of tall three-way arrays. *Psychometrika* **65**(4), 525–532. DOI: 10.1007/BF02296342.

ten Berge, J. M. F. (2004). Partial uniqueness in CANDECOMP/PARAFAC. *Journal of Chemometrics* **18**(1), 12–16. DOI: 10.1002/cem.839.

ten Berge, J. M. F. (2011). Simplicity and typical rank results for three-way arrays. *Psychometrika* **76**(1), 3–12. DOI: 10.1007/S11336-010-9193-1.

ten Berge, J. M. F. and Kiers, H. A. L. (1999). Simplicity of core arrays in three-way principal component analysis and the typical rank of $p \times q \times 2$ arrays. *Linear Algebra and its Applications* **294**(1–3), 169–179. DOI: 10.1016/S0024-3795(99)00057-9.

ten Berge, J. M. F. and Sidiriopolous, N. D. (2002). On uniqueness in CANDECOMP/PARAFAC. *Psychometrika* **67**(3), 399–409. DOI: 10.1007/BF02294992.

ten Berge, J. M. F. and Stegeman, A. (2006). Symmetry transformations for square sliced three-way arrays, with applications to their typical rank. *Linear Algebra and Applications* **418**(1), 215–224. DOI: 10.1016/j.laa.2006.02.002.

ten Berge, J. M. F. and Tendeiro, J. N. (2009). The link between sufficient conditions by Harshman and by Kruskal for uniqueness in Candecomp/Parafac. *Journal of Chemometrics* **23**(7–8), 321–323. DOI: 10.1002/cem.1204.

ten Berge, J. M. F., Kiers, H. A. L., and de Leeuw, J. (1988). Explicit CANDECOMP/PARAFAC solutions for a contrived $2 \times 2 \times 2$ array of rank three. *Psychometrika* **53**(4), 579–583. DOI: 10.1007/BF02294409.

ten Berge, J. M. F., Sidiropoulos, N. D., and Rocci, R. (2004). Typical rank and INDSCAL dimensionality for symmetric three-way arrays of order $I \times 2 \times 2$ or $I \times 3 \times 3$. *Linear Algebra and its Applications* **388**, 363–377. DOI: 10.1016/j.laa.2004.03.009.

TensorFlow Team (2022). *Working with Sparse Tensors*. TensorFlow Guide. URL: www.tensorflow.org/guide/sparse_tensor (accessed July 29, 2024).

Tobler, C. (2012). *Low-Rank Tensor Methods for Linear Systems and Eigenvalue Problems*. PhD thesis. ETH Zurich. URL: http://sma.epfl.ch/~anchpcommon/students/tobler.pdf (accessed July 29, 2024).

Tomasi, G. and Bro, R. (2005). PARAFAC and missing values. *Chemometrics and Intelligent Laboratory Systems* **75**(2), 163–180. DOI: 10.1016/j.chemolab.2004.07.003.

Tomasi, G. and Bro, R. (2006). A comparison of algorithms for fitting the PARAFAC model. *Computational Statistics & Data Analysis* **50**(7), 1700–1734. DOI: 10.1016/j.csda.2004.11.013.

Trefethen, L. N. and Bau, D. (1997). *Numerical Linear Algebra*. Philadelphia: SIAM. DOI: 10.1137/1.9780898719574.

Tucker, L. R. (1966). Some mathematical notes on three-mode factor analysis. *Psychometrika* **31**, 279–311. DOI: 10.1007/BF02289464.

Uschmajew, A. (2010). Well-posedness of convex maximization problems on Stiefel manifolds and orthogonal tensor product approximations. *Numerische Mathematik* **115**(2), 309–331. DOI: 10.1007/s00211-009-0276-9.

Uschmajew, A. (2012). Local convergence of the alternating least squares algorithm for canonical tensor approximation. *SIAM Journal on Matrix Analysis and Applications* **33**(2), 639–652. DOI: 10.1137/110843587.

Vandecappelle, M., Vervliet, N., and De Lathauwer, L. (2020). A second-order method for fitting the canonical polyadic decomposition with non-least-squares cost. *IEEE Transactions on Signal Processing* **68**, 4454–4465. DOI: 10.1109/tsp.2020.3010719.

Vannieuwenhoven, N., Vandebril, R., and Meerbergen, K. (2012). A new truncation strategy for the higher-order singular value decomposition. *SIAM Journal on Scientific Computing* **34**(2), A1027–A1052. DOI: 10.1137/110836067.

Vavasis, S. A. (2009). On the complexity of nonnegative matrix factorization. *SIAM Journal on Optimization* **20**(3), 1364–1377. DOI: 10.1137/070709967.

Vervliet, N. and De Lathauwer, L. (2016). A randomized block sampling approach to canonical polyadic decomposition of large-scale tensors. *IEEE Journal of Selected Topics in Signal Processing* **10**(2), 284–295. DOI: 10.1109/JSTSP.2015.2503260.

Vervliet, N. and De Lathauwer, L. (2019). Numerical optimization-based algorithms for data fusion. In *Data Handling in Science and Technology*. Amsterdam: Elsevier, pp. 81–128. DOI: 10.1016/b978-0-444-63984-4.00004-1.

Vervliet, N., Debals, O., Sorber, L., Van Barel, M., and De Lathauwer, L. (2017). *Datasets: Dense, Incomplete, Sparse and Structured.* TensorLab User Manual. URL: www.tensorlab.net/doc/data.html#sparse-tensors (accessed July 29, 2024).

Vyas, S., Even-Chen, N., Stavisky, S. D., et al. (2018). Neural population dynamics underlying motor learning transfer. *Neuron* **97**(5). DOI: 10.1016/j.neuron.2018.01.040.

Vyas, S., O'Shea, D. J., Ryu, S. I., and Shenoy, K. V. (2020). Causal role of motor preparation during error-driven learning. *Neuron* **106**(2). DOI: 10.1016/j.neuron.2020.01.019.

Welling, M. and Weber, M. (2001). Positive tensor factorization. *Pattern Recognition Letters* **22**(12), 1255–1261. DOI: 10.1016/S0167-8655(01)00070-8.

Williams, A. H., Kim, T. H., Wang, F., et al. (2018). Unsupervised discovery of demixed, low-dimensional neural dynamics across multiple timescales through tensor components analysis. *Neuron* **98**(6), 1099–1115. DOI: 10.1016/j.neuron.2018.05.015.

Williams, V. V., Xu, Y., Xu, Z., and Zhou, R. (2024). New bounds for matrix multiplication: from alpha to omega. In *Proceedings of the 2024 Annual ACM-SIAM Symposium on Discrete Algorithms (SODA)*, pp. 3792–3835. DOI: 10.1137/1.9781611977912.134.

Winograd, S. (1971). On multiplication of 2×2 matrices. *Linear Algebra and its Applications* **4**(4), 381–388. DOI: 10.1016/0024-3795(71)90009-7.

Wright, S. J. and Recht, B. (2022). *Optimization for Data Analysis*. Cambridge: Cambridge University Press. DOI: 10.1017/9781009004282.

Wu, X., Ward, R., and Bottou, L. (2018). *WNGrad: Learn the Learning Rate in Gradient Descent.* arXiv: 1803.02865v1.

Zhang, Z. and Aeron, S. (2017). Exact tensor completion using t-SVD. *IEEE Transactions on Signal Processing* **65**(6), 1511–1526. DOI: 10.1109/tsp.2016.2639466.

Zhao, K., Di, S., Lian, X., et al. (2020). SDRBench: scientific data reduction benchmark for lossy compressors. In *2020 IEEE International Conference on Big Data*. DOI: 10.1109/bigdata50022.2020.9378449.

Zhao, Q., Zhou, G., Xie, S., Zhang, L., and Cichocki, A. (2016). *Tensor Ring Decomposition*. arXiv: 1606.05535.

Zhou, G., Cichocki, A., and Xie, S. (2014). *Decomposition of Big Tensors with Low Multilinear Rank.* arXiv: 1412.1885.

Zhou, S., Vinh, N. X., Bailey, J., Jia, Y., and Davidson, I. (2016). Accelerating online CP decompositions for higher order tensors. In *Proceedings of the 22nd ACM SIGKDD International Conference on Knowledge Discovery and Data Mining (KDD'16)*. DOI: 10.1145/2939672.2939763.

Zhu, C., Byrd, R. H., Lu, P., and Nocedal, J. (1997). Algorithm 778: L-BFGS-B: Fortran subroutines for large-scale bound-constrained optimization. *ACM Transactions on Mathematical Software* **23**(4), 550–560. DOI: 10.1145/279232.279236.

Index

$*$, *see* Hadamard product
$\odot$, *see* Khatri–Rao product
$\otimes$, *see* Kronecker product
$\mathbb{L}$, *see* linear/tuple index conversion
$\mathbb{T}$, *see* linear/tuple index conversion
$\mathcal{O}$, *see* big-O notation
$\circ$, *see* outer product
$\times_k$, *see* TTM

Bernoulli distribution, 259–261, **381–382**
beta divergence, 263–264
BFGS (optimization method), 229, **370**
big-O notation, 319
bilinear form, 277–278
BLAS (basic linear algebra subroutines), 351–353
block coordinate descent, 128, 205, 253, **373**
border rank, 276–277
bound constrained L-BFGS, *see* L-BFGS-B

CANDECOMP, 157, 180,
 see also CP decomposition
CANDELINC (linearly constrained CP), 306–308
canonical polyadic, 157, 180,
 see also CP decomposition
Cauchy–Schwartz inequality, 323
chain rule (multivariate), 358
Chicago crime tensor, 16
 CP-ALS, 213–217
 GCP-OPT, 177–180, 271
Cholesky decomposition (matrix), 206, 207, 210, **337**, 343
column-major (matrix order), 351–352
computational complexity, 319
congruence, *see* Kruskal tensor, similarity
conjugate gradient method, 235, **343–344**
convex function, 366
COO format, *see* sparse tensor, coordinate format
CP decomposition, 19, **157–180**, 302,
 see also Kruskal tensor
 alternating least squares, *see* CP-ALS
 block, 314
 choosing the rank, 165–166
 component, 19, **157**
 component weight, **160**, 171
 expectation maximization, *see* CP-EM
 factor, 157
 factor matrix, 157
 gradient, 222–228
 greedy computation, 296–297
 incomplete data, 169–170, **245–256**
 infinite dimensional, 314–315
 initialization, 166–167
 Jacobian, 234–235
 name origin, 180
 nonlinear least squares, *see* CP-NLS
 nonnegative, 168, 174–176, 230–232
 optimization, *see* CP-OPT
 postprocessing, 167–168
 preprocessing, 167
 rank, 157
 symmetric tensor, 170, 310
 Tucker connection, 304
 Tucker preprocessing, *see* CANDELINC
 uniqueness, *see* Kruskal tensor, uniqueness
 weighted alternating least squares, *see* CP-WALS
 weighted optimization, *see* CP-WOPT
CP-ALS (alternating least squares), 163–164, 171–173, **205–217**, 225
CP-EM (expectation maximization), 169
CP-NLS (nonlinear least squares), 164, **233–244**
CP-OPT (optimization), 164, 176, **219–232**
CP-WALS (weighted alternating least squares), 170, **253–254**
CP-WOPT (weighted optimization), 170, **249–252**, 254–256
cubical, 4
curse of dimensionality, 141, 303

damped Gauss–Newton, 164, 233, **371–372**
descent direction, 363
diagonal (matrix), 322
dimension tree, *see* memoization

Eckhart–Young theorem, 349
EEM tensor, 13–14
 CP-ALS, 171–173
 CP-OPT, 230–232
 CP-WOPT, 254–256
eigendecomposition (matrix), 121, **340–341**
eigenproblem, 311–312
Einstein notation, 88
elementwise product, *see* Hadamard product
essentially unique, 161–162, **191–193**, 304

fast complex multiplication, 278–279
fast matrix multiplication, 161, 280–285
fiber, 8–10
frontal slice, 6–7
full rank (matrix), 327
full reconstruction
 Kruskal tensor, 193–195
 Tucker tensor, 110

gamma distribution, 262–263, **382–383**

Gaussian distribution, 259, **381**
GCP decomposition, 170, 216, **257–271**
  gradient, 266–268
  loss functions, 257–265
  optimization, *see* GCP-OPT
GCP-OPT (optimization), 180, **266–271**
generalized CP, *see* GCP decomposition
global minimizer, 362
  sufficient conditions, 366
gradient, 164, **355**
  CP decomposition, 222–228, 249–251
  GCP decomposition, 266–268
gradient descent, 164, 228, **368**
Gram matrix, 212, 228, **330**

H-eigenpair, 312
Hadamard product, 87, 88, 212, 228, 248, **330–331**
Hessian, **359**, 365–366, 369–370, 374
higher order, 4
higher-order orthogonal iteration, *see* HOOI
higher-order SVD, *see* HOSVD
HOOI (higher-order orthogonal iteration), 71, **98**, 128–131
horizontal slice, 6
HOSVD (higher-order SVD), 96–97, **122–125**, 167
  approximation error, 134–135
  quasi-optimality, 137–138
Huber loss, **264–265**, 269
hyperslice, 7

identity matrix, 322
incomplete tensor, 245
indefinite (matrix), 340
indexing, **4–5**, 21, *see also* linear/tuple index conversion
  Cartesian versus tensor, 11
inner product, 47–48
  Kruskal tensor, 197
  Tucker tensor, 113–114
inner product (matrix), 323
inner product (vector), 322
inverse matrix, 325, *see also* linear system

Jacobian, **356–357**, 371–372
  CP decomposition, 164, **234–235**
  Kruskal tensor, 223, **226**

k-rank, 285–286
Khatri–Rao product, 186, 193–195, 206, **334–336**, *see also* MTTKRP
  linear indexing, 27, **29**
KL (Kullback–Leibler) divergence, 261–262
Kronecker product, 49–54, 106–108, **331–334**, 359
  linear indexing, 26–28, **29**
Kruskal tensor, 181–204, *see also* CP decomposition
  approximation error, 198–200
  component, 182, **184**
  component weight, 184–186
  factor, 182, **184**
  factor matrix, 182, **184**
  format, 182–186
  full construction, 193–195
  Jacobian, 223, **226**
  masked construction, 195–196
  rank, 182, **184**
  renormalization, 186
  similarity, 202–204
  uniqueness, 285–287
  weight vector, 185

L-BFGS (limited-memory BFGS), 164, 229, 251, 268, **371**
L-BFGS-B (bound-constrained L-BFGS), 169, 176, 180, 229, 230, 268, 271, **377**
LAPACK (linear algebra software), 351–353
lateral slice, 6
leading left singular vectors, *see* LLSV
limited-memory BFGS, *see* L-BFGS
line search, 367–368
linear independent (vectors), 326
linear index, 21, *see also* linear/tuple index conversion
linear least squares, 345–348
  choice of solver, 347–348
  CP-ALS, 206–207, **209**
  gradient, 358
  multiple right-hand sides, 348
  normal equations, 345–346
  QR decomposition, 346
  Tucker core, 117–118
  via QR decomposition, 346
  via SVD, 347
linear system, 342–345
  CP-ALS, 207
  iterative methods, 343
  multiple right-hand sides, 343
  nonsymmetric, 344
  symmetric positive definite, 343
linear/tuple index conversion, 21–31
  composition of linearization, 24, **25**
  general ordering, 29–31
  general/natural conversion, 30
  natural ordering, 22–25
  reverse ordering, 25–29
  reverse/natural conversion, 28
  strides, 21
link function, 258
LLSV (leading left singular vectors), 95–96, **120–122**
  HOOI, 128–131
  HOSVD, 122–124, 135
  ST-HOSVD, 125–128, 137
  TT decomposition, 145–146, 149–152
  via eigendecomposition, 121
  via SVD, 120
local minimizer, 362
  necessary conditions, 364–365
  necessary conditions with nonnegativity constraint, 377
  sufficient conditions, 366
logistic regression, 259–261
low-rank matrix approximation, 301–306, **348–351**
LU decomposition (matrix), **337**, 344

matricization, *see* unfolding

matricized tensor times Khatri–Rao product, *see* MTTKRP
matrix, **4**, 321
matrix product, 324–325
matrix product states (MPS), 141
matrix trace, 325
matrix–vector product, 324
`mats2vec`, 220, **221**
maximum likelihood estimate, 258, **380**
maximum rank, 274–275
mean, 379–380
memoization, **71–79**, 131, 211, 228, 241
memory complexity, 5, **320**
memory layout, 33
  mode-k unfolding, 40–41
memory layout (matrix), 351–352
minimization, *see* optimization
Miranda simulation tensor, 11–13
  ST-HOSVD, 100–102
missing data, *see* CP decomposition, incomplete data
mode, 4
monkey BMI tensor, 15–16
  CP decomposition, 174–177
  GCP-OPT, 269–271
MTTKRP (matricized tensor times Khatri–Rao product), **65–71**, 206–212, 223–228, 250–252, 267–268
  Kruskal tensor, 200–201
  sequence, **74–79**, 225, 251
  sparse tensor, 81–83
  Tucker tensor, 115–116
multi-index notation, 258
multi-TTM, **61–65**, 99, 103–104, 112, 114, 115, 123–124
  mode ordering, 64–65
  sequence, **71–73**, 129
  unfolding, 62, **63–64**
multilinear rank, *see* multirank
multirank, **91–92**, 95

Newton's method, 369–370
nnz (number of nonzeros), 79
nonlinear least squares, 362
  CP decomposition, *see* CP-NLS
nonnegative matrix factorization (NMF), 303
nonnegativity constraint, 168, 230–231, 255, **377**
nonsingular (matrix), 325
norm, 48
  Kruskal tensor, 198
  sparse tensor, 81
  Tucker tensor, 114–115
norm (matrix Frobenius), 323
norm (vector), 322
normal distribution, *see* Gaussian distribution
normal equations, 345–346
  CP-ALS, 206

ODECO (orthogonally decomposable), 169, 305
optimization, 361–376
  constrained, 376–377
order, 4
orthogonal (matrix), 328
orthogonal (vectors), **323**, 326
orthogonal projector (matrix), 328
orthonormal (matrix), 328
  factor matrix, 108–109, 304, *see also* ODECO
orthonormal (vectors), 326
outer product, **49–54**, 159, 324
overdetermined (least squares), 345

PARAFAC, 157, 180, *see also* CP decomposition
partial gradient, 356
partial Jacobian, 357
PCA (principal component analysis), 383–387
perfect shuffle
  for matrix, **330**, 333, 360
  for tensor, **43–44**, 223, 234
permutation (of tensor modes), 41–45
permutation ambiguity, 161, **190**
permutation matrix, 329
Poisson distribution, 261, **382**
positive (semi-)definite (matrix), **325**, 340
positive definite, 309
preconditioned conjugate gradient method, *see* conjugate gradient method
principal component analysis, *see* PCA
probability density function, 380
probability mass function, 379
projected gradient, 230, **377**
pseudoinverse, 347

QR decomposition, 338
  orthonormalization, 109
  solving least squares, 207, 346
  SVD computation, 341
quasi-Newton method, 164, 228, **370**
quasi-optimality, 137–140
  HOSVD, 96
  ST-HOSVD, 98, **140**
  TT-SVD, 152

random variable, 379–380
range (matrix), 327
rank, 158–159, 273
  maximum, 274–275
  NP-hardness, 274
  of $2 \times 2 \times 2$ tensor, 289–293
  of $n \times n \times 2$ tensor, 293–294
  typical, 275–276
rank (matrix), 327
rank-1 tensor, 49, **51**, 181–182, 287–289
regularization, 166, 227
  CP-ALS, 207
reshape, 33
row-major (matrix order), 351–352

saddle point, 366
scaling ambiguity, 161, 191
scarce tensor, 169, **245**
Schur product, *see* Hadamard product
score, *see* Kruskal tensor, similarity
sequentially truncated HOSVD, *see* ST-HOSVD
sign ambiguity, 191

simultaneous diagonalization, 165, 294–296
singular (matrix), 325
singular value decomposition, *see* SVD
slice, 5–7
span (of vectors), 326
sparse matrix, 322
sparse tensor, 17, **79–84**, 212–213
  coordinate format, 79, **80**
ST-HOSVD (sequentially truncated HOSVD), 97–98, **125–128**
  approximation error, 136–137
  quasi-optimality, 139–140
stationary point, 364
steepest descent direction, 364, *see also* gradient descent
Strassen's algorithm, 280–281
SVD (singular value decomposition), 302, 305, **338–340**
  computational cost, 341–342
  LLSV, 95
  matrix approximation, 349
  solving least squares, 347
symmetric matrix, 322
symmetric tensor, 308–312

t-SVD (tensor SVD), 312
tensor, 4
tensor completion, 169
tensor contraction, 84–88
  batched, 87
tensor network diagram, 86–87
tensor ring decomposition, 313
tensor times matrix, *see* TTM
tensor train decomposition, *see* TT decomposition
tensor train SVD, *see* TT-SVD
trace (matrix), **322**
transpose (matrix), 322
TT (tensor train) decomposition, 141–154, 302
  formulation, 142–145
TT-SVD, 145–153
TTM (tensor times matrix), 54–61, 96, *see also* multi-TTM
  Kruskal tensor, 201
  Tucker tensor, 115
Tucker decomposition, 19, **91–102**, 301, *see also* Tucker tensor
  approximation error, **94**, 101, 133–140
  compression ratio, **94**, 101
  core tensor, 19, 91
  CP connection, 305
  error decomposition, 133–134
  exact, 95
  factor matrices, 91
  formulation, 92–94
  full reconstruction, 99–100
  optimization problem, 117–120
  partial reconstruction, 100
  symmetric tensor, 310
Tucker tensor, 103–116, *see also* Tucker decomposition
  core tensor, 103, **104**
  factor matrix, 103, **104**
  format, 103–105
  full reconstruction, 110
  nonuniqueness, 108
  orthonormal factors, 108–109
  partial reconstruction, 111
  rank, 103, **104**
tuple index, 21, *see also* linear/tuple index conversion

unfolding, 10–11, **33–41**
  Kruskal tensor, 189
  Tucker tensor, 106–107

variance, 379–380
`vec2mats`, 220, **221**
vector, **4**, 321
vectorization, 31–33
  Kruskal tensor, 188
  Tucker tensor, 106–107
vectorization (matrix), 322

Z-eigenpair, 312